Introduction to Penology and Corrections

EDITORIAL ADVISORS

Introduction to Penology and Corrections

Laura Pinto Hansen

Instructor in Criminal Justice
Department of Sociology, Anthropology, and Criminal Justice
New Mexico Highland University

Professor Emerita in Criminal Justice
Department of Criminal Justice, Sociology, and Social Work
Western New England University

Cover image: rawf8/Shutterstock.com

To contact Customer Service, e-mail customer.service@aspenpublishing.com, call 1-800-950-5259, or mail correspondence to:

> Aspen Publishing
> Attn: Order Department
> PO Box 990
> Frederick, MD 21705

Printed in the United States of America.

1 2 3 4 5 6 7 8 9 0

ISBN 978-1-5438-4635-5

Library of Congress Cataloging-in-Publication Data

Names: Hansen, Laura L. (Laura Lynn), author.
Title: Introduction to penology and corrections / Laura Pinto Hansen,
  Professor Emerita in Criminal Justice, Department of Criminal Justice
  and Sociology, Western New England University.
Description: Frederick, MD : Aspen Publishing, [2023] | Series: Criminal
  justice series | Includes bibliographical references and index. |
  Summary: "Introductory book for Criminal Justice courses on
  penology/corrections"—Provided by publisher.
Identifiers: LCCN 2022020499 (print) | LCCN 2022020500 (ebook) | ISBN
  9781543846355 (paperback) | ISBN 9781543846362 (ebook)
Subjects: LCSH: Corrections. | Corrections—United States.
Classification: LCC HV8665 .H35 2023 (print) | LCC HV8665 (ebook) | DDC
  364.6—dc23/eng/20220518
LC record available at https://lccn.loc.gov/2022020499
LC ebook record available at https://lccn.loc.gov/2022020500

SUSTAINABLE FORESTRY INITIATIVE

Certified Chain of Custody
Promoting Sustainable Forestry

www.sfiprogram.org

ABOUT ASPEN PUBLISHING

Aspen Publishing is a leading provider of educational content and digital learning solutions to law schools in the United States and around the world. Aspen provides best-in-class solutions for legal education through authoritative textbooks, written by renowned authors, and breakthrough products such as Connected eBooks, Connected Quizzing, and PracticePerfect.

The Aspen Casebook Series (famously known among law faculty and students as the "red and black" casebooks) encompasses hundreds of highly regarded textbooks in more than eighty disciplines, from large enrollment courses, such as Torts and Contracts to emerging electives such as Sustainability and the Law of Policing. Study aids such as the *Examples & Explanations* and the *Emanuel Law Outlines* series, both highly popular collections, help law students master complex subject matter.

Major products, programs, and initiatives include:

- **Connected eBooks** are enhanced digital textbooks and study aids that come with a suite of online content and learning tools designed to maximize student success. Designed in collaboration with hundreds of faculty and students, the Connected eBook is a significant leap forward in the legal education learning tools available to students.

- **Connected Quizzing** is an easy-to-use formative assessment tool that tests law students' understanding and provides timely feedback to improve learning outcomes. Delivered through CasebookConnect.com, the learning platform already used by students to access their Aspen casebooks, Connected Quizzing is simple to implement and integrates seamlessly with law school course curricula.

- **PracticePerfect** is a visually engaging, interactive study aid to explain commonly encountered legal doctrines through easy-to-understand animated videos, illustrative examples, and numerous practice questions. Developed by a team of experts, PracticePerfect is the ideal study companion for today's law students.

- The **Aspen Learning Library** enables law schools to provide their students with access to the most popular study aids on the market across all of their courses. Available through an annual subscription, the online library consists of study aids in e-book, audio, and video formats with full text search, note-taking, and highlighting capabilities.

- Aspen's **Digital Bookshelf** is an institutional-level online education bookshelf, consolidating everything students and professors need to ensure success. This program ensures that every student has access to affordable course materials from day one.

- **Leading Edge** is a community centered on thinking differently about legal education and putting those thoughts into actionable strategies. At the core of the program is the Leading Edge Conference, an annual gathering of legal education thought leaders looking to pool ideas and identify promising directions of exploration.

This textbook is the culmination of studying corrections and punishment for over twenty years, as well as teaching corrections courses at universities for over seventeen years. In previous books I have published, I have thanked the usual suspects, including my parents and my brother, along with the college professors who inspired me. The ancestry of my scholarship in corrections lies in the hands of the late Austin Turk, a renowned scholar in the field, who was one of my most influential mentors at University of California Riverside. However, there is only one person I would like to dedicate this book to who sparked my passion for the subject matter and that is to my son, Erik Sundell-Bahrd.

While I was in graduate school, I attended a number of conferences. In 2001, I had an opportunity to present a paper at the annual Pacific Sociological Association conference, held in San Francisco that year. As Erik was turning 13 (a teenager!) at the same time as the conference, I took him with me so we could spend his milestone birthday together. When asked what sights he might want to see while we were in San Francisco, Erik insisted that we visit Alcatraz Island, where the former federal military fort turned prison can now be toured, courtesy of the National Park Services. I was rather lukewarm at the prospect of visiting an old crumbling prison, but it was his birthday wish, so off we went on a boat across the chilly, choppy San Francisco Bay to the island.

At that time in graduate school, I knew I was interested in specializing in criminology, but quite frankly, I found corrections to be, well, depressing. That tour of Alcatraz changed everything for me and the direction of my career. I came to the realization in that visit that the study of prisons and punishment can include the examination of administrative practices and application of organizational theory, in addition to the study of the humanity of prisoners and their guards. Though I am better known for scholarship in other areas in criminology and criminal justice, to date, the study and teaching of corrections and punishment have remained some of the more interesting aspects of my career. More importantly, it opened the door to a wider range of career and volunteer opportunities.

So, thank you, Erik, for making me take you to Alcatraz during that fateful trip. You continue to inspire me every day with your curiosity and intelligence, introducing me always to new subject matter I did not know I wanted to know. You are indeed my pride and joy.

Summary of **CONTENTS**

CONTENTS

CHAPTER **ONE**

THE PURPOSES OF PUNISHMENT: AN INTRODUCTION TO PENOLOGY   **1**

CHAPTER **FOUR**

PRISON ADMINSTRATION   103

CHAPTER **FIVE**

JAIL AND PRISON STAFF PERSPECTIVES — 133

CHAPTER **SIX**

THE PRISONER'S PERSPECTIVE   155

CHAPTER **SEVEN**

PRISONERS' RIGHTS   **193**

CHAPTER **EIGHT**

WOMEN IN JAILS AND PRISONS   233

Contents

CHAPTER **NINE**

JUVENILE DETENTION AND PROBATION   267

CHAPTER **TEN**

VIOLENCE IN PRISON   315

CHAPTER **ELEVEN**

PHYSICAL AND MENTAL HEALTH ISSUES IN CORRECTIONS   347

CHAPTER **TWELVE**

ALTERNATIVES TO INCARCERATION: COMMUNITY-BASED CORRECTIONS   387

Contents

CHAPTER **THIRTEEN**

THE DEATH PENALTY   **423**

CHAPTER **FOURTEEN**

OTHER CONTROVERSIES IN PUNISHMENT AND CORRECTIONS   461

Contents

PREFACE

The criminal justice system in the United States is currently experiencing extreme pressure to make serious and profound social changes. Much of this is motivated by social justice movements, but the system has needed dire restructuring for a number of decades in response to societal and political upheaval outside of jails and prisons, as well as changing attitudes towards existing drug laws. The push for reform extends to demands for changes in corrections. This textbook looks to bridge the traditional views in corrections with those that are rapidly emerging, even as this book goes to press.

One way that I am addressing this push for criminal justice reform is to include discussions of social justice issues as they relate to problems in corrections. For example, instead of merely presenting the sterile facts of Death Row and the death penalty from the perspective of prison administration, I have also included extensive discussions of the moral and ethical ramifications of capital punishment in Chapter 13. In order to offer balanced viewpoints, I have also included separate chapters on the prison experience from the perspective of prisoners and that of prison administration, staff, and officers.

It is important to note that as in the case of any less advantaged group in today's society, the labels we use are changing as well. Whereas the offensive label "mentally retarded" has been relegated to the uninformed past, more kind and better descriptive terms are now in use, including "intellectual disability" or "learning disability." There is currently a push to soften the terminology that we use to describe those who have been convicted and have served their sentence and their debt to society. For example, the Humanity First Movement has suggested that instead of using the term "convict," to alternatively use "formerly incarcerated person" to describe those who have spent time in prison. I have purposely not used that label in this textbook and have instead retained the terminology that is most commonly in use today within the Criminal Justice System so as to not to confuse the reader, as there has not been a wholesale acceptance of some of the new terminology. I wholeheartedly support reform in a number of aspects of corrections, including overturning stigmatizing vocabulary, as long as any reform does not jeopardize the safety of staff or prisoners and detainees. However, I strongly feel that students should familiarize themselves with the terminology commonly used in criminal justice professions, however outdated it may be to those in social justice circles.

Included in vocabulary reform over the years in corrections that has been widely accepted are the terms we now use for those who directly are in charge of detainees and prisoners. Whereas prison staff were historically called "jailers" (from the old Norman French term *gaoler*s) or guards, jail and prison personnel are now more commonly called corrections or correctional officers in the United States, with the exception of some states that use the term "correctional police officer." Of course, there are a number of colorful terms used by prisoners that are far less flattering, including "turnkey" and "hack," along with names that include profanity. Wherever it is historically accurate to use the term "prison guard," we will include it in this text. Whereas in any discussion of modern correctional systems, we will use "correctional officer."

No matter which form of "officer" is used in jails and prisons, it is indicative of the continued push to further professionalize the vocations of those who work directly with prisoners. However, as we will note within this book, there are still jurisdictions in the United States where prison officers as young 18 years old with no experience can apply for positions in jails or prisons, as in the example of the New Mexico Department of Corrections (See https://cd.nm.gov/divisions/training-academy/recruiting/correctional-officers/). There is also the question of the professional standards in private jails or prisons, discussed in this book.

Another difference that sets this book apart from a standard corrections textbook is the extensive discussion of *penology*, the study of punishment and prison management. Though this is not a book on the courts and sentencing, it is not only instructing students on the practicalities of jail and prison administration, but also examines the social and psychological effects of the correctional system on those who occupy space within jails and prisons.

It also provides a peek behind the curtain of systems of punishment in other countries. This is done so as to allow the reader to critically think about how corrections in the United States, as imperfect as it may seem, is more humane (if that is possible in punishment) or less humane, as compared to other places in the world. Of course, it would be an impossible task to include all countries, and the ones chosen here, in some cases, are the most extreme examples on one end or the other of the spectrum of punishment. Most importantly, throughout this book, the reader should be asking themselves, whether examining corrections in the United States or abroad, what are the long term effects of incarceration on individuals, hence inhibiting efforts in rehabilitation and contributing to unacceptably high rates of recidivism. Or as Michel Foucault proposed[1], has contemporary punishment shifted from eroding the body to extinguishing the soul?

---

[1] *Discipline and Punishment: The Birth of the Prison* (1975)

CHAPTER ORGANIZATION

The textbook chapters are designed to offer the richest reading experience for the different styles of learning students have today, including those with various learning disabilities. The organization of the chapters is as follows:

- **Chapter Objectives** to guide the reader to the most important goals of the chapter.
- **Key Terms** to define vocabulary that is commonly used in corrections. Instructors will note that we have also included definitions to some words that we cannot assume students are familiar with that are not related to corrections but will help them better grasp their relevance in the course.
- **Chapter Summaries** that very briefly give a quick overview of the chapter and direct the student to the more important general information contained in them.
- A **Stories from Behind Bars** feature to offer biographical or autobiographical tales of what it is like to be a guard, a detainee, or a prisoner. These are mostly first-hand accounts and so we should approach them as subjective truths of the writers, but their truths nevertheless.
- An **International Perspectives on Punishment and Corrections** feature that will offer cross-cultural, cross-national views, as well as a peek behind prison walls in countries around the world.
- **International Perspectives on Juvenile Justice** in Chapter 9 gives cross-cultural and cross-national views on treatment of juvenile offenders.
- **References and Suggested Readings** at the end of each chapter that are not only intended to cite the sources used but to encourage students to research topics further, as well as give them a start for their research papers in their class.
- **Resources** in some chapters with recommended videos, films, websites, or fictional stories that will offer different ways to understanding the textbook materials and lectures, as well as provide help for those who may be personally affected, as in the example of a list of children's books in Chapter 6 for the offspring of incarcerated parents.

Though it is not the main focus of this book, topics on social justice and criminal justice reform are included. Like other areas in criminal justice, criminology, psychology, social work, and sociology, there are a number of topics that require a closer look, as the public and practitioners increasingly are demanding answers. And our students who take this course will increasingly be asked to come up with solutions to social justice issues when they leave the university and enter their chosen profession, if it is in any field that is even remotely connected to the criminal justice system.

You will note that I have included "trigger warnings" in some chapters. Though we expect students in criminal justice, sociology, and social work to be able to handle the harsh realities of criminals and criminology, I do not want to limit this textbook to those students. In the last several years, I have included a statement in my syllabi that there might be some materials discussed in the course (e.g., juvenile delinquency, child abuse, punishment and corrections) that might be more than unpleasant—they might trigger anxiety in students, particularly those who have been victimized. We cannot talk about corrections and punishment without diving into the unpleasant and disturbing underbelly of society. Nor should we want to avoid these topics, as besides policing, corrections has some of the biggest controversies that we can find in criminal justice. However, we have to present these materials with heightened sensitivity to those that might be affected by them.

Laura Pinto Hansen, Ph.D.
Instructor in Criminal Justice
Department of Sociology, Anthropology, and Criminal Justice
New Mexico Highland University

Professor Emerita in Criminal Justice
Department of Criminal Justice, Sociology, and Social Work
Western New England University

ACKNOWLEDGMENTS

ACLU March for Prisoners' Rights. Copyright © 2017 American Civil Liberties Union. Retrieved from https://www.aclu.org/cases/prisoners-rights/dockery-v-hall.

Alfonso Gonzalez Sanchez, alias "El Chucky," in a Mexican jail's holding cell. Copyright © 1998 AP Photo/Elizabeth Dalziel.

Courtroom Bailiff. Copyright © 2010 Alina555 / iStock.

Display of weapons confiscated from prisoners. Photo by Anna Cabreira. Reprinted with permission from Eric Schatz/Schatz Realty Group.

Duties of Prison Chaplains, survey result. Pew Research Center, Washington, D.C. (2012). https://www.pewforum.org/2012/03/22/prison-chaplains-what-they-do/.

Effects of Parents' Incarceration on Minor Children, graph. From Morsey and Rothstein (2016), "Mass incarceration and children's outcomes." Reprinted with permission from the Economic Policy Institute. Retrieved from https://www.epi.org/publication/mass-incarceration-and-childrens-outcomes/.

Percent of juvenile cases involving black youth by state of proceeding, graph. Used with permission of the School of Government, copyright © 2022. This copyrighted material may not be reproduced in whole or in part without the express written permission of the School of Government, CB# 3330, UNC-Chapel Hill, Chapel Hill, NC 27599-3330, sog.unc.edu.

Example of jail and prison toothbrushes. Reprinted with permission from Security Dental Products.

Execution Methods in the US (1950-2019), graph, from "The Death Penalty is Wrong. What Can President Biden Do About It?" "by Yona Litwin '21, The Science Survey, March 21st, 2021.
Retrieved from https://thesciencesurvey.com/editorial/2021/03/21/the-death-penalty-is-wrong-what-can-president-biden-do-about-it/. Reprinted with permission.

Exterior of Malmaison Oxford Hotel. Copyright © David Jones/ Alamy Stock Photo.

Female prison inmate inside a cell. Copyright © 2013 by Officer Bimblebury at Wikimedia Commons. This work is licensed under CC BY-SA 4.0, https://creativecommons.org/licenses/by-sa/4.0/deed.en.

How an Ignition Interlock Device works. Retrieved from https://www.fightduicharges.com/ignition-interlock-device/. Reprinted with permission from Fight DUI Charges.

Incarceration in the United States, 1925-2018, graph, from "Trends in U.S. Corrections." Reprinted with permission from The Sentencing Project. Retrieved from https://www.sentencingproject.org/publications/trends-in-u-s-corrections/.

Inmates picking up trash. Copyright © 2007 Mikael Karlsson/ Alamy Stock Photo.

Interior of Clink78 Hostel, London, UK. Reprinted with permission from Clink Hostels.

Interior of the Alameda County (CA) Juvenile Justice Center. Reprinted with permission from Judge Trina Thompson.

Jail pat down. Copyright © 2008 lisafx/ iStock.

La Sante Prison. Copyright © 2019 Francois Mori/AP/Shutterstock.

Mental Health Treatment Among Incarcerated Adults, graph. Courtesy of Nursing@ USC, the online FNP program from the University of Southern California, with data from the U.S. Department of Justice. Retrieved from https://nursing.usc.edu/blog/correctional-nurse-career/.

Nashua Street Jail, Boston. Copyright © 2014 Chandra Das/ iStock.

New Mexico State Penitentiary, Santa Fe County. Copyright © 2005 by Shelka04 at en.wikipedia. This work is licensed under CC BY-SA 3.0, https://creativecommons.org/licenses/by-sa/3.0/deed.en.

New York House of Refuge. Courtesy of the Museum of the City of New York, J. Clarence Davies Scrapbook Collection.

One Year of Prison Costs More Than One Year at Princeton, graph. Copyright © 2011 PublicAdministration.net. This work is licensed under CC BY-NC-ND 4.0, https://creativecommons.org/licenses/by-nc-nd/4.0/.

Outward Bound participant. Copyright © 2018 Dalton Johnson/Shutterstock

Overlap of Street Gangs with Prison Gangs. From Mitchell et al. (2016), "Criminal crews, codes, and contexts: Differences and similarities across the code of the street, convict code, street gangs, and prison gangs," Deviant Behavior, 38(10), 1200. https://doi.org/10.1080/01639625.2016.1246028. Copyright © 2016 Taylor & Francis.

Presidio Modelo, a panopticon designed prison at Isla de Juventud, Cuba. Copyright © 2005 by Friman at Wikimedia. This work is licensed under CC BY-SA 3.0, https://creativecommons.org/licenses/by-sa/3.0/deed.en.

Social network transmission of HCV from prison to people on the outside, infographic. From Dalgic et al. (2019), "Improved Health Outcomes from Hepatitis C Treatment Scale-Up in Spain's Prisons: A Cost-Effectiveness Study," Scientific Reports, vol. 9 (2019). https://doi.org/10.1038/s41598-019-52564-0. Copyright © 2022 Springer Nature Limited. This work is licensed under CC BY 4.0, https://creativecommons.org/licenses/by/4.0/.

Sturminster Newton Bridge Warning Sign. Copyright © 2005 Caroline Eastwood/ Alamy Stock Photo.

U.S. Incarcerates a larger share of its population than any other country, infographic. Pew Research Center, Washington, D.C. (2021) https://www.pewresearch .org/fact-tank/2021/08/16/americas-incarceration-rate-lowest-since-1995/.

Introduction to Penology and Corrections

Chapter ONE

The Purposes of Punishment

An Introduction to Penology

If you are going to do something wrong, do it big, because the punishment is the same either way.

— Jayne Mansfield, 1950s American actress and sex symbol

Chapter Objectives

- Introduce the philosophies of punishment through the ages.
- Introduce vocabulary that will be frequently used throughout this textbook and the course.
- Examine the merits and flaws of contemporary purposes of punishment.
- Begin discussing the controversies around punishment and corrections, including the criticisms highlighted in social justice movements.

Key Terms

Banishment
Community corrections
Deterrence
Differential association theory
General deterrence
Incapacitation
Incarceration
"Just deserts"
Norm
Penologists
Penology
Pity booking

Prisoners of war (POWs)
Pure restitution
Recidivism
Rehabilitation
Restitution
Restorative justice
Retribution
Shaming and reintegration
Specific deterrence
Strain theory
Vengeful, vengeance

INTRODUCTION

We can hardly begin a discussion of corrections systems without first establishing the purposes of punishment. In this chapter, we will explore contemporary theories in *penology*, or the study of punishment. Of course, those who are in the penology field do more than just study types of punishment. They also study the effectiveness of different types of punishment in rehabilitating prisoners and preventing them from reoffending. Some penology theories are driven by the findings of researchers. Others are driven by public sentiment or by the agendas of politicians and legislatures.

The study of punishment should not be confused with the profession of penologists. Those who study penology tend to be academic researchers. Working directly with prisons, a *penologist* helps prisoners with their rehabilitation and reentry into society after incarceration (Criminal Justice U.S. Jobs, 2020). However, penologists should not be confused with social workers. Penologists also work with prison management to assess whether punishment is really preventing crime.

The word "corrections" appears in the title of this book and very possibly in the name of your course. Throughout this book, as we are examining the concept of punishment, it is important to ask the question "is punishment corrective?" In other words, are the types of punishment that convicted criminals receive in their sentences through courts systems in the United States and other places in the world really correcting the targeted behavior? If so, then the name is apt. If not, we should consider that the term "corrections" for the different types of punishment (e.g., incarceration) may be misleading. Just the same, we will use the term "corrections" throughout the book because it is the label most often used to describe the part of the American criminal justice system that is responsible for carrying out court-ordered punishment and administering the housing of prisoners.

Defining exactly what we mean by punishment poses a number of considerations. By strict definition, punishment is a penalty imposed when someone has broken a law or rule or, in the case of more ancient societies without formal law, violated a community *norm,* the expected, lawful behavior that society requires of its members and that is generally agreed upon by most people in the population. However, there is also the moral dilemma as to what is in the best interest of the community, while taking into consideration humane treatment of the accused. Many of the social justice issues in the forefront of the push for criminal justice reform include those related to the fairness of sentencing and the perceived inhumanity of prisons.

Throughout written history, there have been documents specifying rules and suggesting specific punishments to fit violations. Religious writings have included lists of punishable offenses, with suggested punishments, often gruesome in their delivery to the offenders, by today's standards. For thousands of years, punishment was imposed by religious leaders, who were, next to rulers, the final authority in

The Code of Hammurabi. (*Source:* Stanford Education History Education Group, Stanford University, retrieved from https://sheg .stanford.edu/history-lessons/hammurabis-code)

communities, when the rulers were not already themselves the religious authorities. The *Code of Hammurabi*[1], a legal text drawn up in the 1700s BCE by the Babylonian king on authority he claimed from the Babylonian god of justice, is one of the earliest sets of laws that has been preserved in stone. It gives 282 Babylonian[2] rules, similar to contemporary civil law, on many aspects of life and the conduct of business, with specific penalties spelled out for breaking any of the rules, including fines and punishment. This was quite unusual in comparison to other ancient civilizations that handed out punishment ad hoc. However, without some form of written record, we can only speculate what types and how consistent punishment was in other cultures.

We should take into consideration the fact that the perceptions of punishment are subjective. For the homeless[3], a *"pity booking"* or arrest and detention in jail on questionable charges on a cold winter's night, may in fact be humane if the shelters are all full. As harsh as jail conditions may be, for those who are living on the street, the roof over the head and predictable meals may be more attractive than the alternative. For some, punishment will make them all the more defiant, a behavior similar to that of children when they have had privileges taken away. There are examples of prisoners whose sentence to incarceration eventually saved their lives because they were able (where available, that is) to get the rehabilitation help they needed. For others, being sentenced to an excessively long prison term on a personal use drug offense, as we saw starting in the 1980s and 1990s, may have undermined their chances for a fulfilling life, as they remain unemployable. Often ties with friends and family have disappeared. In such instances, punishment extends far beyond the actual incarceration.

---

[1] The actual Code of Hammurabi stone can be found at the Louvre Museum in Paris, France.

[2] Babylon was an ancient city whose ruins are in present-day Iraq.

[3] We should note that other terms such as "unhoused" have begun to replace "homeless" to describe individuals who do not have a home. Finding an appropriate label becomes further confusing when describing people who are transient or "couch surfing" or permanently living in a converted van or RV, which has become increasingly popular in recent years.

Some forms of punishment are intended to inflict physical discomfort, as in the case of a child being spanked for misbehaving[4]. Other types of punishment are intended to inflict emotional and psychological pain or deprivation, as in the example of *banishment*. Banishment is a form of social death, where the accused or convicted is separated not only from their family and friends, but also from their community. When a child is given a time-out in their room, as punishment, the time-out may have little meaning if there are sources of entertainment such as television and computer present; however, it functions as a form of deprivation by imposing a temporary separation from the socializing and activities happening elsewhere in the household.

And yet other forms of punishment inflict both physical and psychological torture, as in the example of the Spanish Inquisition and the cruel treatment of people with Jewish, Muslim, and Moorish ancestry in Spain and Portugal, as well as in the Americas. In today's terms, inhumane treatment of prisoners is considered a crime by international consensus (van der Vyver, 2003), yet torture for real or imagined offenses as part of punishment still exists in some parts of the world. Throughout this book, we will also discuss international perspectives on punishment and corrections, as a basis of comparison with the criminal justice system in the United States. Punishment, in particular excessive punishment, is not universally defined the same way. Furthermore, the concept of what exactly is a punishable offense can differ from society to society and from era to era.

CLASSICAL THEORIES OF PUNISHMENT AND IMPRISONMENT

Theories about how to punish offenders, the morality of punishment, and the effectiveness of punishment as a way to deal with those who commit crimes come from a number of disciplines. These include theories that have been developed in philosophy, psychology, sociology, economics, and criminal justice. Whereas some theories address the human toll on the offender, others focus on justice for the victims of crime, and yet others focus on overall, broader societal tolls. Some theorists write discussions of the merits of punishment, while quantitative researchers use statistics to conduct tests in order to see whether the theories hold up with real data. Whatever approach is taken to study punishment, theorists and researchers today are standing on the shoulders of people who wrote essays on penology, in some cases, thousands of years ago.

---

[4] Spanking is no longer as commonly administered or tolerated as a form of punishment for children as it was some 50-odd years ago. Studies have indicated it as having negative psychological effects or possibly leading to further child abuses (Lee et al., 2020). However, studies of contemporary parenting do indicate that two thirds of parents still approve the use of spanking to discipline their children (Smith, 2012).

Ancient Philosophers

As far back as Ancient Greece, philosophers debated about the limits of punishment. Some of their perspectives were fairly advanced and are often revisited today by penology scholars.

Some of the ancient philosophers' views during the 5th and 4th centuries BCE on punishment were seemingly progressive, even by today's standards. Socrates (470-399 BCE) believed that people have free will and so will commit crimes willingly, a theory which runs parallel with contemporary rational choice theories of crime. As such, Socrates believed that punishment was justified, a view which is similar to more conservative views about crime today. The criminal seemingly knows the consequences of their actions.

Most of what we see as far as punishment goes, even leading into the 19th century, is based primarily on religious doctrine. However, earlier in Ancient Greece, there were those who were already thinking more secularly when it came to punishment. Plato (c. 428-c.348 BCE), a student of Socrates and later a teacher to Aristotle (348-322 BCE), suggested that punishment should be based on societal norms rather than on the laws of gods or goddesses (Smith Pangle, 2009). Aristotle returned to Socrates' teachings that proposed that the criminal is a rational actor but also argued that punishment as revenge to satisfy any associated anger directed at the criminal is justified (Konstan, 2003).

Ancient Romans in the Roman Republic (509 BCE-27 BCE) also had distinct views on crime and punishment. Roman writers and philosophers were influenced by the views of Greek philosophers, including those on punishment. We should note that Romans did not take issue to more violent types of punishment, as in the example of accepting domestic violence as being justified (*Law Explorer*, 2015). Up until very recent decades, at least in the western world, domestic violence was largely ignored and affairs that went on between spouses or within the home were largely viewed as private affairs. In some places of the world today, domestic violence is still tolerated and not criminalized. Cicero (106 BCE-43 BCE), a philosopher and Roman statesman, believed there should be equal justice, in that the punishment for specific crimes should be identical and consistent, which is uniform with the push for sentencing guidelines and truth in sentencing in contemporary times. We should note that Cicero himself was assassinated, for alleged political transgressions, without benefit of trial in order to defend himself.

In the late period of the Roman Republic, capital punishment was, curiously, abolished. How much of that was a result of philosophical and moral reasoning is debated. Cicero saw the abolishment of the death punishment as praiseworthy:

What could I more desire than that in my consulship I had removed the execu-
tioner from the Forum, the cross[5] from the Campus? But that praise, Quirites[6],

---

[5] As noted in the biblical history of Jesus Christ, Romans commonly executed criminals by nailing them to a cross.
[6] Citizens of ancient Rome.

belongs to our ancestors, who, when they drove out the kings, kept no trace of royal cruelty among a free people; then to the many brave men who willed that your liberty should not be menaced by harshness of punishments but protected by the mildness of laws. (Green, 1929, p 268)

The speculation of scholars, including Green (1929), is that this change of heart had more to do with the shift in the Roman political system and the sentiment of citizens than any moral reasons. Like other countries that had removed traditional aristocracy and replaced it with democracy, ancient Rome abandoned practices of excessive punishment, including the death penalty. Many contemporary democracies have done the same and replaced it with seemingly more just and humane treatment of convicted criminals, including life in prison without the possibility of parole.

18th- and 19th-Century Social Philosophers, Criminologists, and Sociologists

The 18th and 19th centuries in Europe and in the United States, besides social and political revolutions, brought a shift away from the general belief that criminals were possessed by a demon or the devil. There grew a better understanding that people were more likely to commit crimes due to their own free will and/or because of circumstances beyond their control, like poverty. It is no coincidence that the growth of the new disciplines of sociology and criminology emerged out of the 19th century.

One social philosopher and early criminologist who helped shape the course of punishment, whether he was aware of it in his own lifetime or not, was Cesare Beccaria (1738-1794). To his credit, Beccaria promoted penal reform away from more cruel punishments, including torture and capital punishment. It is important to note that Beccaria is considered the "father of penology" for his then groundbreaking criticisms of the conditions of criminals and prisons, published in *An Essay on Crimes and Punishment* (1764; 2009). Beccaria proposed that punishment should be rational, not emotionally doled out for the sole purposes of vengeance. This was very much a forward thinking philosophy of retribution, considering how arbitrary and often cruel punishment was in the 18th century, both in The American Colonies, later the United States, and countries abroad.

Another familiar name in criminology and punishment is Caesar Lombroso (1835-1909), whose theory about "born criminals" emerged with other xenophobic theories in the 19th century. In his depiction of "born criminals," Lombroso suspiciously included physical characteristics that can be described today as Semitic or raced based. However, for all his xenophobic views, Lombroso also embraced the growing movement for penal reform, including the push for rehabilitation in the late 19th century.

Eighteenth- and 19th-century social philosophers also included some of the founding theorists in sociology. Immanuel Kant and Friedrich Hegel, part of the German Idealist Movement, were among some of these early pioneers to discuss punishment and its limits. To date, there are still a number of debates about their own contradictions of punishment for revenge's sake and the use of punishment as a deterrence (Brooks, 2001), though we should note that these are not mutually exclusive. Vigilantism is founded on revenge, yet also serves to send a message to others who might be inclined to commit the same crimes.

Known in sociology for his writings on the evolution of punishment, among other subjects that were somewhat taboo at the time (e.g., suicide), Emil Durkheim believed that crime and punishment were inevitable in organized social life (Spitzer, 1975). Durkheim however also believed that punishment ends up extending beyond the intended target and strikes the innocents, including family members, children, neighbors, and communities of the convicted. He was one of the first sociologists to address the issues of how not only crime, but punishment, affects society in general.

As social, economic, and political systems underwent upheavals in the 19th century, Karl Marx (1818-1883) emerged as the voice for those looking to upturn class stratification. His views of the purposes of punishment fell in line with his call for awakening the working poor to the disparities between the rich few and the greater mass of people living in poverty in the 19th century. He saw punishment as one more form of class control, where it was built into the disparity of subordination and bourgeois domination. His writings later influenced 20th- and 21st-century penologists and social reformists who argue, rightfully so, that the rich are less likely to receive prison time for the same types of crimes committed by the poor. Or as in the case of white-collar crimes where thousands, sometimes millions, are stolen from fraud victims, conviction may result in much less prison time than that meted out to average perpetrators responsible for the typically smaller monetary losses of conventional crime victims.

Yet other 19th-century sociologists saw punishment as necessary. Max Weber believed that punishment is functional, but should also be impersonal. Weber was the leading theorist then and to this day on the characteristics of bureaucratic structures, of which jails, prisons, and the correctional system are one type. Punishment is rational, according to Weber and similar theorists who study social structures, and is required for the smooth functioning of societies based on bureaucratic organization.

More Contemporary Theories on Punishment

French social philosopher Michel Foucault (1926-1984) wrote not only about contemporary punishment, but also about the purposes of punishment in the 19th century, in *Discipline and Punish: The Birth of the Prison* (1975). In his estimation, any reforms that were proposed within the 19th century towards seemingly more benign punishment were more a function of bringing order to what was, at the time, a chaotic system of punishment. Foucault estimated that reform was focused on reducing the theater of punishment, not at reducing the public shame of the convicted (Foucault, 1975).

David Garland (1955-), a neo-Marxist theorist, believes that there is a connection between property relations and the law, with sanction and punishment determined by the ruling class. He is not off the mark, when we consider that some property crimes convictions result in more time in prison than some physical victimization, including rape and some murders. For example, in California, a first-degree burglary conviction (e.g., home invasion, California Penal Code 459) can result in two to six years in prison and fines up to $10,000 (HG Legal Resources, n.d.). In the same state, a felony conviction on involuntary manslaughter [California Penal Code 192(b) and 1170(h)] can result in a shorter sentence of two to four years in state prison and fines up to $10,000 (Wallin and Klarich Law Corp., n.d.), depending on what weapons are involved. Federal sentencing guidelines for involuntary manslaughter recommend even shorter sentences, with the average time served between 12 and 16 months in jail or prison.

We should note that public executions were still the norm in the 19th century into the early 20th, as one of the earliest forms of scaring the public into following laws, and as a part of *deterrence* strategies, further discussed later in this chapter. The problem with that reasoning, as given the example of Crumlin Road Gaol in Belfast, Northern Ireland, where hangings were public spectacles, is that they were more entertaining than terrifying, with a celebratory atmosphere[7], instead of a solemn event. And in the United States, as Linders noted (2002, p. 607):

> *During the nineteenth century, the execution in America underwent a major transformation from a large and rowdy public spectacle to a hidden and tightly controlled ritual (Fearnow 1996; Lofland 1976, Madow 1995; Masur 1989) Typically described as uncivilized, irrational, and ignorant, the public execution crowd triggered . . . concerns for nineteenth-century reformers.*

Much of what we see today, particularly in the United States, in the way of reforms targeting punishment, is driven by political philosophies. There is an ongoing push-pull between more conservative politicians who generally embrace a "get tough on crime" approach and more liberal politicians who are advocating for rehabilitation and community-based corrections punishment. We should note that this dichotomy is not necessarily based on political parties, as attitudes towards

---

[7] Though only an urban myth that is perpetuated in Belfast tours, the term "hangover" is believed to have its origins in the misery that celebrants experienced the day after watching a hanging, where they may very well have overindulged in alcoholic beverages. In actuality, according to Associate Professor Daniel Van Olmen at University of Lancaster in the United Kingdom, only in the last century has the term segued from representing any leftover business or unresolved issues and gained popularity as representing the after-effects of drinking too much alcohol (Caldera, 2020).

punishment are on a continuum, not strictly divided by the right and left, though it may appear that way in these more divisive times.

PURPOSES OF PUNISHMENT

There are several schools of thought regarding the purposes of punishment, some of which overlap and are not mutually exclusive. Classically, there are five purposes or goals of punishment that include the consequences of being found guilty in a court of law and result in imprisonment, fines, and/or *community corrections*. Community corrections refer to forms of punishment or rehabilitation other than incarceration that is served in the community. These five purposes are *deterrence*, *incapacitation*, *rehabilitation*, *restitution*, and *retribution*. In this chapter, we are adding to the list one more purpose that has grown in popularity in recent decades, *restorative justice*, that isn't a form of punishment per se, but should be part of the discussion, particularly in consideration of restitution to the victim.

Deterrence

As we will see in our discussion of retribution, *deterrence* is one of the oldest forms of crime control. Before the Age of Enlightenment and even after the Age of Reason when Europe emerged from a period of religious fervor, the ultimate deterrence to committing crime was the concept that by doing so, particularly by violating religious laws, perpetrators might be condemning themselves to punishment or, even worse, to a place of eternal suffering after death. One explanation concerning the failure of religious teachings as a deterrence is that in some religions, one merely needs to admit to the crime and repent before their deity or deities in order to be forgiven and, in turn, become eligible for some form of paradise in the afterlife.

One purpose of punishment is to be so horrific that no one will want to commit the same crime and no one who has already committed a crime and been punished, will ever again want to commit another crime. We should also note, however, that torture per se was not technically always a punishment, but rather a means by which to extract religious conversion, confessions, or information, as in the example of the Spanish Inquisition. However, the threat of torture could also serve to prevent crime or coerce conversion as well.

Similarly to the case of trying to define punishment, there are different perspectives as to what a deterrence theory of punishment is. From philosophy, it is not enough to use punishment for deterrence of other potential offenders. The reason for this is that when harshly punishing one perpetrator, that perpetrator is unacceptably and unfairly being *used* as an example of what not to do (Ellis, 2003). We should also consider that there is a difference between *specific deterrence*, where specific crimes are targeted, and *general deterrence*, where crime in general is being targeted.

One punishment that has historically been thought of as a deterrence to certain forms of homicide is the death penalty, which we will discuss in detail towards the end of this book. The death penalty is one of the oldest, if not *the* oldest, forms of punishment in the world. The drug laws in the 1990s that resulted in lengthy prison sentences for drug offenders is another example of the use of deterrence sentencing. If deterrence theories really worked as intended in all cases, there would be no homicides or drug pushers or addicts. But we know that is not the case by crime statistics.

Other definitions see harsh punishment for certain crimes as a form of *"just deserts"*[8] (also known as the "justice model")—that the offender should suffer and deserves the punishment that they have received. The term was first imagined during the European Enlightenment by the 18th-century social philosopher Immanuel Kant, who proposed the "just deserts" where individuals had free choice as to whether they would offend or not, so suffering by the offender was justified. He was certainly not the first to conceive of the notion of the rational criminal who understands the consequences of their actions, as we saw from the examples of Greek and Roman philosophers.

Kant was not without his critics. The criticisms of Kant's philosophy include that there is a question as to whether wrongdoers really suffer in their punishment (Hill, 1999). We certainly see this in cases of white-collar crime, where individuals who have been convicted and even have served prison time, do not set an example for other potential white-collar criminals—otherwise we would not see the continued rash of crimes committed by some individuals working on Wall Street or in political office, even as their fellow offenders are hauled off to jail or pay large fines for their crimes. As we noted, some theories of punishment overlap with others, and "just deserts" is often coupled with retribution theories, which we will discuss further later in this chapter.

From economics, the failings of deterrence theories arise from human errors in convictions and sentencing. In the economic theory of crime deterrence, it is predicted that if someone is wrongly convicted, it could arguably be as detrimental as if someone has been acquitted who, in truth, is guilty (Rizzoli and Stanca, 2012). In which case, as in the example of a suspected cheating spouse, if someone is being accused of infidelity, when in actuality they have been faithful, enough verbal punishment for supposed misconduct may result in someone thinking, "as long as I am being accused of it already, I may as well commit the crime." And as in economics, where risks are calculated in financial transactions, so does the criminal, who does not get caught, calculate the probability of getting caught the next time they commit a crime. They can simply be emboldened.

---

[8] Oddly, we find that "just desserts" is often spelled "just deserts." Deserts are dry, arid regions with lot of sand and little water; desserts are usually tasty finalés to meals, like ice cream or cake. The original meaning of "just desserts" was that an offender would get what they deserve, like in the case of a child who has misbehaved and has had their dessert withheld from them as punishment. Though the phrase originated with Kant as "just desserts", we will use what is more commonly seen in research and academic literature, "just deserts."

Another issue with deterrence theories is the consideration that who you hang out with may result in you receiving grief if you *don't* commit a crime. Worst yet, if you are part of an organized crime family, your life and that of your loved ones might be threatened. There may be too much peer pressure, in comparison to the cost of committing a crime and getting caught. So, deterrence theories may run counter to what Sutherland believed to be true in his *differential association theory*. For those less familiar with Sutherland from a criminology course, he proposed that people are more likely to commit crimes when they hang out with people who are delinquent. You actually feel like the penalty for not doing what your friends and family are doing criminally is greater than the penalty for getting caught, whether it is actually true or not. An example would be how members of a street gang feel, or those who are required to commit a crime as part of gang initiation.

One study of prisoners found that the degree to which *incarceration* was an effective prevention for *recidivism* (reoffending by individuals who have spent time in jail or prison, or on probation) was dependent on who a prisoner might have as a cellmate. Harris et al. (2018) discovered that incarceration as punishment does not work when a prisoner is housed with a more experienced offender and, more so, dependent on peer groups in prison. As we will read later in this textbook, the newly incarcerated oftentimes will self-segregate to find people who will protect them in prison, primarily into groups based on race. In which case, perhaps more credence should be given to differential association than to punishment being a deterrence to the offender and non-offenders alike.

Merton's *strain theory* additionally pokes holes in deterrence theories, where people who are blocked from certain opportunities (education, jobs) may choose to commit crimes as perhaps the only means by which to achieve certain societal goals (status and wealth) in spite of possible consequences. For example, threat of jail time may not be enough of a deterrence for a young person with the opportunity to sell drugs, as compared to taking a legitimate minimum wage job at a fast food restaurant. Or a parent desperate to feed their family that is living in poverty, will turn to crime in order to keep food on the table. We also have to take into consideration the magical thinking of teenagers who often believe that they are the ones who *won't* be caught.

Finally, we should consider that incarceration for the mentally ill, of which there are large numbers in jails and prison, will not serve as a deterrence. Violent offenders who need treatment and medication to control their behavior will not necessarily be deterred from reoffending by the fear of another prison sentence. We will further explore this in our chapter on prisoners' health (Chapter 11).

Incapacitation

Incapacitation likewise has so many meanings. From something more benign like public shunning to the finality of a death penalty, for eons, societies have tried to find ways to stop criminals from being a danger to others, beyond punishing them.

In most cases, in modern times, incapacitation translates to locking an individual up in jail (pretrial) or prison, after being convicted. Or it might mean court ordered home confinement. Even within the prison system, there are ways to further incapacitate the criminal, when they are put in solitary confinement either for disciplinary reasons, because they dangerously do not get along with other prisoners, or because they are a threat to prison personnel. The threat of further incapacitation while incarcerated is in itself considered a deterrence to further crime.

In theory, we would expect that with higher incarceration rates, we would find a subsequent drop in crime. However, the data are mixed. Assuredly, as we saw a rise in incarcerations in the United States, the overall crime rates dropped. But this has not been consistent across age groups. In a study of juvenile delinquents in California, higher rates of juvenile incarceration did not result in a reduction of juvenile offending (Stahkopf et al., 2010).

As we will note in our discussions of white-collar offending, not all punishments are equal. White-collar criminals are far less likely to find themselves incapacitated by a prison sentence and are far more likely to find themselves at the receiving end of a civil lawsuit. They are oftentimes also in a better financial position to post bail, so they often do not have await trial in jail. The punishment in the form of a civil judgement is only as good a deterrence as the amount of the fine and the means that the offender has to pay it.

One concern with incapacitation by imprisonment is that it results in difficulty, in most cases, for the offender to be reintegrated into society once they are released. This is due to a number of factors, the least of which is that ex-convicts generally have a difficult time finding employment after prison. It is one of the concerns that those interested in social justice issues target in their efforts to bring about criminal justice reform.

Rehabilitation

Rehabilitation within sentencing and corrections is exactly what it means. The purposes of rehabilitation for all convicted individuals, whether they are incarcerated or not, is to give them the foundation by which they can successfully reenter or remain in society without reoffending. The idea is that the problems that got them in trouble in the first place are addressed, in hopes that it will help them from living a life that is nothing more than a revolving door to the criminal justice system, as can be the case for habitual offenders.

There are a number of types of rehabilitation that we will explore in more detail later in this book. For now, you are probably already aware of the typical types of rehabilitation that are available to people in and out of the criminal justice system, the most commonly known to address problems of drug and/or alcohol dependency. For prisoners, there is an additional list of rehabilitation programs that are available, depending on the location of the jail or prison. As we will see later in the book, some jurisdictions have a wealth of rehabilitation opportunities. Others do not have nearly enough services for prisoners.

The primary types of rehabilitation programs available to prisoners include:

- Drug and/or alcohol treatment;
- Criminal rehabilitation; and
- Education and job training.

Other rehabilitation programs are faith-based. However, as religious belief is so personal and, in many respects, immeasurable, it is difficult to determine if faith-based rehabilitation works, except to follow recidivism rates. It is not unusual for a prisoner up before a parole board to claim that they have been rehabilitated through their newly-found or rediscovered religious faith. How much of this is sincere and how much of this is being said for the parole board's benefit is hard to say. In recent decades, there has been a shift to treating religious treatment programs as privileges rather than as part of rehabilitation. There have also been concerned of the constitutionality of religious programs, if a condition of drug and alcohol treatment, education, and counseling is dependent on the prisoners agreeing to include Bible studies as part of treatment (Odle, 2007). The argument, according to Odle (2007), is whether in federal facilities or state-funded facilities, this violates separation of church and state, as stated in the Establishment Clause of in the Bill of Rights.

Yet other programs target specific behavioral problems, particularly those of violent offenders. If we consider that much of the negative behavior we see in criminals is a product of their upbringing and exposure to more violent peers, households, or communities, it is the goal of anger management programs to resocialize them into finding alternative, positive ways to cope with anger. Study after study indicate that the inability of some individuals to control their emotions will often, inevitably lead to domestic violence and other forms of assault (Immarigeon, 2016). Resocialization and education may include behavioral modification therapy or mindfulness training and mediation. Some prisons are even incorporating yoga practice.

The reality is that recidivism rates are discouraging. Some correctional facilities report that 65 percent or more of their former inmates will reoffend within three years of release. Other statistics are grimmer, with the U.S. Department of Justice reporting that as many as 83 percent of state prisoners will be arrested at least once within nine years of release (Alper et al., 2018). This mirrors statistics on some types of offenses, where the rearrest rates are discouraging within nine years post-release.

Another harsh reality is that rehabilitation programs often do not work, whether it is someone who is outside of prison or is incarcerated. This is more often the case for the individual who does not voluntarily choose to change their life, which can be the case with court-ordered rehabilitation as in the example of drug addiction treatment programs. Rehabilitation programs that do work to reduce recidivism rates are those that target specific categories of offenders, as in the example of how a GED earned in prison goes a long way in former prisoners being hired in better jobs with higher wages than if the convicted remains a high school dropout (Petersilia, 2011).

Restitution

Restitution, in most cases, means that the criminal has been court-ordered to financially pay for their crimes. Which begs the question: Should payment be made to the victim or to the state? The problem lies in whether or not paying a debt to society with money rather than prison time after offending is punishment. In other words, is it enough to pay one's way out of trouble? If we examine the concept of *pure restitution*, it can only be considered *pure* if (1) it does not carry punitive intent and (2) it replaces all other forms of punishment, including incarceration (Gallagher, 2016; Dagger, 1991).

You may recall that if some purposes of punishment overlap, in theory the offender should feel better after paying their victims, and that in itself should serve as a form of rehabilitation or therapy. The reality is that offenders view fines as severe punishment as they generally have few legitimate sources of income (Gladfelter, et al., 2018). If you think about it, it would be tragically ironic if, to avoid rearrest, the offender has to commit yet more crimes in order to pay their court-ordered fines. Or use ill begotten gains to pay for their fines that they have managed to hide from investigators. And of course, as we have mentioned, court-ordered fines are more painful to some than others, as in the case of a wealthy individual having more than enough means to pay a fine. However, that does not mean that the wealthy necessarily escape civil court judgements to pay substantial restitution to victims in some cases.

Restitution to either victims or to the state is often problematic. In both criminal cases and civil cases, the defendant or respondent has the option to appeal the judgement of a fine, sometimes dragging out payment for years. In most cases, there are low rates of payments of fines because the offenders are not able to pay (Gladfelter, et al., 2018).

If you consider the case of child or spousal support, it is not necessarily in the best interest of the child to take a "deadbeat" parent to court. Technically, someone who fails to pay their child or spousal support during or after a divorce is in contempt of court and can conceivably find themselves in jail. Which in itself makes little sense, as if they are not able to work or worse yet, lose their job as a result of their arrest, there is greater likelihood that support in arrears will never be paid, much less future owed payments. Or more troubling, that individual can go back to the family courts and appeal the support judgement with the argument that they no longer have a means by which to pay support if they have lost their jobs. In which case, child or spousal support may ultimately be greatly reduced as a result.

There have been a number of debates over the years as to how much monetary restitution can replace more traditional types of punishment, like incarceration. For the very wealthy, as in the case of corporations that receive fines for criminal or unethical behaviors, the fine may be more an annoyance rather than a punishment, much less restitution. For the victims, as in the case of class action lawsuits, they may only get a small fraction of what is really owed them, when the financial judgement is shared among many victims, much less with civil attorneys.

Restorative Justice

Philosophies and justifications for punishment tend to swing between more liberal and more conservative stances. Particularly in election years, politicians will frame the dichotomy as differences between being "soft on crime" and being "tough on crime." Just as we saw a steep rise in incarcerations in the 1990s, push for *restorative justice* came to the forefront in the purposes of punishment, largely due to political pressures.

The philosophy behind *restorative justice* is that the convicted has an opportunity to make a public apology to the victim(s) and the community for their transgression. In other words, the criminal is allowed to express their remorse directly to the victim and to other individuals that might have been indirectly affected by the crime. This is similar to peer mediation programs in high schools. An example of what restorative justice looks like in the school setting, as compared to zero-tolerance policies can be found in Figure 1.1. The benefit of

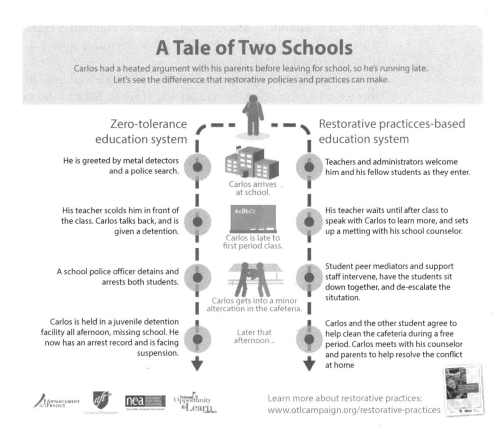

FIGURE 1.1 **Zero-Tolerance vs. Restorative Justice in Schools**
(*Source:* AdvoZ Mediation and Restorative Practices, 2020, retrieved from https://advoz.org/news/a-tale-of-two-schools/)

restorative justice programs is that coupled with community service and probation, the offender, whether adult or juvenile, can remain in their community and with their families.

There are several cornerstones to restorative justice, depending on who you speak to. According to Michigan Virtual, a nonprofit organization that advises on K-12 online instruction, the foundations of restorative justice include respect, accountability, healing, and empathy (AZYEP, 2020). The last feature, empathy, is crucial in the process of restorative justice. It means that the criminal should express (and truly feel) empathy for their victim and that the victim should have an opportunity to forgive the criminal, both for their own sake and for the mental well-being of the offender. So empathy is viewed as a two-way street between offender and victim.

Another cornerstone of restorative justice examines the differences between the viewpoints of traditional criminal justice and that of restorative justice. (See Table 1.1) In Zehr's comparative model (2015, in Figure 1.3), it spells out the differences between the focus on offenders and the focus on victims.

Yet another model sees two triads of relationships, that between the offender, victim, and community, and that between accountability, community safety, and competency development for the offender, as seen in Figure 1.2, where the second triad is embedded within the first.

Shaming and reintegration, which we will talk about later in the textbook, is to a large extent a form of restorative justice. If we go back to the example of a parent disciplining the child, in healthy parenting, the message to the child should be, "I don't approve of or like your behavior, but I still love you." The individual is reprimanded, sometimes publicly, but then is still reintegrated back into the community, rather than sending them away for punishment. This of course, is more likely to happen with less serious crimes and in juvenile cases.

TABLE 1.1. Comparisons between Traditional Criminal Justice and Restorative Justice Viewpoints

Criminal Justice	Restorative Justice
Crime is a violation of the law and the state.	Crime is a violation of people and relationships.
Violations create guilt.	Violations create obligations.
Justice requires the state to determine blame (guilt) and impose pain (punishment).	Justice involves victims, offenders, and community members in an effort to put things rights.
Central focus: Offenders getting what they deserve.	Central focus: Victims' needs and offender responsibility for repairing harm.

Source: Zehr, 2015, p. 21.

FIGURE 1.2 | **Restorative Justice Triads**
(*Source:* University of Wisconsin-Madison Law School, n.d., retrieved from https://law.wisc.edu/fjr/rjp/justice.html)

Other forms of restorative justice include programs by which inmates or released convicts give back to their community, by speaking to the public about the errors of their ways. Some of these programs are extreme, as in the case of Scared Straight, where inmates are expected to frighten children who are delinquent and are therefore at risk of future incarceration themselves, whether through the juvenile or adult systems. Others, as in the case of prisons that allow school visits, prisoners often talk directly and openly to high school and college students about the prison experience and what landed them there in the first place.

One potential backlash of restorative justice programs is that the offender is now marked as a "criminal"[9] to possibly a wider audience within their community. This is much like the character of Hester Prynne in Nathaniel Hawthorne's *The Scarlet Letter*, where she was forced to wear a red letter "A" on her clothing to inform the community of her sin of adultery. Though we do not ordinarily use outward symbols of criminality, like Hawthorne's Hester, there are some who believe that public shaming is beneficial.

However, in this age of social media, a photo or video of the offender being shamed in public going viral online may result in anger and not regret for criminal behavior, as well as marking the individual for public ridicule. For example, Joshua Hill was ordered to spend three days in jail, plus carry a sign four hours a day, for seven days, in front of the courthouse (Earl, 2017). The sign read, "this is the face of domestic abuse, ordered by the North Carolina judge in the case (Earl, 2017). Where the problem lies in shaming is that it does not work without the component of

---

[9] As we have noted in the preface of this book, even the labels "incarcerated," "inmates," and "convicts" are viewed by some, particularly those in social justice circles, as being stigmatizing in themselves.

reintegration. In the case of Hill, would he have benefited more from a meeting with his victim in a closed door hearing with mediation, along with court-ordered anger management training?

Another recent criticism of restorative justice in its current form is that there may be gender differences in treatment of the offender. Females who offend often are treated harsher because as the so-called "fair sex", they are expected to know better than to commit crimes. There have been recent calls for more gender-neutral interventions, instead of additionally shaming and stigmatizing women who offend, as opposed to males who might be given a pass for their behavior, because "boys will be boys" (Hodgson, 2019). Sometimes the stereotype of female offenders is the "woman in trouble", in which case instead of being more harshly treated in the restorative justice process, they may be more leniently forgiven, as it is viewed as chivalry and may not fully require them to acknowledge culpability (Failinger, 2006).

Retribution

The concept of *retribution*, or revenge-based punishment whereby the punishment should be similar to the crime committed, is perhaps as close to biblical, *vengeful* purposes of punishment as we get in the five classical purposes of punishment. It is the earliest motivation for punishing criminals. From Deuteronomy 19:21, in the *Old Testament* (King James version of the *Bible*):

> *And thine eye shall not pity; but life shall go for life, eye for eye, tooth for tooth, hand for hand, foot for foot.*

We should note that this contradicts Romans 12:19, whereby, in religious terms, *vengeance* is supposed to be given out to the offender only by God, not by mere mortals. Keep in mind that since the beginning of recorded history, alleged offenders often where not tried in a court of law, but rather in the court of public opinion. Many times, it was an angry mob that executed the punishment before the authorities even were aware that a crime had been committed.

In biblical times, these punishments were taken quite literally, with maiming or death given as punishment for a wide variety of offenses. To a large extent, these extreme punishments, sometimes for fairly minor infractions by today's standards (e.g., infidelity), were intended to serve as deterrents and to maintain civil order. In classical retributivist theory, punishment is justified because the accused knew better than to commit a crime (Pereboom, 2020). Again, this falls within the rational choice theory framework. Whereas in biblical times, crimes were viewed as being committed against God, since the Enlightenment, the government that made the laws or society in general was more likely to be viewed as the victimized entity.

As we have already noted, attitudes towards the purposes of punishment swing like a pendulum between liberal views focused on rehabilitation and more conservative views focused on retribution. Lacey and Pickard (2015) observed that more recently both in the United Kingdom and in the United States, what should be considered appropriate punishment for particular crimes is blurred by public debate and political discourse, plus in sentencing practices.

There are a number of criticisms of the retribution purposes of punishment. This is largely due to the fact that retribution often comes out of emotional responses to the crime, the most common being anger. As Pereboom proposes (2020, p 89).

> *First, retributivist sentiments may be grounded in vengeful desires, whereupon retribution would have little more plausibility than vengeance as a morally sound as a morally sound policy for action. . . . Second, supposing that the requisite capacity for control is in place, and that basic desert [sic] could be secured as good or right, we can ask whether the state has the right to invoke it in justifying punishment.*

In other words, if the punishment is deserved, is it the right of the state to dole out the punishment? When we discuss the death penalty in this book, we will further explore how this most extreme of punishment is viewed as sanctioned murder by some people and by human rights watch groups.

INTERNATIONAL PERSPECTIVES

Most of us live in a bit of a bubble when it comes to understanding prisoners and their experiences, save those who work in criminal justice professions. The reality is that no society escapes crime and criminals, "no society primitive or modern, no country whether under developed or developing or developed is free from [their] clutches." (Priyadarshi, 2014, p 1). Even so, the general public is generally unaware of prison conditions in the United States, much less, elsewhere in the world (Roberts and Hough, 2005).

In the same way our perceptions of jails and prison in the United States is shaped by popular culture, what we know of foreign punishment and imprisonment is viewed through the sensationalized lens in movies or in the sterilized lens of news. We do not always get good information from foreign countries on their crime statistics, much less how they treat prisoners.

In addition to uncovering the realities of prison life around the world, as compared to portrayals in movies and television, as the world has become more globalized, so have criminal justice systems. Poverty is not specific to any one country, and as there is a high correlation between it and incarceration, it is important to examine corrections in global context. As Garland (2001; Weegels, 2020) noted, crime control is part and parcel with an increasingly globalized culture of control, with the culprit being the failure to address social problems, including poverty.

It is important while reading accounts of prison experiences elsewhere in the world to do so as objectively as possible. After all, there are countries in the world who condemn the alarming rise in incarceration in western societies (Tata, 2016). While we might want to pass judgement on punishment elsewhere on legal, moral, or human rights grounds, what is important to do is to divide justice practices in the world between those that are similar to the United States and those that are different, whether we agree with them or not. Hence the inclusion of international perspectives in each chapter of this book. We will not go into detail of the structures of criminal justice systems around the world, save the corrections arm of those systems.

SOCIAL JUSTICE AND THE CHALLENGES WITH PUNISHMENT

Social justice causes and movements are not new. They were the core of the Civil Rights movement in the 1960s and 1970s. With a rash of abuses of suspects and the incarcerated by some law enforcement and corrections staff coming to light in recent decades, there is a renewed interest in criminal justice reform, including in corrections.

The core goals of social justice movements is to bring fair treatment to all people, regardless of sex, gender identification, race, ethnicity, religion, country of origin, or social economic status. Social justice movements have more recently been gaining recognition after the death of George Floyd he was while in police custody in 2020, in Minneapolis, Minnesota, and the emergence of the Black Lives Matter movement. Social justice, by definition, is the effort to provide not only equal protection under the law when encountering law enforcement personnel, but equal treatment in the courts as well. This can mean the ability to get adequate representation in court, as well as fair punishment, if convicted, that does not take into consideration the social status or wealth of the convicted. The reality is that the defense that a suspected criminal has during their trial is only as good as their legal counsel and their means to hire them.

The difficulty in spreading social justice around in a pluralistic society like the United States is that the individual states have considerable sovereignty in creating laws and punishment that might be more harmful to some groups than another. For example, in southern states, the discriminatory laws created in the Jim Crow Era particularly against Blacks. have been abolished. However, remnants of the era can still be seen in the disproportionate number of people of color who are incarcerated today, as well as discrimination and prejudices that remain in the south. Discrimination may be legislated away, but the prejudices are much more difficult to erase.

One push within the social justice movement and prison reform is addressing the public health issues of the incarcerated. We will be discussing extensively throughout this book about the petri dish that prisons are for disease transmission. In addressing health crises in prisons, it not only tackles the health inequities of the incarcerated, but also helps slow or stop transmission of diseases like HIV/AIDS, tuberculosis, hepatitis C, and others from reaching the community after prisoners are released. Programs like the Prison to Patient (P2P) program in Louisiana prisons are born out of the community pushing for health care reform in prisons (Wennerstrom et al., 2020).

The challenge is to get public opinion on the side of not expecting that punishment should include a large dose of deprivation, including withholding adequate health care. At least in the United States, where health insurance costs have skyrocketing in recent decades, it is somewhat understandable why there might be public resistance to supporting the nearly free health care that prisoners are allowed.

It is still early days in the social justice movement and we have yet to see what prison reforms will be pursued in the coming years, not to mention criminal justice reforms over all.

SUMMARY

The purposes and types of punishment have had a long history, one that more than likely predates written history. Punishment has moved from being gruesome and a public spectacle, to a process often carried out behind prison walls. And as we have noted, philosophies of punishment are contingent on public opinion and political will of legislatures, both on the state and federal levels in the United States.

In contemporary times, there have been five primary purposes of punishment: deterrence, incapacitation, rehabilitation, restitution, and retribution. Some of these are remnants of the past, as in the case of retribution still in use today in some parts of the world, including in the United States, and biblically inspired punishment (e.g., "and eye for an eye"). Some types of punishment today are meant to stop the offender (and others) from reoffending. Other types are meant to take the offender out of society and lock them away where they cannot further harm the community. Yet others are focused on turning around the lives of the incarcerated with programs targeting rehabilitation, including for substance abuse issues, anger management, education, or job training.

In the mix of contemporary purposes of punishment, we are also taking into consideration more recent pushes for criminal justice reform through social justice movements such as the Black Lives Matter movement. Some of the push for prison reform revolves around public health issues, particularly critical during the COVID-19 pandemic. Yet other pushes are intended to help address the problems of disproportionate numbers of people of color who are incarcerated today, not only in the United States, but elsewhere in the world.

STORIES FROM BEHIND BARS

Punishment in Military and POW Camps

Though we will not be spending considerable time discussing military prisons in this book, they are of interest in discussions of corrections, as the incarcerated are there either for misbehaving while serving in the military or because they were caught behind enemy lines and are being held as *prisoners of war (POWs)*. The systems of confinement and punishment are generally under the control of the military, with some distinct differences from penal institutions for civilians. Some of the most horrific stories of punishment come from the Civil War era (1861-1865), World Wars I and II (1914-1918 and 1939-1945, respectively), and more recently from the Vietnam War era (1955-1975).

Punishment in POW camps has a different purpose than in civilian prisons. Those who are captured by the enemy that they are fighting are subjected to punishment with the purposes of degrading, demoralizing, and often, obtaining information of military or political strategies. Interrogations can range from psychological to physical torture, including the controversial use of waterboarding[10] during the question of "enemy combatants" at Guantanamo Bay Camp.

Andersonville Prison. (*Source:* https://www.nps.gov/ande/learn/historyculture/camp_sumter_history.htm)

During the Civil War era and up until the discovery and use of penicillin in the early 20th century, soldiers, including POWs, would be more likely to die from infection and disease than from actual battle wounds, as in the example of what happened to inmates at Camp Sumter. More well known as Andersonville, Camp

---

[10] Waterboarding involves torture by placing the person being interrogated on their backs with their heads lowered, and pouring water on a towel or cloth placed over their faces, including mouth and nose, giving them the sensation of drowning.

Sumter was a Confederate military camp in Georgia that eventually was used to relocate Union soldiers who had been captured, as the battle lines crept further and further south in 1864 (NPS, n.d.).

As the Confederate side faced loss after loss on the battlefield, conditions in Andersonville deteriorated, with no clear lines of authority (Richardson, 2018). Captives were used as prison labor, though they refused to work as clerks for the Confederate officials (Richardson, 2018). The Union soldiers held there suffered more from neglect than anything else, with scarcity of food, crowded living conditions, and being forced to sleep in tents. The stream that ran down the center of the encampment served as a communal toilet, resulting is a cesspool that caused diseases associated with unsanitary conditions to run through the camp population, including dysentery.

Andersonville was not without some code of conduct expected of the prisoners. In July 1864, six Union POWs were found guilty of robbing or killing their fellow captives, resulting in their hanging as their sentence for their crimes (Jacobs, ed., 2020). In a personal account of how he survived Andersonville, First Sergeant Elisha Davis Conklin of the Union army offered his memories in an autobiography of how the POWs kept their spirits up:

> *We would sit and talk and wonder if we would live to get home and tell our folks how lousy we were in here if they would believe us. Then on Sundays we would talk about what a dinner they would be having and us foolish fellows to have enlisted. So that is the way we would pass the time.* (Jacobs, ed., 2020, retrieved from http://eds.b.ebscohost.com.wne.idm.oclc.org/eds/pdfviewer/pdfviewer ?vid=2&sid=001dd841-a2ad-4795-85e4-826320d27a10%40sessionmgr102)

We cannot underestimate the importance of food, particularly when you are being fed either insufficient calories, the same monotonous meals, and/or food of questionable quality. Or when denying food is used as one more punishment. This is true whether we are discussing POWs during the Civil War era or individuals incarcerated today. As Gustavo Alvarez says about food in his more recent prison experience,

> *Eating a meal, no matter how simple, is the essential element of liberty. A moment to savor, be sated, and get refueled. The first thing released inmates look forward to is a meal. Whether it's from Mickey D [McDonalds] or from momma, it means you've survived, you're still human.* (Collins and Alvarez, 2015, p 112)

Since the end of World War II, as the world became more acutely aware of the terrible treatment of prisoners of war from media stories and books that were published, there was a concerted effort to try and come to some world understanding of how to humanely treat enemy combatants held in captivity. In 1949, a treaty was signed establishing the *Geneva Convention relative to the Treatment of Prisoners of*

War (75 U.N.T.S.). In summary, some of the following provisions were included in the treaty (University of Minnesota, Human Rights Library, n.d.):

- People who have taken no active part in fighting, including military personnel who have surrendered their weapons, shall be treated humanely, caring for sickness or wounds.
- Murder of all kinds, mutilation, cruel treatment of POWs is prohibited.
- Humiliating and degrading treatment is prohibited.
- Prisoners of war cannot renounce (give up) any of the provisions for humane treatment spelled out in the Geneva Convention.
- Any treatment that harms, maims, or kills the prisoner of war is prohibited.
- Prisoners of war are not to be subjected to medical or scientific experiments of any kind.
- Any measure of reprisal against a prisoner of war is prohibited.

Though the Geneva Convention has been widely accepted since World War II, it was largely ignored by the North Vietnamese Army in their capture of American prisoners of war. The late Senator John McCain's story of capture and treatment in a Vietcong military prison is similar to those of the 765 other known American POWs (U.S. National Park Services, n.d.). Other accounts put the number at 735, 73 of whom died in captivity (Gamel, 2019).

In October 1967, McCain, a United States Naval aviator, was shot down while on a bombing mission and forced to parachute into the middle of a lake, breaking a leg and both arms in the process (*ABC News*, 2018). Instead of receiving humane treatment, an angry Vietcong mob descended upon him—he was ultimately taken to the infamous Hòa Lò Prison ("Hanoi Hilton"), where he was held for five years before being released (McCain, 2008).

At first, McCain was treated somewhat better than expected and taken to a hospital to treat his injuries, on the basis of his father's reputation, who served in the Navy as an admiral (*ABC News,* 2018). McCain instead told his captors that it wasn't fair to the other POWs, after which McCain was held in solitary confinement, during which he was a victim of repeated beatings and hung by his arms in an excruciatingly painful torture, called the "Vietnamese Rope Trick" (Gamel, 2019; *ABC News, 2018*). This last form of torture is described in the military publication, *Stars and Stripes* (Gamel, 2019, retrieved from https://www.stripes.com/news/special-reports/vietnam-stories/1969/the-torture-stopped-1969-brought-temporary-changes-to-infamous-hanoi-hilton-1.593300):

The method involved binding a prisoner's hands behind his back with manacles to rotate them upward until his shoulders and elbows popped out of their sockets. 'The rope trick hurts like crazy and will get you to say anything,' said Robert Wideman, a Navy pilot who was captured after his jet went down in May 1967.

According to McCain, other prisoners were treated far worse. One fellow American POW, Humbert "Rocky" Versace, a Medal of Honor recipient, was killed by his captors during a torture session when he would not give up or break down and while he was defiantly singing *God Bless America* (Wood, 2018). Once McCain was released from solitary confinement, it was fellow prisoners who nursed him back to health (*ABC News*). American prisoners of war were subjected to years of being locked up, subject to interrogation and regular beatings, except during a brief reprieve of abuses after the death of Ho Chi Minh, the Communist leader of North Vietnam (Gamel, 2019).

After McCain was released from the North Vietnam POW prison, he returned to the states, where he served as a senator from the state of Arizona, from 1987 to the time of his death in August 2018. He never fully recovered from the injuries he sustained during the crash of his plane or the torture he endured at the hands of his captors.

There are a number of military personnel lost during the Vietnam War that are unaccounted for to this day and are listed as missing in action. Every once in a while, skeletal remains are found in Vietnam that are identified as one of these missing men.[11] The "Hanoi Hilton" is now a museum, as tourism to Southeast Asia opened up after the end of the Vietnam War.

More recent controversies surround the high security Guantanamo Bay Detention Camp (also referred to as GTMO or GITMO), a military prison attached to the U.S. Naval base on the island of Cuba. Most of these are centered on possible human rights violations, as well as prohibited treatment of prisoners as listed in the *Geneva Convention*. After the events of September 11, 2001, a number of prisoners identified as "enemy combatants" of foreign nationalities and suspected of terrorism have been held there.

The purpose of holding them in GITMO, instead of a mainland prison, was to avoid U.S. court jurisdiction and to deny them access to U.S. courts, including due process rights (Human Rights Watch, 2018). According to the Human Rights Watch (2018, retrieved from https://www.hrw.org/news/2018/06/27/qa-guantanamo-bay-us-detentions-and-trump-administration),

> As part of the detainees' interrogation, the U.S. military subjected them to torture and other ill-treatment, including putting them in painful stress positions and in extended solitary confinement; threatening them with torture, death, and military dogs; depriving them of sleep; and exposing them for prolonged periods to extreme heat, cold, and noise.

As recently as 2021, President Joe Biden ordered a review of conditions of GITMO, with a goal of closing the camp before he leaves office, with a yet to be determined destination for the remaining 40 detainees (Spetalnick et al., 2021).

---

[11] During the Vietnam War, women were not allowed to hold combat positions in the military.

SOURCES

ABC News (2018) Interview: John McCain on the horrors he endured as a POW. Video. Aug. 26. Retrieved from https://www.youtube.com/watch?v=RYxMRiftYuY.

Collins, C. and G. Alvarez (2015) *Prison Ramen: Recipes and Stories from Behind Doors.* New York: Workman Publishing.

Gamel, K. (2019) 'The torture stopped': 1969 brought temporary changes to infamous Hanoi Hilton. Vietnam at 50. *Stars and Stripes.* Aug, 15. Retrieved from https://www.stripes.com/news/special-reports/vietnam-stories/1969/the-torture-stopped-1969-brought-temporary-changes-to-infamous-hanoi-hilton-1.593300.

Human Rights Watch (2018) Q&A: Guantanamo Bay, U.S. Detentions and the Trump Administration. June 27. Retrieved from https://www.hrw.org/news/2018/06/27/qa-guantanamo-bay-us-detentions-and-trump-administration.

Jacobs, M., ed. (2020) Surviving Andersonville: A Civil War soldier's story. *America's Civil War.* Nov., Vol. 33, Iss. 5:40-49.

McCain, J. (2008) John McCain, prisoner of war: A first person account. *U.S. News and World Report.* Jan. 28. Retrieved from https://www.usnews.com/news/articles/2008/01/28/john-mccain-prisoner-of-war-a-first-person-account.

Richardson, S. (2018) Interview with Angela Zombek: North and South behind bars. HistoryNet. Dec. Retrieved from https://www.historynet.com/interview-angela-zombek.htm.

Spetalnick, M., T. Hunnicutt, and P. Steward (2021) Biden launches review of Guantanamo prison, aims to close it before leaving office. Reuters. Feb 12. Retrieved from https://www.reuters.com/article/us-usa-biden-guantanamo-exclusive/biden-launches-review-of-guantanamo-prison-aims-to-close-it-before-leaving-office-idUSKBN2AC1Q4.

United States National Park Services (NPS) (n.d.) History of Andersonville Prison. Retrieved from https://www.nps.gov/ande/learn/historyculture/camp_sumter_history.htm.

University of Minnesota, Human Rights Library (n.d.) Geneva Convention relative to the Treatment of Prisoners of War, 75 U.N.T.S. 135, entered into force Oct. 21, 1950. Retrieved from http://hrlibrary.umn.edu/instree/y3gctpw.htm.

Wood, M. (2018) This Medal of Honor recipient was executed for singing "God Bless America. Warfare History, *History Collection.* Mar. 26. Retrieved from https://historycollection.com/this-medal-of-honor-recipient-was-executed-for-singing-god-bless-america/2/.

INTERNATIONAL PERSPECTIVES ON PUNISHMENT AND CORRECTIONS: CANADA

Canada is a country made up of number of provinces and territories, including French-speaking Quebec. The correctional system in Canada is run by the Correctional Services of Canada (CSC). On average, there are approximately 38,000 adult prisoners and 700 under the age of 18 in youth custody (World Prison Brief, 2019 statistics, n.d.), in a country with a population of nearly 38 million people by United Nations' estimates (The World Bank, 2020). With a population one-tenth that of the United States, incarceration rates are much lower in Canada.

One side of the coin of prison expansion is that by building new prisons, communities where they are built gain jobs. Canada has not escaped this politically conservative approach to incarceration historically seen in America, with politicians making the claim that money spent on prison expansion results in economic gains for these towns, with research showing otherwise (McElligott, 2017). In a

Canadian study of prison construction (McElligott, 2017), related improvements to prisons and the building of new ones can harm a local community by overloading sewers and taxing road conditions, and the increase in local commerce is minimal to offset the burdens to a town.

Because there is admittedly a prevalence of I.V. drug use among Canadian prisoners, adding to the transmission of HIV/AIDS as well as other infectious diseases, the Canadian government has taken measure to improve prisoners' health. The concern is also the transmission of disease once Canadian detainees or prisoners are released into the community. In 2018, the CSC rolled out the Prison Needle Exchange Program in federal institutions, after pressure from activists (CSC, 2019; Webster, 2018).

Likewise, prison-made tattoos, though technically prohibited, at least in U.S. jails and prisons, is another means by which diseases can be transmitted if not done in as sterile conditions as possible. Of which, jails and prisons are notoriously lacking. Canada, in accordance with U.N. recommendations worldwide, launched a program in which illicit tattooing materials would be seized and allowing for safer tattooing services made available in prison (Tran et al., 2018). By doing so, the prisons are also providing training in a skill that can be used in employment outside of prison (Tran et al., 2018).

An additional area of prison reform, Canada leads countries in humane treatment of women in prisons. With women being the fastest growing prison population, as well as the fact most women in prison are mothers, more prisons in Canada have Mother-Child Programs, in which children may live with their mothers up to the age of seven (Paynter and Snelgrove-Clarke, 2017). In comparison, most similar programs require mothers in U.S. prisons to relinquish care of their children by age one.

Many would attribute the prison reform for women to the high profile death of a baby, at 13 months of age, that had been born to 26-year-old Julie Biolotta in 2012, on the floor of an Ottawa solitary confinement cell (*Postmedia News*, 2015). His death was blamed on the respiratory difficulties he suffered from, that allegedly were due to the crude prison conditions for pregnant and post-partum mothers and their infants (*Postmedia News*, 2015). Knowing the health benefits of breastfeeding of infants, Canadian prisons with the Mother-Child Programs are now offering breastfeeding support to incarcerated post-partum mothers.

SOURCES

Correctional Services of Canada (CSC) (2019) The Prison Needle Exchange Programme. Aug. 28. Retrieved from https://www.csc-scc.gc.ca/health/002006-2004-en.shtml.

McElligott, G. (2017) Investment in prisons: Prison expansion and community development in Canada. *Studies in Social Justice*. Vol. 11, Iss, 1:86-112.

Paynter, M.J. and E. Snelgrove-Clarke (2017) Breastfeeding support for criminalized women in Canada. *Journal of Human Lactation*. Vol. 33, No. 4:672-676.

Postmedia News (2015) Baby born in Ottawa jail cell dies one year after birth, sparking investigation into 'sudden death'. *National Post.* Jan, 25. Retrieved from https://nationalpost.com/news/canada/baby-born-in-ottawa-jail-cell-dies-one-year-after-birth-sparking-investigation-into-sudden-death.

Tran, T. T., C. Dubost, S. Baggio, L. Gétaz, and Hans Wolff (2018) Safer tattooing interventions in prisons: A systematic review and call to action. *BMC Public Health.* Vol, 18:015.

Webster, P. (2018) Canada reveals needle exchange programme in prisons. *The Lancet.* May 26. Retrieved from https://www.thelancet.com/journals/lancet/article/PIIS0140-6736(18)31170-X/fulltext.

World Bank, The (2020) Population total – Canada. *DataBank.* Retrieved from https://data.worldbank.org/indicator/SP.POP.TOTL?locations=CA.

World Prison Brief (n.d.) World Prison Brief data, Canada. Institute for Crime and Justice Policy Research, University of London, Birkbeck. Retrieved from https://www.prisonstudies.org/country/canada.

GLOSSARY

Banishment   Punishment by which the guilty party is ordered to leave the community, generally to never return again, as a form of social death.

Community corrections   Punishment or rehabilitation other than incarceration that is served in the community. Examples would be community service, probation, or court-ordered drug treatment.

Deterrence   In context of punishment, the philosophy that the punishment should be so painful that the guilty will not commit the crime again, nor will others in the community be tempted to commit a similar crime.

Differential association theory   Sutherland's theory suggesting that people become criminals when they hang out with people who exhibit deviant behavior and who do not support or reward good behavior in their friends and companions. These can include family members who have criminal histories.

General deterrence   Punishment or barriers to prevent crimes in general and not any one specific crime.

Geneva Convention   Signed in 1950, a unilateral agreement brought by the United Nations to require that prisoners of war be treated with dignity and not subjected to torture or abuses.

Incapacitation   Punishment that is intended to temporarily stop further criminal behavior, including imprisonment or in extreme cases of violent crimes, the death penalty.

Incarceration   Punishment that includes time in jail or prison as part of sentencing.

"Just deserts"   Kant's philosophy of punishment that criminals get what they deserve, even with harsh sentencing.

Norm   The expected, lawful behaviors that society requires of its members, generally agreed upon by most people in the population.

Penologists   Trained professionals who work in prisons to study the efficiency and effectiveness of incarceration and programs.

Penology   The study of the purposes and types of punishment.

Pity booking   The arrest and detaining of unhoused individuals in jail on extremely cold or hot days/nights. These bookings usually include charges of vagrancy that are often dropped once weather conditions outside improve for the unhoused.

Prisoners of war (POWs)   Individuals who are captured by an enemy in the course of war; POWs can include both civilian and military captives.

Pure restitution   Philosophy of punishment whereby the guilty party is only responsible for restitution to the victims and generally not excessively fined or required to serve time in prison.

Recidivism   Reoffending by individuals who have spent time in prison or on probation.

Rehabilitation   Programs that are directed at the behaviors that land people in prison in the first place.

Restitution   Usually fines paid to victims in civil proceedings. Can also include fines to the state or federal government as a means by which to monetarily pay for a crime.

Restorative justice   Philosophy of punishment by which the act of facing one's crime victim and asking for forgiveness will be beneficial for both the criminal and the victim.

Retribution   Revenged-based punishment whereby the punishment should be similar to the crime committed. Example: An eye for an eye from the Bible.

Shaming and reintegration   Form of restorative justice that requires the guilty party to publicly admit their crime to their victim(s) and to the community so that they may be forgiven and become lawabiding members of the community again.

Specific deterrence   A punishment or barrier that is targeting a specific type of crime. Example: burglar alarms.

Strain theory   Merton's theory of crime and deviance that proposes that if individuals cannot meet societal goals by acceptable, lawful means (e.g., personal wealth), they will find illegal ways to accomplish these goals. Or they may reject the goals and means all together.

Vengeful, vengeance   Punishment that is intended to "get even" with the accused, as in the example of torture before killing a suspect.

REFERENCES AND SUGGESTED READINGS

Alper, M., M. R. Durose, and J. Markman (2018) 2018 Update on prisoner recidivism: A nine-year follow-up period (2004-2015). Office of Justice Programs, *Bureau of Justice Statistics*, U. S. Department of Justice. May. NCJ 250975. 23 pp.

AZYEP (2020) Restorative justice: Is there a way to decrease recidivism within the criminal justice system? KDNK 88 Community Radio. Jul. 13 airdate. Retrieved from https://www.kdnk.org/post/restorative-justice-there-way-decrease-recidivism-within-criminal-justice-system.

Beccaria, C. (1764; 2009) *On Crime and Punishment*. Scotts Valley, AZ: CreateSpace Independent Publishing Platform. Trans. from Italian.

Brooks, T. (2001) Corlett on Kant, Hegel, and retribution. *Philosophy*. Vol. 76, No. 298:561-580.

Caldera, C. (2020) Fact check: 'Hangover' refers to aftereffects, not the practice of sleeping over a rope. *USA Today*. Oct. 23. Retrieved from https://www.usatoday.com/story/news/factcheck/2020/10/23/fact-check-hungover-refers-aftereffects-not-sleeping-over-rope/3732337001/.

Criminal Justice U.S. Jobs (2020) Learn how to be a penologist. Feb. 2. Retrieved from https://cjusjobs.com/penologist-career-guide/.

Dagger, R. (1991) Restitution: Pure or punitive? *Criminal Justice Ethics*. Vol. 10, Iss. 2:29-39.

Earl, J. (2017) "It's the shame effect": Judge orders public humiliation for domestic abuser. *CBS News*. Mar. 31. Retrieved from https://www.cbsnews.com/news/its-the-shame-effect-judge-orders-public-humiliation-for-domestic-abusers/.

Ellis, A. (2003) A deterrence theory of punishment. *The Philosophical Quarterly*. Vol. 53, No. 212:337-351.

Failinger, M. A. (2006) Lessons unlearned: Women offenders, the ethics of are and the promise of restorative justice. *Fordham Urban Law Journal*. Jan. Vol. 33, Iss. 2:487-526.

Foucault, M. (1975) *Discipline and Punish: The Birth of the Prison*. Trans. New York: Pantheon Books.

Gallagher, S. (2016) The limits of pure restitution. *Social Theory and Practice*. Jan., Vol. 42, No. 1:74-96.

Garland, D. (2001) *The Culture of Control: Crime and Social Order in Contemporary Society*. Oxford: Oxford University Press.

Gladfelter, A. S., B. Lantz, and R. B. Ruback (2018) Beyond ability to pay: Procedural justice and offender compliance with restitution orders. *International Journal of Offender Therapy and Comparative Criminology*. Vol. 63, No. 13:4314-4331.

Green, W. M. (1929) An ancient debate on capital punishment. *The Classical Journal*. Jan., Vol. 24, No. 4:267-275).

Harris, H. M., K. Nakamura, K. B. Bucklen (2018) Do cellmates matter: A causal test of the Schools of Crime hypothesis with implications for differential association and deterrence theories. *Criminology*. Feb., Vol. 56, Iss. 1:87-122.

HG Legal Resources (n.d.) Burglary charges under California Penal Code 459. Retrieved from https://www.hg.org/legal-articles/burglary-charges-under-california-penal-code-459-25139.

Hill, T. E. (1999) Kant on wrongdoing, desert, and punishment. *Law and Philosophy*. Vol. 18:407-441.

Hodgson, J. (2019) Feminising restorative justice: A critical exploration of offending girls' experiences participating in restorative justice conferences. Thesis, Liverpool John Moores University.

Immarigeon, R. (2016) Does anger management work? *Offender Programs Report*. Jan./Feb., Vol. 19, Iss. 5:71-80.

Konstan, D. (2003) Strategies of status, in *Ancient Anger: Perspectives from Homer* to Galen, S. Braud and G. W. Most, eds. Yale Classical Studies XXII. Cambridge: Cambridge University Press. 99-120.

Lacey, N. and H. Pickard (2015) The chimera of proportionality: Institutionalising limits on punishment in contemporary social and political systems. *Modern Law Review.* Mar., Vol. 78, No. 2:216-240.

Law Explorer (2015) Crime and punishment. General Law. Nov. 30. Retrieved from https://lawexplores.com/crime-and-punishment/.

Lee, J. Y., A. C. Grogan-Kaylor, S. J. Lee, T. Ammari, A. Lu, and P. Davis-Kean (2020) A qualitative analysis of stay-at-home parents' spanking tweets. *Journal of Child and Family Studies.* Mar., Vol. 29, Iss. 3: 817-830.

Linders, A. (2002) The execution spectacle and state legitimacy: The changing nature of the American execution audience, 1833-1937. *Law and Society Review.* Vol. 36, No. 3:607-656.

Odle, N. (2007) Privilege through prayer: Examining Bible based prison rehabilitation programs under the Establishment Clause. *Texas Journal on Civil Liberties and Civil Rights.* Spring, Vol. 12, Iss. 2:277-312.

Pereboom, D. (2020) Incapacitation, reintegration limited general deterrence. *Neuroethics.* Vol. 13:87-97.

Petersilia, J. (2011) Beyond prison bubble. National Institute of Justice, U.S. Department of Justice, Office of Justice Programs. Nov. 2. Retrieved from https://nij.ojp.gov/topics/articles/beyond-prison-bubble#:~:text=Rehabilitation%20programs%20reduce%20recidivism%20if,to%20get%20jobs%20after%20release.

Priyadarshi, N. (2014) A socio-legal study of prison system and its reforms in India. *International Journal of Enhanced Research in Educational Development.* Nov.-Dec., Vol. 2, Iss. 6:1-5.

Rizzoli, M. and L. Stanca (2012) Judicial errors and crime deterrence theory and experimental evidence. *The Journal of Law and Economics.* Vol. 55, No. 2:311-338.

Roberts, J. V. and M. Hough (2005) The state of prisons: Exploring public knowledge and opinion. *The Howard Journal.* Jul. Vol. 44, No. 3:286-306.

Smith, B. L. (2012) The case against spanking: Physical discipline is slowly declining as some studies reveal lasting harms of children. *Monitor on Psychology.* Apr., Vol. 43, No. 4:60.

Smith Pangle, L. (2009) Moral and criminal responsibilities in Plato's "Laws." *The American Political Science Review.* Vol. 103, No. 3:456-473.

Spitzer, S. (1975) Punishment and social organization: A study of Durkheim's theory of penal evolution. *Law and Society Review.* Summer, Vol. 9, No. 4:613-638.

Stahlkopf, C., M. Males, and D. Macallair (2010) Testing incapacitation theory: Youth crime and incarceration in California. *Crime and Delinquency.* Vol. 56, No. 2:253-268.

Tata, C. and N. Hutton, eds. (2016) *Sentencing and Society.* London: Routledge, Taylor and Francis Group.

United States Department of Justice (2020) Tribal Law and Order Act. Jan. 2. Retrieved from https://www.justice.gov/tribal/tribal-law-and-order-act.

University of Wisconsin-Madison (n.d.) About Restorative Justice. UWM Law School. Retrieved from https://law.wisc.edu/fjr/rjp/justice.html.

van der Vyver, J. D. (2003) Torture as crime under international law. *Albany Law Review.* Vol. 67:427.

Wallin and Klarich Law Corporation (n.d.) Involuntary manslaughter punishment sentencing – California Penal Code 192(b). Retrieved from https://www.wklaw.com/involuntary-manslaughter-sentencing/#:~:text=If%20convicted%2C%20you%20could%20spend,%2C%20three%2C%20or%20four%20years.

Weegels, J. (2020) Prison riots in Nicaragua: Negotiating co-governance amid creative violence and public secrecy. *International Criminal Justice Review.* Vol. 30, No. 1:61-82.

Wennerstrom, A., B. Reilly, M. Sugarman, N. Henderson, and A. Niyogi (2020) Promoting health equity and criminal justice reform: The Louisiana experience. American Journal of Public Health. Jan., Vol. 11, Series 1:39-40.

Zehr, H. (2015) *The Little Book of Restorative Justice: Revised and Updated.* 2d ed. Brattleboro, VT, Good Books.

Chapter TWO

History of Punishment and Corrections in America[1]

For my part I think it is less evil that some criminals should escape, than that the government should play an ignoble part [in their punishment].

—Oliver Wendell Holmes, Jr., Associate Justice, U.S. Supreme Court

Chapter Objectives

- Provide a brief timeline of different philosophies of punishment in America, including rehabilitation trends and "get tough on crime" eras.
- Introduce the history of punishment in the American colonies prior to the end of the Revolutionary War.
- Review 19th-century reforms in American corrections.
- Review 20th and 21st-century corrections in the United States.

Key Terms

13th Amendment	Indentured servant
Antebellum	Lynching
Bail	"New Jim Crow"
Branding	Penal colonies
Buccaneers	Penitence
Corporal punishment	Piracy
Habeas corpus	Privateers

---

[1] **TRIGGER WARNING**: There are a number of sensitive topics discussed in this chapter and drawings, photos that might be disturbing to some readers. We recommend that you discuss with your professor or instructor as to how much or how little of this chapter you will be responsible for.

Seditious libel   Stolen Generation (Australia)
Sentencing Project, The   Waste management model

INTRODUCTION

We sometimes forget that the criminal laws and subsequent punishments did not simply spring up out of the minds of the United States founders. The history of punishment in America starts in western Europe, primarily England, but was also influenced by law from Ancient Rome. Medieval and early modern empires in western Europe, built themselves in the image of Rome, once a mighty empire itself (Kumar, 2012). Though not as influential as Rome, the Ancient Greek Empire also played a role in the shaping of the character of the British Empire (Kumar, 2012). As the colonies in America were viewed as part of empire building in Britain, it stands to reason that British law would be the first to be established. Colonists in America, though wanting to rid themselves of British rule, later as a new nation did not completely jettison the legal models imported from western Europe, including England.

We also have to remember that in 17th- and 18th-century America, much of what we saw in punishment was tied to religion. The persecution of heretics in the 17th century was common, with the Massachusetts Colony Puritans passing laws that banned certain religious groups from their midst, including Catholic priests, missionaries, or Jesuits—the penalty for first offense was banishment; on second offense, the penalty was death (Perrin and Coleman, 1998). Ironically, although some colonists were escaping England because of religious persecution, they themselves imposed religious mandates that were anything but liberating.

The 17th century was also a period of hysteria over supposed witchcraft. A famous example of this is the witch trials in Salem, Massachusetts, where in 1692, 19 men and women were put to death for the supposed practice of witchcraft (Miller, 2012). Religious life and law were one and the same during this period of the American settlement. If you drive through towns established in colonial times in New England, churches with white spires, some erected prior to the 19th century, may be the most striking feature of the landscape, and often are the first thing you see. It wasn't until the late 19th century that power began to shift to town halls as centers for settling criminal and civil legal matters.

In the western United States, when what we know as states now were territories, law was more haphazard and therefore, so was punishment. Vigilante and frontier justice was the rule of the day, and territories left of the Mississippi were justifiably described as the "Wild, Wild West". Even places west of Ohio were considered the untamed wilderness until the later part of the 19th century, early 20th century in the United States. Trials and subsequent convictions, if they did take place, resulted in swift punishment. However, we should consider that banishment or being run out of town did not necessarily mean certain death. Those who were banished could start over elsewhere with changed names and identities, in an era long before Social Security numbers, fingerprinting, and a cyber footprint through social media, texting, and emails.

Moving into the late 19th century, while the west was still a frontier, reformists in the east were pushing for a new model of prisons where rehabilitation was the ideal, with the belief that criminals could be reformed. There was already some semblance of that in the Pennsylvania prison system, including at Eastern Pennsylvania Penitentiary in Philadelphia. Since then, corrections, punishment and views of justice have vacillated between retribution and rehabilitation, up into modern day.

The corrections system in the United States as we know it today is unrecognizable from that of the original British colonies on the eastern shores of America. English criminal justice and punishment was subjective, favoring the wealthy and aristocrats, where one could be sent to the gallows for what we would consider today to be misdemeanors, if the convicted were poor (Friedman, 1993). What has not changed is that the criminal justice still favors the wealthy, where many of the accused to this day can escape justice, with the right defense team and the means to pay them.

COLONIAL PERIOD

Though there were established laws in the American colonies, punishment could be arbitrary, community-based, and often involving the use of *corporal punishment*. These were physical punishments, including whipping. By the 19th century, prison reformers argued that penitentiaries were supposed to be places of rehabilitation, not physical punishment (Smith, 2016). Whereas today we have capital punishment for relatively few defined crimes, during colonization there were legal mass executions for a variety of offenses, including witchcraft and *piracy* (Blackman and McLaughlin, 2014). As in Europe, what was particularly horrific was the additional use of torture, which often inevitably led to death, whether it was the intended outcome or not.

When examining the criminal offenses that one could be convicted of in the Massachusetts Bay Colony where the Puritans established their first home, with legal and religious life inseparable, moral crimes that we would now classify as being outside the privy of the legal system, like adultery and other sexual behavior outside of marriage, as long as it is between consenting adults, had criminal liability resulting in very public punishment. These were punishable crimes not so much as they were committed against others, but rather, as Cotton Mather, a 17th-century Congregational minister in New England promoted, moral crimes were acts against the explicit word of God (Friedman, 1993).

Punishment as Theater

During the Colonial Period, punishment was public spectacle. Public punishments, including executions, have been occurring for millennia, perhaps since the beginning of organized societies. Over time, punishment has increasingly become a private affair and by the early 20th century public executions ceased altogether, conducted behind the walls of prisons (Montagne, 2001).

Some of the more common forms of punishment, most of which were carried out in public, included the following, excluding the death penalty (Perrin and Coleman, 1998):

■ **Tarring and feathering.** As described in Mark Twain's novel, *Adventures of Huckleberry Finn* (1884), the accused would be stripped of their clothing, covered with hot tar, similar to what is used in road construction today, covered with feathers, then driven out of town. As Perrin and Coleman (1998) note, this could result in their death. Tarring and feathering originated in England.

Tarring and Feathering. (*Source:* National Portrait Gallery, Washington, D.C., retrieved from https://www.npg.org.uk/collections/search/portrait/mw61932/Retribution---tarring-and-feathering---or---the-patriots-revenge)

- **Stocks or pillory.** The typical set of colonial stocks were built from heavy timber that could be raised to insert the head and/or the feet and hands of the accused and then locked into place. This was generally on display in the center of town where the public could verbally ridicule the person, throw objects at them, and in extreme cases, lop off parts of their bodies, including their ears. The pillory was devised in medieval Europe, where an upright board had openings for the head and hands: "Often the ears were nailed to the wood on either side of the head-hole" (Perrin and Coleman, 1998, p. 10).

The Stocks. (*Source:* StockMaster, 2017, retrieved from http://www.pilloryhistory.com/law.html)

▪ **Whipping.** Whippings were a favorite punishment in Colonial America. Whipping posts were often placed in a public square, similar to the stocks, so that the whipping took place in public. In a description of the whipping of women on State Street in 18th-century Boston, Samuel Breck recalled,

> *Here women were taken in a huge cage in which they were dragged on wheels from prison, and tied to the post with bare backs on which thirty or forty lashes were bestowed among the screams of the culprit and the uproar of the crowd.* (Perrin and Coleman, 1998, p. 11; Earle, 1896)

▪ **Ducking stool.** Another import from England, ducking involved seating and shackling a person into a chair set across two beams and dragging them underwater through a pond or river (Cox, 2003). This punishment was primarily used on women accused of nagging their husbands or gossiping, though men were occasionally dunked as well. Married couples could also be tied back to back if they were quarrelling. The ducking stool was one form of "trial by ordeal." In the case of suspected witches, if they survived being dunked, they were witches. If they drowned, it was proof of their innocence. Keep in mind that a person who did not know how to swim or hold their breath under water would be at great risk of not surviving the ducking stool.

Ducking Stool. (*Source:* History Collection, retrieved from https://historycollection.com/ 11-unbelievable-trials-by-ordeal-throughout-history/6/; The British National Archives)

▪ **Gagging (or scolding bridle).** Just as it sounds, the mouth is gagged with an object, including a stick or metal apparatus. Again, women were often the recipients of this type of punishment, for any number of verbal offenses, including the use of profanity or nagging. As the accused was forced to wear this out in public, it was clear as to what type of crime they were accused of.

Scolding Bridle. (*Source:* Houghton Library, Harvard University, 2017, retrieved from https://blogs.harvard.edu/houghtonmodern/2017/03/09/scolds-bridle-branks-bridle-branks/)

In many respects because punishment was carried out in public as a deterrence, punishment included taking away the dignity of the accused. Note we use the term "accused" as not everyone who allegedly committed a crime had the benefit of being tried in a court of law. As we noted with the ducking chair, some trials were conducted as tests of endurance. The taking of the dignity of accused criminals was not limited to physical and emotional punishment. It could also mean punishment that included the stripping of the individual's property rights, with property confiscated with no compensation, nor for any legitimate purpose (Acevedo, 2017).

Surprisingly, sex crimes would not always bring the same severity of punishment, as these were not viewed as seriously as property crimes. We should also consider that during the Colonial era through into the mid to late 1900s, women had little to no recourse if they were sexually assaulted, doubly so if they were assaulted by their husbands. It is only recently that sexual assault has been given more serious consideration in the criminal justice system, by arrests, prosecution, and punishment. Beyond property crimes, adultery and other moral offenses, as they were so closely tied to religion, were still very much punishable offenses. These, once again, were brought over to the colonies from English law, and as in the examples of adultery and incest, moral crimes could be classified as felonies (Davis, 1895).

Women in the Colonial Period did not escape more severe or lasting punishment for supposed crimes, as witnessed by witch hunts in New England and Nathaniel Hawthorne's fictional tale of Puritan Hester Prynne in *The Scarlet Letter*. Whereas the fictional Hester had to wear a red letter "A" on her clothing to note that she was an adulteress and gave birth out of wedlock, both Puritan men and women could be branded with a letter, burned into the hand, cheek, or forehead, representing the crime they were accused of, leaving a visible, permanent mark for the everyone to see (Cox, 2003). Some of the more frequently used brands in the colonies included (Cox, 2003),

B for burglary, burned into the right hand for first offense, left for second offense, or on the forehead if the offense was committed on the Sabbath (Sunday).
SL for *seditious libel*, burned into either cheek.
M for manslaughter.
T for thief.

R for rogue or vagabond.

F for forgery.

H for hog stealer, HH if the hog stealer was a slave.

The purpose of *branding* is similar to the literal interpretation of the biblical "eye for an eye," where even in some places in the world today, the maiming of the prisoner's body, as in the example of chopping off the hand of a thief, offers visible proof of guilt for specific crimes.

One solution to punishing criminals in England was to put them on ships bound to one of the colonies, as discussed in our international perspective on Australia in this chapter, though relatively few were sent to New England (Ziegler, 2014). Women convicted in England could be transported to Virginia and Maryland to serve as white bonded labor, working on farms or forced to do unpaid domestic work (Ziegler, 2014). In many cases and similar to child labor arrangements, the women's only crime was poverty.

Highlights in the Chronology of Colonial Laws Affecting Punishment

- **1627**: Petition of Right passed by English parliament; people cannot be imprisoned without hearing the charges against them; *bail* (an amount set by the court that allows the accused to be conditionally released from jail prior to trial) allowed.
- **1641**: Massachusetts prohibits imprisonment of the accused prior to sentencing except in capital cases, cases where the defendant had shown disrespect for the court, only if they provide guarantee that they would appear at trial.
- **1679**: *Habeas Corpus* Act is passed in England requiring that the accused be brought before

a judge within a specific number of days following arrest and providing terms for release on bail within a specified number of days on bailable offenses.[2]

- **1705**: Virginia passes a series of laws that would be adopted by other slaveholding colonies, legislating that all African, mulatto[3], and Native American servants brought to Virginia were slaves and were to be held in permanent bondage, used in commercial trade, punished for infractions, and given no legal standing in the courts.
- **1740**: South Carolina passes the Negro Act[4] legalizing execution of rebellious slaves and

---

[2] Of course that this meant that the wealthy could be released on bail, if and when they were accused, whereas the poor would be left in jail, assuming that they could not make bail.

[3] Mulatto refers to an individual of mixed Black and white ancestry who, by this law, would be viewed as Black, even if their father was a white slave owner.

[4] We should note that the terms "negro" and "colored" have been considered offensive since the 1980s.

Highlights in the Chronology of Colonial Laws Affecting Punishment (Continued)

prohibiting slaves from, among other things, assembling in groups, raising food, earning money, and learning to read English.

- **1786:** Pennsylvania adopts the Wheelbarrow Law, requiring convicts to perform public labor while chained to a cannon ball to

prevent escape and to wear unattractive clothing.[5]

Source: Miller, 2012, pp. xxix-xi.

Punishment for Piracy

Piracy is considered to be the first form of organized crime in the Americas during the Golden Age of Piracy in the 17th and 18th centuries. And with it came new definitions of maritime crimes and punishments. The attacking and robbing of ships on the high seas and along coastlines predates the British colonies in America, but escalated as there was more transport of goods and wealth between England and the colonies.

What we would consider to be pirates or "freebooters" were not always ragtag bands of criminals, as depicted in the beloved *Pirates of the Caribbean* movies (Walt Disney Pictures, 2006-2017) or theme park rides. Some were *privateers* possessing official government commissions or authorizations; others were *buccaneers*, whose exploits sent shockwaves of fear and terror along the American coast and in the Caribbean, as well as in the South Pacific (Payton, 2013). As such, there was a concerted effort on the part of the British Navy and other nations to rid the seas of pirates, buccaneers, and privateers who had turned rogue.

Piracy was an ongoing challenge in colonial times and beyond. Folklore in Lynn, Massachusetts, a town north of Boston settled in 1659, tells a number of stories of pirates, including that there is treasure still buried in the Lynn Woods. There are also stories told about the Blue Parrot, an old tavern that pirates would often frequent in Lynn. Once they were intoxicated and bragging about their exploits under the influence of alcohol, they were locked up in a jail that was above the tavern and, no doubt, if the stories are true, later executed. We should note that the average time spent as a pirate was around 18 months, with death likely to occur due to capture,

---

[5] This is where we get the saying "the old ball and chain" and we still see vestiges of this with chain gangs and Department of Corrections t-shirts with community service trash pickup on highways, so that it is clear who is a convict.

disease, or in battle. Taverns were also a good place to find drunks who could be conscripted to serve on military and pirate vessels. The unsuspecting individual could find themselves waking up to a hangover and out to sea. Like any folklore, we may not know fully where the lines between truth and embellished fiction lie.

Those who have read the history of the British colonies in America will recall that even before the American Revolution, the British Crown had a number of challenges in managing the colonies from afar, including piracy. During the period in which King George II issued The Act of Grace (1717, 1719), pirates were offered the opportunity to receive a pardon from the king if they gave up piracy (Dolin, 2018). These efforts were met with lukewarm responses, as piracy was alleged to be profitable and the later issue of the act in 1719 included a clause offering a reward from the Crown for providing information or capturing a pirate, including a £200 bounty if a sailor turned in their pirate captain (Dolin, 2018). There was a reporting in 1718 of a mass execution of 49 pirates in Charleston, South Carolina, after a swift trial that is shrouded in mystery to this day, considering how sensational the public event was at the time (Butler, 2018). By all accounts, piracy came to a grisly end after 400 pirates reportedly were hung between 1716 and 1726, double that number were hunted down and killed, and numerous deaths occurred in sea battles (Dolin, 2018).

A YOUNG NATION (1781-1850)

Though the intentions of the U.S. Constitution were to provide a broader range of rights to citizens of the newly formed nation, criminal law did not deviate substantially from British law. However, as Friedman (1993) argues, America attempted to shape its emerging laws in its new image, divorced from Britain.

Highlights in the Chronology of Early United States Affecting Punishment

- **1789:** The U.S. Judiciary Act of 1789 specifies which crimes are bailable, plus guidelines for establishing bail.
- **1794:** Pennsylvania law creates the category of first-degree murder for homicides that are planned or particularly heinous, making it the only crime eligible for capital punishment. Those convicted of second-degree murder were sentenced to prison.
- **1841:** John Augustus, a shoemaker from Massachusetts, invents the system of probation, convincing a court to release a homeless man charged with drunkenness into his care.

Source: Miller, 2012, pp xi-xli

Crime and Punishment of Slaves

Slavery was not unique to the Americas, but its practice had a long-term impact on the nation that can still be felt today. Legally, slaves had no rights, and many scholars and social justice activists have argued, justifiably so, that the post-Civil War South, as well as places in the North, have continued to suppress the rights of Blacks, as witnessed in the flurry of voter laws after the 2016 presidential election that are more likely to suppress and disenfranchise people of color.

If we consider that slaves were treated as property and listed as such in inventories of plantations and farms, they were treated as an economic commodity. It could be financially detrimental to the owner if a slave who committed a crime was jailed or executed. It was more likely that punishment was left up to the slave owner and not to a court of law. However, this did not mean that slaves escaped prosecution all together, nor were, in theory, to be denied due process. For example, once Alabama was admitted to the Union (1819), its newly minted constitution stated that "in the prosecution of slaves for crimes of higher grade than petit [petty] larceny, the General Assembly shall have no power to deprive them of impartial trial by petit jury" (The Avalon Project, n.d., retrieved from https://avalon.law.yale.edu/19th_century/ala1 819.asp). The Alabama *Code of 1852* stated that for lesser crimes, the slave should receive nor more than 50 lashes, later increased to 100 (Sellers and Amos Doss, 1994).

Leading up to the end of slavery, abolitionists published horrifying accounts of slaves being beaten, branded, and mutilated, as well as, in some cases, starved (Clark, 1995). Slaves, having suffered for generations did not escape from tyranny at the hands of their owners after the *13th Amendment* passed, abolishing slavery. In the aftermath of the Civil War and during the Reconstruction period, white supremacy groups emerged including the Klu Klux Klan (KKK), whose members took matters into their own hands, sometimes *lynching* (hanging by a mob) Blacks for real or imagined crimes but primarily because of the color of their skin. These were conducted outside of the law, but often the legal authorities in the South turned a blind eye or willfully partook in the illegal execution by hanging of Blacks and other people of color. We should note that it is only in 2022 that an anti-lynching bill was passed by Congress, signed into law by President Joe Biden, to address the continued and horrific illegal practice of lynching in the United States.

19TH-CENTURY REFORMS (1850-1899)

In 1878, Massachusetts was the first state to create a state system for probation, paying officers who were responsible for supervising released convicts (Miller, 2012). As we will see later in this textbook, probation and parole are forms of forgiveness, with the attitude that criminals deserve a second chance and are redeemable. One benefit that we see to this day to the use of probation over incarceration is that the convicted can still be productive members of the community, including the ability to provide for their families, if they are able to keep their jobs after conviction. It also offers a means by which convicts can earn a living and pay for restitution, if fines were imposed in their sentencing.

Capital Punishment

We will address the controversies surrounding capital punishment in more depth in Chapter 13. Here we are examining, briefly, capital punishment prior to the 20th century in America. Legal mass executions, conducted after hasty trials, were allowed through 1865 in the United States and were conducted in public to serve as warning to anyone who dared to commit similar crimes. Approximately one-fifth of mass executions were for war-related crimes, including treason, desertion, mutiny, and espionage (Blackman and McLaughlin, 2004) and about 9 percent involved piracy. Other mass executions were for slave revolts, with convictions easily obtained and appeals nonexistent (Blackman and McLaughlin, 2004).

Not everyone had the stomach for capital punishment in the 19th century. Prior to the Civil War, the roots for the abolishment of the death penalty were growing among the Quakers, as well as among European and American intellectuals. One of the greatest reforms was with the enactment of discretionary death penalty statues in Tennessee (1838), where capital punishment was no longer arbitrary but could only be sentenced in very specific (and horrific) murder cases (Bohm, 1999). Louis Masur's 1849 anti-gallows poem summarizes the spectacle that a hanging was expected to be in the 19th century (Barton, 2014, p 26):

> Put the scaffold on the Common,
> Where the multitude can meet;
> All the schools and ladies summon,
> Let them all enjoy the treat.
> What's the use of being "private"?
> Hanging is a righteous cause;
> Men should witness what you drive at,
> When you execute the laws.

Prison Labor

The concerns for the cost of housing prisoners did not simply begin in the late 20th century in the aftermath of mass incarceration trends. A means by which to have prisoners earn their keep, beyond manual labor outside, began in earnest during the Industrial Revolution. One means by which to cut costs in the care of prisoners was to join in private prison-private sector ventures, where convicts provided, in many cases, free labor to build products that in turn would be sold, with profits shared with prisons to offset their expenses of running their facilities (Durham, 1989). The purposes of prisoner labor were meant to be twofold. Beyond the first function of profiting from convict labor, the second function was to make the prisoner suffer while performing hard labor (Goldsmith, 1999).

Adult corrections was not the only system of punishment that underwent changes in the 19th century. Children were long thought of as small adults until there was better understanding of developmental stages from the early studies in psychology. Until then, juvenile prisoners were housed with adults, leaving them vulnerable to victimization, including sexual assault. Juveniles have not completely escaped these fates today, as children as young as 13 can be charged as adults and given a sentence of life in prison without the possibility of parole in cases of murder. Likewise, children in juvenile detention facilities today can be victimized, but not at the same rates as when they were once housed with adult offenders. Other solutions in the 19th century included placing them in work houses and reformatory schools, similarly to what we saw in the eastern states. As in the case of non-juvenile offenders, conditions were brutal, involving long hours of work, often under dangerous conditions.

Similar to use of prison labor to offset costs, the emerging juvenile justice systems in Europe and in the United States began an industrial school movement that could potentially place children whose only crime may have been poverty in factory settings as a form of punishment and to provide vocational training. We should be reminded that federal child labor laws did not go into effect in the United States until 1938, and it was not uncommon for children to work in factories, sometimes to their peril, as they provided cheaper labor than adult males (U.S. Department of Labor, n.d.).

Prison Factory Labor System, 19th Century. (*Source:* Berrigan, 2015, Retrieved from https://fit-ace-nyccriminal-wp1.azurewebsites.net/?p=70)

New York State Penitentiary, Auburn

In the next chapter, we will go into greater detail about the actual architecture of the Auburn, New York and Pennsylvania penitentiaries. For now, our focus will be on the social reforms that these two prisons brought about within corrections. In the 19th century, increasingly social reform movements pushed the public to see convicts as redeemable, allowing them to be rehabilitated with the possibility of their contributing to building the new republic on the outside of prison (Mullens, 2016). The goal of the Auburn prison in New York, built in 1818, was to put prisoners to work instead of having them lying idle in their cells, with the primary goal of teaching them work skills they could use after incarceration. This was not manual labor solely for the sake of profit. Rather the hope was that by allowing them to work side by side, collectively they would learn both trade and social skills needed to pursue a useful occupation after release from prison (Mullens, 2016).

An honorable mention of 19th-century prisons in New York includes Sing Sing, a correctional facility in Ossining, on the banks of the Hudson River. What makes it remarkable is that the prison was constructed by prisoners from marble they had excavated, finishing construction in 1828 (Sing Sing Prison Museum, n.d.). So, they were virtually building their own prison cells. In a comparison with the Hudson River Valley School art movement (founded in 1825), located in the same region as the prison, while the artists portrayed the area as idealized natural landscape in their paintings, the prison represented the profitable labor that was extracted from prisoners, often by routine beatings (Bernstein, 2013).

Pennsylvania Eastern State Penitentiary

Arguably one of the most important prisons in the United States, if not in the western world, the Eastern State Penitentiary in Philadelphia has been the subject of study by penologists since its inception. The brainchild of the Pennsylvania Prison Society in the early 19th century, Eastern State Penitentiary was intended to provide a more compassionate way by which to house prisoners. We should note that the Pennsylvania Prison Society was founded in 1787 by some of the signers of the Declaration of Independence and the U.S. Constitution, including Benjamin Franklin (Kashatus, 1999; Pennsylvania Prison Society, n.d.). The Pennsylvania Prison Society also led the reform movement for women convicts, advocating that they be housed separate from males (Pennsylvania Prison Society, n.d.).

Shortly after the Auburn prison was opened in New York, the Eastern State Penitentiary was opened in 1829. Unlike the Auburn prison, which was built in rural New York, Eastern State Penitentiary was located right in the city of Philadelphia. Philadelphia was a town that attracted Quakers (The Religious Society of Friends), a religion founded in England and whose members were brought to American shores due to persecution for their faith. The Pennsylvania Eastern State Penitentiary was modeled after Quaker beliefs, which included more focus on *penitence* (regret and apology for wrongdoings, usually with some form of religious request for forgiveness) for the sins of committing crimes. In fact, penitence is the root word of penitentiary. This required inmates to be held in single-person cells, to give them the supposed solitude they needed to reflect on their crimes and mend their ways.

In the Eastern State Penitentiary, prisoners could not see each other, much less communicate with one another. The isolation was intended to remove the prisoner from all contact with the outside world, which was viewed in the Quaker religion as corrupt and contributing to the individual's criminal behavior. French penal reformer, Alexis de Tocqueville, was so enthusiastic about the Eastern State Penitentiary system that he advocated for its adoption in France, reporting after his 1831 visit that "'thrown into solitude, the prisoner reflects, learning to hate his crime.'" (Kashatus, 1999, retrieved from http://paheritage.wpengine.com/article/punishment-penitence-reform-eastern-state-penitentiary-controversy-solitary-confinement/#:~:text=Built%20on%20the%20idea%20that,to%20society%20as%20productive%20citizens) The Pennsylvania Quaker prison system, having been adopted in a number of European countries, still existed in France through the mid-20th century (Cary, 1958).

In addition to solitary confinement, the day in the life of a prisoner in Eastern State Penitentiary was purposefully orderly. It was believed that by establishing a fixed schedule, one that was planned around meals, it would offer the order in their lives they were lacking in their outside lives, that may have led to their committing crimes. In an accounting of what life was like in the prison, their every move during the day was accounted for (Kashatus, 1999, retrieved from http://paheritage.wpengine.com/article/punishment-penitence-reform-eastern-state-penitentiary-controversy-solitary-confinement/#:~:text=Built%20on%20the%20idea%20that,to%20society%20as%20productive%20citizens):

> Prisoners would rise at dawn and eat breakfast at seven o'clock. The fare was simple: corn meal bread and a pint of coffee, cocoa, or green tea. If weather permitted, inmates were allowed on hour of exercise in small individual yards. Alternative exercise periods were scheduled for adjacent cells to assure anonymity and isolation. Dinner[6], the primary meal came at noon and consisted of a pound of beef or pork, a pint of soup, and unlimited servings of potatoes or boiled rice . . . a simple supper was served – often little more than Indian mush sweetened with molasses, sometimes sauerkraut, and tea. Lights went out at nine o'clock.

However, as we see in today's prisons, solitary confinement is not without its critics. Another notable visitor to the Eastern State Penitentiary was the British writer, Charles Dickens, known for his distressing stories of poverty and terrible childhoods. After his visit in 1842 to the Philadelphia prison, he wrote of how appalled he was at the conditions, describing them as "'the picture of forlorn affliction and distress of the mind'" (Kashatus, 1999, retrieved from http://paheritage.wpengine.com/article/punishment-penitence-reform-eastern-state-penitentiary-controversy-solitary-confinement/#:~:text=Built%20on%20the%20idea%20that,to%20society%20as%20productive%20citizens). Today, we know from studies that solitary confinement can

---

[6] In some parts of the country, the midday meal is still called dinner instead of lunch and is a heavier meal than the evening one. It is thought that laborers would need the extra calories to face their afternoon chores, only requiring a lighter meal, called supper, in the evening before heading off to bed.

either exacerbate existing mental illnesses in some people or bring on new ones in others.

Louisiana State Penitentiary

The Louisiana State Penitentiary was built in response to the poor conditions and widespread sickness experienced by prisoners in various jail and prisons scattered throughout the state. Unlike the stories of redemption coming out of both the Auburn prison and Eastern State Penitentiary, the stories out of the Louisiana State Penitentiary were tales of horrible conditions. Though prison conditions were still harsh in the penitentiaries in the east, nothing compared to the hardships that inmates faced in prisons in the south.

Louisiana State Penitentiary, Angola, 1934. (*Source:* 64 Parishes, retrieved from https://64parishes.org/entry/louisiana-state-penitentiary-at-angola; Library of Congress Prints and Photographs Division.)

Incarceration in the south translated to profitability for *antebellum* (pre-Civil War, generally referring to states in the south) state governments in the early part of the 19th century, and to some extent, rehabilitation opportunities for male inmates (Derbes,

2013). The conditions for women and children in the Louisiana State Penitentiary, however, were intolerable. We should note that Louisiana was the only antebellum state that passed laws that required that the children born in prison to enslaved women would be auctioned off, with the proceeds of those sales going to the state (Derbes, 2013).

Emergence of Professionalism in Corrections

By the late 19th century, as the United States approached its 100th anniversary of nationhood, the police and in turn those working in corrections began to look to the professionalization of these jobs[7], soon to be considered true careers by the mid-20th century, with all benefits associated with them, including potential for promotion and retirement pensions. We should note, however, that the criminal justice system was more overtly political in the United States as compared to in England. People working in policing and prisons were far from professionals in the 19th century, with the jobs having no prerequisites beyond having the right family name or political connections (Friedman, 1993).

THE WILD, WILD WEST AND THE AMERICAN FRONTIER (1849-1890)

Though exploration of the west began long before the American Revolution and certainly before the mid-1800s, we start our timeline for the Wild West beginning with the 1849 California Gold Rush. Though California was occupied by the U.S. Army, the local Mexican authorities were allowed to stay in office, with no real consistency in enforcing the law, much less convicting and incarcerating criminals (Ridge, 1999). Settlers were already headed west in advance of the Gold Rush; however, it marked a turning point when there was a surge in violent crime, as many men left their families once they had caught gold fever. It was an era of greed and lawlessness. The so-called Wild West is wrapped in mythology with stories of miners searching for gold and silver. Cowboys, pioneers, Native Americans, and gunslingers, were all nostalgically recalled in the heyday of movie Westerns (Pak, 2020).

Some of the crime associated with the Gold Rush has been blamed on mental illness. San Francisco was the closest city to the California gold fields, and the city grew overnight, from 1,000 residents in 1848 to over 25,000 by 1850, the second year of the Gold Rush (Holiday, 1999; Rawls,1999). Many of the people who landed in California during the Gold Rush did not adjust well to the hardships, resulting in the San Francisco town council left to handle those who were mentally ill (Webb and Brody, 1968). Prior to opening a state hospital for the mentally disturbed, the

---

[7] We should note that by Max Weber's definitions (1922, in *Economy and Society*), jobs are temporary and people can have a series of jobs during their lifetime, possibly in unrelated fields. Careers, on the other hand, are lifelong pursuits with promise of promotion, nurturing commitment to one's chosen profession.

solution was in the acquisition of the prison ship *Euphemia*, as a place to put them, along with criminals, "rowdies," and drunkards, out in the San Francisco Bay (Webb and Brody, 1968).

The Prison Ship Euphemia, San Francisco. (*Source:* Delgado, n.d., from The Annals of San Francisco, 1855, retrieved from https://www.foundsf.org/index.php?title=The_Prison_Ship_%27Euphemia%27)

The west was not completely devoid of jails and prisons. For example, a prison that consisted of a single building was constructed in 1871, in the Montana territory (Edgerton, 2004). According to Edgerton (2004, p xii), in Montana, "there has always existed the will to punish criminals forcefully, even severely. . . . Like many Americans, Montanans have always wanted their prison to be tough places, even places where acceptable, measured violence is meted out, places of no return." The State Penitentiary, in Deerlodge, Montana, is now closed to prisoners, but there is currently a museum that can be visited, preserved by the Powell County Museum and Arts Foundation (*Genealogy Trails*, n.d.).

Before Arizona became a territory in the early 20th century, the punishment for crimes was arbitrary and inconsistent, as similarly seen in the early years of the nation in eastern states. Until 1873, there were no legal executions and the accused could find themselves at the end of a noose, the victim of vigilante justice before there could be a trial (Wilson, 2013).

20TH-CENTURY CORRECTIONS (1900-1999)

The United States faced two major world wars in the first half of the 20th century. The demographic in which we find more risk for offending, young males, were more likely to volunteer or be drafted into the military during those periods. Post-World War I through to the 1970s, the incarceration rates held steady, followed by the rates of imprisonment quadrupling within the following decades in the United States (Travis et al., eds., 2014), as noted in the graph in Figure 2.1.

During the second half of the 20th century, there was a push to close mental health hospitals ("deinstitutionalization") which contributed to the trends of mass incarceration that followed shortly after. With nowhere to go but the streets, many of the mentally ill landed in prison on a number of different charges, beginning with the less serious charges of vagrancy up to violent crimes including assault and homicide. Those who did not have support from family members or friends, did not consistently have access to the medications they needed to stabilize their conditions, or if they had access, often did not take them. We find this to be the case

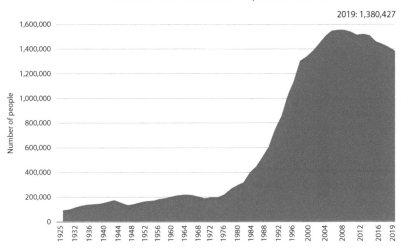

Trends in U.S. Corrections

U.S. State and Federal Prision Population, 1925–2019

FIGURE 2.1 | **Incarceration in the United States, 1925-2018.**
(*Source:* The Sentencing Project, retrieved from https://www.sentencingproject.org/wp-content/uploads/2020/08/US-prison-pop-1925-2018.png)

still today, with estimates of 15-20 percent of those in jail and prison suffering from severe mental illness (Torrey et al., 2014).

Beyond mental illness, we see a similar demographic of individuals incarcerated today in the United States, race aside, as we have historically seen throughout the world. They are primarily people coming from poverty, primarily men under the age of 40, poorly educated with drug and/or alcohol addiction and few work skills—in other words, "their criminal responsibility is real, but it is embedded in the context of social and economic disadvantage" (National Research Council, 2014, *Summary*, p 2).

In the 20th and 21st centuries, we find that housing prisoners is now more expensive than funding public education. According to U.S. Census data and the Vera Institute of Justice, government spending on prison exceeds that which is spent on educating public primary and secondary students, as seen in Figure 2.2.

By the late 1980s, the cost of housing a prisoner rose to an average of $30,000 per year. In some states, the cost is even higher. California's current per-inmate cost exceeds $75,000 a year, or as one journalist notes, the equivalent to the cost of one year of education at Stanford University (Walters, 2018).

Convict labor has not ceased to exist in the 20th and 21st centuries. Nor have convict labor abuses ceased to exist. Both male and female Blacks in the south were

FIGURE 2.2 ‖ **Spending on Public Schools vs. on Prisons.**
(*Sources:* U.S. Census Data; Vera Institute of Justice; Yalen, CNN, retrieved from https://money .cnn.com/infographic/economy/education-vs-prison-costs/)

often sentenced to hard labor on the chain gang in Georgia (LeFlouria, 2015). Black women who had been convicted were exploited, bounced around labor prison camps in both the north and south, and whichever labor camp they landed in, terror and violence would follow them (LeFlouria, 2015). Mass incarceration, as well as sentencing of Blacks to prison labor camps in the 20th century is viewed as an era of "the *New Jim Crow,*" meaning that incarceration is viewed as a means to continue to marginalize people of color after slavery ended, and where, as Alexander (2020) notes, the majority of Black males living in urban centers are either incarcerated or have criminal records.

It was during the 20th century that the last legal public execution was conducted. Rainey Bethea, a 26-year-old Black man, was hanged on August 14, 1936, after being convicted of the rape and murder of a 70-year-old woman (Montagne, 2001; Kageyama, n.d.). It is thought that it was Bethea's hanging and the carnival atmosphere of the massive crowd of approximately 20,000 spectators that witnessed it, that put an end to public hangings (Montagne, 2001). As in the case of social media today, the photograph of the crowd at the hanging brought about public outcry against the inhumanity of public execution, much less capital punishment in general.

By the late 20th century, the shift from rehabilitation to a *waste management model* began in earnest. As the name of the model implies, prisoners are viewed as disposable, to be locked away where others in society cannot view them. This includes where prisons are built. Beginning in the 1980s, there was a dramatic increase in not only the number of incarcerated prisoners, but excessively long periods of solitary confinement used as social control (Lobel, 2020). As we will see later in this textbook, an extended stay in solitary confinement translates into a decreased ability to function in society, particularly after release, as it contributes to deteriorating mental health.

As Black males continue to be incarcerated at alarming rates, Black women also face rates of incarceration that surpass those of white women. According to a 2013 *Sentencing Project* report, 30 percent of women incarcerated in state and federal prison are Black; Black women are three times as likely to face prison or jail as white women (Gaskew, 2014). As the incarceration of Black women declined from 2000-2009, the number Hispanic women incarcerated increased by 23 percent (Gaskew, 2014). By the numbers from the 2020 Census (2021), in the United States, Blacks[8] still only make up about 13 percent of the population, while Hispanics or Latino(a)[9] make up about 18 percent, confirming that incarceration of people of color particularly those in the Black and Latino(a), Hispanic

---

[8] Respondents who identified as Black only, not mixed race.
[9] Respondents who identified as either Hispanic or Latino(a) only, not mixed race.

populations, continues to be disproportionate, in comparison with incarcerated whites or any other race.

With the number of incarcerated individuals increasing, the field of corrections in the United States grew alongside it. The demand for correctional officers increased exponentially, but the Bureau of Labor statistics predicts that that demand will decline have by 7 percent between 2019 and 2029, with the current strains on state and local budgets, particularly after the COVID-19 pandemic (U.S. Bureau of Labor Statistics, 2021). It is too soon to tell if any meaningful criminal justice reform will occur in the near future that will result in a further decline in demand for correctional staff.

Mass incarcerations and longer sentences also meant that corrections officers spent months and years having oversight over convicted individuals, who they might come to know very well over the course of their incarceration. Boundary violations continue to be a challenge for prison officials to prevent within their staff, which can lead to risks of blackmail, smuggling contraband, and in some cases, sexual liaisons between inmates and corrections officers, as they have more unprofessional and personal interactions over the course of time (Cooke et al., 2019).

The news coming out of corrections in the 20th and 21st centuries is not all grim. For example, the Department of Justice, Bureau of Prisons incorporated the elimination of e-waste[10] in federal prisons, participating in environmentally friendly solutions through inmate recycling programs (Conrad, 2011). However, environmentalists and activists are concerned that the toxic materials in electronic devices (e.g., cell phones) may result in adversely affecting the health of inmates (Conrad, 2011). It is important to note that much of what happens with e-waste disposal is exporting it to poorer countries to dismantle and recycle, where they bear more possible exposure to toxic materials in discarded electronics.

There are also increasingly more programs to help ex-convicts transition to life outside of prison, which in turn hopefully reduces recidivism. Though we will discuss the controversies of college for inmates in our last chapter, there are positive findings in research on inmates who participate in college programs from behind bars, including courses on offender reintegration and life skills, employment education during incarceration (Black et al., 1993). There are reentry programs within prison, but the majority of support that ex-convicts get, if available and if they are willing to accept the help, comes from outside prison walls in the community. The one drawback of reliance on community programs is that a number of these are supported by grants, which are not always guaranteed to be renewed and funds can dry up resulting in their being discontinued.

SUMMARY

The punishments used in the Colonies and following the American Revolution were primarily imported from England. Punishment could be brutal and disfiguring, as

[10] E-waste is all the electronics and their components in use today that are environmentally damaging when simply thrown away in the trash.

corporal punishment was common. It could also be fatal. There were special penalties for piracy, the first form of organized crime in America, most often used as deterrence to warn other would be pirates, including the public display of executed pirates. Crime and punishment in some places in the colonies, including in Massachusetts, was dictated by religion, with near strict interpretation of the Christian Bible (e.g., "and eye for an eye").

Perhaps the only remnant of earlier punishment from the colonial era that remains today is capital punishment. However, capital punishment is no longer used for a number of unrelated offenses, but for a more narrowly defined category of crimes, primarily homicides. Punishment for moral indiscretions gave way to secular laws defining what crimes are, without regard to religious doctrine, regulating the types of sentences that the convicted received.

Jails and prisons have likewise evolved over time in the United States. As much as social justice advocacy groups call for prison reform, the jail and prison experience is far more humane today, compared to those witnessed up and into to 20th century. Punishment is no longer theater, as in the examples given of the public humiliation of the stocks and the public spectacle of executions carried out in the open.

As more or organized government moved west following early settlers, so did more formal criminal justice systems. Though we should note that this move west was often to the detriment and decimation of indigenous tribes. This meant that vigilante and arbitrary justice that took place west of the Mississippi River, often without the benefit of trials, eventually gave way to more courts, jails, and prisons built, as territories became states. However, vigilantes did not entirely disappear, as witnessed by anti-lynching legislation passed in 2022.

The late 19th century brought about a number of reforms, including implementing a system of probation, first started in Massachusetts in 1878. Other reforms included building prisons that targeted rehabilitation, as in the examples of the New York State Penitentiary in Auburn and the Eastern State Penitentiary in Philadelphia.

Along with solitary confinement designed to give prisoners an opportunity for quiet self-reflection in hopes that they would reform their criminal ways, they also worked during the day in prison industries in the north. This was designed to keep them occupied as well as to provide some vocational training. However, not all prison labor was meant to be benign and represented profits to companies that hired prisoners, as they were not paid well and wages was funneled right back into the prison. Southern states were even less kind to prisoners, and chain gangs were not uncommon, still in used today in prisons in the south.

Much of what we see today is prisons, from overcrowding to recidivism rates, have been a result of housing those with mental health issues plus stricter anti-drug laws. During the second half of the 20th century, state funded mental hospitals began to close, leaving many with those with mental health issues unhoused and, on the streets, where they were more likely to commit crimes. In addition to the disproportionate number of people with mental health issues incarcerated, we continue to see a larger number of non-white inmates and those coming from poverty. Public funding of jails and prisons continues to outpace that spent on public education, which has those interested in social justice asking if money spent in corrections is better spent on schools and crime prevention programs.

STORIES FROM BEHIND BARS

"The Life and Adventures of a Haunted Convict"—First Known Prison Memoir by an African American[11] in 19th-Century America

As Black males and the Black community in general know all too well, the number of young men of color incarcerated in our prisons today is staggering. Black males are five times more likely to be incarcerated than whites. As Sampson and Lauritsen (1997, p. 312) lamented, "the topic of race and crime still rankles [in research], fueling competing schools of thought such as discriminations versus differential involvement, cultures of violence, versus structural inequality, and empiricism versus critical theory." Bottom line, even scholars disagree as to why there is such a big disparity between Blacks and whites in rates of incarceration. No matter the origins, most scholars would argue that there is institutionalized racism that contributes to the high incarceration rates of Black males.

The subject of our story this chapter is Austin Reed, a self-educated Black man of mixed race, who in the 19th century faced discrimination and incarceration, even though he was not born into slavery. Before the Civil War, the north was not without its own form of slavery, with Reed witness to Blacks being pressed into service against their will, to work all day without rest and without wages, even though it was in "the free North". As Smith notes (2016, Introduction, para. 8) even though slavery was outlawed,

> the Northern States were inventing new ways to [create] instruments of free labor, new sites of confinement, and new patterns of inequality. Reed was caught up in these snares, and he struggled hard against them. He carried the evidence on his body, in the marks of the whip and the flame.

Austin Reed lived in Rochester, New York, coincidentally also the one-time home to Frederick Douglass, himself an escapee from slavery in the south. There the coincidence between the two men ends at their residences in New York.

In Reed's own words, "no sooner had the cold clods covered the remains of my father before I forgot his last blessing and dying prayer with all his advice. I soon broke through the restraints of my mother and fell victim to vice and crime." (Smith, Ch 1, para 1) Hence, like so many lost Black men of his generation, he was aimless

---

[11] There is debate as to whether it is appropriate to use the label, "African American" vs. "Black". This author chose to use the term, "Black" as not all Black people are from Africa, as well as a number of Black authors using the term in describing their own identities. However, research indicates that preferences are still divided between which racial label (a social construct with no basis in biology) is appropriate (Sigelman, 2005). It is also important to note that even though surveys are not always sensitive to racial and ethnic diversity, most will use the term "Black," as in the example of the U.S. 2020 Census.

after his father's death. He was indentured at the Ladd family house, where he was not treated too kindly, with episodes of being tied up like a slave and whipped.

In 1833, still a juvenile at age 12, Reed was convicted for arson of the Ladd family's property. He was eventually sentenced to the New York House of Refuge, the first juvenile reformatory in the United States, until the age of 21. The juvenile facility housed both Blacks and whites in the same dormitory, unlike segregation in the south. Though the intention of the reformatory was to rehabilitate, the promise was far from the reality, and it was not uncommon for children to be locked up in dungeon-like conditions. It was a place of racism, exploited labor, and as Smith (2016) notes from Reed's autobiography, violent cruelty took place against both boys and girls. Conditions were so bad, a former officer at the Refuge, Elijah Devoe, published a critical essay about the juvenile facility, reporting the dehumanizing conditions (Smith, 2016). Reed was incarcerated at the Refuge from 1833 to 1839, when a fire destroyed the facility, after which he was rented out as an *indentured servant*, which in today's terms, means another form of slavery, even if it was in the so-called free North.

New York House of Refuge, First Juvenile Reformatory in the United States. (*Source:* Miller, 2018, retrieved from http://daytoninmanhattan.blogspot.com/2018/06/the-lost-new-york-house-of-refuge-5th.html)

After Reed was able to escape servitude, he made his way back to his mother's house, where his family had fallen on hard times. Reed then took odd jobs in hotels and taverns, where prostitution and gambling took place. Reed contradicts himself in his accountings, in some cases describing himself as a naïve boy taken advantage of by con men and scoundrels; in other cases writing of himself as a hardened criminal (Smith, 2016). Following a series of thefts, he once again found himself convicted, this time sent to adult prison. He eventually landed in a different kind of bondage in the Auburn prison system in New York, beginning with his first of many adult sentences in 1840. While serving several sentences at Auburn, according to the prison's punishment records, he was subjected to whippings, including with the notoriously painful "cat-o'-nine-tails," used to discipline prisoners, soldiers, and sailors (Brown, 2018; Smith, 2016).

Reed would be in and out of the Auburn prison, as well as Clinton Prison, through 1866, caught in the revolving door of incarceration and reoffending. It was somewhere around 1858 that he wrote his articulate memoirs of his life in and out of prison. As Smith (2016) observes of Reed's experiences, he was more familiar with juvenile detention and prison than any other home he had known since he was nine or ten years old.

Post-script: Reed received a pardon in 1876, from then governor of New York Samuel Tilden. He allegedly passed away sometime in 1895, at the age of 72, which in terms of late 19th-century America, was a ripe old age.

As Smith (2016) notes, even before the Civil War, the penal system that currently houses a million Blacks in the north was being built. Ever to be a blemish on the criminal justice system and part of social justice movements' goals long before the tragic George Floyd incident in 2020[12], the mass incarceration of Black males and females is part and parcel of the history of corrections in the United States.

SOURCES

Brown, A. (2018) Suicide and the fear of flogging. Social History Society. Sept. 17. Retrieved from https://socialhistory.org.uk/shs_exchange/suicide-and-the-fear-of-flogging/.

NAACP (n.d.) Criminal justice fact sheet. Retrieved from https://www.naacp.org/criminal-justice-fact-sheet/.

Sampson, R. J. and J. L. Lauritsen (1997) Racial and ethnic disparities in crime and criminal justice in the United States. *Crime and Justice*. Vol. 21 (Crime and Immigration: Comparative and Cross-National Perspectives):311-374.

Smith, C., ed. (2016) *The Life and Adventures of a Haunted Convict, Austin Reed.* New York, NY: Random House. Digital.

INTERNATIONAL PERSPECTIVES ON PUNISHMENT AND CORRECTIONS: AUSTRALIA

Like India, Australia is a former British colony and makes for noteworthy contrast with our history of corrections in the United States. Australia is an interesting anomaly in our mix of countries discussed in international perspectives within this book. It is both a continent and a country. Though the continent is known to have been populated by indigenous Aborigines for millennia, the British, after adding Australia to its growing empire, used the continent as a *penal colony* between 1788

---

[12] 46-year-old George Floyd was killed while taken into custody by Minneapolis police for allegedly passing off a counterfeit $20 while buying cigarettes at a convenience store.

and 1868, as a place to put prisoners from Britain and its colonies. This is similar to the case of British prisoners being sent to the American colonies, with some distinct differences. The prisoners sent to Australia were not always nonviolent offenders. In fact, a number of them had been convicted of homicide and violent theft (Godfrey, 2019). Unlike the United States where relatively few criminals were sent during the Colonial era, countless numbers of people living in Australia today are descendants of those prisoners. Australia, along with many of the other countries we are examining in this book, currently has high rates of incarceration and prison overcrowding.

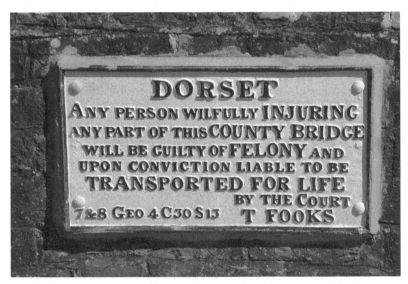

Dorset Sturminster Newton Bridge Warning Sigh, 19th Century, United Kingdom. (*Source:* British Literature Wiki, University of Delaware, n.d., retrieved from https://sites.udel.edu/britlitwiki/the-victorians-and-australian-penal-colonies/)

To understand Australia's penal and corrections systems, it is valuable to understand its roots as a penal colony, similar to how we better understand Russia's by reviewing the history of Gulag prison camps. Between 1850 and 1868, men in Britain who were convicted of similar crimes were offered the choice of whether to serve time in a British prison or go to Australia to serve their sentence, as a means to increase the population in the new colony (Godfrey, 2019). Prior to 1850, the convicted might be shipped off to the Australian penal colony without volunteering to do so. For the non-convict population living in western Australia, they welcomed prisoners as they needed their labor to build their settlements (Godfrey, 2019). In addition to being sent to Australia, British prisoners as young as nine years old were sent to Tasmania penal colonies as well as forced labor (*E2BN*, 2006).

In comparing conditions in British prisons and the Australian penal colony, as harsh as conditions may have been in 19th-century incarceration, there is evidence that Australia was the lesser of two evils. By using prisoners as labor in Australia, it gave rise to an entrepreneurial class, where "laundered" (translation, reformed) convicts eventually made their way into society after release, many of who avoided reoffending with education, training, and employment, as well as the support by family and fellow ex-convicts in Australia (Godfrey, 2019). British prisons were in a habit of not only housing criminals but the poor, creating an endless cycle of hopelessness, sometimes intergenerationally. With convicts in Australia allowed to get married, have children, and eventually be employed for wages, unlike prisoners in Britain at the time, there was far more motivation for ex-convicts in Australia to live conventional lives.

A factor in order to better understand conditions in Australian prisons today is to review the horrific treatment of Aboriginal people since the 19th century. In a misguided program and now described as the *Stolen Generations*, Aboriginal and Torres Strait Islander children were removed from their parents between 1910 and 1969, with some stories placing the time period as actually prior to and after these dates (*Australians Today*, 2020). They were either placed in state homes or placed in adoption with non-Aboriginal families. The intent, similar to what was done to Native American and First Nations children in North America, was to forcibly assimilate them into the dominant white culture in Australia by removing all vestiges of their indigenous culture, including language and religion.

Aboriginals and Islanders who were removed from their families were exposed to (*Australians Today*, 2020):

- Psychological, physical, and sexual abuse while in state care and/or with their adoptive families.
- Efforts to make them feel shamed for their indigenous culture.
- False stories that their parents had been abusive, had died, or had abandoned them as reasons for removing them from their biological families.
- Oppressively controlled environments, where children were punished harshly, were cold and hungry, and denied affection.
- A very low level of education, being expected to work as manual laborers and domestic servants, with no hope of advancing in career or social status.

The effects of the government policy are still felt by Aboriginal people today, by those who were part of the Stolen Generations and their descendants, including unresolved trauma (Larkin, 2020). One grave effect is that members of the Stolen Generations have not only lost their indigenous culture, but their language as well. Their deplorable education while under state or adoptive care was so poor that many of them are unable to help their own children with their schoolwork and education, and experience lifelong economic consequences for both themselves and their offspring (*Australians Today*, 2020). As we know from criminological theory, lower levels of education are highly correlated with crime and in turn, risk for incarceration, as economic opportunities are diminished. It is also correlated with higher rates of recidivism.

Like Native American, First Nations people of North America, Aboriginals are more likely to misuse alcohol than non-Aboriginals (d'Abbs, 2019), a problem that has not been adequately addressed with current policies. Self-harm by alcohol abuse may be contributing to the number of Aboriginals in Australian prisons. Today, in the same way that Black males are over-represented in American jails and prisons, there is over-representation of indigenous people in Australian prisons (Shephard et al., 2016).

Similarly to what we see in the way of prison reform in the United States, not all news coming out of contemporary Australia prisons is grim. Australia is one of the few countries that are including more contemporary organized exercise programs in prison, to aid with the mental and physical wellbeing of prisoners. One such program that involves both yoga and meditation, The Parinaama Prison Project, originated in Mexico and has volunteer instructors trained in a number of different traditions (Prison Mindfulness Institute, 2003). Australia has also implemented yoga for prisoners as a form of well-being intervention. Although some inmates view yoga as "weird," participants report that they were excited and grateful to be participating in the program (Hopkins et al., 2019). Yoga and meditation programs in Australia are viewed as a mean to show concern and compassion for inmates, as well as recognizing their humanity (Hopkins et al., 2019).

SOURCES

Australians Today (2020) The Stolen Generations: The forcible removal of Aboriginal and Torres Strait Islander children from their families. Nov. 17. Retrieved from https://australianstogether.org.au/discover/australian-history/stolen-generations#stolengenref5.

d'Abbs, P. (Jamijin)[13] (2019) Aboriginal alcohol policy and practice in Australia: A case study of unintended consequences. *International Journal of Drug Policy*. Apr., Vol. 66:9-14.

E2BN (2006) Convict life in Australia. *Victorian Crime and Punishment*. Retrieved from http://vcp.e2bn.org/justice/page11384-convict-life-in-australia.html.

Godfrey, B. (2019) Prison versus Western Australia: Which worked best, the Australian penal colony or the English prison system? *British Journal of Criminology*. Vol. 59:1139-1160.

Hopkins, A., L. Bartels, and L. Oxman (2019) Lessons in flexibility: Introducing a yoga program in an Australian prison. *International Journal of Crime, Justice and Social Democracy*. Vol. 8, No. 4:47-61.

Larkin, S. (2020) Addressing the gap within the gap. *Journal of Indigenous Wellbeing*. May, Vol. 5, Iss. 1, Art. 6:72-78.

Prison Mindfulness Institute (2013) Prison yoga in Mexico. Jul. 15. Retrieved from https://www.prisonmindfulness.org/prison-yoga-practice-in-mexico/.

Shepherd, S. M., J. R. P. Ogloff, and S. D. M. Thomas (2016) Are Australian prisons meeting the needs of Indigenous offenders? *Health and Justice*. Vol. 4:13-22.

---

[13] Peter d'Abbes is a member of Jamijin, an Aboriginal tribal group in Australia.

GLOSSARY

13th Amendment   Section 1, Exception Clause, as it relates to corrections: "Neither slavery nor involuntary servitude, except as a punishment for crime. . . ." (*Constitution Annotated*, n.d., retrieved from https://constitution.congress.gov/browse/essay/amdt13_S1_1_2/#:~:text=Thirteenth%20Amendment%2C%20Section%201%3A,place%20subject%20to%20their%20jurisdiction)

Antebellum   In American history, the period prior to the Civil War, usually referring to the southern states.

Bail   An amount set by the court that allows the accused to be conditionally released from jail prior to trial.

Branding   A common punishment during the Colonial Era, involving the use of a hot iron to mark the accused indicating their convict status for life.

Buccaneers   Spanish term for pirates who operated primarily off of the Spanish American coasts, as well as off the coasts of southeastern America.

Corporal punishment   Any form of physical punishment (e.g., whipping, branding).

Habeas corpus   Legal right for someone who has been arrested to be brought before a judge in a timely matter (which is subjective) and provide provisions for release, unless there are legal grounds to detain the accused before trial.

Indentured servant   An individual in Colonial times who voluntarily enters a contract to work for an employer for free, save room and board, in return for payment of travel expenses. Example: An immigrant cannot afford to travel to the American colonies, so promises to work for free in return for the payment of passage to America.

Lynching   An unsanctioned, illegal hanging of an accused individual, whether they are guilty or not of their offense, usually by an angry mob.

"New Jim Crow"   Continued use of a caste system in post-Jim Crow southern states, which disadvantages Blacks and other minorities by discrimination and prejudice.

Penal colony (United States and Australia)   Off shore communities housing prisoners established in more remote parts of the world, as in the example of 19th-century England's Australian penal colony. Not all criminals sent to penal colonies were hardened, violent criminals. Some worked as servants to settlers who could eventually become part of the larger community after serving their time. Others were/are used as forced labor, including on chain gangs.

Penitence   The display of regret and apology for wrongdoings, usually with some form of religious request for forgiveness.

Piracy   The attacking and robbing of ships on the seas and along coastlines, by robbers and pillagers who traveled by sea.

Privateers   Pirates who are operating on the high seas with the blessing of a government, including military activities along with robbery.

Seditious libel   A concept brought over from England to the American colonies, making it a criminal offense to publish or make statements that are anti-government.

Sentencing Project,   From their website, a non-profit that "promotes effective and humane responses to crime that minimize imprisonment and criminalization of youth and adults by promoting racial, ethnic, economic, and gender justice." See https://www.sentencingproject.org/about-us/

Stolen Generation (Australia)   Similar to the practices of Indian Schools in the United States, children of indigenous Aborigines in Australia were taken from their homes from 1910 to the 1970s. Under the guise of the Aboriginal Protection Act of 1869, the policy was instated as a form of horrendous racial genocide with the expectation that the indigenous race would die out with the mixing of races between Caucasian settlers and Aborigines over time. This included the attempted erasure of language, culture, and religious practices of the indigenous people on the continent of Australia and surrounding islands.

Waste management model   A punishment philosophy in the United States that promotes the removal of convicted criminals, sequestering them far from the rest of society, where they and the prisons they are housed in cannot be seen by the general population.

REFERENCES AND SUGGESTED READINGS

Acevedo, J. F. (2017) Dignity Takings in the Criminal Law of Seventeenth-Century England and the Massachusetts Colony. *Chicago-Kent Law Review*. Summer, Vol. 92, Iss. 3:743-767.

Alexander, M. (2020) *The New Jim Crow: Mass Incarceration in the Age of Colorblindness*. New York, NY: The New Press.

Avalon Project, The (n.d.) Alabama: Constitution of 1819. Lillian Goldman Law Library, Yale Law School. Retrieved from https://avalon.law.yale.edu/19th_century/ala1819.asp.

Barton, (2014) *Literary Executions: Capital Punishment and American Culture*, 1820-1925. Baltimore, MD: Johns Hopkins University Press.

Bernstein, L. (2013) The Hudson River School of Incarceration: Sing Sing Prison in antebellum New York. *American Nineteenth Century History*. Vol. 14, No. 3:261-292.

Black, H. L. et al. (1993) "Life after prison": Successful community reintegration programs, reduced recidivism in Illinois. Southeaster Illinois College, Correctional Education Division. Report. May. Retrieved from https://files.eric.ed.gov/fulltext/ED362674.pdf. 19 pp.

Blackman, P. H. and V. McLaughlin (2004) Mass legal executions in America up to 1865, in *Crime, Histoire and Société/Crime, History, and Societies*. International Association for the History of Crime and Criminal Justice. Vol. 8, No. 2:33-61.

Blackman, P. H. and V. McLaughlin (2014) The dog that stopped barking: Mass legal executions in 21st-century America. *Laws*. Vol. 3, Iss. 1:153-162.

Bohm, R. (1999) *Deathquest: An Introduction to the Theory and Practice of Capital Punishment in the United States*. Cincinnati, OH: Anderson Publishing.

Butler, N. (2018) The pirate executions of 1718. Charleston County Public Library. Dec. 8. Retrieved from https://www.ccpl.org/charleston-time-machine/pirate-executions-1718.

Cary, J. H. (1958) France looks to Pennsylvania. *The Pennsylvania Magazine of History and Biography*. Apr., Vol. 82, No. 2:186-203.

Clark, E. B. (1995) 'The sacred right of the weak': Punishment and the culture of individual rights in Antebellum America. *Journal of American History*. Sept., Vol. 82, Iss. 2:423.

Conrad, S. (2011) A restorative environmental justice for e-waste recycling. *Peace Review*. Jul.-Sept., Vol. 23, Iss. 3:348-355.

Cooke, B. K, R. C. W. Hall, S. H. Friedman, A. Jain, and R. Wagoner (2019) Professional boundaries in corrections. *The Journal of the American Academy of Psychiatry and the Law*. Mar., Vol. 47, No. 1:91-99.

Cox, J. A. (2003) Bilboes, brands and branks: Colonial crimes and punishment. Colonial Williamsburg Journal. Spring. Retrieved from https://research.colonialwilliamsburg.org/Foundation/journal/spring03/branks.cfm.

Davis, A. M. (1895) The law of adultery and ignominious punishments with especial reference to the penalty of wearing a letter affixed to the clothing. *Proceedings of the American Antiquarian Society*. Vol. 10, Iss. 1:97-126.

Dolin, E. J. (2018) Turning the tide against piracy in America: Pardons, punishments, British Naval Power, and plenty of hanging. *Crime Reads*. Oct. 15. Retrieved from https://crimereads.com/turning-the-tide-against-piracy-in-america/.

Durham, A. M. (1989) Managing the costs of modern corrections: Implications of Nineteenth-Century privatized prison-labor programs. *Journal of Criminal Justice*. Vol. 17:441-455.

Earle, A. M. (1896) *Curious Punishments of Bygone Days*. New York: Macmillan. Available at https://www.gutenberg.org/files/34005/34005-h/34005-h.htm

Edgerton, K. (2004) Montana Justice: Power, Punishment and the Penitentiary. Seattle, WA: University of Washington Press.

Friedman, L. M. (1993) *Crime and Punishment in American History*. New York, NY: Basic Books.

Gaskew, T. (2014) *Rethinking Prison Reentry: Transforming Humiliation into Humility*. Latham, NY: Lexington Books.

Genealogy Trails (n.d.) History of Montana's State Penitentiary. Powell County, Montana: Genealogy and History. Retrieved from http://genealogytrails.com/mon/powell/prison.html.

Goldsmith, L. (1999) "To profit by his skill and to traffic on his crime": Prison labor in Early 19th-Century Massachusetts. *Labor History*. Vol. 40, No. 4:439-457.

Holiday, J. S. (1999) *Rush for Riches: Gold Fever and the Making of California*. Oakland, CA: Oakland Museum of California; Berkeley, CA: University of California Press.

Kageyama, B. (n.d.) America's last public execution. *History of Yesterday*. Retrieved from https://historyofyesterday.com/americas-last-public-execution-bb4b86c019ed.

Kashatus, W. (1999) "Punishment, penitence, and reform": Eastern Penitentiary and the controversy over solitary confinement. *Pennsylvania Heritage*. Winter. Retrieved from http://paheritage.wpengine.com/article/punishment-penitence-reform-eastern-state-penitentiary-controversy-solitary-confinement/.

Kumar, K. (2012) Greece and Rome in the British Empire: Contrasting role models. *Journal of British Studies*. Jan., Vol. 51, No. 1:76-101.

Lobel, J. (2020) Mass solitary and mass incarceration: Explaining the dramatic rise in prolonged solitary in America's prisons. *Northwestern University Law Review*. Vol. 115, Iss.1:159-209.

LeFlouria, T. L. (2015) *Chained in Silence: Black Women and Convict Labor in the New South.* Chapel Hill, NC: The University of North Carolina Press.

Miller, W. R., ed. (2012) Introduction, in *The Social History of Crime and Punishment in America: An Encyclopedia.* London, UK: SAGE Publications, Inc.

Montagne, R. (2001) The last public execution in America. NPR, *Morning Edition.* May 1. Retrieved from https://legacy.npr.org/programs/morning/features/2001/apr/010430.execution.html#:~:text=Rainey%20Bethea%20was%20hanged%20on,last%20public%20execution%20in%20America.

National Research Council of the National Academies (2014) *The Growth of Incarceration in the United States: Exploring Causes and Consequences.* Retrieved from https://www.nap.edu/read/18613/chapter/1. Summary:2.

Pak, E. (2020) 10 iconic Wild West figures. *Biography.* Apr. 30. Retrieved from https://www.biography.com/news/wild-west-figures

Payton, J. M. (2013) Alexander Oliver Exquemelin's The Buccaneers of America and the disenchantment of Imperial history. *Early American Literature.* Spring, Vol. 48, Iss. 2:337-364.

Pennsylvania Prison Society (n.d.) Our history. Retrieved from https://www.prisonsociety.org/history.

Perrin, P. and W. Coleman (1998) *Crime and Punishment: The Colonial Period to the New Frontier.* Carlisle, MA: Discovery Enterprises, Ltd.

Rawls, J. J. (1999) *A Golden State: Mining and Economic Development in Gold Rush California.* Berkeley, CA: University of California Press.

Ridge, M. (1999) Disorder, crime, and punishment in the California Gold Rush. *Montana: The Magazine of Western History.* Autumn, Vol. 49, No. 3 (Gold Rush Issue):12-27.

Sellers, J. B. and H. E. Amos Doss (1994) Crimes and punishments of slaves, in *Slavery in Alabama.* Tuscaloosa, AL: University of Alabama Press. Ch. 7.

Sigelman, L., S. A. Tuch, and J. K. Martin (2005) What's in a name: Preference for "black" versus "African American" among Americans of African descent. *Public Opinion Quarterly.* Fall, Vol. 69, No. 3:429-438.

Sing Sing Prison Museum (n.d.) History. Retrieved from http://www.singsingprisonmuseum.org/history-of-sing-sing-prison.html.

Smith, C., ed. (2016) *The Life and Adventures of a Haunted Convict, Austin Reed.* New York, NY: Random House. Digital.

Torrey, E. F., M. T. Zdanowicz, A. D. Kennard, H. R. Lamb, D. F. Eslinger, M. C. Biasotti, and D. A. Fuller (2014) *The Treatment of Persons with Mental Illness: A State Survey.* Treatment Advocacy Center. Apr. 8. Retrieved from https://www.treatmentadvocacycenter.org/storage/documents/treatment-behind-bars/treatment-behind-bars.pdf.

United States 2020 Census (2021) Quick facts. Retrieved from https://www.census.gov/quickfacts/fact/table/US/PST045219.

United States Department of Labor (n.d.) Child labor. Wage and Hour Division. Retrieved from https://www.dol.gov/agencies/whd/child-labor#:~:text=The%20federal%20child%20labor%20provisions,well%2Dbeing%20or%20educational%20opportunities.

United States Department of Labor (2021) Correctional officers and bailiffs. Occupational Outlook Handbook. Apr. 9. Retrieved from https://www.bls.gov/ooh/protective-service/correctional-officers.htm#:~:text=in%20May%202020.-,Job%20Outlook,to%20keep%20order%20in%20courtrooms. .

Walters, D. California's per-inmate cost has skyrocketed to $75,000 a year. The Mercury News. May 21. Retrieved from https://www.mercurynews.com/2018/05/20/walters-why-californias-per-inmate-cost-has-skyrocketed-to-about-75000-a-year/.

Webb, W. F. and S. A. Brody (1968) The California Gold Rush and the mentally ill. *Southern California Quarterly.* Mar., Vol. 50, No. 1:430-50.

Wilson, R. M. (2013) *Crime and Punishment in Early Arizona.* Sacramento, CA: Stagecoach Publishing.

Ziegler, E. M. (2014) *Harlots, Hussies, and Poor Unfortunate Women: Crime, Transportation, and Servitude of Female Convicts, 1718-1783*. Tuscaloosa, AL: University of Alabama Press.

SUGGESTED NONFICTION AND FICTIONAL ACCOUNTS OF PUNISHMENT IN AMERICA

Dead Man Walking: An Eyewitness Account of the Death Penalty in the United States. Sister Helen Prejean (1993)

In the Belly of the Beast: Letters from Prison. Jack Henry Abbott (1981)

In the Place of Justice. Wilbert Rideau (2010)

No Beast So Fierce. Edward Bunker (2011)

Orange is the New Black. Piper Kerman (2010)

The Birdman of Alcatraz. Robert Stroud (1962)

The Brethren. John Grisham.

The Executioner's Song. Norman Mailer. (1980)

The Scarlet Letter. Nathanial Hawthorne (1850)

Solitary: Unbroken by Four Decades in Solitary Confinement. Albert Woodfox (2019)

Chapter THREE

Prison Architecture and Structure

> *No one truly knows a nation until one has been inside its jails. A nation should not be judged by how it treats its highest citizens but its lowest ones.*
>
> — Nelson Mandela

Chapter Objectives

- Review the classification systems of prisons.
- Explore the form and function of jail and prison architecture.
- Introduce the challenges to building jails and prisons, including the "Not in my backyard" (NIMBY) mentality of locals and stakeholders.
- Review new eco-friendly practices in today's prisons.

Key Terms

Administrative-level security	"Not in my backyard" (NIMBY)
Biophilic design	Protective custody
High security prisons	Sally port
Infirmary	Solitary confinement
Low security prisons	"Supermax" prisons
Medium security prisons	Units or pods

INTRODUCTION

In this chapter we examine not only the physical space of jails and prisons, but the psychological effects of jail and prison design on the incarcerated. Some of the jails and prisons still in use today that are discussed in this book were built several decades ago and may have outlived their usefulness. Others are brand new, built with the latest technology and based on the most recent punishment philosophies, implementing an eco-friendly design. And still others have simply been built in response to the rise in mass incarceration that required an investment of more state and federal money in their construction (Nadel and Mears, 2020).

As much as clinical settings like hospitals and medical facilities can be cold, impersonal, and intimidating, there is perhaps no setting more intimidating than a jail or prison, even in the most progressive countries. Punishment is built into the harshness of the accommodations, as even the not-yet-convicted who are living in jails are meant to feel that they are separated from society in more ways than one:

> To confine, secure, rehabilitate or punish: the prison has several, sometimes contradictory aims, but however humane its approach, penal architecture is essentially cruel . . . The Marquis de Sade wanted to beat his brains out against them [referring to the cell walls], Jean Genet was moved to kiss them. The walls of prisons are invested with a strange kind of energy: whether implacable or erotic, they are never simply structural. (Wilkinson, 2018, retrieved from https://www.architectural-review.com/essays/typology/typology-prison)

Jails and prisons are specifically designed for control and surveillance of all activities of detainees and prisoners. Perhaps the most intimidating humiliation that inmates experience, beyond body cavity searches, is the loss of privacy when using a toilet or shower. There is very little in the way of modesty allowed in jails and prisons, with all bodily functions taking place in front of witnesses. This is not to purposefully humiliate detainees or prisoners, but to assure that they are not retrieving contraband from some orifice of their body or conducting any other prohibited activities outside the view of corrections officers.

We will be speaking a bit later in this chapter about the Suffolk County Sheriff's Department in Boston which houses the Nashua Street Jail, which has open air basketball courts (one chainlink-fenced wall, at least) where the detainees and convicted can get the only fresh air in the place. However, their privileges to use the basketball courts can be taken away if they start shouting at or try to communicate with any pedestrian below, or if there are any disputes over basketball possession. As one corrections officer working at Nashua Street Jail explained, there are times when there is only one basketball to serve 60+ detainees or inmates.

We also need to talk about the practicalities of managing jails and prisons and how their design can help facilitate the smooth running of operations. Corrections in general became more bureaucratic after WWII (Woodruff, 2017), which in turn had an effect on design. Unlike the older prisons in the United States discussed in Chapter 2, contemporary jails and prisons utilize technology that can greatly increase security for both the incarcerated and staff. What prison design today has in common with prisons of yesteryear is that they are still built based on whatever current philosophies of punishment and rehabilitation are in vogue at the moment.

There cannot be discussion of jail and prison designs without examining their effects on detainees and prisoners, as well as staff. We know from our some of own needs for personal space, that our surroundings can have a large impact on our mental well-being. Except perhaps for the prisoner who is in and out of jail or prison on a regular basis, sometimes intentionally when they cannot cope in the outside world, prison will never feel like home. And for good reason—it shouldn't.

As much as we may find that the designs of prisons are inherently made to provide discomfort to inmates, they are a far cry from the jails and prisons prior to the 19th century. Early jails and prisons, lacking any real offender management, typically consisted of unventilated, cold, and miserable places located in the bowels of a castle, crowded, disease-ridden cages, or prison ships (Waid and Clements, 2001). For the accused, this might translate to a death sentence, no matter how minor the offense, if they died from the conditions of jail or prison.

The ideal is to have inmates serve their debt to society, be released, then get on with their lives on the outside. The reality is that there are some convicts who function better in prison than they do in society. Or even after release, continue to be threats to society, where their time in prison has not served as a deterrence to reoffending. The jails and walls of prisons become all too familiar for the chronic offender. Like adult children who cannot bring themselves to leave their parental units' home, there are some convicts who purposely reoffend to find themselves back in familiar surroundings, as intimidating as prison may seem to the rest of us.

PRISON CLASSIFICATION SYSTEMS

The design of prison is dependent on the level of security needed in any facility. It is very appropriate to consider the classification of a prison in our discussion of prison architecture, as security level is one key component in deciding the design. Typically, there are *low* or *minimum security*, *medium security*, *high security*, and "*supermax*" prisons, though the names may be different, depending on the state. Along with these more typical types of prisons, there are also juvenile, psychiatric, and military prisons. Of course, we tend to see juvenile facilities labeled with much softer terminology, such as "juvenile detention facility." We will go into more depth on the labels used for prison facilities for juveniles in Chapter 7.

A *low* or *minimum security* prison may be called a "camp" and is generally set up in dormitory style housing. Most commonly used to house white collar offenders and low level, nonviolent felony convicts, like those who have been convicted of recreational drug possession, these have had a history of appearing to be to "luxurious" for inmates, in comparison to traditional prisons. Martha Stewart was sentenced to serve time in Alderson Federal Prison Camp in connection with an illegal ImClone stock trade. The prison, located in West Virginia, had been nicknamed "Camp Cupcake" for its seemingly resort-like atmosphere. A photo of a minimum security prison that once was a hospital in Cranston, Rhode Island, can be seen in the next photo, with a similar reputation as the Alderson Federal Prison Camp. As compared to more secure prisons, the Rhode Island prison, at least from the outside, resembles a hotel, more than a place that houses convicts.

Minimum Security State Facility, Cranston, RI. (*Source*: State of Rhode Island, Department of Corrections, retrieved from http://www.doc.ri.gov/institutions/facilities/minimum.php)

With public backlash, some prison camps have done away with luxuries like tennis courts, that could be misconstrued as going too easy on convicts. Federal facilities like Alderson Federal Prison Camp have also been nicknamed, "Club Fed," as in the case of the Federal Correctional Institution in Dublin, California. Actress Felicity Hoffman of "Varsity Blues" college admissions scandal fame briefly stayed there after pleading guilty to charges against her of paying to have her daughter's SAT scores inflated (Gonzales, 2019). The Dublin facility has been rated as one of most cushy of prisons, and resembles, again, a summer camp, at least in physical design. Depending on their behavior, prisoners can be transferred from a higher security prison to a lower security prison if they have longer sentences, and based on good behavior.

A *medium security* prison is intended to house prisoners who require stricter schedules and confinement than found in minimum security prisons. These are prisoners who do not require close supervision, but do not meet the criteria for a minimum security prison (Petek, 2019). There is, of course, the risk of misclassification of prisoners, as was the case in the Colorado state prisons where, a decade ago, there was a rise in prison violence in medium security facilities, partially attributed to the presence of convicted gang members (Harmon, 2010). A spokesperson for the Colorado Department of Corrections, Katherine Sanguinetti, stated that "It was the wrong offender in the wrong bed and we need to get the right offender in the right bed." (Harmon, 2010, retrieved from https://go-gale-com.wne.idm.oclc.org/ps/i.do?v=2.1&u=mlin_w_westnew&it=r&id=GALE%7CA217514840&p=GPS&sw=w). An example of a medium security facility, which resembles the prisons that we expect to see, can be found in the next photo of the federal prison in El Reno, Oklahoma.

Medium Security Federal Correctional Institute, Three Rivers, TX. (*Source*: https://en.wikipedia.org/wiki/Federal_Correctional_Institution,_Three_Rivers#/media/File:ThreeRiversNewBOPimage.jpg)

In a *maximum security* prison, you find primarily the most serious offenders. However, there are times when judges wish to make an example of a white collar nonviolent offender by sending them to a maximum security facility to serve time alongside murders, rapists, and other violent offenders. To some extent, the sentencing of the convicted to one type of facility or another can be arbitrary, based on the preferences of the judge and the amount of pressure from the public or victims.

There is an additional level of security beyond maximum security that the U.S. Federal Bureau of Prisons uses. *Administrative-security level* facilities, or ADXs, house a mixed population of prisoners, including those who have special medical needs to the containment of dangerous, violent inmates, or those who are escape-prone, as well as those who are pretrial on federal offenses (U.S. Federal Bureau of Prisons, n.d.). An infamous inmate of an ADX facility was Bernie Madoff, who was convicted on charges of running a Ponzi scheme[1] and served time at the administrative-security level federal prison located in North Carolina until his death from natural causes in April, 2021.

---

[1] A Ponzi scheme is a white collar criminal offense where older investors are being paid with new investors' money.

A super maximum security prison, more commonly referred to as a *"super-max"* is a prison that employs even more corrections officers than a maximum security prisons. Supermax facilities house the most dangerous and violent of offenders, as well as high profile inmates who committed particularly heinous crimes, many of whom are serving time on death row. Unlike most maximum security prisons, inmates spend much of their time in their cells as they pose particularly high security risks to other inmates and to staff. There are both state and federal supermax prisons. An example of a federal supermax, ADX prison is the U.S. penitentiary in Florence, Colorado, seen in the next photo.

Federal ADX (Supermax) Prison, Florence, CO. (*Source*: Beckman, KRCC, 2019, retrieved from https://www.cpr.org/2019/06/27/investigative-report-alleges-human-rights-abuses-at-colorados-supermax-prison/)

Some of the more famous inmates sent to the federal supermax in Colorado include:

- Timothy McVeigh, convicted of domestic terrorism and the 1995 bombing of the federal building in Oklahoma City. Executed on June 11, 2001, at the U.S. Penitentiary in Terre Haute, Indiana.
- Ted Kaczynski, the so-called "Unibomber," convicted of domestic terrorism after he delivered homemade bombs to, targeted universities and college professors.
- Robert Hanssen, convicted of espionage and sharing classified government information with Russia.

The classification of a prisoner is not the only determining factor in where they might be housed. At least in the case of decisions made on where to place someone who has been convicted on federal charges, the location of the prison is also taken into consideration on a number of other factors:

The Bureau of Prisons shall designate the place of the prisoner's imprisonment, and shall, subject to bed availability, the prisoner's security designation, the prisoner's programmatic needs, the prisoner's mental and medical needs, any request made by the prisoner related to faith-based needs, recommendations of the sentencing court, and other security concerns of the Bureau of Prisons, place the prisoner in a facility as close as practicable to the prisoner's primary residence, and to the extent practicable, in a facility within 500 driving miles of that facility. (BOP, U.S. Department of Justice, 2019, retrieved from https://www.bop.gov/policy/progstat/5100_008cn.pdf)

The classification of prisons has an effect on both prisoners and staff. In a study of prison corrections officers in Indiana state facilities, prison staff reported more job satisfaction working in medium security prisons, given their ability to have more control over their work-related activities, as compared to those working in maximum security prisons (Roy et al., 2012). We can also guess that the happiest prison staff are those who work in minimum security prisons, where there are fewer concerns for personal safety, based on the types of more trusted prisoners housed there.

FORM AND FUNCTION

There is the reality for prison architects and state and federal corrections administration that in most cases, the public does not want to see a prison built in their community, particularly in more urban or suburban communities. In fact, "*not in my backyard*" or *NIMBY* can be applied aptly to where prisons are constructed. One concern is for what will happen once the detained or convicted are released into the community. One fear, whether real or imagined, is that crime will somehow seep into the community with the presence of a jail or prison. Of course, some larger police departments located in the middle of communities already have holding cells for people who are arrested, in which case, technically jail facilities are in many neighborhoods that have police departments, without the residents necessarily being aware of their proximity.

According to the *Independent Lens* (PBS, 2017), 70 percent of prisons are built in rural areas. Prisons can provide a number of economic advantages for smaller communities, particularly for those that had been dependent on industries such as manufacturing that, due to technological advances, moved operations to urban areas or overseas for cost-saving benefits (Swenson, 2019). The reality is that jobs are disappearing from rural areas in the United States and building prisons in them is an attractive proposition for many rural residents. So, there are in some cases a "yes, in my own backyard" or "YIMBY" mentality,

FIGURE 3.1 | **Rural America's Economic Dependence on Prisons**
(*Source*: Independent Lens, PBS, 2017, retrieved from https://www.pbs.org/independentlens/
blog/prison-economy-how-do-prisons-affect-the-places-we-live/)

where new prison construction is welcomed because of the jobs and commerce that will result from it. If a rural area is dependent on the jobs and commerce that a prison brings to the community, then any threat of closure will adversely affect the local economy as demonstrated in Figure 3.1. So, in the case of rural areas, prisons are not necessarily viewed as a liability, but as an opportunity for economic survival in the face of the migration of other industries to urban settings or overseas.

Much of what jails and prisons look like on the outside, in contemporary terms, has to do with where they are located. For example, from the outside, the Nashua Street Jail in Boston looks like any other office building, right down to bars on the windows that look like vertical blinds to persons passing by. Considering the relatively expensive residential homes and high-rise condominium complexes just across the Charles River, potential buyers would hardly want to invest in a property that has a view of a jail that distinctly looks like a correctional facility. We should also note that the world-renowned medical facility Brigham and Women's Hospital is right across the street from the jail as well. The esthetics in the architecture of the jail fits in seamlessly with the surrounding area.

Nashua Street Jail, Suffolk County Sheriff's Department Boston. (*Source*: Inmate Aide, n.d., retrieved from https://www.inmateaid.com/prisons/suffolk-county-nashua-street-jail)

In other cases, because of the remote location, the architect does not hide the fact that it is a prison. For example, the medium security prison for men in Chino, California, was built solely for function and is spartan in any sense of creative design. Built in 1941, the builders could not have anticipated that the surrounding area of the city, some 41 miles southeast of Los Angeles would eventually be the location of the primarily upper middle class community of Chino Hills (California Department of Corrections, n.d.). In the 1940s, prior to the urban sprawl of Los Angeles, Orange, and Riverside Counties, the area was primarily made up of cow pastures and other agricultural enterprises. It wasn't until after World War II, and more so during the 1970s and 1980s, that Southern California became wall-to-wall residential areas, businesses, and freeways. The average cost of a home in Chino Hills was $761,114 in 2021 (*Zillow*, 2021), and some of them overlook the prison. Were the same facility being built today, it is more likely that the California Institute for Men (CIM) in Chino would be disguised in some fashion.

Perhaps the most important consideration is cost. Size is an important factor in the cost of building a new prison, but there are other contributing factors including design configuration, number of stories, and security level (Nadel and Mears, 2020). Whether jails or prisons are public or private, they essentially have to be run like businesses. This requires that operating costs be reduced as much as possible. Another consideration is that operating spending is dependent on state or federal budget constraints. Design alone can have certain upfront costs, as in the case of using sophisticated technologies to keep detainees and prisoners contained. However, in the long run, that investment in the latest technologies can result in fewer overall costs, including requiring fewer staff or substituting inmate labor wherever possible (e.g., kitchen and housekeeping staff) (Nadel and Mears, 2020; Wener, 2012).

Bottom line, no matter where a jail or prison is built, its primary goals in design are function and efficiency. It is not enough to simply "buy a jail," as Simme et al. (2011) warn. Leaving out the development process of building a new facility means that any existing deficits of a building being purchased, that were factors in why it was abandoned in the first place might not be considered or addressed. Jails are intended to keep the accused and the convicted behind bars and walls in the most cost-effective ways possible, keeping the public safe, as well as serving as part of punishment.

JAIL ARCHITECTURE

For good reason, jails are constructed to hold a variety of suspected offenders. Though there is classification of detainees based on their alleged offenses, jails have to be built to hold the most dangerous offenders, included accused serial killers, rapists, and the criminally insane. Because there are a number of philosophies on the aesthetics of jails, considering that a good portion of those who are housed there are awaiting trial, it becomes the moral dilemma as to whether jail, like prison, should be a miserable experience.

Assuming that the mantra of "innocent until proven guilty" from the U.S. criminal justice system is true, jails should, in theory, be secure, but at least offer some creature comforts. The reality is that from the time someone is arrested to when they have their day in court, they are treated as if they are indeed guilty, whether they are or not, at least when they are housed in jail pretrial.

For good reason, as our communities are varied in their design, so are local jails. In smaller towns, jails are part of a system of criminal justice services, and are included in the same building as a police or sheriff's department and courthouse. Others in larger cities, where more than half of all jailed individuals are housed, resemble prisons separate from law enforcement offices, where the primary function of the building is to serve as a jail to the accused and prison for those convicted who have shorter sentences. As Zimmerman (1916, p 717) pointed out, there is really no model jail:

To be asked to speak on a model jail, without the location of the building being stated, is an architectural subject which is broad and somewhat vague, for it is evident that a model jail for one district administered under the laws and ordinances of one community may be far from serving the purposes of some other locality.

Though Zimmerman was speaking to jail design more than a century ago, what he said then still holds true today. Even though the arrest to conviction ratios might vastly differ from a century ago, Zimmerman notes that jails are peculiar places where most of the people held are there for relatively minor offenses and a limited number will be convicted, at least within the area of jails Zimmerman studied.

Communities vary so much in size that a design for one community will not work for another. If a town is rural or small, the jail staff may know their detainees and convicts, especially those who have shorter sentences, very well. That scenario has been the subject of sitcoms, as in the case of *The Andy Griffith Show*[2] that ran from 1960 to 1968 (CBS Productions). In that television series about a small town sheriff and his bumbling deputy, the character Otis Campbell (portrayed by actor Hal Smith) was the stereotypical town drunk who would, when he was intoxicated, let *himself* into a jail cell until he sobered up. Then he simply grabbed the key, which was within reach of the cell, and let himself out. That, of course, is unheard of in real life.

Though small towns may see the "usual suspects" arrested on a number of charges, this does not mean that they have the same free access to a jail cell when they are inebriated. Larger cities may also have a revolving cast of repeat offenders rotating in and out of their jails, but it is much less likely that the jail staff will know as many of them personally, as in smaller towns.

The bottom line in the construction of jails is that they are made to be as secure as possible to house a wide variety of offenders. What can sometimes be difficult, and will be discussed in our chapter on women in prison, is that there are far fewer female offenders. So depending on the size of the community and jail needs, it may be a challenge to find housing for female detainees. When starting from scratch with a new jail, designers need to consider what their population looks like in that jurisdiction, determine how staff can be best served, and examine all money-saving options that can reasonably be taken while building (Kimme et al., 2011).

PRISON ARCHITECTURE

There are a number of theories as to what is the most effective way to build a prison in order to keep an eye on detainees and prisoners. Another consideration is whether it is better to house prisoners together in communal housing spaces or to segregate prisoners. Earlier prison designs that included single occupant cells were intended to allow prisoners to have time to silently contemplate their misdeeds and to repent for their transgressions. In the 19th century, behavioral change was believed to be achieved with penitence and reflection that could only be achieved in isolation (Nadel and Mears, 2020; Fairweather and McConville, 2000).

---

[2] The Andy Griffith Show can still be seen in syndication and streaming online.

In today's prisons, with overcrowding, except in segregation units discussed later in this chapter, it is impractical to offer detainees or prisoners single occupancy cells. Overcrowding has become so commonplace that places in jails and prisons that have other intended uses, such as gymnasiums, have been at times turned into dormitories to house more people.

JUVENILE FACILITIES

As we have noted elsewhere, jails and prison that are intended to hold juveniles have softer names, such as "juvenile detention centers." However, the same considerations that go into building adult jail and prison facilities have to go into the building of juvenile corrections centers. First concern is the safety and well-being of children being held by youth authorities. Second is that the facility is secure so as to discourage escape.

More recently there have been greater efforts to make juvenile detention facilities less foreboding, as compared to adult jails and prisons. Though rehabilitation is sometimes an afterthought in adult prisons as far as architecture goes, the focus in juvenile detention center design has shifted to designs that provide more natural daylight, restorative surroundings, and calming acoustics with the goal that juveniles who are still undergoing developmental and cognitive changes can still thrive (HMC Architects, 2018).

To facilitate rehabilitation of juveniles, HMC Architects (2018, retrieved from https://hmcarchitects.com/news/juvenile-correctional-facility-design-that-encourages-rehabilitation-2018-10-17/) recommend that the following design elements be included in juvenile correctional facilities, giving the example of Alameda County Juvenile Justice Center in California:

- **Open communal areas** so as to make the facility feel more open, encouraging juveniles to leave their rooms.
- **Flexible furnishings** that are inviting and encourage group discussion or can be arranged for one-on-one, smaller group counseling.
- **Daylighting** to include floor-to-ceiling windows and skylights to let natural light into spaces, giving them a less confining feeling.
- **Central control stations** placed at ground level so as to encourage juveniles to talk to staff, promoting more positive interactions with custodial staff.
- **Outdoor spaces** where juveniles can spend more time in green, non-threatening spaces that encourage outdoor programs, including sports.
- **Durable, familiar materials** that do not appear "institutional."
- **Peaceful features** including soft LED lighting instead of the harsher fluorescent lighting usually found in corrections facilities.
- **Calming acoustics** by including sound-absorbing materials on walls.

- **Convenience** of on-site courtrooms so as to allow juveniles to appear before judges on site.
- **Personalized details** where juveniles are empowered to make their spaces their own, within reason, including choices for bedding color and arrangement of furniture.

Of course, we cannot ignore the fact that in some, thankfully, infrequent cases, children are tried as adults. One example is Lionel Tate, who in 2001, at age 13, was accused and convicted of first-degree murder of a 6-year-old relative. Tate was one of the youngest juveniles to be sentenced to adult prison in Florida.[3] In which case, they are housed, like Tate, with adults and often require protective custody, so as to not be victimized by older inmates.

Interior, Alameda County Juvenile Justice Center, CA. (*Source*: Thompson, Alameda County Probation Department Juvenile Field Services, 2016 retrieved from https://www.law.berkeley.edu/wp-content/uploads/2016/09/Juvenile-Services-Overview-Powerpoint-Judge-Thompson-Edition.pdf)

PRISON DESIGNS

Beyond the need to build prisons specific to security levels, there are some classic designs that have been used, in some cases, for decades, if not for centuries. The list of designs included here are not exhaustive, but offer the best sampling of common designs.

---

[3] In 2006, while on post-incarceration probation, Tate robbed a pizza delivery person at gunpoint, resulting in a 30-year extension of his sentence and a return to adult prison (Aguayo, 2006).

Earlier jails and prisons were communal and did not segregate by age or sex, including in debtors' prisons, first discussed in Chapter 2 on the history of prisons in America. This led to a number of problems, including the sexual exploitation of incarcerated children. As prison reforms came to fruition in the 19th century, improvements were made in the United States and elsewhere in the following ways (Woodruff, 2017, retrieved from https://www.lexipol.com/resources/blog/prison-reform-origin-contemporary-jail-standards/):

- Segregation of prisoners by age, sex, and severity of offense;
- Individual cells instead of common rooms;
- Salaried staff to prevent extortion of prisoners;
- Provisions of adequate clothing and food; and
- Hiring chaplains and doctors.

Contemporary jails and prisons are focused on the practicalities of direct (human) or indirect (technological) supervision and are more likely to have units with separate cells that are clustered around a central monitoring station (Woodruff, 2017). With the technologies discussed in this chapter, this not only becomes a more efficient way to keep an eye on detainees and prisoners (except in maximum security and supermax prisons), but requires less prison staff. The various types of prisons and the philosophies behind their design are summarized in Table 3.1.

TABLE 3.1. Purposes and Goals of Prison Architecture

Safety	Primary concern in prison design and operations.
Security	Mechanisms in place for surveillance or restraint; used to exert control over inmates.
Deterrence	Prisons are designed to be unpleasant so as to act as a deterrence for offending or reoffending.
Rehabilitation	Prisons keep the convicted away from the influences that got them there in the first place. Rehabilitation is a tool to reform and control behavior.
Retribution	The convicted deserve the punishment of live in the discomfort of prison.

Source: Nadel and Mears, 2020.

Panopticon Design, Jeremy Bentham, 18th Century

Jeremy Bentham in the late 18th century proposed a prison design that would separate guards[4] from the inmate population, while assuring that they were secured in

---

[4] We used the term "guard" here as the panopticon design predates the more contemporary term, corrections officer. We do the same elsewhere in this chapter, where it is historically accurate to do so.

their cells and still under surveillance. The key feature of the circular or panopticon design is a large guards' station in the center, with the outer edges of the interior room consisting of rows of prison cells several stories high (Nadel and Mears, 2020; Casella, Evans). Cells face the center of the room were all in the line of sight of a single guard occupying the center station. Bentham also envisioned the design for hospitals and other institutional settings.

This design was cost effective, as it reduced the number of guards needed, while still keeping them safe (Johnston, 2000; Semple 1993). As Casella observed (2007, p. 19; Nadel and Mears, 2020), the design was created to force the "physical and psychological subjugations of its inhabitants." Or as Foucault noted (1977; Nadel and Mears, 2020) about prison design, creates a cruel and ingenious cage, as seen in the next photo. The panopticon design is not generally in use today in contemporary prison design.

Abandoned Panopticon Designed Prison, Cuba. (*Source:* WebUrbanist, n.d., retrieved from https://weburbanist.com/2014/05/15/real-life-panopticons-deserted-dystopian-prisons-in-cuba/)

Radial Design

A radial, star-shaped prison looks something like a wagon wheel, with a central control center and wings built out from it. This, like the panopticon design, is meant to efficiently use guards, where at the central station, activities in all wings can been seen, more or less. Used primarily in England and Ireland, the chief architect of the radial design was William Blackburn (Waid and Clements, 2001). Cells were designed for single occupants and were large enough that inmates could still perform prison labor, while at the same time preventing prisoners to see or talk to one another (Waid and Clements, 2001). An example in the United States is the Eastern State Penitentiary in Philadelphia, discussed in the last chapter. The following photo is an example of a radial-design prison, in the bird's eye schematic of Eastern State Penitentiary.

Bird's Eye View, Eastern State Penitentiary, PA. (*Source*: Inmate Aid, 2021, retrieved from https://www.inmateaid.com/prisons/la-doc-louisiana-state-penitentiary)

Telephone-Pole Design

As the name implies, there is a long central corridor in the telephone-pole design, with the other corridors branching off perpendicular to it. Similar to the radial prison design, this allowed for wings of the prison to be devoted to specific purposes like prison industries and rehabilitation, as well as providing ease of segregation of prisoners by classification (Waid and Clements, 2001; Travisono, 1978). The telephone-pole design eventually replaced the radial design in the early 19th century (Johnston, 2000).

Designed by Alfred Hopkins, interiors in the telephone pole design were more spartan, with fewer design embellishments (Davies, 2007). Because of the design, it required more guards, as each wing required separate supervision. This increased the overall surveillance of prisoners, as well as providing more control over their movements (Bosworth, 2005; Waid and Clements, 2001). The next photo gives an example of the telephone-pole design, as given the example of Louisiana State Penitentiary, Angola.

Louisiana State Penitentiary, Angola, 1934. (*Source*: Inmate Aid, 2021, retrieved from https://www .inmateaid.com/prisons/la-doc-louisiana-state-penitentiary)

Courtyard Design

The courtyard prison design is perhaps the most utilitarian of all prison designs. Built as a square or rectangle building, the center of the prison is open. This is conducive to allowing prisoners recreation time, while keeping them confined more securely than exterior fences or walls. With an open layout, research has indicated that the courtyard design improves inmate-corrections officer relationships (Jacobs, 2017) and is more likely to be used in contemporary prison design.

An example of the courtyard design can be found at the Minnesota Correctional Facility, Oak Park Heights, seen in the next photo.

Courtyard Prison Design, Minnesota Correctional Facility, Oak Park Heights. (*Source*: Minnesota Department of Corrections, n.d., retrieved from https://mn.gov/doc/about/photos-videos/photo-galleries/oak-park-heights.jsp)

Campus Style Design

Depending on the design of your college campus, the campus-style prison will look similar to your college or university. Except for the walls, fences, or barbed wire, of course. Another name for this type of design layout for a prison is "cottage," which again, like "campus style design", is a mislabeling as it is far from being as quaint as the name implies. Campus or cottage designs consist of a number of free standing buildings, each one having a number of cells with communal living area and guard station (Nadel and Mears, 2020; Beijersbergen et al., 2014).

Campus Style Prison Facility, Las Colina Detention Center and Rehabilitation Facility, San Diego, CA. (*Source:* BSCC California, 2021, retrieved from https://hmcarchitects.com/portfolio/civic/las-colinas-detention-and-reentry-facility/)

There is some merit, at least for minimum or medium security facilities, to be built in the campus style design. They tend to be less sterile places than traditional prison designs, as evident by the photo of newly renovated Las Colinas Detention and Reentry Facility, San Diego County, California on the previous page. What was once a dark, crowded, and foreboding facility, now boasts welcoming landscape and openness lacking in most jails around the country. As noted by the Board of State and Community Corrections, California (BSCC) (2021), the design of the women's jail has received national recognition for its resemblance to a community college campus, rather than a jail. As the BSCC also noted (2021), it is an unusual design for a jail, meant to reduce the psychological trauma of incarceration, as well as to reduce recidivism.

High Rise Design

As the name implies, high rise jails and prisons perhaps have the easiest time blending into the surrounding urban landscape. These are buildings, several stories high, that make for efficient land use when real estate is scarce and at a premium. The concern is that unlike surrounding commercial or residential high rise properties, the budgets to build jails are not anywhere on the same scale and they can appear to look, as Wainwright describes (2019, retrieved from https://www.theguardian .com/cities/2019/dec/09/new-yorks-high-rise-prisons-what-could-go-wrong), like a "vertical human storage facility."

Further criticism is that the brutalist[5] architectural style of high rises for prisons is further emphasizes the mass-incarceration, "waste management" model of corrections. The New York City Department of Corrections, a perfect example of trying to manage the jail population in a very expensive real estate market, by considering the building of four jails in the city, as seen in the previous photo of a mockup of the designs.

Perhaps the one redeeming feature of highrise designs is that highrise structures are difficult to destroy, which is fine when you are looking for long-lasting durability

Mockup of Highrise Jail, at Originally Proposed 45 Stories. (Source: Wainwright, 2019, The Guardian, Retrieved from https://www.theguardian.com/cities/2019/dec/09/new-yorks-high-rise-prisons-what-could-go -wrong; NYC Department of Corrections)

---

[5] Brutalist architecture as part of the brutalism movement of the early 20th century is recognized by their resemblance to ultra-modern, cold towers that are generally not thought of as welcoming.

in a jail or prison. But the nearly indestructible construction becomes problematic when a high rise has to be demolished to make way for some other building project.

Tent Cities

The most controversial of all jail or prison designs are the so-called tent cities. The most notorious of these was the Tent City Jail in Maricopa County, Arizona. On the surface, a tent city may seem like a benign way of housing offenders. However, detainees and prisoners in Tent City Jail lived outdoors in tents surrounded by a high chain link fence with barbed wire strung on the top and were exposed to the elements, including harsh winters and blistering heat in the summer. There is no mistaking that this was a place of incarceration. On top of living under these harsh outdoor conditions, the male detainees and inmates were forced to wear striped convict uniforms, reminiscent of chain gangs in the south, as well as pink underwear as a form of humiliation by emasculation (Kennedy, 2017).

After considerable public criticism of the questionable treatment of the incarcerated and of former Maricopa County Sheriff Joe Arpaio, a major proponent of the jail, the tent city was eventually torn down in 2017. In 2017, Arpaio, a "tough on crime" politician, ironically was convicted himself on charges of criminal contempt. He faced prison time when he failed to stop racial profiling on a judge's order, but was pardoned by President Donald Trump that same year (Kelly, 2017; Dwyer, 2017).

For obvious reasons and the controversies, this is not a jail or prison design that has been in wide use, at least in the United States. It would be difficult to find year-round weather conditions anywhere in the United States that would be favorable for tent cities as a solution to incarceration, including problems of overcrowding.

Cells and Units

Like in the design of jails, there are a number of variations on the configuration of cells in the interior of a jail or prison. In many cases there are a number of two-person cells contained in individual units, called by some, "pods." The practicality of having units is that offenders or alleged offenders who have committed similar crimes can be housed together. For example, a unit might be comprised of those awaiting trial on nonviolent drug charges. It also helps to segregate more vulnerable populations as well, as in the case of gang members who are attempting to leave gang life, without necessarily putting them in more confining solitary confinement. It also gives prison staff an opportunity to separate detainees or inmates who are not getting along. Another reason to house certain individuals together is if they are in specific rehabilitation programs.

Prison Unit, Central Utah Correctional Facility, Gunnison. (*Source*: Utah Department of Corrections, retrieved from https://corrections.utah.gov/index.php/home/alerts-2/1132-new-unit-at-central-utah-correctional-facility)

Jail and Prison Designs of the Future

Prison architects and designers are rethinking the one-person, two-person and dormitory forms of incarceration. Just as universities and colleges have rethought what the modern dormitory should look like with the traditional two-person rooms, some designers are looking to technology in creations of suites, rather than cells. In the Netherlands, a high-tech prison has six-person cells, where electronic wristbands are used to track the movement of inmates, as a cheaper alternatives to more traditional unit and cell configurations (Kenis et al., 2010). This can only work if the individuals placed in these suites can form a functioning and stable social structure—prisoners cook together as well as socialize with one another more than in a traditional cell setting (Kenis et al., 2010), better preparing them for life outside of prison.

A less commonly known jail and prison design is the *monolithic dome*, similar to ones that were part of a residential building craze in the 1960s and 70s:

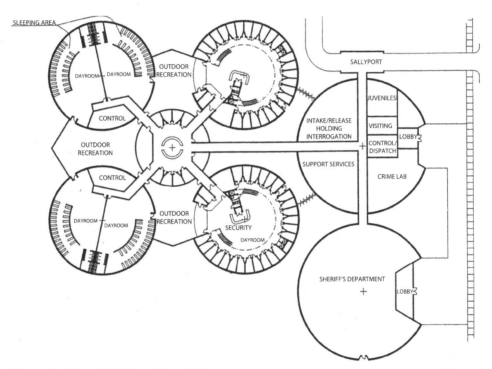

Schematic, Monolithic Dome Prison Design. (*Source*: South, 2009, Monolithicdome.com, retrieved from https://www.monolithic.org/commercial/monolithic-domes-make-perfect-jails-and-prisons)

As South (2009) argues, there are many practicalities to the dome design over conventional prisons:

- They are less expensive to build and operate, and are energy-efficient for heating and cooling.
- The interiors can be open, free of any feature that could be a hiding place for prisoners, including the absence of pillars, columns, or interior walls, giving corrections officers a clear view of prisoners at all times.

▪ The steel-reinforced concrete shells are fireproof and cannot be damaged; inmates cannot simply chisel or knife their way out to an escape.

The monolithic dome design has never really caught on, possibly, some think, because the radical departure from traditional designs may be hard for most jurisdictions accept; or, as others believe, there may be a concern that monolithic domes, long thought of as "hip" residential designs that are best located in lovely wilderness places like ski resorts, may get a bad name if associated with prisons (South, 2009).

As noted, detainees and prisoners who are not in minimum or medium security prisons pretty much have little opportunity to get outside and commune with nature. Prisoners experience more mental health issues than the non-prison population and studies have shown that getting out into the fresh air and sunshine does considerable good to the psyche, whether one is incarcerated or not. Any college student who has stayed inside day after day, either due to the COVID-19 pandemic or because of a heavy course schedule requiring a lot of time at the computer and not outdoors, can attest to that. Or anyone who has endured the long dark winters of Alaska or Antarctica will tell you that living indoors constantly and indefinitely is not good for any human being.

Prisons do not necessarily require expansive outdoor space to provide the benefits of getting outside. Incorporating *biophilic design* with natural greenery and outdoor spaces in jails and prisons can contribute to better mental well-being (Söderlund and Newman, 2017). However, some of the elements in a garden or recreational area outside have to be modified in prisons so as to discourage escape attempts, as in the case of having a climbing wall as are popular in some gyms outside of prison, available for inmates that is too close to the peripheral walls. There are also the humanitarian and public health issues associated with continued indoor living, where we see greater outbreak of diseases and epidemics in poorly designed buildings (Asim and Shree, 2020).

Biophilic Design Elements for Prisons. (*Source*: Asim and Shree, 2019; Frumkin, 2001, retrieved from file:///Users/laurahansen/Downloads/preprints201907.0323.v1%20(1).pdf)

PRISONS WITHIN PRISONS

If you consider that even medium security prisons have to have separate accommodations for when prisoners become unruly, there are more secured units in prisons for this purpose. In many ways, these can be considered prisons within prisons, as segregation units (sometimes called special units) do not allow the same freedoms as elsewhere in the prison. Inmates are locked down up to 23 hours a day in single-person cells, with little social contact with other inmates or the staff.

In many cases, prisoners are placed in segregation for their own safety. This includes detainees, in jails or prisons where inmates want to leave gangs or have been an inside informant. Also, segregation may be necessary in the case of detainees and inmates who are experiencing psychotic episodes or other mental illness deterioration. They are unfit to be placed in the general population and have to be segregated. Sometimes detainees or prisoners volunteer to go into segregation, requesting *protective custody,* which often translates into *solitary confinement* (placement in cells with single-person occupancy). As in the example of Pelican Bay in California, solitary confinement can take place in cells with no windows.

Others labeled as being "difficult" may be placed in segregation simply because they just can't get along with other detainees or prisoners (McGeachan, 2019). Being placed in segregation is not necessarily a permanent condition. Some are put in special units briefly, either until medication stabilizes their mental state or until they have calmed down and no longer appear to be a threat to others or to themselves.

Inmates that have been convicted of a capital offense, either in a state that has the death penalty or of a federal capital offense, will be kept in a separate unit, informally called *death row.* We will be talking in more depth about the death penalty in Chapter 13. Death row is a difficult place for both inmates and the corrections officers who work there.

EFFECTS OF PRISON DESIGN ON INMATES

Just like the design of the home you live in has an effect on your daily life in so many ways, so does the design of prisons on inmates. Studies have shown that prison architecture can have a direct or indirect effect on inmate behavior (Morris and Worrall, 2014). As we mention in our introduction to this chapter, the loss of privacy built into jail and prison design can have a big impact on how people survive the experience of being incarcerated.

Though prison design has some effect on prisoner misconduct, particularly in the case of the more informal, campus model with dormitories, design aside, one of the biggest factors that will contribute to violent behavior or any rule violations is overcrowding, a theme we shall see running throughout this book. Conditions beyond the control of staff or prisoners can also have an effect on prisoner conduct.

For example, during the COVID-19 pandemic, some people coped better with forced isolation than others. For the happily introverted individual, it may have not been difficult to have to stay away from people. However, it is still too early in the research process in studying the pandemic and there is little empirical evidence at the writing of this book that introverts have mentally survived the pandemic better than more extroverted people.

We cannot assume that an introverted person will survive isolation better under the condition of prison. A prisoner who is extremely introverted may also suffer from neurosis that can cause instability while isolated behind prison walls, particularly in segregated units (Gujonsson et al., 2004). We should also note that introverted people don't necessarily dislike people. They simply need time away from people in order to decompress. However, as Corsetti (2020) notes, social distancing is not the same as solitary confinement. Prison also means being isolated from the outdoors and nature (*National Geographic*, 2016) as well as being restricted from using the digital means by which to connect with people when we want to, as in video chatting, text messaging, and cell phone calls.

In a similar vein, we cannot assume that extroverted people will do better in the confines of prison. Nor is it predictable as to whether the prisonization process might in turn make an otherwise extroverted person more introverted as they find fewer people they can trust than on the outside. There is the assumption that people universally need social contact, which is incorrect. Typically, individuals still need to feel that they have control over when and where they interact with other people, even if they are extroverted (Wener, 2012). They lose that control the minute that they are arrested and subsequently placed in jail, if not released. We will be discussing more of the effects of prisonization in Chapter 10 on detainees and prisoners' perspectives on incarceration.

Jails and prisons, by their nature, are generally built in a fashion so as to be an unpleasant experience for the accused and the convicted. The color palette of jail and prisons is institutional, leaving no question that one is incarcerated. The same is true for the complete lack of cheerful, homey decorative touches, except in the case of child-friendly rooms that are available in some prisons and designated for visitation with family members. Even rooms set aside for conjugal visits tend to be stark and uninviting, which in turn can bring on feelings of shame to the visiting spouse.

ANCILLARY SERVICES IN JAILS AND PRISONS

There are a number of considerations for where to place ancillary services, like the *infirmary* (medical facilities), kitchen, and laundry facilities. In many cases, detainees and prisoners work in these areas, which means that they need to be as secure as anywhere else in the facility. When designing these spaces, there has to be a means by which jail and prisoners can do their work without being a risk to themselves, others, or to prison staff. For example, prisoners could hardly be asked to work in the kitchen with plastic utensils. Knives in particular can easily be stolen if not chained down to work stations.

TECHNOLOGY IN TODAY'S JAILS AND PRISONS

The saving grace of jails and prisons today is that staff are aided with a number of innovations that have helped to make these institutions safer. Corrections officers no longer have to manually open and close cell doors most of these function replaced by computers. In some jails and prison, officers are allowed to use oleoresin capsicum (OC), better known as pepper spray in order to squash and minimize physical altercations with violent inmates (DeFranco and Duncan, 2017). Some jails and prisons also use K-9 dogs to control inmates (DeFranco and Duncan, 2017), though the K-9 unit are not really technology and not necessarily a new form of control. K-9 units help in not only controlling inmates, but can also be helpful in finding contraband in cells. Officers in K-9 units, whether in or out of correctional facilities, are required to take additional training beyond the academy.

For the seasoned veteran, these innovations previously unavailable, save the use of dogs, help immensely in providing them with ways to protect themselves and colleagues. Prior to these, correctional staff had to resort to brute strength alone, though they still have to do so from time to time when an inmate is particularly difficult to control.

OTHER PRACTICAL CONSIDERATIONS

Depending on the age of a facility, jails and prisons can be very noisy places. More recently jail and prison design have incorporated buffer zones in order to cut down on the noise pollution from ordinary conversation and the shouting of detainees or inmates when they become frustrated, angry, or are suffering from mental illness, besides the ambient sounds coming from televisions. Some ways to muffle sound are by using storage areas or program service areas as puffers, and with insulated partitions (Kimme et al., 2011).

Though these strategies are helpful, it does not cut down on the noises that can be transmitted by drainage pipes or of greater concern, communication between prisoners by tapping out code against the cell walls. In many ways, the ability to communicate to another human being is greatly restricted in jails and prisons yet the human need to connect for those who need to do so, does not change while incarcerated. If we take the example of the covert ways that American POWS in Vietnam communicated to one another, including hearing news from home from new arrivals, there is good evidence that the ability to secretly "talk" to one another may have been key to keeping them sane (Corcoran, 1991).

Jails and prison also have to be designed to minimize a number of challenges that can crop up within the incarcerated population (Kimme et al., p 4):

- Accommodations for smaller or special populations, including women and intoxicated inmates, or those with behavioral problems that require specialized mental health care.
- Assaults against staff and inmates.
- Suicides and suicide attempts.
- Fires.
- Vandalism.
- Personal injury lawsuits.
- Contraband passage.
- Standards compliance.

Other design considerations include the safe transport through the *sally port,* a double door entrance into the facility, as well as creating safe passage within the jail or prison. There has to be enough safety built into the security features, like surveillance cameras and locking doors, so as to minimize the chance of injury or escape.

In addition to handling detainees and prisoners with mental disabilities, with an aging prison population, increasingly inmates have special dietary and medical needs. Prison cells are not generally built to accommodate wheelchairs or other medical equipment and this is a serious consideration when designing new jails and prisons. There is also the consideration of the detainee or prisoner who is terminally ill. Specialized medical care has to be provided, though it comes at the expense of inconveniences to staff. There is also the concern as to whether medical equipment, like crutches, can be used to hide contraband or can be used as weapons against other prisoners or corrections staff. Some countries, like those in the United Kingdom, are addressing the problem of an aging prison population by pushing for the development of "age-friendly cities and communities" of prisoners (Codd, 2020, p. 1).

Jails and prisons have also been challenged during the COVID-19 pandemic where in many cases, social distancing is impossible due to current design. Except for in maximum security or supermax facilities, there is communal living and much more opportunity for disease and infection transmission. The saving grace is that jail and prison populations, along with corrections staff, were some of the earliest to get vaccinated for the COVID-19 virus. It is still early in the recovery phase of the pandemic to know whether jail and prison designers will rethink the current architectural models in response to the pandemic.

SUMMARY

What we have introduced here is only a sampling of possible jail and prison designs. Most of what we have presented is commonplace, as in the campus style or telephone-pole design. Another are less commonly seen, as in the notorious tent city in Arizona that closed down in 2017. There are efforts by architects and social progressives to change the look of jails and prisons, as in the example of the women's jail in San Diego County, California.

The most important things to consider when building a jail or prison is the safety of inmates and corrections staff. Another important consideration directly related to the incarcerated is that the facilities are escape proof. Punishment is built into the structure of jails and prisons, where the physical structure restricts the movement and activities of the inhabitants. But this also means that the design of jails and prisons can also have negative psychological effects on corrections officers as well.

There are a number of challenges to corrections departments that will have to be addressed in the coming years. We have an aging population, with increased longevity, which in turn means that there is an aging prison population as well. This means that facilities have to meet the standards of the Americans with Disabilities (ADA) with cells, units, and hallways that can accommodate any number of physical or medical disabilities associated with aging.

Another challenge is how do you house the detained or convicted, without placing them in harm's way in the middle of a pandemic? It has not been nearly as easy to employ social distancing requirements, as recommended by the Centers for Disease Control and Prevention, particularly with jail and prison overcrowding. There are additional challenges, which will be further discussed in Chapter 6 on women in prison, who have some distinct needs that men do not require, including adequate housing during pregnancy and birth.

Prison architecture is a varied and interesting subject, to scholars and to designers. It continues to be a partnership between the dreamers (architects), researchers in the social sciences, engineers, and prison administrators.

STORIES FROM BEHIND BARS: ART IMITATING LIFE

Prison Architect[6]

We deviate somewhat in this chapter in our *Stories from Behind Bars* section. This story comes from *outside* prison walls. Debuting in 2001, the simulation game, *Prison Architect*[7], allows the player to plan, design, and construct a fictional prison in the United States, after which they are expected to run its operations (Keary, 2015; Porche, 2015). Within the first two weeks of the games release, there were

---

[6] This is not an endorsement of or advertisement for the game by the author and it is presented here for educational purposes. Like other online and downloaded games, there are costs associated with playing *Prison Architect*.
[7] Chris Delay, designer. Paradox Interactive, Introversion Software, Double Eleven, publishers. Available on a number of platforms.

over 2,000 copies sold; in relatively short order, there were one million players (Keary, 2015).

As we would expect with a video game, though well-researched by the game developers, it does not show all the realities of running a jail or prison, just the more gruesome aspects. As Keary said in their review of the game (2015, retrieved from https://www.theguardian.com/technology/2015/oct/09/prison-architect-review-once-youre-in-you-cant-get-out),

> . . . the prison system is effectively a business, and it's a business that involves death. The studio [that developed the game] has scrupulously researched the U.S. prison system, talking to both wardens and prisoners and reading up on the theory of prison architecture.

Chris Porche, a correctional officer employed with the Maricopa County Sheriff's Office in Arizona (of Tent City notoriety mentioned in this chapter), reviewed the game for its authenticity. In Porche's estimation there are some accuracies to the game, including in the case of contraband control:

> There are many ways your prisoners can acquire contraband. They may get drugs passed to them through visitation; or they may steal a knife from the kitchen, or tools from the workshop. To keep things in check, the player may place metal detectors and K9 handlers in high traffic areas, interview confidential informants and order the occasional shakedown. (Porche, 2015, retrieved from https://www.corrections1.com/corrections/articles/a-correctional-officer-reviews-prison-architect-4o1d2DreIXnyp9RV/)

As Porche (2015) notes in his review, the game is so authentic, it includes a number of realistic details, including classification, visitation, and parole hearings. What is interesting about the more recent edition of the game is that it requires to player to use environmentally sound design, in their "Going Green" version.

SOURCES

Delay, Chris (2001) *Prison Architect*. Video Game. Stockholm, Sweden: Paradox Interactive, Introversion Software, Double Eleven. Available at https://www.prisonarchitect.com/.

Keary, I. (2015) Prison Architect review—once you're in you can't get out. *The Guardian*. Oct. 9. Retrieved from https://www.theguardian.com/technology/2015/oct/09/prison-architect-review-once-youre-in-you-cant-get-out.

Porche, C. (2015) A correctional officer reviews *Prison Architect*: How does the popular game stack up to really running a prison. From *Under the Phoenix Sun*, published at Corrections1. Apr. 28. Retrieved from https://www.corrections1.com/corrections/articles/a-correctional-officer-reviews-prison-architect-4o1d2DreIXnyp9RV/

INTERNATIONAL PERSPECTIVES ON PUNISHMENT AND CORRECTIONS: MEXICO

We should preface our discussion of Mexican prisons with the dynamics of employment in that country as a police officer or prison staff. Unlike the professionalization of the criminal justice work in law enforcement and in corrections that we see elsewhere in North America, with few exceptions, those who chose law enforcement professions in Mexico rarely see it as a career. And as the BBC reports, Mexican citizens are not rushing to law enforcement jobs as they have the great risk of being deadly in the face of drug cartels, with the number of officers killed on and off the job on the rise (Martinez, 2019). Even Mexican politicians and judges are threatened and killed when they attempt to stop the drug cartels and drug trafficking.

Holding Cell, Mexican Jail. (*Source*: Center for Latin America Studies, University of California, Berkley, retrieved from https://bit.ly/3jWCL9H)

Though we have been primarily focused on the construction of prisons in this chapter, we should acknowledge that architecture and the experiences of prisoners, prison staff differs around the globe. One universal condition that can strike a percentage of corrections officers is burnout, no matter how well designed prisons are.

If you consider that for all their power in controlling prisoners, many spend their days being verbally abused and, in some cases, having feces and body fluids flung at them by prisoners from time to time. With the great number of people incarcerated with mental illness, few officers are well equipped to handle the unpredictable fallout from this class of prisoners.

In Mexico, particularly as prison staff are not as well trained as in the United States, there are high rates of exhaustion. This, coupled with officer indolence, it gives the impression that being lazy on the job is a coping mechanism and results in feelings of guilt, putting Mexican prison staff at risk for deteriorated mental health (Gil-Monte et al. 2013). In addition to low morale, there is the risk of corruption, as bribery is reportedly commonplace in Latin American countries, throughout their criminal justice systems. It is difficult to combat it in law enforcement circles and prison facilities, when corruption reaches every level of the judiciary, including prosecutors and judges (Ríos-Figueroa, 2012). And it is not uncommon for police officers to be paid bonuses for the number of arrests they make, putting into question how many innocent people have been jailed or prosecuted in Mexico (Sanger, 2009).

As is rapidly becoming a pattern throughout most of the world, some Mexican prisons are impossibly overcrowded. According to a 2019 report by the National Human Rights Commission in Mexico, a third of federal and state prisons are overcrowded; two-thirds are deficient in hygienic measures (Vivanco, 2020), which is particularly troubling when considering the risk of transmission of the COVID-19 virus and other communicable diseases.

As much as we may hear of complaints of prison conditions in the United States, Mexican prisons are considerably worse. As Felbab-Brown reports, translated from an article by La Reforma's *Mexico Today*,

> *46% of the imprisoned shared their cell with at least five other inmates; 13% with more than 15. They lack adequate food, water, hygienic facilities, and health care. To obtain daily necessities, many prisoners depend on relatives to bring them food, toiletries, and money to purchase essentials, including water: In theory, water should be provided free, but in practice, it is monetized along with other commodities and aspects of life within the large illicit economy that dominates Mexican prisons.* (2020, retrieved from https://www.brookings.edu/blog/order-from-chaos/2020/05/26/mexicos-prisons-covid-19-and-the-amnesty-law/#:~:text=Mexican%20prisons%20are%20notoriously%20overcrowded,hygienic%20facilities%2C%20and%20health%20care.)

There are certainly a number of anecdotal stories of Americans who landed up in Mexican jails and prisons while on vacation. In some cases, they committed no crime but had the bad fortune of running into corrupt police officers. However, with the amount of smuggling of drugs, weapons, and people between the borders of Mexico and United States, American citizens who are involved in these illegal (and dangerous) activities can find themselves in the wrong country when arrested.

American citizens can be thrown into prisons, built for 300 prisoners, that now house upwards to 1,200 inmates, even with the intervention of the American Consulate in Mexico (Neary and Siegel, NPR, 2002). Some creature comforts can be purchased, including renting a larger cell, small refrigerators, televisions, and where available, window-unit air conditioners (Neary and Siegel, NPR, 2002). However, these items are generally unavailable, except to gang leaders who enjoy special privileges: "A statement by the Nuevo Leon state prosecutor's office said Zetas [gang] leader Ivan Hernandez Cantu had his cell equipped with a king-size bed, a luxury bath and a huge television." (BBC, 2016, retrieved from https://www.bbc.com/news/world-latin-america-35578390). Unless an American who has been thrown into a Mexican jail or prison has cash on them, they have to endure the same squalid conditions that Mexican citizens who have been arrested or convicted and without means face. Often their only hope in this case is if a relative or friend can intervene with cash.

As compared to the United States, Mexico is similar in the enforcement of gender roles, where women become sole caregivers of children when their partners are incarcerated. Women are also expected to visit their partners in prison, and when able to do so, bring personal items and money (Agoff et al., 2020). Male prisoners in Mexico relinquish or voluntarily walk away from all financial responsibility of their children no matter what their financial situation might be, but romanticized their roles as caring fathers and as being emotionally supportive while they are incarcerated, in particular how they have transformed from being "bad" to "good" fathers by the experience (Agoff et al., 2020; Sandberg et al., 2020). They believe that they can still protect and educate their children from prison (Sandberg et al., 2020), which is rarely the case in reality. This isn't to say that there is no benefit to this type of self-reflection that might be therapeutic towards planning for release and reuniting with their families.

Conditions are not impossibly bad in every one of the prisons in Mexico. They are one of the few countries in the world where mindfulness, meditation, and yoga practice can be found in some facilities. For example, there have been yoga programs as a part of rehabilitation in Mexican juvenile detention centers, with an eye on preventing these to be "universities" of crime (AFP News Agency, 2013). The yoga classes also offer an opportunity for certified yoga instructors in the Parninaama tradition[8] to teach classes behind bars, perhaps inspiring former inmates to do the same (AFP News Agency, 2013; Prison Mindfulness Institute, 2013). The program encourages prisoners to teach yoga outside of prison, once they are released, and acts as a different kind of vocational training program as well (Camarena, 2017).

Likewise, some (but not all) prisons in the United States have yoga programs for rehabilitation, including San Quentin Prison in California (Prison Yoga Project,

---

[8] Parninaama yoga and the Parninaama Yoga Institute founded by Ann Moxey, is specifically dedicated to transformation, teaching prisoners that they are more than their bodies, but that they also possess a spirit and soul (Camarena, 2017).

2021). As the Prison Yoga Project professes (2021, retrieved from https://prisony oga.org/), "Most incarcerated people have a history of complex, interpersonal trauma. Unless this unresolved [issue is] addressed the tendency to re-offend will remain." So, yogá practice serves as both a means to achieve mental and physical wellness and vocational training for prisoners in Mexico, the United States, and in the handful of countries around the world that recognize this. In the case of the Mexico program it provides jobs post-incarceration.

SOURCES

AFP News Agency (2013) Mexico: Yoga classes to steer young offenders away from crime. Sept. 30. Video. Retrieved from https://www.youtube.com/watch?v=2LcK2lPOVao&t=6s.

Agoff, C., S. Sandberg, and G. Fondevilla (2020) Women providing and men free riding: Work, visits and gender roles in Mexican prisons. Victims and Offenders. Nov. 19. Available at https://www.researchgate.net/profile/Sveinung_Sandberg/publication/346979143_ Women_Providing_and_Men_Free_Riding_Work_Visits_and_Gender_Roles_in_Mexi can_Prisons/links/5fd74409299bf140880a87e1/Women-Providing-and-Men-Free-Rid ing-Work-Visits-and-Gender-Roles-in-Mexican-Prisons.pdf.

British Broadcasting Company (BBC) (2016) Mexico dismantles 'luxury cells' in Topo Chico riot jail. Feb. 15. Retrieved from https://www.bbc.com/news/world-latin-america -35578390.

Camarena, P. (2017) Yoga as a tool for rehabilitation. Fairfly Project. Apr. 25. Retrieved from https://www.fairflyproject.com/yoga-as-a-tool-for-rehabilitation/.

Felbab-Brown, V. (2020) Mexico's prisons, COVID-19, and the amnesty law. *Order from Chaos*, The Brookings Institute. May 22. Retrieved from https://www.brookings.edu/ blog/order-from-chaos/2020/05/26/mexicos-prisons-covid-19-and-the-amnesty-law/ #:~:text=Mexican%20prisons%20are%20notoriously%20overcrowded,hygienic%20fac ilities%2C%20and%20health%20care.

Gil-Monte, P. R., H. Figueiredo-Ferraz, H. Valdez-Bonilla (2013) Factor analysis of the Spanish Burnout Inventory among Mexican prison employees. *Canadian Journal of Behavioural Science*. Vol. 45, No. 2:96-104.

Martinez, M. (2019) Deadly job: No rush to join Mexico's new police force. News, *British Broadcasting Company* (BBC). Sept. 11. Retrieved from https://www.bbc.com/news/ world-latin-america-49551033.

Neary, L. and R. Siegel (2002) Profile: Conditions inside Mexican prisons, and how they dif-fer from those in American prisons. *All Things Considered*, National Public Radio, Inc. (NPR) June 25.

Prison Mindfulness Institute (2013) Prison yoga in Mexico. Jul. 15. Retrieved from https:// www.prisonmindfulness.org/prison-yoga-practice-in-mexico/.

Ríos-Figueroa, J. (2012) Justice System institutions and corruption control: Evidence from Latin America. *The Justice System Journal*. Vol. 33, No. 2:194-214.

Sandberg, S., C. Agoff, and G. Fondevilla (2020) Stories of the "good father": The role of father-hood among incarcerated men in Mexico. Punishment and Society. Nov. 5. 0(0):1-21.

Sanger, M. E. (2009) Mexico: Presumed guilty: Based on an untrue story. Berkeley Review of Latin American Studies, Center for Latin American Studies, University of California, Berkeley. Retrieved from https://clas.berkeley.edu/research/mexico-presumed-guilty -based-untrue-story.

Vivanco, J. M. (2020) Covid-19: The risk in Mexican prisons. Human Rights Watch and *El Universal*. June 4. Retrieved from https://www.hrw.org/news/2020/06/04/covid-19-risk -mexican-prisons.

GLOSSARY

Administrative-security level A facility, generally in the federal corrections system, that houses a mixture of inmates, including those needing specialized medical care, those prone to escape, and more violent offenders needing more supervision.

Biophilic design A prison design that allows for more green spaces, natural light, and open concept interiors.

High security prisons Correctional facilities that house the most violent offenders, those with gang affiliations, and the criminally insane that are not housed in psychiatric hospitals. Inmates need the highest degree of supervision at all times, many of whom are kept in solitary confinement.

Infirmary Another name for the medical facilities within a jail or prison.

Low security prisons Prisons intended for low level offenders, including nonviolent drug offenders and white collar criminals.

Medium security prisons Prisons for inmates who do not need as much supervision as in a high security facility but cannot necessarily be trusted in a low security facility.

"Not in my backyard" (NIMBY) The concerns of residents and business have when faced with the possibility of a jail or prison being built in the community, the fear being that it will negatively affect property values and bring crime to the area.

Protective custody Solitary confinement or special unit placement of inmates who are at risk of being harmed by fellow inmates if held in general population.

Sally port "Sally" meaning to go out and "port," the French word for door, together are still used today to describe the double doored entrance by which the arrested and prisoners are escorted in and out of jail or prison. Most sally ports today lead directly to the processing (or intake) offices of the facility. Like other terms used in corrections, sally port comes from the military, used for the gate or door that soldiers went out of during a siege.

Solitary confinement Cells with single-person occupancy, used either in protective custody, or as discipline when there has been serious rule violations or violence committed by an inmate. Prisoners with extreme mental disorders are also housed in solitary confinement for their safety and the safety of others.

"Supermax" prisons Highest security level prisons where inmates generally spend up to 23 hours in their cells.

Units or pods   A collection of jail or prison cells, used to keep similar offender populations together, whenever possible, of those who are undergoing rehabilitation.

REFERENCES AND SUGGESTED READINGS

Aguayo, T. (2006) Youth who killed at 12 gets 30 years for violating probation. *New York Times.* May 19. Retrieved from https://www.nytimes.com/2006/05/19/us/youth-who-killed-at-12-gets-30-years-for-violating-probation.html.

Asim, F. and V. Shree (2020) Biophilic architecture for restoration and therapy within the built environment: A review. Visions for Sustainability. Vol. 15. Retrieved from https://www.preprints.org/manuscript/201907.0323/v1.

Beijersbergen, K. A., A. J. E. Dirkzwager, P. H. van der Lann, and P. Nieuwbeerta (2014) A social building? Prison architecture and staff-prisoner relationships. *Crime and Delinquency.* Vol. 62:1-32.

Board of State and Community Corrections (BSCC) A new kind of jail inspires staff, offenders alike. The State of California. Retrieved from https://www.bscc.ca.gov/s_countyfacilitiesconstruction/.

California Department of Corrections (CDCR) (n.d.) Details and history, California Institute for Men (CIM). Retrieved from https://www.cdcr.ca.gov/facility-locator/cim/.

Casella, E. C. (2007) *The Archeology of Institutional Confinement: An American Experience in Archeological Perspective.* Gainesville, FL.: University Press of Florida.

Codd, H. (2020) Prisons, older people, and age-friendly cities and communities: Towards an inclusive approach. *International Journal of Environmental Research and Public Health.* Dec. 9, Vol. 17, No. 24:1-14.

ConflictNerd (2018) Prison Architect/Strong Foundations (#1). Video. Sept. 25, retrieved from https://www.youtube.com/watch?v=qWSbVZbVxRE.

Corcoran, C. S. (1991) Communication: The key to survival for American prisoners of war in Vietnam. *Air Power History.* Vol. 28, No. 4:48-54.

Corsetti, G. (2020) Social distancing – not an introvert's dream. Blog. *Mental Agility.* Mar. 24. Retrieved from https://mentallyagile.com/blog/2020/3/24/social-distancing-not-an-introverts-dream.

Davies, K. (2007) Telephone pole design, in *Encyclopedia of Prisons and Correctional Facilities,* M. Bosworth, ed. Sage Publications. Newbury Park, CA: SAGE Publications

Defranco, J. and T. Duncan (2017) *Life as a Jailer.* Morrisville, North Carolina: Lulu Publishing Services.

Dwyer, C. (2017) Ex-sheriff Joe Arpaio convicted of criminal contempt. NPR. Jul. 31. Retrieved from https://www.npr.org/sections/thetwo-way/2017/07/31/540629884/ex-sheriff-joe-arpaio-convicted-of-criminal-contempt.

Fairweather, L. and S. McConville, eds. (2000) *Prison Architecture: Policy, design, and experience.* Woburn, MA: Reed.

Foucault, M. (2007) *Discipline and Punish: The Birth of the Prison.* A. Sheridan, trans. New York, NY: Random House.

Gonzales, R. (2019) Felicity Huffman begins prison term at 'Club Fed' in East Bay in College Admissions Scandal. KQED, NPR. Oct. 19. Retrieved from https://www.kqed.org/news/11780480/felicity-huffman-begins-prison-term-at-club-fed-in-east-bay-in-college-admissions-scandal.

Gundjonsson, G. H., J. F, Sigurdsson, O. O. Bragason, E. Einarsson, and E. B. Validiarsdottir (2004) Compliance and personality: The vulnerability of the unstable introvert. *European Journal of Personality.* Jul./Aug., Vol. 18, Iss. 5:435-443.

Harmon, T. (2010) Violence on the rise in state prisons: Problem is attributed to gangs and high security inmates in medium-security prisons. *Pueblo Chieftain*. Jan. 27. Retrieved from https://go-gale-com.wne.idm.oclc.org/ps/i.do?v=2.1&u=mlin_w_westnew&it=r&id=GALE%7CA217514840&p=GPS&sw=w.

Independent Lens (2017) The prison economy: How do prisons affect the places we live? Public Broadcasting Service (PBS). May 5. Retrieved from https://www.pbs.org/independentlens/blog/prison-economy-how-do-prisons-affect-the-places-we-live/.

Jacob, R. (2017) How prison architecture can transform inmates' lives. *Pacific Standard Magazine*. May 3. Retrieved from https://psmag.com/news/jail-prison-architecture-inmates-crime-design-82968.

Johnston, N. (2000). *Forms of Constraint: A history of Prison Architecture*. Chicago, IL: University of Illinois Press.

Kelly, A. (2017) President Trump pardons former Sheriff Joe Arpaio. NPR. Aug. 25. Retrieved from https://www.npr.org/2017/08/25/545282459/president-trump-pardons-former-sheriff-joe-arpaio.

Kenis, P., P. M. Kruyen, J. Baaijens, and P. Barneveld (2010) *The Prison Journal*. Vol. 90, No. 3:313-330.

Kimme, D. A., G. M. Bowker, and R. G. Deichman (2011) Jail Design Guide, 3d ed. National Institute of Corrections, U.S. Department of Justice. Mar., NIC Accession Number 04806. Champaign, IL: Kimme and Associates, Inc.

McGeachan, C. (2019) "A prison within a prison"? Examining the enfolding spatialities of care and control in the Barlinnie special units. *Area*. Jun., Vol. 51, Iss. 2:200-2007.

Morris, R. G. and J. L. Worrall (2014) Prison architecture and inmate misconduct: A multi-level assessment. *Crime and Delinquency*. Vol. 60, No. 7:1083-1109.

Nadel, M. R. and D. P. Mears (2020) Building with no end in sight: The theory and effects of prison architecture. *Corrections*. Vol.5, Iss. 3:188-205.

National Geographic (2016) Stories of Life in Solitary Confinement/Short Film Showcase. Aug. 6. Retrieved from https://www.youtube.com/watch?v=Q7ajzsh-i54.

Petek, G. (2019) *Improving California's Prison Inmate Classification System*. Legislative Analyst's Office, California Department of Corrections and Rehabilitation. May.

Roy, S. and A. Avidija (2012) The effect of prison security levels on job satisfaction and job burnout among staff in the USA: An assessment. *International Journal of Criminal Justice Sciences*. Jul.-Dec., Vol. 7, No. 2:524-538.

Semple, J. (1993). Bentham's Prison: A Study of the Panopticon Penitentiary. New York, NY: Oxford University Press.

Söderlund, J. and P. Newman (2017) Improving mental health in prisons through biophilic design. *The Prison Journal*. Vol. 97, No. 6:750-772.

South, D. B. (2009) Monolithic domes make perfect jails and prisons. Commercial Monolithic Dome Structures, Momolithicdomes.com. May 26. Retrieved from https://www.monolithic.org/commercial/monolithic-domes-make-perfect-jails-and-prisons.

Swenson, D. (2019) Opinion: Dwindling population and disappearing jobs is the fate that awaits much of rural America. *Market Watch*. May 24. Retrieved from https://www.marketwatch.com/story/much-of-rural-america-is-fated-to-just-keep-dwindling-2019-05-07.

Thompson, T. (2016) Arrest, detention, and beyond juvenile probation overview. Power Point presentation. Alameda County Probation Department Juvenile Field Services Division. Courtesy of Berkeley Law, University of California. Sept. Retrieved from https://www.law.berkeley.edu/wp-content/uploads/2016/09/Juvenile-Services-Overview-Powerpoint-Judge-Thompson-Edition.pdf.

Travisono, A. P. (ed.) (1978) *The American Prison: From the Beginning: A Pictorial History*. College Park, MD: American Correctional Association.

United States Bureau of Prisons (BOP) (n.d.) About our facilities: Administrative-level security. U.S. Department of Justice. Retrieved from https://www.bop.gov/about/facilities/federal_prisons.jsp#:~:text=Administrative%20facilities%20are%20institutions%20with,%2C%20or%20escape%2Dprone%20inmates.

United States Bureau of Prisons (BOP) (2019) Change Notice: Inmate security designation and custody classification. U.S. Department of Justice. Sept 4. Retrieved from https://www.bop.gov/policy/progstat/5100_008cn.pdf.

Waid, C. A. and C. B. Clements (2001) Correctional facility design: Past, present and future. American Correctional Association, Inc., *Corrections Compendium*. Nov., Vol. 26, Iss. 11:1-29.

Wainwright, O. (2019) New York's high-rise jails: What could go wrong? The Guardian. Dec. 9. Retrieved from https://www.theguardian.com/cities/2019/dec/09/new-yorks-high-rise-prisons-what-could-go-wrong.

Wener, R. E. (2006) Effectiveness of direct supervision system of correctional design and management: A review of the literature. *Criminal Justice and Behavior*. Vol. 33:392-410.

Wener, R. E. (2012) *The Environmental Psychology of Prisons: Creating Spaces in Secure Settings. Environment and Behavior* series. Cambridge: Cambridge University Press.

Wilkinson, T. (2018) Typology: Prison. *The Architectural Review*. June 11. Retrieved from https://www.architectural-review.com/essays/typology/typology-prison.

Woodruff, L. (2017) Prison reform: The origin of contemporary jail standards. *Lexipol*. Feb. 22. Retrieved from https://www.lexipol.com/resources/blog/prison-reform-origin-contemporary-jail-standards/.

Zillow (2021) Chino Hills home values. Feb. 28. Retrieved from https://www.zillow.com/chino-hills-ca/home-values/.

Zimmer, W. C. (1916) Model jail architecture. *Journal of the American Institute of Criminal Law and Criminology*. Jan., Vol. 6, Iss. 5:717-713.

Chapter FOUR

Prison Administration

> *The organization of offices follows the principle of hierarchy ... each lower office is under the control and supervision of a higher one.*
>
> — Max Weber, notable 19th-century sociologist

Chapter Objectives

- Review the concepts of bureaucracy, under which structure prisons are run.
- Explore the various careers within corrections.
- Examine what goes right and what goes wrong in bureaucratic structures as applied to jails and prisons.
- Review jail and prison hierarchies.

Key Terms

Bureaucratic control	Micromanage, micromanagement
Bureaucracy	Nepotism
Chain of command	Paramilitary
Detention officer	Simple control
Iron Cage of Bureaucracy	Span of control
Jurisdictional roles	Technical control

INTRODUCTION

In this chapter, our focus will be primarily on how prisons are supposed to run in an ideal world. This means understanding what a "bureaucratic structure" is and the importance of each of its characteristics within jail and prison systems. Later in Chapter 5, we will discuss the actual work experiences of jailers and prison staff. For now, we will concentrate on the expectations for prison administration and corrections personnel.

We are approaching this chapter as a source of practical information on not only the structure of jails and prisons, but also as an informative tool in exploring the various careers available to pursue in corrections.

BUREAUCRACY

Max Weber (1864-1920) is perhaps the best-known theorist who dissected the characteristics of *bureaucracy* (organizational operating features such as specialization, written records, and a clear hierarchy). Weber wrote about the characteristics of *bureaucratic control* (a system where control of workers and the running of an organization is built into the rules and regulations) in *Economy and Society* (1922). Writing primarily in the late 19th century, Weber was observing the later years of the Industrial Revolution, where we began seeing distinct specializations in professions. Much of what Weber based his observations on were the military and the emerging business community of the late 19th century. As bureaucratic structures, all aspects of corrections, including probation, parole, jails, and prisons, run on similar principles to provide order and smooth operations.

Weber's characteristics of bureaucracy (printed posthumously in 1922) and how they can be applied in corrections are as follows:

1. *Fixed Jurisdictional areas.* People who work in correctional settings have specific jobs with specific job descriptions. For example, someone who is hired specifically to work in prison units would not also be asked additionally to work in the kitchen. There are trained chefs, food service managers, and nutrition specialists who are hired to oversee prison labor in kitchens.
2. *Office hierarchy.* There is a clear chain of command with no ambiguity of who is in charge and who is to follow instructions from their superiors ("the line").
3. *Written documents* ("files"). Records are to be maintained on not only detainees in jails and convicts in prison but also for budgeting purposes, personnel issues, and other staff-related matters. These days documents are primarily managed electronically.
4. *Specialization with training.* Rarely, if ever, are people hired in corrections without formal education and training before they enter their profession. For example, you would not want someone with only high school diploma or general educational development (GED) diploma take a position as a substance abuse counselor without the appropriate training, credentials, and licensing.

5. *Full working capacity.* Most positions in probation, parole, jails, and prison are full-time. On the most part, hours are fairly predictable, except in the rare occasion of extra shifts having to be covered due to personnel shortages or in the case of jail or prison lockdown. However, these are not always 9-to-5 daytime positions. A number of personnel have to work nights and early mornings.

6. *General rules.* Both detainees and prisoners have to follow rules or they will be written up in discipline reports that can affect sentencing or parole. Failing to follow rules can have an effect on work assignments as well. Likewise, corrections personnel are given an employee handbook with rules that they need to follow in order to keep their jobs or to avoid disciplinary action themselves. By having all rules and policies in writing, there can be no ambiguity as to what is expected. So it goes also for detainees and prisoners.

Weber did not always have glowing words to say about bureaucratic structures, as much as he seemed to think it was the most efficient way to run an organization. He describes the *Iron Cage of Bureaucracy* as being the stifling number of rules, as well as all the red tape one has to go through to run an organization, including correctional facilities. For any of you who plan on going on to a career in one of the criminal justice professions, you will encounter a great deal of paperwork, mostly provided on line to fill out, civil service exams in most cases, and training. This will take time and patience on your part and also creates mounds of paper work (again, mostly electronic these days) for the people who plan to hire you.

THE PRISON HIERARCHY

The structures of jails and prisons are very similar to what you see in the military. In fact, corrections is often described as *paramilitary* operations. It helps explains why military veterans are attractive candidates for jobs in corrections. In order to have jails and prisons operate as efficiently as possible, there cannot be any ambiguity as to what responsibilities belong to what position in the facility. This is particularly true in the case of emergencies, as in the examples of disturbances or riots, where everyone has a specific role to play in order to restore peace.

Job descriptions within corrections hierarchies are very specific, with lists of duties and responsibilities for each position in corrections. In our next section of this chapter, we will be discussing some of the types of jobs available in corrections.

As much as people may dislike the red tape of bureaucracy, hierarchy, whether in the military or in corrections, is the most efficient way to spell out the *chain of command* (clearly delineated lines of leadership and front line staff). Ranks of correctional personnel are clearly spelled out, as shown in the following example of an organizational chart from U.S. Bureau of Prisons. (See Figure 4.1)

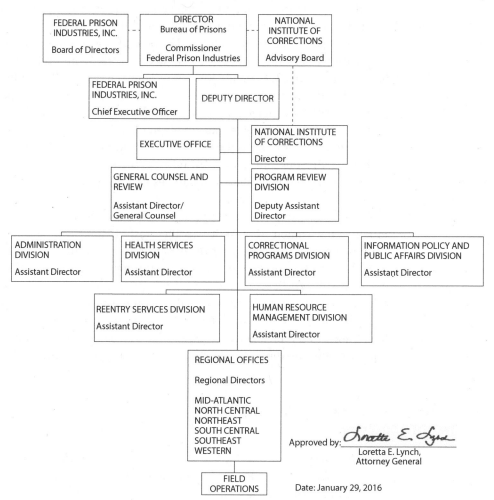

FIGURE 4.1 ┃ **Organizational Chart from U.S. Bureau of Prisons**
(*Source*: Retrieved from https://www.justice.gov/jmd/page/file/1104056/download)

The needs of prison administrators, in reality and in what they need from their workforce are innumerable. According to Russo (2019, retrieved from https://nij.ojp .gov/topics/articles/workforce-issues-corrections#figure1), there are five key themes to the systematic needs of administrators, as reported by the RAND Corporation and University of Denver, in order to address the shortages in correctional personnel:

- Clarify the mission of the corrections sector.
- Improve staff competencies.
- Improve staff training.

- Improve work environment and conditions.
- Develop [mentor] future leaders.

As much as jail and prison administrators attempt to adhere to bureaucratic ideals in their institutions, the ongoing shortage of corrections staff is the Achilles' heel of their operations.

TECHNICAL CONTROL

Richard Edwards, a prominent organizational theorist in the 1970s, proposed that there were three main types of control that employers have over their employees: Simple control, technical control, and bureaucratic control. *Simple control*, similar to what we see in small companies and those primarily hiring family members and friends, is personal and direct, and can sometimes be arbitrary in following a set of rules, if they even exist in writing (Edwards, 1979). This would not do well in the prison setting. Prisons use a combination of controls, including the rationality of bureaucracy, as described by Weber and *technical control*, as Edwards noted (1979) where control is built into the physical structure of the building. Though Edwards was discussing how factories control the pace of work on assembly lines, we can just as easily apply his theories to the running of a prison. Beaurcratic control, as we have discussed from Weber earlier in this chapter, means that written rules are strictly adhered to.

Most jails and prisons have a number of safeguards against escape. There are several reinforced doors between the jail and prison population and the outside world, often controlled by a number of electronic or computerized panels, that can easily shut cells and units down in the event that the incarcerated become unruly. It is also more difficult for detainees and prisoners to communicate with one another with more contemporary cell designs, though not impossible. Older jails and prisons still have the classic cells with bars, which makes it more difficult for corrections staff to monitor communications between cells. If you will recall that we reviewed the evolution of prison design in Chapter 3.

What makes a jail or prison unique in regard to technical control is that staff, detainees, and inmates are all controlled by the physical structure. Detainees and prisoners could hardly be controlled by the limited number of corrections officers generally found in the average prison. For example, according to federal law governing private prisons (2008, 28 CFR §97.14), when transporting violent prisoners, there must be at least one corrections officer for every four transportees (Legal Information Institute, n.d.). By limiting the movement of corrections staff, intentionally or not, jail and prison personnel in maximum security facilities are less free to wander off for an unscheduled break or make a personal phone call, as compared to minimum or low security facilities. Keep in mind also that jails are inherently high security, as there are a variety of criminals being detained or incarcerated, from minor offenders to the potentially violent criminal. Inherently, the technical control has to be substantial.

Blue Shirts, White Shirts

We are borrowing the blue shirts, white shirts reference from the way by which officers are divided by rank at Suffolk County Sheriff's Department in Massachusetts, and these are the colors commonly used in a number of correctional facilities to signify rank. Of course, different jurisdictions have different hues to distinguish higher ranked officers from the rank and file, usually somewhere in the color palette of white, gray, brown, black, or blue. The hierarchy is more simplified in local prisons jail or prison setting than we see in the organizational charts at the federal and state levels. As we have noted, with corrections facilities running as paramilitary operations, the position titles and patches[1] worn on uniforms are nearly identical to what we see in the military, given the example in the photo from the New Hampshire Department of Corrections.

| Corrections Officer | Corrections Corporal | Corrections Sergeant | Corrections Lieutenant | Corrections Captain |

Example of Ranks in Corrections, NH Dept. of Corrections. (*Source*: New Hampshire DOC, retrieved from https://nhdocjobs.com/careers-in-corrections/opportunities/)

If you think of a jail or prisons like a business, the warden acts as the CEO or president of the operations. Beneath the warden will be a number of officers who in some facilities are called "white shirts" on the basis of their uniform shirts. Rank and file corrections officers at the bottom of the hierarchy are the "blue shirts." We can see this in the example of the Suffolk County Sheriff's Department, which includes the main jail facility in Boston, in the following photo. This way one can easily distinguish between higher ranked officers, including lieutenants and sergeants. If you note in the photo, the "white shirt" officer is in the foreground, further designating his more prestigious rank among the three officers.

One cannot simply move up the ranks in law enforcement or in corrections on the basis of length of time on the job or whether you are well-liked. Attaining most supervisory positions in jails and prisons requires passing exams that test

---

[1] Badges of correctional officers are now patches, rather than metal. This is for the safety of the officers as a metal badge can be used as a weapon.

the candidate's qualifications. This process mirrors exactly what Weber refers to as specialization, where people do not simply get promoted based on years on the job or by *nepotism*. Nepotism is the practice of hiring based on familial or friendship relationships, without necessarily being qualified for the job.

An important point that Slyker (2020) makes in this chapter's Stories from Behind Bars section is that once someone is promoted, they should be transferred to a new institution. This way once promoted, they are not supervising their friends which could ultimately become awkward and unprofessional when a subordinate needs to be disciplined. However, this is much easier to do at the federal level than at the state level. The U.S. Federal Bureau of Prisons has an easier time transferring employees in and out of facilities and locations (Slyker, 2020).

Any one supervisor can only have so much control over those they are managing, dependent on the number of those who have to be under their careful eye. In modern jails and prisons, much of the control is technical (*technical control*) where, as we noted from Edwards's theories, the opening and closing of doors, bars, and barriers between units can be handled at a computerized or mechanical control panel. Even with technical help, people working in jails and prisons can only manage so many detainees or prisoners at a time. We call the number of people that one supervises, whether in government, business, or a correctional facility, the *span of control*. As we will note in the comparison of private and public correctional facilities, there are fewer officers per individuals they need to guard in private prisons than in state or federal institutions.

Studies also indicate that the more advanced training, including formal education that workers have, the more that management does not have to *micromanage* their employees (Blau, 1968). Same holds true in corrections and is one reason that correctional agencies are requiring their new hires to have some college education. More recently, an additional reason to insist on the professionalization of corrections personnel is to address issues of corruption and inhumane treatment of prisoners (Jurik and Musheno, 2006).

CAREERS IN PRISONS AND CORRECTIONS

Some positions in corrections are entry-level and require no more than a high school diploma or GED. Others require college degrees and in some cases postgraduate diplomas and/or certificates. For obvious reasons, people in the mental health fields, nurse practitioners, and physicians require advanced degrees and state licensing. Even for individuals with high school and college degrees, additional training is required, including academy training similar to law enforcement training that new corrections officers have to complete once they are hired.

Job descriptions are so specific that, without formal training, corrections officers and other corrections professionals would not be able to do the jobs they are expected to do. After initial training, there might be continuing education that officers might have to complete. For example, from an advertisement for a *detention officer* in Bernalillo, New Mexico, within one year of hire, officers are also expected to obtain the following:

- Detention/Corrections Certification in the State of New Mexico;
- CPR/First Aid/AED[2] Certificate; and
- Mental Health First Aid Certificate
  (*Government Jobs* 2021, retrieved from https://www.governmentjobs.com/care ers/sandovalcountynm/jobs/3314590/detention-officer?utm_campaign=google_ jobs_apply&utm_source=google_jobs_apply&utm_medium=organic.

As a side note, New Hampshire is ranked as one of the two best states for safety in their correctional facilities (U.S. News and World Report, n.d.; National Institute of Corrections, n.d.). Hawaii leads the United States in the same rankings (U.S. News and World Report, n.d.; National Institute of Corrections, n.d.). This could be due to a combination of the types of prisoners housed in New Hampshire and Hawaii, as well as level of training.

If you, the reader, have not been put off or scared by the stories contained in this chapter (or in this book, for that matter), here are some pieces of advice on how to become a corrections officer or other professional in a jail or prison system (Rasmussen University, retrieved from https://www.rasmussen.edu/degrees/ justice-studies/blog/corrections-careers/). The viewpoints offered from Rasmussen University in this book are on the wide variety of careers available at the federal, state, and local levels in corrections, in the United States:

Correctional Officer

From this course and textbook, you should have a pretty good understanding of what correctional officers do. What you may not know is the salaries in corrections. In the following map below, you can find which states are paying higher wages for correctional officers and jailers. Keep in mind that the cost of living varies from state to state. For example, California pays their personnel more than some of the Midwestern states. However, it takes considerably more income to put a roof over your head in California than in Kansas or Oklahoma.

Depending on the area and the demand for state or federal corrections personnel, education requirements can range from a high school diploma or equivalent (e.g., GED) to 2-year or 4-year college degree. In some places, like with police departments, applicants with military or law enforcement experience may get preference in hiring. What college degree you possess may not be important in

---

[2] AED stands for training on an automated external defibrillator used to revive patients, in this case, detainees or prisoners, who have suffered an apparent cardiac arrest.

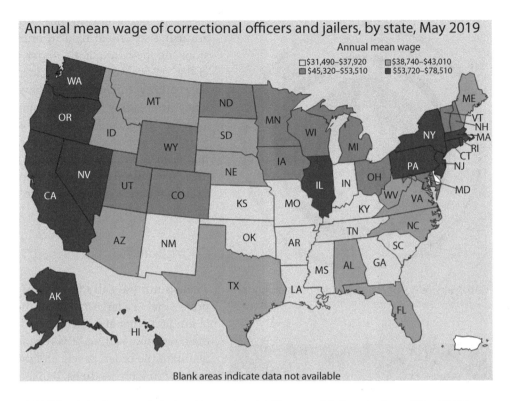

FIGURE 4.2 | **Average Salaries, Correctional Officers and Jailers, by State (May 2019)**
(*Source*: Bureau of Labor Statistics, 2019, retrieved from https://www.bls.gov/oes/current/oes333012.htm)

some prisons as the fact that you have the education. There can be applicants with degrees in a number of different disciplines, but largely come from criminal justice and other related college majors.

The general age requirement to become a corrections officer is 18 years old, however, some states or jurisdiction require that their applicants be at least 21 years old (Correctional Officer Education, n.d.). If you consider that the frontal cortex of the brain is not fully developed until around age 25, the ability to make good, quick decisions on the job may very well be dependent on more maturity and life experience. Of course, personal character and physical fitness are also taken into consideration.

Pretrial Service Officer

This corrections profession focuses on detainees who have been charged with crimes and are in jail awaiting trial. It is the job of the pretrial service officer to research the defendant's background before trail and whether they are candidates for pretrial release on bond or on their own recognizance. The pretrial service officer then advises the court as to whether the accused is a flight risk.

Pretrial Service Agency Logo, District of Columbia, US
(*Source*: https://www.psa.gov/)

Courtroom Bailiff. (*Source*: Bryant and Stratton College, retrieved from https://www.bryantstratton.edu/global/bryantstratton/jobs/bailiff).

It is important to note that more judges are using statistical data in order to make decisions on how much of a risk a defendant is, either pretrial or at sentencing. A pretrial service officer today should have some competency in reading data and statistical analysis. There is an excellent TedTalk on the very subject (*Why smart statistics are the key to fighting crime*, Anne Milgram, 2012, available at https://www.ted.com/talks/anne_milgram_why_smart_statistics_are_the_key_to_fighting_crime/up-next).

Court Bailiff

Though not typically thought of as a corrections profession, to a large extent the duties of the bailiff is similar to that of a corrections officer, but within the courtroom setting. It is the job of the bailiff to maintain the order, peace, and safety of the courtroom during proceedings, deliver documents, and escort witnesses and defendants to and from the courtroom. Court bailiffs are the main source of security in the courtroom. It is also the job of a bailiff to make sure that attorneys, defendants, and witnesses do not attempt to influence jurors outside the courtroom.

Probation Officer

As you know by now in this course and textbook, not all convicted criminals are required to remain in jail or spend any time in prison. It is not uncommon for offenders with lesser charges, like first time *DUI* (or *DWI*) offenders, to be given probation for a period of time, in lieu of jail or prison, and as long as they follow the conditions of their probation. It is the job of the probation officer to have regular visits with the probationer, or as they are commonly called, client[3], in order to make sure that they are adhering to the conditions of their probation. Probation officers

---

[3] Probationers are more commonly called clients as this helps destigmatize the condition of being a convicted criminal. That way it sounds more like the client is working with a social worker (which, in truth, they sort of are), rather than someone who is part of the corrections or criminal justice system.

also help in determining what types of rehabilitation or job training, career help their clients might require to prevent them from reoffending.

Probation Officers, Santa Barbara CA. (*Source*: Santa Barbara Probation Department, https://www .sbprobation.org/sbcprob/index.html)

Probation, parole, and other correctional treatment specialists are expected to have a college degree in criminal justice, psychology, social work, or other related disciplines. However, there are a variety of majors one can pursue in college and become a probation officer. The median annual salary of probation officers and other correctional specialists was around $54,000 as of May 2019 (Bureau of Labor Statistics, 2020b). Of course, salaries vary from region to region.

Depending on the jurisdiction, a probation officer can expect to have a sometimes impossible number of clients to supervise. Some clients only need to check in once in a while. Others are under intense supervision and constitute to about 10 percent of probation officers' appointment load. It is not uncommon for those convicted of relatively minor crimes to simply be on probation, with no requirement of meeting with a probation officer.

Parole Officer[4]

Whereas probation usually front ends or replaces a prison sentence, parole is on the back end. Parole officers are assigned clients[5] who have just been released from prison and who, as a condition of parole, are required to meet with a parole officer on a regular basis. In some jurisdiction, a parole officer is required to be as physically fit as police and corrections officers, as in the course of their duties, they may have to restrain one of their clients.

---

[4] Not one of the ten professions published by Rasmussen University, but should be included in this lists of jobs in the corrections field.
[5] Like in the case of probation officers, parolees are called clients to lessen the stigma of being ex-convicts.

Parole Officer Confronting a Parolee. (*Source*: Careers in Psychology, retrieved from https://careersinpsychology.org/parole-officer/)

Sometimes parole officers have to apprehend parole violators, rather than first calling the police to do so. As in the example of home visits, it may require chasing them down if they run out the backdoor when the officer makes an unannounced visit and/or the client is known to be breaking some condition of their parole (e.g., drug and/or alcohol consumption, hanging around with known criminals, etc.). In which case, parole officers have the authority to arrest a suspected parole violator.

Substance Abuse Counselor

Working in or out of jails and prisons, the substance abuse counselor is a trained and licensed mental health professional. The primary role of counselors is to provide support, treatment, and rehabilitation options to inmates with drug and/or alcohol abuse issues. The focus is on teaching addicts the skills they need in order to change the destructive behavior that may have very well landed them in trouble in the first place.

Individuals who are substance abuse counselors generally have a four-year degree in psychology, preferably with specific training. As mental health professionals, they are also expected to work closely with psychiatrists, psychologists, and social workers, in the case of corrections, those working with the prison population, probation or parole clients. According to Destination Hope (2012), an addiction recovery program, some of the very best substance abuse counselors are those who are former addicts that remain in recovery as they offer a level of empathy that can only be fully felt by someone who has dealt with addiction.

Corrections Nurse

As part of their rights as detainees or prisoners, the incarcerated have the right to adequate health care. This is subjective and differs in quality of care from jurisdiction to jurisdiction. In order to work in a prison as a nurse, unless you are currently in a nursing program, you will have to get additional education and training as either a registered nurse (RN) or as a licensed practical nurse (LPN). In addition to medical training, nurses benefit from having training and education in criminal justice, though not required. This could include a course in corrections, as it makes them doubly well equipped to handle the rigors of handling the wide range of illness and health problems of the incarcerated.

Federal Prisons, Nurse Practitioner. (*Source*: Federal Bureau of Prisons, retrieved from https://www.bop .gov/jobs/positions/index.jsp?p=Nurse%20Practitioner)

We should note that medical doctors and psychiatrists work in prisons as well. They generally do not make as much money as if they worked for a hospital or in a managed care program (e.g., HMO, PPO), or are in private practice. Medical personnel who work in prisons have to be dedicated to the profession, as not only is the pay not as high as outside the prison, they are working with very difficult populations, with a number of behavioral and health problems.

What the Rasmussen University list is also missing and should be mentioned here is that nurse practitioners are often employed in jails and prisons. Nurse practitioners hold degrees in nursing, including Master of Science degrees and Ph.Ds., giving them nearly the same capabilities to treat patients as a medical doctor, including prescribing medication. What nurse practitioners can or cannot do, including in the prison setting, varies from state to state, depending on their licensing requirements (*Nurse Practitioner Schools*, 2020). Generally, nurse practitioners can be employed as a cost savings to the institution, as their salaries tend to be lower than for physicians.

Case Manager

A case manager or correctional treatment specialists can either be a civilian or a corrections officer, depending on the setting. The role of the case manager is similar to a social worker in that they assist inmates and probationers in their efforts in rehabilitation, including connecting them with the services that they need. One critical role of the case manager working within a jail or prison is to prepare the prisoner for reentry, including contacting halfway houses or group homes for released convicts, if warranted, drug treatment facilities, and employment agencies.

Chaplain

A prison chaplain provides religious counseling and education to prisoners. They can be affiliated with any religion or denomination, but have to be adept at providing religious guidance through any religious doctrine. It is not uncommon for prisoners to seek spiritual guidance while in prison, either from other inmates or from the prison chaplain. As noted in our previous chapters, religion is one of the oldest forms of rehabilitation, including penitence, conversion and prison fellowship. Chaplains and other religious professionals may be volunteers and not necessarily paid employees of a prison.

A chaplain performs a number of services to detainees and prisoners that go beyond religious support, as indicated in Table 4.1.

TABLE 4.1. Duties of Prison Chaplains

Percent Saying They Perform Each of the Following:	%
Administer/organize religious programs	93
Personally lead worship and other services	92
Work with external faith-based groups	92
Advise correctional staff on religious issues	92
Supervise/train volunteers	91
Provide support/counseling for staff	85
Supervise inmates to help maintain safety and security	78
Facilitate interfaith dialogue	74
Administer educational or other secular rehabilitation services	42
Follow up with former inmates after release	33

Source: Pews Research Center, 2012, retrieved from https://www.pewforum.org/2012/03/22/prison-chaplains-what-they-do/

Group Counselor

Group counselors are mental health professionals with degrees in psychology that work with inmates, parolees, or those on probation. The clients they work with are generally some of the same that substance abuse counselors work with, including those with addictions, behavior disorders, and/or mental illnesses. Group counseling has several benefits in that it provides peer support, allows for the treatment of several clients at one time, and is a cheaper alternative to one-on-one benefit. However, there are some individuals who benefit more with more personalized counseling.

Group Therapy, Substance Abuse Treatment. (*Source*: Federal Bureau of Prisons, retrieved from https://www.bop.gov/inmates/custody_and_care/substance_abuse_treatment.jsp)

Michelle Edmark, Warden, NH State Prison for Men.
(*Sources*: New Hampshire Department of Corrections, retrieved from https://www.nh.gov/nhdoc/facilities/concord.html)

Warden

The warden of a prison is the most senior position at the facility. Their work is similar to that of a CEO or president of a company, where their focus is on management of the prison, including budgets, supervision of officers and staff, and training. An added responsibility of warden is public relations, as wardens tend to be the face of the institution. If anything goes wrong and leaked to the public via news or social media, it is generally the warden that is blamed, even if the event is beyond their control. Some prisons even have public relations staff who work closely with the warden, politicians, and the public and who are the official spokespersons for the prison.

PRISON ADMINISTRATION MANAGEMENT STYLES

There are a handful of main types of administrators, whether we are discussing jails and prisons or any other organization. However, we can adapt these typologies to what we see in corrections:

- *The Autocrat* An autocrat in a jail or prison, generally the warden, wants complete and total control of their workforce. This style can be problematic if it requires coercive control, which, as Edwards (1979) would describe it, is abusive. This can include bullying behavior as well. The autocrat is not necessarily the warden. Correction officers in prison with more advance ranks may abuse those who work underneath them in the hierarchy; corrections officers at the bottom ranks can bully prisoners. It is one of the least effective management types that can lead to rebellion, passive-aggressive behavior, or the ousting of the manager when there is enough unhappiness among the ranks. Up until fairly recently, these types of managerial behaviors went largely unchecked. There is today much more aware- ness of workplace abuses, though some autocrats still exist in corrections.
- *The Bureaucrat* A strictly bureaucratic leader will always refer to and defer to the rules and regulations within the corrections setting. They will also defer to their superiors, in this case, the Department of Corrections administrators for wardens. It may not always be the most efficient way of running a jail or prison, as some decisions have to be made quickly and there might not be time to consult the rule book or those higher up in the hierarchy. However, it is one of the safest ways to assure that there are no questions about violations, either by personnel or by the incarcerated. Plus it offers both prisoners and corrections personnel recourse if something is seriously amiss.

  This is not always practical in the jail or prison setting, as we have mentioned the limitations of the red tape of bureaucracies, particularly if they are public enti- ties that have to answer to taxpayers, legislatures, governments, and larger agencies like the federal Bureau of Prisons. However, it is the best management type for con- sistency, especially in the case of when wardens retire or leave their positions for any reason. The rule book and policies will live on after their departure.
- *The Democratic Leader* A democratic leader in corrections will not make deci- sions without discussing the alternatives with their employees. It is possible to be both a bureaucratic leader, following the rules, while still consulting with staff. This management type is seen as the easiest to work under, as personnel find that when they have a voice in decisions made at the institutional level, they are more invested in the work they do. Of course, a number of decisions are beyond the control of even the warden and are left to the state and federal Departments of Corrections or policy makers, including politicians.
- *The Laissez Faire Manager* Coming from the French, translated loosely to "let them do" or "let them be," the laissez faire manager will pretty much leave peo- ple alone while they are working, as long as they are doing their job, or at least

appearing to do so. The downside of this type of management style is that there is the risk that things may indeed be going wrong but they have either not been detected as yet or have been swept under the rug. In extreme cases, there is corruption going on right under the nose of higher ranked jail or prison administrators. This is perhaps the least functional of the four types of jail or prison administrators we discuss here.

Of the four, as we have noted, the democratic leader that combines their management style with following bureaucratic rules and regulations is the most effective type in the jail or prison setting and in most organizational settings in general.

PROFESSIONALISM AND ETHICS IN JAILS AND PRISONS

Once upon a time, there were no real requirements to become corrections officers in jails and prisons. The same applied to police officers. In the United States, there was a movement to push for law enforcement reform beginning in the late 19th century, with the real push for formal police professionalization not coming until the 1960s (Sklansky, 2011). To some extent, the professionalization of corrections personnel predates that of the police.

With professionalization, the expectation is that with more education, corrections personnel are less likely to walk the fine line between ethical and unethical behavior in the correctional setting, as well as being better trained to handle the social and psychological issues that are associated with jails and prisons. As we will see in Chapter 5 on the jail and prison experience from the perspective of corrections staff, this is not always an easy line to walk.

Part and parcel of American values is the social construct of the work ethic. Comparatively speaking, Americans have a wildly different approach to work as people elsewhere in the world, including working longer hours, taking fewer vacations, and socializing less on the job (Abadi, 2018). It would only stand to reason that this strong (and unusual) work ethic would carry over into the corrections professions. However, having a strong work ethic is not without its drawbacks, including creating strain in one's personal life and leading to physical and emotional exhaustion.

On the individual level, in order to remain professional in one's career, one has to have already developed some form of positive core values. In studies of training both in the profession and in professional ethics, the more enlightened that students become, the more likely that individuals will tap into these core values and reject unethical decision-making for themselves or peers (Craft, 2013).

We would assume that people entering the law enforcement and criminal justice professions have strong moral compasses. However, as we will see in Chapter 5, the allure of money can corrupt. The starting salary for corrections officers in some places is only in the high $20,000 to low $30,000 (more likely in private prisons) range, which is hardly a living wage for such a dangerous occupation in today's terms. To put this into perspective, the 2021 poverty guidelines reported by the U.S. Department of Housing and Human Services (2021) for a family of four was $26,500. It is why law enforcement and corrections personnel who receive lower wages could be at risk for bringing in drugs or other contraband into jails and prisons, in exchange for cash or gifts from associates of detainees or prisoners who on the outside. They are also at greater risk for other forms of bribery.

When there is a case of illegal activities being conducted by prison personnel, it becomes a logistical and public relations nightmare for administrators. However, in the case of the laissez faire manager in a jail or prison, if unethical behavior is not called into question, it may be interpreted as administrators endorsing it. This is why ethics education is crucial either prior to or during training.

Surprisingly enough and as we will see in Chapter 6, prisoners themselves have a pretty strong code of ethics. Most of this comes from informal training, with more experienced inmates teaching new prisoners what will and will not be tolerated, but it also can be imported into the prison from the streets. Likewise, there can be informal training for corrections officers, where more seasonal veterans teach younger officers about the unpublished "rules" and expectations.

PRIVATE vs. PUBLIC PRISONS

Private prisons are not a new invention. The use of the private sector to perform governmental duties has been ongoing for centuries (King, 2012). Private prisons were a common practice in some countries in Europe in the 17th century (Blakely and Bumphus, 2004). However, they are relative newcomers in American corrections. There was a boom of private prisons in the United States, beginning in the 1980s (Sigler, 2010).

There are some disadvantages to working in the private prison system, as compared to public prisons. The philosophies between not-for-profits (e.g., state and federal public prisons) vs. for-profits (e.g., privatized, private sector prisons) are radically different, though both must pay attention to budgets. Early studies as to whether there is real cost savings if a state or the federal government pays private prisons to house prisoners, found that there are really no financial benefits of private over public prisons (Pratt and Maahs, 1999). As other studies have likewise come to the same conclusions, there are a lot of discussions in both academic and social justice circles centered on how ethical it is to use for-profit prisons. Like in the case of a hotel, if they do not maintain close to full capacity, it hurts the bottom line, eating away at the profit margin.

There are concerns that private prisons may not hold the same professional standards for their personnel as for public jails and prisons. State and federal jails and prisons require that prospective correctional officers take civil service exams, as well as psychological and physical fitness tests. The Federal Bureau of Prisons go one step further and require a bachelor's degree, unless they have three years of work experience in corrections, as do many state corrections systems these days. Military veterans are often given preference in hiring, largely due to their extensive training they have received already. Some veterans have in fact served as military police during their service, making them particularly attractive candidates for policing and corrections jobs.

However, this does not mean that state departments always have stringent requirements for their correctional staff candidates. If we used the example of the New Mexico Corrections Department (NMDC), the minimum requirements to become a state correctional officers in some states are to be at least 18 years old, be a high school graduate or have a GED, be a U.S. citizen, and have no felony convictions, though candidates can be disqualified if they have more recently used certain drugs, including marijuana (*Correctional Officer Education*, n.d.). This does not mean that every candidate who meets the minimum requirements are good candidates, particularly with the number of people (including perhaps yourself) who have earned either a two-year or four-year degree in criminal justice and might be competing for the same jobs. And as we have more recently learned about the development of the human brain, the frontal lobes, responsible for impulse control among other functions, is not fully developed until around the age of 25 (Sowell et al., 1999), meaning that corrections officers who are older are more likely to have the maturity to handle the psychological rigors of the job.

There is also the criticism that because private juvenile facilities prisons are profit-motivated, they would encourage mass incarceration rather than probation for the convicted. What is of particular concern is when judges are successfully bribed to encourage them to sentence convicted criminals to private prisons. In other words, there is illegal financial incentive to sentence as many people as possible to private prisons in order to fill them up, for some corrupt individuals. In 2011, a federal judge in Pennsylvania, Mark Ciavarella, Jr., was convicted of taking bribes to the tune of $1 million from the developers of juvenile detention center in a case that was known as "kids-for-cash" (Peralta, 2011). Ciavarella's 28 year sentence was upheld on appeal in 2020 (Rubinkam, 2020). This is unfortunately not the only case where a judge took bribes in return for sentencing people to private juvenile detention centers and prisons.

As a preview of our focus on the perspectives of prison staff in Chapter 5, one important fact of what we know about private prisons is that corrections officers who work in them are often not part of unions. This means, as we previously noted, that they are not paid as well as they would be in publicly funded jails and prisons, often close to or below the national poverty line. If you stop and think that a for-profit prison will find cost-saving strategies where they can, one place they can find it is in lower salaries for personnel. The other disadvantage is that officers in private prisons do not necessarily get as rigorous training as those who are required to go through the academy.

Besides not paying as well, nor offering the same benefits as public jails and prisons, private prisons require a higher prisoner to corrections officer ratio (Blakely and Bumphus, 2004). This makes sense, as being for-profit, a private prison will try to manage with as few personnel as possible. However, this puts the corrections personnel in greater danger of being attacked by prisoners.

ACTIVATING NEW JAILS AND PRISONS

If you can imagine, it is challenge enough to handle the day to day operations, as well as manage jail and prison personnel in existing facilities. A particular challenge to the U.S. Bureau of Prisons (BOP) is to build and activate a new facility. If you are familiar with what a charter school is, similar to when a brand new school opening is announced offering modern facilities and more resources, personnel want to flock to newly built jail or prison. It can result in a talent drain from older facilities, where because the desirability of working with latest technology, clean environment, at least initially, can result in the ability to hire only the best and most qualified corrections staff in newer jails and prisons, just as in the case of teacher hiring practices in charter schools.

The desirability of a new facility is particularly apparent when the BOP restricts the number and type of prisoners who will be accepted into new prisons. As the BOP reports, in order to allow for the smooth transition of moved prisoners to a new prison, certain inmate characteristics have to be met, including reports of good conduct, no gang affiliation, and good health (U.S. Bureau of Prisons, 2014). Clearly, transferred and new prison staff will be working with a more desirable population of prisoners.

SOCIAL JUSTICE AND PRISON MANAGEMENT

The older an organization is, the harder it is to change it. People get stuck in their ways, including seasoned jail and prison administrators. With jails and prisons slow to respond to changes, including more awareness of the transsexual transgender community, a rise in mental health issues in the general population that spills over into prisons, as well as a number of emerging dietary restrictions (e.g., gluten intolerance, peanut allergies), prison management has no choice but to confront these issues with reform, often reluctantly. As one of the main duties of prison administrators is to assure the humane treatment of detainees and prisoners, including those who are from special populations, they cannot ignore for long changes that need to be made in response to public outcry.

Prisoners themselves are not clueless to pushes for social reform. Once upon a time, prisoners had to put up with whatever treatment they received while incarcerated. As we will see in our chapter on prisoners' rights, this is no longer the case. Prisoners have rights, though limited, on taking recourse in cases where they are being unfairly or cruelly treated while incarcerated.

As we have mentioned in this textbook, wardens and other prison administrators cannot simply look inward to their institutions. Public opinion and sentiment, plus pressure from politicians can be a large part of what they deal with on a near daily basis. Social media has also put a spotlight on prison reform that cannot be ignored. However, public sentiment and the views of politicians swing like a pendulum, back and forth between tough on crime attitudes and push for making jails and prisons more humane. We will see in the sections in the book providing international comparisons, some countries are more advanced in address social justice issues, some are still relatively oppressive. The United States, subjectively, falls somewhere in the middle of those extremes at the moment.

Like everything else in criminal justice, treatment of the incarcerated is under the microscope with more recent push for social justice reform. Since the death of George Floyd during his arrest, as well as other questionable actions by law enforcement, much of the focus has been on police reform. Slow to follow is social justice reform in prisons, with most of the focus on easing overcrowded conditions. As we see in our international comparisons of corrections, this is a universal theme around the world.

Attempts at prison reform are not new, by any means. As early as the 19th century, there have been movements to improve prison conditions, along with working conditions of officers. However, most of the reforms have been directed at rehabilitation, and not always with benevolent goals in mind. For example, in the early 20th century, prison reform translated in more efficient use of prison labor, in some cases with a for-profit motive, as we currently see in private prisons:

> If 75,000 men, mostly unskilled, but the majority able at all times to do good work, were at our disposal and you had absolute control over their employment and the proceeds thereof, your only outlay would be to supply them with ample food, clothing, and shelter. . . . It can easily be shown that the principal sources of [financial] loss in prison is unemployment, and the inefficiency of convict labor. Remove these and you make prison profitable. (Smith, 1921, p 587)

It is more difficult, as we note elsewhere in this book as well, to front end social problems with money than it is to get funding for the back end of social problems and crime, including the exponential growth of new prisons in recent decades. This has more to do with the priorities in state and federal budgets. It is similar to the spending on disaster preparedness. Whether we are discussing corrections or emergency management, prevention is difficult to find funding for. As the saying goes, it's hard to close Pandora's Box once it has been opened. However, study after study confirms that the costs for prevention are far lower than the costs to pay for prisons in the long run.

Recently, social workers have been more aware of their role in improving prison conditions. As a study in Ireland concluded, in order to promote social justice in prisons, social workers should be better informed on what can be done to create better conditions, including pushing for the reduction of the inhuman and degrading conditions that prisoners live under (News Staff Editor, *Politics and Government Business*, 2016). However, social workers and corrections administration do not always speak the same language, nor share the same goals.

One roadblock to real reform in jails and prisons is the ongoing personnel shortage that correctional administrators face. Russo observes (2019) that with the rank and file officers as the backbone of corrections, the difficulty is in dealing with a shortage of officers, as well as the ongoing difficulty in finding and retaining corrections staff. Russo also reports (2019) that the turnover rate for some state prisons is as high as 55 percent, which means that administrators are left with hiring people who may or may not be adept to change, nor as socially aware.

We should note that improving working conditions for officers may in turn improve prison conditions for inmates. Correctional facilities are notoriously noisy, many lack air conditioning, and both officers and the incarcerated have little access to natural light, as they spend most of their time indoors (Russo, 2019). Officers' saving grace is that they are allowed to leave the facility at the end of their shift, as long as no crisis has occurred that warrants a lockdown.

As of the publication of this textbook, there has been much talk of reform in criminal justice, including prisons. Whether any suggestions for reform come to real fruition is yet to be seen. It is too early to see which way the pendulum will swing and is dependent on a number of factors, including public sentiment, budgets, the state of the economy, and crime statistic trends. The political environment as well, at the state level and in Washington, D.C., have an impact on just how fast reform can be achieved.

SUMMARY

As we have seen in this chapter from the information that Rasmussen University provides, there are a number of jobs in jails and prisons, in the corrections field in general. Though corrections officers may only be required to have a high school diploma, with more students graduating from college and a better understanding of the need for job candidates to have some background in psychology or sociology, more state departments of corrections are requiring their employees to have at least graduated from a two-year college. At the federal level, officer candidates are expected to have completed a four-year degree, though those with a military service record are also a highly sought out for employment.

Some corrections careers require working directly with detainees or inmates. Others, like probation officers, parole officers, and case workers are in the business of trying to keep the convicted out of jail, as well as keeping them from going in and out of the revolving door of the criminal justice system. There are also careers in the medical and psychiatric fields to help detainees and inmates.

There are a number of differences in public and private jail and prison facilities. There is a higher prisoner to corrections officer ratio, leaving possibly more dangerous conditions for those who work in private jails or prisons. Correction officers who work in private facilities do not have bargaining power, as they are not members of a union, unlike those working in public facilities. And they are also paid less and reportedly receive less preparedness for the job, than those who are required to complete academy training to work in state or federal facilities.

Prison administrations have a number of responsibilities, some of which include keeping an eye on public sentiment and the political environment. They also habitually deal with overcrowding in their facilities, as well as with staff shortages due to turnover and officer burnout. All of these have become increasingly taxing on administrators in the new era of social justice reform, which includes the outcry for reforms in the whole criminal justice system, including corrections. These administrative headaches are not unique to the United States. They are also seen almost universally throughout corrections systems in the world, with few exceptions.

Perhaps the most challenging problem for prison administration is the public outcry for social justice reforms. Though as we noted, it is more readily seen in law enforcement, there are a number of critics of the corrections system in the United States who want to see change, the least of which is dealing with problems of overcrowding. The demands for social justice in corrections are not new, but have simply become more vocal in recent years.

STORIES FROM BEHIND BARS

On the Outside, Looking In

We begin Chapter 5 with the consideration that during their shifts on the job, corrections officers are also serving time, but for eight-hours (or more likely, longer) at a time. In this chapter's Stories from Behind Bars, we will focus on the experiences of a former prison administrator, Joseph Slyker, who spent 29 years in a career working for the U.S. Federal Bureau of Prisons. He was in a unique position, as most prison administrators, to understand the experiences from the bottom up of the hierarchy.

Slyker's early interest in criminal justice and specifically in corrections started—in much the same way as many of your experiences that might have influenced you to pursue criminal justice courses—during his childhood watching movies and television shows about fictional police officers. These included *Dragnet* (Mark VII Productions, NBC), *The F.B.I.* (Warner Bros., ABC), and *Adam 12* (Warner Bros., ABC).[6] In his early teens, he belonged to the Police Cadets, a program for juveniles, out of the Kansas Police Department which further solidified his interests in law enforcement.

---

[6] You can find these television shows currently streaming in a number of places online.

Slyker's serious career interests were in policing after he served as a Marine during the Vietnam War. He was discouraged after discharge from the Marine Corps when applying to a police department close to home and was told that he should go back to school, even though he was a veteran. The exact words he was told by the Overland Park Police Department, Kansas were "We are trying to professionalize." (Slyker, 2020, p. 65). This was in the 1970s, when it was still generally unheard of that police officers were more attractive candidates if they possessed either two-year or four-year college degrees, as compared to returning veterans. But as the growth of criminal justice programs in colleges and universities began in earnest in the 1960s, and with as many returning veterans from the Vietnam War taking advantage of the VA education benefits, it stands to reason that criminal justice would be one of the more attractive majors and in turn offered better educated candidates to police departments who were hiring.

Eventually earning a bachelor's degree with a focus in corrections, it was a logical step in Slyker's early career in criminal justice to work in jails or prisons. Depending on where the police department is that you wish to work at, the competition may be so fierce that one back door entry into the department is through first working in corrections. After completing a couple of corrections internships at the state level, which in itself is a testament to the importance of internships in deciding whether to pursue a career in corrections, he was able to gain permanent employment with the Federal Bureau of Prisons (BOP). He eventually ended up working at USP Leavenworth, a maximum security prison in Kansas.

During his years at Leavenworth, Slyker, like other new officers, learned that intuition plays a huge part in how one adapts to employment in the corrections setting: "How you behave there may appear challenging, send subtle signals, or possibly be interpreted the wrong way. Image then becomes very important as to other things like sensitivity, perspective, insight, tolerance, and more." (Slyker, 2020, p. 380) His introspective approach to the job would serve him well later on as he moved up the ranks, leaving USP Leavenworth as a case manager of prisoners.

In the federal prison system, it is relatively easy as an employee to move from one position to another between facilities. After USP Leavenworth, Slyker worked at the Allenwood Federal Prison Camp. Later he was transferred to the Leavenworth Prison Camp where he gained a different experience and perspective in a minimum security facility with primarily nonviolent white collar criminals. What came with that experience was a different prisoner code, a set of informal rules among inmates (discussed in detail in Chapter 6), that did not uniformly apply in a minimum security facility:

A convict in a maximum-security facility would not openly snitch on another convict or steal another convict's property for fear of severe retribution as one would possibly retaliate with a weapon for a perceived wrong. These camp inmates on the other hand would not hesitate to tell on or complain openly to staff about another inmate or steal from each other, and they would fight each other as a last resort. (Slyker, 2020, p. 480)

Slyker said that the same rules apply to both correction officers and prisoners. No one likes a snitch. Like the prison code, there is a "blue code" that requires officers to refrain from reporting fellow corrections staff for indiscretions or unethical behavior. As Slyker lamented, "this culture will continue [the "blue code"] because there will be those who condone this unprofessional behavior or simply choose to say nothing as I did." (Slyker, 2020, p. 514). In retrospect, he believes that inappropriate behavior, including not reporting on fellow corrections officers when they are abusive or otherwise unprofessional, should not be tolerated.

In 1979, he traded in his uniform for a suit and tie and was promoted to case worker. Even with a number of years under his belt, Slyker was naive about the politics of promotion. He acknowledges that there might have been more qualified candidates, but it may be due to a friend working as a case worker putting in a good word for him that had more weight in the promotion decision, than his qualifications.

In Slyker's new position as a case worker, he was responsible for running scheduled meetings of prisoners, including check-ins on their vocational or education progress. No longer was he referred to by prisoners and inmates as "officer," but as either Mr. Slyker or "sir." This career shift to a corrections supervisor moved him from GS-7 to GS-11[7], which included a substantial increase in salary. Slyker bitterly explains that just because these are higher ranks with more income attached to them, does not necessarily mean that it requires a college degree: "If you were to look at the qualifications of a unit manager [in a prison] you would find that this job would require no more than a high school diploma or GED certificate. . . . I wondered why a GS-12 earned a lot more than someone with a college degree." (Slyker, 2020, p. 582).

As in any career, Slyker advises that the means by which to be promoted not only has to do with luck and who you know, but on building a reputation at being really good at your job. He also found from his own experiences that it is not necessarily a good thing to stay at the same facility for the length of your career. This may, as in Slyker's case, means uprooting your family to relocate. He would leave his position behind as a case worker and moved on to the Federal Prison Camp[8] in Allenwood, Pennsylvania, as a unit manager.

---

[7] General Schedule or GS ratings in the federal government designate rank and pay grade. The 2021 locality pay scale can be found at the U.S. Office of Personnel Management, available at https://www.opm.gov/policy-data-oversight/pay-leave/salaries-wages/2021/general-schedule/.

[8] The camp has since been renamed to Federal Correctional Institution. There has been movement to rename prison camps as they still sound, to the public, too much like country clubs or resorts than prisons, even though they are minimum or low security facilities.

Making the shift to a supervisory position in a unit meant that attention had to be given to more than just managing programs. The sanitation of the unit was also one of Slyker's new responsibilities, which meant management of prisoners' personal habits, including their handling of their bedding and clothing, personal items, and general clutter. Because of the types of privileges that prisoners in a minimum security prison have, the expectations for keeping cubicles clean was high. Slyker found that he not only had to keep expectations high for prisoners, but that he had also to do so with those who worked under him. He supervised by example, from the way he dressed, to the extra hours he might put in beyond an eight-hour shift, to maintaining good morale.

As difficult as it was working as an officer at USP Leavenworth, where he saw inmate abuses, suicides, and inmate on inmate violence, he was not prepared for the ultimate despondency he began feeling at FPC Allenwood. Some of this depression was due to do with what was happening in his personal life, but most reflected what he was experiencing on the job:

> *I was unfortunately faced with other hurdles both at work and at home. . . . Pennsylvanians did not seem to be as friendly and accepting as those in the Midwest. . . . At work I was questioning the work ethic of some staff compared to the work ethic of Midwesterners. . . .* (Slyker, 2020, p 849)

Ultimately, Slyker asked for assistance in relocating his family back to the Midwest, citing the number of hardships his family faced, including the difficulties in traveling back and forth to Kansas to visit relatives. To Slyker's good fortune, there was a Disciplinary Hearing Officer (DHO)[9] at the North Central Regional Office of the Federal Bureau of Prisons who wanted to return to the Northeast and a trade was made. Slyker packed up his family and after training in Colorado for the new position, he started his new job as a DHO. He would remain in that position until 2005 when he retired from his career in corrections.

As last thoughts and reflections on his career, Slyker said the following, sentiments that could hold true about any career, in or out of criminal justice:

> *We must never forget that our number one job is to our family and to ourselves; everything else is and should be secondary. I lost track of that along the way and have my regrets of time not spent with family. I do not, however, regret taking this journey of personal reflection and say to anyone who reads this [book] to follow your own path and if it is the right one, you will know it.* (Slyker, 2020, p. 1028)

---

[9] A Disciplinary Hearing Officer (DHO) is responsible for fact-finding and recommendations for discipline of inmates, as well as assisting in training staff on inmate discipline.

SOURCE

Slyker, J. E. (2020) *Outside Looking In: Navigating My 29 Year Career as a Federal Employee of the Federal Bureau of Prisons.* Kindle Edition. New Providence, NJ: Bowker

INTERNATIONAL PERSPECTIVES ON PUNISHMENT AND CORRECTIONS: EGYPT

Much of what we know of punishment and prison in Egypt today stems from the military coup against the democratically elected president, Mohamed Morsi, in 2013. There are an estimated 60,000 political prisoners after the military coup who have reportedly been subjected to cruel treatment and in the extreme, execution (*The Guardian*, 2019). One ongoing serious concern is for the radicalization of prisoners, as prisons fill and conditions deteriorate (Fadel, 2016).

Curiously, there has been little recent academic research on the conditions in Egyptian prisons, yet there was a flurry of journal articles published in the late 19th century on the subject. This was a period in history when the British Empire expanded into Egypt and there was more contact between Europe and the African continent. According to Major Arthur Griffiths, Her Majesty's [Queen Victoria] Inspector of Prisons, the function of 19th century prisons in Egypt was to provide labor (Griffiths, 1897, p. 283):

> *Convicts do much good work sometimes of a superior kind. Now and again a trained handicraftsman is found who is willing to put forward his best skill, and there is always a smart man or two who will act as leader and foreman to the rest, very much as is found with convicts all over the world.*

To date, using prison labor has changed little around the world since the 19th century.

Like other countries, including the United States, prisons in Egypt are reportedly overcrowded. Reports from former prisoners and in letters smuggled out of prison give accounts of inmates having to sleep in shifts as there is not enough floor space to accommodate them (NPR, 2014).

The biggest concern in housing so many political prisoners in Egyptian prisons is there is the risk of martyrdom. More recently, in their efforts to combat terrorism, Egyptian authorities are jailing individuals for their Facebook® posts or their involvement in protests (NPR, 2016).

Some of the overcrowding has been a function of cracking down on certain supposed crimes, including criminal charges that are politically motivated. For instance, journalists in Egypt are fearful of the military-led regime that has targeted journalists, including allegedly fictitious charges against them, accusing the reporters of providing support for terrorism (Hersh, 2014). This makes Egyptian prisons atypical in that they house a large number of political prisoners alongside conventional criminals. Political prisoners are often housed separate from ordinary convicts as there is again a concern that there might be radicalization of the inmate population.

SOURCES

Fadel, L. (2016) As Egypt's jails fill, growing fears of a rise in radicalization. Broadcast, NPR, *Morning Edition.* Aug. 24. Retrieved from https://www.npr.org/sections/parallels/2016/08/24/491170122/as-egypt.

Griffiths, A. (1897) Egyptian prisons. *The North American Review.* Sept., Vol. 165, No. 490:276-287.

Guardian, The (2019) The Guardian view on Morsi's death in Egypt: shocking because foreseen. *Editorial.* Jun. 18. Retrieved from https://www.theguardian.com/commentisfree/2019/jun/18/the-guardian-view-on-morsis-death-in-egypt-shocking-because-foreseen.

Hersh, J. (2014) Journalism becomes a crime in Egypt. The New Yorker. Jan. 31. Retrieved from https://www.newyorker.com/news/news-desk/journalism-becomes-a-crime-in-egypt.

National Public Radio, Inc. (NPR) (2014) A view on the torture and terror of Egyptian prison. Broadcast, *All Things Considered.* Mar. 21. Retrieved from https://go-gale-com.wne.idm.oclc.org/ps/i.do?p=LitRC&u=mlin_w_westnew&id=GALE%7CA362745818&v=2.1&it=r&sid=ebsco.

GLOSSARY

Bureaucracy   According to Weber (1922), the most efficient way to run an organization, including the military, or in this case, corrections. Bureaucracy has a number of characteristics, which include hiring people with expertise and specialization, keeping written records, and clear hierarchy. (See *Chain of command*)

Bureaucratic control   From Edwards (1979) and Weber (1922), a system where control of workers and the running of an organization is built into the rules and regulations.

Chain of command   As demonstrated by an organizational chart, the chain of command shows the clear lines of leadership and front line staff.

Detention officer   Synonymous with corrections officer.

Iron Cage of Bureaucracy   Weber's concept of bureaucracy becoming so rule-bound that it becomes difficult to get anything accomplished. Same thing as the proverbial "red tape."

Jurisdictional roles   Same as "job descriptions" that clearly state exactly what duties someone has in a particular position.

Micromanage, micromanagement   An inefficient, hands-on approach to management where a supervisor wants to handle all aspects of operations themselves. A more efficient way of managing is to trust your employees and that you have hired the best people for their jobs.

Nepotism Practice of hiring family and friends, even though they may not be qualified for the job they are filling.

Paramilitary Not to be confused with extremist groups, paramilitary operations, like in jails and prisons, are organized similarly as the military with a clear chain of command and ranks. (See *Chain of command*)

Simple control Management style described by Edwards (1979) in smaller operations where supervision is up close and personal; it can at times can be arbitrary, as in the example of a family-run business.

Span of control The number of people that someone can effectively supervise. That number is dependent on the industry. In corrections, it refers to the number of staff that a supervisor can manage or the number of prisoners that a corrections officer can safely handle.

Technical control Edwards's term (1979) where control of employees, and in this case, the incarcerated as well, is built into the physical structure of the building. In jails and prisons, this includes mechanized or computerized security doors and cells.

REFERENCES AND SUGGESTED READINGS

Ababi, M. (2018) 11 American work habits other countries avoid at all costs. Business Insider. Mar. 8. Retrieved from https://www.businessinsider.com/unhealthy-american-work-habits-2017-11.

Blakely, C. R. and V. Bumphus (2004) Private and public sector prisons—A comparison of select characteristics. *Federal Probation*. Vol. 68, No. 1:27-31.

Blau, P. (1968) The hierarchy of authority in organizations. *American Journal of Sociology*. Vol. 73, Iss. 4:453-467.

Craft, J. L. (2013) Living in the gray: Lessons on ethics from prison. *Journal of Business Ethics*. Vol. 115:327-339.

Edwards, R. (1979) *Contested Terrain: The Transformation of the Workplace in the Twentieth Century*. New York: Basic Books.

Government Jobs (2021) Detention officer: Job description. Retrieved from https://www.governmentjobs.com/jobs/2914094-0/detention-officer?utm_campaign=google_jobs_apply&utm_source=google_jobs_apply&utm_medium=organic.

Jurik, N. C. and M. C. Musheno (2006) The internal crisis of corrections: Professionalization and the work environment. Justice Quarterly. Vol. 3, Iss. 4:457-480.

Legal Information Institute (n.d.) 28 CFR §97.14—Guard to prisoner ratio. Cornell Law School. Retrieved from https://www.law.cornell.edu/cfr/text/28/97.14.

National Institute of Corrections (n.d.) Corrections rankings: Measuring the efficiency of state prison systems. U.S. Department of Justice. Retrieved from https://nicic.gov/corrections-rankings-measuring-efficiency-state-prison-systems.

News Staff Editor (2016) Researchers at National University of Ireland, Galway target social work. *Politics and Government Business*. Jan. 14. P. 144.

Peralta, E. (2011) Pa. judge sentenced to 28 years in massive juvenile justice bribery scandal. *The Two-Way*. NPR. Aug 11. Retrieved from https://www.npr.org/sections/thetwo-way/2011/08/11/139536686/pa-judge-sentenced-to-28-years-in-massive-juvenile-justice-bribery-scandal.

Rubinkam, M. (2020) Kids-for-cash judge loses bid for lighter prison sentence. *The Washington Post*. Aug 26. Retrieved from https://www.washingtonpost.com/national/kids-for-cash-judge-loses-bid-for-lighter-prison-sentence/2020/08/26/a8e82fea-e7a8-11ea-bf44-0d31c85838a5_story.html.

Russo, J. (2019) Workforce issues in corrections. National Institute of Justice, U.S. Department of Justice. Dec. 1. Retrieved from https://nij.ojp.gov/topics/articles/workforce-issues-corrections#figure1.

Sklansky, A. (2011) New perspectives in policing. Harvard Kennedy School, Program in Criminal Justice Police and Management; National Institute of Justice. Mar. Retrieved from https://www.ojp.gov/pdffiles1/nij/232676.pdf.

Smith, B. (1921) Efficiency vs. reform in prison administration. *Journal of the American Institute of Criminal Law and Criminology*. Feb., Vol. 11, Iss. 4:587-597.

Sowell, E. R., P. M. Thompson, C. J. Holmes, T. L. Jernigan, and A. W. Toga (1999) In vivo evidence for post-adolescent brain maturation in frontal and striatal regions. *Nature Neuroscience*. Vol. 2, No. 10:859-861.

Suffolk County Sheriff's Department (2018) Common ground. Newsletter. Apr. . Retrieved from http://www.scsdma.org/wp-content/uploads/2018/04/1804.pdf.

U.S. Bureau of Labor Statistics (2020) Probation officers and correctional treatment specialists. Sept. 1. Retrieved from https://www.bls.gov/ooh/community-and-social-service/probation-officers-and-correctional-treatment-specialists.htmd.

United States Bureau of Prisons (BOP) (2014) Management of new prison activations can be improved. U.S. Government Accountability Office. Aug. Retrieved from https://www.gao.gov/assets/gao-14-709.pdf#?.

United States Department of Housing and Human Services (HHS) (2021) Annual update of the HHS poverty guidelines. Feb. 1. Retrieved from https://www.federalregister.gov/documents/2021/02/01/2021-01969/annual-update-of-the-hhs-poverty-guidelines.

U.S. News and World Report (n.d.) Corrections rankings: Measuring the efficiency of state prison systems. Retrieved from https://www.usnews.com/news/best-states/rankings/crime-and-corrections/corrections?src=usn_tw.

Weber, M. (1922, 1978) *Economy and Society: An Outline of Interpretive Sociology*. Vols. 1&2. Berkeley, CA: University of California Press.

Chapter FIVE

Jail and Prison Staff Perspectives

> *The fastest growing occupation in the private sector is security guards. The fastest growing occupation in the public sector is prison guards.*
>
> — Robert Reich, Economist and former Secretary of Labor, 1992

Chapter Objectives

- Examine jail and prison staff attitudes towards prisoners and detainees.
- Review the different career options in the corrections system from Chapter 4.
- Note what stresses correctional staff face in working with prisoners and detainees.
- Compare new prison and jail staff with more seasoned correctional staff.
- Introduce the protections that unions provide for corrections personnel.

Key Terms

De-escalate	Lockdowns
Emotional labor	Post-traumatic stress disorder (PTSD)
Infirmary	"Staties"

INTRODUCTION

One of the main paradoxical challenges in being a part of jail or prison staff is how to maintain one's humanity while working with a population that for the most part has no desire to be incarcerated. This conundrum is on top of having the primary job of maintaining order and making sure that both personnel and prisoners follow institutional rules (Ibsen, 2013). According to Ibsen (2013), the study of the lives and social roles of jail and prison staff have long been a tradition in sociology, including work by Sutherland (1931; 1955), Cloward et al. (1960), Goffman (1961), and Blau et al. (1986), and yet as much as we know about the practical aspects of the profession, we still know less about what the job of reconciling the contradictions does to the psyche.

In the last chapter, most of our discussion was focused on the ideal ways to run jails or prisons. In this chapter, we will be discussing the realities of life in the corrections professions. Even in the United States, where corrections staff are professionals, many with college degrees, the turnover rate for officers is notoriously high, at around 16 percent according to Lommel (2004), as well as high absenteeism rates (Kaufman, 2019). Federal prisons, with lower turnover rates, do not feel the shortage of corrections personnel as acutely as state jails and prisons, where the turnover rates are twice as high (Kaufman, 2019).

On average, there were 254 work-related injuries per 10,000 officers from assaults and violent acts (2013 data), as well as higher than average work-related fatalities for corrections officers (International Corrections and Prisons Association, n.d.), in comparison to other criminal justice professions, on top of high burnout rates. The U.S. Bureau of Labor Statistics (2020) reports that correctional officers are subject to more injury and illness, as compared to most other professions. It takes substantial commitment, training, and intestinal fortitude to make corrections a life-long career. However, based on salaries at state and federal facilities, plus attractive benefit packages including medical insurance and retirement pensions, it is understandable why corrections continues to be an attractive route for those interested in the criminal justice professions, in spite of the perceived drawbacks.

As in any profession, there are inside jokes shared among prison staff. One of these include, "I'm serving time, but 8 hours at a time" referring to the fact that corrections officers specifically are occupying the same space as prisoners during their workdays, but have the freedom to go home after their shift is completed. Of course, there really isn't a typical shift for the rank and file who work in jails or prisons. The typical shift that corrections officers work may not be 8 hours long, with the expectation that this will not be a stereotypical 9-to-5, Monday through Friday profession. Prisons are 24-hour operations, much as police departments, fire stations, and hospitals are. This means that jails and prison have to be adequately staffed 24 hours a day, 7 days a week. Some facilities have 12-hours shifts, in which case an officer can typically expect to work 3 days on with 2 days off (*Chron* Contributor, 2020).

Another common joke among those who work in corrections is that the initials for the Department of Corrections, DOC, really stand for "**d**ivorced **or c**heating," referring to the strain that the prison occupations put on the personal lives and families of employees. Part of that strain is due to the unusual shifts they work. Other strains come from prison personnel bringing the stress of working with accused and convicted offenders home with them. There are little current data to support the idea that divorce rates among correctional officers, much less law enforcement personnel in general, is different than in other occupations (Gold Buscho, 2019; McCoy and Aamodt, 2010). However, older studies indicate higher divorce rates, particularly among supervisors in corrections (Cheek and Dimiller, 1983). The reality is that in order to be an effective corrections officer in jails or prisons, it is critical that work life is in balance with home life (Koonce, 2012). This holds true for most professions.

One cannot work for a prison without acquiring a different perspective of society in general. Corrections officers, like police officers, when dealing with the most hardcore criminals, can easily become cynical about humanity in general. As one corrections officer put it, he couldn't even go out to dinner without worrying whether he might run into a former inmate from his facility. This might have been due to the unpleasantness of a possible encounter or for fear that they might be attacked, if recognized by a former inmate. It's why we find that corrections officers and convicts alike may very well sit with their backs to a wall and facing the front door in public spaces.

We should also consider that regardless of whether you work in jails or in prisons, the detainees and prisoners are not there voluntarily and they generally have little to do each day but to watch corrections staff go about their business. As one former jailer explains, detainees and prisoners "watch us do our job and in some cases watch officers who aren't doing their jobs, and to try and figure out how to beat you out of whatever their scam is. . . that can range from getting an extra dinner roll to planning an escape or riot." (Defranco and Duncan, 2017, p. 12) It is bad enough to be under the scrutiny of supervisors. It's another thing all together to be constantly watched by alleged or convicted criminals.

We need to preface this chapter with the fact that there is little academic research that has been done studying the lives of corrections officers. There is more that we learn from anecdotal stories told by the officers and staff themselves. As such, like we caution in the next chapter on prisoners' perspectives of incarceration, that many of the stories we tell in this chapter are subjective, firsthand accounts. That does not mean that the experiences are not valid, but that they are personal and may or may not reflect the feelings of most officers.

Like some other criminal justice professions, to a large extent it is a closed society, where what happens on the job, stays on the job—until it gets so intolerable and it spills out into one's personal life. It is a profession that has historically been hypermasculine with few officers wanting to share their stories. What we do know, is that like a number of first responder professions, correctional officers experience high rates of burnout on the job that results in physical and mental exhaustion (Harizanova and Stoyanova, 2020).

We also need to note that there is even less research that separates the attitudes and experiences of jailers from those of correctional officers. As we recall from earlier chapters, the people who are housed in jail are those awaiting trial (detainees) and those who have been sentenced to shorter sentences that do not warrant the bother to move them to a prison facility. It is practical from a housing standpoint, if within a jurisdiction, as there may not be enough detainees at any given time to warrant the bed capacities of local facilities. So as compared to prisons, the "residents" are there short term bringing a different orientation for correctional officers. Jailers, in particular females and younger corrections officers, are more likely to fear that that detainees and inmates alike will undermine the officers' authority, and in some cases, may be more abusive towards detainees and inmates, as compared to prison staff who are male and/or more seasoned in the job (Cook and Lane, 2014).

For many people working in corrections, it is a lifetime career. For others, the choice of the profession is viewed as a stepping stone into the state police, particularly in states where the "*staties*"[1] are viewed as elite law enforcement, as in the case in some of the states in New England. And yet others work in corrections for a brief period of time, walking away from the career when the burnout becomes intolerable.

Much of the work that corrections officers perform is routine. In fact, there can be tedium interspersed with emergency situations where they have to deal with unruly inmates, depending on the level of security at a prison. The monotonous tasks that corrections officers perform include mediation between prisoners, paperwork, inmate counts, and hazard checks (*Chron* Contributor, 2020). Prison and jail personnel may also be called on to transport prisoners to and from court, as well as be prepared to work overnight, weekends, and holidays in the event of sudden staff shortages and *lockdowns* (emergency events in jails or prison when there is a real or reported threat of violence, rioting, or escape and detainees and inmates are locked in their cells until the emergency has passed).

THE ROOKIE

The first time a new correction officer enters a secured facility, it is the same experience that you might feel when going on a jail or prison tour for your class. Keep in mind that corrections officers do not carry guns, for good reason. With the ratio between corrections officers and prisoners what it is, it would be too easy to be overpowered and have your service revolver taken. Defranco and Duncan (2017) ask their readers to imagine going into the worst neighborhood where there are a lot of criminals, as in the case of gang-infested areas and hanging around there all day on the job without a weapon. In their estimation, police officers are not even exposed to that much risk. As DeFranco and Duncan (2017) note, there are a number of emotions felt by people who enter jails and prisons for the first time, even if they know that they will be allowed to leave when their shift is done:

> *I guess one of the best ways I could try [to explain the feelings] is by asking you to go to prison tomorrow how do you think you would feel once you walked in, what type of emotions would yo3u be feeling, how heightened would your senses be and what types of thoughts do you think would be racing through your mind? Well the Corrections Officer is no different; now you may see oh*

---

[1] According to the Urban Thesaurus (https://urbanthesaurus.org/synonyms/state%20trooper), some of the more flattering names for state police or troopers include "smooth trooper," "trooper mike," and "smokey bear." Out of respect for the profession, we are not including the more disparaging names for state law enforcement personnel.

you're trained you're an officer that's your job and that's my point although we're still human as you, we are professionals and deal with that scenario every day we go to work. (Defranco and Duncan, 2017, p. 36)

One of the biggest mistakes that a new correction officer can do is to try and be a friend to detainees or prisoners. Those housed in jails and prisons are notoriously manipulative, whether convicted or awaiting trial. If you can consider how much time they have on their hands, it is no mystery as to how they think up ways to either torment new correction officers or try and get illegal activities past them.

According to *Corrections1.com* (2019) the most common mistakes that rookie correctional officers make are

1. Inability to say no, so inmates will manipulate them.
2. Not understanding what they don't know, which sets them up for potential injury due to foolish mistakes.
3. Failing to ask questions and listening to more experienced coworkers.
4. Making friends with inmates, including giving personal information about themselves.
5. Basing their preconceptions of what prison is like by what they see on television or movies.
6. Failing to learn how to de-escalate a potentially dangerous situation.
7. Failing to document everything that goes on under their watch in their logbooks and reports.

When they start out in their careers, even the most well-educated correctional officers are ill prepared for what they will see behind bars. Defranco and Duncan (2017) believe that it takes working in a jail or prison for at least one year – if the rookie even lasts that long—before there is an understanding what the job is really like.

THE SEASONED VETERAN

Not all corrections officers or wardens are jaded with negative views of prisoners. Some have joined the ranks hoping to truly help prisoners. Though this is difficult to do without crossing the line into friendships with inmates, as we see to be a rookie mistake mentioned in the previous section of this chapter. Nevertheless, a good percentage of officers are working to help make conditions better in jail or prison, at least in areas that are within their control.

One risk that comes with being a seasoned veteran in corrections is that apathy may set in over time. Apathy is an occupational hazard in a number of criminal justice professions, on the basis of the clientele that employees work with. This can come from becoming jaded at the things that prison staff see and hear, sometimes on a daily basis, that would not be tolerated outside of jails or prisons.

Apathy or indifference can also be derived from the tedium of some of the more mundane tasks performed by officers, which can, in turn, result in neglect.

Chief Deputy Hart of the Santa Cruz Sheriff's Office in Northern California emphasizes the importance of taking routine welfare checks of detainees in jail seriously, regardless of how boring that task might be. Officers who are not engaged in their work may skip hourly checks, or may miss some life-threatening situation, if they do not adequately check on detainees (Sultan, n.d.). There have been charges of neglect of infamous inmates while they were in jail or prison, including in the cases of James "Whitey" Bulger, Jr., the notorious organized crime boss, suspected of having been murdered while incarcerated, or Jeffrey Epstein, who committed suicide in jail while awaiting trial on a number of charges of sex trafficking of minors.

One ongoing concern within the last few years is that both federal and state prisons are reporting an alarming number of veteran correctional officers are either quitting or retiring. This has left prisons to scramble to find personnel to guard inmates, reportedly resorting to using cooks and medical staff to fill in the gaps (AP, 2021; Jenkins, 2021). As in any industry, when there is an alarming exit of experienced personnel, without a concerted effort, there can be some chaos until there are promotions and hiring of new correctional officers.

EMOTIONAL LABOR OF CORRECTIONS PERSONNEL

Any profession that requires you to deal with the public requires that you put personal feelings aside while on the job. The same goes for people who work in criminal justice professions. The individuals that corrections staff primarily deal with are troubled and in trouble, in some cases with violent tendencies and often suffering from mental illness. No matter how much someone working in a jail or prison may dislike, or in fact loathe, any individuals, including the occasional colleague, personnel have to remain professional and not let their personal feelings get in the way of their job. This is not easily accomplished.

In Arlie Hochschild's famous research, published in *The Managed Heart: Commercialization of Human Feeling (*1983), she discusses the phenomena of *emotional labor*. Emotional labor, simply put, means that the worker is being paid to be cheerful or display a positive attitude. Hochschild (1983) uses the example of flight attendants she interviewed who, no matter how lousy they might feel, how much they might not like the behavior of passengers on a plane, or how heartbroken they might be in their personal lives, had to put on a smile and be courteous to everyone. Another example would be someone who works at one of any number of amusement park resorts. You could hardly be a Disney cast member and greet the public with a gloomy disposition, unless you worked the Haunted Mansion attraction where it would be expected to be part of the ambiance of the ride. Though Hochschild applies this concept to the service industry where people have to display a specific positive emotions as part of the job, we can also apply it to people who work in corrections.

As Hochschild and others have noted (e.g., Kruml and Geddes, 2000), this constant performative labor where employees have to act in a way that may be counter to their true feelings is exhausting. This in turn can contribute to burnout and high turnovers rates, particularly in the more difficult parts of the prison to work, including death row. Political views as well, beyond state of emotions, have to be and should be set aside while working with the most challenging populations, including death row inmates. Again, because of the nature of the job, this can be difficult to do.

CORRECTIONS OFFICERS UNIONS

Unions, in general, have lost their power since the 1970s in the United States; more so since the Reagan administration's war on unionization in the 1980s. However, there are some unions that still have a good deal of power, unions for corrections personnel as an example. In fact, corrections unions are some of the most powerful in the country. Three of the best known in the United States are the Correction Officers Union and National Correctional Union, and the American Federation of State, County, and Municipal Employees (American Corrections United, ACU). There are a number of other, more local unions for corrections employees as well. There are also unions that serve employees in broader careers at the state and federal level, as in the example of the American Federation of Government Employees (AFGE).

Unions have historically been subject to corruption from time to time. Some of this is due to their ties to the political machinery, itself also historically corrupt, as in the examples of Chicago and New York cities. There have also been alleged ties between unions and organized crime, as in the case of Jimmy Hoffa and the Teamsters in the 1970s.

POWER, CONTROL, AND RESPECT

Though they seem to be interchangeable terms, power and control have two distinct meanings. If we look at power to mean legitimate power, correctional officers are charged with the power and responsibility to keep detainees and prisoners in line. The varying degree to which they exercise this power is dependent on the individual. For example, some correctional officers may turn a blind eye to minor rule breaking, like inmates bartering with commissary goods, if it helps keep the peace in a jail or prison. Some correctional officers will abuse their powers, as in the case of physical mistreatment of prisoners, similar to what is reported of some police officers, which serves no purposes whatsoever and can end up creating more tensions in what is already a tense situation for prison staff.

Control, on the other hand, is getting people to do what you want them to do, even when they don't want to. So, in other words, you could have the formal authority and power to give orders, but unless anybody follows them, it's impotent authority. Control is a large part of what correctional officers are dealing with on a daily basis with detainees and prisoners. As we saw in our discussions of the rookie officer, sometimes in the process of trying to be likeable to prisoners, they not only can lose control, but also lose respect from prisoners and colleagues alike. It is a fine line between humanely handling detainees and prisoners and crossing the line into being too "soft" on inmates.

Unfortunately, some people who enter criminal justice professions, including corrections officers, are seeking the power, control, and respect that they perceive they have not experienced outside of work. This could be due to their experiences growing up, their experiences in school, or experiences in their adult lives. Fortunately, there are not large numbers of these misguided individuals. Generally, they find themselves out of a job if their efforts to seek these three goals results in mistreatment of prisoners or constant conflict with superiors and colleagues. Sometimes they are even weeded out during their academy training when instructors see potential for problems down the road.

RESPONDING TO CRISES IN JAILS AND PRISONS

Up to 85 percent of detainees and prisoners are suffering from varying degrees of mental illness, which means that at any given moment, a prisoner will not respond to requests to follow rules. As King (2020, p. 1) states in his manual for deescalating volatile situations, "demonstrating genuine care and concern for another human being in crisis is not always easy." It is precisely this reason that it is critical for all prison and jail staff be trained in responses to not only medical emergencies, but to psychological crises as well. King (2020) offers 15 "laws" on how to respond to a crisis situation, including in prisons or jails:

1. Care for the people you are helping in a crisis, even if it seems like it is more than they deserve.
2. Be the first to try and find a solution, including letting the involved parties know that you are there to help.
3. Pay attention to what isn't being said, including body language.
4. Aim for harmony, not balance, as you may not be able to achieve equitable treatment. Example: In an assault, usually someone throws the first punch and is more culpable.
5. Listen to what is being said and adapt changes to your own behavior if warranted.

6. Understand that there is a difference between what you think and what you know. Don't assume you know everything about a situation before acting.

7. Work on your *Emotional Intelligence* (EQ or EI).

8. Separate your emotions and personal experiences from the crisis you are trying to resolve.

9. As we mentioned in the "rookie" section of this chapter, as the mediator, be friendly, but do not be friends with the prisoners.

10. Though the person or persons you are dealing with may appear to be out of control and "crazy," for many who are in crisis, this is a temporary situation. Do not be so quick to label an inmate as "insane" while dealing with their crisis.

11. Master your own emotions and mindset before attempting to de-escalate a crisis.

12. Do not appear to be a threat when mediating by acting angry, loud, or aggressive.

13. Try to find a connection with the person or persons in crisis—like a hostage negotiator, try to find a way to get them to trust you.

14. Primary focus should be meeting the needs of the individual or individuals (e.g., medications, getting them to safety).

15. Provide options to detainees and prisoners. Part of the crisis they are experiencing is related to their sense of helplessness in the face of having no choices. These should include asking them as to whether they need to see a chaplain or medical, psychiatric staff member.

King also suggests following the 3 Cs (2020, p. 54):

> *Cooperation* vs. Confrontation;
> *Coordination* vs. Control; and
> *Communication* vs. Criticism

It is difficult for corrections officers to always remember that the goal is to *de-escalate* (defuse) a potentially violent situation between prisoners and not to necessarily resort to physical force as a first response. One important reason to use communication tactics is that when prisoners (or anyone for that matter) are physically restrained, this will result in residual resentment and the originating problem never gets solved. Of course, there are times when correctional staff have no choice but to physically restrain detainees or prisoners, particularly if there is a chance they will hurt themselves, others who are incarcerated, and/or staff.

Corrections officers can become jaded to the assaults they have to witness within the course of their jobs. As DeFranco and Duncan note (2017, p. 2) from their experiences as jailers, violence is "something you get used to . . . It's just another day at work for the Corrections Officer." This can mean that the officers might dangerously ignore a spat between prisoners that can escalate into something more serious, if not put in check.

JAIL, PRISON STAFF, AND MENTAL HEALTH ISSUES

The mental health issues of jail and prison staff tends to be overlooked in academic research as well. However, it has been well documented by rehabilitation resources, including by the American Addiction Centers (2022), that corrections officers are at risk for substance abuse issues, and even suicide. Historically, the four most commonly cited stressors for officers include understaffing, overtime demands, shift work, and supervisor demands (Finn, 1998).

As Sultan (n.d.), an expert on criminal justice and mental health, reminds us,

> *When we think about corrections – we need to think about all of the people behind the wall. Incarcerated individuals are a piece of this world, but they are not the entire group. There is a population of individuals of correctional officers, health care workers, and other professionals [working in prisons] that undergo reentry on a daily basis. Those working in corrections live between two worlds – prison life and life over the wall.* (n.d., retrieved from https://www.psychalive.org/working-behind-the-wall-mental-health-of-correctional-based-staff/#:~:text=Twenty%2Dfive%20percent%20of%20correctional,report%20hopelessness%20and%2For%20worthlessness.)

As we noted at the beginning of this chapter, prison staff are "serving time" in their jobs, but for eight hours (or longer) at a time. Unless they are interacting on the outside with people who understand what it likes to work in a jail or prison, they may find themselves isolated when they leave work at the end of their shift. Though recommendations for high stress professions include the suggestion that work and home life be kept separated, it is difficult to do so for people in criminal justice careers.

We will be discussing at some length in a later chapter the mental issues that prisoner may face. Yet, we know that both law enforcement personnel and prison staff face a number of stressful situations in the course of their work. Likewise, though there is mental health screening of prisoners on a regular basis, except for the purposes of initial applications and academy training, prison staff rarely, if ever have mental health check ins themselves. This mainly occurs when they seek out treatment on their own or are required as a condition of continued employment to undergo therapy due to some specific work-related incident.

Just like combat soldiers and law enforcement personnel, as well as other first responders, correction officers are at risk for developing post-traumatic stress disorder (PTSD). Some studies indicate that corrections officers suffer from PTSD at greater rates than military personnel (American Addiction Centers, 2022). Finn (2000) notes that research and anecdotal evidence indicate that one of the biggest stressors for correctional officers is the threat of violence against them, as well as experiencing actual instances of violence. In addition to violence, correctional officers are likewise stressed by inmate demands and manipulation, as well as conflict between co-workers (Finn, 2000).

Another stressor for jail and prison staff is that work shifts may not be predictable. New officers may have overnight shifts that not only affect themselves, but their families as well if they are in a committed relationship and/or have children. Staff that have young children may find that they have limited time with them if they work weekend shifts (Grant, 1995). In turn, the stresses of what they feel at home may spill over into staff's work lives, which sets them up for a vicious cycle of finding no relief from stress, either at home or on the job. Captain Frank Dwyer, a 28-year veteran of New York City's Rikers Island, reports that jail culture can bleed into daily life and he credits his wife for offering him the support he needed to keep him sane (Sultan, n.d.).

Mental health issues are not exclusive to correctional officers in the United States. In a study conducted in France, researchers found that there were higher instances of depression, anxiety, and sleep disorders among prison staff, as compared to other occupations (Goldberg et al., 1996). If we consider that this study was conducted just at the cusp of research on stress in professions and more admissions, diagnoses of mental disorders in general, we can assume that the instances reported of mental illness, if the same study was conducted today, may be far higher. This especially at the height of the COVID-19 pandemic, where jail and prison staff were considered essential workers and were required to work in particularly precarious circumstances.

PRISONERS' PERCEPTIONS AND TREATMENT OF PRISON STAFF

In our next chapter on prisoners' perspectives about incarceration, we will go into more detail on their introspective experiences. In this section of this chapter, we will focus more on the prisoners' perceptions of prison staff.

Because prisoners and prison staff live in close quarters, any disagreements between inmates is known pretty much throughout a cellblock and by prison staff. The reverse is also true. Inmates will pick up on any tensions between prison personnel. Things can get so out of hand between corrections officers, that inmates may feel ignored because of verbal and sometimes physical fights that happen between jail or prison personnel (Trammell and Rundle, 2015).

Prisoners are known for their efforts to manipulate personnel in prison infirmaries. Drug-seeking behavior by addicts is found inside and outside of prison or, in prison, by those who wish to spend their time in prison "zoned out" on drugs. This means that staff can end up either wittingly or unwittingly complacent in prisoner drug-seeking behaviors.

143

SUMMARY

We have to remember that most people who work in the correctional setting are well-meaning people. A small percentage will choose the career, whether it be police officer or corrections officer, because they believe that it will give them the power, control, and respect that they are otherwise lacking in their lives. These individuals tend to be weeded out very quickly in academies or in the course of their careers. Others genuinely believe that they can do some good for detainees or prisoners; some of them will become burned out on the job quickly or find themselves manipulated by inmates if they attempt to be friends with them. Others yet choose the profession for the substantial benefits, including pensions funds, at least in public jails and prisons.

Professions in corrections are subject to worker burnout at a greater rate than many other professions. Some of this can be attributed to the emotional labor involved, where jail and prison personnel cannot show their true feelings. They are not allowed, though this is difficult to do, to show preferential treatment of prisoners, unless it is used as a reward for good behavior. Likewise, they are not allowed to show their disgust for any single detainee or prisoner, no matter how they might be appalled by their words or behavior. They of course can show displeasure when rules are broken, but they theoretically should not be showing any personal animosity towards individuals housed in their facility. There is also the difficulty of remaining professional around colleagues that they cannot get along with, which can happen in the highly charged environment in correctional institutions.

Prison personnel, whether they work in the *infirmary* (medical facilities) or in the cell blocks, are exposed to the potential for violence from detainees and inmates. This too can be one of the contributing factors for depression, anxiety, and apathy. Most studies and anecdotal stories from corrections officers themselves show that the best protection against any of these three factors is to maintain a balance between home life and work life. Another contributing factor to mental health issues is the varying shifts that correctional staff have to keep, including weekends and holidays, plus unexpected lockdowns. This can make it difficult to create and maintain family time at home.

STORIES FROM BEHIND BARS

Life in the "Bing" — Central Punitive Segregation Unit, Rikers[2] Island, New York

Rikers Island in New York, a maximum security prison built in the 1930s and expected to close later in this decade, makes the list for one of the top ten notoriously dangerous jails and prisons in the United States. Rikers Island is the jail system that serves New York City and consists of several separate jails (Garcia, 2020; *News Talk 1450*, *Worldnews* Staff, n.d.). It is virtually on an island in the East River. Prater (2021) observed that conditions in Rikers Island have been deteriorating in the last few years, beyond being the unpleasant place that the public expect jails and prisons to be. Prisoners have been without access to adequate medical or mental healthcare, at times warehoused in large rooms that have no toilets or showers (Prater, 2021).

Rikers Island, NYC. (*Source*: John Moore/Getty Images, *The Guardian*, 2020, retrieved from https://www.theguardian.com/us-news/2020/feb/25/rikers-island-harvey-weinstein-prison-brutality)

Though most former corrections officers writing about their experiences of working behind bars will emphatically state that working in jail or prison is nothing like what you see in movies or television, Jose Garcia, a former Rikers Island corrections officers disagrees. This is how he describes the experience (Garcia, 2020, p. 14):

> *For a Corrections Officer at Riker's Island their version of training day.[2] Much like in the movie starring Denzel Washington and Ethan Hunt, when Ethan Hunt's character gets high, most of your day can be a blur due to working a double (working an additional 8 hour shift because of low staffing), after you have already worked an 8 hour shift for your third day straight. Or you feel as if you're on an episode of SpikeTV's Gangland where it's you and 60 other gang members in a housing area and all you have is OC spray[3], and a radio.*

[2] Garcia is referencing the 2001 movie, *Training Day* (Warner Bros. Studio), about a veteran police officer working with a rookie in the LAPD narcotics division.
[3] From Chapter 3, oleoresin capsicum, commonly known as pepper spray.

> *But sometimes it's a reality TV show where inmates can come up with creative ways to cook or make a meal.*

Some of the more infamous detainees and prisoners who were unfortunate to find Rikers Island their temporary or permanent home after conviction include (Neuman, 2021; Barr, 2020):

- Tupac Amaru Shakur, rapper
- Sid Vicious, English musician
- David Berkowitz, "Son of Sam" serial killer
- Foxy Brown, rapper
- Lil Wayne, rapper, singer, songwriter
- Dominique Strauss-Kahn, French politician and former director of the International Monetary Fund (IMF)
- Plaxico Burress, former NFL wide receiver
- Jayson Williams, former NBA player
- Harvey Weinstein, former movie producer and studio head.

Corrections officers are not the only ones who have been greatly affected by their time working at one of the Rikers Island jail facilities. Homer Venters, the former Chief Medical Officer at Rikers Islands, describes the toll of the jails on detainees and prisoners housed there (2019, p. 2):

> *Correctional health services like ours see every day how jail harms our patients, and we also possess the resources and skills to group together many health outcomes like injuries or sexual assaults and identify trends and risk factors. . . Detainees are beaten and threatened to prevent them from telling the truth about how they are injured, health staff are pressured to lie or omit details in their own documentation. . . .*

For a physician who has taken the Hippocratic Oath upon becoming a doctor and pledges to "first, do no harm," Rikers Island is an alienating environment to work in. It is assumedly so for all health care workers in the jail system. Venters (2019) does admit that one of the problems in treating the sick and injured in jail is that they often have preexisting conditions that predate their time in custody.

To add to the difficulties of working at Rikers Island, there have been recent reports of corruption among the ranks of jailers. An example of a corrupt corrections officer is Norman Seabrook, the former president of the New York City correction officers' union. Seabrook was arrested in 2017 and accused of pilfering the retirement fund held through the Corrections Officers Benevolence Association (COBA). Gary Heyward, another Rikers Island corrections officer, was convicted of smuggling drugs into the jails and admittedly ran a prostitution ring inside, calling the jailhouse sex workers "copstitutes" as they were recruited among female law enforcement officers (Connelly, 2015; Heyward, 2015). For officers and staff who are legitimately doing their jobs in the jail, this is demoralizing.

Rikers Island was investigated by the U.S Justice Department in 2014 for irregularities at the facilities. Their report found that the jail system had a culture of violence where there is regular use of force by corrections officers in order to maintain control of the violently out of control complex (Gonzalez, 2020; U.S. Department of Justice, 2014). Of particular concern was the physical and emotional trauma experienced by adolescent males housed on Rikers Island (U.S. Department of Justice, 2014). Though the dates of closure continue to be moved, Rikers Island is currently reported to be officially closed sometime in 2027.

To put this into perspective, some 8,000 correctional officers, plus all ancillary staff, including health care workers, will be out of a job. Hopefully they will be relocated to the planned four borough-based jails that are expected to replace Rikers Island (Gonzalez, 2020). Their saving grace is that the demand for jail and prison workers has been steadily increasing for a number of decades.

SOURCES

Barr, J. (2020) Harvey Weinstein leaves Rikers Island for state prison facility. *The Hollywood Reporter.* Mar. 18. Retrieved from https://www.hollywoodreporter.com/thr-esq/harvey-weinstein-leaves-rikers-island-state-prison-facility-1284504.

Connelly, S. (2015) Ex-Rikers guard, who served time for selling drugs to inmates, also pimped out female officers as 'copstitutes': book. *Daily News.* Mar. 14. Retrieved from https://www.nydailynews.com/new-york/nyc-crime/ex-rikers-guard-sold-drugs-pimped-female-officers-book-article-1.2149561.

Garcia, J. (2020) *Riker's Island: Patrolling the toughest precients [sic] in New York City, as a CO: Life in the Bing (Central Punitive Segregation Unit).* Apr. 30. New York: Self-published, Amazon Kindle Edition.

Gonzalez, K. (2020) A timeline on the closure of Rikers Island. *City & State New York.* Oct. 20. Retrieved from https://www.cityandstateny.com/articles/policy/criminal-justice/timeline-closure-rikers-island.html#:~:text=Alongside%20New%20York%20City%20Council,and%20smaller%20criminal%20justice%20system.

Heyward, G. L. (2015) *Corruption Officer: From Jail Guard to Perpetrator Inside Rikers Island.* New York: Atria Books.

Neuman, A. E. (2021) 13 famous prisoners of Rikers Island. Unspeakable Times, *Ranker.* Feb. 26. Retrieved from https://www.ranker.com/list/famous-prisoners-at-rikers-island/tread lightly.

News Talk 1460 (n.d.) Top 10 most notorious prisons in the U.S. . KION (AM radio), Worldnews Staff. Salinas, CA. Retrieved from https://woldcnews.com/944822/top-10-most-notorious-prisons-in-the-u-s/

Prater, N. (2021) 'It's hard to find the words to describe how bad it is right now'. Intelligencer, *New York Magazine*. Sept 27. Retrieved from https://nymag.com/intelligencer/2021/09/hard-to-find-the-words-to-describe-how-bad-it-is-on-rikers.html.

U.S. Department of Justice (2014) Manhattan U.S. attorney finds pattern and practice of excessive force and violence at NYC jails on Rikers Island that violates the Constitutional Rights of adolescent male inmates. Press release, U.S. Attorney's Office, Southern District. Aug. 4. Retrieved from https://www.justice.gov/usao-sdny/pr/manhattan-us-attorney-finds-pattern-and-practice-excessive-force-and-violence-nyc-jails.

Venters, H. (2019) *Life and Death in Rikers Island.* 1st ed. Baltimore, MD: Johns Hopkins University Press.

INTERNATIONAL PERSPECTIVES ON PUNISHMENT AND CORRECTIONS: ANTARTICA

Antarctica is an unusual continent when it comes to crime and punishment. The primary inhabitants of the frozen land at the bottom of the globe are a rotating cast of scientists, the military, and civilian support staff.[4] The residents, mostly temporary, are truly international. Few stay through the harsh, dark winter and it is primarily in the summer months (October through February in Southern Hemisphere) that there are a greater number of personnel. The indigenous population in Antarctica is long gone (Dittman, 2003). Antarctica does not belong to any one nation, but rather is managed by a collaborative number of countries. To simplify things, what we will discuss in this section is the jurisdiction of the United States in criminal matters.

Basic psychology and sociology, for people who live in small villages similar to what the scientific community in Antarctica looks like, indicates that there is a tendency to self-govern. Everyone pretty much knows everyone else and there is less temptation to step out of line and break social norms, including committing crimes.

However, the psychology of living in confined quarters, working in extreme environmental conditions, dictates that people will inevitably undergo both physiological and psychological changes (Anton-Solanas et al., 2016). This means that there may be inevitable tensions, similar to what we see in reality television series (e.g., *Big Brother*, *CBS*; *The Bachelor* franchise during the COVID-19 pandemic, *ABC*) that may lead to criminal behavior. Each year, psychologists working for the U.S. Antarctic Program travel to Antarctica in order to conduct around-the-clock psychological evaluations on personnel who spend the six-month period of near darkness during the winter (March through August in the Southern Hemisphere) (Dittman, 2003).

---

[4] In the 1980s, the author's then husband, who is a master mechanic on Caterpillar® machinery, had two job offers, one in Alaska and one in Antarctica. We chose the Alaska job as the Antarctica position was seasonal.

There are claims that there is a history of violence in Antarctica during the early years of research, including "one unconfirmed story reported in Canadian Geographic, [where] a scientist working at Russia's Vostok Station in 1959 snapped after losing a chess game and murdered his opponent with an axe," after which chess was banned in Antarctica (Debczak, 2019, retrieved from https://www.ment alfloss.com/article/579732/mysterious-death-rodney-marks-scientist-who-was-poisoned-antarctica).

When there is a fatality in Antarctica, it generally is due to a tragic freak accident. There is, however, an unsolved mystery of the suspected homicide in 2000 of Rodney Marks, a research scientist. Marks, an Australian national, was an astrophysicist working at the National Science Foundation's South Pole station, which is under the control of the United States (Mervis, 2006), when he suddenly became ill and died. His death, initially attributed to natural causes, was later announced as being due to methanol poisoning. During the coroner's inquest conducted in New Zealand, Detective Senior Sergeant Grant Wormald accused the U.S. authorities of not cooperating with the investigation at the time of Marks's suspicious death (Mervis, 2006).

More recently in 2018, a Russian engineer, Sergey Savitsky, stabbed a colleague after having a psychological breakdown, immediately after which he was arrested and placed under house arrest before facing attempted murder charges in Russia (Daley, 2018). His case was dismissed when Savitsky pleaded guilty to the charges and reconciliated with the victim, Oleg Beloguzov. Both Savitsky and Beloguzov continued to work at the Institute of the Arctic and Antarctic after the incident (*Terrible Things Happening in Cold Places*, 2019).

The only law enforcement for U.S. interests in Antarctica is a special deputy with ten weeks of training in crime investigation and evidence collection, who also serves as the National Science Foundation Station Manager (Christian, 2002). When people who are part of the U.S. Antarctic Program do commit crimes in Antarctica, they are not housed in jail but rather confined to a hut until they can be transferred to a jail to await trial off the continent (Christian, 2002). A hut for crime suspects in Antarctica is not as we envision from the movies, but rather a well-insulated building separate from other housing.

SOURCES

Anton-Solanas, A., B. V. O'Neill, T. E. Morris, and J. Dunbar (2016) Physiological and cognitive response to an Antarctic Expedition: A case report. *International Journal of Sports Physiology and Performance*. Vol. 11:11053-1059.

Bilder, R. B. (1966) Control of criminal conduct in Antarctica. *Virginia Law Review*. Vol. 52, No. 2:231-285.

Christian, E. R. (2002) TIGER in Antarctica: Crime and punishment. National Aeronautics and Space Administration, Goddard Space Flight Center. Retrieved from https://asd .gsfc.nasa.gov/archive/tiger/crime.html.

Daley, J. (2018) Russian researcher charged with attempted murder in Antarctica. Smithsonian Magazine. Oct. 25. Retrieved from https://www.smithsonianmag.com/smart-news/russian-faces-antarctica-attempted-murder-charge-180970632/.

Debczak, M. (2019) Death at the South Pole: The mystery of Antarctica's unsolved poisoning case. *Mental Floss.* June 25. Retrieved from https://www.mentalfloss.com/article/579732/mysterious-death-rodney-marks-scientist-who-was-poisoned-antarctica

Dittmann, M. (2003) Braving the ice: Psychologists journey to Antarctica to evaluate those stationed there during the severe winters. *Monitor on Psychology.* Mar., Vol. 34, No. 3:56.

Mervis, J. (2006) South Pole death probed. *Science.* Dec. 22., Vol. 314, Iss. 5807:1861.

Terrible Things Happening in Cold Places (2019) The Bellingshausen stabbing: An update and some background. Aug. 24, 7:33 pm. Retrieved from http://www.terriblethingshappeningincoldplaces.com/bellingshausen-stabbing-update.

GLOSSARY

De-escalate (or de-escalation)   To defuse a potentially violent or deadly situation, in this case in a jail or prison. Learning techniques to de-escalate a situation takes specialized training, generally in psychology.

Emotional labor   Based on Hochschild's research (1983), when part of the conditions of working requires the display of certain emotions, as in the example of prison personnel having to not only look "tough" but also impartial.

Infirmary   Borrowed from military terms, the medical facilities in a jail or prison.

Lockdowns   Emergency events in jails or prison when there is a real or reported threat of violence, rioting, or escape. Detainees and inmates are required to be locked in their cells until the emergency has passed and prison administration end the lockdown.

Post-traumatic stress disorder (PTSD)   Psychological disorder that is experienced by some people who have lived through traumatic events in their lives. For example, veterans who were actively engaged in war.

"Staties"   The term used in law enforcement circles that refers to state police. In some states, they are considered to be the elite of the elite in law enforcement at the state level. County and State Police are generally responsible for running local jails.

REFERENCES AND SUGGESTED READINGS

American Addiction Centers (2022) Corrections officers: Addiction, stressors, and problems they face. By ed. staff. Jan 31. Retrieved from https://americanaddictioncenters.org/rehab-guide/corrections-officers.

Associated Press (AP) (2021) Federal prisons forced to use cooks, nurses to guard inmates due to staff shortages. *U.S. News*, NBC News. May 21. Retrieved from https://www.nbcnews.com/news/us-news/federal-prisons-forced-use-cooks -nurses-guard-inmates-due-staff-n1268138.

Blau, J. R., S. C. Light, and M. Chamlin (1986) Individual and contextual effects on stress and job satisfaction. *Work and Occupations*. Vol. 13, No. 1:131-156.

Cameron, J. (2021) Cooks, nurses, helping to guard inmates in US prisons amid shortage. *The Hill*. May 21. Retrieved from https://thehill.com/homenews/news/554741-cooks-and -nurses-helping-to-guard-inmates-in-us-prisons-amid-officer-shortage.

Cheek, F. E. and M. S. Di Miller (1983) Experience of stress for correction officers:

Double-Bind Theory of correctional stress. *Journal of Criminal Justice*. Vol. 1, Iss. 2:105-120.

Chron Contributor (2020) What kinds of hour shifts do correctional deputies work? Work/ Career Advice/Frustrations at Work, *Chron*. Oct. 15. Retrieved from https://work.chron .com/kind-hour-shifts-correctional-deputies-work-24189.html

Cloward, R. A., D. R. Cressey, G. H. Grosser, R. McCleery, L. E. Ohlin, G. E. Sykes, and S.E. Messenger (1960) *Theoretical Studies in Social Organization of the Prison*. New York City, NY: Social Science Research Council.

Cook, C. L. and J. Lane (2014) Professional orientation and pluralistic ignorance among jail correctional officers. *International Journal of Offender Therapy and Comparative Criminology*. Vol. 58, No. 6:735-757.

Correctional Officer Education (n.d.) Corrections officer jobs in New Mexico. Retrieved from https://www.correctionalofficeredu.org/new-mexico/.

Correctional Officer Education (n.d.) Job requirements for state and federal corrections officers. Retrieved from https://www.correctionalofficeredu.org/correctional-officer-requirements/ #:~:text=General%20Requirements,high%20school%20diploma%20or%20GED.

Corrections1 (2019) 7 mistakes that rookie correctional officers consistently make. Nov. 25. Retrieved from https://www.corrections1.com/corrections-jobs-careers/articles/7-mista kes-that-rookie-correctional-officers-consistently-make-OTfsx0ixwIkkvIBw/.

Defranco, J. and T. Duncan (2017) *Life as a Jailer*. Morrisville, North Carolina: Lulu Publishing Services.

Destination Hope (2012) Recovering addicts as addiction counselors. Nov. 1. Retrieved from https://destinationhope.com/recovering-addicts-as-addiction-counselors/.

Finn, P. (2000) Addressing correctional officers programs and strategies. U.S. Department of Justice Office of Justice Programs, NCJ Number 183474. Dec. Retrieved from https:// www.ojp.gov/ncjrs/virtual-library/abstracts/addressing-correctional-officer-stress-progr ams-and-strategies.

Finn, P. (1998) Correctional officer stress: A cause for concern and additional help. Federal Probation. Vol. 62 Iss. 2:65-74

Goffman, E. (1961) *Asylums: Essays on the Social Situation of Mental Patients and Other Inmates*. New York City, NY: Anchor Books (Doubleday)

Gold Buscho, A. (2019) Divorce, emergency responders, and special circumstances. *Psychology Today*. Nov. 11. Retrieved from https://www.psychologytoday.com/us/blog/ better-divorce/201911/divorce-emergency-responders-and-special-circumstances.

Goldberg, P., S. Simone, M. F. Landre, M. Goldberg, S. Dassa, and R. Fuhrer (1996) Work conditions and mental health among staff in France. *Scandinavian Journal of Work, Environment, and Health*. Vol. 22, No. 1:45-54.

Grant, B. A. (1995) Impact of working rotating schedules on family life of correctional staff. Forum on Corrections Research. May, Vol. 7, Iss. 2:40-42.

Harizanova, S. and R. Stoyanova (2020) Burnout among nurses and correctional officers. *Work.* Vol. 65, No. 1:71-77.

Hochschild, A. (1983) *The Managed Heart: Commercialization of Human Feeling.* Berkeley: University of California Press.

Ibsen, A. Z. (2013) Ruling by favors: Prison guards' informal exercise of institutional control. *Law and Social Inquiry.* Vol. 38, Iss. 2:342-363.

International Corrections and Prisons Association (n.d.) Time to better protect our corrections and prison officers. Retrieved from https://icpa.org/time-to-better-protect-our-corrections-and-prison-officers/.

Kaufman, C. (2019) Solutions to a national problem of correctional officer turnover in the U.S. *Brief Policy Perspectives.* Dec. 18. Retrieved from https://policy-perspectives.org/2019/12/18/solutions-to-a-national-problem-correctional-officer-turnover-in-the-u-s/.

King, B. (2020) *The 15 Fundamental Laws of De-Escalation: How to Put Out Fires, Not Start Them.* Self-published.

King, M. T. (2012) A history of private prisons, in *Prison Privatization: The Many Facets of a Controversial Industry*, Vol. 1, B. E. Price and J. C. Morris, eds. Westport, CT: Praeger Publishers.

Koonce, L. (2012) *Correction Officer's Guide to Understanding Inmates.* Atlanta, GA: Koonce Publishing.

Kruml, S. M. and D. Geddes (2000) Exploring the dimensions of emotional labor. Management Communication Quarterly. Aug., Vol. 14, No. 1:8-49.

Lommel, J. (2004) Turning around turnover. *Corrections Today Magazine.* Vol. 66, Iss. 5: 54-57.

McCoy, S. P. and M. G. Aamodt (2010) A comparison of law enforcement divorce rates with those of other occupations. Mar., Vol. 25, No. 1:1-16.

Nurse Practitioner Schools (2020) Nurse Practitioner vs. Doctor (Physician). Staff Writers. Oct. 26. Retrieved from https://www.nursepractitionerschools.com/faq/np-vs-doctor/.

Peralta, E. (2011) Pa. judge sentenced to 28 years in massive juvenile justice bribery scandal. National Public Radio (NPR). Aug. 11. Retrieved from https://www.npr.org/sections/the-two-way/2011/08/11/139536686/pa-judge-sentenced-to-28-years-in-massive-juvenile-justice-bribery-scandal.

Pratt, T. C. and J. Maahs (1999) Are private prisons more cost-effective than public prisons? A meta-analysis of evaluation research studies. *Crime and Delinquency.* July, Vol. 45, Iss. 2:358-371.

Rubinkam, M. (2020) Kids-for-cash judge loses bid for lighter prison sentence. AP, *The Washington Post.* Aug. 26. Retrieved from https://www.washingtonpost.com/national/kids-for-cash-judge-loses-bid-for-lighter-prison-sentence/2020/08/26/a8e82fea-e7a8-11ea-bf44-0d31c85838a5_story.html.

Sigler, M. (2010) Private prisons, public functions, and the meaning of punishment. *Florida State University Law Review.* Article 4. Vol. 38, Iss. 1:149-178.

Sultan, B. (n.d.) Working behind the Wall: Mental health of correctional-based staff. *PsychAlive.* Retrieved from https://www.psychalive.org/working-behind-the-wall-mental-health-of-correctional-based-staff/#:~:text=Twenty%2Dfive%20percent%20of%20correctional,report%20hopelessness%20and%2For%20worthlessness.

Sutherland, E. H. (1955) *Principles of Criminology*, revised by D. R. Cressey. New York City, NY: J B Lippincott Co.

Sutherland, E. H. (1931) The prison as a criminological laboratory. *Annals of the American Academy of Political and Social Sciences.* Vol 157:131-136.

Trammell, R. and M. Rundle (2015) The inmate as a nonperson: Examining staff conflict from the inmate's perspective. *The Prison Journal*. Vol. 95, No. 4:472-492.

United States Bureau of Labor Statistics (BLS) (2020) Correctional officers and bailiffs — Work environment. Sept. 1. Retrieved from https://www.bls.gov/ooh/protective-service/correctional-officers.htm#tab-3.

United States Department of Housing and Human Services (HHS) (2021) Annual update of the HHS poverty guidelines. Feb. 1. Retrieved from https://www.federalregister.gov/documents/2021/02/01/2021-01969/annual-update-of-the-hhs-poverty-guidelines.

RESOURCES AND PUBLICATIONS FOR CORRECTIONS OFFICERS AND PRISON STAFF

Correctional Officer Education (n.d.) Job requirements for state and federal corrections officers. Retrieved from https://www.correctionalofficeredu.org/correctional-officer-requirements/#:~:text=General%20Requirements,high%20school%20diploma%20or%20GED.

Corrections Today. Trade publication for the American Correctional Assocation (ACA). Available at http://www.aca.org/ACA_Prod_IMIS/ACA_Member/correctionstoday.

Corrections1 (2019) Seven mistakes that rookie correctional officers consistently make. Nov. 25. Retrieved from https://www.corrections1.com/corrections-jobs-careers/articles/7-mistakes-that-rookie-correctional-officers-consistently-make-OTfsx0ixwIkkvIBw/.

Defranco, J. and T. Duncan (2017) *Life as a Jailer*. Morrisville, North Carolina: Lulu Publishing Services.

Garcia, J. (2020) *Riker's Island: Patrolling the toughest precients [sic] in New York City, as a CO: Life in the Bing (Central Punitive Segregation Unit)*. Apr. 30. New York: Self-published, Amazon Kindle Edition.

Grant, B. A. (1995) Impact of working rotating schedules on family life of correctional staff. Forum on Corrections Research. May, Vol. 7, Iss. 2:40-42.

King, B. (2020) *The 15 Fundamental Laws of De-Escalation: How to Put Out Fires, Not Start Them*. Self-published.

INTERVIEWS WITH CORRECTIONAL STAFF (VIDEOS)[5]

A Day in the Life of a Correctional Officer (2015) Lexington County Sheriff Department, SC. Available at https://www.youtube.com/watch?v=9-VgEymhKSY.

Behind Bars: Rookie Year: Is it Worth It (2019) A&E. Available at https://www.youtube.com/watch?v=Ugz5xFLlnkc.

Behind Bars: Rookie Year: Little Lilly Shows She's Tough (2019) A&E. Available at https://www.youtube.com/watch?v=6mrsWuOPdDs.

Rikers Correction Officer/A Day in the Life (2016) *ABC News*. Available at https://www.youtube.com/watch?v=4X0xKSBvqvE.

---

[5] Trigger Warning: There are some scenes of violence in some of these videos, as well as use of profanity and racially charged terms by detainees and prisoners.

What's It Like Being a Female Correctional Officer? (2020) *Tier Talk.* Available at https://www.youtube.com/watch?v=dk0clnB7vL4.

What's it Like to be a Jailor? (2019) Henrico County Sheriff's Office, VA. Available at https://www.youtube.com/watch?v=8ZddzDXa140.

What's It Like Being a Prison Guard in America? (2017) BBC Three. Available at https://www.youtube.com/watch?v=9-VgEymhKSY.

Chapter SIX

The Prisoner's Perspective

Time to empty our slop pails and run a little water over our faces,
then back to our cells for the entire day. With nothing to do, no news
and in terrible solitude, we were 100 unfortunates awaiting our fate.
I had no illusions about myself. If I could only escape, run away....

— A Man Escaped (1956, Gaumont Film Company)

Chapter Objectives

- Introduce the prison experience through the lens of detainees and prisoners.
- Introduce prison culture, including how it differs from popular images in media, including television and movies.
- Identify the challenges for prisoners in negotiating their way through the prison culture.
- Identify the illegal, underground economy in prison.
- Discuss the challenges of reentry.

Key Terms

Blackout cells
Cliques
Conjugal visitation
Crew
Inmate (convict) code
Jailhouse snitches
Lifers
Master status

Prison slang
"Pruno" or "hootch"
Situational homosexuality
Social identity theories
Total institutions
Transgender
"Tree jumper school"

INTRODUCTION

The opening quote to this chapter is from a 1956 French/German film about prisoners of war during WWII. Though the film depicts soldiers who were captured by the enemy during wartime, the sentiment is similar to those of today's prisoners who, on the most part, live lives of monotony in corrections systems throughout the world.

From anecdotal stories, there are two times when detainees and prisoners are most likely to feel a heightened sense of dread or fear. The first time is in the initial days of adjusting to jail or prison life, particularly with respect to the seemingly permanent loss of liberties, even when the sentence is short, and when negotiating their way through the prison culture and code.

An individual who is arrested, detained, and refused or not able to afford bail may have to go through these fear and adjustment cycles a number of times. When first entering jail and if convicted, sentenced to a longer sentence, the fear of what prison will be like inevitably sets in, even for the experienced convict. From the time someone is placed in police custody, there is inevitably the fear of the unknown, even when someone is a repeat offender. However, there are those who no matter how awful the prison experience, once they have spent a substantial time behind bars may reoffend so as to return to what they know and is predictable in prison.

The second scariest period of a prisoner's life are the weeks and days leading up to release. There are a number of things to be realistically afraid of. Will they survive on the outside with the stigma of being an ex-con? Have all family and friends deserted them? After having every part of their lives dictated by prison rules, including when to get out of bed, when to eat, when to sleep, how will they handle the newfound freedom?

Another reason to be afraid as one reaches the end of their sentence or is facing parole, is that jealousy of other prisoners may bubble over and result in trouble being instigated so that the soon to be released prisoner has their release date delayed due to some altercation. Worse yet, parole is revoked. This is why a number of prisoners who are about to be released on parole prefer to lay low and spend their last days behind bars in their cells with minimal contact with other prisoners.

With average recidivism rates as high as 70 percent in some places, there is also the concern as to whether after spending time in prison, the ex-con can even make a successful transition to life beyond prison walls. Two out of three convicts will end up behind bars within three years of release (Tangney, 2014). In the movie, *American Me* (Universal Pictures, 1992), based on a true story, the protagonist, Santana, went to juvenile detention at age 17. While there, he murdered a fellow juvenile delinquent in self-defense after being brutally raped. Once he aged out of the juvenile system, he was moved up to the adult prison system to finish his subsequent sentence for murder. By that time, he already had gained a reputation of being the leader of an in-prison gang. When he was finally released in his 30s, he had no idea how to function as an adult, was clueless on normative romantic relationships, and had no understanding of how to make a living without breaking the law. Without giving away the entire plot of the movie, Santana eventually was sent back to prison on a parole violation.

Between day one and when a prisoner is released, there is a lot of monotony, broken up only by visitors, when they are allowed or willing, plus programs, including rehabilitation. Some, but not all will be put on work detail that likewise breaks up the seemingly never ending days of incarceration. It is no wonder that so many become exercise enthusiasts, as that is yet another way to break up the boredom, as well as resulting in them becoming intimidating specimens of physical strength.

With little exception, prisoners' lives are heavily regulated. Just like children, every waking moment is more or least orchestrated by prison managers. With what they can watch on TV, if they even have access to one, to what they are allowed to read, everything is heavily censored behind prison walls.

The detained and incarcerated are not without means to voice their objections to any aspect of prison life. As we note in our chapter on prisoner's rights, prisoners have a number of ways to share their experiences in prison. One means is through journalism, another by memoir. A more recent and curious way by which to describe the prison experience is by leaving a review of a prison or jail on Yelp®, the online platform more commonly known for reviews of services, shopping, and restaurants. For example, if you look up prisons and jails in Los Angeles, California, on Yelp.com, you can find reviews such as this from both visitors and the formerly held:

> LA County Jail. Food is great and the shower are [sic] warm. Beds are small and a little hard. They need to work in [sic] their customer service tho [sic]. (5 stars, from Luis C. Los Angeles, CA, retrieved from https://www.yelp.com/biz/la-county-jail-los-angeles?hrid=bKn_ydZ0MMXCpeT00arW9w&osq=Jails+%26+Prisons)

This is but one example of reviews that can be found on *Best Jails & Prisons in Los Angeles, CA* page, Yelp.com (available at https://www.yelp.com/search?find_desc=Jails%20%26%20Prisons&find_loc=Los%20Angeles%2C%20CA). One reviewer even cheekily said about the Santa Monica, California, jail after a stay for a DUI, that the facilities were so modern, clean, and efficient that, "if next I break the law, may I do so within your jurisdiction." (A.L. of La Mirada, CA, 2007, retrieved from https://www.yelp.com/biz/santa-monica-jail-santa-monica?hrid=_J8uoqZdUtMbXCj2Ntk7vw&osq=Jails+%26+Prisons). It may seem like an oddity for a website that is primarily devoted to reviews of restaurants and services to also include reviews of jails and prisons. But it gives us yet another subjective peek behind the curtain of jail or prison life.

We will be focusing, on the most part, on men in prison in this chapter. The culture that is unique to women's prisons is extensively discussed in Chapter 8 on incarcerated women. Likewise, we will cover there how women prisoners are portrayed in popular culture. We caution the reader that any prisoners' accounts of their experiences are mostly their words and as much reality as may be in those words, their perspectives are subjective. When the accounts are being told to reporters and writers, we have to also be aware that those writers may lend their own voice and opinions in articles and books.[1]

PRISONS IN POPULAR CULTURE

We should probably start this chapter by pointing out what you, the reader, are most familiar with as far as prison culture goes. Assuming that you are a consumer of books, movies, and shows about criminal justice issues, you have no doubt read or seen scenes on the small and big screen, in which prison is portrayed. In fact, you may have even read books or seen television shows, movies that take place almost entirely in prison, as in the cases of *Orange is the New Black* (Netflix, 2013-2019) and *Oz* (HBO, 1997-2003). But just how true to real life are these depictions of life in jail or prison?

Prisons and jails have long been settings used in literature, television, and movies. Earlier films were titillating, cautionary tales out of the melodramatic imagination of Hollywood, with titles like LeRoy's 1932 film, *I Am a Fugitive from a Chain Gang* (Whissel, 2015). There is always the question as to how accurate the portrayal of incarceration is in fiction, as in comparison to the harsh realities. For anyone who studies prisons for living, either as a scholar or practitioner, it is sometimes frustrating to read or watch fictional accounts of prison life, without having a few or more criticisms for the writers.

For example, in the popular television show, *How to Get Away with Murder* (ABC, Shonda Rhimes, producer), there is a scene in one episode in which an inmate housed in a maximum security prison has visitors and was allowed to readily hug them in long embraces, with no corrections officer in sight. Prisoners in most states and facilities are only allowed to briefly hug or kiss their visitors and certainly under the watchful eye of prison staff and video surveillance.

In most, if not all contemporary maximum security prisons, physical contact with prisoners is limited as there is the real possibility that contraband can be exchanged, including drugs. As this inmate in the *How to Get Away with Murder* episode had a violent past, it would also be unusual for him to be unshackled, much less in the physical presence of his visitors, without some barrier between them (e.g., a window to a separate room).

At least one visitor in the *How to Get Away with Murder* scene was wearing a number of pieces of jewelry as well. Generally, visitors are asked to remove all

---

[1] Books can also be often written by "ghost writers", meaning that the majority of the work is done by a professional writer outside of the officially acknowledged first author.

items of value from their persons, including jewelry and watches, phones, etc., before entering a jail or prison. Though even with prisoners, there are exceptions, as in the case of the wearing of religious jewelry. Again, the fear is that items could be smuggled in and used for bartering in the informal economy behind bars, including exchanging them for prison-made alcohol or drugs that have been smuggled in.

Another thing that fiction often gets wrong: there are no surprise visitors, though these are interesting plot devices. The visitor will need to contact the prisoner prior to visiting so as to be placed on a visitors' list, in fact most facilities require the visitor to fill out an application before the visit can take place (PrisonPro, n.d.). Another common plot twist is when visitors and prisoners get into shouting matches during their visit. As the Bureau of Federal Prisons instruct, visits are expected to be quiet and orderly and the prisoner or visitor can be asked to cut the visit short if either are not acting appropriately (Federal Bureau of Prisons, n.d.).

In television and movies, visitors are indiscriminately admitted to prison facilities. In reality, there are a number of reasons why a jail or prison would not allow just any visitor to be admitted (PrisonPro, n.d., retrieved from https://www.prisonpro.com/content/visiting-inmate-answers-common-questions-things-you-should-know):

- You have provided false information on your application.
- You are a convicted felon.
- You have served time in a correctional institution.
- You have outstanding warrants.
- You have a protective order out against you or the inmate.
- You are deemed a security risk by the facility.
- You are on probation or parole, though there are some exceptions that can be made to this.
- You are on another inmate's visitation list at the same institution already, though again, there are exceptions, as in the case where family members are housed in the same facility.

Visitors are also rejected from entering a facility if they are wearing clothing that doesn't meet the dress code, including tight clothing, gang-related logos, and hooded sweatshirts. In federal facilities, it is the prisoner's responsibility, not the prison's to notify the potential visitor if their application for a visit has been rejected (Federal Bureau of Prisons, n.d.).

As many prison scenes are filmed in actual prisons, though they are no longer in use to house prisoners, the Federal Bureau of Prisons has some discretion on what will and will not be allowed to be filmed. For example, the Federal Bureau of Prisons collaborated with Hollywood's censorship policies during the filming of the *Birdman of Alcatraz* (Millar and Trosper, producers, 1962), depicting the life of murderer Robert Stroud who had been housed in Alcatraz Penitentiary, which is now part of the U.S. National Park Services since its closing in 1963 (Eldridge, 2016). At the time of filming, Alcatraz was still actively used as a federal prison.

So, the realities of prison life can be downplayed in television and film if script approval has to be met by the Federal Bureau of Prisons.

Prisoners and former prisoners are perhaps the best critics of fictionalized prison scenes. In the words of one former prisoner regarding the authenticity of prison movies, "they've almost always been lousy." (Nussbaum, 1973, p.45). On the subject of which films could be watched by prisoners as a form of recreation, in Nussbaum's case, at Leavenworth, a military prison facility and the U.S. Penitentiary at Marion, Illinois, at the time, there was little discretion or censorship; likewise, the films allowed had little educational value (Nussbaum, 1973). There is far more censorship of films and television by jails and prisons today.

One film that Nussbaum (1973) reports to have seen while incarcerated at the Marion facility was *Sexual Communication* (Shangri-La Productions, 1971), one that he considered to be hard-core pornography. We should note that technically all forms of pornography are prohibited in U.S. jails and prisons, though it can be smuggled in. We should also note that one of the more popular book genres among prisoners is romance novels, which can contain passages that can only be described as "soft" pornography.

Film censorship has come a long way from the 1970s when there were looser guidelines in and out of prison. Today, allowing prisoners to watch television and movies is viewed as a means by which to restore prisoners' sense of humanity, remain updated on popular culture trends outside of prisons, however inaccurately portrayed, and to help alleviate loneliness, at least briefly (Griffiths, 2016). But as we noted, these are now shown at the discretion of the facility staff.

There is a listing of fictional accounts on prison life at the end of this chapter, which is by no means an exhaustive list.

DAY ONE

The incarcerated's new life and realities begins at arrest. In some cases, it starts with an indictment prior to arrest. As one white collar criminal described it on hearing of his own indictment,

> *Immediately I felt the surge of a deep wave of anxiety produced by the various chemicals in my body. I was physically conscious of having shifted, in the space of several seconds, from a state of feeling light, relaxed, and focused on the idle pleasures of good times and traveling, to having suddenly entered a dark and ominous tunnel, and feeling a profound sense of dread in the pit of my stomach. My appetite completely disappeared and I felt mild nausea rapidly coming on.* (Teal, 2020, p. 9)

Whether placed—or sometimes roughly stuffed—into a squad car, brought down to a police station, booked, strip searched, and placed in a cell, or allowed to walk into a police station and turn themselves in, a suspect may not fully appreciate the circumstances they have just entered, particularly on a first arrest. A recently arrested former college professor, ironically teaching criminal justice in Northern California, was accused of setting a series of devastating fires. As reported by *NPR* (Chappell, 2021, retrieved from https://www.npr.org/2021/08/11/1026700103/for mer-college-professor-arson-charges-california-dixie-fire), the suspected arsonist, after being told that along with a charge of violating state laws forbidding entering a closed emergency area, he was also being charged with federal felony arson, allegedly shouted[2], "I'm going to kill you, f***ing pig! I told those f***kers I did not start any of those fires!" As is so many times the case during arrest and booking, suspects are not only shocked, but angry, expressing their anger, no matter how serious the charges.

For relatively minor offenses and misdemeanors, the accused may be released on their own reconnaissance, if they do not pose a flight risk. Others may have bail set and if they can afford it, can live on the outside in advance of their trial. For the unlucky, either bail is not allowed, depending on the seriousness of their crime or even if it is set, they may not be able to pay it in order to be released. For these unfortunate souls, they will be remanded to the custody of a jail.

After arrest, prisoners undergo a number of humiliating booking rituals, the least of which are being fingerprinted and photographed. Detainees and prisoners are strip searched for contraband, including drugs and weapons. This is for the safety of not only prison guards, but for the safety of other prisoners. Once arrested, detainees are not even allowed to shower or use a toilet without being seen by others, including corrections staff and other detainees or prisoners. For some, this may be the first time since childhood or a high school gym class, where what are normally private bodily functions and hygiene practices are so publicly displayed.

To a large extent, detainees and prisoners go through the same processes of grieving after arrest as someone who has lost a loved one. The symptoms of this process may include, based on the Kübler-Ross and Kessier model (2005):

- *Denial*, including denial of injury to their victim.
- *Anger*, primarily at the criminal justice system and/or at their victim.
- *Bargaining*, where "magical thinking" takes place and a belief that they will be found not guilty, even though there might be a preponderance of evidence against them.
- *Depression*, while thinking about all the losses associated with incarceration.
- *Acceptance*, when the detainee leans into the process, particularly the "lifer," and in some cases has come to grips with just how messed up their lives have just become.

---

[2] This was included in the affidavit filed in the U.S. District Court for the Eastern District of California, available at https://www.npr.org/2021/08/11/1026700103/former-college-professor-arson-charges-california-dixie-fire.

Of course, the process may occur out of order for some. It can start all over again from scratch once convicted and sent to prison. And unfortunately, prisoners often do not have access to adequate psychological therapies to help them cope with their new status.

Along with grief, the prisoner may feel guilty, not so much for the crime they have committed, but for the fact that they got caught. In many cases they may defiantly feel that their crime is justified. The guilt they may experience is from the thought of what they have done to their friends and families, including the shame that they believe has befallen them. Though it is difficult to know the actual numbers of how many prisoners feel guilty about what they have done to their victims, it is safe to assume some are actually remorseful. It is not uncommon for prisoners who go before parole boards express remorse, whether real or feigned. What the research does indicate that prisoners who are truly remorseful about their crimes are much less likely to end up back in jail or prison (Tangley, 2014).

Beyond grief and anger, the new detainee or prisoner can feel mentally drained and emotionally exhausted. Part of that is a result of the seemingly nonstop adrenalin running through their bodies in response to the unknown. The other part is the necessity of absorbing and processing the prison culture and also the sleep disruption some might experience while incarcerated.

For prisoners, the process of adapting and learning to function within the prison culture, in addition to learning and understanding the larger, administrative rules, may be compared to the experience of navigating the hyperreality of a theme park with its created environment. At a theme park, visitors spend much time and energy making decisions, reacting to unusual stimuli, and being thwarted by long lines, which requires a lot of thinking, learning, and memory (King and O'Boyle, 2011). Things may seem intentionally or unintendedly distorted, including interactions with others. And as we learn in social psychology, everyone lives in their own reality, so a good part of the exhaustion of being a new detainee or prisoner can be contributed to all the mental exercises of anticipating the worst in prison.

PRISON CULTURE

We turn to the classic definition of culture from sociology in order to understand the unique characteristics of prison life from a prisoner's perspective. Culture can be defined as "a shared set of beliefs, symbols, institutions, artifacts, values, and norms transferred from one group. . . to another." (Trammell, 2012, p 5). Experienced prisoners and released convicts will pass on their prison culture to the newly incarcerated or to those who anticipate being incarcerated.

There are several aspects to prison culture from the prisoner's prospective. Some have to do with survival and others have to do with entrepreneurship. Others yet are a natural byproduct of what happens to people when they share the same experiences.

Prison culture is not unlike the culture of any "total institution." For those of you who have had exposure to Erving Goffman's work (1961) on mental hospital patients, you may recall that a *total institution* is one where all activities of its captives are regulated by the authorities and administrators. This includes when to wake up, when to eat, and when to go to bed. It is not unlike the limited freedoms that children have in early childhood. In Goffman's studies, he also included the military, monasteries, and nursing homes in his list of other total institutions, beyond prisons, where except for the employees, the occupants do not have the freedom to come and go at will.

Where prisoners can find control of their lives, they will work to do so. Like students in high school who are forced to wear uniforms find ways to express their individuality in footwear, hair styles, etc., prisoners create their own world with specialized rules, language, and rituals.

If we put this into an international perspective, the characteristics of prison cultures are not universal, just as punishment around the world can be decisively different, depending on the part of the globe. What prison cultures do have in common is that all prisons are self-contained communities (Dervan, 2011).

Not all inmates buy into the prison culture. However, the more they buy into it, the more likely they will discover collective resistance to the formal rules of the prison with their fellow prisoners within the informal inmate culture. As Haslam and Reicher note (2011; 2006; Taifel and Turner, 1979), *social identity theories* dictate that the level of social identification while incarcerated is dependent on whether a prisoner retreats into his own world, avoiding the drama of the prison culture, and to the extent that prisoners can band together to resist, as best they can, plus the rigidity of prison life. Keep in mind that the *master status* (the main identity that one identifies with) of an accused, from the moment of arrest, whether they have had their day in court or not, is that of "prisoner" or "criminal," at least to the criminal justice system and the outside world.

We should note that even though we sometimes use "inmate" and "convict" interchangeably, prisoners see a distinct difference. It makes intuitive sense that a person who is an inmate is, indeed, a convict. Or in otherwords, all inmates are convicts, not all convicts become inmates. An example would be a person who is indicted, released on their own recognizance or immediately on bail, and found guilty at their subsequent trial, yet never sentenced to actual time in jail or prison, given some other form of punishment, like fines or community service. This is not uncommon in white collar crime convictions.

For prisoners, inmates are a faceless bunch of individuals who are told what they cannot do and who they are by the jail or prison (Sanders, n.d.). A convict, on the other hand, at least in the eyes of prisoners and not by standard legal definition, is more complex, always aware of their surroundings (Sanders, n.d.) and able to quickly learns the inmate code, discussed in the next section of this chapter. Whether identified as an inmate or a convict, depending on perspective, all who find themselves behind prison walls have to learn two sets of rules: Those dictated by the institution and those followed by detainees and prisoners. This holds true for both the incarcerated and the staff.

Convict Code

Just as on the street, people who are incarcerated do what little they can to control their peers' perceptions of them. What a "new fish" or newly incarcerated detainee or prisoner has to figure out very early on is the inmate, convict, or prisoners' code. The three terms are synonymous, in theory. The *inmate code* is "the adoption of the normative element of prison culture." (Wellford, C. 1967, p.197) Learning the convict code is necessary for survival and happens immediately once one is arrested and brought to jail. Think of it as a distorted code of honor, where similarly as on the outside of prison, an individual's identity and reputation is very important to them.

One fascinating aspect of the inmate code is its purpose to keep the peace in prison, beyond the efforts of prison staff. There is self-regulation over the way that the underground economy is run, so as to not create conflict among prisoners that could bring attention from corrections staff on illegal activities (Trammell, 2009).

According to Daniel Harris, a convict with experience being incarcerated in Tennessee Colony prison in Texas, claims the "real" convict code includes the following (Harris, n.d., retrieved from https://prisonwriters.com/convict-code-of -conduct/):

1. A true convict is incapable of snitching.
2. No convict is ever a bully.
3. The convict's word is more binding than any contract.
4. It is a convict's nature to seek out peaceful compromises whenever possible.
5. A convict would rather die fighting than live running.
6. Convicts stand by their friends unto death.
7. You'll never see a convict trying to impress anyone; he just does.
8. Never does a convict choose to lead, others just choose to follow.
9. Convicts buy what they need before they buy what they want—and what they don't have, they do without.
10. All convicts are polite and courteous. They have nothing to prove to anyone.

As we see in the list, there are contradictions in the convict code, as in the example of seeking peaceful solutions to disagreements yet advocating violence. According to Harris (n.d.), one cannot ever become a true convict unless they live by this code. But as we know from accounts from prison, both from staff and prisoners, there are a good number of inmates who violate one or more of the items in this particular list.

Some scholars argue that there really isn't a unique inmate code. Hassine (2007, p.175), an author who was himself an inmate and died in prison, argued that prisoners bring their habits, norms, and values into prison:

> *Convicts coming to prison bring with them a moral and ethical code of conduct that they learned and developed from their individual street experiences. For example, members of the Mafia bring with them a Mafiosos' code, street-gang members bring their own gang code, and drug addicts bring a junkie's code of conduct.*

Hassine's observations aside, many of those who are jailed or sent to prison are not members of gangs or organized crime groups, at least in advance of their incarceration, and they have to learn the code in order to negotiate their way through the prison culture.

As we will revisit in our section on white collar criminals in this chapter, the prohibition of discussion between prisoners on how they got there is also part of prisoner code. This makes sense, particularly for those who are detained in jail, as even discussing charges may be interpreted as an admission of guilt. And at least early on in the detainment process, one may not yet know who might be a "jail house snitch." As John Teal has observed during his term in prison, referring to any talk of crimes or convictions,

> *This was a delicate affair. On one hand, I had read, it is considered poor form to ask another inmate about his charge. On the other hand, many of us were eager to have someone to discuss it with, since who else could commiserate and empathize as well as another convict?* (Teal, 2020, p. 51)

The longer that someone is incarcerated, the more likely the inmate code becomes a permanent part of a convict's identity in much the same way as what happens with any good or bad habit over time. Research indicates that it takes, on average, around 66 days for a behavior to become habit (Gardner et al., 2012). For most detainees in the United States, if they are not allowed to be released on bail before their trial, they could be spending a substantially longer period of time than 66 days behind bars before acquittal or conviction, meaning that the convict code can become permanently ingrained in their psyche.

Once an individual leaves jail or prison, the inmate code follows them out into the community.[3] There is some overlap between street code and convict code, as indicated by studies conducted by Mitchell et al. (2017). We will have further discussion of these overlaps in the section on gangs in prison, in this chapter.

Prison Slang

Prison slang is a very colorful and distinct vocabulary that exists in prison culture. Prisoners create this informal way of speaking to one another as a means by which to keep their conversations secret in the very public prison environment. This is not unlike any exclusive organization where words are used that may not be part of the general vocabulary of nonmembers. For instance, a graduate student in sociology may say, as in the case of this author, "I'm in orgs and crim" or "I do crime." This

---

[3] The author of this book recalls a criminal justice student she had in one of her classes who always had to sit in the back of the class, back to the wall. It turned out that this student had previously served five years in prison and one thing they learned was that you always have your back to the wall, facing the door. As it was explained to this author, this was because there is the fear that a fellow prisoner could jump you at any time.

refers to a student studying organizations and criminology. Hopefully the graduate student is NOT actually doing crime, but rather it is their area of concentration in their program. Similarly, prisoners create shortcuts in their speech that in many cases gets carried over into the streets when they are released from prison.

In some cases, prisoners learn and use obscure languages in order to similarly "talk in code" so that either other prisoners or corrections officers will not understand what they are talking about, many times about illegal activities they are planning or have committed. For instance, some inmates in New Mexico use the ancient Aztec language (Najuatl, Spanish náhuatl, or Nawatl) with letters and messages being sent within and in and out of prison, including over phone calls (*KOAT*, 2012). Prison officials have tried to stop this practice by prohibiting prisoners from receiving books unless they are written in English (*KOAT*, 2012). This in itself may violate prisoners' rights (so-called *Library Bill of Rights*, American Library Association[4]), if a prisoner's first and best known language is Spanish, particularly in the written word. This could be the case in a state like New Mexico, where there are large Hispanic and LatinX populations, some of which are non-English speakers, including those disproportionately incarcerated.

Prison Slang

There are several places where you can find glossaries of prison slang. From the publication *Mental Floss*, some of the following terms are used in jails and prisons (Soniak, 2012, retrieved from https://www.mentalfloss.com/article/12794/50-prison-slang-words-make-you-sound-tough-guy):

- **All day and a night**—Life without parole.
- **Back door parole**—To die in prison.
- **Brake fluid**—Psychiatric meds.
- **Bug**—A prison staff member who is considered untrustworthy.
- **Cell warrior**—An inmate that puts up a tough front or runs their mouth when locked in their cell, but is submissive or cowardly when interacting with prisoners in the open.
- **Cowboy**—A new correctional officer. "Cowboy" backwards is the acronym YOBWOC, meaning, for prisoners, "young, obnoxious, bastard we often con."
- **Dance on the blacktop**—To get stabbed.
- **Ding Wing**—A prison's psychiatric unit.
- **Duck**—A correctional officer who reveals information about prison staff to inmates.
- **Fire on the line (or fire in the hole)**—A warning—"correctional officer in the area."

---

[4] Available at http://www.ala.org/advocacy/intfreedom/librarybill.

Prison Slang (continued)

- **Grandma's (or Grandma's house)**—A prison gang's headquarters or meeting place, or the cell of the gang leader.
- **Jacket**—(1) An inmate's information file or rap sheet or (2) An inmate's reputation among other prisoners.
- **Jackrabbit parole**—To escape from a facility.
- **Kite**—A contraband letter.
- **Monster (or "the Ninja")**—HIV.
- **Peels**—The orange jumpsuit worn by prisoners in some facilities.

- **Prison wolf**—An inmate who is normally straight on "the outside," but engages in sexual activity with men while incarcerated ("situational homosexuality").
- **Ride with**—To do favors for a fellow convict, often including sexual ones, in exchange for protection, contraband, prison currency, or commissary items.
- **Stainless steel ride**—Death by lethal injection.

Of course, like any vocabulary, specific prisons may have their own special words. Two terms that are pretty much widely used in prison culture that are not included in the *Mental Floss* list are "*pruno*" and "*hootch*," both referring to alcohol beverages made in prison, usually made from stolen yeast from the kitchen or with bread and some kind of fruit.[5] Of course, any alcoholic beverage, even for religious ceremonies, is prohibited in prison.

If you are interested in further exploring prison vocabulary, you can visit the following websites:

- Prison Slang Glossary from *Prison Diaries*, available at https://prison-diaries .com/prison-slang-glossary-2/.
- How secret languages thrive behind bars, from PBS (2019), available at https:// www.pbs.org/newshour/arts/how-prison-languages-flourish-behind-bars

There are also a number of videos that demonstrate prison lingo:

- How to TALK like a prisoner (2017), available at https://www.youtube.com/ watch?v=EAnTkMCEVDk
- Former Convict Breaks Down Prison Slang (2020), available at https://www .youtube.com/watch?v=d8fgZabvEuo

---

[5] This is NOT something that should be tried at home! The way prisoners make alcoholic beverages does not control for alcohol % and can potentially cause neurological damage or have lethal consequences.

"Tree Jumpers"

As much as some prisoners have committed heinous crimes, there are no crimes considered so horrible that even prisoners will reject the perpetrators, with the following exception. Prisoners who are considered pariahs both in society and in prison are those who commit crimes against children. It is because of this, those accused of crimes against children are often kept in protective custody or housed in a separate area of a jail or prison.

The term *"tree jumpers"* is often given to prisoners who have been accused of child molestation or rape. Also, prisoners who have not been convicted of sexually molesting a child, but have killed them nonetheless, also have a difficult time in general prison population. Of course, the definition of "child" is fluid in prison and is dependent on how horrendous the crime is against a juvenile.

If the child sex offender is housed in general population, they are a target for a number of abuses by fellow prisoners. They may be subject to degradation pranks, like having their clothes hidden after a shower (Mann, 2012). As one prisoner stated (Mann, 2012, p.351):

> In this prison, your offence could quite literally get you into trouble because it's a mixed prison which can obviously be very dodgy, with an undercurrent of mistrust and aggro [sic] when it comes to sex offenders. . . . I've had abuse thrown at me but I've always stood my ground and fought back and I can take most of them youngsters.

The older sex offender who is held in protective custody may actually find that their time in prison is tolerable, although research conducted on child sex offenders is contradictory as to whether protective custody is isolating. What does seem to be consistent is that this population is different than the general prison population and tends to be more self-confident, have better communication skills, and have better coping skills in adapting to prison life (Mann, 2012).

Short-Termers vs. Lifers

Ironically, studies indicate that young males who have shorter sentences because of minor charges are most likely to attempt an escape from prison. Logic would dictate that people who have been sentenced to life without possibility of parole would feel that they had nothing to lose and would be more likely to make an escape attempt.

Another irony is that convicts prefer to serve short sentences than to complete community service as part of their sentence. In a study commissioned by the Prison Governor's Association and the Howard League for Penal Reform consisting of 44 interviews with inmates and 25 staff at three prisons in the United Kingdom and Wales, found that offenders believed that shorter prison sentences (< 12 months) were easier to complete than seemingly more punishing community service (Travis, 2011). If you consider the stigma of wearing a brightly colored Department of

Corrections shirt while picking up trash by the side of the road, it may not only be a question of the labor involved in completing community service, but the embarrassment of doing so under the scrutiny of the community.

For those who are destined to spend a relatively short time in prison, say under two years, there may still be an opportunity, however slim, to maintain relationships with people on the outside. However, the longer the sentence, the more likely the inmate will be deserted by family and friends. For women, it is more likely, if they are married or in a serious romantic relationship prior to sentencing, that incarceration will put an end to it, as compared to male prisoners. And the shorter a sentence is, the more likely a prisoner is better equipped to re-enter society after incarceration, though there are few guarantees for the convicted.

For prisoners with longer sentences, including for those who are "*lifers* (individuals who have been sentenced to life in prison)," the best strategy that they can adopt is to settle into the routine of prison, making the best of a terrible situation.

Jailhouse Snitches

One way that a prisoner can ingratiate themselves with prison staff is to inform on their fellow prisoners. The informants can gather information about prisoners who break rules or smuggle contraband in. They can also gather information for ongoing criminal investigations. Prisoners who are in custody and inform on their cellmates and fellow detainees or prisoners, are often referred to as *jailhouse snitches*.

There are a number of issues surrounding jailhouse snitches. Since prosecutors can be dependent on the information that informants gather, there can be compensation to the snitch by way of reduced sentences or dropped charges. Because of this, activists who work against wrongful convictions of innocent people call for greater restraint in the use of inmate testimony (The Justice Project, 2007).

Like some sex offenders, informants or suspected informants eventually need to be protected while in custody, particularly after word gets out that they may have made a deal with prosecutors. As we have discussed in the treatment of criminals who have harmed children, it is part of the convict moral code that they do not snitch on their fellow prisoners.

Sex in Prison

Except for *conjugal visitation*, any form of sexual intercourse is strictly forbidden in jails and prisons. Study after study of illicit sex in jails and prisons, clandestine sex does indeed occur behind bars.

A conjugal visitation is a scheduled, permitted visit between spouses, when one of them is in prison. The philosophy behind allowing for conjugal visitation is that it may be a means to keep a marriage intact. The second, and perhaps the most salient of reasons given is to reduce the instances of male prison rape (Wyatt, 2006). However, as many prison studies are deemed inaccurate due to incomplete data on sexual relationships in prison, the focus should be on increasing inmate responses to surveys in order to fully understand whether conjugal visitations reduce instances of prison rape or lower recidivism rates. What we do know about sex in prison is more antidotal, coming from accounts of life behind prison walls. There is not a complete absence of data on sex in prisons, but due to the sensitive subject matter and the fact that prisoners are considered a special population[6] for research purposes, an accurate picture is almost impossible for researchers to get.

Some inmates, both male and female, even though they may identify as heterosexual outside of prison, will enter into sexual relationships with fellow inmates of the same sex while incarcerated. The terms used in this case are *situational homosexuality*, where in the absence of the opposite sex, heterosexual inmates will have intercourse or engage in other sexual behaviors with same sex partners. Inevitably this results in some self-questioning by heterosexual convicts of one's sexual orientation on release from prison.

Sexual relationships are not always simply between inmates. There have been a number of cases of women behind bars entering into sexual liaisons with male corrections officers. These may go undetected, until a woman becomes pregnant while incarcerated.

In the Civil Rights case, *Graham v. Sheriff of Logan County et al.*, the plaintiff, Stacey Graham, sought damages in a complaint against two corrections officers (Jefferies and Mendez) and the county, citing a violation of her Eighth Amendment rights ("cruel and unusual punishment") as she had sex with the correction officers while in solitary confinement (United States Court of Appeals, Tenth Circuit, 2013). From the court proceedings, it was noted that

> *Sometime between July 2009, Jefferies started speaking to Ms. Graham over the jail intercom system. . . . Over time they began to talk about having sexual intercourse. . . . The two also exchanged explicit notes. One note she wrote to him, but never delivered, stated: 'Hey Sexy, Damn you look good in that uniform. I just want to rip it off of you. . . .'* (United States Court of Appeals, Tenth Circuit, 2013, retrieved from https://cases.justia.com/federal/appellate-courts/ca10/12-6302/12-6302-2013-12-20.pdf?ts=1411095953)

Sex between corrections staff and inmates is generally considered technically and legally rape due to the power dynamics, even if both staff and inmate are willing participants. Judge Hartz in the Graham case ruled in favor of the defendants/appellees on appeal as it was determined that it was consensual sex (Justia.com, United States Court of Appeals, Tenth Circuit, 2013). As happens in many rape cases, the victim's demeanor is put on trial, all the more difficult when the victim is a prisoner.

---

[6] As we noted elsewhere in this book, as prisoners are institutionalized, special care is taken in conducting studies and surveys using the incarcerated, following the rules laid out in the Belmont Report on the ethical research when using human subjects.

Rape, in prison, is unfortunately inevitable, without intervention by prison or jail staff. As we know from the literature on rapes outside of prison, rape is never a romantic act, but rather one of violence, whether it is committed against a male, female, or other variants of gender identification. Prison officials often underestimate the numbers of actual rapes, as in some cases, the sexual relationships in prison are coercive and not necessarily a violent assault per se, which is still technically considered rape (Wyatt, 2006). As one prosecutor stated in court to defendant Matthew Vaca, sentenced to life in prison, she stated,

> I want you to understand what you have to look forward to [in prison]. You will be beaten repeatedly. And you will be brutally raped. And you will lose every ounce of dignity that you have left in your body. And you will live in terror . . . for every minute for the rest of your life. (Wyatt, 2006, p. 613)

We should note that Vaca plead guilty to truly horrific crimes, including the stabbing death of Elizabeth Reiser, age 17, and attempted sexual assault on her friend, Brandi Hicks, age 18 (Greene, 2000).

We will go into greater detail on sexual assault in prison in Chapter 10, on prison violence.

Transgender Prisoners

In recent decades, the transgender population has gained more attention both in public discourse and in research. Someone who identifies as *transgender* is an individual who feels that their gender identity differs from the sex they were assigned at birth (GLAAD, n.d.). A transgender male is someone who was assigned the female sex, but lives and identifies as male; transgender females are assigned the male sex at birth, but live and identify as females (Ledesma, et al., 2020).

As a refresher of sociology and psychology basics, gender and sex are different: Biological sex is based on genitalia identified at birth, gender includes the roles we are expect to take by society, based on biological sex. There is substantial research that indicates that for transgender individuals, there is a disconnect between their biology and the gender that they believe they truly belong to. For these individuals, life is difficult in and out of prison, to the extent that their very lives may be in danger. In prison, as on the outside as well, their psychological well-being is threatened, as they are often housed in solitary confinement, ordinarily reserved for prisoners convicted of violent crimes.

Jails and prisons, on the most part, identify the incarcerated by their sex assignment, though institutions in some states are becoming more progressive in how they house transgender prisoners. For example, in 2020 the State of California announced that transgender detainees and prisoners would be housed based on their gender identification, with the caveat in the law that it would be done, only if there are no management or security concerns (Beam, 2020).

In 2012, the Obama administration addressed the housing of transgender prisoners, by enhancing protections given prisoners under the 2003 Prison Rape Enforcement Act (PREA). In 2018, the Bureau of Prisons reversed a number of these protections, including the requirement of prison officials to no longer consider gender identity of prisoners when making prison housing decisions (Moreau, 2018). In response to the changes, Brenda Smith, the former Commissioner of the National Prison Rape Elimination Commission (NPREC) with others stated in a letter of protest,

> The Trump Administration's decision to change the BOP [Bureau of Prisons] for transgender inmates puts these inmates at significant risk of sexual abuse, assault, and other types of discrimination. . . . This policy is in direct conflict with Prison Rape Act (PREA) and its Standards and will likely only exacerbate the occurrence of sexual abuse and violence in prisons. (American University Washington College of Law, n.d., retrieved from https://www.wcl.american.edu/impact/initiatives-programs/endsilence/research-guidance/nprec-says-bop-policy-change-endangers-transgender-people-in-custody/)

Transgender prisoners may or may not have yet undergone sex reassignment treatment and/or surgery. There is considerable debate whether sex reassignment should be undergone while incarcerated. In the case of the transgender individual who is undergoing sex reassignment before incarceration, it is an additional challenge. Bianca Lucrecia, born male, who had begun female hormone therapy, had developed breasts, and had testicles removed, was forced to be housed in a cell with non-transgender males in a federal prison, forbidden to wear female underwear, and was required to dress so as to conceal her emerging female physical characteristics (Ledesma and Ford, 2020).

Of the two, transgender females are subjected to more threats, sexual abuses, and abuses in male prisons, as compared to transgender males in female prisons (Au, 2016). Transgender prisoners are not just subject to abuses by fellow prisoners. Beyond the physical dangers, transgender prisoners are also at risk for a number of health problems. Transgender people in general are at greater risk for HIV, other sexually transmitted diseases, mental health issues including those leading to suicide, and greater rates of substance abuse, which is argued to be exacerbated in prison, depending on housing designation (Ledesma and Ford, 2020).

Cliques and Prison Gangs

It is a natural social phenomenon that we tend to gravitate to people with whom we share similar values, interests, and social backgrounds. Out of groups, inevitably subgroups or *cliques* will form. In some cases, these cliques are welcoming and will allow outsiders or new people to join. In other cases, cliques can be exclusive, either denying entry to newcomers or requiring them to prove themselves in some fashion before they are allowed to join. An example would be a Facebook® group devoted to some sort of fandom, like sports or famous people, that won't allow you to join their page without first answering specific questions and being vetted by the person or persons managing the group. This, of course, is a benign example, as compared to the initiation prisoners might be required to endure in order to join a clique or gang.

One means by which criminal organizations, form, as in the example of street gangs, is along ethnic or racial lines. Whatever racial divide exists in society is unfortunately amplified in prison. There is considerable peer pressure to hang out with one's own race or ethnic group and this happens immediately on arrival to prison (Paperny, 2016).

Of more serious concern is prison gangs and their initiations. It is not uncommon for the convicted sentenced to prison to already be affiliated with a gang. It is also not uncommon for individuals who are not attached to a street gang on the outside, to join once they are incarcerated. This only amplifies the reputation of prisons being "schools for criminals."

Established street gangs, like the Crips, Bloods, Latin Kings, and MS-13, can be imported into prison. Some gangs were actually started in prison, as in the example of La Nuestra Familia (also known as Nuestra Familia, La Familia) that was founded in Soledad Prison in California. Created by rural Mexican inmates, the gang was formed in order to counteract urban Mexican inmates, including the Mexican Mafia (Lewis, 1980).

There is a great divide between prison administrators and gangs in prison. As in the case of police on the street misidentifying individuals as being gang affiliated based on some superficial criteria (e.g., clothing style), prisoners may be misclassified as gang members on subjective measures.

We cannot assume that groups or gangs of similar race or ethnicity will get along on the streets or in prison. For example, the Crips and Bloods have had decades long, infamous conflicts in and out of prison, even though both gangs are made up of Black members. Likewise, as we noted in California, there is a divide between Hispanic gang members in Northern California (e.g., La Neustra Familia) and Southern California Hispanic gangs (e.g., Mexican Mafia), even though they share the same ethnic roots.

Once established in and out of prison, prison gangs, even when members are incarcerated, can run gang activities on the outside as well. These can even include ordered hits on rival gang members who are not incarcerated. In some gang suppression tactics, mass incarceration of gang leaders can only contribute to the criminal pipeline between prison and street gangs.

One lesser studied phenomenon in prison is when people who know others from their neighborhoods or even from their own families, and who do not have prior gang affiliation, are incarcerated together. They may come from the same *crew*, a type of neighborhood group that may or might be involved in organized criminal activities. They have some characteristics similar to gangs, with noted differences. First, they tend to be neighborhood-oriented (Hansen, 2005). Second, there is more likelihood, due to the transience of populations in poor neighborhoods—where most families are renting rather than own their home—that individuals may have affiliation with more than one crew that are not in competition with one another (Hansen, 2005). Third, they are less likely to be involved in big criminal enterprises and tend to, if involved in crime at all, participate in lesser crimes, like small scale drug sales, and are more loosely organized (D.C. Metropolitan Police Department, n.d.). Like gangs, crews can be found in prison as well. It is not unusual for prisoners to be housed together who come from the same neighborhoods, particularly in jails.

Both crews and gangs adhere to street code and convict code. In the Mitchell, et al. (2017, p. 1200) model, we can see where these overlap with street and prison gangs, in Figure 6.1.

For researchers, there is a reliance on prison records in order to study gangs. However, as much as prison records are easier to obtain, they may not reflect the reality of gangs in prison. Self-identification with gangs while in prison or on the streets does not necessarily indicate *real* membership (Pyrooz et al., 2020). Though more challenging to obtain on many levels, interviews of incarcerated or recently released gang members may give us a better picture of the realities of gang life in

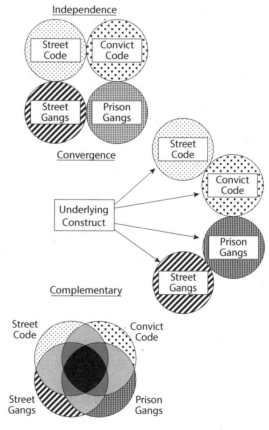

FIGURE 6.1 ‖ **Overlap of Street Gangs with Prison Gangs.**
Source: Mitchell et al., 2017, p. 1200.

prison. It is difficult for researchers to infiltrate gangs in order to conduct studies, with exception with scholars like Sudhir Venkatesh (*Gang Leader for a Day*, 2008). Again, as prisoners are considered a "special population" in human studies, it is also a challenge to get access to prisoners, much less incarcerated gang members.

As we already alluded to in this chapter, the social dynamics of men and women in prison are distinctly different. Except for the fact that women will likewise form cliques in prison, there are fewer antagonistic relationships of gangs. This is not to say that women won't self-segregate into groups by race and/or ethnicity. But the divide is less noticeable as in men's prisons.

WHITE COLLAR CRIME CONVICTS

Sentencing for white collar criminals is not equal, by any means. While some are sent to more comfortable, minimum security prisons, some judges want to make an example of elite criminals and send them to medium or maximum security prisons.

Much publicity was generated when actresses Felicity Hoffman and Lori Laughlin were given and served relatively short sentences for their involvement in the Varsity Blues college admissions scandal. Both women expressed trepidation in advance of incarceration, but neither one spent more than two months in federal prison following their plea deals (Levinson and Mossburg, 2020). White collar criminals, even when sentenced to minimum security prisons, no less face prison with fear similar to their conventional crime counterparts.

One piece of advice that a white collar criminal gave about incarceration is to not complain, particularly to fellow prisoners. As Justin Paperny, a former stockbroker who pleaded guilty to securities fraud in 2007, cautions:

> There's nothing worse than a white collar offender who surrenders for a 3 or 4 year prison term or 18 months or a year and a day, and from that 1st day, 2d or 3d day, they're immediately spending their days complaining about the prosecutor, their attorney who might have screwed them or whatever it is. . . . Then you immediately get checked [by fellow prisoners] . . . you're stepping into an environment where men have lived 2, 5, 10, 15, 20, 30 years. (2016, retrieved from https://www.whitecollaradvice.com/white-collar-101-life-in-federal-prison/)

For however long a white collar criminal's sentence might be, most will not compare to the nonviolent drug offender who might be spending decades in prison for crimes that are far less egregious in comparison to cases of fraud that have bilked victims out of thousands, sometimes millions of dollars.

What may come as a surprise to new prisoners convicted of white collar crime is that it is not all dreary in prison. The minimum security prisons that they are generally housed in offer more liberties and in turn, allow for more joviality among prisoners. On the other hand, as in the case of the clinically depressed comedian, humor may actually be covering up the anger prisoners feel about their circumstances. Teal (2020, p.49) found that:

> *This was a world with more laughter in it than one might expect. We joked around a lot. But the purpose of the joking was often to help cover up the anger. There were a lot things to be angry about.*

White collar criminals are not always elites from the business world. But when they are, between their means by which to defend their charges and the privileged lives they enjoyed prior to incarceration, the anger (or dismay?) that they might feel can be explained. According to Lam of *The Atlantic* (2016), there are even therapists who devote their practices to preparing elite criminals for their prison sentences, including coping with their feelings of shame and anger. Of course, we have to note that elite convicts are uniquely in a position to afford to pay a therapist to help them prepare for the prison. The rest of convicts facing jail or prison time without the financial means have to depend on blogs on line and published articles, books to get some sense of what prison is really like.

PRISONERS' RESISTANCE

There are a number of ways that prisoners can resist the will of administrators. In the extreme, resistance is clear, as in the case of riots, which is explored further in Chapter 10 on prison violence. In other cases, the resistance is subtler.

One way that prisoners can resist individually or collectively is through hunger strikes. One example of hunger strikes are those conducted by the incarcerated suffrage activists who had been arrested during protests. This was prior to the 19th Amendment passing in 1920, giving women the right to vote in the United States. One of the first to do so was suffragette Marion Wallace Dunlop who refused food while imprisoned (Purvis, 2009). In the case of suffragists, hunger strikes were often ineffectual, as guards[7] would force fed them.

Today, given the example of the hunger strike at Guantanamo Bay by alleged terrorists, there are accounts in medical records of prisoners who were force-fed while strapped in restraint chairs. There is debate as to whether a hunger strike is a human right, even as it is detrimental to the health of the prisoner (Annas, 2006). Remember, that one of the responsibilities of corrections administrators is to look after the physical well-being of the detained and imprisoned, at least in the United States. However, in reading accounts from the hunger strikes of suffragists and Guantanamo Bay prisoners, unless medically justified, force-feeding sounds

---

[7]At the time that the suffragists were jailed, the term "guard" is more historically accurate. Corrections officer was not in use as yet.

more like torture, with the use of restraining chairs (Annas, 2006). The practice of force-feeding prisoners on hunger strike continues to be a legal gray area.

Of concern for prison staff is the fact that resistance and disrespect for authority landed many prisoners behind bars in the first place. Defiant prisoners are not suddenly born in jail or prison. As noted in Mary Heinen McPherson's account (Moughni and Krinitsky, 2020) of her experiences in the Detroit House of Corrections beginning at age 22, no amount of religious training and parental intervention prior to incarceration changed the fact that from a very early age, she did not like to be told what to do by anyone. The extreme of McPherson's attitude transcended normal juvenile rebellion, similar to that of criminals in general. Prisoners with histories of rebellious behavior have a difficult time with rehabilitation, and are less likely to be eligible for early release.

WORKING THE PROGRAMS

Not all prisoners actively find ways to defy the system. Some are truly contrite and use the time in prison to attempt to reform. One way to do so is to take advantage of what programs are available to prisoners. Not only does it look good to parole boards, but we have evidence that people who complete their education, even high school, while behind bars, have more work options when they are no longer incarcerated.

If you consider that an awful lot of time in prison is boring and monotonous, having the opportunity to participate in therapy, whether one is willing or not, is one way to break away from the otherwise strict schedule. One advantage of "working the programs" is that they fill time. This means that an inmate may seek out any and every program just to get out of their cells. Whether it is an anger management or alcohol, drug treatment program, even if the prisoner is reluctant to reform they antisocial behavior, the programs can break up the endless days behind bars.

We should also note that not every prisoner who "finds religion" while incarcerated is insincere in their conversion. As faith is an intangible, save the behavior of people, we really don't know how many claim to have become spiritual in prisons, particularly at parole board hearings, are being sincere. If we think of religion as one of the oldest forms of social control, it is a type of service to prisoners that is on the most part beneficial, save the conversion to extreme sects that have beliefs counter to rehabilitation, as in the case of some cults that might be lurking behind prison bars.

PREPARING FOR REENTRY

As we note in our chapter on community corrections, an inmate can leave prison in a number of ways. They can have their sentence overturned in appeal, they can have served the entirety of their sentence, they can be paroled, or in extreme cases, they can die while in prison. In rare cases, they can have their sentence shortened by commutation or erased in a gubernatorial or presidential pardon. For those who are released on parole, they are still part of the system: "For an inmate, being paroled not only means serving the remainder a sentence outside prison, it also represents a triumph over seemingly insurmountable institutional forces." (Lacombe, 2013, p.13).

We have already established in this chapter that there are two times when prisoners are most fearful. One is when they enter jail or prison. The second is when prisoners are preparing to reenter society. The success of reentry is highly dependent on the resources that prisoners have in order to do this triumphantly. Sadly, the reentry resources in most communities are scarce, except in the most progressive prisons. As we will see in our *Stories From Behind Bars* section of this chapter, some prisoners, even given a number of advantages, will still fail to successfully become reintegrated in the community.

The numbers are grim for recidivism. Half of all prisoners released from prison will be reincarcerated within three years (Doleac, 2019; DuRose et al., 2014). Depending on the type of offenses, the recidivism rates can be as high as over 80 percent.

How well that convicts can adjust to reentry after incarceration is a function of how well they are prepared while behind bars or during community corrections. It is also a function of what support systems are in place in the community that they released to. This can be by immersion in programs described in this chapter and in other places in this book.

The vast majority of male prisoners are not married, but consider themselves to be in relationships with people outside of prison (Comfort et al., 2018). Intimate partners and family members can play a part in how well or how badly a convict adjusts to reentry. The newly released are highly dependent on family and partners for financial and emotional support (Comfort et al., 2018; Bobbitt and Nelson, 2004).

Of course, instinctually we may assume that a great deal contributing to successful reentry after incarceration has to do with the mental health condition of the prisoners. However, a study conducted in Massachusetts found that of those prisoners who had been treated for mental illness while incarcerated, that variables like older age at time of release, parole supervision and the seriousness and type of charges for which they were incarcerated were better predictors of whether they would re-offend than their mental illnesses (Hartwell et al., 2016). Meaning that treatment in prison and subsequent follow up during reentry is key to success for a number of released convicts.

SUMMARY

The experiences of prisoners is decidedly different than those of prison staff, even though they occupy the same spaces. For prisoners, it is a 24 hours a day, 7 days a week existence. For correction officers, as we discussed in detail in Chapter 5, they have the luxury of leaving jails and prisons at the end of their shift, as long as no trouble is brewing requiring them to stay longer, as in the example of lockdowns. That does not mean to say that they leave their jobs behind when their shift ends. Particularly after difficult days, no doubt their job follows them home. Similarly, those who have been detained or incarcerated can have the experience haunt them long after they have been allowed to leave the institution.

There are two times when prisoners are generally the most fearful. The first time is when newly arrested or incarcerated and entering a jail or prison facility. The second time is just before being released. Prisoners who serve their entire sentence do not have parole hanging over their heads, where parolees are still essentially part of the criminal justice system, just on the outside. However, both parolees and people who serve their entire sentences before release can be equally fearful of a future full of the unknown, including reestablishing relationships with people, finding employment, and securing a place to live.

In order to cope with the jail and prison experience, the accused and convicted who are incarcerated have to adapt quickly to the culture behind bars. Those living in the less oppressive conditions of minimum security prisons still have an inmate code to follow. There are a number of characteristics to the prison culture, including the formation of cliques, the emergence of leaders, and the formation of a crude underground economy; also, particularly in women's prisons, pseudo families are created. Though sex is prohibited behind bars, prisoners do engage in sexual relationships and in some cases, use rape and sexual assault as weapons against their enemies. They may use it for coercion or use sex in prohibited bartering transactions. These characteristics of sex are a distorted mirror of what we see on the outside.

And not all those incarcerated are treated equally by their fellow prisoners. Even the convict has a minimal line that should not be crossed criminally, particularly the harming of children. Prisoners who have crossed that line are often housed away from the general population in what inmates term as the "tree jumper school," referring to child rapists.

The transgender prison populations are another group that has to be protected while behind bars. With only a handful of states that allow prisoners to be housed based on their gender identification, most transgender individuals are categorized by their designated sex at birth. Transwomen, individuals who are identified as male by their sex, but identify with the female gender, are at great risk for sexual assault and general abuse if housed in male prisons. They can also be ostracized if housed in women's prisons. Transgender prisoners who have been undergoing sex reassignment treatments prior to arrest may find that their treatments are disrupted.

Gangs likewise create tensions, where leaders or violent gang members may have to be housed in solitary confinement in order to maintain peace in prison. Though the incarcerated have the shared experience of lost freedoms, whatever symbolic or real power they can gain in prison, they will attempt to achieve.

In order to protect themselves, prisoners will quickly be forced either by coercion or general peer pressure to join groups, mostly divided along racial or ethnic

179

lines. Whatever racism exists outside of prison is exacerbated behind bars. Some of these groups, primarily gangs, are already formed outside of prison and affiliations continue on the inside, as in the examples of street gangs or white supremacy groups. In some cases, nongang members will become newly affiliated with a gang once in jail or prison.

White collar criminals, when they are sentenced to time in prison, have somewhat different experiences than conventional criminals behind bars. They can often be housed in minimum security prisons with nonviolent offenders, most of whom are incarcerated because of drug charges. Prisoners with shorter sentences, including white collar convicts, are cautioned that they should not complain about their sentencing or any aspect of their cases, as they can be housed with others with much longer sentences.

There are a few ways by which a prisoner can cope with prison life. One way that is beneficial in preparation for release is to "work the programs." In other words, whatever programs that an inmate qualifies for is taken advantage of, including anger management, substance abuse treatment, and education towards a high school GED or college degree. By taking part in programs behind bars, prisoners can break up the monotony of prison life. An additional way to cope is to overmedicate themselves, either with prison doctor prescribed drugs or with drugs that are obtained illegally through the underground prison economy.

The bottom line, is that prisons operate as societies with similar characteristics to what we see on the outside. Detainees and prisoners create their own culture, including their own vocabulary. They will self-segregate, mostly along racial lines, and any racism we witness in general society is amplified behind bars. The difficulty is when prison culture is carried over into the lives of the released once they are on the outside.

STORIES FROM BEHIND BARS

In the Belly of the Beast: Letters from Prison (Jack Henry Abbott, 1981)

There is perhaps no better example of the effects of the prisonization experience than in the case of a juvenile who is incarcerated and ends up spending the greater portion of their lives in prison. The poster child for lifelong incarceration and the "state-raised" criminal is Jack Henry Abbott. We should caution the reader that in Abbott's case, as in the case of accounts written by prisoners, the perceptions are subjective. Nevertheless, it does not make their experiences in prison any less real.

Abbott started his life as a foster child almost from birth in 1944. In the 1940s on and into the 1970s, there was very little progress in treating delinquent children differently than criminal adults. By age 9, Abbott began to spend long periods of time in juvenile detention. As a result, he didn't even complete sixth grade, during a time when a high school diploma became increasingly more important in finding a job. By age 12, Abbott was sentenced to the Utah State Industrial School for Boys.

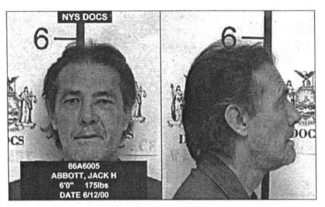

Jack Henry Abbot's Booking (June 1, 2000). (*Source*: Find A Grave, retrieved from https://www.findagrave.com/memorial/18523947/ jack-henry-abbot.)

As an adult, by age 18, Abbott was released from juvenile detention. According to Abbott (1981) it was only a few months later that he was sent to the Utah State Penitentiary with an indeterminate sentence up to 5 years, for bouncing a check for nonsufficient funds. We should note that prior to sentencing guidelines, judges could send convicts to prison for an unknown amount of time, with release dependent on behavior, or in many cases, the political climate of the times. Abbott wrote (1981, p.7), from age 12 to 37, "I have been free the sum total of nine and a half months. . . served many terms in solitary [confinement]." If we consider that the formative years of figuring out what it means to be an adult comes from puberty through young adulthood, Abbott was virtually set up for failure from birth through middle age.

In describing how life in prison is during long sentences, Abbott wrote (1981, p. 3):

> To be in prison so long, it's difficult to remember exactly what you did to get there. So long, your fantasies of the free world are no longer easily distinguishable from what you 'know' the free world is really like. So long, that being free is exactly identical to a free man's dreams of heaven.

One form of solitary confinement that has been used in the past and is, in theory, not in use today is the *blackout cell*. A blackout cell has no windows and once the door is closed, there is no visible light and the prisoner is thrown into complete darkness. Solitary confinement of this type, and of any kind, results in mental health issues including anxiety and stress and physical effects including headaches, deterioration of eyesight, digestive disorders, and dizziness (Leonard, 2020). We saw this to be the case at Alcatraz, first described in Chapter 2.

Abbott was confined in blackout cells at various times of his incarceration. He describes the experience as the following (1981, pp. 27-29):

> My eyes hungered for light, for color, the way someone's dry mouth may hunger for saliva. . . . I counted twenty-three days by the meals. . . . I rose, thirsty, felt my way to the sink. . . . I raised the cup [of water] carefully to my lips and tilted it back to drink. I felt the legs, the bodies of many insects run up my face, over my eyes, and into my hair. . . . I heard someone screaming far away and it was me.

Norman Mailer, the writer to which Abbott sent letters between 1978 and 1981, encouraged him to publish his letters. Mailer additionally lobbied the parole board to release him, with parole coming to fruition for Abbott in 1982 when he was released to a halfway house in New York, given a $500 suit, good shoes, and a job as a $150/week researcher by Mailer (*Washington Post*, n.d.).

Postscript

Abbott's published letters to Mailer became a national best seller, still in print today. Sadly, for all the efforts of writer Mailer to get Abbott released from prison, his subsequent freedom was short lived. Abbott was paroled in 1981, only to kill a waiter six weeks later (Worth, 2002). After the murder, Abbott was arrested and recommitted to prison for violation of parole and consequentially was sentenced to 15-years to life for manslaughter. In February 2002, Abbott, then 58 years old, was found hanging in his prison cell in the maximum-security facility at Wende Correctional Facility, in New York (Worth, 2002). Conceivably, he was close to being paroled, assuming it would be granted. We will never know exactly why Abbott took his own life, even with the possibility of parole, from the contents of his suicide note.

Abbott's experiences in prison are echoed by others, including suicide in some cases where the experience is so intolerable.

SOURCES

Abbott, J. H. (1981) *In the Belly of the Beast: Letters from Prison*. New York: Random House.

Leonard, J. (2020) What are the effects of solitary confinement on health? *Medical News Today*. Aug. 6. Retrieved from https://www.medicalnewstoday.com/articles/solitary-confinement -effects.

Washington Post (n.d.) Prison writer Jack H. Abbott dies. Retrieved from https://www.was hingtonpost.com/archive/local/2002/02/12/prison-writer-jack-h-abbott-dies/b12e2969-a2e7-4530-bc72-d78af089023f/.

Worth, R. F. (2002) Jailhouse author helped by Mailer found dead. *New York Times*. Feb. 11. Retrieved from https://www.nytimes.com/2002/02/11/nyregion/jailhouse-author-hel ped-by-mailer-is-found-dead.html.

INTERNATIONAL PERSPECTIVES IN PUNISHMENT AND CORRECTIONS: TURKEY

Americans in Turkish Prisons — The Billy Hayes Story

For those of you students who are reading this book, you are probably not that much younger or older than Billy Hayes, an American, where he made the serious mistake of strapping two kilos (a bit over four pounds) of hashish onto his body in an attempt to smuggle the drug out of Turkey in 1970. Having dropped out of Marquette University (Milwaukee, Wisconsin) at the beginning of his senior year, he said that he was bored and unfocused (Krajicek, 2015). In 1970, Hayes told his parents that he wanted to travel to Turkey for excitement and adventure (Gupte, 1975).

The 1970s was a period of time in world travel where airfares were extremely inexpensive and youth hostels[8] abundant for young American travelers, primarily college-aged students, who for some included the rite of passage of backpacking trips overseas (Popp, 2018). Some of these backpacking young Americans found themselves in prison, largely due to their ignorance (and foolishness) of not knowing drug laws in foreign countries, where as bad as the penalties were in the United States, could translate into a death penalty elsewhere for even cannabis.

Traveling to Turkey for the purposes of smuggling drugs out of the country seemed like a good idea to Hayes at the time, with the potential of making good money on the sale of the hashish in the United States. Instead, at age 23, on his fourth attempt to smuggle drugs out of Turkey (he had successfully done so in three of his four trips), he was caught at the Istanbul airport, arrested, and sentenced to 30 years in prison, later reduced by the Turkish government with a scheduled release date of 1978 (Quinn, 2015; Gupte, 1975).

In Hayes case, he was not a mere tourist. Based on interview with Hayes in 2012, a friend of his had talked to him about the ease of purchasing hashish on the streets of Istanbul (*Newsday*, 2012). And even though there were increased airport inspections after the Palestine Liberation Army (PLO) executed a number of successful hijackings and terrorist acts on airlines beginning in 1967 (Israel Ministry of Foreign Affairs, 2013; *Newsday*, 2012), Hayes thought it was, as in his own words, a good idea to travel to Turkey for the purpose of purchasing hashish to sell in the United States. Allegedly, as a journalism major in college, he wanted to go out in the world and have some life experiences so as to make his writing more "real" and authentic (*Newsday*, 2012).

Ron Emmons, another American who spent time in Sağmalcılar Prison with Hayes, including over a year as his cellmate, described his experience as follows (Fitzpatrick and *Chicago Sun Times*, 1979, retrieved from https://www .washingtonpost.com/archive/lifestyle/1979/03/11/ten-years-locked-up/98de988b -22a1-42b5-a227-c63e7a130c64/):

> *Fear has a way of locking your emotions inside, making it impossible to fully relate to those around you. . . . 'It all began for me just 10 years ago in Istanbul. I was barely 20 years old. . . . I was restless so I decided to tour Europe. . . .then I ran out of money. I decided the way to get enough money to make it was to sell some hashish. . . . I picked the worst possible time to be in the hashish business. . . . they [Turkish police] caught me in my hotel room with more than a kilo of hash in my suitcase. First they beat me, then they threw me into their prison in Instanbul called Sağmalcılar. (Fitzpatrick and Chicago Sun Times,*

---

[8] Hostels are reasonably cheap dormitory style housing that can be found around the world, including in the United States, that many times include kitchen facilities in order to further reduce the costs of living while traveling.

1979, retrieved from https://www.washingtonpost.com/archive/lifestyle/1979/ 03/11/ten-years-locked-up/98de988b-22a1-42b5-a227-c63e7a130c64/)

Emmons, only 20 years old at the time of his arrest, described the treatment in the Turkish prison in his interview with the *Chicago Sun Times* a number of years after his release:

> *It wasn't just a matter of the beatings. They wouldn't feed you. There was no way to stay clean. During cold weather there was no way to stay warm. And then there were the relationships with other prisoners. Most were Turks, of course, and they hated us for being what they called 'turistes.' I knew that with all the beatings there was a possibility I might be maimed. I knew I might leave prison in a wheelchair.* (Fitzpatrick and *Chicago Sun Times*, 1979, retrieved from https://www.washingtonpost.com/archive/lifestyle/1979/03/11/ten -years-locked-up/98de988b-22a1-42b5-a227-c63e7a130c64/)

Emmons was released after just over three years of the Turkish prison and returned to the United States. He stated in his interview that the terror of the experience continued to follow him long after release (Fitzpatrick and *Chicago Sun Times*, 1979).

Having already spent four years in prison, including his pretrial detainment, Hayes heard rumors that the Turkish government had plans to overturn his original sentence, and resentence him to life in prison. In spite of Hayes's attorney being in the middle of negotiations to have Hayes sent to the United States to serve out the remainder of his sentence, Hayes, who kept fit with yoga and was an expert swimmer, decided to attempt an escape from the Imrali Prison located on an island, after Hayes used a bribe to obtain a transfer from Sağmalcılar Prison and where there was more freedom of movement for prisoners:

> *At dark on Oct. 2 [1975], after 1,821 days [in prison]. . . . Hayes slipped into the sea, swam to a tethered rowboat, and stroked his way clear. . . . He reached shore eight hours later.*
>
> *With help from people he knew from prison, Hayes was able to pose as a Turk and travel by bus about 100 miles west to the Maritsa River, Turkey's border with Greece. . . . [he] surrendered to a U.S. consulate in Greece.* (Krajicek, 2015) retrieved from https://www.nydailynews.com/news/crime/ hed-hed-article-1.2264795)

Following a few weeks of red tape with the U.S. consulate in Greece, Hayes was able to return to the United States in late 1975 (Krajicek, 2015).

Hayes's story about his experiences in a Turkish prison were made known to a wider audience when the critically acclaimed, Oscar-winning film, *Midnight Express*, based on Hayes's best- selling autobiography, was released in 1978 (Colombia Pictures). The title of the movie comes from the slang name given the prisoners' escape routes from prison (Flynn, 2013). When the movie came out, as immune as theater goers had become to the gore of *Jaws, The Exorcist*, and the horrors of the film *Deliverance*, when *Midnight Express* was released, it was "a movie so harrowing that the words 'Turkish prison' still have the power to terrify." (Lawrence, 2020, retrieved from https://www.reviewjournal.com/rj-magaz ine/meet-the-summerlin-resident-whose-drug-arrest-led-to-midnight-express-1966 972/).

We should note that in 21st-century terms, the movie has been critiqued as including Orientalism, where Turkey and Turkish people are portrayed as "evil, masochistic and ignorant, [while] the film rationalizes Western characters as good-natured, clever people, who just happen to be at the wrong place at the wrong time." (Akkan, 2018, retrieved from https://www.iscap.pt/cei/e-rei/n6/artigos/ Goksu-Akkan_Midnight-Express-Hollywood.pdf.). Hayes as himself in interviews and his book, and as he was portrayed by Brad Davis in the film, was presented more as a folk hero than the criminal that he was.

Hayes became a writer, theater director, and actor in Los Angeles, following his Turkish prison escape, after which he relocated to Las Vegas in 2014 (Lawrence, 2020; Flynn, 2013).

Females who are American citizens have not escaped imprisonment in Turkey on the basis of their sex. Maisha Yearwood, a playwright and screenwriter who currently teaches at Hofstra University in Hempstead, New York, was held in Bakırköy Prison in Istanbul, after nine grams of hashish were said to have been found in her pocket during a layover at the Istanbul airport in 2009, allegedly a trumped-up charge (Gross, 2017; *9 Grams*, n.d.). She stated in an interview that she hadn't anticipated that she would be searched again, having already gone through airport security in Israel (*Bric TV*, 2017). Yearwood, Black, and a lesbian gender nonconformist, was kept in solitary confinement because the corrections staff thought she might be "disruptive" to fellow prisoners because she was too "masculine," according to her own words (D.A., 2017; *Bric TV*, 2017).

Unlike Hayes, Yearwood was held in prison for just three months before she was released. Granted, whether the charges were real or not, nine grams of hashish is *considerably less* than the two kilos Hayes attempted to smuggle out of Turkey, or the one kilo attempt by Emmons. In turn, Yearwood wrote an award winning play, *9 Grams*, in which she also performs, based on her experiences in the Turkish prison (*9 Grams*, n.d.). One of Yearwood's interviews can be found on Youtube.com at https://www.youtube.com/watch?v=DODkhcpQa30 (*Bric TV*, 2017). In her *Bric TV* interview, Yearwood speculates that she was targeted with racial profiling because the Black women in prison were primarily from Africa and were generally involved in drug trafficking (*Bric TV*, 2017).

In the most recent decade, a number of Americans have been detained or imprisoned in Turkey for political reasons. In 2016, there was a failed coup, of which a number of Americans have been accused of taking part in. How many of those are still detained or incarcerated is unknown, as the Turkish government has been secretive with the actual numbers. One suspect, Andrew Brunson, a pastor who believes he was arrested for his religious beliefs in a Muslim country, was facing 35 years in prison, until the Trump administration intervened, threatening further sanctions, after which he was released (Hacaoglu, 2018; Zauzmer, 2019).

Regarding Turkey or any other foreign country outside of the United States, American tourists sometimes believe that they are impervious to other countries' laws on the basis of their citizenship. As noted earlier in this section, the best thing that any tourist can do is have a basic understanding of local customs and laws. What might appear to be rather harmless, and assuredly, drug trafficking is not by any means, can result in a stay at the local jail or prison for an indefinite time, with no guarantees that a U.S. consulate, or a president of the United States for that matter, will intervene on your behalf.

SOURCES

Akkan, G. (2018) *Midnight Express* as a product of Hollywood Orientalism. *E-Revista de Estudos Interculturais do CEI—ISCAP (E-Journal of Intercultural Studies)*. May, No. 6:1-6. Retrieved from https://www.iscap.pt/cei/e-rei/n6/artigos/Goksu-Akkan_Midnight-Express-Hollywood.pdf.

BricTV (2017) Maisha Yearwood's "9 Grams" retells the story of being locked up abroad. June 12. Retrieved from https://www.youtube.com/watch?v=DODkhcpQa30.

D.A. (2017) Midnight express: A black lesbian's play tackles her time in a Turkish prison. *Advocate*. Oct./Nov., Iss. 1092:29.

E2BN (2006) Convict life in Australia. *Victorian Crime and Punishment*. Retrieved from http://vcp.e2bn.org/justice/page11384-convict-life-in-australia.html.

Fitzpatrick, T. and *Chicago Sun Times* (1979) Ten years locked up. *The Washington Post*. Mar. 11. Retrieved from https://www.washingtonpost.com/archive/lifestyle/1979/03/11/ten-years-locked-up/98de988b-22a1-42b5-a227-c63e7a130c64/.

Flynn, B. (2013) Expect to be caught. . and do yoga in jail, Midnight Express author to tell Fringe. *The Times* (London, England). Aug. 22. Retrieved from https://go-gale-com.wne.idm.oclc.org/ps/i.do?v=2.1&u=mlin_w_westnew&it=r&id=GALE%7CA340354709&p=GPS&sw=w.

Gupte, P. (1975) Escapee from Turkey describes return. *The New York Times*. Oct. 25. Retrieved from https://www.nytimes.com/1975/10/25/archives/escapee-from-turkey-describes-return.html.

Hacaoglu, S. (2018) U.S. pastor faces 35 years in Turkish prison as coup suspect. *Bloomberg*. Mar. 13. Retrieved from https://www.bloomberg.com/news/articles/2018-03-13/u-s-pastor-faces-life-in-turk-prison-as-coup-suspect-tv-saysj.

Israel Ministry of Foreign Affairs (2013) 1967-1993: Major Terror Attacks. Retrieved from https://mfa.gov.il/mfa/aboutisrael/maps/pages/1967-1993-%20major%20terror%20attacks.aspx.

Krajicek, D. J. (2015) How a hippie hash runner from Long Island escaped from Turkey's Alcatraz and inspired 'Midnight Express'. *New York Daily News*. June 20. Retrieved from https://www.nydailynews.com/news/crime/hed-hed-article-1.2264795.

Lawrence, C. (2020) The ride of his life: Billy Hayes never tires of telling tale that inspired film 'Midnight Express'. Las Vegas Review-Journal Magazine. Mar. 15. Retrieved from https://www.reviewjournal.com/rj-magazine/meet-the-summerlin-resident-whose-drug-arrest-led-to-midnight-express-1966972/.

Newsday (2012) Interview: Billy Hays revisits *Midnight Express*. June 22. Video. Retrieved from *Newsday*, 2012.

Popp, R. K. (2018) From *Marrakesh Express* to *Midnight Express*: Backpackers, drug culture, and incarceration. *Journalism and Communication Monographs*. Vol. 20, No. 3:248-253.

Quinn, K. (2015) Billy Hayes: Convicted drug smuggler tells the true story of *Midnight Express*. *The Sydney Morning Herald*. Mar. 24. Retrieved from https://www.smh.com.au/entertainment/movies/billy-hayes-convicted-drug-smuggler-tells-the-true-story-behind-midnight-express-20150324-1m6ole.html.

Zaumer, J. (2019) Released from Turkish prison, Pastor Andrew Brunson urges Congress to heed others being held. *The Washington Post*. Feb. 6. Retrieved from https://www.washingtonpost.com/religion/2019/02/06/released-turkish-prison-pastor-andrew-brunson-urges-congress-heed-other-prisoners/.

GLOSSARY

Blackout cells   Prison cells used for solitary confinement that do not have any windows and where the prisoner is held in nearly, if not complete, blackout conditions with no light.

Cliques   A subgroup or alliance of individuals who are part of a larger group whose members have the same values, beliefs, and/or goals. Gangs within in prisons are an example of a clique.

Conjugal visitation   Visits sanctioned to prisoners by spouses where sexual relationships are allowed. Held in housing separate from the main prison facility.

Crew   A subgroup similar to gangs, but generally more neighborhood oriented. Not all crews are demonstratively criminal, as compared to street gangs.

Inmate code   The set of rules made up by prisoners themselves on how to behave in prison.

Jailhouse snitches   Individuals who will act as informants to report criminal activities of prisoners or inform on prisoners who are suspected of being involved in criminal activities yet to be reported to prosecutors or authorities.

Lifers   Individuals who have been sentenced to life in prison. This could include individuals with life with or without the possibility of parole.

Master status   The main identity that we identify with. For prisoners, whether they commit to that status or not, prison staff see them, generally, as only detainees or prisoners, guilty of their crimes.

Prison slang   A special vocabulary that has been created by prisoners or, in some cases, brought in from the outside.

"Pruno" or "Hootch"   Homemade alcoholic beverage that is made in prison cells illegally with little no control over the percentage of alcohol contained.

Situational homosexuality   Same-sex relationships that occur when individuals who ordinarily identify as heterosexual are housed with only the same sex.

Social identity theories   Sociological and social psychological theories that address issues around how we identify ourselves on the basis of what groups we belong to.

Total institutions   Places where there are limited liberties for the individuals who are housed there voluntarily or involuntarily, e.g., prisoners, the institutionalized mentally ill, the military, and monasteries.

Transgender   Individuals who are identified at birth as one sex, but identify with the gender, gender roles of the opposite sex.

"Tree jumper school"   Protective custody housing for individuals who have been convicted of certain sex crimes, including sexual abuse and/or murder of children.

REFERENCES AND SUGGESTED READINGS

A.L. (2007) Review, Santa Monica Jail. *Yelp.com*. Mar. 29. Retrieved from https://www.yelp.com/biz/santa-monica-jail-santa-monica?hrid=_J8uoqZdUtMbXCj2Ntk7vw&osq=Jails+%26+Prisons)

American University Washington College of Law (n.d.) Project on addressing prison rape. Retrieved from https://www.wcl.american.edu/impact/initiatives-programs/endsilence/research-guidance/nprec-says-bop-policy-change-endangers-transgender-people-in-custody/.

Annas, G. J. (2006) Hunger strikes at Guantanamo—Medical Ethics and Human Rights in a "Legal Black Hole." *The New England Journal of Medicine*. Vol. 355, No. 13:1377-1382.

Au, J. (2016) A remedy for male-to-female transgender inmates: Applying disparate impact to prison placement. *American University Journal of Gender, Social Policy and the Law*. Vol. 24, Iss. 3:371-399.

Beam, A. (2020) California will house transgender inmates by gender identity. Associated Press. Sept. 26. Retrieved from https://apnews.com/article/prisons-gender-identity-california-gavin-newsom-archive-14cd954b06360d21349b77233318369e.

Bobbit, M. and M. Nelson (2004) The front line: Building programs that recognize families' role in reentry. Vera Institution of Justice. Sept. Retrieved from https://www.prisonpolicy.org/scans/vera/249_476.pdf.

Chappell, B. (2021) A former college professor accused of serial arson is denied bail in California. *NPR*. Aug. 11. Retrieved from https://www.npr.org/2021/08/11/1026700103/former-college-professor-arson-charges-california-dixie-fire.

Comfort, M. K. E. Krieger, J. Landwehr, T. McKay, C. H. Lindquist, R. Feinberg, E. K. Kennedy, and A. Bir (2018) Partnership after prison: Couple relationships during reentry. *Journal of Offender Rehabilitation*. Vol. 57, No. 2:188-205.

Dervan, L. E. (2011) Symposium: Prison policy: American prison culture in an international context: An examination of prisons in America, the Netherlands, and Israel. *Stanford Law and Policy Review*. Vol. 22:413.

District of Columbia (D.C.) Metropolitan Police Department (n.d.) Understanding and avoiding Gangs. DC.gov. Retrieved from https://mpdc.dc.gov/page/understanding-and-avoiding-gangs#:~:text=What%20is%20a%20Gang%20or,often%20based%20on%20a%20neighborhood.

Doleac, J. L. (2019) Wrap-around services don't improve prisoner reentry. *Journal of Policy Analysis and Management*. Mar. Vol. 38, Iss. 2:508-514.

DuRose, M. R., A. D. Cooper, H. N. Snyder (2014) Recidivism of prisoners released in 30 states in 2005: Patterns from 2005 to 2010. Bureau of Justice Statistics, NJS 244205.

Eldridge, D. (2016) Bennett, Breen, and the Birdman of Alcatraz: A case study of collaborative censorship between the Production Code Administration and the Federal Bureau of Prisons. Film History. Vol. 28, No. 2:1-31.

Federal Bureau of Prisons (n.d.) General visiting information. Retrieved from https://www.bop.gov/inmates/visiting.jsp.

Gardner, B., P. Lally, J. Wardle (2012) Making health habitual: the psychology of 'habit-formation' and general practice. British Journal of General Practice. Vol. 62, No. 605:664-666.

Gay and Lesbian Alliance Against Defamation (GLAAD) (n.d.) What does transgender mean? Retrieved from https://www.glaad.org/transgender/transfaq.

Goffman, E. (1961) Asylums: Essays on the Social Situation of Mental Patients and Other Inmates. New York: Doubleday.

Greene, B. (2000) The executioners who live among us. Chicago Tribune. July 16. Retrieved from https://www.chicagotribune.com/news/ct-xpm-2000-07-16-0007160138-story.html.

Griffiths, A. (2016) "For the amusement of the shutins": The vicissitudes of film viewing in prison. Film History. Vol. 28, No. 3:1-23.

Hansen, L. L. (2005) "Girl 'Crew' Members Doing Gender, Boy 'Crew' Members Doing Violence: An Ethnographic and Network Analysis of Maria Hinojosa's New York Gangs." Western Criminology Review. Vol. 6, No. 1:134-44. Available at http://www.western-criminology.org/documents/WCR/v06n1/article_pdfs/hansen.pdf

Harris, D. H. (n.d.) The Convict Code of Conduct—From a True Convict. Prison Writers. Retrieved from https://prisonwriters.com/convict-code-of-conduct/.

Hartwell, S. W. Fisher, X. Deng, D. A Pinals, and J. Siegfriedt. (2016) Intensity of offending following state prison release among persons treated for mental health problems while incarcerated. Psychiatric Services. Jan., Vol. 67, No. 1:49-54.

Haslam, S. A. and S. D. Reicher (2006) On the agency of individuals and groups: Lessons from the BBC Prison Study, in Individuality and the Group: Advances in Social Identity, T. Postmes and J. Jetten, eds. London, UK: Sage. 237-257.

Haslam, S. A. and S. D. Reicher (2012) When prisoners take over the prison: A social psychology of resistance. Personality and Social Psychology Review. Vol. 16, No. 2:154-179.

Hassine, V. (2007) Life Without Parole: Living in Prison Today. R. Johnson and A. Dobrzanska, eds. Oxford: Oxford University Press.

Justice Project, The (2007) Jailhouse snitch testimony: A policy review. Retrieved from https://www.pewtrusts.org/~/media/legacy/uploadedfiles/wwwpewtrustsorg/reports/death_penalty_reform/jailhouse20snitch20testimony20policy20briefpdf.pdf.

King, M. J. and J. G. Boyle (2011) The theme park: The art of time and space, in Disneyland and Culture: Essays on the Park and Their Influences, K. M. Jackson and M. I. West, eds. Jefferson, North Carolina: McFarland and Co., Inc. Ch 1.

KOAT, Channel 7, New Mexico (2012) Inmates using Aztec language to speak in code. Apr. 19. Retrieved from https://www.youtube.com/watch?v=8O9iRUWWMbQ.

Kübler-Ross, E. and D. Kessler (2005) On Grief and Grieving: Finding Meaning of Grief Through the Five States of Loss. New York: Scribner.

Lacombe, D. (2013) "Mr. S., you do have sexual fantasies?" The parole hearing and prison treatment of a sex offender at the turn of the 21st Century. Canadian Journal of Sociologie/ Cahiers Canadièn de Sociologie. Vol. 38, No. 1:33-63.

Ledesma, E. and C. L. Ford (2020) Health implications of housing assignments for incarcerated transgender women. American Journal of Public Health. May;110(5):650-654.

Levinson, E. and C. Mossburg (2020) Lori Loughlin released from prison after 2-month sentence for college admissions scam. *CNN*. Dec. 28. Retrieved from https://www.cnn.com/2020/12/28/us/lori-loughlin-prison-release/index.html.

Lewis, G. H. (1980) Social groupings in organized crime: The case of La Nuestra Familia. Deviant Behavior. Vol. 1, Iss. 2:129-143.

Mann, N. (2012) Ageing child sex offenders in prison: Denial, manipulation and community. *The Howard Journal of Criminal Justice.* Sept. Vol. 51, No. 4:345-358.

Mitchell, M. M., C. Fahmy, D. C. Pyrooz, and S. H. Decker (2017) Criminal crews, codes, and contexts: Differences and similarities across the Cod of the Street, Convict Code, street gangs, and prison gangs. *Deviant Behavior.* Vol. 38, No. 10:1197-1222.

Moreau, J. (2018) Bureau of prisons rolls back Obama-era transgender inmate protections. May 14. Retrieved from https://www.nbcnews.com/feature/nbc-out/bureau-prisons-rolls-back-obama-era-transgender-inmate-protections-n873966.

Moughni, N. and N. Krinitsky (2020) Incarcerated body, liberated mind: The life of Mary Heinen McPherson. *Story Maps*, Carceral State Project: Documenting Criminalization and Confinement. Dec. 28. Retrieved from https://storymaps.arcgis.com/stories/d2552b27f3784308a25ff6273242bb1c.

Nussbaum, A. F. (1973) Let me tell you about prison movies. *Cinéaste*. Vol. 5, No. 4:45-47.

Paperny, J. (2016) White Collar 101: Life in federal prison. *White Collar Advice.* Dec. 18. Retrieved from https://www.whitecolladvice.com/white-collar-101-life-in-federal-prison/.

PrisonPro (n.d.) Visiting an inmate: Answers to common questions and things you should know. Retrieved from https://www.prisonpro.com/content/visiting-inmate-answers-common-questions-things-you-should-know

Purvis, J. (2009) Suffragette hunger strikes, 100 years on. *The Guardian.* July 6. Retrieved from https://www.theguardian.com/commentisfree/libertycentral/2009/jul/06/suffragette-hunger-strike-protest.

Pyrooz, D. C., S. H. Decker, and E. Owens (2020) Do prison administrative and survey data sources tell the same story? A multitrait, multimethod examination with application to gangs. *Crime and Delinquency.* Vol. 66, No. 5:627-662.

Sanders, J. (n.d.) Convict or inmate? (There's a huge difference, by the way.). Prison Writers. Retrieved from https://prisonwriters.com/convict-or-inmate/.

Soniak, M. (2012) 50 prison slang words to make you sound like a tough guy. *Mental Floss.* Oct. 17. Retrieved from https://www.mentalfloss.com/article/12794/50-prison-slang-words-make-you-sound-tough-guy

Taijfel, H. and J. C. Turner (1979) An integrative theory of intergroup conflict, in *The Social Psychology of Intergroup Relations,* W. G. Austin and S. Worchel, eds. Monterey, CA: Brooks and Cole.

Tangney, J. P. (2014) After committing a crime, guilt and shame predict re-offense. Association for Psychological Science. Feb. 11. Retrieved from https://www.psychologicalscience.org/news/releases/after-committing-a-crime-guilt-and-shame-predict-re-offense.html.

Teal, J. A. (2020) *My Journey to Prison: A Story of Failure, Struggle, Discipline, and Gratitude.*

Trammell, R. (2009) Values, rules, and keeping the peace: How men describe order and the inmate code in California prisons. *Deviant Behavior.* Vol. 30:746-771.

Trammell, R. (2012) Enforcing the Convict Code: Violence and Prison Culture. Boulder, CO: Lynne Rienner Publishers.

Travis, A. (2011) Short jail sentence preferable to community service, say prisoners. The Guardian. June 7. Retrieved from https://www.theguardian.com/society/2011/jun/08/prisoners-prefer-jail-sentence-to-community-service

United States Court of Appeals (2013) Stacy Graham v. Sheriff of Logan County; Rahmel Frances Jefferies; Alexander Alicides Mendez. Tenth Circuit. Dec. 20. Retrieved from https://cases.justia.com/federal/appellate-courts/ca10/12-6302/12-6302-2013-12-20.pdf?ts=1411095953

Wellford, C. (1967) Factors associated with adoption of the inmate code: A study of normative socialization. *The Journal of Criminal Law, Criminology, and Police Science*. Vol. 58, No. 2:197-203.

Whissel, K. (2015) The spectacle of punishment and the "melodramatic imagination" in the classical-era prison film: *I am a Fugitive from a Chain Gang* (1932) and *Brute Force* (1947), in *Punishment in Popular Culture*. C. J. Ogletree, Jr. and A. Sarat, eds. New York: New York University Press. Ch. 3.

Wyatt, R. (2006) Male rape in U.S. prisons: Are conjugal visits the answer. *Case Western Reserve Journal International*. Vol. 37, Iss. 2, Art. 20:579-614.

FICTIONAL ACCOUNTS OF PRISON LIFE IN BOOKS AND MOVIES

American History X (New Line Cinema, The Turman-Morrissey Co., 1998) Movie.

American Me (Universal Pictures, 1992) Movie.

Charriere, H. (2006) *Papillon*. New York William Morrow Paperbacks.

Delaney, J. (2013) *Ghost Prison*. Sourcebooks Fire. Naperville, ILL: Sourcebook Fire. Juvenile Fiction.

Ferranti, S. (2013) *Prison Stories*. Rock Hill, SC: Strategic Media Books.

Informer, The (Thunder Road Pictures, 2019) Movie.

King, S. (2020) *Rita Hayworth and Shawshank Redemption*. New York City, NY: Scribner. Movie adaptation: *Shawshank Redemption* (Castle Rock Entertainment, 1994).

King, S. (2017) *The Green Mile,* Illustrated edition New York Pocket Books. Movie adaptation: *The Green Mile* (Warner Bros. and Universal Pictures, 1999)

Chapter SEVEN

Prisoners' Rights

> *A prison that deprives prisoners of basic sustenance . . . is incompatible with the concept of human dignity and has no place in civilized society.*
>
> — Justice Anthony M. Kennedy, U.S. Supreme Court, *Brown v. Plata,* 2011

Chapter Objectives

- Introduce key passages and amendments in the U.S. Constitution, plus legislation that provides the guidepost for prisoners' rights.[1]
- Discuss advocacy groups, including the American Civil Liberties Union, and their roles in improving prison conditions.
- Provide a balanced view between the needs and wants of prisoners versus the concerns of the public and prison officials.
- List the current human and civil rights of the incarcerated in the United States.
- Provide a list of notable civil liberties and human rights cases involving prisoners.

Key Terms

First Amendment
Fourth Amendment
Eighth Amendment
Fourteenth Amendment
ACLU National Prison Project
American Civil Liberties
   Union (ACLU)
Apartheid (South Africa)
Estelle v. Gamble

Habeas privileges
Model Sentencing and Corrections
   Act (1978)
Nelson Mandela Rules (South Africa)
Prison Litigation Reform Act (PLRA),
   1996
Procunier v. Martinez (1974)
Pro bono
Pro se

---

[1] We will be revisiting these later in this textbook, where they apply.

"Publisher only" rule
Strip-search
Summary discipline

"Three strikes" rule, PLRA
Vitek v. Jones
Work-release programs

INTRODUCTION

In our opening quote from Justice Kennedy, we have, in a nutshell, the concerns of activists for the legal rights of prisoners, most importantly, for their human dignity. These are not necessarily popular opinions, as convicts, whether inside of prisons or out, are viewed by the general public and the uninformed as people who have lost all their legal rights the second they committed a crime. Statistics show that as many as 83 percent of ex-prisoners in communities will return to prison within three years of release, facing rejection when seeking work, with the common belief that they are dangerous and bad people, even if they have been convicted of nonviolent or victimless crimes (Kyprianides, 2019).

Though jail and prison facilities serve the same purpose of incarcerating either the accused or the convicted, they have to provide, in theory, distinctly different approaches to how they treat the people they house. The accused who are not yet convicted are, by United States law, considered innocent until proven guilty, regardless of appearances, including their detention behind bars pretrial. The reality is that with few exceptions, the detained are treated the same way as the convicted. If you consider that a jail can have convicts with shorter sentences serving time alongside those who are awaiting trial, the lines are understandably blurred.

Even detainees forfeit some, but not all of their Constitutional rights, once they have been arrested. Additionally, whether one is in jail or prison, an individual's rights will vary slightly depending on where they are incarcerated as well as whether or not they are in the pretrial stage. Detainees cannot be punished, nor can they be treated as guilty before they are convicted in a court of law (HG.org, n.d.). This is not to say that the jailed can't be disciplined if they misbehave. And they can certainly add to their current charges, if they commit another crime while in prison, as in the examples of assaulting a fellow detainee or convict, attacking prison staff.

In a dissenting opinion written by Justice William Rehnquist in *Bell v. Wolfish* (441 U.S. 50, 1979), he condemned the conditions and practices at the jail facility in New York City (Jacobs, 1980). In the case, the U.S. Supreme Court rejected a Court of Appeals case in which there was the demand for standardized review of jails, in order to investigate whether "pretrial detainees could be 'subjected to only those restrictions and privations'[2] which inhere in their confinement itself or which was justified by compelling necessity of jail administration.'" (Jacob, 1980, p. 430).

---

[2]Privations simply means that basic human needs are either lacking or in severe shortage. For example, in some prisons, inmates do not get adequate supplies of fruit and vegetables with their meals, which is a privation of the necessary nutrients for good health.

However, the majority opinion of the Supreme Court judges in that case was that jails only had to show that their practices are reasonably related to a legitimate government objective (Jacob, 1980, p. 430), which set a less restrictive standard for jails to be upheld. In laypersons' terms, it essentially was one more example of where the courts have decided to treat detainees and prisoners exactly the same, with the same shared prisoners' rights.

Nevertheless, no matter how the general public, or politicians for that matter, may feel about the accused or convicts, prisoners who are in the corrections system, those held in jail pending their trial, and those on probation or parole, have certain legal rights. Their rights are not all lost the moment they are arrested, though it may feel that way to the accused. Since the Civil Rights movement in the 1960s sparked discussions of legal rights in general, it would stand to reason that jail and prison reformers would also be pushing to do the same in corrections, though little progress has been made within that part of the criminal justice system.

For the better part of the first half of the 20th century, prisoners had virtually no rights, except to basic shelter and food, which themselves were of questionable quality, depending on the location, and the incarcerated had nearly no legal leg to stand on to protest or sue for any unfair treatment (Yanofski, 2010). As some have noted in historical research on prisons, including Yanofski (2010), from the 19th century through to mid-20th century, prisoners were treated no better than slaves to the state or federal government. In reality, any move in the direction of protecting prisoners' rights has only gained modest traction in recent decades and not immediately on the heels of the Civil Rights movement of the 1960s.

For all the progress we have seen in improving the lives of prisoners and safeguarding their rights, we have to also understand that law, even Constitutional law, can be ambiguous. This means that it is subject to interpretation, which can further be made inconsistent on the basis of the political whims in the courts. After all, judges are appointed or elected, and in some cases, though not always, may feel the need to be beholden to the wants and needs of the politicians and voters who put them on the bench.

Adults and children in correctional facilities are to be, again, in theory, treated differently. As we will see in our chapter on juvenile detention, the language used in the juvenile justice system is "softer," using words that are intended to decrease the stigma of conviction and sentencing to a juvenile facility. The best example of how the language is different is how we sentence adults to jail or prison, and we sentence juveniles, if appropriate, to juvenile "detention," camps, and group homes. The rights of adult prisoners and those of adjudicated juveniles are different as well. Except in the case of a juvenile tried as an adult and sentenced to an adult facility, juveniles are further restricted based on their status as minors. We will cover the rights of juveniles, both in and out of prison, in Chapter 9.

One important distinction between what prisoners are or are not entitled to is in their classification, based on the seriousness of their crime. A defense attorney can argue one type of facility over another, but ultimately, that is up to the full discretion of the judge and prison officials after conviction. For instance, a convict could hardly demand that they be placed in a minimum security facility, whether they have committed a white collar crime or a violent conventional crime, though they can request specific placement through their attorneys. It is not uncommon for a convicted individual to request being placed in a facility that is close to home, family, and friends so as to reduce some of the burden of their prison visits. It is also to the discretion of prison staff and administration to determine if a convict requires intensive supervision, solitary confinement, or protective custody, whether requested or not, no matter the wishes of the prisoner (*LII*, Cornell Law School, n.d.).

U.S. FEDERAL BUREAU OF PRISONS TITLE 28 PRISONERS' RIGHTS

It is understandable if there is some confusion as to exactly what rights prisoners are entitled to. There are the rights as they are spelled out in the Constitution, though vague as they may be as far as how they apply to prisoners. There are the rights that civil and human rights watch groups believe that prisoners are entitled to. However, perhaps the most important are the rights and responsibilities that the U.S. Bureau of Prisons lists in Title 28 CFR 541.12 (Mitchell, 2003, p. 248; Cripe, 1997, pp. 180-182):

- The right to expect that as a human being you will be treated respectfully, impartially, and fairly by all personnel.
- The right to be informed of the rules, procedures, and schedules concerning the operation of the institution.
- The right to freedom of religious affiliation and voluntary religious worship.
- The right to health care, which includes nutritious meals, proper bedding and clothing, a laundry schedule, an opportunity to shower regularly, proper ventilation for warmth and fresh air, regular exercise period, toilet articles, and necessary medical and dental treatment.
- The right to visit and correspond with family members and friends and correspond with members of the news media in keeping with department rules and institution guidelines.
- The right to legal counsel from an attorney of your choice.
- The right to participate in the use of law libraries and reference materials to assist in resolving legal problems.
- The right to reading materials for educational purposes and enjoyment.
- The right to participate in education, vocational training, and employment as far as resources are available.
- The right to use your momentary funds as one pleases, if in compliance with security and good order of the institution.

In addition to these rights, women are entitled to prenatal and postnatal care. However, this is not always under the best of conditions, even though the American

Bar Association (ABA) standards call for female prisoners be able to see obstetricians outside of the prison, whenever possible (Mitchell, 2003). States can draft their own lists of rights as well supplement the ones that are written by the U.S. Bureau of Prisons.

As we will see throughout this chapter, there are certain restrictions and conditions to nearly every one of these rights. For example, though prisoners may have a right to legal counsel, if they cannot afford an attorney, they will have to rely either on the kindness of lawyers who will take the case *pro bono* (free of charge) or rely on a public defender that they may not even see until the day of their trial.

AMERICAN BAR ASSOCIATION'S STANDARDS ON TREATMENT OF PRISONERS

The American Bar Association (ABA), the professional organization for attorneys, provides further guidance on the treatment and rights of prisoners, as we saw above with respect to the rights of pregnant women in prison. In addition to the Title 28 provisions by the U.S. Bureau of Prisons, the ABA also recommends the following general principles, summarized here (Standard 13-1.1, ABA, 2011)[3]:

- A correctional facility should be safe and orderly.
- Imprisonment should prepare prisoners for life after release, including reintegration into free society.
- A correctional facility should protect prisoners from harm from other prisoners and staff.
- Correctional staff should respect the human rights and dignity of prisoners.
- For the convicted prisoner, loss of liberty and separation from society should be sole punishment.
- A correctional facility should be adequately staffed.
- Correctional officials should conduct internal assessments and inspections in order to improve the facility.
- Correctional facilities should be monitored and inspected by independent government entities.
- A lack of resources should not be an excuse for lack of treatment or conditions that violate a prisoner's constitutional rights. The government should provide sufficient resources.
- Private providers (e.g., medical services) should comply with these standards and ensure compliance.

---

[3] Commentary originally published in *ABA Standard for Criminal Justice: Treatment of Prisoners*, Third Edition circa 2011, American Bar Association.

What the ABA would like to see in prisons and what the U.S. Bureau of Prisons and state departments of correction can provide may be in conflict with one another. It is not uncommon for programs to be cut when there is a state budget crisis or when overcrowding makes resources scarcer. And we always have to consider, as we note throughout this chapter, that many of these conditions can be subjectively interpreted.

THE PRISONER HUMAN RIGHTS MOVEMENT

The first wave of the Prisoner Human Rights movements began in the 1960s and, as we noted in the introduction, did not gain traction until more recently. Any movement in the direction of reform stagnated between 1975 and the 1990s, during a period when the "get tough on crime" and "war on drugs" stances drowned out the voices of activists.

The Prisoner Human Rights Movement is not unique to the United States. Other countries, particularly those in the West, have worked to make prison conditions more humane, as well as getting prisoners access to what they need, including, as an example, up to date law materials to help them with their defense or appeals. This is intended to prevent, in the case of the United States, a violation of a number of the amendments to the Constitution that are discussed in this chapter, and to provide the most humane treatment possible under conditions of being punished.

The National Prison Project

The *American Civil Liberties Union* (ACLU) is one of the primary forces behind fighting for both civil liberties and human rights for prisoners. Spearheading the *ACLU National Prison Project*, the ACLU's mission is to assure that jails and prisons comply with the Constitution, domestic law, and international human rights recommendations, with a focus on the health, safety, and human dignity of prisoners (ACLU, n.d.). The key goals of the National Prison Project are as follows (ACLU, n.d., retrieved from https://www.aclu.org/other/aclu-national-prison-project):

- Substantially reducing the incarcerated population, especially among people of color, people with mental disabilities, and other vulnerable populations.
- Increasing public accountability and transparency of jails, prison, and other places of detention.
- Ending cruel, inhuman, and degrading conditions of confinement.
- Expanding prisoners' freedom of religion, expression, and association.

The inconsistency pointed out and the argument that detractors make is that the ACLU advocates and litigates on a principle that the incarcerated should be afforded the same human rights as free people, but that is a near impossibility, as many of the civil liberties they are demanding are difficult to extend to people who have broken the law. For example, at the end of this chapter, in our Stories from Behind Bars, the discussion will be about marriage between inmates. Unless someone on the outside is underage and needs to have permission from their parents or guardian to get married before the age of 18, adults are free to marry without permission beyond a marriage license from the state, as long as they are not currently legally married, in which case they would be committing the crime of bigamy. Prisoners, on the other hand, in most cases, have to seek permission from prison officials in order to marry other inmates or even marry someone who is not incarcerated. In this way, the prison administration very much acts like a parent or guardian to detainees and prisoners.

THE UNITED STATES CONSTITUTION, AMENDMENTS, AND LAWS THAT PROTECT THE RIGHTS OF PRISONERS

From the inception of the United States, rights were intentionally written into the Constitution in hopes that the citizens of the newly formed nation would enjoy more freedoms than previously experienced as subjects of the British Crown. However, these rights were intended in the beginning and well into the 1960s, to provide protections primarily to white males with property and those from the upper echelon of society. Women could not own property in their own name until 1889, and were not even allowed to apply for credit without a male cosigner until the 1980s in America.

Likewise, Blacks did not gain citizenship until after the Civil War ended, even if the Emancipation Proclamation in 1863 gave them their freedom from slavery, at least in Northern states. It is only in recent decades that there has been a concerted and successful push to have at least some of the Constitutional rights of people living outside of prison extended to those who are behind bars.

Basic Human Rights in the United States

The basis of basic human rights in the United States lies in the language of the Constitution. However, there are times when that language is challenged or when it is not inclusive enough as it relates to the rights of prisoners. Women have often been at the forefront of efforts to make changes in prisons. For example, female prisoners in New York State Prison, Bedford Falls, organized a 1974 uprising protesting conditions in their prison, as well as spearheading litigation; their activist work is the foundation of the right of prisoners today to litigate their grievances (Baylor, 2018). However, some prisoners' rights activist groups have feared that any uproar made on behalf of women prisoners would drown out the voices of male prisoners, who make up the vast majority of the inmate population (Barry, 2000).

First Amendment

The *First Amendment* to the United States Constitution offers a broad range of rights related to the freedoms of expression. Of these, there are three freedoms that are most often argued by attorneys on behalf of prisoners: (1) free speech, (2) religious practices, and (3) ability to sue the government, if necessary, for unfair or cruel treatment:

Congress shall make no law respecting an establishment of religion, or prohibiting the free exercise thereof; or abridging the freedom of speech, or of the press; or the right of the people peaceably to assemble, and to petition [in this case, sue] the Government for redress of grievances. (First Amendment, U.S. Constitution)

Prisoners have freedom to express their religion, within reason. Rituals, ceremonies, or religious meetings cannot be disruptive to the operations of the prison. The U.S. Supreme Court maintained that religious rights are limited for prisoners, as prison officials are not required to provide exceptional accommodations on the basis of individuals' beliefs, if it is in conflict with the routine of the prison (*Harvard Law Review*, 2013).

Even the type and value of religious jewelry is restricted. According to Sestanovich (2015), the only two pieces of jewelry that inmates are allowed to wear in federal prisons are a wedding band and necklaces with religious medallions (e.g., crucifix or Star of David). However, there are some further restrictions including that the necklace be nonmetal, worn underneath clothing, and cost less than $100 because expensive jewelry can be used in illegal bartering. This is also for safety reasons, as depending on the design of the necklace pendant, it could be used as a weapon. Permitted jewelry can only be purchased from approved outside vendors (Sestanovich, 2015). So, the scenes in movies where a loved one passes over a religious necklace to an inmate under the nose of a corrections officer during visitation is inaccurately portrayed, unless it fits into the guidelines of what is permitted.

Freedom of speech is also restricted for prisoners, including access to media outlets and reporters. Mail can be read and censored, whether it is going in or coming

Religious Service in Prison. (*Source*: Johnson, n.d., Sagamore Institute, retrieved from https://sagamoreinstitute.org/jailhouse-religion-spiritual-transformation-and-long-term-change/)

out of jails or prisons. In some cases, it will be destroyed if has been found to contain narcotics, weapons, or escape plans (Mitchell, 2003). This isn't meant to be additional cruel punishment. In *Procunier v. Martinez* (1974), the courts determined that any prisoners' mail leaving a federal prison can be read if it poses a threat to prison security (Temko, 2013). As gang members, as well as other organized crime figures, have become increasingly clever with their prison correspondences, it is all the more imperative to scrutinize outgoing mail, as there can even be death threats and orders to assassinate rivals on the outside or behind prison walls. Letters can be encrypted, as noted in the following photo, so that prisoners may write prohibited information to people on the outside, including instructions about hiring hitmen and conducting illegal operations (e.g., drug sales) from prison.

Encrypted Letter from Gang Member in Prison to Friend on the Outside. (*Source*: Federal Bureau of Investigation, 2011, retrieved from https://www.fbi.gov/news/stories/breaking-codes-to-stop-crime-part-1.)

You should note that in our list of those rights that prisoners have fought for, the one that is purposely omitted is the freedom to peaceably assemble. For security reasons, except in cases such as religious services or group therapy sessions held with the permission and supervision of prison officials, prisoners are not allowed to meet on their own to protest or air grievances. This isn't to say it doesn't happen in the privacy of cells between cellmates or in exercise yards. However, any form of vocal protest, peaceful or not, is not sanctioned by prison officials.

From time to time we hear of hunger strikes as a form of protest. In the past, prison officials would resort to prisoners being fed through feeding tubes forced down their throats, as in the example of women suffragists who had been arrested during their protests for the right to vote and who refused to eat while incarcerated. Hunger strikes as a symbolic form of protest are argued to be protected by the First Amendment and any attempt to force-feed a prisoner may also be a violation of their right to refuse medical treatment (Kanaboshi, 2014). This creates a dilemma for prison staff. On the one hand, they are responsible for the physical well-being of those in their custody; on the other hand, they are faced with concerns of over-stepping boundaries and violating prisoners' protected civil and Constitutional rights. In most prisons, hunger strikes are largely ignored, but during detention at Guantánamo Bay prison camp, one detainee reported the following experience when he refused to eat (Hodgson, 2014, p. 8):

> *I was sick in the prison hospital and refused to be fed, a squad of eight military police officers in riot gear burst in. They tied my hands and feet to the bed. They forcibly inserted an IV into my hand. I spent 26 hours in this state. Later, they began feeding me by nasal catheter. . . . I hope that the politicians will understand that this is not about food. I cannot stand being here any further, so I am sacrificing myself.*

Fourth Amendment

Like other laws that protect prisoners' rights, the *Fourth Amendment* is somewhat ambiguous. We ordinarily think of ambiguity in laws affecting business and commerce as being purposefully ambiguous, allowing for wiggle room in interpretation; we don't ordinarily see this with the rights of everyday people. Laws that rule our everyday lives are pretty clear cut. However, the Fourth Amendment language does not consider the types of searches that correctional staff are required to do for the safety and well-being of both staff and prisoners, not to mention preventing rule-breaking by prisoners.

The Fourth Amendment, passed by Congress in September 1789, ratified in December 1791, reads as follows:

> *The right of the people to be secure in their persons, houses, papers, and effects,* ***against unreasonable searches and seizures***, *shall not be violated, and no Warrants shall be issued without probable cause, supported by Oath or affir-mation, and particularly describing the place to be searched, and the persons or things to be seized.* (Fourth Amendment, U.S. Constitution)

Where the controversy and ambiguity lie is in the fact that prisoners can have contraband on their bodies and in their jail or prison cells. Hence the strip-searches along with routine cell inspections. A *strip-search* can be a limited inspection of a person's body visually up to the much more invasive inspection of body cavities (i.e., genital and rectal areas) (Babbar, 2021). This, unfortunately for prisoners, is humiliating but necessary. There are untold numbers of stories in corrections of strange things hidden on the bodies of detainees and prisoners, including drugs and weapons. One correctional officer at Suffolk County Sheriff's Department in Boston reported that one prostitute who was regularly detained at the jail inevitably was found with food products in their packaging during body searches, secured under the folds of skin on her ample body.

The concerns are about illegal strip-searches, particularly those conducted on women and underage children. Other concerns are about non-private searches, conducted in front of other detainees and prisoners. Females report feeling more traumatized by the searches than males, especially if they are menstruating or lactating[4], describing the experience as a form of forced "self-rape" (Babbar, 2021). Transgender individuals are also traumatized, because they are forced to reveal their genitals which, unless they have had sex reassignment surgery, are in conflict with their identities (Babbar, 2021). And studies have indicated that strip-searches with body cavity inspections to be equally traumatizing, whether the offender is in jail for the first time or has been in prison for a number of years (Babbar, 2021).

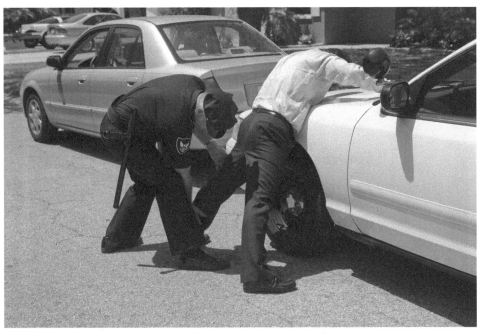

Police Pat Down. (*Source*: Albert Cobarrubias Justice Project, 2012) retrieved from https://www.istockphoto.com/photo/police-pat-down-gm117163895-6688338)

Even visitors to jails and prisons have been illegally subjected to strip-searches and pat downs. When Jeannette Reynoso visited her husband at Rikers Island jail complex in 2015, she had anticipated the metal detectors as well as having to wait hours to see him, but she had never expected to be made to stand naked in front of two corrections officers as they inspected her body cavities for smuggled contraband

---

[4]Lactating is the process of producing breast milk just prior to and after giving birth, subject to leaking onto clothing.

(Ransom, 2018). She had consented to a pat down frisk, that only requires removing outerwear, but was also ordered to remove all her clothing (Ransom, 2018). Strip-searches, along with body cavity searches of visitors to state and federal jails or prisons, are prohibited. Reynoso eventually sued the city over the humiliating incident. In this book, we discuss how punishment extends beyond the accused to family and friends. This is but one example of how this happens.

The bottom line is that Constitutional scholars, including some judges on the United States Supreme Court, have agreed that invasive strip-searches that include body cavity inspections violate the Fourth Amendment, as well as legal commitments to preserving the dignity of prisoners. However, in a recent decision by the United States Supreme Court, the majority ruling stated that correctional institutions can conduct routine strip-searches of all detainees and prisoners, even if they are being stopped for or incarcerated for minor offenses, and that such a search does not violate the Fourth Amendment (Garvey, 2012; Albert Cobarrubias Justice Project, 2012).

The difficulty is in the fact that detainees and prisoners can and will hide contraband on their bodies, making the invasive searches necessary, unfortunately, for detainees and prisoners. It is critical in maintaining the safety of those who either live or work behind prison walls, as the types of things that are hidden on prisoners' bodies can be lethal, including makeshift weapons. However, the practice of strip-searches will no doubt continue to be the subject of litigation now and in the future, in spite of any U.S. Supreme Court ruling.

Fifth Amendment

Most of what we read in the Fifth Amendment of the U.S. Constitution pertains to charges and trial procedures. However, the due process clause has a direct impact on detainees as they await trial, as well as on prisoners:

> *[shall not] be deprived of life, liberty, or property, without due process of law* (Fifth Amendment, U.S. Constitution)

There is considerable confusion around how the Fifth Amendment protects people once they are incarcerated. In *Bell v. Wolfish*, the U.S. Supreme Court, for the first time, specifically ruled on what rights under the Constitutions that detainees give up before their trial (Supreme Court Review, 1979). There were a number of practices commonly followed in the New York City short-term facility, Metropolitan Correction Center (MCC), that restricted detainees' right to liberty and were struck down in the case. Among these were the following (*Bell V. Wolfish*, 441 U.S. 520, Justia, 1979, retrieved from https://supreme.justia.com/cases/federal/us/441/520/), deemed by the U.S. Supreme Court to not violate the due process clause of the Fifth Amendment:

- "Double-bunking" where there is detainee overcrowding.
- Punishment of detainees who misbehave in jail pretrial, which was argued to contradict the presumption of innocence.

- Body cavity searches on detainees after they have had visitors.
- Requiring detainees to give up their privacy interests while in jail is necessary.
- Corrections staff are allowed to do what is necessary to assure that the smooth day-to-day operations, including requiring the detainee to stand outside their cells while an inspection is underway. Cell searches are necessary for the safety of facility.
- *"Publisher only" rule* (requirement that both detainees and prisoners only receive publications from the outside directly from the publisher) does not violate the First Amendment rights of the MCC inmates.
- Restriction against the receipt of packages from outside the prison, as they are handy devices for smuggling of contraband (e.g., weapons, drugs).

None of the restrictions in the *Bell v. Wolfish* case were viewed as "punishment," but rather as necessary to assure the safety and well-being of detainees, inmates, and prison staff.

Though disciplinary proceedings are not part of criminal proceedings, there is a form of due process by which a prisoner is punished for bad behavior or breaking rules while in prison. Because the awarding and forfeiture of good-time credit towards release is subject to the behavior of prisoners, they have the right to a fair and measured hearing on why they are being disciplined with the loss of credit (Legal Information Institute, n.d.).

Eighth Amendment

Again, like the Fifth Amendment, pretrial rights are included. However, much of what is contained in the *Eighth Amendment* applies to the convicted:

> Excessive bail shall not be required, nor excessive fines, imposed, nor cruel and unusual punishment inflicted. (Eighth Amendment, U.S. Constitution)

Much of what we see in Eighth Amendment challenges related to prisoners' rights are centered on medical care. With the rising cost of medical care in the United States, in the debate of whether to implement a single payer medical insurance program, supporters argue that prisoners get health care paid for, while the ordinary citizen does not (Paris, 2008). This is inaccurate, in that prisoners are still required to pay the equivalent to a managed health care plan copay. The Eighth Amendment guarantees that prisoners will receive the minimum of care, or prison administrators, the state, or the federal government run the risk of facing civil liability. In particular, withholding of medical care is interpreted as cruel and unusual punishment.

One case in point is in the death of Joseph Jones, who died while in custody, after he had first been hospitalized for an asthma attack, released with special treatment instructions, which the prison staff failed to properly follow for his condition after he was admitted to the prison infirmary (Marder-Spiro, 2020). After Jones's death, his mother filed a lawsuit against the prison, arguing that his Eighth

Amendment rights were violated (Marder-Spiro, 2020) on the basis that it was the responsibility of prison staff to assure that he was receiving adequate medical care.

As the Eighth Amendment is often also applied to discussions of the death penalty, we will save more in depth discussion of amendment again in Chapter 13. We will also cover the Eighth Amendment further as it applies to other health issues of prisoners, in Chapter 11.

Eighth Amendment and Medical Research on Prisoners

One thing that students of corrections may not be aware of as yet from other courses, is that prisoners are a protected population when it comes to studies using them as research subjects, even for something as innocuous as a survey. Prisoners who are used in research are part of the list of special populations that include children, those who have diminished mental capacity, and anyone who is institutionalized (e.g., in a hospital or nursing home), including detainees and prisoners. This means that extra care is taken to make sure that they are not involved in research against their will and without their permission.

On the other hand, this does not mean that prisoners have free access to volunteering in clinical trials of new medications or medical procedures. Which, some have argued, violates the Eighth Amendment right to adequate medical care while incarcerated. In *Estelle v. Gamble* (1976), the Supreme Court acknowledged that as detainees and prisoners cannot medically care for themselves, it is a public duty that they be cared for while they are incarcerated (Lee, 2012). For example, if you or I were to feel under the weather or suspected that we were suffering from a serious condition, we would simply either call our personal doctor for advice, run down to the local pharmacy to pick up over the counter medications, or fill a prescription for our symptoms. Prisoners cannot as easily seek out medical care.

Detainees and prisoners also do not have freedom to seek out medical treatment or advice from any medical personnel of their choosing—they are limited to who they have access to in the jail or prison infirmary. The Supreme Court also argued in *Estelle v. Gamble* that prisoners do not have the right to automatically obtain access to clinical trials, even when they are made available (Lee, 2012), whether it would benefit them or not in the long run. This stands to reason when you consider that even individuals outside of prison cannot readily have access to clinical trials and may have to join a long list of people seeking experimental treatment. Detainees and prisoners are allowed to participate in clinical trials if the researchers specifically seek them out as subjects for their studies and with the permission of prison administrators.

Fourteenth Amendment

There is a lot to unpack in the *Fourteenth Amendment* of the U.S. Constitution, as it applies to detainees and prisoners, and it is sometimes a source of legal confusion:

No State shall make or enforce any law which shall abridge the privileges or immunities of citizens of the United States; nor shall any State deprive any person of life, liberty, or property, without due process of law; nor deny to any person within its jurisdiction the equal protection of the laws. (Fourteen Amendment, U.S. Constitution, Section 1)

Of first concern is that there can be a disconnect between federal rights and states' rights. In theory, federal rights supersede states' rights. But we see a number of places where they are in conflict. For example, increasingly states are legalizing recreational marijuana use, yet it still remains a serious criminal offense on the federal level.

Conversely, where we might be given provisional rights at the federal level, we may have more restrictions at the state level. Where this applies to prisoners, under the Fourteenth Amendment, is that they are entitled to *habeas privileges,* meaning they can make challenges at the federal level, sometimes ultimately through the Supreme Court, about the lawfulness of their captivity or treatment in a state facility, when they cannot seek recourse through their state's court system (Kovarsky, 2014).

Along the same lines, the due process clause of the amendment safeguards prisoners from being involuntarily transferred to a psychiatric hospital without notice or a hearing, as argued in the Supreme Court (and won) in *Vitek v. Jones* (1980) (Knochel, 1980). Convicts also cannot be held indefinitely in a psychiatric hospital without civil commitment proceedings promptly commencing (*Vitek v. Jones*, §83-180, 1980).

Under the Fourteenth Amendment, prisoners also have the right to refuse medical treatment, within limitations. People in hospitals may have to be given a sedative or antipsychotic drug against their will, under circumstances where they may harm themselves or others. Prisoners may likewise be medically treated for psychiatric illnesses without their permission. For example, in *Washington v. Harper* (1990), the U.S. Supreme Court found that inmates can be given antipsychotic drugs against their will, but ideally, after a judicial hearing, under the procedural protections of the due process clause (Sindel, 1991).

The Model Sentencing and Corrections Act of 1978

The equal protection clause in the Fourteenth Amendment also applies to prisoners, against whom discrimination on the basis of race, religion, sex, or national origin is prohibited. This was reinforced in the *Model Sentencing and Corrections Act of 1978,* along with fortifying other constitutional rights of prisoners.

There are a number of provisions in the act that addresses some limitations to protections for prisoners, when it is in the best interest of others or the prison, briefly summarized here (Article 4, Part 1, Section 104, Model Sentencing and Corrections Act, U.S. Department of Justice, 1979[5]):

---

[5] The Model Sentencing and Corrections Act (1978) in its entirety can be found at https://www.ojp.gov/pdffiles1/Digitization/55600NCJRS.pdf.

- A warden can limit freedoms of prisoners in the event of an emergency in a facility (e.g., rioting, general unrest).
- In the event of an emergency that requires restriction of prisoners' freedoms, the warden has to provide a written report to their governor, including what measures were taken to get the facility back under control of prison staff.
- A warden has the power to classify material as being prohibited (e.g., drugs, pornography).
- A warden and their employees may use limited force in the event that they believe it is in the best interest of safety or security.

Americans with Disabilities Act of 1990 (ADA)

The Americans with Disabilities Act (ADA) has had a profound impact on infrastructures everywhere, including on jail and prison facilities. Title III of the ADA requires that there must be reasonable accommodations to meet the needs of disabled detainees or prisoners held in state or federal facilities (Greifinger, 2006). However, "reasonable accommodations" can be subjectively interpreted, considering that primary functions of jails and prisons is safety and security. ADA accommodations go beyond physical access to cells and other spaces in the facility. It also requires that jails and prisons provide medical equipment, like wheelchairs, and offer adequate medical and psychiatric programs for those in need.

Not all who are jailed or in prison come to the facilities in good health. In fact, a good portion arrive with a number of mental and medical ailments, much of which is discussed in Chapter 11. Coupled with an aging prison population on the heels of the "war on drugs" and longer sentences, it stands to reason that the normal disabilities one experiences as one ages, including decreased mobility, would affect older inmates. Of course, age is relative to how one feels, but there is enough evidence that the experience of being in prison prematurely ages people. If we look specifically at former prisoners of war or concentration camp survivors, there are higher instances of chronic illness as they age (*Jablònski*, et al., 2015; *Creasey*, et al., 1999), including cardiovascular changes and skeletal dysfunctions, which worsen by the length of stay.

In addition to normal or accelerated aging processes affecting detainees and prisoners, since the HIV/AIDS epidemic took hold in mid-1980s and COVID-19 pandemic in 2020, increasingly communicable, including sexually transmitted diseases, have been argued to be conditions that should fall under the umbrella of the ADA. Dalrymple-Blackburn (1995) noted that those who are HIV-positive (and assumedly, for those who test positive for COVID-19 or other communicable diseases) who are anywhere in jail, prison, probation, or parole have to be treated within the criminal justice system.

The ADA also applies to those released from prison and on parole. In *Crowell v. Massachusetts Parole Board* (2017), the Massachusetts Supreme Judicial Court determined that adequate post-incarceration treatment options designed to reduce recidivism are required for those who are on parole and mentally disabled, whether that disability was in advance of incarceration or a result of it (Massachusetts Supreme Judicial Court, 2018).

PRISON GRIEVANCES PROCEDURES

Prisoners have the right to complain about the conditions that they are living under. Prison officials prefer to keep the problems within prison walls and handle them administratively, rather than through civil courts. However, there are times when the conditions in prison, whether real or perceived as being intolerable, result in civil lawsuits.

Though we would think that reforming the avenues for airing prisoner grievances from within jail and prison walls would benefit the incarcerated, critics state that it has done the opposite. Because prison officials will argue that there are grievances procedures in place that are deemed fair, it has further limited the abilities of prisoners to exercise their First Amendment rights to free speech in order to effect social change, where they can individually or jointly bring their complaints to the public or to the courts (Hughett, 2019).

Prison Litigation Reform Act (PLRA)

For the better part of the 1970s and 1980s, on the heels of the Civil Rights movement, the courts were inundated with cases filed by prisoners. Inmates would challenge every aspect of prison life, including programs and practices, creating, as Jacobs (1980, p. 429) termed it, "a battlefield where prisoners and prison administrators, led by their respective legal champions, engaged in mortal combat." As we moved into the more politically conservative 1980s and 1990s, there were efforts by legislatures and U.S. Congress to curb the number of civil rights cases filed by inmates, resulting in the passing of the *Prison Litigation Reform Act (PLRA)* in 1996.

After a flurry of cases that were deemed to be a meaningless waste of the courts' time, the Prison Litigation Reform Act (PLRA) of 1996 began to curtail prisoner litigation, as courts were tired of frivolous lawsuits against prison officials. Ordinarily if the court believes that the lawsuit is nothing but a nuisance, with no legal merit, the person filing the claim can be penalized and even fined for a frivolous or malicious law suit, whether they are prisoners or ordinary citizens. Though the ability for prisoners to file any number of lawsuits is dependent on individual state rights, for prisoners held in state facilities. For instance, Connecticut historically has not had specific rules on the type or number of lawsuits that a prisoner can file (Reinhart, 2003).

The PLRA severely limited the ability of poor people to sue in cases of mistreatment or grievances while incarcerated. One of the key provisions of the act was to prohibit indigent[6] inmates who have already filed three seemingly frivolous lawsuits from ever doing so again, in the *"three strikes" rule*[7] (Reilly, 2021). It is less clear as to the ability of prisoners with financial means to do so, can continue to file lawsuits, whether interpreted as frivolous or not. Judges may be prone to subjective interpretation of the law where what might be labeled frivolous in one court, may not be labeled the same in another. The "three strikes" rule has greatly reduced the number of inmate lawsuits, at least in federal courts, but has also resulted in conflicting interpretations (Reilly, 2021). Prisoners, with or without the means to pursue a civil lawsuit, are also required by the PLRA to report their grievances to prison officials before they can file a lawsuit, which in turn prisoners fear there might be retaliation, further inhibiting them from airing their complaints through prison channels (Tempko, 2013).

Access to the Courts

Prisoners, for all the restrictions that the PLRA places on their ability to sue in civil court, do have some rights to file civil lawsuits. They also have the right to have access to whatever legal materials they need, as well as legal representation, whether for their criminal or civil cases. In *ex parte Hull*, U.S. Supreme Court case 312 U.S. 546 (1941) and in *White v. Ragen,* (case 324 U.S. 760), the Court ruled that prisoners must have access to law libraries and lawyers and other people trained in the law (Legal Information Institute, n.d.).

Prisoners who do have cases where they can afford to pay the court costs or whose lives are in eminent danger, are not limited on the number of cases they file, even if some are later deemed frivolous (Reilly, 2021). However, that does not guarantee that the prisoner who can afford an attorney will necessarily get the best representation in either their criminal or civil cases. As Umphres (2019) notes, the restrictions that the PLRA places on the fees that attorneys can collect for their services to a client who is a prisoner deters many lawyers from taking these cases.

Most prisoners will file their claims *pro se*, meaning that they will represent themselves in court. This puts them at a distinct disadvantage and clogs up the courts, even in cases with merit (Umphres, 2019). Prisoners who represent themselves have to be self-taught and with their general ignorance of court proceedings, it slows down the process as the courts often have to educate them on proper courtroom etiquette and protocol in the middle of trials. There are on occasion

---

[6] Someone who is indigent is poor and with no visible financial means. Example would be someone who is unhoused, living on the streets, not by choice, but due to poverty or jobless. Though we must note that many of these individuals are also suffering from drug or alcohol addiction and mental illness. Not all prisoners are technically living below the poverty line before incarceration, but many lose what little financial means they had in the first place due to legal fees and loss of income.

[7] The "three strikes" rule in the PLRA should not be confused with the "three strikes" laws in some states, where individuals who on their third felony offense will be sentenced to 25 years to life in prison (e.g., California, Washington states).

the proverbial "jailhouse lawyers," detainees or prisoners who can adeptly find their way around the law sources they have available. But there can also be fellow detainees or prisoners who are offering bad or inaccurate advice as well to those who file *pro se.*

We do have a number of illustrations of truly nonsensical and frivolous lawsuits brought by prisoners. For example, there was the case of Lawrence Bittaker, in San Quentin Prison, California, who sued over a lunch that he was served where the sandwich was soggy and his cookie was broken. There was also the case of Joseph Gonzalez in Sing Sing Prison, New York, who sued claiming that he was losing sleep and suffering from headaches and chest pains after being given what he thought was a bad haircut. These cases are often cited as illustrations for why there is a need for the PLRA (Raine, 2012). Yet another case was that of Kenneth Parker, an inmate in the Nevada State Prison, who sued over a mistake in his prison canteen order, where he received one jar creamy and one jar chunky peanut butter, instead of the two jars of chunky peanut butter that he had ordered (Raine, 2012). Their basis for the lawsuits? They claimed that their civil rights had been violated.

Most prisoner rights cases are currently filed by civil rights groups or advocacy groups and organizations (Schlanger, 2016). However, even prisoners who have access to or the support of civil rights groups may be reluctant to file a lawsuit, regardless of how legitimate their complaints may be because they fear being penalized or targeted by prison staff for retaliation (Raine, 2012).

Access to Computers and the Internet

One running theme in punishment of the convicted and certainly of those condemned to death is that from the time of arrest to incarceration, and in the case of death penalty recipient or those sentenced to prison without possibility of parole, prisoners lose nearly every right to freely communicate with people on the outside. Even their contact with a select few, including other inmates, spouses, family members, and friends is censored, during visitation and in any written communication. Inmates are severely restricted from exchanging information and getting in touch with people that the rest of us have taken for granted for the past several decades, including through computers and smart phones (Jewkes and Johnston, 2009). To a large extent, their least restricted communication is with their attorneys.

Just imagine what it would have been like to be a convict sentenced to 25 years in prison in 1975. The changes in technology between the time that convict entered prison and their release have been substantial. Not only are computers commonplace, but you would be hard pressed to find a pay phone anywhere since 2000. Prisoners who are incarcerated for a long period of time are at a distinct disadvantage if not allowed to keep up with these exponentially fast technological changes. As Jewkes and Johnston (2009, p. 132) describe by the title of their article, prisoners become "cavemen in an era of speed-of-light technology" once they are incarcerated.

Since the rise of the Computer Age in the last quarter of the 20th century, the gap between prisoners and those on the outside grew even wider. As more and more resources are digitalized, including law documents, computer illiteracy further inhibits prisoners on the inside and more importantly, on the outside once released, as they seek employment. There are few occupations today that do not use some form of computer technology. Teaching inmates computer technology, even the basics, is imperative. The fact that distance learning is conducted entirely on the Internet is yet another reason why knowing computer basics is critical to those who are incarcerated, as more and more education options are offered online.

Having unrestricted free access to all that is available on the Internet is an entirely different issue and controversy. Before we discuss what access to the Internet that detainees and inmates, we need a basic understanding of the different realms of the World Wide Web and beyond. There are three primary locations where content can be posted, stored, accessed, etc.

Put in simple terms, the **surface web**[8] is open to everyone with access to the Internet, as in the example of major news organization (e.g., CNN); the **dark web** includes websites that require passwords, like in the example of your email (Hansen, 2020). The dark web is where hacking crimes often occur, as in the example of someone accessing your personal bank account.

It is the **deep web** that we are most concerned about when it comes to cybercrimes, including potentially committed by prisoners, which while it requires specialized software and apps in order to access websites there, it is the place where criminal enterprises can be plotting their next crimes (Hansen, 2020). We have to remind ourselves that some prisoners are incarcerated because of the cybercrimes they have committed, making them a special security risk when they have access to the Internet.

A prisoner does not have to be sophisticated in computer skills to offend from behind bars, using a computer as their weapon. If given full access to the Internet, including email and social network websites (e.g., Facebook™), they can either stalk their victims, perspective jurors, past jurors, or any number of possible targets, including prosecutors and defense attorneys, with the potential of threatening them from behind bars. As reported by the Secure World news team (2018), there have been a few cases where prisoners have managed to hack computers and commit identity theft. The main concern for detainees and prisoners having access to the Internet, besides all the questionable content published there, including sites that promote violence and other crimes, is that if they are indeed computer savvy, prisoners can have the opportunity to reoffend from behind prison walls, committing cybercrimes, like fraud or hacking, either within the dark or deep webs.

Even those on probation or on parole, as a condition of their release, may be limited in their access to computers and the Internet, depending on their conviction. In the case of Paul Thielemann, convicted for receiving online child pornography, as part

---

[8] In bold here as these are terms that do not refer directly to the subject of corrections and are provided here for informational purposes only.

of his condition of a ten-year term of supervised release, was prohibited from owning or operating a personal computer with Internet access (Gillett, 2010). Such restrictions are argued to be a violation of First Amendment rights to free speech. And again, this can limit the number of job opportunities that someone like Thielemann might have.

The invention of the tablet (e.g., Apple's iPad™) has dramatically changed the lives of prisoners. Easily configured so as to allow inmates to exchange emails with people on approved lists, while still blocking Internet use, it has allowed prisoners to have more access to the outside world, as in the example of Marvin Worthy who was able to stay in contact with his son this way, keeping their relationship intact (Kruzman, 2018). However, while some states provide the tablets for free, as in the examples of Colorado, New York, and Virginia, others charge for services, including for use of emails, video calls, and downloads of various entertainment media, creating yet another gap between the prisoners with and those without means (Kruzman, 2018).

RIGHTS OF NONCITIZEN DETAINEES AND PRISONERS IN U.S. JAILS AND PRISONS

Noncitizens who find themselves in U.S. jails or prisons do not have the same rights as those who are convicted and are U.S. citizens. Most notably, a citizen in the United States who has been detained, convicted, or, sentenced to prison can be released either on pretrial bond, probation, parole, or after they have finished out their complete sentence from behind bars. Noncitizens, regardless of their visa status, can be detained beyond the terms of their sentence and are not generally released on bond pretrial, or as they additionally await deportation hearings and likely deportation out of the United States to their country of origin.

The status of detainees and prisoners who are not citizens has been a topic of controversial debates primarily since the 9/11 terrorist attacks in New York City and Washington, D.C. The administration of President George W. Bush moved to charge people, many of whom were not American citizens, as "enemy combatants." While those who are awaiting trial in jail for conventional or white collar crimes will sooner or later have a definitive court date for their trial, those detained on terrorist charges can be detained indefinitely with no trial or hearing set, as in the case of the detainees in Guantánamo Bay prison camp in Cuba.

When trials were set for the alleged 9/11 terrorists housed at Guantánamo Bay, it had been nearly 10 years since the attacks on New York and Washington, D.C. Delays pushed back trial dates to August 2021 (Pfeiffer, 2020), and then the pandemic pushed the dates back again. Pretrial negotiations are still ongoing with prosecutors and as of this writing, court date in most of the remaining trials are still waiting to be set. Of the roughly 780 original detainees, 38 remain, with 10 of the cases scheduled for trial and two convicted (*The New York Times*, 2022). There are recommendations that in 19 of the cases, the detainees should be deported, rather than stand trial (*The New York Times*, 2022). Some, but not all, of the delay was due to the backlog of court cases in the face of the COVID-19 pandemic. It is nearly unheard of for anyone to be detained for so long a time for ordinary crimes, as the average processing time from arrest to felony conviction in non-terrorist cases has historically been around six months (Levin, et al., 2000), before the pandemic.

Foreign detainees in the United States do have protection under the Fourteenth Amendment against cruel and unusual punishment. Humanitarian organizations have claimed that conditions in the past few years in detention centers at the southern borders of the United States for those attempting to enter the country there have violated the Constitution. Judge David Bury, a federal judge in Arizona, agreed, ruling in February 2020 that the conditions in detention cells at the border holding both children and adults, "have been 'substantially worse than detainees face upon commitment to either a [typical] civil immigration detention facility or even a criminal detention facility, like a jail or prison.' " (Da Silva, 2020, retrieved from https://www.newsweek.com/judge-says-conditons-us-border-holding-cellsviolated-consituion-monumental-ruling-1488281.

Others have argued that families that have crossed the borders and have had their children separated from them have been dealt with in an unusually cruel way.

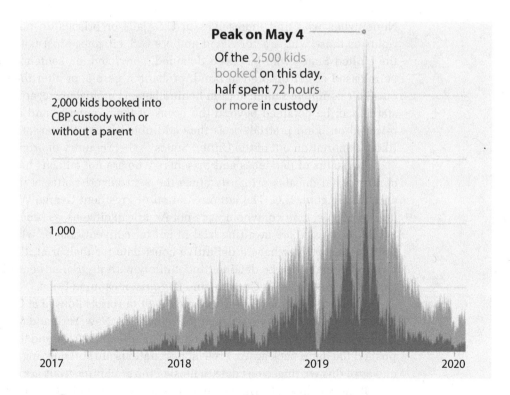

FIGURE 7.1 | **Number of Unaccompanied Minors Booked into U.S. Customs and Border Protection Custody**
(*Source*: Flagg and Calderon, 2020, retrieved from https://www.themarshallproject.org/2020/10/30/500-000-kids-30-million-hours-trump-s-vast-expansion-of-child-detention.)

In 2014, the border patrol detained approximately 40,000 children; by 2019, that number had skyrocketed to nearly 250,000 (Flagg and Calderón, 2020). In a number of cases, the children have been lost in the system and have yet to be reunited with their parents, some of whom have already been deported. This too has been argued to be unconstitutional, with women and children sometimes held in frigid conditions with inadequate sanitation (Human Rights Watch, 2018). An alarming trend is the number of unaccompanied minors crossing the border, who, if caught, will also be detained. (See Figure 7.1)

There is no easy solution in solving the problem of illegal immigration. There are likewise few solutions for how to house so many who cross over the border illegally and are caught, without violating Constitutional rights that protect noncitizens.

OTHER NOTABLE PRISONERS' RIGHTS CASES

We cannot, for obvious reasons, cover every law case involving the treatment or rights of prisoners. However, we have chosen a few notable, groundbreaking, or interesting cases to include in this book. They are presented here in chronological order so the reader can follow the timeline of progress, or in some cases, regression of prisoners' rights laws.

Robinson v. California (1962)

Certainly not the first case heard on the question of drug use, the U.S. Supreme Court's decision in *Robinson v. California* helped pave the way to distinguishing between recreational drug use and addiction. In the early 1960s, there was a California statue making it a punishable misdemeanor offense to be addicted to narcotics, with the possibility of prison time, if convicted (Superior Court of California, *Robinson v. California*, 1962). We have to realize that at the time, we were just beginning to understand the mechanics of addiction. The complainant, Lawrence Robinson, had been convicted and sentenced to prison in California on the addiction statue, even though he had never used or possessed narcotics in the state and failed to have the conviction overturned on appeal (Superior Court of California, *Robinson v. California*, 1962; Oyez, n.d.).

In a 6-2 decision by the U.S. Supreme Court, Justice Potter Stewart wrote that it is unlawful and unconstitutional to convict a person who is addicted to an illegal drug, as it was in violation of both the Eighth and Fourteenth Amendments (Oyez, n.d.). Justice Stewart likened it

> *to making it a criminal defense 'to be mentally ill, or a leper, or to be afflicted with a venereal disease . . . [and] argued that the state could not punish person merely because of their 'status' of addiction. The Court noted that the law was not aimed at the purchase, sale, or possession of illegal drugs.* (Oyez, n.d., retrieved from https://www.oyez.org/cases/1961/554)

After a period of even more punitive drug laws in most states, recently, due to overcrowding and continued research on drug addiction, plus public outcry, more states are now adopting a drug court framework focused on rehabilitation. States have also been moving to either decriminalize or legalize marijuana use, as well as making other adjustments to drug laws. Some states have even reclassified all drug possession from felonies to misdemeanors, except in the cases of intent to distribute illegal drugs (Elderbroom and Durnan, 2018).

Ruiz v. Estelle (1979)

In *Ruiz v. Estelle*, the state maximum security penitentiary in Texas, a complaint was filed that covered four areas of grievances, claiming that there were violations of the Eighth and Fourteenth Amendments (Justice, 1990) including: (1) brutality, (2) poor medical care, (3) overcrowding, and (4) *summary discipline* (arbitrary punishment without purpose). In addition to the questionable conditions highlighted, the case also made the argument that *work-release programs* (where the convicted work in the community during the day but need to return to prison after their shift), which at the time were only available to a limited number of inmates, were much more cost effective, as well as relieving overcrowding, at least for part of the time during the day (*Ruiz v. Estelle*, U.S. District Court, Southern District of Texas, Justia, 1980).

As we have noted, most prisoners who bring lawsuits to civil court have to represent themselves, unless they can find an attorney who will take the case *pro bono*, if the prisoner has the financial means to hire an attorney, or they can find an advocacy group that will champion their case. *Ruiz v. Estelle* not only brought to light the conditions in the Texas penitentiary, in the opinion of Judge Justice, prisoners (or anyone for that matter) who has to come before the court and represent themselves is at a distinct disadvantage, creating a number of procedural problems, resulting in further injustices (Justice, 1990).

At the time of the case, inmates held by Texas Department of Corrections had the following additional disadvantages[9] (*Ruiz v. Estelle*, U.S. District Court, Southern District of Texas, Justia, 1980):

- 41 percent were under the age of 25;
- The mean intelligence quotient (IQ) of inmates was 93.92, on the lower end of the average IQ in the United States;
- Upwards of 10-15 percent were developmentally disabled;
- 85 percent were high school dropouts, most of which had less than a seventh grade education; and
- 68 percent were mentally disturbed.

---

[9] We should note that this was according to expert witnesses in the case.

We can safely assume that this prevents prisoners, as Judge Justice argued, from mounting a substantial defense in their criminal cases, much less diminish their ability to represent themselves in civil cases.

The Civil Rights movement in the 1960s put the jail and prison systems under the microscope. According to Marquart and Crouch (1985), there was also a due process revolution with the courts expanding the constitutional rights of prisoners, essentially rejecting that prisoners are socially disposable, with little to no oversight on corrections officers' treatment of them. Increasingly with civil lawsuits, the judiciary stepped in and prisons became more bureaucratic in response (Marquart and Crouch, 1985), as a means of preventing more lawsuits that are in the long run costly to both finances and reputations. The final Supreme Court decision in the *Ruiz v. Estelle* case has been argued to be an important change agent in reform, with a broad condemnation of Texas jails and prisons (Marquart and Crouch, 1985). Following the case, it has often been cited in a number of civil rights lawsuits (Newman and Scott, 2012). Reportedly (Chase, 2021), in spite of the civil rights victory in *Ruiz v. Estelle*, some states, including Alabama, are increasingly overcrowded, understaffed, with higher than national averages in prison violence, including verified homicides.

Brown v. Plata (2011)

As we note throughout the course of this book, one of the running themes that contributes to the criticism of jail and prison conditions is overcrowding. Argued in front of the U.S. Supreme Court in 2010, decided in 2011, California prisons that were designed to hold under 80,000 inmates and had almost double that number incarcerated, with two thirds of inmates double to cells intended for one (Newman and Scott, 2012; *Brown v. Plata, Oyez*, 2011).

This was not the first case, as we see from our discussion of *Ruiz v. Estelle*, that challenged overcrowded conditions in prisons. What makes this case particularly interesting and somewhat unusual is that the primary complainant in the case was then Governor of California Jerry Brown who at the time was appealing the decision by a panel of judges to reduce the prison population in the state.

The Prison Litigation Reform Act (PLRA) includes provisions for how decisions are made to reduce prison populations. It is a two-pronged approach that calls for sentencing fewer people to prison and early release programs for the current prison populations. It is not simply a matter of the governor of a state to order a reduction in prison. It requires a three-judge panel to make the decision to do so (Newman and Scott, 2012).

Some of what was included in the final decision handed down by the U.S. Supreme Court in the case, in compliance with the provisions in the PLRA, were the following (Newman and Scott, 2012):

- California prisons were putting the safety of correctional staff and inmates at risk with severe overcrowding.

- Overcrowding impedes meeting the medical needs of prisoners and violates the Eighth Amendment.
- Overcrowding also contributes to greater risk for serious illness or injury, as well as indifferences to these on the part of corrections staff, again violating the Eighth Amendment.
- Upheld three-judge panel order to decrease the population of prisoners in California by approximately 46,000. Note, this would still mean that the prison population would be 137.5 percent of capacity.
- There were inadequate medical personnel, including physicians and psychiatrists.

Dockery v. Hall (2019)

In a number of places in this book, we discuss the controversy surrounding private prisons. Case in point: the scathing reports submitted by the ACLU, and a number of other civil rights organizations that claimed that East Mississippi Correctional Facility (EMCF), a private prison in Mississippi operated by Management and Training Corporation, was a violent, dangerous, unsanitary place with inadequate medical or psychiatric care for those with chronic mental disabilities (ACLU, 2017). EMCF is intended for the treatment and housing of severely mentally ill prisoners (*Dockery v. Hall,* 2018). The Mississippi Department of Corrections countered this with their own report from their experts that contradicted the civil rights violation claims made by ACLU and others (ACLU, 2017).

ACLU March for Prisoners' Rights. (*Source*: ACLU, 2017, retrieved from https://www.aclu.org/cases/prisoners-rights/dockery-v-hall.)

The complaints of inmates at EMCF, beginning with the first civil lawsuits in 2013, included the following (*Dockery v. Hall*, 2018, pp. 4-5):

- Inadequate medical care, including dental, presented a substantial risk of serious harm and injury.
- Solitary confinement in EMCF presented a substantial risk of harm and injury due to inadequate exercise and nutrition, unsafe environmental conditions, and conditions of extreme social isolation and sensory deprivation.
- Correctional staff inflicted excessive force.
- EMCF failed to protect prisoners from violence, ignored emergency situations, and enabled violent attacks on prisoners.
- Prisoners were exposed to vermin (e.g., rats, mice), smoke and other toxic substances, filthy cells and fixtures, broken plumbing, inoperable lighting, constant illumination, and inadequate ventilation.
- Nutrition was inadequate to maintain health and food was served in an unsanitary and unsafe manner.

As described by inmates, EMCF was "hell on earth" (Takei, 2018).

After complaints, lawsuits, and appeals, EMCF conceded to contract with a new company to provide mental health care, and established an in-house pharmacy to facilitate better administration of medications (*Dockery v. Hall,* 2019). However, an additional lawsuit was filed in the U.S. District, even after changes were being made to the facility, of which the court ruled in favor of the prison, stating that medical and psychiatric care, as well as the cleanliness issues, had been addressed by EMCF:

> *The changes made at the prison are evident from the record, and from the tour of the facility that was made during the trial. The Court was surprised with respect to the cleanliness and condition of the prison in particular after seeing photographs of the facility that were take prior to the lawsuit's having been filed before trial, and hearing the anecdotal evidence presented by the prisoners who testified at trial. (*Dockery v. Hall*, U.S. District Court, 2019, p. 22)*

By the 2019 case, the U.S. District Court ruled in favor of the defendants on all complaints brought by the prisoners and ACLU, other interested parties. Though prisoners did not appear to win in civil lawsuits, in the long run they were victorious, as EMCF acted to address the well-placed grievances of inmates.

As a postscript to *Dockery v. Hall,* in January 2021, 27-year-old Cortez Wooten (sentenced to 35 years for manslaughter and armed robbery) was found unresponsive in his cell and later pronounced dead at the same California facility (WTOK Staff, 2021a). In May 2021, EMCF found itself under the microscope once again as two inmates at EMCF were found dead, in separate incidents (WTOK Staff, 2021b). On May 1, at 4:00 p.m., 65-year-old Fritz Garcia (sentenced to life for homicide) was found dead in his cell; at 8:15 the same evening, 46-year-old Terry Walker (sentenced to 15 years for armed robbery) was found unresponsive on his cell floor and pronounced dead after receiving CPR by paramedics (WTOK Staff, 2021b). No foul play was suspected, but the deaths were under investigation.

We should note that the COVID-19 pandemic had hit prison facilities particularly hard in 2020 and 2021, and there were a record number of deaths reported of prisoners in general at that time.

SUMMARY

When it comes to the legal rights of the incarcerated, we need to distinguish between detainees (those who are awaiting trial) and prisoners (those who are already convicted). Because of the presumption of innocence, detainees are, in theory, not supposed to be punished. However, in a number of court rulings, jailers are allowed to discipline them in the event that their behavior is disruptive to the operations of the facility.

In addition to court rulings, the U.S. Bureau of Prisons sets a standard for prisoners' rights and treatment, as does the American Bar Association, and activist groups like Human Rights Watch and the American Civil Liberties Union. Though there is considerable overlap in all these lists, they are subject to interpretation and in many cases, complaints will be resolved in civil lawsuits, not always in favor of prisoners.

Though the general public tend to believe that those who are jailed and prisoners lose all rights when they are incarcerated, this is a myth. They retain some of their civil and Constitutional rights while behind bars:

- **First Amendment.** Some free speech is allowed; however, mail, and correspondences are closely monitored and those in custody do not have free access to reporters with the press or media.
- **Fourth Amendment.** Those who are in jail or prison must submit to searches of their bodies and cells, for the safety of those in the facility, including correctional staff. However, strip-searches and body cavity searches are argued to be excessively invasive.
- **Fifth Amendment.** Often argued in debating the ethics on the death penalty, certain practices in jails and prisons may violate the Fifth Amendment rights, including in cases of overcrowding.
- **Eighth Amendment.** The most common challenges to this amendment by the incarcerated are centered on health care, or more precisely the lack of it in correctional facilities. Being deprived of adequate mental or medical treatment is argued to be a form of cruel and unusual punishment. Likewise, it is also argued in death penalty cases.
- **Fourteenth Amendment.** Also used in civil lawsuits involving mental or medical care, prisoners cannot be disciplined or transferred without being informed and without a hearing.

There are a number of pieces of legislation since the Civil Rights Act that have provided prisoners with additional protections under the law. These include the Model Sentencing and Corrections Act of 1978 and the Americans with Disabilities Act of 1990. In recent years, one of the biggest concerns of prisoners has been access to adequate mental and medical health care, particularly after the world was struck with the AIDS/HIV (1980s), COVID-19 (beginning in 2020) pandemic and with an aging prison population. This has made it additionally challenging for prisons to meet the medical needs of prisoners, on top of chronic overcrowding.

Though the incarcerated do have the right to have access to the courts in order to file civil lawsuits against jail and prisons, as well as states or the federal government, their ability to do so has been curtailed since the Prison Litigation Reform Act (PLRA) of 1992. This was primarily legislated to reduce the number of frivolous lawsuits, like our examples of prisoners complaining about a lousy meal or being delivered the wrong type of peanut butter. However, it has made it equally difficult for those with legitimate complaints to file civil lawsuits. This is also exacerbated by the fact that in the vast majority of these cases, the prisoners are representing themselves in court, unless they can find an activist group or attorney who is willing to foot the cost of a trial and provide their services for free.

Reading materials have always been a source of contention, with people in jail and prison limited to what they can get directly from publishers. To add to the controversy, in recent decades it has become imperative for prisoners to have access to computers, not only for job training, but for the vast quantities of educational and legal materials that can only be found digitally in this day and age. It is also a means by which to stay in touch with friends and loved ones, as fewer and fewer people are using letters for correspondences. However, their access to the Internet has to be limited because of the amount of online materials that are inappropriate for anyone, much less for prisoners.

Finally, in this chapter we briefly addressed the issue of noncitizens who find their way into the criminal justice system in the United States, whether they are here legally or illegally. They have their personal freedoms further curtailed, in that they are at risk for being deported after they serve their prison sentences, if convicted. And detainees held on terrorist charges may find themselves in jail or prison camp awaiting trial indefinitely, as in the case of the detainees held at Guantánamo Bay.

There is also the controversy of the number of people who have crossed over the U.S. border through Mexico from a number of different countries, some of whom are unaccompanied minors. As we have noted, there is no easy solution on how to humanely detain this population as they are placed in temporary facilities until a solution can be found for those legitimately seeking asylum or they can be deported.

Prisoners' rights are forever evolving, dependent on interpretation of the Constitution as well as the political climate. They are further challenged with changing conditions, including the Computer Age and pandemics. It is yet to be seen if new reforms to prisoners' rights come to fruition, along with pushes for reform in other areas of the criminal justice system.

STORIES FROM BEHIND BARS

Inmate Marriages

Love blossoms, just about anywhere, including in prison. Or at least something that resembles love. We should consider that for prisoners, any form of affection, or attention for that matter, that they receive, even from a distance, is generally welcomed. As much as we believe that prisoners are isolated, there are means by which they can connected with the outside world. Or more likely to happen, the outside contacts them. For example, while Scott Peterson was on trial for the homicide of his wife, Laci Peterson and their unborn baby, his boyish good looks attracted a number of female fans, even though he was on trial for murder with special circumstances in California.[10] Or the Menendez brothers, Lyle and Erik, who are behind bars in California, convicted of killing their parents in 1996, who have both married women who they met after incarceration, with Lyle marrying twice since being in prison (Murtha, 2021). To date, they have exhausted all appeals in their cases and most likely will spend the rest of their lives in prison, with no possibility of parole for either one of them and being united with their spouses on the outside (Murtha, 2021).

There are also a number of websites, including WriteAPrisoner.com, where people on the outside who are not related in any way to inmates on the inside, can initiate and carry on pen-pal correspondences with them. The website states that inmates benefit from the correspondence as it helps them with their social adjustment, emotional well-being, and reintegration into free society (WriteAPrisoner. com, n.d.). To their credit, these websites provide opportunities for potential employers to reach out to inmates. However, they also provide an avenue for someone with unrealistic or romantic notions of reforming a prisoner to become emotionally attached to them, which can have unintended (or intended) consequences, both for the prisoner and the person corresponding with them. Trickier yet are romances struck up between inmates.

In some cases, such correspondences result in marriages from behind bars. In other cases, couples who were together before the incarceration of one or both of them may wish to petition to get married. For example, Niccole Wetherell, serving a life sentence for first-degree murder in 1998 and Paul Gillpatrick, serving a 55-90 year sentence for second-degree murder in Nebraska in 2009, had met prior to their incarceration, became engaged in 2012, and petitioned the courts for the right to marry, citing the landmark case *Turner v. Safley* (1987) as reason enough for them to be allowed to do so (Armstrong, 2019), although they were incarcerated in different facilities. In a postscript, even though a U.S. District court ruled in favor of the couple, the state appealed the decisions and Wetherell died in February 2021 from an undisclosed medical condition before there could be a final ruling (The Associated Press, 2021).

---

[10] California has since overturned Peterson's death sentence, ordering a new trial, on the basis of a juror who may have committed "prejudicial misconduct" (Levine, 2020).

Turner v. Safley, 482 U.S. 78 (1987)

In the U.S. Supreme Court case, a class action lawsuit was brought against the State of Missouri on the basis of inmates being prohibited to marry. This was predicated on the prohibition of inmates corresponding with other inmates. Of course, these types of correspondences can and do occur against prison rules, but the case was brought forth to fight for the legitimate right of inmates to correspond with one another, particularly in the case of spouses.

The Court's decision in *Turner v. Safley* was that Missouri put unnecessary burdens on prisoners, stating that marriages are constitutionally protected relationships. Missouri's argument was that by prohibiting marriages, there was less likelihood of "love triangles" that could lead to violent inmate confrontations, an argument that the Court found did not have merit. After all, love triangles can occur even without the benefit of a legally recognized relationship. This led the way for marriages to be permitted between inmates, with the caveat that prison officials have the discretion as to when and where a marriage ceremony will take place.

How to Marry a Prisoner

We should first note the difference between a marriage ceremony and a wedding ceremony. A marriage ceremony can be a civil service that essentially creates a legal, binding relationship between two people. A wedding ceremony, on the other hand, may or may not have religious significance.

You can have a marriage ceremony without clergy, as long as the person who is performing the ceremony is licensed in the state to perform the ceremony. However, a religious wedding ceremony is only legal if there is a marriage license issued by the state and the ceremony is performed by a licensed person. In prison, it is to the discretion of a warden to approve inmates' requests to marry (U.S. Federal Bureau of Prisons, 2011). Likewise, they may approve or disallow a marriage ceremony if it poses a threat or excessive burden to the facility to provide security.

Depending on the state, prisoners in the same prison facility can marry where permitted, as long as they abide by the rules and regulations of the facility. As same-sex marriages are now legal, prisoners of the same sex are permitted to marry as well.

Using Michigan Department of Corrections as an example, the first point of contact for those wishing to get married is the prison chaplain (Michigan Department of Corrections, 2021). What may be confusing to prisoners is that a marriage license has to be issued in the county in which you reside. Using the Michigan example, this means that if a prisoner is housed, say in Detroit, but they are actually from Flint, they would need to get the marriage license in Wayne County where Detroit is, rather than Genessee County where Flint is located. Regulations for inmate marriages may vary from state to state as far as required steps to take.

As we noted, the *Turner* case makes marriage possible between inmates if incarcerated in Michigan. But "weddings are scheduled on the availability of time, space, and staff schedules. The couple getting married are responsible for providing an officiant and two witnesses, who must complete LIEN [approved visitor] clearances . . . the prisoner's ring cannot be more than $75 and must be a plain band (without stones or insignia)." (Michigan Department of Corrections, 2021, retrieved from https;//www.michigan.gov/corrections/0,4551,7-119-9741_12798-228401--,00.html). As a basis of comparison, in 2021, the average cost of a bride's engagement ring and band was $6,113; in 2020, the average cost of a groom's ring was $468 (Wedding Stats, 2021). For anyone who has ever gotten married outside of prison, these restrictions may present bumps in the road but are not insurmountable.

Planning the Wedding

Though any marriage should not be entered into without a certain amount of caution, marriage with an inmate or between inmates carries an added burden of concerns. The main concern is long-term planning, as in the event that the inmate is released from prison, which requires considerable lifestyle adjustments (Stritoff, 2019) and may jeopardize the rehabilitation process with added stressors when couples have never lived together previously.

Whereas a future bride or groom may be working with a wedding planner, inmates are required to work with prison staff, in most cases, with a prison visit coordinator (Stritoff, 2019) after permission has been given. The cost of a prison wedding is, on average, $150-$175 for documents, fees, etc. (Stritoff, 2019).

As we have noted, in the Michigan case, you cannot simply have anyone stand up for you at your wedding if you are incarcerated. It is recommended that visitors who have already been approved at the prison for visitations serve as witnesses to a prison wedding (Stritoff, 2019). For obvious reasons, there is no traditional reception with friends and family after the wedding and certainly no alcoholic beverage is present to toast with. There will generally be no cake and certainly no honeymoon. As in the example of Gigi and Carlos Colon's wedding while he was serving time in Dixon Correctional Center in central Illinois, the groom wore his prison uniform to the ceremony and they were only allowed to kiss for two minutes after the ceremony (Owens-Schiele and Eldeib, 2011).

Divorce Rates Among Prisoners

We cannot discuss prison marriages without also discussing divorce rates among prisoners. Even without getting married while incarcerated, prisoners are at greater risk for divorce in general. In a study conducted by Florida State University criminologists (Siennick, et al., 2014), they found the following alarming, but unsurprising statistics:

▪ Though males in prison are more likely to be unmarried, if they are married at time of incarceration, they are more likely to get divorced during their incarceration.
▪ Divorce rates are higher than in the general population for prisoners who are released from prison, even if their marriage is intact during incarceration.

- The longer that an inmate is in prison, the greater likelihood their marriage will end in a divorce by 32 percent.

Bottom line from the Siennick, et al. study (2014), incarceration is hard on marriages.

SOURCES

Armstrong, M. (2019) In sickness and in health—and in prison. *Looking Back, The Marshall Project.* Aug. 19. Retrieved from https://www.themarshallproject.org/2019/08/19/in-sickness-in-health-and-in-prison.

Federal Bureau of Prisons (2011) Marriages of Inmates. U.S. Department of Justice. Sept. 22. Retrieved from https://www.bop.gov/policy/progstat/5326_005.pdf.

Michigan Department of Corrections (2021) Marriage—Marrying a Prisoner. Retrieved from https://www.michigan.gov/corrections/0,4551,7-119-9741_12798-228401--,00.html.

Murtha, E. (2021) Menendez brothers case back in spotlight thanks to TikTok teens: Reporter's notebook. News, ABC13. Apr. 3. Retrieved from https://abc13.com/menendez-brothers-now-abc-2020-lyle-erik-2020-episode/10480073/#:~:text=The%20brothers%20have%20now%20served,t%20changed%20all%20too%20much.

Owens-Schiele, E. and D. Eldeib (2011) Prisoners of love: Marrying an inmate brings challenges. *Chicago Tribune.* Dec. 21. Retrieved from https://www.chicagotribune.com/news/ct-xpm-2011-12-21-ct-x-1221-prison-wives-20111221-story.html.

Siennick, S. E., E. A. Steward, and J. Staff (2014) Explaining the association between incarceration and divorce. *Criminology.* Vol. 52, No. 3:371-398.

Stritoff, S. (2019) How to marry a prisoner. Aug. 4. Retrieved from https://www.thespruce.com/how-to-marry-a-prisoner-2300890#:~:text=Regulations%20for%20marrying%20a%20prisoner,permission%20to%20marry%20the%20prisoner.&text=Once%20the%20forms%20are%20completed,facility%20with%20the%20requested%20fees.

U.S. Supreme Court (1987) *Turner v. Safley,* 482 U.S. 78. Justia. Retrieved from https://supreme.justia.com/cases/federal/us/482/78/.

Wedding Stats (2021) Finance: Average cost of a wedding band. Jan. 16. Retrieved from https://www.weddingstats.org/cost-of-a-wedding-ring/.

INTERNATIONAL PERSPECTIVES ON PUNISHMENT AND CORRECTIONS: THE REPUBLIC OF SOUTH AFRICA

There is perhaps no better example of how social activism changes the complexion of punishment than in the African nation of South Africa. Long under colonial rule, first by the Netherlands, then Great Britain, South Africa has a long and controversial history in penology. Historically South African prisoners, as other African prisoners, faced cramped, dirty quarters, were given insufficient food allotments, and were provided with little to no clothing (Sarkin, 2008). In the late 19th century, within the colonized nations of Africa, prisons not only housed the victims of colonial oppression, they also were a mirror of European views of white superiority—torture and capital punishment of native Africans was sanctioned, as Europeans viewed them as uncivilized and savage (Sarkin, 2008; Peté and Devenish, 2005).

The most notable case of a South African prisoner is the incarceration of Nelson Mandela, who was a political prisoner for 27 years, convicted for his human rights activism against *apartheid* (a policy that calls for institutional racial segregation, where there is discrimination against nonwhite people, even if they are in the majority by population numbers). Mandela, once released, and at the end of apartheid in South Africa, was eventually elected president of the African nation in the 1990s. Originally modeled after the British prison system, there has perhaps never been a greater transformation of prisons within the past century as in South Africa, including the release of political prisoners, the use of community corrections, and the end of inmate segregation based on race beginning in the 1990s (Luyt, 2008).

More recently, in the midst of the pandemic starting in the 2020, we have heard news out of South Africa of a new, more virulent and potentially deadly form of the COVID-19 virus. This, of course, has been a grave concern in prisons around the world. However, South Africa is also home to some of the highest rates of HIV and tuberculosis in the world (Keehn and Nevin, 2018). Up until the pandemic, these have been the most serious health issues in the prison population.

Exacerbating the public health concerns in South African jails in prison is over-incarceration, including excessive pretrial detention and life sentences (Keehn and Nevin, 2018). Even with the prison reforms in the 1990s, there continued to be mass incarceration, similar to what we have witnessed in the United States. Like the argument some activists make that mass incarceration in the United States is the "new Jim Crow," likewise critics say that in South Africa, the same phenomenon is fueled by institutional racism and xenophobia.

Some of this overcrowding in South Africa has been somewhat alleviated by the implementation of the *Nelson Mandela Rules* for the treatment of prisoners. The rules are used in a number of countries around the world and originally adopted by the United Nations in 2015 as the Revised Standard Rules for Minimum Treatment of Prisoners and renamed in honor of Mandela (McCall-Smith, 55 International Legal Materials 1180, 2016). The main theme of the rules is human dignity of prisoners.

In comparing the nuances of sentences in South Africa and in other African nations, a South African prisoner sentenced to life is automatically eligible for parole after 25 years—a life sentence does not mean an indeterminate period of time as it does in the United States (Mujuzi, 2009).

SOURCES

Keehn, E. N. and A. Nevin (2018) Health, human rights and the transformation of punishment: South African litigation to address HIV and tuberculosis in prisons. *Health and Human Rights Journal*. Vol. 20, No. 1:213-224.

Luyt, D. (2008) Governance, accountability, and poverty alleviation in South Africa. Paper, United Nations Social Forum. Sept. 2. Geneva, Switzerland.

McCall-Smith, K. (2016) Introductory Note to United Nations Standard Minimum Rules for the Treatment of Prisoners (Mandela Rules). 55 International Legal Materials 1180/ International Legal Materials. Vol. 55, Iss. 6:1183-1205.

Mujuzi, J. D. (2009) The evolution of the meaning(s) of penal servitude for life (life imprisonment) in Mauritius: The Human Rights and jurisprudential challenges confronted so far and those ahead. *Journal of African Law.* Vol. 53, No. 2:222-248.

Peté, S. and A. Devenish (2005) Flogging, fear, and food: Punishment and race in colonial Natal. *Journal of African Studies.* Vol. 31, No. 1:3-21.

Sarkin, J. (2008) Prisons in Africa: An evaluation from a human rights perspective. *International Journal of Human Rights.* Jan. Retrieved from https://sur.conectas.org/en/prisons-in-africa/.

GLOSSARY

First Amendment As it relates to detainees and prisoners, they have the rights to freedom of religion, freedom of speech, and freedom to sue the government, all of which have certain restrictions for prisoners where the safety and security of the facility is concerned.

Fourth Amendment Usually cited in cases where detainees believe that there has been an unreasonable search of their cell or during a strip-search or pat down. (See *strip-search*)

Eighth Amendment The most commonly used clause in prisoners' civil lawsuits is prohibition of cruel or unusual punishment.

Fourteenth Amendment. Cited for equal protection of detainees and prisoners under the law, as well as depriving a person of life, as in the case of the death penalty. (See Chapter 15)

ACLU National Prison Project An initiative and cause of the American Civil Liberties Union to protect and defend prisoners' civil, human, and Constitutional rights. (See *American Civil Liberties Union*)

American Civil Liberties Union (ACLU) Founded in 1920, the ACLU's mission is to work with lawmakers to protect individual rights (See ACLU faqs [sic] at https://www.aclu.org/faqs#:~:text=The%20American%20Civil%20Liberties%20Union,laws%20of%20the%20United%20States.)

Apartheid (South Africa) A policy that calls for institutional racial segregation, where there is discrimination against nonwhite people even if they are in the majority by population numbers, as in the example of South Africa, from 1948 after the National Party took over with an all-white government, until negotiations to end apartheid finalized in 1994.

Estelle v. Gamble (1976)   Eighth Amendment case brought by an inmate, J. W. Gamble, against the Texas Department of Corrections after he was not given proper care after a back injury while doing prison work and instead was placed in solitary confinement when he refused to return to light work, citing the Eighth Amendment for cruel and unusual punishment. (For further information, see https://www.oyez .org/cases/1976/75-929)

Habeas privileges   From the Constitution, habeas corpus is the right to be brought before a judge before being detained or imprisoned. This is why arraignments and formal charges brought against a suspect and have to take place quickly after some-one has been arrested.

Model Sentencing and Corrections Act (1978)   Legislation that was intended to unify correctional systems, in order to more efficiently use scarce resources. (See https://www.ojp.gov/pdffiles1/Digitization/55600NCJRS.pdf.)

Nelson Mandela Rules (South Africa)   United Nations policies and rules that are given to mandate the expected treatment of prisoners, including prohibiting tor-ture, excessive time in solitary confinement, and denial of health care. Named for Nelson Mandela, who served 27 years in South African prisons for being an anti-apartheid activist. Mandela was later elected President of South Africa after his release from prison.

Prison Litigation Reform Act (PLRA, 1996)   Legislation that was intended to stop or at least slow down the number of frivolous lawsuits that were taking up court time as well as court resources.

Procunier v. Martinez (1974)   Case that defined the freedoms and limits of inmates' First Amendment rights to free speech.

Pro bono   The offer of an attorney to provide legal services free of charge.

Pro se   Representing oneself in a court of law or in a legal matter.

"Publisher only" rule   Requirement of both detainees and prisoners to only receive publications from the outside directly from the publisher.

Strip-searches   Searching a person's body while they are either partially or fully undressed.

Summary discipline   Punishment that does not have purpose; is arbitrary.

"Three strikes" rule, PLRA   After inmates have had three civil lawsuits denied on the basis of being frivolous, they are not able to file further lawsuits, unless they can prove that it is an emergency or that they are in eminent danger.

Vitek v. Jones   U.S. Supreme Court case that requires inmates who are going to be transferred to mental hospitals or facilities to be notified and given a hearing, under the due process clause of the Fourteenth Amendment.

Work-release programs   Prison programs where the convicted are allowed out in the community to work during the day, but need to return to prison after their shift, typically at night and have to be incarcerated over the weekend and/or their days off from work.

REFERENCES AND SUGGESTED READINGS

Albert Corbarrubias Justice Project (2012) Supreme Court rules any offense, however minor, allows for a strip search. Apr. 3. Retrieved from https://acjusticeproject.org/2012/04/03/supreme-court-rules-any-offense-however-minor-allows-for-a-strip-search/.

American Bar Association (2011) Criminal justice standards: Treatment of prisoners.

American Civil Liberties Union (ACLU) (n.d.) ACLU National Prison Project. Retrieved from https://www.aclu.org/other/aclu-national-prison-project.

American Civil Liberties Union (ACLU) (2017) *Dockery v. Hall*. Mar. 2. Retrieved from https://www.aclu.org/cases/prisoners-rights/dockery-v-hall.

Associated Press, The (2021) Nebraska inmates' fight to wed ends after one of them dies. *ABC News*. May 24. Retrieved from https://abcnews.go.com/US/wireStory/nebraska-inmates-fight-wed-ends-dies-77877572.

Babbar, M. (2021) The Fourth Amendment stripped bare: Substantiating prisoners' reasonable right to bodily privacy. *Northwestern University Law Review*. Vol. 115, Iss. 6:1737-1779.

Barry, E. M. (2000) Women prisoners on the cutting edge: Development of the activist Women's Prisoners' Rights Movement. *Social Justice*. Vol. 27, Iss. 3:168-175.

Baylor, A. (2018) Centering women in prisoners' rights litigation. *Michigan Journal of Gender and Law*. Vol. 25, Iss. 2:109-159.

Da Silva, C. (2020) Judge says conditions at U.S. border holding cells violated the Constitution in 'Monumental' ruling. *Newsweek*. Feb. 20. Retrieved from https://www.newsweek.com/judge-says-conditions-us-border-holding-cells-violated-constitution-monumental-ruling-1488281.

Elderbroom, B. and J. Durnan (2018) Reclassified: State drug law reforms to reduce felony convictions and increase second chances. *Urban Institute*. Oct. Retrieved from https://www.urban.org/sites/default/files/publication/99077/reclassified_state_drug_law_reforms_to_reduce_felony_convictions_and_increase_second_chances.pdf.

Constitutional Center (2021) Fourth Amendment: Search and Seizure. Retrieved from https://constitutioncenter.org/interactive-constitution/amendment/amendment-iv#:~:text=The%20right%20of%20the%20people,and%20the%20persons%20or%20things

Chase, R. T. (2021) VOICES: Prison violence like Alabama's demands a national reckoning. *Facing South*. June 18. Retrieved from https://www.facingsouth.org/2021/06/voices-prison-violence-alabamas-demands-national-reckoning.

Creasey, H., M. R. Sulway, O. Dent, G. A. Broe, A. Jorm, and C. Tennant (1999) Is experience as a prisoner of war a risk factor for accelerated age-related illness and disability? *Journal of American Geriatrics Society*. Vol. 1, No. 1:60-64.

Cripe, C. A. (1997) *Legal Aspects of Corrections Management*. Gaithersburg, MD: Aspen Publishers, Inc.

Dalrymple-Blackburn, D. (1995) Comment: AIDS, prisoners, and the American Disabilities Act. *Utah Law Review*. Vol. 1995, No. 3:839-886.

Flagg, A. and A. Calderón (2020) Million hours: Trump's vast expansion of child detention. *The Marshall Project*. Oct. 30. Retrieved from https://www.themarshallproject.org/2020/10/30/500-000-kids-30-million-hours-trump-s-vast-expansion-of-child-detention.

Garvey, T. M. (2012) Routine strip-searches upheld. *Sexual Assault Report*. Vol. 16, No. 2:28.

Gillett, G. (2010) A world without Internet: A new framework for analyzing a supervised release condition that restricts computer and Internet access. *Fordham Law Review*. Oct., Vol. 79, Iss. 1:217.

Greifinger, R. (2006) Disabled prisoners and reasonable accommodations. *Criminal Justice Ethics*. Winter/Spring, Vol. 25, Iss. 1:2-55.

Hansen, L. P. (2020) *White Collar and Corporate Crime: A Case Study Approach*. Riverwoods, IL: Wolters Kluwer United States, Inc.

Harvard Law Review (2013) Recent cases: First Amendment – Free exercise in prison – Fifth Circuit holds that prison's prohibition on all objects over twenty-five dollars did not violate prisoner's First Amendment rights or substantially burden his religion under RLUOPA – *McFaul v. Valenzuela*, 684 F.3d 564 (5th Cir. 2012). Feb., Vol. 126, Iss. 4:1154-1161.

HG.org (n.d.) Do inmates have rights? If so, what are they? *Legal Resources*. Retrieved from https://www.hg.org/legal-articles/do-inmates-have-rights-if-so-what-are-they-31517

Hodgson, J. (2014) Guantánamo Bay: The hunger strikes: Based on the personal statements of five detainees at Guantánamo prison camp. *Art Journal*. Vol. 73, No. 2:5-12.

Hughett, A. B. (2019) A "safe outlet" for prisoner discontent: How prison grievance procedures helped stymie prison organizing during the 1970s. *Law and Social Inquiry*. Nov., Vol. 44, Iss. 4:893-921.

Human Rights Watch (2018) In the freezer: Abusive conditions for women and children in US immigration holding cells. Feb. 28. Retrieved from https://www.hrw.org/report/2018/02/28/freezer/abusive-conditions-women-and-children-us-immigration-holding-cells#.

Jablonski, R. K., J. Leszek, J. Rosinczuk, I. Uchmanowicz, and B. Panaszek (2015) Impact of incarceration in Nazi concentration camps on multimorbidity of former prisoners. *Neuropsychiatric Disease and Treatment*. Vol. 11:668-674.

Jacobs, J. B. (1980) The Prisoners' Rights Movement and its impact, 1960-1980. *Crime and Justice*. Vol. 2:429-470.

Justice, W. W. (1990) Origin of Ruiz v. Estelle. *Stanford Law Review*. Vol. 43, Iss. 1:1-12. Retrieved from https://www.ojp.gov/ncjrs/virtual-library/abstracts/origin-ruiz-v-estelle.

Justia (2021) *Bell v. Wolfish*, 441 U.S. 520 (1979). Retrieved from https://supreme.justia.com/cases/federal/us/441/520/.

Lee, V. (2012) Prisoner participation in clinical research trials: A fundamental right under the Eighth Amendment. *Journal of Legal Medicine*. Vol. 33, Iss. 4:541-ii.

Legal Information Institute (n.d.) Rights of prisoners. Cornell Law School. Retrieved from https://www.law.cornell.edu/constitution-conan/amendment-14/section-1/rights-of-prisoners#fn1266amd14.

Levin, D. J., P. A. Langan, and J. M. Brown (2000) State court sentencing of convicted felons, 1996. Office of Justice Programs and Bureau of Justice Statistics, U.S. Department of Justice. Feb. Retrieved from https://www.bjs.gov/content/pub/ascii/scscf96.txt#:~:text=*%20Average%20elapsed%20time%20from%20date,trials%20took%20about%206%20months.

Levin, E. (2020) California Supreme Court orders Scott Peterson's murder conviction reexamined. *New England Public Media*, NPR. Oct. 15. Retrieved from https://www.npr.org/2020/10/15/923995078/california-supreme-court-scott-peterson-murder-conviction.

LII (n.d.) Prisoners' rights: Overview. Cornell Law School. Retrieved from https://www.law.cornell.edu/lii/about/who_we_are.

Kanaboshi, N. (2014) Prison inmates' right to hunger strike: Its use and its limits under the U.S. Constitution. *Criminal Justice Review*. Vol. 39, No. 2:121-139.

Kang, R. (n.d.) Welcome to the dark web: A plain English introduction. International Association of Privacy Protection. Retrieved from https://iapp.org/news/a/welcome-to-the-dark-web-a-plain-english-introduction/.

Knochel, K. S. (1980) Fourteenth Amendment. Due process for prisoners in commitment proceedings. *The Journal of Criminal Law and Criminology*. Vol. 71, No. 4:579-592.

Kovarsky, L. (2014) Prisoners and habeas privileges under the Fourteenth Amendment. *Vanderbilt Law Review*. Vol. 67:609.

Kruzman, D. (2018) In U.S. prisons, tablets open window to outside world. Reuters. July 18. Retrieved from https://www.reuters.com/article/us-usa-prisons-computers/in-u-s-prisons-tablets-open-window-to-the-outside-world-idUSKBN1K813D.

Kyprianides, A. (2019) We need to rethink the way we treat ex-prisoners. Character and Context, Society for Personality and Social Psychology. June 12. Retrieved from https://www.spsp.org/news-center/blog/kyprianides-exprisoners.

Marder-Spiro, J. (2020) Special factors counselling action: Why courts should allow people detained pretrial to bring Fifth Amendment *Bivens* claims. *Columbia Law Review*. June, Vol. 120, Iss. 5:1295-1331.

Marquart, J. W. and B. M. Crouch (1985) Judicial reform and prison control: The impact of *Ruiz v. Estelle* on a Texas penitentiary. *Law and Society Review*. Vol. 19, No. 4:557-586.

Massachusetts Supreme Judicial Court (2018) Americans with Disabilities Act and parole – Massachusetts Supreme Judicial Court Observes that Americans with Disabilities Act applies to parole. *Harvard Law Review*. Jan., Vol. 131, Iss. 3:910-917.

Mitchell, D. (2003) Prisoners' constitutional rights. *Criminal Justice Studies*. Vol. 16, Iss. 3:245-264.

New York Times, The (2022) The Guantánamo docket. Mar 11. Retreived from https://www.nytimes.com/interactive/2021/us/guantanamo-bay-detainees.html.

Newman, W. J. and C. L. Scott (2012).*Brown v Plata*: Prison overcrowding in California. *Journal of the American Academy of Psychiatry and Law*. Vol. 40, No. 4:547-52.

Oyez (n.d.) Robinson v. California. Retrieved from https://www.oyez.org/cases/1961/554.

Paris, J. E. (2008) Why prisoners deserve health care. Medicine and Society, *AMA Journal of Ethics*. Feb. Retrieved from https://journalofethics.ama-assn.org/article/why-prisoners-deserve-health-care/2008-02.

Pfeiffer, S. (2020) Trial of Sept. 11 defendants at Guantánamo Bay delayed until August 2021. *Investigations*, NPR. Sept. 30. Retrieved from https://www.npr.org/2020/09/30/918454831/trial-of-sept-11-defendants-at-guant-namo-delayed-until-august-2021.

Raine, G. (2012) Inmates' "ridiculous" lawsuits rile officials. *San Francisco Gate*. Feb. 8. Retrieved from https://www.sfgate.com/news/article/Inmates-ridiculous-lawsuits-rile-officials-3151589.php.

Ransom, J. (2018) Women describe invasive strip searches on visits to city jails. *The New York Times*. Apr. 26. Retrieved from https://www.nytimes.com/2018/04/26/nyregion/strip-search-new-york-city-jails-lawsuits.html.

Reilly, S. B. (2021) Where is the strike zone? Arguing uniformly narrow interpretation of Prison Litigation Reform Act's "three strikes" rule. Vol. 70, Iss. 3:755-796.

Reinhart, C. (2003) Prisons and prisoners; litigation. OLR Research Report, State of Connecticut. Oct. 10. Retrieved from https://www.cga.ct.gov/PS98/rpt%5Colr%5Chtm/98-R-0822.htm.

Schlanger, M. (2016. The just barely sustainable California Prisoners' rights ecosystem. *The Annals of the American Academy of Political and Social Science*. Vol. 664, 62. https://advance-lexis-com.wne.idm.oclc.org/api/document?collection=analytical-materials&id=urn:contentItem:5JCP-HD70-00CV-J160-00000-00&context=1516831.

Secure World News Team (2018) 2 cases of cybercrime behind bars. July 30. Retrieved from https://www.secureworldexpo.com/industry-news/cybercrime-behind-bars.

Sestanovich, C. (2015) Prison bling. *The Marshall Project*. Apr. 3. Retrieved from https://www.themarshallproject.org/2015/04/03/prison-bling#:~:text=The%20Rule%3A%20Inmates%20are%20only,or%20a%20Star%20of%20David).

Sindel, P. E. (1991) Fourteenth Amendment—the right to refuse antipsychotic drugs masked by prison bars. *The Journal of Criminal Law and Criminology.* Winter, Vol. 81, No. 4:952-980.

Superior Court of California (1962) *Robinson v. California*, No. 554. Appellate Department, Los Angeles County. Decided June 25. Retrieved from https://tile.loc.gov/storage-servi ces/service/ll/usrep/usrep370/usrep370660/usrep370660.pdf.

Takei, C. (2018) The East Mississippi Correctional Facility is 'hell on earth.' *Speak Freely*, American Civil Liberties Union (ACLU). Mar. 5. Retrieved from https://www.aclu.org/ blog/prisoners-rights/medical-and-mental-health-care/east-mississippi-correctional -facility-hell.

Temko, D. (2013) Prisoners and the press: The First Amendment Antidote to civil death after PLRA. *California Western Law Review.* Article 3, Vol. 49, No. 2:195-229.

Umphres, E. (2019) 150% wrong: The Prison Litigation Reform Act and attorney's fees. *American Criminal Law Review.* Winter, Vol. 56, Iss. 1:261-293.

United States District Court (2018) Dockery v. Hall, Civil Action No. . 3:13-cv-326-WHB-JCG. Southern District Mississippi, Northern Division. Filed Aug. 24. 11 pp.

United States District Court (2019) *Dockery v. Hall*, Civil Action No. 3:13-cv-326-WHB-JCG. Southern District Mississippi, Northern Division. Decided Dec. 31.

WriteAPrisoner.com (Correspondence and Reintegration) (n.d.) Why write a prisoner? Retrieved from https://writeaprisoner.com/why-writeaprisoner.

WTOK Staff (2021a) Autopsy ordered after inmate death at EMCF. News Center, ABC 11. Jan. 16. Retrieved from

WTOK Staff (2021b) Inmate deaths under investigation at EMCF. News Center, ABC 11. May 2. Retrieved from https://www.wtok.com/2021/01/16/autopsy-ordered-after-inmate-death -at-emcf/.

WTOK Staff (2021b) Inmate deaths under investigation at EMCF. News Center, ABC 11. May 2. Retrieved from https://www.wtok.com/2021/05/02/inmate-deaths-under-investigat ion-at-emcf/.

Yanofski, J. (2019) Prisons v. prisons: A history of mental health rights. *Psychiatry.* Vol. 7, No. 10:41-44.

RESORCES FOR PRISONERS' RIGHTS

American Bar Association (ABA) Treatment of Prisoners: https://www.americanbar.org/ groups/criminal_justice/publications/criminal_justice_section_archive/crimjust_ standards_treatmentprisoners/

American Civil Liberties Union (ACLU), National Prison Project: https://www.aclu.org/ issues/prisoners-rights?redirect=prisoners-rights

Center on Juvenile and Criminal Justice: http://www.cjcj.org/index.html

Legal Services for Prisoners with Children (LSPC): https://prisonerswithchildren.org/

Prison Activist Resource Center (PARC): https://www.prisonactivist.org/

The Sentencing Project: https://www.sentencingproject.org/

Chapter EIGHT

Women in Jails and Prisons[1]

> *Prisons do not disappear social problems, they disappear human beings. Homelessness, unemployment, drug addiction, mental illness, and illiteracy are only a few of the problems that disappear from public view when the human beings contending with them are relegated to cages.*
>
> — Angela Davis, activist, former detainee, Marin County, California

Chapter Objectives

- Introduce the key issues that women face in jails and prisons.
- Provide a list the social psychological challenges unique to female convicts, including stigma based on female stereotypes.
- Expose the challenges with pregnancy and motherhood in jails and prisons.
- Explain why there are few drug and alcohol rehabilitation programs or vocational education options for women in jail or prison.

Key Terms

Benevolent sexism
Dysphoria
Gender dysphoria
Intimate partner violence (IPV)
Occupational therapy
Patient-to-prisoner pipeline

Pseudo-families
Social capital offenders
Stigma
Transgender
Yellow journalism

---

[1] **TRIGGER WARNING**: There are a number of sensitive topics discussed in this chapter that might be disturbing to some readers. We recommend that you discuss with your professor or instructor as to how much or how little of this chapter you will be responsible for.

INTRODUCTION

Women are often overlooked as research subjects in a number of disciplines, including medicine. This is true as well in the study of female inmates. Part of the reason for the absence of studies on women in prison is the fact that there are far fewer incarcerated females than males. Only about 7 percent of those incarcerated in state and federal prisons are women (U.S. Federal Bureau of Prisons, 2021). Yet women include the fastest-growing segment of prisoners in the Western world (Day et al., 2018; Jeffries and Newbold, 2016). The number of females who are incarcerated has risen exponentially since 1980, largely due to "get tough on drugs" campaigns, but girls and women still represent only a tiny fraction of all those incarcerated.

Ask corrections officers who they would prefer to supervise and most would reply that males are easier to manage in jails and prisons. Some of this has to do with the fact that jails and prisons are built and run on a male model of incarceration. But much of this has to do with the unique challenges that women face in jail and prisons that male inmates do not necessarily face. The way jails and prisons are managed also is due to the stereotypes held by many, including that females get "overly emotional and hysterical" while males displaying the same behavior (e.g., shouting, lashing out), are simply viewed as angry. Given the choice between dealing with a so-called hysterical female and an angry male, male corrections officers in particular prefer the latter.

WHY WOMEN GO TO JAIL AND PRISON

Predictably, the American Civil Liberties Union (ACLU) believes that there is over-incarceration in the United States, including women (ACLU, 2021). As the quote at the beginning of this chapter indicates, the same social ills that plague men and send them to prison will likewise do so for women as well. However, there are challenges that are unique to women who are incarcerated, including for some, pregnancy. This runs counter to our societal expectations of women. For example, we might ask why a woman would, by commiting a crime, risk losing her children but we don't always ask the same question about men who are criminals. The answer as to why women commit crimes may lie in who goes to prison. According to Alexander (2017, para 6),

> *Our women's prison are filled with people from the poorest, most vulnerable and marginalized segments of our society, whose offenses are often a consequence of their circumstances: lack of access to employment, familial stability, drug treatment, and protection from sexual and physical abuse.*

Similar to males who are arrested, a good portion of females are picked up on drug charges. Both women and men landing in prison often have histories of poverty and drug and/or alcohol abuses or addiction. Women who end up in prison are disproportionally also victims, as compared to male offenders. Where they particularly diverge in why they go to jail or prison, women are more likely to have been victims of *intimate partner violence* (IPV) by 43 percent, with 18 percent of female inmates convicted of killing their abuser (van der Leun, 2021). In other words, the female prisoner may be both an offender and a survivor (Day et al., 2018). This is not to say that some males experience the same phenomenon, but rather women offenders are more likely to have been victimized. As one female prisoner convicted of murder shared in an interview, she had been "brutalized for decades" and "that morning he [the victim] said, 'One of us is going to die'. . . I just snapped." (van der Leun, 2021, p. 33).

Women are also often arrested as accessories to crimes committed by males, rather than as the primary perpetrators. Seemingly they are at risk of receiving longer sentences than males for the same crime, in certain instances, again due to the antiquated expectation by society that women should be better behaved than men. For example, Christine Sayesva, charged as an accessory in a Pueblo, Colorado, murder case, received 2,191 days in prison (about six years) for the same crime for which six other defendants with similar charges in the same jurisdiction received probation (Malone, 2008). However, studies contradict the anecdotal stories, indicating that women receive lighter sentences than their male counterparts. Men receive, on average, 63 percent longer sentences than females, discounting racial disparities, but only in cases where the woman is heterosexual (Starr, 2012; Rehavi and Starr, 2012). Rehavi and Starr (2012) describe this as *benevolent sexism* based on patriarchy in sentencing, where sentencing judges may be overly protective, holding positive perceptions of the female defendants before them, particularly if they appear to meet society's expectations for them, aside from their crimes. Same holds true for juries.

In maximum-security prisons housing women, we find, as we do in high security prisons for men, that the most serious female offenders in most cases are the primary perpetrators. In a study in a maximum security facility, DeHart (2018) found that there were five distinct groups of incarcerated women. These could be classified as (1) aggressive career offenders, (2) women who killed or assaulted persons in retaliation or self-defense, (3) women who abused or neglected children, (4) women who are substance-dependent (e.g., drugs, alcohol) experiencing intimate partner violence (IPV), and (5) *social capital offenders* (DeHart, 2018). More specifically, in DeHart's study (2018, p. 1469) of the convictions of women,

> *women were incarcerated [in maximum security] for current offences including murder (12%); cocaine or crack manufacture, distribution, or trafficking (12%); homicide by child abuse (10%); forgery (8%); burglary (7%); arson (5%); shoplifting (5%); kidnapping[2] (3%); assault and battery (3%); felony DUI (3%); child neglect (3%); lewd act on a child (2%); grand larceny (2%); and financial transaction card theft (2%). . . . Sixty percent of the women had prior convictions.*

---

[2] Kidnapping charges can include the taking of one's own child, if you are not the legal custodial parent.

It may be surprising to know that not all women, and probably not all men, come to jail or prison completely against their will, particularly in the case of offenders who are not adjusting well to living outside prison walls. It is not altogether uncommon for some of those released after prison to they find themselves so uncomfortable on the outside that they may purposely reoffend in order to be able to go back to what they consider to be a predictable, safe haven. In Japan, where the elderly population is twice that of the United States, female seniors, most of them widowed, may resort to committing relatively minor crimes (e.g., shoplifting) for which they will be convicted and incarcerated because they are economically disadvantaged and actually see prison as a means by which to pay for their medical costs, room, and board without becoming a burden on their families (Fukada, 2018). Prison, with its predictability and because it meets basic needs, however meager they may be, may seem like an reasonable alternative to the harsh realities of poverty on the outside. This is especially true in a country like Japan, where expectations run high that the younger generation will take care of the older one as they age.

SOCIAL STIGMA OF BEING A FEMALE CONVICT

Social *stigma* (negative attitudes towards and discrimination against individuals who do not appear to conform to society's norms, standards, and expectations) plagues most people who do not conform to what society expects of them, unless they can find a place where they are accepted for who they are, along with their unconventional behavior. Erving Goffman (1963; 2009) limited his typologies of stigma to three main types, including mental illness, physical deformity, or disability, plus racial or ethnic differences, or religious beliefs that run counter with mainstream society. We can just as easily apply his theories to the convicted criminal. Goffman's views of stigma (1963; 2009) include the management of one's self once one's reputation has been tarnished in some fashion. Reputation, in many respects, is the primary thing that needs to be rehabilitated for individuals who have been convicted of a crime. Again, this can be more difficult for a female than a male convict, due to the expectations of stereotyped gender roles.

During the Edwardian Age in England (c. 1901-1919) and beyond, some of the most sensationalized stories told about females in the news were about the "fallen woman" or "bad woman." These were mostly fictionalized accounts of women, made to appear to be about real people, and intended as cautionary tales of what happens if women do not follow social convention, particularly when it comes to sexuality. In Jane Austen novels of an earlier period and in the widely popular television show, *Bridgerton* (2020, *Netflix*), set during the 1800s, women who even kissed a man before matrimony were expected to marry them, assuming that the men would have them, at least in the upper classes. Premarital kissing was considered to be a reason enough for a woman to lose her reputation as a "good girl." An indiscretion could even bring shame upon her family. If something as simple as a kiss prior to engagement could ruin the reputation of a woman (note: not that of a man), we can only imagine the stigma attached to women who commit crimes, including prostitution, during the same time period as Jane Austin's heroines.

The stereotype of the fallen woman is based on a patriarchal system, where women were (and are) expected to be submissive and their behavior answerable to their male relatives, including their fathers, brothers, and husbands. As El-Saadawi (2018) proposes in the Foreword to *Unveiling Desire: Fallen Women in Literature, Culture, and Film*, "Women and slaves were and are used by their [male][3] masters: physically, spiritually, sexually, economically, socially, morally, and religiously." Up until later in the 19th century, women were not allowed to own property. If a woman's husband passed away, his wealth would be transferred to the next male heir, even if it was a distant relative, often leaving women and her female offspring destitute. As late as the late 1970s, women in the United States could not apply for credit in their own name without a male co-signer.

If males are stigmatized by arrest, conviction, and incarceration, females are doubly so. While growing up, boys can get away with certain bad behavior because "boys will be boys" but girls cannot necessarily equally misbehave. They are expected, even to this day, to follow societal norms on gender role expectations and possess better social manners than their male counterparts. As Eisenchlas (2013) and Kunda and Sherman-Williams (1993) note, in the absence of any other information, the expectation for how people should behave automatically is guided by specific, binary gender stereotypes.

The world has slowly become somewhat more egalitarian, but there are still a good portion of people who adhere to strict gender conformity. Views on gender equality is split down political party lines, with those with more conservative views more likely to be resistant to changing gender roles (Horowitz et al., 2017). Add to that the complex layers of belonging to an additional minority group, based on race and/or ethnicity, plus poverty, or poor education, women often have fewer options than males when they leave prison, save the unrealistic expectation that they will settle down, possibly marry if not already married, and become domesticated, focused on running a household rather than pursuing work outside of the home. Yet so many women in prison, if they have children, are head of a single parent household. The reality is that due to the stigma of being a convict (or even a detainee, if charges are dropped or there is an acquittal), it is doubly hard for females who are released from jail or prison to resume what is considered a "normal life" by society's standards.

---

[3] El-Saadawi (2018) is referring to male relatives and not slavery.

237

WOMEN CONVICTS IN THE MEDIA

The Victorian Era (mid- to late 19th century) and the early 20th century ushered in a new kind of *yellow journalism* (news based less on fact than on sensationalism in order to garner a larger audience) including cautionary tales in which inevitably, at the end of the story, the fallen woman has repented and subsequently dies from some awful disease or fate. In many respects, similarly to how female convicts are viewed in society, in cautionary tales fallen women are expected to confess their sins and simply go away, never to be allowed back into so-called proper society. In many respects, females who have been arrested or incarcerated become invisible, to this day (Belknap, 2020).

Women who refused to follow convention were often hidden away, sent off to convents or distant relatives with the intention of "straightening them out," or kept housebound. In many cultures, womanhood demands domesticity, docile behavior, and asexuality (Khan, 2018), all attributes that are seen to be the opposite of how women convicts are perceived. Whether the attributes are real or not, female convicts are portrayed in the media as untamed, unruly, and very likely sexually promiscuous, whether true or not.

In a way that is similar to what we saw in literature since the 19th century, in the 20th century we see female convicts in film unrealistically portrayed as tragic, comical, overly sexualized, as in the case of exploitive B-movies[4] of the 1950s. For a more recent example, in the fictionalized account of Aileen Wuornos (*Monster*, 2003, Newmarket Films)[5], a prostitute turned serial killer who was put to death in Florida in 2002, she is written as a victim of circumstances with whom the audience might sympathize rather than be horrified by her crimes. Screenwriters may claim poetic license in the film portrayal of Wuornos; however, in actuality her crimes were brutal and premeditated in some cases.

Though some stories and films look to tell a story of a woman reformed, others, like *Caged* (Warner Brothers, 1950), ask the question as to whether formerly incarcerated females can ever be reformed. The film interprets female inmates as having passions that are easily "ignited" due to their incarceration, resulting in exploding tempers that neither they nor their correction officers can keep in check (Bouclin, 2009). Because of the stigma associated with females who commit crimes, doubled with the media portrayal, it is difficult to shed the shame associated with being a currently or previously incarcerated woman.

---

[4] A B movie is one that is the second to be shown during a double feature, back in the days when you would see two movies in the theaters. The second film showed was generally a much inferior one to the first feature. It is similar to how when you would buy a vinyl record and the A side had a really good song, the B side was usually just not that great. B movies have the reputation of being low-budget, poorly produced with inferior acting by lesser known actors.
[5] Charlize Theron, who portrayed Wuornos in the film, won the 2004 Oscar for Best Actress for her performance.

Women convicted of murder are more often reported in the media than women committing lesser crimes; the same holds true for cases of males suspected or convicted of murder. Their activities are more likely to be sensationalized if they are convicted of a capital crime, as in the case of Aileen Wuornos. Often in the crimes committed by women that are reported in the news, there is a romantic twist, as in the case of Shabnam, a school teacher set to be executed in India, who while pregnant, single, and in love with unemployed Saleem who did not belong to her same caste[6], murdered seven of her family members with an axe, including a 10-month-old child (Mitra, 2021). She leaves behind her now 13-year-old son, who is portrayed as an additional victim (but rightfully so) in the media.

Sentencing for women who commit a crime of passion run parallel with sentencing of other crimes, as compared to their male counterparts. What is interesting to note is that in a study conducted by Ragatz and Russell (2010), males are more likely to receive longer sentences than women for crimes of passion where a cheating lover or spouse has been murdered. This is an oddity as we would expect males to be more sympathetic characters when their female spouse is having an extra-relational affair, as cheating women again are seen as flying in the face of societal norms, more so than when men cheat.

PSEUDO-FAMILIES AND SOCIAL NETWORKS IN WOMEN'S PRISONS

Whereas male inmates will often self-segregate by race and ethnicity, women inmates, including women of color, view themselves first and foremost a minority by their sex. This is not to say that divisions by race do not occur in women's prisons, but they are far less pronounced. Whereas they might be territorial based on street divisions on the outside, as in the case of female gang members, women will create interpersonal networks and groups in prison that resemble families (Kolb and Palys, 2018). As they are not families by legal definition, they are described as *pseudo-families*. These are central to the character of the prison culture in facilities housing females.

Part of the reason that women create pseudo-families in and out of prison is that compared to men, they are more likely to identify with their roles within their families than men do. Men more closely identify with their work role, which is why they often have a more difficult time than women in transitioning to retirement (Gradman, 1990). It can also devastate men when they are arrested and incarcerated, if they were employed in an industry with prestige, as in the example of white collar criminals holding executive positions in financial institutions (Hansen, 2020).

---

[6] Caste system is social stratification in India requiring females to marry within or above their caste, never below. Even in marrying above their caste, they set themselves up for ridicule by their bridegrooms' family, friends. Failure to marry within one's community and caste can result in violence or honor killings for the alleged shame brought to the family (Mitra, 2021).

Even when women work outside of the home, they tend to more closely identify with their roles as spouses and/or mothers than that of their work roles.

Pseudo-families in prison do not always provide the same supportive and positive dynamics that one ordinarily associates with family ties. It is true that pseudo-families can provide emotional and economic support—as in the exchange of goods from the commissary—but they can also be a source of coercion, aggression, and intimidation, as well as incidences of interpersonal violence (Forsyth and Evans, 2003). What may be more functionally positive for women are prison programs with supervision that nurture communities of general support among female offenders, creating social networks to help with the adjustment to prison life and separation from family (Collica, 2010).

MOTHERS IN PRISON

Parenthood, at best, can be trying, particularly for first-time parents. For women, it is additionally challenging because for most mothers, the greater burden of child-drearing rests on their shoulders. Women in jails and prisons report that the separation from their children is the most traumatizing of experiences while incarcerated (Corston, 2007).

Of course, we must acknowledge that fathers who are incarcerated are often affected as well when they are separated from their children. But we also have to consider that females, including those who are convicted of crimes, as we noted, are more likely to be single heads of household in the United States. This plus the increasing number of children born out of wedlock, either by design or unplanned, the greater number of parents who are incarcerated who provided primary child care and had custody of their children prior to prison are female.

Childbirth in Prison

It is, for most people, startling to hear that there are women who have given birth in jail or prison. However, justice does not necessarily standby in most cases to allow pregnant women to give birth before they are arrested or serve their sentence, if they have committed a crime that warrants jail or prison time. According to Clarke and Simon (2013) and Clarke and Adashi (2011), between 5 and 10 percent of women enter jail or prison pregnant and approximately 2,000 babies a year are born behind bars. This creates a number of ethical and medical dilemmas.

Any woman who has given birth will tell you that it can be stressful during the time leading up to and during birth. Because women who give birth in jail or prison are incarcerated, they are shackled while giving birth. This does not necessarily make for the healthiest or easiest delivery, as in some cases labor lasts hours. Being deprived of the ability to get up and move around during labor may in itself cause birth complications. According to Ondeck (2019), women who are allowed to be mobile during their labor, including being allowed to be in an upright position as well as walking around during labor rather than lying down, have shorter labors, fewer cesarean births, and less severe pain than those who are lying down during the entirety of labor.

With the COVID-19 pandemic, mothers and mothers-to-be face added concerns. It is the responsibility of jails and prisons to keep both mothers and their babies safe, even though prisons are inherently unsafe for pregnant women and their unborn children (Delap, 2020). Again, the problem continues to be imposing the male model of incarceration on the female prison population, even in the case of pregnant inmates.

Raising Infants in Prison

Most women who give birth in prison will not be able to raise their newborns. Some female prisoners will not even be given the opportunity to nurse their babies, much less bond with them. However, there are a number of state jails and prisons in the United States that are more progressive, recognizing the importance of babies to bond with their mothers. Of course, this is easier to accomplish when the mother is in jail or prison for a shorter sentence. As examples, Washington Corrections Center for Women (WCCW), in Gig Harbor, Washington, has a program for new mothers (Corley, 2018), as does Bedford Hills Correctional Facility, a maximum security prison in New York with accommodations for 26 mothers and their infants (Chuck, 2018). Infants behind bars have also been the subject of documentaries, including A&E's television series, *Born Behind Bars*, which follows young mothers in the Wee Ones nursery program at Indiana Women's Prison in Indianapolis (Riley, 2019; A&E, 2018).

However, these programs have drawn certain criticisms, including (1) that allowing women to keep their infants and toddlers with them during incarceration diminishes the mothers' punishment for their crimes and (2) that as the child is technically behind bars as well, the arrangement is argued to be unconstitutional for the children, as they have not committed a crime themselves (Chuck, 2018). On the other side of the argument, proponents of nursery programs argued that to separate a mother from their newborn is unethical and in violation of the 8th Amendment[7] prohibiting cruel and unusual punishment (Beit, 2020). We should also note that there is a limit to how long a child can stay with their mother in prison. Even in programs that have nursery units, the longest time a child can stay with their mother is 30 months or at 2 ½ years old (Riley, 2019), after which the child will have to go live with relatives or enter foster care.

---

[7] We covered the 8th Amendment in Chapter 7 and will do so more extensively in Chapter 13 in our discussions on the death penalty.

Unfortunately, there are few programs in the United States that allow mothers to keep their child with them during incarceration, even for those with shorter sentences. Being pregnant in jail or prison is far from holding a guarantee for mothers that they will be allowed to nurse their infants for any length of time after delivery. We should note that this is not in the best interest of the infant, as nursing not only serves the purpose of creating bonds between mother and child, but also passes on some immunity to viruses and bacterial infections, results in fewer ear infections and digestive disorders, and lower rates of infant mortality such as those due to Sudden Infant Death Syndrome (SIDS) (Cleveland Clinic, 2018).

Allowing women who have shorter sentences to care for their infants while incarcerated also eases their transition to life on the outside, rather than the alternative of having a family member or friend have temporary custody of their child and then learning to care for them once they are released from prison. Studies have also indicated that recidivism rates are lower for incarcerated mothers who have been allowed to keep their children with them after birth (Beit, 2020).

It is a whole different story for the newborns of women who have been sentenced to longer time in prison. In such cases, the newborn inevitably has to go to live with the father or other family members, be placed in foster care, or be put up for adoption. Typically, the newborn is taken from its mother within 48 to 72 hours (Chuck, 2018).

To paraphrase Hillary Clinton (2012), former First Lady, senator, and Secretary of State, it takes a village to raise a child. Even under the best of circumstances of a two-parent household, the extended family of grandparents, aunts, uncles, etc., as well as a community support system of friends, neighbors, and clergy is the ideal when there is a newborn involved. These social ties can be extremely helpful in the exhausting and seemingly endless job of parenting, particularly in the early years when infants and toddlers are the most dependent. Realistically, incarcerated parents often lose their support systems, if they had them in the first place, particularly if their family members and friends abandon them after arrest or sentencing.

Parenting from Prison

It is challenging for any parent who is away from their children for any length of time to effectively be a part of their upbringing. This is true whether the parent is away from home due to employment, as in the example of military deployment, or if they are incarcerated. Over half the inmates in state and federal prison are parents (Kjellstrand, 2012). A number of studies indicate that frequency of visits with family members reduces the risk of reoffending, once released from prison (Baker et al., 2021; Friedman, 2014; Shanahan and Agudelo, 2012; Martinez and Christian, 2009). Both parent and child benefit with routine contact, even if it is within a prison setting. It is more challenging for women to maintain a relationship with their children while incarcerated. Due to the fewer numbers of women in prison, they are often housed a greater distance from their homes and receive fewer visits from their families, as compared to male prisoners (Balahur and Ichim, 2019).

There is also the possibility that the children do not want to see their incarcerated parent, due to embarrassment, anger, and a range of other emotions. For a number of children of the incarcerated, their lives prior to the arrest of their parent or parents included exposure to poverty, domestic violence, drug and/or alcohol abuse, and neglect (Saunders, 2017; Stanley and Goddard, 2004). For some, their parent or parents being arrested and convicted may very well result in a happier outcome for them. However, even children in the worst living conditions are negatively affected when their parents are taken away from them, even when the removal is in the best interest of the child.

Some of loss of regular contact is actually a function of where the parent is incarcerated. As noted earlier, incarcerated women may often find themselves at greater distances from home. We can often see this in cases in California and Texas, larger states by landmass, where families may have an impossible commute to a prison to visit a loved one. This is true for both male and female inmates. In 63 percent of the cases in the United States, the commute between families and their incarcerated loved ones is over 100 miles (Lockwood and Lewis, 2019; La Vigne, 2014). Lockwood and Lewis (2019, retrieved from/www.themarshallproject.org/2019/12/18/the-long-journey-to-visit-a-family-member-in-prison) relate the stories of women who had to go to great lengths to visit their family members who were in prison:

- Jodi Calkin has been visiting her son and her son's father in separate prisons for decades. Calkin's travels 1,250 miles from her home in West Virginia, driving three hours to the Pittsburgh International Airport in order to fly to Dallas, where she has to rent a car to get to the prison, which takes an additional hour. (Total time commuting one-way: 10 hours).
- Romanethia Porter visits her husband in Solana State Prison in Northern California, a 500 mile commute from her home in Southern California. She makes the trip twice per month, requiring a round trip Amtrak® ticket costing about $106, on top of the $60 cost of taking an Uber® each way from train station to prison.

Compound that with the difficulty of a commute to a prison with children, visitation is a grueling routine that take an additional toll on families. An arrest of a parent can also leave crippling financial burdens associated with court costs, legal fees, and the expense of visiting a jail or prison. When those factors combine to a point where the family may no longer be able to stay connected with incarcerated family members, a further erosion of family ties results (*Washington Corrections Watch*, 2021). The COVID-19 pandemic placed yet another burden on families, as beginning in 2020, families were limited to or prohibited altogether from visitations at prisons and travel was severely curtailed. In Alabama, Mississippi, and Virginia, even visits from attorneys were prohibited during the pandemic (The Marshall Project, 2020).

In some cases, when the families are impoverished or live in cities where people don't generally own cars and rely instead on public transportation, visitation may require a long commute by bus or train. There is also the possibility that after a long commute to a prison, family members may show up at the prison gates only to be turned away on arrival because the facility is in lockdown. Or the inmate in question is being disciplined by temporarily prohibiting visits from family. This further erodes trust for children who may not fully understand why they are being kept from their parents, particularly after a long commute to see them.

As incarceration rates have risen in the past few decades, so has the number of children with an incarcerated parent. Children whose parents are in prison also suffer. When parent-child visitations can be arranged, there is an opportunity to reduce the potential long-term effects on both the parents and the children (Haverkate and Wright, 2020). How well either parent or child adapts to the inevitable changes is also dependent on the developmental stage of the child and the abilities of the parent to be an active part of their child's life, even from a distance.

The most alarming experience for absentee parents, beyond missing developmental milestones, is not being there to assist with the inevitable changes in behavior of their children. Of grave concern is the fact that children of incarcerated parents are at greater risk for juvenile delinquency and adult offending (Haverkate and Wright, 2020). Beyond the threat of offspring of the incarcerated become convicted criminals themselves, there are a number of physical and mental health issues that can plague them, as seen in Figure 8.1.

We generally think of younger children as being more adaptable to change, which simply is not the case when it comes to the offspring of the incarcerated. Visits to parents who are incarcerated, for younger children, can be cold, intimidating, and overwhelming events. In order to reduce the trauma of visiting a parent in prison, some, but not all correctional facilities allow parent-child visitation in

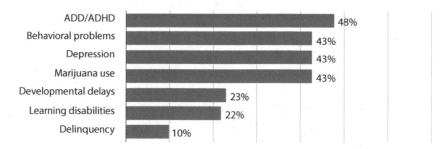

Children with either parent incarcerated

Economic Policy Institute

FIGURE 8.1 ||| **Effects of Parents' Incarceration on Minor Children.**
(*Source*: Morsey and Rothstein, 2016, retrieved from https://www.epi.org/publication/mass-incarceration-and-childrens-outcomes/)

warm surroundings that include non-institutional colors other than the usual drab green, gray, beige with harsh florescent lighting. There can also be activities planned for incarcerated parents and their children to participate in, as in the example of including an arts and craft table in the visitation room.

There have been some recent efforts to normalize prison visits. The U.S. Bureau of Prisons, in collaboration with local communities, has attempted to reduce the stress of prison visitations by providing special programs, like the Universal Children's Day, a visiting event where inmates and their families could get together and participate in various activities and workshops (U.S. Bureau of Prisons, 2013). Unfortunately, these types of programs, though well-meaning, are not consistent and are dependent on interested parties investing time and resources to the prison population and their families, and can often be largely neglected. When they are grant funded, they can quickly disappear when funding ceases.

At the end of this chapter, there are resources provided for children who have a parent or parents in jail or prison and for the caregivers who raise them, in their parents' absence.

Children of Incarcerated Parents Bill of Rights

The creation of a Bill of Rights for the children of incarcerated parents was initiated in San Francisco in 2005, not by the California Department of Corrections, but by a nonprofit organization. It has been subsequently adopted in one form or another by other states, including New York (The Osborne Association, n.d.). The primary goal of the Bill of Rights is to nurture the relationships between children and their parents who are incarcerated. It is also designed to reduce the likelihood that the children themselves slip through the cracks and possibly end up in the foster care, resulting in the increased risks of intergenerational offending. A list of the rights can be found in Figure 8.2.

1. I have the right to be kept safe and informed at the time of my parent's arrest.
2. I have the right to be heard when decision are made about me.
3. I have the right to be considered when decisions are made about my parent.
4. I have the right to be well cared for in my parent's absence.
5. I have the right to speak with, see and touch my parent.
6. I have the right to support as I face my parent's incarceration.
7. I have the right not to be judged, blamed or labeled because my parent is incarcerated.
8. I have the right to a lifelong relationship with my parent.

FIGURE 8.2 ‖ **Children of Incarcerated Parents Bill of Rights.**
Sources: Cramer, et al., 2017, retrieved from https://www.urban.org/sites/default/files/publication/89601/parent-child_visiting_practices_in_prisons_and_jails.pdf; San Francisco Children of Incarcerated Parents Partnership, 2003

PSYCHIATRIC AND HEALTH ISSUES UNIQUE TO FEMALE DETAINEES AND PRISONERS

Beyond pregnancy, there are other health issues that women face. For instance, while most healthy men only have to see a general physician or family doctor once a year, healthy females should also have annual gynecological exams, including routine breast examinations, mammograms, and pap smears to detect for cancer. Though males increasingly need additional types of routine yearly examinations as they get older (e.g., to check for prostate cancer and, in rare instances, breast cancer), females should have routine medical exams beyond the standard general physical, beginning at a much younger age than males, and doubly so if they are pregnant or post-partum.

The health of the reproductive system of women involves more than pregnancy. Women in menopause[8] or post-menopause can experience a number of symptoms that if unpleasant or debilitating enough, can be treated. There is rarely treatment available in prison for the symptoms of menopause.

If women are still menstruating, they are often given inadequate supplies of sanitary napkins and tampons are prohibited in some facilities in the United States. We will see this type of neglect repeated in our section on women's prisons in Thailand in this chapter. Up until recently, supplies for periods were considered "luxury items" in public schools, prisons, and homeless shelters, not acknowledged as being as necessary as toilet paper for women in prison (Marusic, 2016). Marilyn Sanderson, a prisoner in a Colorado facility described in our *Stories from Behind Bars* section of this chapter, reported that female inmates were allotted one roll of toilet paper in the first week, with any other toilet paper after that, plus soap, shampoo, and other basic feminine hygiene items having to be purchased from the prison store (Sanderson, 2017). Without funds, a prison job, or help from the outside, inmates have to resort to the illegal underground prison economy, described in more detail in Chapter 6, in order to get these items.

There are a number of roadblocks to women receiving medical or psychiatric treatment while incarcerated. This includes the suspicion that women are seeking medication in order to get high, even when they are suffering from legitimate ailments (Jaffe et al., 2021). This is a reasonable concern for prison medical staff, as drug seeking behaviors happen in both men's and women's jails and prisons, particularly by addicted inmates. Women are also notably more likely to be over-medicated in prison, with some women in a described "zombie-like" state while incarcerated, to treat supposed "hysteria" which is part of the female stereotype we

---

[8] Menopause is the period of time in which women's menstrual cycles become sporadic and stop all together, naturally happening sometime after age 45 (Hadizadeh et al., 2014). Some of the normal symptoms of perimenopause, menopause, and post-menopause include hot flashes, night sweats, insomnia, and mood changes (Mayo Clinic, n.d.). If symptoms are severe enough, there are treatments that inmates may or may not have available to them.

discussed earlier in the chapter. If an incarcerated woman will not calm down, they will be made to calm down by forcible administration of a sedative.

Just as men have health issues unique to their sex (e.g., prostate cancer), women suffer as well from health crises that males are much less likely or not likely to experience, including breast and reproductive organ disorders (e.g., cervical, ovarian cancer). Study after study indicate that jails and prisons fail to meet the basic health needs of incarcerated women beyond prenatal care, including for the elderly (Roush, 2021). As women, on average, enjoy longer lifespans than men, a life sentence can translate into a greater number of years in prison as an elderly inmate for female convicts.

Women are also statistically more susceptible to depression and anxiety disorders, though the true numbers for males suffering from the same is underreported. Inside and outside of prison women are more likely than males to seek medical or psychiatric help, largely due to the belief that if a male does the same, he will be perceived as weak or effeminate. As a result, inmates with mental illnesses, including depression and anxiety disorders, are often caught up in the *patient-to prisoner-pipeline*, if they cannot be adequately cared for in the community (Onah, 2018).

Like male inmates, female prisoners also face the risks of HIV/AIDs transmission, along with other communicable diseases. Among these are hepatitis and tuberculosis, a function of living in close proximity with infected individuals as in the example of the close quarters of prison. And as in the case of men's prisons, the COVID-19 pandemic took its toll on female prisoners prior to widespread vaccination. However, female prisoners were viewed as an overlooked population in the criminal justice system when it came to the pandemic, with deaths from the virus more likely to be explained away as the result of preexisting medical conditions rather than an outcome of the inadequate precautions taken in women's prisons (Aspinwall et al., 2020).

Self-injury is of additional concern for prison administrators. Whether in the example of cutting behavior where a sharp object is used to repeatedly harm oneself or the more tragic suicide while serving time in prison, incarcerated women are more susceptible to self-injury. The risk factors, along with the function of self-injury and a sample of therapeutics can be found in Table 8.1.

More alarming, self-injury has disproportionately increased among incarcerated women, requiring a number of therapies noted in the previous table that are not always available in prison (Wakai et al., 2014).

VOCATIONAL PROGRAMS FOR WOMEN IN PRISON

Jail and prison systems tend to either impose a male model of incarceration on women convicts or rely on stereotypical gender roles when creating vocational programs for women in prison. These are geared towards training in lower-paying feminized professions, like food services and housekeeping (Young and Mattuci, 2006).

TABLE 8.1. Risk Factors, Psychological Function, and Interventions for Self-Injury, Prisoners*

Risk Factors	Functions	Interventions**
Race: White	Relief from negative mood states	Individual assessment
Age: Young	A distraction	Collaborative management between medical, mental health, and custodial staff
Marital status: Single	A cry for help	
Sex: Female	Express anger or guilt	
Family history of self-harm and/or suicide	Dissociating from situation or negative emotion	Correctional staff training
		Evidence-based therapy approach
Limited social support	Relief from boredom	Cognitive behavioral therapy (CBT)
Longer prison sentences	Coping mechanism	Talk therapy
Inability to tolerate emotional distress		Motivational interviewing (MI)
		Motivational Enhancement Therapy (MET)
Drug/alcohol use		
Eating disorders		
Depression		
Anxiety		
Anger issues		
Low self-esteem		

Source: Wakai et al., 2014.

* If you or someone you know self-injures, a crisis text line is available at
https://www.crisistextline.org/topics/self-harm/#what-is-self-harm-1

** This is not an exhaustive list of all therapies available for patients who suffer from self-injury.

Worldwide, women in prison have similarly had a more difficult time gaining access to academic programs, which require strong commitments from community partnerships, including those that are willing to assist with reentry (Ryder, 2020).

For all inmates, one concern is how to train those with learning or mental disabilities in anything other than lower-paying skills? Women prisoners on average are already poor, under-educated, and lacking in job skills (Hayes, 2007; Lewis and Hayes, 1997). Unless there is widespread reform of women's prisons in general, those with disabilities will suffer in the long run from the inadequate programs available in prison for those with special needs (Hayes, 2007). Female inmates with intellectual and developmental disabilities who have the opportunity to participate in *occupational therapy* (exercises that help in their abilities to negotiate the activities of everyday life) quickly show improvement in their work capabilities and potential (Stelter and Evetts, 2020).

As women on the outside are increasingly joining male-dominated fields in the 21st century, some prisons recognize that there are some job training programs that offer more promise for women after prison, as compared to more traditional ones. In a study of vocational programs for women in state prisons in New York, women were offered an opportunity to take a 16-hour, hands-on course in pre-plumbing skills, preparing them for further instruction in basic maintenance (Young and Mattucci, 2006). As plumbing is one career that has the potential for a comfortable income, in comparison to more feminized jobs, with the median earning potential being over $50,000/year, according to the Bureau of Labor Statistics (BLS, 2021), it is a profession that offers opportunities for women to escape poverty and dependence on a spouse or other family members after incarceration. It is also a profession that is more forgiving of a criminal record, depending on the severity of the crime, including the ability to obtain a plumber's license (Jobs for Felons Hub, 2021).

SEXUAL ABUSE, VIOLENCE, AND COERCION IN WOMEN'S PRISONS

We do not ordinarily think of rape as being an issue in women's prisons, as most people think that the act has to be associated with nonconsensual heterosexual intercourse. This is not the case, as there are a number of ways and means that a woman can be sexually assaulted that can still be defined as rape. Sexual assault is largely viewed through the lens of masculinity, where female inmate-on-inmate aggression is often overlooked in prisons that are mostly operated by men, even though rape laws reform in the 1970s and 1980s included gender-neutral language (Moss, 2009).

Surprisingly, though there are rapes of female prisoners by male correction officers, it is not the primary way that female inmates are sexually assaulted (Moss, 2009). Moreover, inmate-on-inmate sexual assault is more likely to be relational in women's prisons, as compared to men's, where the violence between women is an extension of the complex relationships, including pseudo-families, in the female prison culture.

The Human Rights Watch has stated that sexual abuse damage goes beyond the initial assaults. A rape or sexual assault in prison is compounded by the inability to escape the abuser, poorly executed investigations, lack of employee accountability, and ignorance or little concern on the part of the public (*American Law and Legal Information*, 2021; Human Rights Watch, 1996). This is true whether the perpetrator is a fellow inmate or a correction officer.

TRANSGENDER FEMALES

We will go into more detail about *transgender* males and females later in the book, but we would be remiss in not beginning the discussion in this chapter. Individuals who identify as transgender suffer from gender *dysphoria* (feelings of unhappiness, unease, or dissatisfaction with life). If forced to remain in the incongruent sex they are born with, they can experience various levels of distress (Bizic et al., 2018). Transgender individuals already suffer from greater rates of anxiety and depression, along with other mental health issues (Klemmer et al., 2021), without the added stresses of incarceration.

The uncomfortable (and disturbing) truth is that transgender females will almost always be housed with males, which puts them at added danger of violence based in homophobia, including sexual assault. And the concern is not simply for the risk of being targeted for violence by fellow inmates. There have been accounts of corrections staff raping transgender females as well, though we do not have adequate data on how often this might occur, as prison rapes in general are underreported (Au, 2016).

The corrections systems on the federal and state levels have been slow to acknowledge the unique challenges of housing individuals within a prison population that they cannot identify with by gender. Besides the risks of assault, transgender females in male jails and prisons are subjected to verbal and psychological abuses. In order to survive in a male prison, transgender females often have to conceal their femininity, which further adds to their anxieties while incarcerated (Baker, 2017).

Transgender inmates who are in the process of transitioning from male to female, including undergoing female hormone therapy or breast augmentation, may be forced to undress and shower in front of male inmates, exposing formed breasts (Au, 2016). In *Farmer v. Brennan* (U.S. Supreme Court, 1994) and *Inscoe v. Yates* (U.S. District Court, California, 2015), the plaintiffs, transgender females, charged that corrections officers and administrators were either ignoring the risks of transgender sexual assaults or were actively participating, in violation of their 8th Amendment rights. According to Ledesma and Ford (2020), when transgender inmates are assigned to the wrong jail or prison and subsequently raped while incarcerated the question arises as to whether they can claim that it violates Section 1983 of the Civil Rights Act or the 8th Amendment, of the U.S. Constitution prohibiting cruel and unusual punishment.

Of added concern is that if a transgender female was undergoing sex reassignment treatments prior to arrest, they may very well not have access to them once arrested. Disruption of hormone treatments will inevitably result in regrets on the part of the transgender individual, as physicians generally will not start gender reassignment treatments unless they feel with 100 percent certainty that it is in the best interest of the patient (Bizic, 2018). Having to regress in the process of transitioning, even briefly, can add additional psychological strain, along with physical discomfort.

SUMMARY

There are a number of similarities between female and male inmates, including a background of poverty, minority status, or drug and alcohol addition, among others. There are, however, a number of differences, including rates of offending and unique physical and mental health needs of women. These are not always addressed adequately in women's prisons, because in general, the male prison model is imposed on female inmates. The media does not help this, especially with movies or television shows with fictionalized accounts of women's prisons where women are portrayed as being either helpless or over-sexed and beyond rehabilitation, redemption, or reform.

In order to cope with prison life, women often form pseudo-families that replicate the dynamics of family life on the outside, including emotional and economic interdependence. As women are less likely to divide themselves by race as male inmates, these pseudo-families can have more racial diversity within them. However, pseudo-families can also be sources of IPV and coercion, which makes programs that encourage formation of strong social ties between prisoners, with supervision, a more successful way for women to cope with prison life.

Challenges to women who are incarcerated with families are two-fold. One, because of the lower numbers of female inmates, they are often housed in facilities that are far from their homes, making it difficult for family members to visit, particularly if those on the outside are impoverished and dependent on public transportation to get to the prison where their loved ones are serving their sentences. Second, a good portion of females in prison are mothers, sometimes pregnant at the time of their arrest and giving birth in jail or prison. Or they may have dependent children at home at the time of their arrest and subsequent conviction. Some facilities do allow mothers to have their newborns in prison with them, generally up to the age of one, but most do not allow female convicts to keep their babies with them.

For the children with mothers who are incarcerated, it is imperative for their own mental well-being that a relationship can be maintained with their parent, unless they were the victim of abuse at their mother's or both parents' hands. Studies indicate that children are much better adjusted if they can continue contact with their incarcerated parent. Studies also find that there are lower recidivism rates for inmates who have frequent visits from their family members, including their children. This also holds true for formerly incarcerated women who have been able to raise their infants in prison after giving birth behind bars.

Women face unique health issues that men do not similarly deal with, beyond childbirth, including menstrual cycle disorders and the symptoms that can accompany menopause. Prisons are slow to respond to these, and in many cases, will not even provide adequate sanitary napkin supplies when women are experiencing their periods. Women can also be stereotypically viewed as more emotional, even hysterical, as compared to male inmates, in which case they are at greater risk of being ignored or overmedicated, when in fact, they may be suffering from serious psychological distress, beyond the normal stressors of prison, that requires immediate therapeutic intervention.

Women who were born with female genitals are not the only population in prisons facing a number of issues based on sex and gender. The transgender community is generally placed in prisons that do not reflect their actual gender identity, including trans women placed in male prisons, where they are subject to sexual and psychological abuses by other inmates and even correction officers.

Because there are so few women in prison, they are also often overlooked in research. This is compounded by the fact that their needs are also overlooked by the criminal justice system in general. They are, indeed, as Belknap (2020) proposed, invisible women, once arrested, tried, and convicted.

STORIES FROM BEHIND BARS

"I messed up. Do I deserve to live in fear?" (Chase, 2017, para 26)

As women convicts so rarely have a voice, instead of focusing on one female inmate or former inmate experience, we are introducing a number of autobiographical accounts in this chapter's Stories from Behind Bars section. Whether these women have names here or not, their stories mirror those of countless, faceless women in jails and prisons.

What makes these women unique together is that they were able to survive the prison experience, the first two women in our stories taking the extraordinary steps to not only avoid reoffending, they were able to become productive, law-abiding members of their communities, countering the false stereotype that female convicts (or any convict, for that matter) cannot be redeemed.

What they have in common as far as their offenses go, can be found in Merton's Strain Theory, where he proposed that when confronted with a number of road-blocks to what society expects of you, there is the risk of turning to a life of crime in order to meet those goals. In some cases, the crimes were committed out of desperation as they try to dig themselves out of a life of perpetual poverty. In others, they were committed crimes because they were addicted to drugs and/or alcohol.

Olivia Hamilton, formerly incarcerated

Olivia started her early life in ways similar to those of many women who find themselves incarcerated. Abandoned by her parents during her childhood, pregnant in her teens, Olivia gave birth in prison to her youngest child, delivered by a medically unnecessary Cesarean section (C-section)[9], while serving a six-month

---

[9] A Cesarean section or C-section as it is more commonly called, is the surgical removal of a fetus or infant through the abdomen in the event of emergencies occurring during birth or in the event that the woman's pelvis is too small to safely deliver their baby vaginally. As it involves major abdominal surgery, there can be more complications that can occur than with a routine vaginal birth, though C-sections have become fairly routine as well in recent decades. Recovery time after birth takes longer, typically from six to eight weeks. Needless to say, giving birth at all in prison is not ideal, more so in the case of a C-section preformed in prison.

sentence for embezzlement, a nonviolent white collar crime. She was chained to the operating table during the procedure. Her pregnancy during incarceration was not without risks:

> The [prison] doctor complained that I wasn't getting enough water, vitamins, or fresh fruits, and that it could affect my baby's brain. The county doesn't give you fruits, and it's not like I could buy them. So I just tried to drink as much water as I possibly could. (Hamilton, 2017, para 22)

At the time of her arrest, Olivia, unmarried, already had two other children and was working two jobs, one at Kmart, the other at Pep Boys, an auto parts and repair store. To compound the challenges of poverty in her life, she and her boyfriend had been displaced, living in FEMA housing after Hurricane Katrina devastated New Orleans in 2005.

By Olivia's account, she had a friend come through her checkout at Kmart and she did not ring her up for all the items, including diapers that Olivia needed. The embezzlement was caught on video tape, she was arrested, fired from her job, and the store pressed criminal charges. Olivia claims she took about $300 in merchandise, which would have been a misdemeanor, while the store claimed it was closer to $1,200, which made it a felony embezzlement conviction in Georgia. In Olivia's mind at the time of offending, she had no criminal record and expected that the worst that could happen to her was probation, if convicted.

Postscript: Olivia eventually married her then boyfriend and has since mended the relationship with her mom following release.

Maria Taylor, formerly incarcerated

Maria Taylor was a juvenile when she was involved in a drug deal that turned violent, resulting in an adult sentence for second-degree murder. She grew up in a single-parent household in Pittsburgh, Pennsylvania, in a gang-infested neighborhood. It was rare for girls in her neighborhood, particularly if they were Hispanic, to complete their education beyond middle school. Girls as young as twelve years old would get pregnant, ending up in the welfare system. Maria herself was pregnant by age twelve, a victim of the landlord. Her mother took her to have an abortion, and she left school by the ninth grade. At fourteen, she had a job at a mall in a clothing store. When the cash register came up $380 short one day, even though she was not accused of embezzling, because of her position as the assistant to the assistant manager, she was held accountable for the missing money. Maria has no memory of ever being happy in her childhood.

After 16 years in prison for second-degree murder, Maria was suddenly called up before the parole board. During her incarceration, by her account, she had become stronger and to a large extent, a vocal activist, who initiated class action litigation against the prison for incidences of sexual abuse and rape by correction officers. Being called before the parole board meant early release, news that can be a cause of both joy and fear:

> *All that mattered was that the parole board wanted to see me. Then my happiness turned to fear, because a staff member knew that the parole board wanted to see me. Now I was even more of a target. . . . Every prisoner who goes to the parole board gets picked on by guards and other prisoners. . . . So my happiness immediately turned to extreme fear. I didn't want to be in the shower because I was afraid someone was going to come in and try to hurt me. I didn't want to leave my room.* (Taylor, 2017, para 43)

Eventually Maria received a commutation by the governor of Pennsylvania after she actively petitioned to have her sentence reduced.

Postscript: Maria was released in 2009 and completed college, including graduate school, starting a program in her community that is focused on at-risk girls and women. She attributes her successful reentry to the people who mentored her, including those in her graduate program, and in turn, has devoted her life to helping other girls and women in need.

Marilyn Sanderson, currently incarcerated for second-degree murder

Marilyn is the product of a broken home in Colorado, with parents that divorced when she was six years old. This in itself is far from unusual with a divorce rate of over 50 percent in the United States, but tragically her mother's second husband sexually abused her from the time she was 8 years old, saying "it's our little secret," an all too frequent mantra of sexual predators of children. A year later her mother remarried again, this time to an alcoholic. By age 16, Marilyn went to live with her biological father and stepmother in Kansas. From there, as a young adult, she moved in with her aunt and uncle in the San Francisco Bay area of California. As Marilyn describes it, things got a little fuzzy around this time as she began taking drugs, including methamphetamine, which is highly addictive.

After a series of boyfriends and two children later, she met Tony, who became abusive. At the time, she was taking prescription Xanax, which, like the methamphetamine, by her account, made her memory hazy of events leading up to Tony's death and her part in his murder. Her brother and his friend disposed of the body after which Marilyn went to the police with a made up story which led them back to her brother as a suspect. He confessed to his role in removing the body. Marilyn was ultimately charged with first-degree murder, conspiracy to commit murder, and kidnapping. She was told by the prosecutors that unless she took a plea agreement, most likely she would lose her two children with no chance of seeing them again. The plea agreement essentially accomplished the same thing, as she accepted the deal to serve 60 to 80 years in prison for second-degree murder, even though she has no recollection of killing Tony herself. She has not seen her children since they were two and five years old.

Marilyn is currently approaching her 50s and has experienced a number of health problems while incarcerated, including a required hysterectomy[10]. She has found that the prison staff is slow to respond to medical issues of inmates:

> *If you have an obvious emergency or an injury, the prison staff will deal with you immediately. Otherwise, you submit a 'kite,' which is a medical request form. You turn it in with your problem, and you may or may not hear back, and you may or may not get scheduled. You definitely won't hear for at least a couple of weeks; it's at the prison's discretion.* (Sanderson, 2017, para 37)

The most alarming medical emergency Marilyn has experienced while incarcerated was when she woke up one morning to find that her face was drooping and she couldn't form her words, usually signs of a stroke. After seeing a neurologist outside of the prison who ordered a CT scan and MRI, they were followed by a spinal tap after a couple of unidentifiable spots on her brain were discovered in the previous tests.

Ordinarily when someone undergoes a spinal tap, they are required to lie still afterwards for a few hours to prevent headaches. In Marilyn's case, they put her in the back of the prison transport vehicle fairly quickly after the procedures and drove her back to the prison over bumpy roads, resulting in a severe headache. To date, she is still experiencing difficulty with words, and even though she is still experiencing stroke symptoms, was not allowed to see a neurologist again, stating that since there was no definitive diagnosis, there was no need.

Postscript: In spite of the length of her sentence, Marilyn holds out hope she will eventually be released from prison. She does not accept the fact that she is most likely facing a lifetime in prison. Her biggest regret is that her brother was also incarcerated after his confession to his role in the murder. She is one of the fortunate few with a longer sentence with a mother who is very much still a part of her life and gives her hope that she will eventually be able to build a relationship with her own children.

SOURCES

Alexander, M. (2017) Forward: Standing without sweet company, in *Inside This Place, Not of It: Narratives from Women's Prisons*, R. Levi and A. Waldman, eds. Voice of Witness© (VOW). Brooklyn, NY: Verso Books. Kindle ed.

Chase, S. (2017) Sarah Chase, in *Inside This Place, Not of It: Narratives from Women's Prisons*, R. Levi and A. Waldman, eds. Voice of Witness© (VOW). Brooklyn, NY: Verso Books. Kindle ed.

Hamilton, O. (2017) Olivia Hamilton, in *Inside This Place, Not of It: Narratives from Women's Prisons*, R. Levi and A. Waldman, eds. Voice of Witness© (VOW). Brooklyn, NY: Verso Books. Kindle ed.

---

[10] Surgical removal of the uterus, due to cancer or other reproductive disorders.

Levi, R. and A. Waldman, eds. (2017) *Inside This Place, Not of It: Narratives from Women's Prisons.* Voice of Witness©. Brooklyn, NY: Verso Books. Kindle ed.

Sanderson, M. (2017) Marilyn Sanderson. *Inside This Place, Not of It: Narratives from Women's Prisons.* Voice of Witness©. Brooklyn, NY: Verso Books. Kindle ed.

Taylor, M. (2017) Maria Taylor, in *Inside This Place, Not of It: Narratives from Women's Prisons,* R. Levi and A. Waldman, eds. Voice of Witness© (VOW). Brooklyn, NY: Verso Books. Kindle ed.

INTERNATIONAL PERSPECTIVES ON PUNISHMENT AND CORRECTIONS: THAILAND

Thailand is a contradiction in laws, with reportedly thriving sex tourism existing side-by-side with severe punishment for seemingly innocent crimes, as well as for more universally serious offenses. According to Iverson (2017), in an article to inform tourists of obscure laws in Thailand, the following offenses can land you in a Thai jail or prison (or worse):

1. Any criticism of the royal family, including during the daily ritual of the national anthem being played, can result in jail time, where both citizens and tourists alike are expected to stand still for a moment and pay tribute to the country.
2. Going without underwear ("going commando") outside of the home is illegal.
3. There are a number of places where tourists will be arrested and receive prison time if they drink alcoholic beverages, including places of worship and public parks.
4. Even if tourists are of legal age to drink alcoholic beverages in Thailand (age 20), purchase of liquor is prohibited between 2 and 5 p.m. and midnight to 11 a.m., plus election day, on the birthdays of the Queen and King of Thailand, and some religious holidays.[11]
5. It is illegal to drive a motorcycle or car shirtless, resulting in a fine.
6. Though the recommendation for tourists anywhere in the world is to carry some form of identification at all times while traveling, it is illegal to not do so in Thailand.
7. Thailand, like many other countries in the world, will sentence tourists and Thai citizens to death if they are caught carrying a substantially large quantity of drugs.

In 1999, 20th Century Fox studio[12] released a motion picture, *Brokedown Palace*, in which two fictional American women, loosely based on a composite of

---

[11] We should note that some states in the United States have a "blue law" where it is illegal to do any secular activities on the Sabbath, including selling or buying alcoholic beverages on Sunday (e.g., before noon on Sunday in Massachusetts).

[12] After the Walt Disney Company purchased the studio in 2020, the film making portion of the old 20th Century Fox was renamed 20th Century Studio.

real women, were arrested and thrown into a Thai prison after unwittingly taking part in a drug smuggling operation. The conditions of the prison were depicted as nightmarish, including prisoners being forced to sleep on woven mats on a dirt floor in an open air cell. The American women did not know the language, nor customs, and had to quickly to learn the prison culture from the more generous of fellow prisoners. Audiences were left wondering how much the film accurately portrayed real conditions in Thai prisons for women.

We specifically include Thailand in this chapter, as it reportedly has the highest incarceration rate of females in the world (Jeffries, et al., 2020; Castillo, 2019; Chokprajakchat and Techagaisiyavanit, 2019). Reported conditions in women's prisons in Thailand seem to accurately mirror what we see in the movie. Fifty women are made to sleep on mats, sometimes served rotting food for their meals (Castillo, 2019). And as we see worldwide, overcrowding in women's prisons in Thailand continues to be a chronic problem. Thai women's prisons can be at 94 percent to 652 percent of capacity, even in model prisons (International Federation for Human Rights, 2019). Even so-called "model" prisons operate well below international standards for humane treatment in corrections (International Federation for Human Rights, 2019).

As we have seen in the United States and elsewhere, a good portion of the offenses in Thailand are drug-related convictions for women (Jeffries, et al., 2020). Also similar to what we see in the United States, women's victimization experiences, including childhood abuse and domestic violence, tend to be common themes in female offending in Thailand (Jeffries, et al., 2020) More incarcerations translates to more female ex-prisoners returning to their communities, creating a new set of cultural challenges.

One theme we see in Thai jails and prisons, echoed elsewhere in the world and in this chapter, is the ignorance of prison administrators who are primarily male to recognize that women do not universally experience menstruation the same way. If a woman does not have an adequate supply of sanitary napkins or tampons during menstruation, it can result in embarrassment and humiliation. For women in Thailand, body searches during menstruation, as well as long commutes without bathroom breaks when they are being transferred between facilities, is further debilitating, further violating women's right to dignity (Wongsamuth, 2020).

It is bad enough to be given a limited allotment of sanitary napkins for those who experience heavier bleeding during their periods, it is another all together to withhold providing any products altogether to menstruating women. For cultural reasons, tampons are not readily available in Thailand.[13] Wongsamuth (2020) reports that women in Thai prisons are required to purchase sanitary napkins and when they run out, will not be provided any more by prison staff, particularly

---

[13] According to Goldberg (2018), women in federal prisons prior to 2018 could not afford tampons, with the average price $5.50 for two tampons. To put this into perspective, Settembre, (*Market Watch*, 2018) a monthly subscription for tampon delivery to the home, including an 18-pack, starts at $6.50/mo.

when there is already a shortage of other hygiene products for the women. They are not seen as a priority in prison budgets, even in women's prisons. The Corrections Department in Thailand is dependent on donations of sanitary supplies from individuals and non-governmental organizations (NGOs), but these donations are not guaranteed (Wongsamuth, 2020).

One curiosity in the list of prison facilities for women in Thailand are the Women Correctional Institution Vocational Training Centers (also known as Women's Massage Centers by Ex-Prisoners[14]), with several locations in the country. The "ex-prisoner" portion of the centers alternative title is deceiving, as these women are still incarcerated. Most women who have been incarcerated on drug charges who exit Thai prisons have a difficult time finding work afterwards, and many result to selling drugs again as they find few who will hire people with criminal records (Castillo, 2019). The massage centers are intended to provide rehabilitation to female prisoners, and Eaton (2015) reports that the masseuses are nonviolent offenders and that the settings are pleasant, some including beautiful gardens and restaurants for clientele. This is the antithesis of how women's prison settings are generally described in Thailand, including in the fictional account told in *Brokedown Palace*.

SOURCES

Castillo, T. (2019) Incarcerated women in Thailand face issues seen worldwide. *Filter Magazine.* Nov. 26. Retrieved from https://filtermag.org/incarcerated-women-thailand/.

Chokprajakchat, S. and W. Techagaisiyavanit (2019) Women prisons in North-Eastern Thailand: How well do they meet international human rights standards? *International Journal for Crime, Justice, and Social Democracy.* Vol. 8, Iss. 4:123-136.

Eaton, K. (2015) This is what it's like to get a massage in a Thai prison. *NBC News.* May 8. Retrieved from https://www.nbcnews.com/news/asian-america/what-its-get-massage -thai-prison-n348986.

Goldberg, E. (2018) Women often can't afford tampons, pads in federal prisons. That's about to change. *Huffpost.* Dec. 20. Retrieved from https://www.huffpost.com/entry/the-new -criminal-justice-bill-provides-free-tampons-pads-in-federal-prisons_n_5c1ac0a0e4b08 aaf7a84ac38.

International Federation for Human Rights (2019) Not so model: The reality of women incarcerated in Thailand's 'model' prisons. Nov. 12. Retrieved from https://www.fidh .org/en/region/asia/thailand/not-so-model-the-reality-of-women-incarcerated-in -thailand-s-model.

Iverson, K. (2017) A guide to Thailand's strange laws. *Culture Trip.* Feb. 16. Retrieved from https://theculturetrip.com/asia/thailand/articles/a-guide-to-thailands-strange-laws/.

Jeffries, S., C. Chuenurah, and T. Russell (2020) Expectations and experiences of women imprisoned for drug offending and returning to communities in Thailand: Understanding women's pathways into, through, and post-imprisonment. *Criminology and Criminal*

[14] More information on the centers can be found at the Dignity Network, available at https://dignity network.org/womens-massage-center/.

Justice. June 2020. Open Access. Available at https://www.mdpi.com/2075-471X/9/2/15/htm.

Settembre, J. (2018) For less than $7 a month you could never run out of tampons again. *Market Watch*. Aug. 1. Retrieved from https://www.marketwatch.com/story/for-less-than-7-a-month-you-could-never-run-out-of-tampons-again-2018-08-01-888812.

Wongsamuth, N. (2020) In prison, with periods and no pads: Life in a Thai jail. Reuters. Nov. 26. Retrieved from https://www.reuters.com/article/us-thailand-prison-women-trfn/in-prison-with-periods-and-no-pads-life-in-a-thai-jail-idUSKBN2861HT.

GLOSSARY

Dysphoria   Feeling very unhappy, uneasy, or dissatisfied with life. (See *Gender dysphoria*)

Benevolent sexism   Overly positive and affectionate attitudes towards females, promoting male superiority (Ragatz and Russell, 2010).

Gender dysphoria   The disconnect between the sex that one is identified as at birth and the expected gender roles linked to that sex, resulting in a number of psychological disorders, including depression and distress. Transgender individuals who have not as yet allowed themselves or are not allowed by others to manifest the gender that they identify with are said to suffer from gender dysphoria. Treatments include hormone therapy and sex reassignment surgery. (See *Transgender*).

Intimate partner violence (IPV).   Domestic violence, stalking, sexual assault, or psychological harm perpetrated against or between romantic partners and/or spouses.

Occupational therapy   For adults, it is the combination of exercises targeting mental, physical, and psychological disabilities that help in their abilities to negotiate the activities of everyday life, including holding a job.

Patient-to-prisoner pipeline   Not to be confused with the school-to-prison pipeline described in our chapter on juveniles in custody, the patient-to-prison pipeline is the path that many people with mental illness take if they do not have intervention and/or help from family or friends (Onah, 2018).

Pseudo-families   A group of people who are not related by the legal definition of family by blood, marriage, or adoption, but for all intents and purposes, consider themselves to be a family unit. Examples would be a house full of roommates or a cohabitating couple, who, even though they are not legally related, still rely one each other for financial and emotional support within the household, similarly to the way that legal families do.

Social capital offenders   Women who grew up in rural settings in poor households, with low victimization histories, serving time for drug offenses (DeHart, 2018).

Stigma   The negative attitudes and discrimination against individuals who do not appear to conform to society's norms, standards, and expectations. Stigma is difficult to get rid of as whatever it is, it is viewed as the master status of the individual. Example: Ex-convict.

Transgender   An individual whose self-identification by sex and gender is in conflict with the sex they were born with. For instance, a trans woman is born male, but identifies as female; a trans male is born female, but identifies as male. (See *Dysphoria, Gender dysphoria*)

Yellow journalism   News that is based less on fact than on sensationalism and exaggerations in order to draw a bigger audience, and in turn, generate more revenue for the source.

REFERENCES AND SUGGESTED READINGS

American Civil Liberties Union (ACLU) (2021) Facts about the over-incarceration of women in the United States. Retrieved from https://www.aclu.org/other/facts-about-over-incarceration-women-united-states.

Arts and Education (*A&E*) (2018) *Born Behind Bars*. Television series. Season 1. Retrieved from https://play.aetv.com/shows/born-behind-bars.

Aspinwall, C., K. Blakinger, and J. Neff (2020) What women dying in prison from COVID-19 tell us about female incarceration. The Marshall Project. May 14. Retrieved from https://www.themarshallproject.org/2020/05/14/what-women-dying-in-prison-from-covid-19-tell-us-about-female-incarceration.

Au, J. (2016) A remedy for male-to-female transgender inmates: Applying disparate impact to prison placement. *American University Journal of Gender, Social Policy and the Law*. Vol. 24, Iss. 3:371-400.

Baker, S. U. (2017) *Transgender behind prison walls*. Hook, Hampshire, UK: Waterside Press.

Baker, T., M. M. Mitchell, J. A. Gordon (2021) Prison visitation and concerns about reentry: variations in frequency of visits are associated with reentry concerns among people incarcerated. *International Journal of Offender Therapy and Comparative Criminology*. Electronic publication. May 4: 306624X211013516

Balahur, D. and G. M. Ichim (2019) Women and gendered penalties: Risks and needs of female prisoners. *Scientific Annals of Al. I. Cuza University*, Department of Sociology and Social Work. Dec., Vol. 12, Iss. 2:15-24.

Beit, C. (2020) Legal, ethical, and developmental considerations concerning children in prison nursery programs. *Family Court Review*. Oct., Vol. 58, Iss. 4:1040-1048.

Belknap, J. (2020) *The Invisible Woman: Gender, Crime, and Justice*. Newbury Park, CA: SAGE Publishing. 5th ed.

Bizic, M. R., M. Jeftovic, S. Pusica, B. Stojanovic, D. Duisin, S. Vujovic, V. Rakic, and M. L. Djordjevic (2018) Gender Dysphoria: Bioethical aspects of medical treatment. *BioMed Research International*. June 13. Retrieved from https://www.ncbi.nlm.nih.gov/pmc/articles/PMC6020665/.

Bouclin, S. (2009) Women in prison movies as jurisprudence. Canadian Journal of Women and the Law. Vol. 21, Iss. 1:19-34.

Bureau of Labor Statistics (BLS) (2021) Plumbers, pipefitters, and steamfitters. Apr. 9. Retrieved from https://www.bls.gov/ooh/construction-and-extraction/plumbers-pipefitters-and-steamfitters.htm.

Chuck, E. (2018) Prison nurseries give incarcerated mothers a chance to raise their babies – behind bars. *NBC News*. Aug. 17. Retrieved from https://www.nbcnews.com/news/us-news/prison-nurseries-give-incarcerated-mothers-chance-raise-their-babies-behind-n894171.

Clarke J. G. and E. Y. Adashi (2011) Prenatal care for incarcerated patients: A 25 year old woman pregnant in jail. *Journal of the American Medical Association*. Vol. 305, No. 9:939-929.

Clarke, J. G. and R. E. Simon (2013) Shackling and separation: Motherhood in prison. *American Medical Association Journal of Ethics*. Sept., Vol. 15, No. 9:779-785

Clinton, H. (2012) *It Takes a Village*. New York, NY: Simon and Schuster.

Collica, K. (2010) Surviving incarceration: Two prison-based peer programs build communities of support for female offenders. *Deviant Behavior*. Vol. 31:314-347.

Corley, C. (2018) Programs help incarcerated moms bond with their babies in prison. *National Public Radio* (*NPR*). Dec. 6. Retrieved from https://www.npr.org/2018/12/06/663516573/programs-help-incarcerated-moms-bond-with-their-babies-in-prison.

Corston, J. (2007) *The Corston Report: A review of women with particular vulnerabilities in the criminal justice system*. HM Department of Corrections (UK). Retrieved from https://www.nicco.org.uk/directory-of-research/the-corston-report#:~:text=The%20Corston%20Report%20is%20a,2006%20by%20Baroness%20Jean%20Corston.&text=The%20Corston%20report%20is%20useful,having%20a%20mother%20in%20prison

Day, A., A. Gerace, C. Oster, D. O'Kane, and S. Casey (2018) The views of women in prison about help-seeking for intimate partner violence: At the intersection of survivor and offender. *Victims and Offenders. Vol.* 13, No. 7:974-994.

DeHart, D. D. (2018) Women's pathways to crime: A heuristic typology of offenders. *Criminal Justice and Behavior*. Oct., Vol. 45, No. 10:1461-1482.

Delap, N. (2020 What does COVID-19 mean for new mothers in prison? *British Journal of Midwifery*. Aug., Vol. 28, No. 8:460-461.

Eisenchlas, S. A. (2013) Gender roles and expectations: Any changes online? *SAGE Open*. Oct.-Dec.:1-11. Retrieved from https://journals.sagepub.com/doi/pdf/10.1177/2158244013506446.

El-Saadawi, N. (2018) Foreword, in *Unveiling Desire: Fallen Women in Literature, Culture, and Film*. D. Das and C. Morrow, eds. New Brunswick, Camden, Rutgers University Press.

Forsyth, C. J. and R. D. Evans (2003) Reconsidering the pseudo-family/gang gender distinction in prison research. *Journal of Police and Criminal Psychology*. Vol. 18:15-23.

Friedman, A. (2014) Lowering recidivism through family communication. *Prison Legal News*. Apr. p. 24.

Goffman, E. (1969; 2009) *Stigma: Notes on the Management of Spoiled Identity*. New York, NY: Touchstone Books.

Gradman, T. J. (1990) *Does Work Make the Man: Masculine Identity During the Transition to Retirement*. Santa Monica, CA: Rand Corporation.

Haverkate, D. L. and K. A. Wright (2020) The differential effects of prison contact on parent-children relationship quality and child behavioral changes.

Horowitz, J. M., K. Parker, and R. Stepler (2017) Wide partisan gaps in U.S. over how far the country has come on equality. Pews Research. Oct. 18. Retrieved from https://www.pewresearch.org/social-trends/2017/10/18/wide-partisan-gaps-in-u-s-over-how-far-the-country-has-come-on-gender-equality/.

Hansen, L. P. (2020) *White Collar and Corporate Crime: A Case Study Approach.* Riverwoods, IL: Wolters Kluwer.

Hayes, S. C. (2007) Women with learning disabilities who offend: What do we know? *British Journal of Learning Disabilities.* Sept., Vol. 35, No. 3:187-191.

Human Rights Watch (1996) All too familiar: Sexual abuse of women in U.S. state prisons. Report. Dec. Retrieved from https://www.hrw.org/reports/1996/Us1.htm.

Jafari, F., M. H. Hadizadeh R. Zabihi, and K. Ganji (2014) Comparison of depression, anxiety, quality of life, vitality and mental health between premenopausal and postmenopausal women. *Climacteric.* Vol. 17:660-665.

Jaffe, E. F., A. E. L. Palmquist, A. Knittel (2021) Experiences of menopause during incarceration. *Menopause: The Journal of The North American Menopause Society.* Vol. 28, No. 7:1-4.

Jeffries and Newbold (2016) Analysing trends in the imprisonment of women in Australia and New Zealand. *Psychiatry, Psychology and Law.* Vol. 23:184-206

Jobs for Felons Hub (2021) Can a felon become a plumber? Apr. 20. Retrieved from https://www.jobsforfelonshub.com/rights/can-felon-become-plumber/.

Khan, H. N. (2018) The trope of the "fallen women" in the fiction of Bangladeshi women writers, in *Unveiling Desire: Fallen Women in Literature, Culture, and Film.* D. Das and C. Morrow, eds. New Brunswick, Camden, Rutgers University Press.

Kjellstrand, J., J. Cearley, J. M. Eddy, D. Foney, C. R. Martinez (2012) Characteristics of incarcerated fathers and mothers: Implications for preventive interventions targeting children and families. *Child Youth Services Review.* Dec. 1:2409-2415.

Klemmer, C. L., S. Arayasirikul, H. F. Raymond (2021) Transphobia-based violence, depression and anxiety in transgender women: The role of body satisfaction. *Journal of Interpersonal Violence.* Vol. 36, No. 5-6:2633-2655.

Kolb, A. and T. Palys (2018) Playing the part: Pseudo-families, wives, and the politics in women's prisons in California. *Prison Journal.* Dec., Vol. 98, Iss. 6:678-699.

Kunda, Z. and B. Sherman-Williams (1993) Stereotypes and the construal of individuating information. *Personality and Social Psychology Bulletin.* Vol. 19:90-99.

La Vigne, N. G. (2014) The cost of keeping prisoners hundreds of miles from home. Urban Institute. Feb.3. Retrieved from https://www.urban.org/urban-wire/cost-keeping-prisoners-hundreds-miles-home#:~:text=For%20state%20prisoners%2C%20the%20distance,but%20averages%20about%20100%20miles. .

Ledesma, E. and C. L. Chandra (2020) Health implications of housing assignments for incarcerated transgender women. *American Journal of Public Health.* May, Vol. 110, No. 5:650-654.

Lewis, K. and S. C. Hayes (1998) Intellectual functioning of women ex-prisoners. *Australian Journal of Forensic Science.* Vol. 30:19-28.

Lockwood, B. and N. Lewis (2019) The long journey to visit a family member in prison. The Marshall Project. Dec. 18. Retrieved from https://www.themarshallproject.org/2019/12/18/the-long-journey-to-visit-a-family-member-in-prison.

Malone, P. (2008) Long sentence goes against precedent: Woman gets six years for accessory to murder; six others charged this decade for same crime got far lighter sentences. *Pueblo Chieftain.* Sept. 3.

Marshall Project, The (2020) How prisons in each state are restricting visits due to coronavirus. Mar. 17. Retrieved from https://www.themarshallproject.org/2020/03/17/tracking-prisons-response-to-coronavirus.

Martinez, D. J. and J. Christian (2009) The familial relationships of former prisoners: Examining the link between residence and informal support mechanisms. *Journal of Contemporary Ethnography.* Vol. 38, No. 2:201-224.

Marusic, K. (2016) The sickening truth about what it's like to get your period in prison. *Women's Health Magazine*. July 7. Retrieved from https://www.womenshealthmag.com/life/a19997775/women-jail-periods/.

Mayo Clinic (n.d.) Understanding menopause and discover relief from symptoms. Retrieved from https://www.mayoclinic.org/landing-pages/womens-health-menopause?mc_id=google&campaign=12413826146&geo=9001666&kw=menopause%20symptoms&ad=504867715813&network=g&sitetarget=&adgroup=125043279344&extension=&target=kwd-52076033&matchtype=p&device=c&account=6033656803&invsrc=consult&placementsite=minnesota&gclid=Cj0KCQjw4ImEBhDFARIsAGOTMj_nBPjyGX2oKrJoiTkqHD27Ltz1nCw4v9lzhO8REKKhj9APM9N-ydAaAuC0EALw_wcB.

Mitra, E. (2021) She killed 7 members of her own family while pregnant. Now her son could be orphaned by execution. KAKE, Wichita, KS, ABC. Apr. 25. Retrieved from https://www.kake.com/story/43744092/she-killed-7-members-of-her-own-family-while-pregnant-now-her-son-could-be-orphaned-by-execution.

Moss, H. (2009) Invisible aggression, impossible abuse: Female inmate-on-inmate sexual assault. *Georgetown Journal of Gender and Law*. Vol. 10, Iss. 3:979-985.

Onah, M. E. (2018) The patient-to-prisoner pipeline: The IMD exclusion's adverse impact on incarceration in the United States. *American Journal of Law and Medicine*. Vol. 44, No. 1:119-144.

Ondeck, M. (2019) Healthy birth practice #2: Walk, move around, change positions throughout labor. *The Journal of Perinatal Education*. Vol. 28, Iss. 2:188-193.

Ragatz, L. L. and B. Russell (2010) Sex, sexual orientation, and sexism: What influence do these factors have on verdicts in a crime-of-passion case? The Journal of Social Psychology. Vol. 150, No. 4:341-360.

Rehavi, M. M. and S. B. Starr. Racial disparity in federal criminal charging and its sentencing consequences. University of Michigan Law and Economy, Empirical Legal Studies Center, Paper No. 12-002. June 2. Retrieved from https://papers.ssrn.com/sol3/papers.cfm?abstract_id=1985377.

Riley, N. S. (2019) On prison nurseries. National Affairs. Spring. Retrieved from https://www.nationalaffairs.com/publications/detail/on-prison-nurseries.

Roush, K. (2021) Prison health services fail to meet the needs of incarcerated women. *American Journal of Nursing*. Apr. Vol. 121, Iss. 4:14.

Ryder, J. A. (2020) Enhancing female prisoners' access to education. *International Journal for Crime, Justice, and Social Democracy*. Vol. 9, Iss. 1:139-149.

Saunders, V. (2017) Children of prisoners – children's decision making about contact. *Child and Family Social Work*. Vol. 22:63-72.

Shanahan, R. and S. V. Agudelo (2012) Family and recidivism. *American Jails*. Sept./Oct.:17-24.

Starr, S. B. (2012) Estimating gender disparities in federal criminal cases. University of Michigan Law and Economy, Empirical Legal Studies Center, Paper No. 12-018. Aug. 29. Retrieved from https://papers.ssrn.com/sol3/papers.cfm?abstract_id=2144002

Stelter, L. and C. Evetts (2020) The impact of an occupational-based program for incarcerated women with intellectual and developmental disabilities. *American Journal of Occupational Therapy*. Aug., Vol. 74, Iss. 2, Sup 1.

Supreme Court of the United States (SCOTUS) (1994) *Farmer v. Brennan*. United States Court of Appeals for the Seventh Circuit. No. 92-7247.

United States Bureau of Prisons (BOP) (2013) BOP holds first ever Universal Children's Day. Dec. 11. Retrieved from https://www.bop.gov/resources/news/20131210_childrensDay.jsp.

United States Bureau of Prisons (BOP) (2021) Inmate gender. Statistics. Apr.10. Retrieved from https://www.bop.gov/about/statistics/statistics_inmate_gender.jsp.

United States District Court (2009) *Inscoe v. Yates.* Eastern District of California, 9th Circuit. Case 1:08-cv-01588-DLB PC.

van der Leun, Justine (2021) "No choice but to do it": Why women go to prison. *New Republic.* Jan./Feb., Vol. 252, Iss. 1-2:28-37.

Wakai, S., S. Sampl, L. Hilton, and B. Ligon (2014) Women in prison: Self-injurious behavior, risk factors, psychological function and gender specific interventions. *The Prison Journal.* Vol. 94, No. 3:347-364.

Washington Corrections Watch (2021) *Punishing Relations: How WA DOC's Collateral Damage and Hidden Costs Imprison Families.* Report. Jan. Retrieved from https://washingtoncorrectionswatch.files.wordpress.com/2021/01/punishing-relations-e28093-how-wa-docs-hidden-costs-and-collateral-damage-imprison-families-2.pdf

Young, D. S. and R. F. Mattucci (2006) Enhancing the vocational skills of incarcerated women through a plumbing maintenance program. *Journal of Correctional Education.* Vol. 57, No. 2:126-140.

BOOKS AND ONLINE RESOURCES FOR CHILDREN OF DETAINEES, PRISONERS, AND EX-CONVICTS

Books

Acosta, L. (2015) *Please Don't Take My Daddy!* Bloomington, IN: Xlibris US (ages 3-7)

Butterworth, O. (1993) *A Visit to the Big House.* Boston, MA: Houghton Mifflin Harcourt (ages 7-10)

Cain, S. and M. Speed (1999) *Dad's in Prison.* London, UK:A&C Black (ages 7-10)

Levy, J. (2004) *Finding the Right Spot: When Kids Can't Live With their Parents.* Washington, D.C.: Magination Press (ages 3-7)

Caple, L. (2004) *Mama Loves Me From Away.* New York, NY: Astra Publishing House (ages 2-5)

Ellis, D. (2007) *Jakeman.* Markham, Ontario, CA: Fitzhenry and Whiteside (ages 7-10)

Higgins, M. (2014) *The Night Dad Went to Jail: What to Expect When Someone You Love Goes to Jail (Life's Challenges).* Bloomington, MN: Picture Window Books (ages 2-5)

Mayo, B. (2015) *Growing up on 21st Street, Northeast Washington, DC: A Memoir.* Scotts Valley, CA: Createspace Independent Publishing Platform (ages 10+)

Spanne, A., N. McCarthy, and L. Longhine (2010) *Wish You Were Here: Teens Write About Parents in Prison.* New York, NY: Youth Communication, New York Center (ages 10+)

Stauffacher, S. (2009) *Harry Sue.* New York, NY: Yearling Books (ages 7-10)

Walker, J. (2006) *An Inmate's Daughter.* Norris, MT: Raven Publishing (ages 10+)

Walker, J. (2015) *Romar Jones Takes a Hike.* Gig Harbor, WA: Plicata Press, LLC (ages 10+)

Witthold, M. (1998) *Let's Talk about when Your Parent Is in Jail.* New York, NY: Power Kids Press (ages 7-10)

Support Groups

7 Helpful Programs for Children of Incarcerated Parents:
https://web.connectnetwork.com/programs-for-children-of-incarcerated-parents/

MeetUp.com – Support groups for families of prisoners:
https://www.meetup.com/topics/support-group-for-families-of-prisoners/

Prison Families Anonymous:
https://www.pfa-li.com/

Parents with Incarcerated Children:
http://prisonmoms.net/index.php

Children of Incarcerated Parents:
https://youth.gov/youth-topics/children-of-incarcerated-parents

Chapter NINE

Juvenile Detention and Probation

Juvenile justice is probably the area that's most ripe for reform, in the nice liberal sense of the word, simply because there's no getting around the fact that a teenage brain is not an adult brain.

— Robert Sapolsky, Neuroendocrinology Researcher, Stanford University

Chapter Objectives

- Review the basics of juvenile justice system.
- Compare and contrast the adult system with the juvenile justice system, including facilities that house children.
- Review probation alternatives for juveniles.
- Introduce the alternatives for housing adjudicated juveniles.
- Discuss the consequences of children tried as adults.

Key Terms

Alternative school

Case petitioning

Child Protective Services (CPS)

Cognitive Behavioral
    Therapy (CBT)

Differential Association Theory
    (Sutherland)

Evidence-based programs

Food insecurity

Individuals with Disabilities
    Education Act (IDEA)

Intake

Juvenile boot camps

Labeling Theory (Tannenbaum)

National Survey of Youth in
    Custody (NSYC)

Office of Juvenile Justice and
    Delinquency Prevention (OJJDP)

Self-fulfilling prophecy (Merton)

Shaming and reintegration

Social Learning Theory (Akers)

Strain Theory (Merton)

Technical violation
Wards of the Court

Wilderness programs
Wraparound programs

INTRODUCTION

As our opening to this chapter implies, the brain of a juvenile is just not the same as the fully developed brain of an adult. In addition to recognizing this, the field of juvenile corrections requires many complex and specialized services, the least of which is education. Children are greatly affected by separation from their families, even if their families are dysfunctional and have contributed to their delinquency, and they require specialized psychiatric treatment. Separation anxiety is compounded with a number of other psychiatric disorders in detained juveniles, including psychosis, attention deficit, anxiety, and obsessive-compulsive disorders (Abram et al., 2003). Admittedly, some of these disorders may have landed them in juvenile detention in the first place, but incarceration can exacerbate preexisting psychological conditions.

We saw in our chapter on the history of corrections that juvenile offenders historically were housed with adults in the United States and Western Europe, sometimes in co-ed conditions, until late in the 19th century. Some of the solutions for juvenile delinquents or homeless children during Colonial America included sending them to almshouses, placing them in indentured servitude, apprenticing them out into a trade, placing them in orphanages and, to the extreme, in jails with adults. We have already noted that this was not simply a function of space, but rather because until fairly recently there was only a limited understanding of developmental psychology and the brain of a child. The juvenile courts with a separate juvenile justice system from adults did not come into being in the United States until 1899 in Illinois, with all 50 states following suit by 1919 (Burton, 2019; Mennel, 1973).

In the 19th century, reforms by activist groups like the Child Saver movement combined Judeo-Christian values and practices with the development of self-worth within children. However, then as now, not all children were uniformly viewed as "childlike." Minorities and the poor are in many cases still stereotyped today as devious and threatening, even when they have not yet reached adulthood (Burton, 2019). At around the turn of the 20th century, poor immigrant groups (e.g., Italian, Irish, Jewish) and, by extension, their children, were often viewed as degenerate and hence not as "redeemable" as more affluent white Anglo-Saxon Protestants. (Burton, 2019). We see remnants of this class, race, and ethic disparity in the current juvenile justice system in the United States.

Parents or guardians who can afford to do so can hire expensive attorneys or send their children off to private rehabilitation centers rather than having them swept up into the juvenile justice system, depending on the severity of their delinquency. Worse yet, even poor white children are less likely to be suspended from

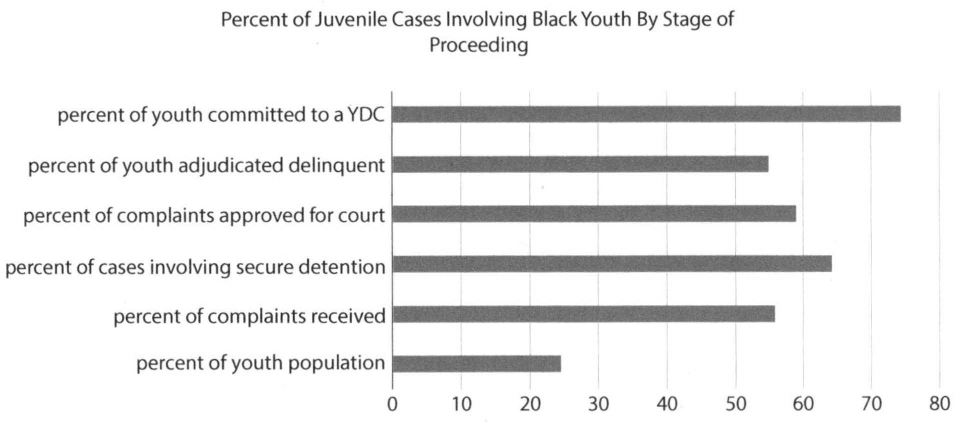

Percent of Juvenile Cases Involving Black Youth By Stage of
Proceeding

FIGURE 9.1 | **Percent of Juvenile Cases Involving Black Youth by Stage of Proceeding.**
(*Source*: Greene, 2020, Race and Ethnicity in Juvenile Justice: North Carolina, North Carolina Criminal Law, retrieved from https://nccriminallaw.sog.unc.edu/race-and-ethnicity-in-juvenile-justice-north-carolinas-numbers/)

school or sent to juvenile detention as compared to Black children who come from wealthy families, with race disparity existing today in the juvenile justice system, as it similarly does in the adult system (Ward, 2012). This can be witnessed in the disproportionate number of juvenile cases involving Black youth that end up in youth detention centers (YDC), as depicted in Figure 9.1.

Even the terms "youth," "juvenile," and "minor" are not uniformly used in all 50 states. In fact, the whole concept of "childhood" is a relatively new one, with some confusion as to when a child really is a child, by chronological age. Whereas we generally think of the cutoff of a juvenile is on the 18th birthday, states disagree on the highest age at which the misconduct of a child can be considered delinquent rather than criminal.

One challenge to the juvenile justice system is whether detention may actually result in graduating some children into the adult system as more hardened criminals. Prison has often been called a "school for criminals," similarly as it is depicted in Fagan's youth gang in Dickens's novel, *Oliver Twist*. In other words, will delinquency engender more delinquency and adult offending for juvenile offenders if sent to juvenile detention? Sutherland predicted this in his theory of *Differential Association*, when there are anti-social influences that are stronger than positive ones, and it is more likely that peer pressure will result in criminal behavior and co-offending.

There are a number of theories that we can attach to juvenile delinquents, their experiences in detention, and to their life courses. We do not, by far, offer an exhaustive list. In fact, we encourage the reader to think about other plausible explanations as to why juvenile detention fails in many cases and why a number of delinquent children end up aging into the adult prison, after exiting the juvenile justice or child welfare systems.

In being formally charged and sent to a detention center, might the following conditions result?

- Individuals, including children, who commit crimes are perceived as "bad" or "evil" people, in which case it may be difficult for them to find positive social role models and find a way to hang out with the "right" crowd (Tannenbaum's *Labeling Theory*[1]).
- Juvenile detention increases any strain the child is already experiencing and may result in additional blocked educational and vocational opportunities (Merton's *Strain Theory*[2]).
- Self-labeling: "I must be bad; everyone says I am" resulting in committing the very crimes and behaviors that are already expected from them, whether they had the propensity to reoffend or not (Merton's *Self-Fulfilling Prophecy*[3]).
- By being in juvenile (or adult) detention, juveniles will learn more serious and creative ways to commit crimes from fellow juvenile delinquents (Aker's *Social Learning Theory*[4]).

Running counter to the data found in adult convictions, the number of juveniles held in youth detention has declined steadily since the 1990s. During the same period, adults in prison increased by 23 percent (Bureau of Justice Statistics, 2019). State officials and policy makers would like to give credit to juvenile justice reforms, resulting in fewer out-of-home placements handed out to adjudicated minors (Evans et al., 2020). The statistics are deceptive, as we have likewise seen a decline in the number of younger people, as birth rates dropped in the United States during the same period of time. Birth rates in 2020 had dropped to their lowest, estimated to be a consequence of the COVID-19 pandemic (Chappell, 2021). It would stand to reason, with everything else held constant, that crime rates among juveniles and youth detention would continue to drop as well.

There is something inherently challenging in guarding juveniles as compared to adults. Increasingly juvenile correction hires are expected to have completed an undergraduate degree in a related field that offers classes in juvenile delinquency and developmental psychology, including criminal justice, social work, sociology, or psychology. One of the risks that correctional staff face is that they may become too emotionally invested in the children that they work with. One key finding in the Critical Incident Survey from the 1990s is that juvenile corrections staff members who become emotional during a crisis will lose control of the situation and may be left with feelings of humiliation due to their loss of control in front of juveniles and

---

[1] In Tannenbaum, F. (1938) *Crime and the Community*. Boston: Ginn.
[2] In Merton, R. (1938) Social structure and anomie. *American Sociological Review*. Vol. 38, No. 4:319-361.
[3] In Merton, R. (1948) The self-fulfilling prophecy. *The Antioch Review*. Vol. 8, No. 2:193-210.
[4] In Akers, R. L. (1985). Deviant behavior: A social learning approach (3d ed.). Belmont, CA: Wadsworth.

colleagues (Farmer, 1990). It is why juvenile corrections staff are advised to have specialized training, including continuing education courses and workshops on juvenile correction issues.

Though generally more progressive youth justice policies may have contributed to the decline of crimes since the 1990s, states that were more liberal did not find significantly lower rates than those that had more conservative policies (Evans et al., 2020). What may be one of the key variables to the decline in juvenile confinement may be the fact that arrests have decreased as well (Evans et al., 2020). Another key variable is unemployment rates—where they were higher, rates of offending are higher as well (Evans et al., 2020).

OVERVIEW OF THE JUVENILE JUSTICE SYSTEM

If we consider the harsh labels for adult incarceration—convicted, criminal offense, etc.—there is at least some attempt to soften the terms that are used within the juvenile justice system. Most juvenile cases are treated in a similar fashion as civil court, rather than the criminal proceedings for adult offenders. Even the courtrooms themselves are somewhat less intimidating than courtrooms for adult cases, including those where juveniles are being tried as adults.

Figure 9.2 is a side by side comparison of the juvenile justice system language with the language used in adult prosecution, conviction, and incarceration.

The most important distinction is that children and adolescents are not convicted, they are found to be *delinquent*. And except under extraordinary

FIGURE 9.2 Comparing Terms Used in Juvenile Justice System with the Adult System. (*Source*: Hansen, *Criminal Justice 342: Juvenile Delinquency*, lecture slide, Western New England University)

circumstances, their juvenile records are sealed once they reach adulthood, with these circumstances described under the section of this chapter that discusses the rights of juveniles in detention.

Similar to how the language used in juvenile justice differs from the terminology of the adult criminal justice system and corrections, the types of offenses that children are adjudicated for include bad behavior or habits that we don't ordinarily treat as "criminal" in adults. For example, a juvenile who runs away from home can be held by law enforcement until a solution can be found, including return to parents or guardians or entering the child welfare system or foster care. Generally, adults who disappear from home and whose whereabouts are unknown are simply reported as missing. If subsequently found, unless they misled law enforcement in their disappearance (e.g., by faking their death), they will not be detained nor forced to return home. Likewise, if a college student skips classes regularly (something we do not recommend), they will not be taken in by authorities for truancy, unlike in the case of children due to compulsory education laws for juveniles, even if they are old enough to officially drop of school before graduating high school.

Parental Rights

What many parents are not aware of is that the ultimate authority over children is the state. Guardians, having been appointed by the courts, are more aware of their rights and responsibilities, as well as the limitations of their authority. This

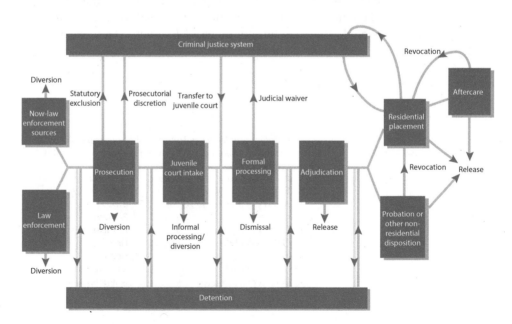

FIGURE 9.3 | **Case Flow Chart, Juvenile Criminal Justice System.**
(*Source*: Office of Juvenile Justice and Delinquency Prevention (OJJDP) (n.d.) retrieved from https://www.ojjdp.gov/ojstatbb/structure_process/case.html)

is mainly for the protection of children, where the state can intervene when there are reports of an unfit or abusive parent or step-parent. Even guardians and foster parents, as much as they might be vetted, can be found to be unfit. The state can also intervene even if it is only one parent who is abusive.

In the United States, parental rights can be a complex issue in the law, as they differ from state to state. And as Senate Bill S.984 (104th Congress, 1st Session, 1995) argued, some decisions in both federal and state courts treat parental rights as not being part and parcel of general fundamental rights and freedoms in the United States, with some decisions resulting in more dire conditions for both parents or guardians and their children or wards. This can include decisions made in juvenile courts.

Few, if any, parents want to be called unfit to care for their own children or to relinquish their care, regardless of how dysfunctional their own lives may be. Once a child has been taken into custody and entered the juvenile justice system the message perceived by the parents or guardians is that they are, basically, failures as parents, whether that is factual or not.

It is possible for parents or guardians to relinquish their rights to care for their children or adolescents. For juveniles in detention centers, the only place for them to go after their sentence is served may be either to relatives' homes or into foster care, or detrimentally to their well-being, if they run away from home, to the streets. By terminating parental rights, the parent or guardian loses the following capabilities of care and decision making for their child:

- All rights and responsibilities towards the child.
- Any legal right to see or visit the child, have custody of the child, or be involved in any decisions made regarding the child's future.
- Any authority to decide when and how to end the legal rights of the parent, as this is ultimately for the courts to decide once the process begins.

This does not mean that parents or guardians cannot petition to resume their parental rights. But it is generally an expensive, uphill battle to face once they have relinquished their rights in the first place. The courts can intervene in the following scenarios to remove parental rights, including juveniles within the juvenile corrections system (Miller-Perrin and Perrin, 2013):

- Dependence on *Child Protective Services* (CPS); e.g., multiple calls to the home. CPS is responsible, along with the courts, to remove juveniles from the homes of unfit parents, relatives, or guardians;
- Court has ordered services, but problem continues, including abuse and/or delinquency;
- Child has been out of home care for a number of months, a number which is different from state to state;
- There is little likelihood that conditions have or will improve in the home once a juvenile is released from detention; and

- The continued relationship between parent and child will make finding a permanent home more difficult.

Rights of Juveniles at Intake

Juvenile *intake* is the process by which a juvenile is referred to the juvenile justice system, to determine what type of programs may be appropriate. Much of what we find to be the rights of juveniles is similar to that of adults. In fact, with a few exceptions, they are exactly the same. Because of the importance of Constitutional Rights in the United States for the detained and incarcerated, they bear repeating here as well (Umpierre, 2014):

- **Free speech (1st Amendment).** Speech is limited in juvenile detention centers and adult prisons, to the extent that speech does not interfere with the security of the facility. The classic example is someone shouting "Fire!" in a crowded theater when, in actuality, there is no fire, resulting in a number of injuries or even death and the occupants frantically trying to exit the building.
- **Freedom of religion (1st Amendment).** The caveat to this freedom for both juveniles and adults who are detained or incarcerated is that it requires sincerely held religious beliefs, not rituals or practices that are disruptive the routines or rules of the facility, as decided in *Ford v. McGinnis* (2003)[5]. However, as we have noted in the case of adult prisoners, sincerity of belief is difficult to measure.
- **Equal protection under the law (5th Amendment).** There are a number of areas where juveniles in custody are given equal protection under the law. These include non-discriminatory treatment and compliance with Title VI of the Civil Rights Act of 1964 and Executive Order 13166, where staff are required to take steps to make sure that non-English speaking detainees have access to interpreter and translation services. Materials written in their native or primary language must be made available for juveniles in detention. . Juveniles cannot be discriminated against on the basis of sex, race, ethnicity, or religion. This is, of course, what is legal. In reality, biases and prejudices are everywhere, whether acted on consciously or unconsciously.

    Staff is also required to treat LGBTQIA+[6] juveniles equally. This, in particular is crucial, as juveniles in childhood or adolescence, even those in young

---

[5] In *Ford v. McGinnis*, the plaintiff, a self-identifying practicing Muslim, claimed that he was served a meal for the Islamic holiday Eid ul Fitr over a week after the festival ended, which the court found to be a reasonable oversight, as Ford was in the process of being transferred from one facility to another during the festival and also because participation was not mandated by Muslim law or teachings – it is described as a family event, according to arguments in the court records (*Ford v. McGinnis*, 352 F. 34e 582, Court of Appeals, 2d Circuit, 2003).

[6] There are a number of variations and abbreviations of this acronym. LGBTQIA+ is the most inclusive and represents the lesbian, gay, bisexual, transsexual or transgender, question or queer, intersex, asexual, and any other non-heterosexual, non-cisgender individuals.

adulthood may still be in a phase of figuring out their gender and/or sexual identity and LGBTQIA+ youth are at great risk in and out of detention for psychological distress, bullying, assault, and suicide. It cannot be emphasized enough that staff needs to be specifically trained to help juveniles who identify with one or more of these categories.

- **Right to seek legal counsel (6th Amendment).** Similar to adults, juveniles being prosecuted in either the juvenile or adult systems have the right to have access to an attorney and it is the responsibility of the facility staff to allow them access, including to meetings and by phone. It is safe to assume that if parents or guardians are actively involved in the juvenile's defense, they may also be active in facilitating these meetings and phone calls.

- **Freedom from cruel and unusual punishment (8th Amendment).** There are two conditions attached to whether treatment of juveniles or adults is out of bounds. First, the condition or incident has to be assessed as to whether it imposes a substantial risk of serious harm, and second, it has to be determined whether detention center staff acted with deliberate indifference or recklessness (*Estelle v. Gamble*, 429 U.S. 87, 104, 1976; *Farmer v. Brennan*, 511 U.S. 825, 1994; *Wilson v. Seiter*, 501 U.S. 294, 1991).

- **Due process of law (14th Amendment).** Due process includes the prohibition of punishment before adjudication of guilt while juveniles are detained. In itself, this is a challenge for staff, as even in the course of disciplining a minor in the home, punishment may be necessary, as in the example of withholding privileges when the juvenile misbehaves.

Beyond the Constitutional Rights of juveniles in detention, juvenile records are to remain strictly confidential. This is true as well of juveniles participating in community-based programs. Like medical (HIPAA[7]) and school records (FERPA[8]), any records that are generated at most detention and correctional facilities for juveniles are kept private, as the laws are intended to reduce the stigma of participating in court-ordered programs, including drug or alcohol rehabilitation.

Unlike adult criminal cases, juvenile records are private, and kept from the public eye and media. This is why you will only see a juvenile named in a court case if they are being tried as an adult and only in the case of an exceptionally heinous crime, like homicide. We should note that privacy rights do not extend to law enforcement agencies' right to search and seizure in the event that a crime has been committed or suspected, nor for probation officers that suspect that a probation violation has occurred.

---

[7] HIPAA is the law that requires that medical, psychological, and psychiatric patient records must be kept confidential and cannot be released unless there is written consent from the individual.
[8] The Federal Education Rights and Privacy Act (FERPA) prohibits release of school records without the permission from the individual. That is why your own school records, including your grades, cannot be released to your parents or guardians, or anyone else (e.g., prospective employer) without *your* permission, even if they are paying for your college education.

There are specific exceptions to the privacy of the criminal records of minors, as in the case where certain people are allowed access (Nolo, n.d.):

- Parents or legal guardians;
- Defense attorneys;
- Federal, state, or city attorneys;
- School officials;
- Child protective services; and
- Academic or institutional researchers.

In most states, juvenile records are sealed at age 18, but it can differ from state to state. If an individual who has a juvenile record becomes an adult offender, the courts can order the records unsealed for the purposes of establishing a pattern of criminal behavior. Though in theory, what is done during childhood or adolescence allows for the juvenile offender to have the opportunity for a new start in adulthood, without the stigma of a juvenile delinquency record.

Case Processing

As noted in the flowchart earlier in the chapter, there are a number of major crossroads in juvenile justice where decisions have to be made on the welfare of the juvenile and for the community as a whole. At any point, there can be a decision to either release or detain a suspected juvenile offender (Burke, retrieved from https://openoregon.pressbooks.pub/ccj230/chapter/13-20-the-structure-of-the-juvenile-justice-system/#:~:text=The%20juvenile%20justice%20process%20involves,placement%2C%20including%20confinement%20in%20a):

1. Arrest;
2. Referral to court;
3. Diversion;
4. Secure detention;
5. Judicial waiver to adult court;
6. Case petitioning;
7. Delinquency finding and adjudication;
8. Probation; and/or
9. Residential placement.

RISKS FOR DELINQUENCY

Though this chapter is not specifically about the causes of juvenile delinquency, we would be remiss if we did not discuss the risks that contribute to it. Without addressing those risks, it is difficult to curb recidivism in juvenile offenders. Any or all of these risks can contribute to juvenile delinquency, including gang membership and violent crimes.

Poverty

When we are discussing the key variables that contribute to crime, poverty is right up there at the top of the list of variables that scholars point a finger to. However, we should be cautioned that there is contradiction in research, from Wilson's (1987) and others' contention that poverty is a major contributor to crime, to Hipp and Yates's study (2011) as well as Kuang et al. (2019) challenging the importance of poverty as a variable in offending, where even in some areas where there are very high poverty rates, crime will not be exponentially higher. Much of the discrepancies we see in studies of poverty and crime have to do with research methodology, including other variables that researchers test for, and level of analysis (e.g., levels of support in a community; local programs and policies).

In the United States, a relatively wealthy nation, approximately 1 out of 5 children live in poverty even though the United States had reached a record low for poverty in 2019. These numbers have been reversed in light of the COVID-19 pandemic and rising unemployment and eviction rates (Bartash, 2020). During the pandemic, one in seven families with children reported that they didn't have enough to eat in their households, one in five households with children are unsure if they can make their next rent or mortgage payment on time, and one in eight families lack health insurance, all leading to increased depression and feelings of hopelessness (Annie E. Casey Foundation, 2020). Again, there are many factors in how we define poverty; some conditions may be more powerful in contributing to crime than others (e.g., divorce, single parent household).

Food Insecurity

A byproduct of poverty is that an unacceptable and alarming number of families and individuals live without knowing where their next meal will come from. When this becomes a chronic problem, we say that the family or individual is living with *food insecurity*. As in anything else, food security is on a spectrum.

Again, the pandemic created a gap in food delivery, when children who would ordinarily be getting at least one government-subsidized meal a day at school now had to do without when they were forced to take instruction at home. According to the *New England Journal of Medicine*, for children of low income households, the snacks and meals they receive at school makes up 2/3 of their daily dietary intake, and are generally healthier than what they receive at home (Dunn et al., 2020). In a Baltimore City study, food insecurity experienced in 14-to-19-year-old adolescents resulted in girls turning to prostitution and boys turning to drug sales or stealing to get money for food (Mmari et al., 2019).

School (Dis)engagement

As much as we like to think that the United States is at the forefront of education, it falls far behind a number of other countries in the world. Once a child is discouraged in school due to drug or alcohol use, family dysfunction, or untreated mental health issue, they are at greater risk to drop out. If you consider that 68 percent of all males in prison in the United States do not have a high school diploma (Hanson and Stipek, 2014), completing a high school education, at the very least, appears to be one crucial key in preventing juveniles from transitioning into the adult prison system. The earning potential of a high school graduate, never mind someone who has a college degree, is exponentially higher than that of a dropout, as seen in Figure 9.4.

There is also the question about whether a formal education offers practical life skills training. These should include instruction in goal-setting, personal finances, sexuality, healthy lifestyles and relationships. Unfortunately, often these courses are lost in curriculum, offered as optional rather than required for graduation. Approximately 25 percent of high school students have no knowledge of how to manage personal finances, with 68 percent having no understanding of credit scores; 40 percent of adults do not have a $400 emergency expense savings and 59 percent of the employed cite that financial stress is their number one concern (Cooks, 2020; *EverFi*, n.d.). As education is correlated with employment and earning outcomes in reducing crime, it seems that one solution to reducing juvenile crime, and after the fact, recidivism, is mandatory life skills curriculum.

One *evidence-based program, Positive Action*, offers life skills training that begins in pre-Kindergarten and is reinforced through the end of high school, which might be transforming for the potential juvenile delinquent. Their research found that educators who use the *Positive Action* curriculum achieved the following positive

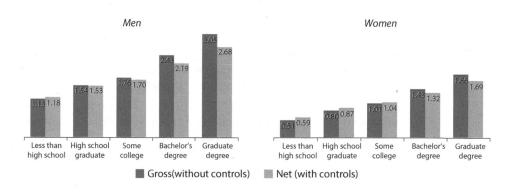

FIGURE 9.4 **Comparing Men and Women, Estimated Lifetime Earnings by Educational Attainment, in Millions of Dollars.**
(*Sources*: Tamborini, et al. (2015); Social Security Administration (SSA), (n.d.), retrieved from https://www.ssa.gov/policy/docs/research-summaries/education-earnings.html)

outcomes in their students (*Positive Action*, n.d., retrieved from https://www .positiveaction.net/life-skills-curriculum-program):

- 63% reduction in substance abuse;
- 28% reduction in absenteeism;
- 27% improvement in self-control;
- 22% improvement in self-concept;
- 21% improvement in physical health; and
- 23% improvement in total development.

Positive Action notes that their curriculum is also suitable for students with physical and intellectual disabilities (*Positive Action*, n.d.).

Zero-Tolerance Policies

Up through the 1980s, if a child misbehaved in school, the worst that could happen would be a trip to the principal's office and having to face the parental units. Corporal punishment (e.g., spanking by teachers or administrators) was not unheard of, but has been banned from use in public schools in some states, beginning with Massachusetts in 1971. Beginning in the 1990s, schools began to implement *zero-tolerance* policies, taking punishment out of the hands of teachers and administrators (Black, 2016). Under zero-tolerance policies, if a student breaks school rules, it may result in penalties, suspension or expulsion, and a referral to law enforcement (Winter, 2016). This means that instead of a trip to the principal's office, the misbehaving child can end up in the custody of police and the juvenile justice system.

At-Risk Communities

Beyond impoverished communities, there is also the consideration of the degree to which there is exposure to gang-related crime that contributes to delinquency. 47 percent of incarcerated juveniles are active gang members, in comparison to 2 percent in the general population of minors (MST Services 2019[9]). Community-based violence can contribute to delinquency. Juveniles who live in communities where they are at risk for victimization are more likely to engage in risky behavior themselves, including substance abuse and delinquency (Bountress, 2021).

Child Maltreatment

One of the problems with defining child maltreatment is that by legal definition and the fact that laws might differ from state to state. Most definitions are based on

---

[9]MST stands for multisystemic therapy for juveniles. For more information, see https://www .mstservices.com/.

physical injury outcomes. This is the very reason why physicians, school nurses, and teachers are legally obligated to report any visible signs of physical or sexual abuse. However, a number of types of abuses might be hidden, including psychological abuse or neglect.

Yet another consideration is the fact that certain family dynamics, including step-parenting, can contribute to an increased risk of child maltreatment. There are also a number of myths about the risks for child maltreatment:

- *Myth*: "Stranger danger."
  Reality: The greatest risk is in the home for being sexually abused, not outside of the home, with the victim knowing their abuser.
- *Myth*: Risk factors always lead to child maltreatment.
  Reality: There are a number protective measures, including a strong family network, even if risk factors exist (e.g., poverty, single-parent household).
- *Myth*: Minor acts of child maltreatment are trivial and inconsequential.
  Reality: All forms of maltreatment of children, however minor, have long-term consequences, including psychological disorders, delinquency, poor school performance, and dysfunction in adulthood.

There is good evidence that a strong correlation exists between child maltreatment and neglect with violent lifelong antisocial behavior in the victim (Baglivio et al., 2020). It stands to reason that a number of these children end up in juvenile custody.

JUVENILE PROBATION

Juvenile probation is front-end adjudication that is intended, as in the case of adult probation, to keep the offender out of a corrections facility and allow them to remain in the community. The *Office of Juvenile Justice and Delinquency Prevention* (OJJDP), a government agency whose mission it is to prevent delinquency and improve the juvenile justice system in the United States, describes probation as the cornerstone of juvenile justice since the 1990s (OJJDP, n.d.). But as in adult probation, this by no means represents leniency necessarily, as it also is practical. Juveniles who are placed on probation can become *wards of the court* (taken under the protection of the court with parental or guardian rights being diminished) for the duration of their probation, depending on the jurisdiction and the severity of the crime. Typically, juvenile probation can last anywhere from six months to one year, with the discretion of the courts to require juvenile probation up to the age of 21, up to age 25 on more serious offenses (Kraut, n.d.).

Juveniles, like adults on probation, have a number of conditions that they must meet. However, as they are minors, there are additional conditions that adults do not have to meet (e.g., school attendance). Some of the general conditions include the following, most of which are common sense, for juvenile probationers:

- Do not associate with known criminals, including gang members.
- Do not use non-prescription street drugs or illegally obtained prescription drugs or alcohol while on probation.
- Maintain a curfew, as set by the Courts.
- May include mandatory drug and/or alcohol testing.
- May be required to submit a DNA sample (e.g., California).
- May have to complete court ordered community service hours.
- Maintain good school attendance and behavior while at school and at home.
- May be required to attend frequent court dates during probation in order to provide updates on progress (Kraut, Child Crime and Prevention Center, n.d.).

As juvenile detention centers are required to offer a broader range of services than in adult prison, including compulsory education, depending on the juvenile offenders' ages, it is both in the interest of the minor and the juvenile justice system in general, to avoid detention wherever possible. Education is only one facet of the cost factors involving the housing of juvenile offenders. Given the example of New York State, detaining juvenile offenders can approach nearly $900,000 per year (Yoder, 2020), as compared to the much lower costs of probation, including rehabilitation services and assessed fees that are passed on to parents or guardians, along with the costs of room, board, and clothing of the minor in their own home. The typical costs of housing juveniles in detention centers in 2020 was reported to be anywhere from $100,000 and $500,000, depending on location (Justice Policy Institute, 2020). Of states that charge a supervision fee, seven states charge the fee directly to the child, eight charge both the child and the parents or guardians, which is argued to exacerbate race and economic disparities (NJDC, 2017). Or in the case of children under child welfare custody, requiring the foster care system to foot the bill for the care of a juvenile offender in their care.

Another often-cited advantage of juvenile probation, unlike juvenile detention facilities, is that the capacity of the probation system, in theory, is limitless (OJJDP, n.d.). In reality, historically the parole and probation professionals have been overwhelmed as well, making some question how effective they can be in their jobs if they have too many clients. There are high rates of job-related burnout among juvenile probation officers because of the demands of the job, including large caseloads and the emotional energy needed in order to work with minors (White et al., 2015).

There are a number of other limitations to juvenile probations, beyond probation officer burnout. As in the case of adult probation, juveniles can violate their probation on the basis of a noncriminal event. As we will see in Chapter 12 on the topic of alternatives to adult incarceration, juveniles can either violate their probation by committing a new crime, breaking one of the conditions of probation (e.g., underage drinking or other delinquency), or by a *technical violation*. Technical violations are "noncriminal, nondelinquent incidents in which an individual fails to meet the terms of his or her probation." (Dir et al., 2021, p. 283; Leiber and Peck, 2013; Smith et al., 2009).

There are race differences in the rates at which technical violations occur, with Blacks more often cited on a technical violation and sooner in the probation process than white juvenile delinquents (Dir et al., 2021). Race aside, probation is not automatically revoked in the case of a technical violation. The juvenile probationer may be let off with a warning or stricter guidelines will be added to their existing probation conditions. However, we should note that even though the courts recognize that juveniles have underdeveloped cognitive abilities, juvenile courts hold probationers to absolute compliance, meaning that they are more likely to violate their probation on some minor condition (NJDC, n.d.).

Juvenile probation officers have considerable control over their clients and their families. One would expect that the parents or guardians of a delinquent juvenile would become stricter under the circumstances. A surprising research finding is that the reverse happens during probation: Rule-setting is loosened by parents or guardians, curfews are not necessarily enforced, and parental or guardian monitoring of the child is reduced (Fine et al., 2020). We can speculate that this may be partially due to fact that some parental controls are being handed over to probation officers, which may unintentionally send the message that the probation officers are the primary agents of change and socialization in the juvenile offender. We see a similar phenomenon in education, where teachers are increasingly expected to be the primary source of positive socialization.

Similar to what we see in adult corrections and discussed in Chapter 12, there are a number of types of probation, including from minimal surveillance to intensive supervision. As states differ in their classifications, we will give the system used in the state of California as one example. The Code Sections in the list below refers to California Welfare and Institutions Code (Kraut, Child Crime Prevention and Safety Center, n.d., retrieved from https://childsafety.losangelescriminallawyer.pro/supervised-juvenile-probation.html#:~:text=Possible%20terms%20and%20conditions%20of,driver's%20license%20restrictions%2C%20fines%20and):

- Section 725(a)—Under this section, a minor can be placed on probation without being declared a ward of the court. The period of supervision cannot exceed six months.
- Section 725(b)—Under this section, the minor is declared a ward of the court and is placed under the supervision of the probation department for six months or less.
- Section 790—this is a deferred-entry of justice ("DEJ") program aimed at first time felony-level juvenile offenders. The minor would admit to the allegations in the petition and the charges would be dismissed upon successful completion of a 12 to 36-month program.
- Section 602—Under this section, the minor is declared a ward of the court and is placed on formal supervised probation.
- Section 727—Under this section, a minor can be place on unsupervised probation with special conditions as dictated by the Court.

JUVENILE DETENTION AND CORRECTIONAL FACILITIES

We would hope that juvenile detention or custody, as it is called in some jurisdictions, would be a last resort. Unfortunately, as we have noted earlier, often the choice to incarcerate a juvenile boils down to race and economic circumstances. Juvenile detention is understood to be

> the temporary and safe custody of juveniles who are accused of conduct subject to the jurisdiction of the court who require a restricted [residential] environment for their own or the community's protection while pending legal action. (Clark, 2004, retrieved from https://info.nicic.gov/dtg/node/4)

Formal Structure of Detention Centers

There are a number of formal functions of juvenile detention centers (Clark, 2014):

- Maintain public safety;
- Maintain the safety of children placed in detention centers;
- Maintain humane and constitutional conditions of confinement; and
- Fulfill the requirements of the specific facility.

Whereas contemporary adult corrections depend on the warehousing of criminals in the "waste management model" of incarceration, the primary goals of juvenile facilities is rehabilitation and therapy. Based on the Balanced and Restorative Justice (BARJ) model,

> the operation of juvenile facilities rests on the assumption that the best way to improve public safety is by changing an offender's behavior. Success in doing so, however, is people-driven and therefore expensive with staff costs for salaries, benefits, and training constituting a large part of operational costs. (Roush and McMillen, 2000, retrieved from https://www.ojp.gov/pdffiles1/ojjdp/178928.pdf)

Educational Services in Juvenile Detention Centers

Though there are any number of federal legal judgements, including *Brown v. the Board of Education* where the U.S. Supreme Court determined that racial segregation was unconstitutional, it is left to states to manage their schools. This does not turn out to mean equal quality of public education, particularly in juvenile detention centers. The importance of education in preventing juvenile delinquency has been proven time and time again in studies; however, the implementation of education programs within juvenile centers varies widely by states and within individual states, often with little evidence to support their promise of success (Sullivan, 2018).

When standardized testing was implemented with President George W. Bush's Leave No Child Left Behind program, New Jersey and Massachusetts ranked at the top in student scores and states in the South and Southwest, including Mississippi and New Mexico, ranked at the bottom. (*U.S. News and World Report*, 2021; World Population Review, 2021). The rankings are based on both testing scores and drop-out rates. It is safe to assume that there is a relationship between the general quality of education in a state and the quality provided in juvenile detention centers because both are equally tied to publicly funded budgets.

Unlike in adult prison, education can be compulsory up to a certain age, depending on the state, for a number of minors housed in juvenile detention centers. A number of states even require minors to attend school up to age 18 (Lohman, 2000). Unfortunately, in a study conducted by Joseph Doyle, an economist at the Massachusetts Institute of Technology (MIT) who reviewed the records of 35,000 research subjects over the course of ten years, teenagers who have been incarcerated are less likely to finish high school and worse yet, more likely to go on to adult offending and prison (Dizikes, 2015). And as we have already noted, education is highly correlated with lifetime earnings.

Of special concern in educating children in detention is that a disproportionate number of them have documented and undocumented learning and cognitive disabilities. Though the federal government, under the *Individuals with Disabilities Education Act* (IDEA), mandates special education services for students who need them, studies indicate that these needs are not being adequately met in short-term and long-term juvenile detention centers. In some cases, juveniles in detention have been denied their legally mandated individual education plan (IEP) and placed in a general classroom. As one Utah mother complained, they are not always given the materials they need, including books, paper and pencils, nor access to tutors (Morris and Thompson, 2008).

All is not lost in education programs in juvenile delinquency centers. Studies indicate that one type of educational programming that seems lead to more positive outcomes for detained youth is a combination of computer-assisted instruction as well as personalized learning for all students, not just those in special education (Steele et al., 2016).

Race and Juvenile Detention

As in adult prisons, racial differences and tensions are amplified in juvenile detention centers. One promising piece of research (Williams and LaTess, 2020) indicates that exposure to cultural awareness helps in deflecting the racial tensions in juvenile detention. This is yet one more component in the complexities of detention that, if addressed, has the potential to reduce the bullying and violence in facilities housing juveniles (Williams and LaTess, 2020).

Mirroring what we see in adult prisons, minorities are disproportionately represented in the juvenile detention populations. Children of color are more likely to be arrested and detained, as compared to white children committing similar crimes. Same can be found in the racial makeup of children who are suspended or expelled from school.

Gangs in Juvenile Detention

As we earlier noted, a good number of juveniles in custody are affiliated with gangs. It is imperative that staff working at juvenile detention centers are aware of gang affiliation during intake, as it speaks to the safety of the facility (MST Services, 2019). If you consider that juvenile facilities have little control over rival gang members being admitted, as in the case of adult prisons, they may have to be segregated to prevent intergang violence. We go into greater detail about the consequences of the presence of gangs in correctional facilities in Chapter 6 on prison culture and in Chapter 10 on violence in jails and prisons. Much of what is contained in those chapters can be applied to juveniles.

As on the streets, there is always the concern that once incarcerated, a juvenile who previously had no gang affiliation may feel compelled to join one. There are a number of reasons why joining may be appealing. First, one of the attractions of gangs is that they offer the promise to provide protection. Second, if someone does not join a gang, there may be a greater fear of victimization by gang members. Finally, juveniles, particularly adolescents, are in the developmental phases of figuring out exactly who they are and what they believe in. With the degradation and possible shame of being held in a juvenile detention center, gangs offer a place to find a sense of belonging and pride, however misplaced that might be under the circumstances.

Keeping violence from being imported from the streets to juvenile facilities is a challenge for staff. Gang members are more likely to resort to violence, as well as engage in violent behavior while incarcerated (Scott, 2018; Decker et al., 2013; Tasca et al., 2010; Delisi et al., 2004). Preventing violence from occurring in juvenile detention centers requires specialized staff training in conflict resolution, as well as gang awareness. It is suggested that one means to distract juveniles from gang recruitment is to keep them busy—but with less restricted supervision, as this can reduce both gang and non-gang related violence in facilities, while giving juveniles some sense of autonomy and independence (Scott, 2018).

MENTAL HEALTH ISSUES AND JUVENILE DETENTION CENTERS

There have been many concerns, as in the adult prison system, that juvenile detention centers are now the place to warehouse children with mental health issues. In a hearing before the Committee on Governmental Affairs of the U.S. Senate,

Senator Susan Collins questioned in her opening statement (U.S. Senate, 2004, para 3) whether "another consequence of our tattered safety net for children with mental illness. . . is the inappropriate use of juvenile detention centers as holding areas for people who are waiting for mental health services."

Not all of the mental health issues occur in advance of juvenile detention. Like adult offenders, these may come after incarceration. Two common emotions of children housed in juvenile detention are discouragement and hopelessness (Lubben, 2019). No amount of treatment will work without addressing the mental health issues that arise, if not preexisting, in youth who are incarcerated. However, as we see in this section, juveniles are not always appropriately treated for their illnesses by staff.

Post-Traumatic Stress and Violence Exposure

Post-traumatic stress disorder (PTSD) can be found in both the adult and juvenile populations. Approximately 5 percent of the general adolescent population (that we know of) suffer from the disorder (Grasso et al., 2019; Merikangas et al., 2010), with higher rates found in youth who have been exposed to the juvenile justice system (Modrowski et al., 2017) and child welfare services (Ko et al., 2008). Trauma and PTSD is more likely to be present in juvenile detainees, as compared to children in the general community or those who have been given probation (Abrams et al., 2005).

In some juvenile detention centers, there is little that can be done to stop violence from breaking out, similarly to adult prison. In fact, in some cases, corrections officers and staff ignore it; worse yet, encourage it. In a study of girls in juvenile facilities in California (Flores, 2013), staff members rely on the "tough" reputation of some of the adjudicated to keep order in the facility by condoning violence, which can run counter with the goals of detention.

Psychotropic Medications in Juvenile Detention Centers

Children can be inappropriately (and involuntarily, in violation of their rights and those of their parents or guardians) overmedicated with psychotropic drugs[10]. The purpose of overmedication of juveniles in detention, and adults in prison for that matter, is an attempt to suppress their violent or emotional tendencies in detention, in something that Flores (2019) terms, *pharmaceutical violence*, with three phases:

---

[10] Psychotropic drugs are a class of pharmaceuticals that target a range of disorders and include anti-anxiety medication, anti-depressives, stimulants, and other mood stabilizing drugs (National Institute of Mental Health, n.d.).

Phase 1: Diagnosis and treatment, or in this case, overtreatment, where drugs are prescribed haphazardly.

Phase 2: Talk therapy with staff creating structural arrangements that made sure that juvenile in detention comply with taking their medication.

Phase 3: Once released, juveniles have to deal with the long term effects in the community of having taken medication behind bars.

Sexual Abuses and Assaults in Juvenile Detention

Statistics on adult victimization are imperfect, as there can be underreporting, particularly in the case of rape or sexual assaults. Data on juvenile victimization is even more difficult, As a protected, special population in research, extra care is taken when surveying juveniles and it can be a challenge for researchers to capture the real statistics. Our best estimates in the United States on incidences of sexual assault and victimization of minors comes from the *National Survey of Youth in Custody (NSYC)*, which gathers data on sexual assault and abuses in juvenile facilities, and from the National Institute of Science (NIS), where approximately 9.5 percent of youth in detention centers report having experienced sexual assault or other forms of victimization, a figure that is twice that of reported victimization in adult prisons (Ahlin and Barberi, 2019). Sexual abuses and assaults contribute to yet more physical and mental health issues that add to the complexity of protecting juvenile populations in detention.

The following is a list of 2018 key findings in the NSYC, as they apply to juveniles in custody (Ahlin and Barberi, 2019):

- Although there has been considerable research on adults in prison, there is less on youth in jail, and even less on youth in detention centers.
- There is little research on sexual assault and victimization of girls and women in correctional settings.
- There are some similarities and differences (e.g., race, history of abuse) between adult and juvenile victims, while in custody. The risk factors for victimization, in order, are

  (1) LGBTQIA+ juveniles.
  (2) History of sexual victimization.
  (3) Younger age (in adult prisons only).
  (4) Length of time spent in facility (decreases risk in adults, increases risk in juveniles).
  (5) Physically smaller, slighter stature (in adult prison only).
  (6) Gang membership (decreases risk in adults, increases risk in juveniles).

- Surprisingly, juveniles in adult custody experience less victimization, with 1.8 percent reporting sexual assault or other victimization. Again, we do not know how accurate that rate really is, with suspicions that the actual number is higher.

- The survey reinforced current research on developmental differences between juveniles and adults, including emotional maturity, which means that individual responses to victimization will be different.

As is the case for adults in prisons, juveniles are not only at risk for sexual assault and victimization by fellow incarcerated juveniles, although there fewer reported incidents of guards sexually abusing inmates in juvenile facilities as there are in adult prisons. In both juvenile and adult correctional settings, because of the power dynamics between guards and prisoners, any sexual relations are considered abuse, regardless of whether or not they are consensual.

ALTERNATIVES TO DETENTION FOR JUVENILE OFFENDERS

As is the case in adult corrections, there are always efforts to figure out what might work to correct criminal behavior, with somewhat more urgency in the case of children. Probation alone is not always the answer, especially not blanket detention for all juvenile offenders. A number of alternatives have been tried, some with good success, others that fail. In some cases, the alternatives are viewed by some as brutal, as in our first alternative discussed, juvenile boot camps.

The criticisms of juvenile detention are many and universal. From studies conducted in England, the following have been used as arguments against youth custody and for efforts to find alternatives (Muncie, 2021; Willow, 2015; Prison Reform Trust and INQUEST, 2012; Annie E. Casey Foundation, 2011; Jacobsen et al., 2010; Howard League, 2008; Children's Society, 1989):

- Approximately 70 percent of juveniles who have been sent to youth detention will reoffend within a year of release.
- A juvenile in custody cannot make restitution or reparation to the victims or to the community.
- Prison and detention centers provide protection from criminals, but a good portion of juveniles sentenced to detention do not pose a threat to society.
- Detention and custody only further breaks ties to family, friends, and community.
- With upwards of 40 percent or more of juveniles vulnerable to abuses while in custody, juvenile detention is not safe.
- The bottom line is that juvenile detention is dangerous, ineffective, unnecessary (in a number of cases), financially wasteful, and inadequate.

Like adults, juvenile offenses run a broad range, from petty theft and simple assault to the unspeakable cases of children who commit homicides. However, a good portion of juvenile offenses are relatively minor and as we have already noted, many have been status offenses, rather than actual criminal offenses. The following sections address a representative sample of alternatives to juvenile detention, with some being better than others.

Some of the programs discussed are evidence-based, whereas others have gained traction largely due to networking and word of mouth among corrections professionals. In some cases, "the cure can be worse than the cold." Abusive programs that outside of detention will not effectively correct criminal behavior; if anything, may simply anger the juvenile offender further, as well as cause post-traumatic stress disorder (PTSD).

Juvenile Boot Camps

One alternative to traditional juvenile detention is *juvenile boot camps*, which are military-styled residential programs for juvenile delinquents or at-risk youth, focused on physical fitness, behavioral modification, and discipline. It is not a new concept, as juvenile boot camps operated from 1938 into the 1970s in England and in the United States and they have generally been used for first time, nonviolent offenders (Csukai and Ruzsonyi, 2018). Residential camps are intended for short time detention and are not meant for extended stays, as in the case of the time served by more serious juvenile offenders in traditional juvenile detention centers. Personnel wear military style uniforms and use military terms, with drill sergeants submitting residents to the same type of degradation rituals and verbal confrontation experienced by recruits in authentic military boot camps (Csukai and Ruzsonyi, 2018).

According to the Office of Juvenile Justice and Delinquency Prevention (OJJDP), juvenile boot camps in the United States were reestablished in the 1990s in response to an increase in juvenile arrests (Peters et al., 1997). Three distinctly different pilot programs[11] were initiated by the OJJDP and the U.S. Department of Justice in the cities of Cleveland, Ohio, Denver, Colorado, and Mobile, Alabama, with the following common components (Peters et al., 1997):

- Military style discipline, with regimented schedule, focused on discipline, physical training, and work (some hard labor, community service).
- Rehabilitation.
- Participant's perception that the boot camp was an alternative to incarceration.
- Residential phase in camp of six months or less.
- Six key components: Education, job training, and placement; community service; drug/alcohol treatment; medical and mental health care; individualized case management; and intensive aftercare services integrated/coordinated with the residential program.

---

[11] Pilot programs are used in order to evaluate research design with the intention of correcting mistakes, if any, and eventually run a full program with improvements. They are also used to collect preliminary data on intended research subjects to further improve the study.

In a way that is similar to the sentencing of adults to brief stints in jail, residential juvenile boot camps are a form of shock incarceration intended to instill discipline as well as to scare young offenders, in the hopes that they will be reformed. Boot camps are also used for "troubled" juveniles who have yet to enter the juvenile justice system, but are at high risk for committing crimes. These are generally privately run and children are placed there at the insistence of their parents or guardians and not by the courts.

An OJJDP experimental pilot study of juvenile boot camps had mixed results. For the Cleveland and Denver groups who participated in the program, they actually had higher recidivism rates, including new adjudicated offenses, than the control groups[12] (Peters et al., 1997). Mobile, Alabama had slightly better results, with 28 percent of the boot camp participants reoffending, as compared to 31 percent of the control group and two sites experienced better educational outcomes (Peters et al., 1997). Worse yet, all three experimental groups reoffended at a much faster pace than the control groups, with higher costs associated with the boot camps and aftercare in the case of the Cleveland and Denver programs (Peters et al., 1997). The following lessons were learned in the juvenile boot camp studies (Peters et al., 1997):

- Staff were inadequately trained, including understanding the program phases and how they are connected. This may have been a function of high staff turnover.
- Clearly defined roles and responsibilities need to be established for the camp personnel.
- Phases of the boot camps and aftercare need to be integrated and continuous so that every staff member is working on the same assumptions, philosophies and procedures.
- Data collection should be uniform across both experimental groups and control groups.
- Outcomes should not only be focused on recidivism but on other measurable successes like educational attainment.

Bottom line, the experimental boot camps did not provide the juvenile delinquency solutions that the program designers had hoped for in any of the experimental sites. In general, the aggressive and hostile tactics taken by boot camp staff where only military style discipline is implemented has not been found to promote rehabilitation. It also can result in endangering the physical health of the participants by imposing overly strenuous physical exercises that have even resulted in the death of some juveniles in boot camp care (Csukai and Ruzsonyi, 2018).

---

[12] In social psychological experimental research, a control group is one that does not receive treatment or participate in a program that is designed to change behavioral outcomes. That way researchers can see if interventions really work. In the case of this study of pilot juvenile boot camps, the interventions in Cleveland and Denver worsened recidivism rates.

Wilderness Programs

Wilderness programs (or wilderness camps, wilderness therapy) have become popular in recent decades in the corporate world, used as executive retreats. Based on the two premises that being in the great outdoors is good for the soul and that getting away from life's routines facilitates team building, organized wilderness programs are viewed as beneficial for boosting self-confidence and self-awareness. Most scouting groups for juveniles incorporate some form of camping experience and outdoor adventures in their curriculum so that members can earn badges and, in the case of the Boy Scouts and Girl Scouts, move up in the ranks by, for example, becoming an Eagle Scout.

Wilderness programs have also been used for "troubled youth" or "troubled teens." This does not require the juvenile to be adjudicated in the courts in order to participate in residential wilderness programs. Often, like with boot camps, juveniles are referred there by parents, guardians, and/or therapists. However, they have also been used as yet another alternative to detention. What makes this different than the typical summer youth camp is that there is concerted focus on changing negative attitudes and behaviors. The target population varies by location, but on average, the participants range in ages from 11 to 17, with the vast majority older teenagers (OJJDP, 2011; Fuentes and Burnes, 2002).

Outward Bound Intercept Program. (*Source*: Outward Bound, n.d., retrieved from https://shutr.bz/3uE6t9s)

As many of these programs are operated by private organizations, hence many for profit, there is no consistency in treatment. More so, there is also no uniform definition of the residential programs that would help in distinguishing one program from another (OJJDP, 2011). There are some general similarities in that the camps are located in natural environments (e.g., mountains, forest, desert, seashore), with a number outdoor activities available like hiking, obstacle courses, and rock climbing.

Programs also can include individual and/or group therapy and family counseling sessions focused on rehabilitation (OJJDP, 2011; Roberts, 2004). Team building exercises aim at improving interpersonal interactions and requiring communication in a group setting, which may be at the core of the juvenile's disruptive behavior (OJJDP, 2011). Whereas the research studies on military-style boot camps fail to indicate that they reduce recidivism rates, there are much more promising results coming out of studies of wilderness camp experiences (OJJDP, 2011).

Alternative School Placement

One way to keep juveniles out of custody for status offenses (e.g., truancy) or less serious behavioral problems in school is to send them to an *alternative school* (a school where students who have been expelled from or referred to for behavior problems can go to complete their compulsory education). This is an option instead of suspension or expulsion. It is not a perfect solution, as it both places juveniles with other misbehaving children and labels them, including the misconception that they are somehow less intelligent than children in traditional public schools. Alternative schools are not limited to juvenile delinquents but also enroll students with a variety of special needs or circumstances, such as being married or having children (Verdugo and Glenn, 2006).

Alarmingly, again, a disproportionate number of minorities find themselves in an alternative school as compared to their demographic representation, instead of being allowed to continue their studies in a traditional school after being disciplined. In general, Black and Hispanic students are much more likely to be disciplined with suspension or expulsion, with Black students at greatest risk.

We have to remind ourselves that lacking in school engagement is by no means a measure of intelligence. In many cases, students in alternative schools could function in traditional schools, given the right support services (Verdugo and Glenn, 2006). Placement in alternative schools is largely a function of other factors in a child's life, including undiagnosed learning disabilities. However imperfect, alternative schools represent a means by which to keep at least a portion of at-risk youth out of the juvenile justice system and keep them in school.

Substance Abuse Treatment, Rehabilitation, and Wraparound Programs

Treatment for drug and/or alcohol abuse and addiction often is a condition of probation, incarceration, or aftercare after release. In order for treatment to be successful, the juvenile has to be willing to make the changes, or, as in the case of addicts, be willing to give up drugs and often alcohol as well. This is why substance abuse treatment plans and rehabilitation come as part of *wraparound programs* for juvenile offenders. Addiction can be just one symptom of a number of dysfunctions in a minor's life. Wraparound programs can be incorporated in rehabilitation plans at any phase that the juvenile is in the juvenile system.

According to the Center on Juvenile and Criminal Justice in San Francisco, California (n.d.), a continuum of social services, as part of a wraparound program, targets juveniles and young adults who are already involved in the criminal justice system, between the ages of 14 and 24. The bed capacity of the Center of Juvenile and Criminal Justice to serve juveniles and their families is 15 juvenile detainees, as it requires intensive work by the counselor staff. In many ways this leaves this particular wraparound program deficient in serving as many at-risk juvenile offenders as possible. The greatest disadvantage is that there are not enough services available for juveniles that need them. Considering that it also works on the basis of referrals by probation officers and other juvenile welfare agencies, the competition is stiff as to who will be accepted into the program.

In the example of the Wrap Rehabilitation Program offered by the Center on Juvenile and Criminal Justice, the following services are fairly typical for these types of intensive programs (Center on Juvenile and Criminal Justice, n.d.):

- 24/7 crisis management;
- Academic support and tutoring;
- Multidisciplinary therapies;
- After school programs;
- Vocational training; and
- Family location services.

Cognitive Behavioral Therapy (CBT)

Besides traditional forms of treatment for behavioral problems, including talk and group therapy, there are a number of other respected therapies in the treatment of juvenile delinquents. One of the relative newcomers in the treatment of behavioral problems is *cognitive behavioral therapy* (CBT). CBT focuses on social rehabilitation, where distorted thoughts, feelings, and perceptions that lead to criminal behavior are corrected, so that they are more aligned with reality (Siemionow, 2020). Juveniles and adults who successfully complete treatment experience less distress and will function better in society (Siemionow, 2020). CBT is used in a number of psychiatric disorders, not simply those related to potential criminal behavior (e.g., anxiety, depression, panic disorders).

Holistic Family Treatment

In most cases, treatment of mental health issues is targeted at the individual. However, in the case of juveniles, it takes the entire family, including siblings, to successfully maintain the mental health of the affected individual. It is also not uncommon for other members of the family to suffer from the same disorders, particularly those where there is a genetic predisposition. We identify this as a holistic approach, where the whole family will receive therapy, not only in how to manage a mentally ill family member but to develop coping skills to maintain their own mental well-being. It also requires looking at the environment beyond the family home, including factors that may be beyond the control of parents or guardians, such as the neighborhood and the school their child or children attend.

Shaming and Reintegration

In many respects, *shaming and reintegration* is not a new concept. The offender is expected to take their punishment with public humiliation or confession, repent in the process, and then be reintegrated into general society with the community welcoming them back in (in theory). Shaming was once commonplace, as in the example of the stocks in Colonial America discussed in Chapter 2. It is also perhaps one of the oldest forms of community-based punishment, having biblical antecedents as a tool for societal integration. It may have its roots in how early cultures responded to violations of norms although we have little information on punishment in prehistoric communities based on archaeological evidence short of what we understand of ritualistic curses, banishment, or death (Riyad, 2021).

There is a definitive cultural component to shaming and reintegration strategies. It does not work in every community or in every cultural setting. In smaller communities offenders may have a higher profile and be known by more residents, making it more difficult to get away with criminal behavior without "everyone" knowing about it. In contrast, one can become anonymous, and in many ways, invisible in a large city, hiding the shame of a current or past criminal life. This does not mean that the ex-convict in a large city will have an easier time getting a job. It simply means that they may not be interacting with as many people who are aware of their offenses or criminal past as they would if they lived in a small town.

Peer Mediation

As an alternative to school discipline, including expulsion and referral to law enforcement for less serious delinquency, *peer mediation* is a solution that is similar to shaming and reintegration tactics, with some distinct differences. In peer mediation, a panel of fellow students, supervised with teacher and guidance counselor staff oversight, reviews conflicts between students that have the potential for escalation, possibly into violence and/or suspension or expulsion. Peer mediation has been in schools for a number of decades and can be found in both primary and secondary schools. Generally, a peer mediation session consists of the following components (Region 13 Education Service Center, 2019):

1. Parties agree to mediation.
2. Parties are allowed to tell their side of the story.
3. Parties focus on interests and needs, rather than on punishment.
4. Mediators work towards a win-win situation for both parties.
5. Parties are given options to resolution.
6. Parties enter into an agreement, if possible.

Student peer mediators in schools are required to undergo training. They are expected to be neutral, with the role of helping with conflict resolution and not taking sides. Because the offending juveniles or juveniles in conflict are in discussion with their peers, there is the possibility that they will be more open to disclosure and reform, than if being lectured to by an adult. There are a number of additional benefits to peer mediation (Lithoxoidou et al., 2021):

- It resolves student conflicts.
- It improves school performance.
- It acts as both intervention and prevention.
- It teaches essential life skills, including interpersonal communication skills for both the offender and the peer mediators, as well as empowering students and increasing their self-esteem.
- It encourages students to resolve their own conflicts, instead of resorting to violence.
- It teaches citizenship and democratic processes.

FEMALE JUVENILE OFFENDERS IN THE SYSTEM

Though males have traditionally been more violent and have committed more violent crimes than females, females are catching up with males, particularly in the case of female gang members (Hansen, 2005). Violence seems almost unavoidable in juvenile detention centers for females. What is alarming is that research suggests that juvenile detention staff seem to promote violence and other problematic behaviors, creating an environment where violence is inevitable (Flores, 2016).

As in the case of adult females in prison, females in juvenile detention have likewise historically been neglected as research subjects. As much as males who are in prison have restricted access to a number of things, females in juvenile facilities are often marginalized with even more restricted access to material and social resources. What they receive in treatment and rehabilitation is largely based on their perceived race and class, with white females who come from more privileged classes receiving better treatment (Brewster and Cumiskey, 2017). As is the case for females outside of the juvenile justice system, success on the basis of gender requires programs behind bars that empower females, rather than diminishing them into stereotypical passivity and submissiveness that is far from today's norms (Brewster and Cumiskey, 2017). In a 2009 study (Zahn et al.), 85 percent of females who were allowed to actively participate in the accountability for their crimes reported achieving the goals that they themselves defined, as compared to those who had goals imposed on them. So self-efficacy is critical in the rehabilitation of female juvenile offenders.

There are a number of challenges unique to females leaving juvenile detention. Whereas males can often be forgiven for their "boyish exploits," females are more greatly stigmatized for their "unladylike" criminal behavior. Keys to success in release back home are the perceptions that resources are available to help, including a family support system in the home. What seems to work with released juveniles, and girls in particular, based on successful programs in Illinois and Missouri that reduce recidivism rates, is intensive pre-release planning for females (Herman and Sexton, 2017). Pre-release planning should include (Herman and Sexton, 2017)

- Use of specialized parole officers who establish a relationship with the juvenile while they are incarcerated.
- Reenrollment in school outside of detention.
- Family involvement.
- Identification of employment opportunities.
- Established curfews.
- Positive reinforcement instead of negative punishment while incarcerated.
- Intensive therapy.
- Short-term furloughs while incarcerated.
- Establish a behavioral contract prerelease.

It is important to note that similar to adult female offenders, juvenile offenders who are female are likely to be both offender and victim. A number of girls in juvenile detention are there due to victimization. For example, juveniles who participate in prostitution, like adults, will be treated as criminals by the system. However, as children are attractive targets to sex traffickers, juvenile prostitutes are often unwilling participants in the sex trade. In a study reported by the *New York Times* (Ubrina, 2009), about one third of runaways or children who are kicked out of their homes will inevitably exchange sex for money, food, drugs, and/or a place to stay. As these are self-reported statistics, that number may very well be much higher. Estimates on the number of sexually exploited children are unreliable, and in some cases, contradictory (Salisbury et al., 2015; Mitchell et al., 2010).

Consider that a juvenile without job skills or completed education, friends, or a family network to help them, has little in the way of anything to exchange for their basic needs, including food and shelter, besides sex. As one 14-year-old girl reported, who was already in the child welfare system, she

> *ran away from her group home in Medford, Ore., and spent weeks sleeping in parks and under bridges. Finally. . . . [she] grew [so] desperate that she accepted a young man's offer of a place to stay. The price came later. . . . one day he threatened to kick her out if she did not have sex with several of his friends in exchange for money. She agreed, fearing she had no choice. "Where was I going to go?"* (Urbina, 2009, retrieved from https://www.nytimes.com/2009/10/27/us/27runaways.html)

These children, primarily girls, often get caught in the tangle of the juvenile justice system with few alternatives beyond detention, and few options after detention. As Salisbury et al. (2009) recommend, juveniles who are arrested for prostitution, and no doubt can be proven to be victims of sexual exploitation, should be diverted to social services instead of incarcerated.

PRIVATE JUVENILE DETENTION FACILITIES

Increasingly juvenile offenders are being referred to private juvenile detention centers in the past several decades. Since Congress passed the Juvenile Justice and Delinquency Prevention Act in 1974, private prisons have become increasingly the norm, which was not the intention of advocacy groups looking for alternatives to traditional incarceration of juveniles (Bayer and Pozen, 2005). By 1989, 40 percent of juvenile delinquents were being held in private juvenile facilities (McDonald, 1992). Yet there is relatively little research conducted comparing the effectiveness of private over public juvenile detention centers, beyond the argued cost savings for the state.

As we will see in the last chapter of this book that includes controversies in corrections, private juvenile detention centers have attracted negative publicity. The fact that there have been cases of judges accepting bribes for sentencing juveniles to detention instead of alternatives to incarceration, as in the "kids for cash" scheme we will discuss in Chapter 14, private prisons in general do not have the best of reputations for correctional facilities.

Whether we are discussing public or private juvenile detention, the most important thing continues to be results. Does one type of facility produce juveniles that are less likely to reoffend, over the other type? At least in a Florida study (Bayer and Pozen, 2004), for-profit private facilities experienced 5.3 percent less recidivism among former juvenile detainees within a year, nonprofit private facilities experienced 6 percent less recidivism, as compared to juveniles released from public, state-run facilities. For all the criticism of private facilities, they may show more promise for long term rehabilitation of juveniles, though there has been little in the way of more recent research to demonstrate that one is better than the other.

JUVENILES IN THE ADULT SYSTEM

As we have already noted, juveniles are only charged as adults in extreme cases. Since the 1990s, during the "get tough on crime era," 45 of 50 states had passed laws and amended legislation making it far easier to prosecute juveniles in adult courts (Austin et al., 2000). Until 2005, juveniles were allowed to be executed in the United States, until the Supreme Court limited death sentences for juveniles. Children as young as 13 could still be sentenced to life in prison without possibility of parole (Equal Justice Initiative, n.d.). In *Miller v. Alabama* (2012)[13], the U.S. Supreme Court handed down a decision that mandatory life without the possibility of parole is unconstitutional in the case of those who had committed a homicide as juveniles, this in spite of the increase in murders committed by offenders under the age of 18 (Khachatryan et al., 2016). However, arrests for violent crimes by juveniles have decreased, following a spike in the early 1990s. As to be predicted, the number of juveniles sentenced to adult prisons and jails has also decreased. Juveniles who received life sentences prior to *Miller v. Alabama* became eligible for resentencing under the new sentencing guidelines (Heilburn, et al., 2018). Yet with the restrictions placed on sentencing minors to death or to life without the possibility for parole by federal mandate, 19 states still permit the execution of adults who have been convicted of violent crimes they committed at age 16 or 17 (ACLU, 2021).

One of the biggest concerns of sentencing juveniles to adult prison, beyond risks for victimization, is that adult prisons are not equipped to meet the needs of a juvenile who is still going through the developmental stages of childhood and adolescence. Worse yet, they are ill equipped to care for juveniles with mental or learning disorders, as their developmental, education, health care, and rehabilitation needs are different than that of adults or juveniles without cognitive disabilities (Wills, 2017).

As we well know, public perception of juvenile offenders and their potential for rehabilitation, appropriate sentencing, and the realities may contradict one another. The general public have historically believed that longer sentences are appropriate for older youths (Cochran et al., 2003), where as if given a greater number options in

---

[13] In the case of *Miller v. Alabama* (567 U.S. 460, 2012), it was determined that the 14-year-old juvenile offender sentenced to life in prison without the possibility of parole for a murder was too young and their underdeveloped sense of responsibility led to their recklessness. The U.S. Supreme Court decided on the bases that the sentencing violated the 8th Amendment for cruel and unusual punishment. (SEE Dwyer, 2012, available at https://www.cga.ct.gov/2012/rpt/2012-R-0290.htm).

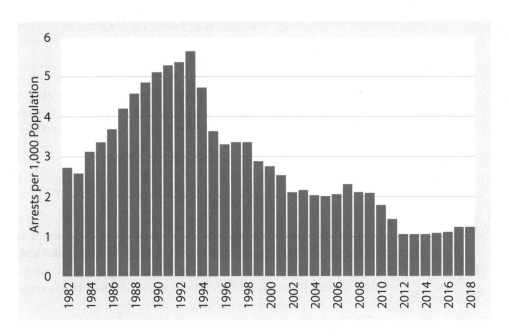

FIGURE 9.5 | **Number of Juvenile Arrests for Violent Crimes, 1982-2018, per 1,000 Population.**
U.S. Office of Financial Management, 2020, retrieved from https://ofm.wa.gov/washington -data-research/statewide-data/washington-trends/social-economic-conditions/ juvenile-arrests-violent-crimes)

sentencing, the public is more inclined to rethink the appropriateness (or fairness, ethics) of a sentence of life without the possibility of parole for juveniles (Heilbrun et al., 2018). Like in the case of marijuana laws in states versus federal law, sentencing of juveniles to adult facilities by states can run counter with federal sentencing guidelines for juveniles.

Blended Sentences

In some cases, juveniles who offend in their youth must serve time in both juvenile and adult facilities, depending on the severity of the crime or if there is reoffending while in a juvenile detention facility. The film, *American Me* (1992, Universal Pictures), depicts this well, where the main character, Santana, committed a minor crime as a juvenile, but while in detention, killed a fellow juvenile offender after he was raped by him. This resulted in a new sentence, where he was remanded to adult custody at Folsom State Prison in California, once he aged out of the juvenile system.

This is a completely different scenario than a juvenile being sentenced as an adult. But as in the case of fictional character of Santana, and real life person, Jack Abbott, who was in and out of detention and adult prison his whole life from the time he was a young teen, the film *American Me* accurately depicts a child aging into the adult system during some of the most critical developmental years. We will discuss Abbott's experiences further, later in this book.

The reality is that young violent offenders cannot always be easily reintegrated into society. If there is any good news out of blended sentences, there is little evidence that in transferring a juvenile to adult prison once they age out of the juvenile system will result in higher rates of recidivism, once released from adult custody (Trulson et al., 2020).

SUMMARY

For anyone interested in working in juvenile corrections, there are so many more complexities than in the adult system. First and foremost, the brain of a juvenile is not fully developed. Juveniles have additional needs, as compared to incarcerated adults. Juveniles are required to attend school up to a certain age which is dependent on the state that they are residing. There are also more complexities in treating juveniles with mental health issues, including involving parents and guardians in treatment plans.

Even the language we use for juveniles in the juvenile court system is different. Terms are "softer" and are intended to be less stigmatizing, than the terms used in adult court. Juvenile Justice courtrooms are designed, generally, to not be as intimidating as those found in adult criminal court, though any courtroom is intimidating, no matter how much effort is put into making them less so.

Factors that lead to delinquency include many of those that contribute to adult offending, such as poverty, drug abuse, and alcohol abuse. There are other risk factors as well for juvenile offenders, including poor school performance and engagement and child abuse victimization. Because of all the possible combinations of risk factors that not only affect the juvenile, but the family as well, in order to address problems that lead to delinquency and juvenile detention or referral to child services, it is beneficial to treat the whole family and not just the individual offender.

Both parents/guardians and juveniles retain some constitutional rights. However, once a child becomes a ward of the state, which does not happen in every juvenile case, parents/guardians are required to give up much of the decisions made for their child, including education. Juveniles are given the same Constitutional Rights as adults, including those protected within the 1st, 5th, 6th, 8th, and 14th Amendments. However, as we have seen in our section on juveniles in adult facilities, there are inconsistencies and contradictions in what states allow versus what federal sentencing guidelines mandate for juvenile offenders.

Sentencing for juvenile offenders is as complex as the combination of sanctions that adults receive when they are found guilty in criminal court. There are a number of different ways that juveniles can be sentenced once they have been found delinquent in a juvenile court. Many of the options are similar to adult sentencing, including incarceration, probation, restitution, community service, and court-ordered rehabilitation. There are differences in that there are more diversion program options available for juveniles, though many are not evidence-based and have mixed results. Also, in the case of juvenile offenders, court fees, fines, and restitution most often falls of the shoulders of parents or guardians.

In the extreme, the alternatives to incarceration can be brutal. Military-style boot camps have not been found to reduce reoffending and can result in injury, even death when the exercise regimes are too aggressive. Wilderness camps may seem a more benign option for at-risk youth and delinquents, but those are inconsistent in their programs and staff training.

Recidivism rates for juvenile offenders vary, depending on offenses and facilities where they have been placed. There is some evidence that private nonprofit and for-profit juvenile detention centers have lower one-year recidivisms rates, as compared to public. However, as we will see in Chapter 14, there are a number of controversies surrounding private prisons and "kids-for-sale" schemes where courts disproportionately can sentence juveniles to private facilities, even when probation is a more reasonable option, both based on costs and outcomes.

Most researchers agree that there is far too little research conducted on juveniles in detention centers. More so is the case for female juvenile offenders. Much of this is the challenge of studying children in general, as they are part of a vulnerable population as research subjects and extra care has to be taken to assure that studies are ethically conducted. Prisons are difficult research labs; juvenile facilities, doubly so.

STORIES FROM BEHIND BARS

Mothers of Juvenile Offenders

Family members of the accused and the convicted often feel punished for their children's crimes, even if they do not serve time behind bars and have not been charged with any offenses. If a child becomes delinquent, the blame often falls squarely on the mother, even when there is an intact family with a father or at least a father figure present. Mothers are the most likely to be punished by society, even in contemporary times where they are not necessarily expected to or can be the primary caregiver or source of socialization for their offspring. Even in academic research, a number of studies point fingers at maternal "coldness" towards their children or perceived neglect as a root cause of delinquency, including Cavanaugh and Cauffman (2017), Bisby et al. (2017), and Kremer and Vaughn (2019), rather than placing any blame at the feet of fathers.

They may not be behind bars when their children are adjudicated, but in many respects, the mothers (and other family members) are figuratively stuck behind invisible prison walls themselves, in some cases for life, due to the stigma. Besides having hopes and dreams for your offspring dashed in the face of juvenile offending, there is the added burden of visiting children in juvenile detention at the discretion of the facility staff. What is still worse, as we will see in the stories below, is when your child is tried as an adult, convicted, and sent to adult prison.

Women who work have often been cornered into feminized professions that require nurturing skills similar to those expected in motherhood, including the education and nursing professions. Juvenile justice reformers and practitioners often place blame on working mothers as being key factors in juvenile offending, even though only a small portion of the general public agrees (Pickett, 2017) with that outlook. On the basis of the traditional roles of women, females are expected to focus on raising children and maintaining household harmony. When their children are juvenile delinquents, they are viewed as failures in these roles, even if the delinquency is due to mental health issues beyond the control of the parent or the child (e.g., schizophrenia, bipolar disorders), save psychiatric interventions that don't always work.

The effects of juvenile offending on mothers begins with first contact with law enforcement. We know that police contact has a negative effect on the mental health of juveniles. Until recently, we had little information on the effects it has on mothers. In a 2021 study conducted by Jackson and Turney (2021), researchers found that mothers of children who had been stopped by the police report higher rates of depression and sleep disruption, with the greatest increases of these found in the urban Black community. What is a surprising finding is that the mothers of daughters stopped by police experience depression-related sleep disruption, but when their sons are stopped, they are more likely to have anxiety-related sleep difficulties (Jackson and Turney, 2021).

Jackson and Turney (2021) explain these differences as being due to the sadness regarding the long-term prospects of life chances for a female juvenile offender, as compared to the anxiety that is caused by impulsive, risk-taking behavior of males. Though not stated in the Jackson and Turney (2021) study, for parents of young urban Black males, we can assume that a great deal of the anxiety experienced when their child have an encounter with the police is associated with the seemingly all too often reports of unarmed Black males being killed by police.

Having a child face criminal charges and juvenile adjudication is one type of anxiety. When they are charged as adults, this brings on a whole different set of challenges and worries for the parent. Even if their child is approaching their late teens, there is the fear that they are more likely to be victimized in an adult prison than a juvenile facility, whether true or not, plus the anxiety that they will be housed with more serious offenders.

The following are examples of what mothers feel like when their sons are incarcerated in adult prison (Susi, 2020; Hillman and Caballero, 2017):

▪ Corrine Broadbridge's son, Chris, was convicted at age 14 of murder, not at his own hands, according to her account, but due to a homeowner who shot Chris' friend dead in the course of a burglary he had participated in. As he was tried as an adult, Chris' face and full name and age were published in the paper: *"There is nothing in this world that can prepare you for how devastating this feels as a Mum.*[14] *It felt like Chris had died and in a way his childhood had died."* (Broadbridge, 2017, retrieved from http://www.campaignforyouthjustice.org/voices/item/mother-s -day-series-being-mum). Chris served six of the eight years he was sentenced to, coming out of adult prison at 21 years old with no life skills and PTSD.

- Michelle Hanneman's son was convicted as a sex offender in the adult justice system, for a crime he committed at age 15. It took 3 ½ years from his arrest to sentencing. The experience of going through the trial, conviction, and incarceration made Michelle go into hiding in her community: *"The simple task of grocery shopping, errands or going to church became daunting because I hoped I would not see anyone I knew because I was afraid of possible questions, looks and judgement. Always feeling this way yet pretending everything was going to be okay for my family. Helpless."* (Hanneman, 2017, retrieved from http://www. campaignforyouthjustice.org/voices/item/mother-s-day-series-2).

- At 15 years old, Marcus Bullock and a friend were caught committing a carjacking. In spite of Marcus' age, he was tried as an adult and served eight years in prison. During Marcus' incarceration, his mother Sylvia questioned her role as a mother, as well as her place in her own community: *"You know, here you are trying to help everybody else, and you can't even minister to your own. . . . Initially it was a sense of feeling alone. . . . I stopped making dinner, but what kept me truly alive and focused was being to write to you* [letters to Marcus in prison]." (Hillman and Caballero, 2017, retrieved from https://www.npr.org/2017/08/11/ 542648319/as-a-boy-in-an-adult-prison-his-mothers-letters-were-everything).

Incarceration of juveniles is difficult on all members of the family, but especially difficult for mothers who are left behind and stigmatized. As every good academic journal article ends with, more research needs to be done on the long-term effects of juvenile incarceration on mothers, beyond the blame and shame placed on their shoulders.

SOURCES

Bisby, M., E. Kimonis, and N. Goutler (2017) Maternal warmth mediates the relationship between emotional neglect and callous-unemotional traits among juvenile offenders. *Journal of Child and Family Studies.* Vol. 26, No. 7:1790-1798.

Broadbridge, C. (2017) Mother's Day Series: Being Mum. Campaign for Youth Justice. May 4. Retrieved from http://www.campaignforyouthjustice.org/voices/item/mother-s-day-series -being-mum.

Cavanaugh, C. and E. Cauffman. Longitudinal association of relationship quality and reoffending among first-time juvenile offenders and their mothers. *Journal of Youth and Adolescence.* Vol. 46, No. 7:1533-1546.

[14] Corrine is British, hence the spelling "Mum" instead of "Mom."

Hanneman, M. (2017) Mother's Day Series: Mad, overwhelmed, trying, helpless, emotional, resilient. Campaign for Youth Justice. Retrieved from http://www.campaignforyouthjustice.org/voices/item/mother-s-day-series-2.

Hillman, K. and A. Caballero (2017) As a boy in an adult prison, his letters 'were everything'. *Morning Edition*, NPR. Aug. 11. Retrieved from https://www.npr.org/2017/08/11/542648319/as-a-boy-in-an-adult-prison-his-mothers-letters-were-everything.

Jackson, D. B. and K. Turney (2021) Sleep problems among mothers of youth stopped by police. Journal of Urban Health. Vol. 98:163-171.

Kremer, K. P. and M. Vaughn (2019) College aspirations among incarcerated juvenile offenders: Importance of maternal education and neglect. *Youth Violence and Juvenile Justice*. Vol. 17, No. 4:431-447.

Pickett, J. T. (2017) Blame their mothers: Public opinion about maternal employment as cause of juvenile delinquency. *Feminist Criminology*. Available at https://doi.org/10.1177/1557085115624759

Susi, M. (2020) Stories from mothers of incarcerated youth. Campaign for Youth Justice. May 7. Retrieved from http://www.campaignforyouthjustice.org/news/blog/item/stories-from-mothers-of-incarcerated-youth.

INTERNATIONAL PERSPECTIVES IN JUVENILE JUSTICE[15]: THE REPUBLIC OF CABO VERDE

The plight of children in prison is particularly dire in some countries of Africa. Beyond overcrowding and violence, there are reports of human trafficking of children through some African prisons (Sarkin, 2008). This chapter offers a perspective from an island nation with a colonial past, similar to the example of British occupation in Zambia. In this piece, we examine the former colony of Portugal, Cabo Verde.[16]

Unlike a number of countries in Africa and elsewhere, Cabo Verde had no established law as the islands were uninhabited before the Portuguese colonized the islands, imposing their legal system (Bogdan, 2000). The legal system in the now independent republic is still influenced by Portuguese law. Though not physically part of the African continent but still of it, Cabo Verdeans do not consider themselves "African" but rather European, though a good portion of the population have African roots due to slavery. Subsequent servitude replaced slavery, after it was selectively prohibited beginning in the mid-19th century, completely banned in 1878.

According to the U.S. State Department, conditions in Cabo Verde prisons are harsh. There are five prisons in the country to serve a population of little over half a

---

[15] As noted in the Preface at the beginning of this book, we are deviating from the usual section titles, "International Perspectives on Punishment and Corrections," for this chapter only.

[16] The author is of Portuguese descent, with her grandfather migrating to the United States from Cabo Verde at age seven. Hence the use of the Portuguese spelling of the nation consisting of a chain of islands in this textbook, that is generally used in that country. The country is known elsewhere by three names: Cabo Verde, Cape Verde, and Cap-Vert.

million (2020 figures, *World Population Review)*, meaning that there is roughly one prison for every 100,000 inhabitants of the islands. In comparison, Louisiana, a state with the highest incarceration rates in the United States, has approximately 20 federal and state facilities for rate of about 4.7 million, or one prison in 235,000 residents.

Tarrafal Concentration Camp, Cabo Verde (Cape Verde). (*Source*: World Monument Fund, retrieved from https://commons.wikimedia.org/w/index.php?search=Tarrafal+Concentration+Camp&title=Special: MediaSearch&go=Go&type=image)

Cabo Verde is also the home of a former concentration camp at Tarrafal. Built by Portuguese dictator Antonio de Oliveira Salazar, Tarrafal prison held political and "social" prisoners, as well as African rebels, including juveniles. Most of the inmates were working class men in their 20s and 30s (Hixson and Mitchell, 2019; World Monuments Fund, n.d.). Punishments included prisoners being left in wretched conditions of no heat or light, tortured and often left to starve, and the facility was described as a "concentration camp of 'slow death.'" (Hixson and Mitchell, 2019, retrieved from https://www.wsws.org/en/articles/2019/04/09/ port-a09.html) After temporary closure in 1954, the prison camp was subsequently reopened, with permanent closure not to come until 1974. The former concentration camp was eventually transformed into a museum.

The more pressing issue in recent decades is the increase in juvenile delinquency and gang violence on the islands (Zoetti, 2014). As a result, the Cabo Verde prison population has more than doubled, with more juveniles serving long sentences for drug and gang related offenses (Zoetti, 2014). This runs counter with the islands' cultural reputation for "morabeza," loosely translated to mean "gentleness." The government of Cabo Verde has recently worked with the UN and Portugal to overhaul the juvenile justice system, in the face of increases in juvenile offending. The purposes of reform measures is to make improvements in the juvenile justice system, including protecting the rights of incarcerated juveniles and finding alternatives to juvenile detention (UN Office on Drugs and Crime, n.d.).

SOURCES

Bogdan, M. (2000) The law of the Republic of Cape Verde 25 years of independence. *Journal of African Law.* Vol. 44, No. 1:86-95.

Hixson, C. and Paul Mitchell (2019) "Tarrafal Never Again!" exhibition in Lisbon exposes horrors of Portugal's fascist concentration camp. *World Socialist Web Site*, International Committee of the Fourth International (ICFI). Apr. 9. Retrieved from https://www.wsws.org/en/articles/2019/04/09/port-a09.html.

Sarkin, J. (2008) Prisons in Africa. *International Journal on Human Rights.* Jan. Retrieved from https://sur.conectas.org/en/prisons-in-africa/.

World Monuments Fund (n.d.) Tarrafal Concentration Camp. Retrieved from https://www.wmf.org/project/tarrafal-concentration-camp.

World Population Review (2020) Cape Verde Population. Retrieved from https://worldpopulationreview.com/countries/cape-verde-population.

Zoetti, P. A. (2014) *Morabeza*, cash or body: Prison, violence and the state in Praia, Cape Verde. *International Journal of Cultural Studies.* Vol. 19, No. 4:391-406.

GLOSSARY

Alternative school Also called continuation school in some places, these are schools where students who have been expelled from a traditional school or have been referred to for behavior problems can go to complete their compulsory education.

Case petitioning Court procedure in which the court is asked to assume jurisdiction over an alleged juvenile delinquent, allowing them to be transferred to criminal court for prosecution. (See Glossary of Terms, OJJDP, available at https://ojjdp.ojp.gov/sites/g/files/xyckuh176/files/pubs/jcs96/glos.html)

Child Protective Services (CPS) The term for a number of agencies (names differs from state to state) that are responsible, along with the courts, to remove juveniles from the homes of unfit parents, relatives, or guardians. The juveniles removed may become wards of the state, in which case they may be placed in foster care or, in extreme cases, put up for adoption. (See *Wards of the Court*). In the case of foster care, removal of the child may be temporary. In the case of adoption, the severing of legal ties between parent or guardian and the child is permanent.

Cognitive Behavioral Therapy (CBT) A form of behavior therapy that targets negative thinking by teaching patients how to recognize their distortions of reality. Example: Understanding the differences between real and perceived threats in anxiety and panic disorders. (See American Psychological Association, n.d., available at https://www.apa.org/ptsd-guideline/patients-and-families/cognitive-behavioral)

Differential Association Theory (Sutherland) In summary, Sutherland's theory that if individuals, in this case, juveniles, hang around with criminal or deviant family or friends, they themselves will become criminal or deviant, because they are more likely to be rewarded with acceptance when they commit crimes, than if they have good behavior, where they might be teased or bullied.

Evidence-based programs Programs that have been tested in pilot programs or have been demonstrated to provide their intended outcomes, as in the example of programs that target recidivism.

Food insecurity The condition of not having predictable or having limited access to enough food to maintain an active, healthy life. (See Hunger and Health, Feeding America, n.d., available at https://hungerandhealth.feedingamerica.org/understand-food-insecurity/)

Individuals with Disabilities Education Act (IDEA) 1997 law that requires that a free, appropriate public education must be made available for eligible children with disabilities, including special education with individualized learning plans. (See Individuals with Disability Act, U.S. Department of Education, n.d., available at https://sites.ed.gov/idea/about-idea/)

Intake Process by which a juvenile is referred to the juvenile justice system, including screening to determine what type of programs may be appropriate, as well as other strategies to avoid juvenile detention, whenever possible.

Juvenile boot camps Military-styled residential programs for juvenile delinquents or at-risk youth, focused on physical fitness, behavioral modification, and discipline.

Labeling Theory (Tannenbaum) Theory that proposes that once someone is stigmatized (e.g., labeled a juvenile delinquent), it is very difficult to get rid of the negative reputation in society.

National Survey of Youth in Custody (NSYC) A survey conducted by the Bureau of Justice Statistics (BJS) as part of the BJS's National Rape Statistics program, which gathers data on sexual assault and abuses in juvenile facilities. (See NSYC, BJS, available at https://bjs.ojp.gov/data-collection/national-survey-youth-custody-nsyc)

Office of Juvenile Justice and Delinquency Prevention (OJJDP) U.S. government agency established as part of the Juvenile and Delinquency Prevention Act of 1974 and the Juvenile Justice and Delinquency Prevention Act Reauthorization (2018) whose mission is to prevent delinquency and improve the juvenile justice system in the United States. (See OJJDP, available at https://ojjdp.ojp.gov/about)

Peer mediation   Programs in primary and secondary schools where fellow students, with adult supervision of teachers and guidance counselors, stand in objective judgement when there is conflict between students. Used in conflict resolution to avoid further escalation of interpersonal issues into violence.

Self-fulfilling prophecy (Merton)   Social psychological phenomenon where other people's expectations of the individual, whether positive or negative, eventually result in that individual living up to those expectations. Example: If a child is constantly accused of stealing, even when they are not doing so, they may begin to start stealing.

Shaming and reintegration   Process by which the offender is confronted with their offense and given a chance to make amends to their victim, repent, and be welcomed back into the community. The goal is to condemn the offense without condemning the offender.

Strain Theory (Merton)   A multifaceted theory where individuals who cannot meet society's goals or find the means by which to achieve those goals, may find alternative, deviant goals and/or means to do so. Other responses may be to reject society's goals and means and become, as Merton termed them, "retreatists."

Social Learning Theory (Akers)   A theory that can be applied to both juvenile and adult offenders, where the environment and who you associate with, including family members and peer groups, may result in learning how to be deviant and/or delinquent. Similar to Sutherland's *Differential Association Theory.*

Technical violation   A violation of a condition of probation or parole that is not criminal, but can still result in having probation or parole revoked and the juvenile or adult taken into back into custody, sent to a detention center, jail, or prison to complete their original sentence. Examples: Continually violating court ordered curfews, missing hearings for updates on progress.

Wards of the Court   Used in both cases of juvenile delinquency and child maltreatment, the juvenile will be taken under the protection of the court and parental or guardian rights are diminished. Similar to becoming a *ward of the state,* which has broader implications, such as having a guardian assigned or being referred to child protective services.

Wilderness programs   Outdoor programs set in the mountains, seaside, or desert that are intended to foster self-esteem, team building, and interpersonal communication skills. An example would be Outward Bound, a program that targets both adults and juveniles.

Wraparound programs   Multipronged approach to reducing juvenile delinquency that includes treating both the offender and the family in community-based corrections (e.g., probation) and rehabilitation.

REFERENCES AND SUGGESTED READINGS

Abram, K. M, L. A. Teplin, and G. M. McClelland (2003) Comorbid psychiatric disorders in youth in juvenile detention. *Archives of General Psychiatry.* Vol. 60, No. 11:1097-1108.

Abram, K. M., L. A. Teplin, and D. R. Charles. (2004) Posttraumatic stress disorder and trauma in youth in juvenile detention. *Archives of General Psychiatry.* Vol. 61, No. 4:403-410.

Ahlin, E. M. and D. Barberi (2019) Addressing sexual assault and victimization in detention facilities: Fifteen years post-PREA. *Juvenile Justice Update.* Winter, Vol. 24, Iss. 4:9-18.

American Civil Liberties Union (ACLU) (2021) Juveniles and the death penalty. Retrieved from https://www.aclu.org/other/juveniles-and-death-penalty#:~:text=The%20United%20 States%20Supreme%20Court,death%20sentences%20have%20been%20imposed.

Annie E. Casey Foundation (2011) *No Place for Kids: The Case for Reducing Juvenile Incarceration.* Baltimore, MD: Anne E. Casey Foundation.

Annie E. Casey Foundation (2020) New reports finds many families with children are depressed, uninsured, hungry and at risk of foreclosure or eviction. Dec. 4. Retrieved from https://www.aecf.org/blog/new-report-finds-many-families-with-children-are -depressed-uninsured-hungry.

Austin, J., K. D. Johnson, and M. Gregoriou (2000) *Juveniles in Adult Prisons and Jails.* NCJ 182503. Washington D.C.: Institute on Crime, Justice and Corrections at George Washington University and National Council on Crime and Delinquency.

Baglivio, M. T., K. T. Wolff, M. DeLisi, and K. Jackowski (2020) The role of adverse childhood experience (ACEs) and psychopathic features on juvenile offending criminal careers to 18. *Youth Violence and Juvenile Justice.* Vol. 18, No. 4:337-364.

Bartash, J. (2020) U.S. poverty rate fell to record low in 2019 but the coronavirus is revers- ing the gains. Market Watch. Sept. 15. Retrieved from https://www.marketwatch. com/story/us-poverty-rate-fell-to-record-low-in-2019-but-the-coronavirus-is-revers ing-the-gains-2020-09-15.

Bayer, P. and D. E. Pozen (2004) The effectiveness of juvenile correctional facilities: Public versus private management. Center Discussion Paper No. 863. Economic Growth Center Yale University. New Haven, CT: Yale University. Retrieved from http://www.econ.yale .edu//growth_pdf/cdp863.pdf.

Bayer, P. and D. E. Pozen (2005) The effectiveness of juvenile correctional facilities: Public versus private management. *Journal of Law and Economics.* Vol. 48, Iss. 2:549-589.

Black, D. W. (2016) *Ending Zero Tolerance: The Crisis of Absolute School Discipline.* Families, Law, and Society Series. New York, NY: New York University Press.

Bountress, K., S. H. Aggen, and W. Kliewer (2021) Is delinquency associated with subsequent victimization by community violence in adolescents? A test of risky behavior in a pri- marily African American sample. *Psychology of Violence.* May, Vol. 11, No. 3:234-243.

Brewster, K. R. and K. M. Cumiskey (2017) Girls in juvenile detention facilities: Zones of abandonment, in *Gender, Psychology, and Justice: The Mental Health of Women and Girls in the Legal System,* C. C. Datchi and J. R. Ancis, eds. New York, NY: New York University Press. Ch. 6.

Burke, A. S. (2021) The structure of the juvenile justice system, in *Introduction to the American Criminal Justice System,* A. S. Burke, D. Carter, B. Fedorek, T. Morey, L. Rutz-Burri, and S. Sanchez, contributors. Ch. 10, Section 10. Open Oregon Education Resources. Available at https://openoregon.pressbooks.pub/ccj230/

Burton, C. S. (2019) Child savers and unchildlike youth: Class, race, and juvenile justice in the early twentieth century. *Law &Social Inquiry.* Nov., Vol. 44, Iss. 4:1251-1269.

Center on Juvenile and Criminal Justice (n.d.) Wraparound Program. San Francisco, CA. Retrieved from http://www.cjcj.org/Direct-services/Wraparound-Program.html.

Chappell, B. (2021) U.S. Birthrate dropped by 4% in 2020 hitting another record low. NPR. May 5. Retrieved from https://www.npr.org/2021/05/05/993817146/u-s-birth-rate -fell-by-4-in-2020-hitting-another-record-low#:~:text=The%20number%20of%20 babies%20born,according%20to%20the%20provisional%20data.

Children's Society (1989) *Penal Custody for Juveniles: The Line of Least Resistance*. London, UK: Children's Society.

Clark, P. (2014) Types of facilities, in *Desktop Guide to Quality Practice for Working with Youth in Confinement*. National Partnership for Juvenile Services and Office of Juvenile Justice and Delinquency Prevention (OJJDP). Ch. 2. Retrieved from https://info.nicic .gov/dtg/node/4.

Cooks, S. (2020) Students need more life skills courses. *Pulse*, Kenosha Unified School District, Wisconsin. Oct. 29. Retrieved from https://www.kusd.edu/indiantrailpulse/ ?p=8522.

Csukai, M. and P. Ruzsonyi (2018) Juvenile boot camps in the shadow of tragedies. *Academic and Applied Research in Military and Public Management Science*. Vol. 17, No. 1:5-12.

Decker, S., C. Melde, and D. C. Pyrooz (2013) What do we know about gangs and gang members and where do we go from here? *Justice Quarterly*. Vol. 30, No. 3:369-402.

Delisi, M., M. T. Berg, and A. Hochstetler (2004) Gang members, career criminals and prison violence: Further specification of the importation model of inmate behavior. Criminal Justice Studies. *A Critical Journal of Crime, Law and Society*. Vol. 17, No. 4:369-383.

Dir, A. L., L. A. Magee, R. L. Clifton, F. Ouyang, W. Tu, S. E. Wiehe, and M. C. Aaslma (2021) Diminishing returns in juvenile probation: Probation requirements and risk of technical probation violations among first time probation-involved youth. *Psychology, Public Policy, and Law*. Vol. 27, No. 2:283-291.

Dizikes, P. (2015) Study: Juvenile incarceration yields less schooling, more crime. MIT News. June 9. Retrieved from https://news.mit.edu/2015/juvenile-incarceration-less-school ing-more-crime-0610.

Dunn, C. G., E. Kenney, S. Fleischhacker, and Sara N. Bleich (2020) Feeding low-income children during the COVID-19 pandemic. *New England Journal of Medicine*. Apr. 30. 382:e40. Retrieved from https://www.nejm.org/doi/full/10.1056/nejmp2005638.

Equal Justice Initiative (n.d.) Children in adult prison. Retrieved from https://eji.org/issues/ children-in-prison/.

Evans, D. N., G. Moreno, K. T. Wolff, and J. A. Butts (2020) Easily overstated: Estimating the relationship between state justice policy environments and falling rates of youth confinement. John Jay College of Criminal Justice Research and Evaluation Center. Jan. 1. Retrieved from https://johnjayrec.nyc/2020/01/01/easilyoverstated2020/#findings.

EverFi (n.d.) The state of financial literacy. Retrieved from https://everfi.com/financial-edu cation/.

Farmer, J. A. (1990) Juvenile exploitation of juvenile correctional workers: A content analysis. *Journal of Correctional Education*. Vol. 41, Iss. 3:118-119.

Fine, A. D., Z. R. Rowan, and E. Cauffman (2020) Parents or adversaries? The relation between juvenile diversion supervision and parenting. *Law and Human Behavior*. Vol. 44, No. 6:461-473.

Flores, J. (2013) "Staff here let you get down": The cultivation and co-optation of violence in a California juvenile detention center. *Signs*. Vol. 39, No. 1:221-241.

Flores, J. (2016) *Caught Up: Girls, Surveillance, and Wraparound Incarceration*. Oakland, CA: University of California Press.

Goldson, B. (2002) New punitiveness: The politics of child incarceration, in *Youth Justice: Critical Readings*. J. Muncie, G, Hughes, and E. McLaughlin, eds. London, UK: SAGE Publishing.

Grasso, D. J., C. Doyle, and R. Koon (2019) Two rapid screens for detecting probable post-traumatic stress disorder and interpersonal violence exposure: Predictive utility in a juvenile justice sample. *Child Maltreatment.* Vol. 24, No. 1:113-120.

Hansen, L. L. (2005) Girl "crew" members doing gender, boy "crew" members doing violence: An ethnographic and network analysis of Maria Hinojosa's New York gangs. *Western Criminology Review.* Vol. 6, No. 1:134-144.

Hanson, K. and D. Stipek (2014) Schools v. prisons: Education's the way to cut prison population. Stanford Graduate School of Education; *San Jose Mercury News.* May 16. Retrieved from https://ed.stanford.edu/in-the-media/schools-v-prisons-educations-way-cut-prison-population-op-ed-deborah-stipek.

Heilbrun, K., K. Durham, A. Thornewill, R, Schiedel, V. Pietruszka, S. Phillips, B. Locklair, and J. Thomas. (2018) Life-sentenced juveniles: Public perceptions of risk and need for incarceration. *Behavioral Science and the Law.* Vol. 36, No. 5:587-596.

Herman, J. W. and J. S. Sexton (2017) Girls leaving detention: Perceptions of transition to home after incarceration. *Journal of Juvenile Justice.* Spring, Vol. 6, Iss. 1:33-47.

Hipp, J. R. and D. K. Yates (2011) Ghettos, thresholds, and crime: Does concentrated poverty really have an accelerated increasing effect on crime? *Criminology.* Vol. 49, No. 4:955-990.

Howard League (2008) *Growing Up, Shut Up Factsheet.* London, UK: Howard League.

Jacobson, J., B. Bhardwa, T. Gyateng, G. Hunter, and M. Hough (2010) *Punishing Disadvantage: A Profile of Children in Custody.* London, UK: Prison Reform Trust.

Justice Policy Institute (2020) *Sticker Shock 2020: The Cost of Youth Incarceration.* July. Retrieved from https://www.justicepolicy.org/uploads/justicepolicy/documents/Sticker_Shock_2020.pdf.

Khachatryan, N., K. M. Heide, E. V. Hummel, M. Ingraham, and J. Rad (2016) Examination of long-term postrelease outcome of juvenile homicide offenders. *Journal of Offender Rehabilitation.* Vol. 55, No. 8:503-524.

Ko, S. J., N. Kassam-Adams, C. Wilson, J. D. Ford, S. J. Berkowitz, M. Wong, and M. J. Brymer, C. M. Layne (2008) Creating trauma-informed systems: Child welfare, education, first responders, heath care, juvenile justice. *Professional Psychology, Research and Practice.* Aug, Vol. 39, No. 4:396-405.

Kraut, M. E. (n.d.) Supervised juvenile probation. Child Crime Prevention and Safety Center. Retrieved from https://childsafety.losangelescriminallawyer.pro/supervised-juvenile-probation.html#:~:text=Possible%20terms%20and%20conditions%20of,driver's%20license%20restrictions%2C%20fines%20and.

Kuang, X., H. Liu, G. Guo, and H. Cheng (2019) The nonlinear effect of financial and fiscal poverty alleviation in China—An empirical analysis of Chinese 382 impoverished counties with PRSR models. *Plos One.* Nov. 5. Retrieved from https://journals.plos.org/plosone/article?id=10.1371/journal.pone.0224375#:~:text=In%20the%20nonlinear%20models%2C%20the,as%20the%20transition%20functions%20diminish.

Lithoxoidou, A., E. Seira, A. Vrantsi, and C. Dimitriadou (2021) Promoting resiliency, peer mediation and citizenship in schools: Outcomes of a three-fold research intervention. *Participatory Education Research.* Vol. 8, No. 2:109-128.

Lohman, J. (2000) School dropout age. *OLR Research Report,* 2000-r-0503. Apr. 24. Hartford, CT: Connecticut General Assembly.

Lubben, T. (2019) Caring for youth in juvenile detention centers: A story of hope. *The Permanente Journal.* May, Vol. 23:18-203.

McDonald, D. C. (1992) Private penal institutions. *Crime and Justice.* Vol. 16:361-419.

Mennel, R. (1973) *Thorns and Thistles: Juvenile Delinquents in the United States, 1825-1940.* Hanover, NH: University of New Hampshire.

Merikangas, K. R., J. P. He, D. Brody, P. W. Fisher, K. Bourdon, and D. S. Koretz (2010) Prevalence and treatment of mental disorders among US children in 2001-2004 NHANES. *Pediatrics*. Vol. 125:75-81.

Miller-Perrin, C. L. and R. D. Perrin (2013) *Child Maltreatment: An Introduction*. 3d ed. Newbury Park, CA: SAGE Publishing.

Mmari, K., A., S. G. Offiong, and T. Mendelson. (2019) How adolescents cope with food insecurity in Baltimore City: An exploratory study. Cambridge University Press. May 24. Retrieved from https://www-cambridge-org.wne.idm.oclc.org/core/journals/public-hea lth-nutrition/article/how-adolescents-cope-with-food-insecurity-in-baltimore-city-an -exploratory-study/ED0FFEE3A73B015CEBE66C7EEAC891BC.

Modrowski, C. A., D. C. Bennett, S. D. Chaplo, and P.K. Kerig (2017) Screening for PTSD among detained adolescents: Implication of the changes in the DSM-5. *Psychological Trauma: Theory, Research, Practice, and Policy*. Vol. 9:10.

Morris, R. J. and K. C. Thompson (2008) Juvenile delinquency and special education laws: Policy implementation issues and directions for future research. *Journal of Correctional Education*. June, Vol. 59, No. 2:173-190.

MST Services (2019) Detention Centers. Nov. 6. Retrieved from https://info.mstservices. com/blog/gang-presence-juvenile#:~:text=Of%20the%20general%20population%20wit hin,having%20a%20place%20to%20belong.

Muncie, J. (2021) *Youth and Crime*. 5th ed. London, UK: SAGE Publishing.

NARCO (2003) A Failure of Justice: Reducing Child Imprisonment. London, UK: NARCO.

National Juvenile Defender Center (NJDC) (n.d.) Violation of probation. Retrieved from https://njdc.info/violation-of-probation/.

National Juvenile Defender Center (NJDC) (2017) The cost of juvenile probation: A critical look into juvenile supervision fees. Issue brief. Retrieved from https://njdc.info/wp-cont ent/uploads/2017/08/NJDC_The-Cost-of-Juvenile-Probation.pdf.

Nolo (n.d.) Exceptions to confidentiality of juvenile court records. *Legal Encyclopedia*. Retrieved from https://www.nolo.com/legal-encyclopedia/exceptions-confidentiality -juvenile-criminal-records.html.

Office of Juvenile Justice and Delinquency Prevention (n.d.) Case flow diagram: Juvenile justice system structure and process. Office of Justice Programs, U.S. Department of Justice. Retrieved from https://www.ojjdp.gov/ojstatbb/structure_process/case.html.

Office of Juvenile Justice and Delinquency Prevention (2011) Wilderness camps. *Literature Review*: A product of the Model Programs Guide. Mar. Retrieved from https://ojjdp.ojp .gov/sites/g/files/xyckuh176/files/media/document/Wilderness_Camp.pdf.

Peters, M., D. Thomas, C. Zamberlan, and Caliber Associates (1997) *Boot Camps for Juvenile Offenders: Program Summary*. Washington, DC: Office of Juvenile and Delinquency Prevention, U.S. Department of Justice.

Positive Action (n.d.) Research outcomes, Evidence-based life skills curriculum and program. Retrieved from https://www.positiveaction.net/life-skills-curriculum-program.

Prison Reform Trust/INQUEST (2012) *Fatally Flawed: Has the State Learned Lessons from the Deaths of Children and Young People in Prison?* London, UK: Prison Reform Trust.

Region 13 Education Service Center (2019) What is peer mediation? *Behavior*. Mar. 18. Retrieved from https://blog.esc13.net/what-is-peer-mediation/#:~:text=Peer%20mediat ion%20is%20a%20process,ways%20of%20resolving%20a%20conflict.

Riyad, Z. A. E. (2021) Ritual curse in Egypt during prehistoric and early dynastic periods. *Journal of General Union of Arab Archaeologists*. Vol. 22, Iss. 1:125-155.

Roush, D. and M. McMillen (2000) Construction, operation, and staff training for juvenile confinement facilities. *Bulletin*, Juvenile Accountability Incentive Block Grants Program, U.S. Department of Justice, Office of Justice Programs. Jan. Retrieved from https://www .ojp.gov/pdffiles1/ojjdp/178928.pdf

Salisbury, E. J., J. D. Dabney, and K. Russell (2015) Diverting victims of commercial sexual exploitation from juvenile detention: Development of the InterCSECt Screening Protocol. *Journal of Interpersonal Violence*. Vol. 30, No. 7:1247-1276.

Scott, D. (2018) A comparison of gang- and non-gang-related violent incidents from the incarcerated youth perspective. *Deviant Behavior*. Vol. 39, No. 10:1336-1356.

Siemionow, J. (2020) A model of social rehabilitation treatment for juveniles: Cognitive and behavioral perspective—practical aspects. *Juvenile and Family Court Journal*. Mar, Vol. 712, Iss. 1:31-44.

Skiba, R. J., R. S. Michael, A. C. Nardo, and R. Peterson (2000) *The Color of Discipline: Sources of Racial and Gender Disproportionality in School Punishment*. Bloomington, IN: Indiana Education Policy Center, University of Indiana.

Steele, J. L., R. Bozick, and L. M. Davies (2016) Education for incarcerated juveniles: A Meta-analysis. *Journal of Education for Students Placed at Risk* (JESPAR). Vol. 21, No. 2:65-89.

Sullivan, K. (2018) Education systems in juvenile detention centers. *Education and Law Journal*, Brigham Young University. Vol. 2018, Iss. 2:71-100.

Tasca, M., M. L. Griffin, and N. Rodriguez (2010) The effect of importation and deprivation factors in violent misconduct: An examination of black and Latino youth in prison. *Youth Violence and Juvenile Justice*. Vol. 8, No. 3:234-249.

Trulson, C. R., J. M. Craig, J. W. Caudill, and M. Delisi (2020) The impact of adult prison transfer on the recidivism outcomes of blended-sentenced juvenile delinquents. *Crime and Delinquency*. Vol. 66, Nos. 6-7:887-914.

Umpierre, M. (2014) Rights and responsibilities of youth, families and staff, in *Desktop Guide to Quality Practice for Working with Youth in Confinement*. Washington, D.C.: National Partnership for Juvenile Services and Office of Juvenile Justice and Delinquency Prevention. Ch. 5.

United Nations Office on Drugs and Crime (2018) Cabo Verde cooperation with Portugal and UNODC on strengthening its juvenile justice system. Retrieved from https://www.unodc.org/westandcentralafrica/en/2018-02-23-cabo-verde-in-portugal-justice.html.

United States Court of Appeals, Second Circuit (2003) *Ford v. McGinnis* 352 F.3d 582, Docket No. 02-0205. Decided Dec. 15. Retrieved from https://scholar.google.com/scholar_case?case=8144509061522185362&hl=en&as_sdt=6&as_vis=1&oi=scholarr.

U.S. News and World Report (2012) Best states 2021: How they rank. Mar. 9. Retrieved from https://www.usnews.com/news/best-states/articles/methodology.

United States Senate (1995) *Senate Bill S.984*. 104th Congress, 1st Session. June 29. Retrieved from https://www.congress.gov/104/bills/s984/BILLS-104s984is.pdf.

United States Senate (2004) *Juvenile Detention Centers: Are They Warehousing Children with Mental Illness?* Hearing before the Committee on Governmental Affairs. One Hundred Eighth Congress, Second Session. Washington, DC: U.S. Government Printing Office.

Urbina, I. (2009) For runaways, sex buys survival. *The New York Times*. Oct. 26. Retrieved from https://www.nytimes.com/2009/10/27/us/27runaways.html.

Verdugo, R. R. and B. C. Glenn (2006) Race and alternative schools. Conference paper, annual meeting of the Alternatives to Expulsion, Suspension, and Dropping Out of School Conference. Feb. 16-18, Orlando, FL. Washington, DC: Office of Justice Programs. Retrieved from https://www.ojp.gov/pdffiles1/ojjdp/grants/226234.pdf.

Ward, G. K. (2012) *The Black Child Savers: Racial Democracy and Juvenile Justice*. Chicago, IL: University of Chicago Press.

White, L. M., E. D. Holloway, M. Aalsma, and E. L. Adams (2015) Job-related burnout among juvenile probation officers: Implications for mental health stigma and competency. *Psychological Services*. Aug, Vol. 12, No. 3:291-302.

Williams, S. N. and S. A. LaTess (2020) Increasing cultural awareness in detained youth: Implications for intergroup relationships. *Professional Psychologist: Research and Practice*. Vol. 51, No. 3:291-296.

Willow, C. (2015) *Children Behind Bars: Why the Abuse of Child Imprisonment Must End.* Bristol, UK: Policy Press.

Wills, C. D. (2017) Caring for juveniles with mental disorders in adult prisons. *International Review of Psychiatry.* Vol. 29, No:25-33.

Wilson, W. J. (1987) *The Truly Disadvantaged: The Inner City, the Underclass, and Public Policy.* Chicago, IL: University of Chicago Press.

Winter, C. (2016) Spare the rod: Amid evidence zero tolerance doesn't work, schools reverse themselves. *APM Reports.* Aug. 25. Radio Broadcast. Retrieved from https://www.apm reports.org/episode/2016/08/25/reforming-school-discipline.

World Population Review (2021) Public school rankings by state 2021. Retrieved from https://worldpopulationreview.com/state-rankings/public-school-rankings-by-state.

Yoder, S. (2020) Sticker shock: The cost of New York youth prisons approaches $1 million per kid. Youth and Family News, *The Imprint.* Nov. 22. Retrieved from https://imprintn ews.org/justice/sticker-shock-cost-new-york-youth-prisons-approaches-million/49580.

Zahn, M. A., J. C. Day, S. F. Mihalic, and L. Tichavsky (2009) Determining what works for girls in the Juvenile Justice System: A summary of evaluation evidence. *Crime and Delinquency.* Vol. 55, No. 2:266-93.

Chapter TEN

Violence in Prison[1]

Ricky Knight: *"I'd just got out of prison."*
Hugh: *"Prison? What was that for?"*
Ricky Knight: *"Mainly violence."*

— *Fighting with My Family,* 2019, MGM Studios

Chapter Objectives

- Identify types and sources of violence in prison.
- Discuss the physical and psychological effects of violence.
- Identify vulnerable populations in prison.
- Illustrate extreme cases of violence in prison, including murders and riots.
- Highlight the role of mental health issues on incidences of violence in prison.
- Describe how gangs contribute to prison violence.

Key Terms

Knuckleduster
Importation Theory
Intimate partner violence (IPV)
Mace
Prison Rape Elimination
    Act (PREA)

Prisonization Theory
Protective custody
Riots
Sap
Shank
Shiv

---

[1] **TRIGGER WARNING**: The topics we are discussing in this chapter may be disturbing to some readers. We recommend that you discuss with your professor or instructor as to how much or how little of this chapter you will be responsible for.

INTRODUCTION

Though many films and television shows depict jails and prisons as places of non-stop confrontation and violence, in reality much of what detainees and inmates experience is boredom. If you will recall from earlier chapters, detainees (those who have been arrested and denied bail) are held in jail, not prison. They are awaiting trial or have not had their arraignment in court yet after arrest. In other words, they have yet to be convicted of the crime for which they are being held. Between detainees and inmates, common sense would say that detainees have far more incentive to behave themselves while in jail. However, violence does occur between both inmates and detainees, or is directed at corrections staff, both in jail and in prison. In this chapter, we will also discuss self-inflicted violence, as in the example of detainee or prisoner suicide.

Anyone who has lived through the COVID-19 shutdowns might well understand how the tedium in jail or prison can be maddening. Even those of us who experienced intensive self-quarantining at home probably occupied a space considerably bigger than a prison cell and had sources of entertainment available with which to fill the time, including television, video streaming, and whatever hobbies we could pursue from home. Whatever was not readily available could be ordered from any number of online shopping sites. Even during quarantine, in most cases, we could at least get outdoors for a walk. We could also talk or video chat with friends and family on a regular basis, if we wanted to. Even so, the restrictions on our normal way of life pre-pandemic could at times be suffocating. Prisoners in most cases do not have the same luxuries that were available to most of us throughout the pandemic. To the extreme, prisoners in maximum security facilities are denied a great number of creature comforts that those of us outside of jail and prison sometimes take for granted. In an extreme case of tempers bubbling over during the pandemic, the protests and riot that took place at a Bogota, Columbia, prison in March 2020 resulted in 24 prisoners killed and 107 people injured, including corrections officers (Human Rights Watch, 2020).

Jail and prison assaults of all kinds, including those that result in manslaughter or homicide, are defined legally exactly the same as they are in the outside world. However, unlike life outside of prison walls, assaults inside are much more difficult to hide—or to hide *from*. As one inmate put it, "You don't have to do anything to become a victim and there's no one man who is strong enough to come against a group of five or six." (Kamaminski, 2004, p. 1; Toch, 1992, pp. 64-65). This reality, coupled with the sharp increase in the number of offenders incarcerated for violent crimes (1951-2011 data, Skarbeck, 2014), widens the ratio between nonviolent and violent offenders and increases the probability that assaults will occur behind bars.

A couple of people may throw some punches at one another outside of prison and if there is no law enforcement intervention, it will largely be ignored as long as no one has been seriously injured or the violence doesn't escalate. Because of almost constant surveillance, most violence that occurs in jail and prison, if not reported by the detainees or inmates themselves, will be witnessed firsthand by prison staff or captured on videotape. More recent data indicate that approximately 12 assault incidents per 5,000 inmates occur in publicly operated prisons (Bureau of Prisons, 2020), as compared to approximately 12.5 aggregated assaults per 5,000 population that occur outside of prison (statista.com, 2019). Though a number of sources, including the media, indicate that there is more violence in prisons, this may only be a perception as the rates for assaults in and out of prison are fairly similar. However, we also have to keep in mind that there is far more surveillance of individuals in prison, so if we consider that there are corrections officers present, the number of assaults in prison is alarmingly high.

Reports of violence in private prisons are somewhat less transparent than in public prisons. However, reports coming out of these prisons allege that there is more violence and may be related to the fact that corrections officers have less training, are poorly paid, and are fewer in numbers, in comparison to public sector corrections. What we do know from data coming out of England and Wales, the fact that there is more violence reported in private prisons overseas (156 out of 1000 prisoners or 47% more violence) raises the question of whether for-profit prison are adequately protecting both corrections officers and prisoners from assaults (Lovlie et and P. Guruli, 2021; Grierson and Duncan, 2019).

In most prisons, even though there is boredom, there is also the heightened tension of having to continually look over your shoulder to make sure that you do not become a victim of a violent assault. This holds true for both prisoners and corrections staff. For some inmates, this state of being constantly on the watch can be psychologically exhausting. The same can be said of corrections officers during their shifts. Detainees or inmates, due to frustration, anger, and/or mental health issues, given the opportunity, will lash out at fellow inmates or correction staff. Fortunately, for most facilities, even if the inclination to commit a violent act is there, there are a number of safeguards to prevent prison violence. However, they are not fail-proof.

TYPES OF VIOLENCE IN JAILS AND PRISONS

Assaults

In cases where prisoners have been prosecuted and convicted for serious assaults that took place in prison at all security levels, the rates have fluctuated between 1 in 10,000 and 2 in 10,000 between 2016 and 2020 (Bureau of Prisons, 2020). As to be expected, when we examine only high security prisons in the same Bureau of Prison data (2020), the rates are higher, to as many as 12 in 10,000 prisoners in April 2018. Of course, these only include the data for cases where the prisoner is found guilty of assault in a court of law, which no doubt extended that individual's time in prison. This is particularly difficult for the accused inmate who is close to release, whether it results in new charges or disciplinary action.

Serious assaults on corrections officers are less common, even though they are essentially unarmed while working in jail or prison units. Between 2016 and 2020, the Bureau of Prisons (2020) reported that rates for assault on staff fluctuated between .06 in 10,000 and .88 in 10,000 inmates. Again, these are assaults where the prisoner was prosecuted and found to be guilty. It does not include unreported assaults or cases where the prisoner has been found not guilty in their trial. Though it is safe to assume that assaults against corrections personnel are more likely to be reported, prosecuted, and result in guilty verdicts, than assaults occurring between inmates.

As the case with crime in general, untold numbers of assaults go unreported. There are two explanations for this. One, the prison staff may feel that the assault is not serious enough to go beyond administrative sanctions, as in the example of a few punches thrown or a bit of shoving taking place. Second, the detainees and prisoners themselves may not report the assault for fear that there may be retribution from fellow inmates for "snitching." Another fear is that they may feel that they will appear weak in front of other detainees or prisoners if they do report the assault.

Prisoners are not the only ones who can find themselves accused of assault in prison. Though not reportedly common, at times prisoners can be unfairly, and in

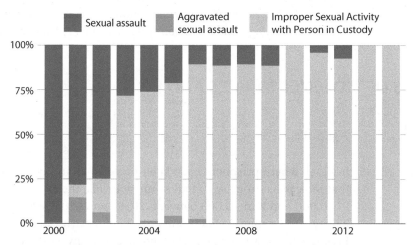

Charges against Texas prison workers in sex cases, 2000-2014

In recent years, Texas officials have increasingly relied on a charge criminalizing consensual sexual relationships between prison staff and inmates rather than assault charges that carry harsher penalties.

SOURCE: TEXAS DEPARTMENT OF CRIMINAL JUSTICE AND SPECIAL PROSECUTION UNIT

FIGURE 10.1 **Charges Against Texas Prison Workers in Sex Cases, 2000-2014.**
(*Source*: The Marshall Project, 2015, retrieved from https://www.themarshallproject.org/2015/06/17/preying-on-prisoners)

some cases, criminally harmed by corrections officers. These can include sexual assaults as noted in the previous graph that includes data on Texas prison staff abuse of prisoners (Fig. 10.1). Again, we have to be cautious as to what the real statistics are, as assaults by prison staff may very well be underreported. Detainees or prisoners who have been assaulted may fear being further victimized or being written up for disciplinary action if they report incidences of excessive force committed by corrections staff. The detained or convicted, by their very statuses, are rarely seen as victims by society when they have been assaulted while incarcerated, whether by fellow inmates or prison staff.

There have been a number of cases where corrections officers have used excessive force on inmates, resulting in assault charges brought against them. In 2020, two former Cuyahoga County Jail corrections officers in Ohio were sentenced in a case of beating an inmate suffering from mental health issues, who had been strapped into a chair during the assault (Cleveland.com, 2020). Both will be required to serve time behind bars in *protective custody* (segregated portion of a jail or prison that is reserved for detainees or prisoners who have to be protected from other inmates), which is customary in cases of former lawyers, judges, law enforcement, and corrections officers or other criminal justice professionals who have been sentenced to jail or prison.

Sexual Assault

There are a number of victim studies on rape and sexual coercion outside of prison walls. Ignored in research and society is the discussion of sexual coercion in prison (Struckman-Johnson, 1996). Officially, as we have noted in other chapters, sexual activities of any kind are prohibited in jail and prison, coerced or otherwise. However, the stories coming out of prisons paint a different picture of what is actually taking place or unofficially permitted.

Like assaults, rapes in prison go largely unreported, so it is difficult to provide statistics that are accurate. Out of the 80,000 prisoners each year who are suspected to have been sexually victimized, only an estimated 8 percent report it to prison staff (Kubiak et al., 2017). A Bureau of Justice survey of former state inmates conducted in 2012 found that 10 percent reported having been sexually assaulted at least one time; 31 percent reported having been victimized three or more times while incarcerated (Beck et al., 2013). Most researchers contend that prison rape rates in even major studies with large numbers of participants are low estimates (Eigenberg, 1994; Struckman-Johnson et al., 1996).

As we discuss rape in this chapter, we are speaking to sexual assault, not situational homosexual behavior or other forms of consensual sex in prison. Consensual sexual behavior was presented in Chapter 6 in discussions of jail and prison cultures among the incarcerated. We should keep in mind that the act of rape is always a violent act, in some cases used as a weapon, with no romantic meaning attached to it. Even prisoners who identify as heterosexual might use rape as a way to retaliate against fellow prisoners or as a form of intimidation.

It is important to note that when prison staff are involved in sexual relationships with inmates, even if it is consensual, it is not viewed as being so by prison authorities and society on a whole. Because of the power dynamic between corrections officers and prisoners, as much as a sexual relationship may been deemed consensual by the both parties as we discussed in Chapter 8 with women in prison, prisoners are always viewed as being coerced as they are seen as powerless to say no to the sexual advances of prison staff.

Before 2003, in the United States, there was little protection for detainees and prisoners against rape while incarcerated. In 2003, the *Prison Rape Elimination Act (PREA)* was passed, with the focus on analyzing the rates and effects of rape in all types of facilities, including federal, state, and local jails and prison, in order to reduce the prevalence of sexual violence in corrections facilities (Ratkalkar and Atkins-Plunk, 2020; National PRE Resource Center, n.d.). Some of the concerns for reducing the incidents of sexual assault in prison have to do with general health concerns, including the reduction of sexually transmittable diseases, including HIV/AIDS.

Detainees and prisoners are not equally vulnerable to sexual assault. Younger and weaker inmates are viewed as easy prey by sexual predators in correctional facilities, as they are less able to fend off unwanted advances. Individuals who identify as gay or bisexual and inmates with a history of childhood sexual abuse are twice as likely to report fearing that they will fall victim to a sexual assault while incarcerated (Ratkalkar and Atkins-Plunk, 2020). It is unknown how much of this fear is due to real threats, PTSD from the childhood abuses, or media perceptions. Whether the threat of being victimized is real or imagined, it is one more extreme stressor added to a long line of stresses experienced in jail or prison.

Likewise, women are not excluded from being victimized by sexual assault while incarcerated. Not surprisingly, as in the case of research on incarcerated women in general, there is little in the way of data to give an accurate picture of how prevalent assaults are. When victimized by prison staff, there are a number of factors that predict whether they will report sexual assault. Among them are victim's age, socioeconomic status, degree of physical injury, and the relationship between the victim and the perpetrator (Kubiak et al., 2017). Women inside and outside of prison are less likely to report a rape if the offender is known to them (Kubiak et al., 2017). Some of this reluctance comes from the real vulnerability to victim blaming, particularly in the case of acquaintance rape, whether it takes place in or outside of prison (Gravelin et al., 2019; Bieneck and Krahé, 2011; Gordon and Riger, 2011.

Increasingly the transgender population behind bars has gained attention as a vulnerable population that is at greater risk of being victimized while incarcerated. The LGBQT+ community, on a whole, is at greater risk of assault in and out of prison. With the greater visibility and growing acceptance of this community in recent decades, we sadly also have a better picture of the rates of sexual assaults on non-heterosexual individuals. However, there are still calls to advance the research understandings of LGBQT+ populations who are incarcerated (Brown and Jenness, 2020).

What we do know is that the most vulnerable of this population are transgender women, most of whom are housed in jails and prisons for men to which they have been incorrectly placed due to genital-based assignment (Sumner and Jenness, 2014). Some transgender inmates may be housed in protective custody, but most are placed in general population, often assigned to the incorrect gender facility.

In *Farmer v. Brennan* (1994), Dee Farmer, a transgender woman, testified that she was repeatedly beaten, raped, and eventually infected with HIV while incarcerated at the men's prison in Terre Haute, Indiana (Brown and Jenness, 2020). In another account of having been assaulted, while serving time in a maximum security men's prison in New York, Glaysa, a transgender female, reported the following horrific experiences:

> *I have faced violence where I have been beaten and raped because of my being transgender with female breasts and feminine (sic). I have been burned out of a cell block and dorm because I wouldn't give an inmate sex. I have been slapped, punched, and even threatened because of my being a transgender that told another inmate 'No' when they wanted sex from me or my commissary buy. . . . I've been subjected to all kinds of verbal harassment from 'look at that inmate scumbag transgender' all the way to threats and sexual harassment physically as well as verbally.* (Brown and Jenness, 2020, retrieved from https://oxfordre.com/criminology/view/10.1093/acrefore/9780190264079.001.0001/acrefore-9780190264079-e-647; Sylvia Rivera Law Project, 2007, p. 25)

Juveniles are particularly vulnerable to sexual assault while in detention[2]. According to the Bureau of Justice Statistics, in 2018, 5.8 percent of children in custody reported sexual misconduct by staff; 1.9 percent reported sexual victimization by another child in youth detention (Smith, 2019). Again, we may never know the actual numbers, due to the unknown rates of coerced, consensual sex between staff and juveniles in custody, as well as the number of sexual assaults that go unreported.

Some of the characteristics of sexually aggressive inmates are as follows (Brown and Jenness, 2020, retrieved from https://oxfordre.com/criminology/view/10.1093/acrefore/9780190264079.001.0001/acrefore-9780190264079-e-647):

- Between the ages of 27 and 45
- Medium to large build and possessing physical strength
- Aggressive in nature

---

[2] A reminder that we are not referring to detention that is imposed by a school for academic or behavioral problems in the classroom. Detention in the juvenile justice system refers to the housing of juveniles after they have been adjudicated in court, sentenced to time in a juvenile facility.

- Having limited ties to outside family and friends and having no outside means of financial support
- Incarcerated for sex offenses or other violent offenses
- More streetwise and gang affiliated
- More accustomed to prison life
- May have difficulty controlling anger
- May display poor coping skills/strategies
- May exhibit voyeuristic/exhibitionistic behavior
- Doing a substantial amount of time
- Established [themselves] by power and strength within the prison inmate hierarchy

Homicide Behind Bars

Though far less common than assaults and rapes, manslaughter and homicides do occur behind bars. These are statistics that are nearly impossible to hide and we have perhaps the most accurate picture on the actual numbers as compared to other forms of violence in jails and prisons. Between 2001 and 2016, there were 1,024 homicides reported in state and federal facilities (Carson and Cowhig, 2020). According to a Bureau of Justice Statistics report, between 2015 and 2016 rates of deaths in state prisons increased from 296 to 303 deaths per 100,000 inmates (Widra, 2020). The leading cause of death in state prisons continues to be chronic illness (Widra, 2020).

We should not conclude that all murders that occur in prison are documented. There are stories of inmates dying from assumedly natural causes when in actuality it may have been the result of a violent act. For example, a prisoner with an intimate knowledge of human physiology can fashion a weapon so fine, that they could potentially stab a fellow inmate in the kidney and it only feels like a pinch. The resulting infection would not be detected until it is too late. Prison officials are reluctant to report a death as "suspicious" if they can possibly help it, particularly those that might be suspected as a result of an assault by an inmate on a fellow detainee or prisoner.

There are a number of famous documented cases of prisoners who were clearly murdered by fellow prisoners, as in the case of Jeffrey Dahmer, the serial killer who had been sentenced to life in prison and murdered by fellow inmate Christopher Scarver while both were in prison. Scarver reportedly crushed Dahmer's head with a metal bar because he was disgusted with Dahmer's habit of fashioning prison food into the shape of human limbs and covering them with ketchup, along with Dahmer's lust for human flesh (Malatesta, 2015). For those of you unfamiliar with the Dahmer case, he was convicted on counts of multiple murder, accused of dismembering his victims and storing their remains in his refrigerator, which police suspected that Dahmer was cannibalizing. As in the case of Dahmer's death, a murder often takes place in prison because fellow prisoners find that the victim's crimes are considered to be the worst of the worst among criminals.

Same with the death of James "Whitey" Bolger, the infamous Boston mob boss, who was killed while incarcerated. But this case was less about the crimes that Bolger committed than the enemies he made while being involved in organized crime. At the time of his murder while he was in custody, Bolger was wheelchair bound and helpless to fend off his attacker(s), who beat him senseless with a so-called *sap* (a makeshift weapon where a hard object like a bar of soap or a lock is placed in a sock and used against a fellow detainee or prisoner; in Bolger's case, it was a lock). We also have a number of documented case of possible suicides in jail and prison, more recently that of Jeffrey Epstein, a convicted sex offender and wealthy financier, who was found dead in his cell, leaving some to question whether it was really a homicide (*60 Minutes*, CBS News, 2020).

Homicide in prison is also viewed as an unfortunate byproduct of prison conditions. Prisons that are overcrowded, coupled with competition for resources, the bad health care received, including mental health counseling, along with conditions of isolation, all can result in more violence, including murder behind bars (Drago et al., 2011). For the victim, if they are aware they are targeted beforehand, because of close quarters in prison, their only option may be to request protective custody.

MAKESHIFT WEAPONS IN PRISONS

The most obvious weapons that prisoners have handy are their fists. A great number of assaults in prisons involve prisoners throwing punches, usually at one another. Sometimes the assault is directed at corrections officers or other prison employees, including those working in the infirmary.

Keeping in mind that detainees and inmates have a lot of time on their hands, there are surprisingly a great number of ordinary everyday things that can be made into weapons. As mentioned above, something as simple as a bar of soap in a sock ("*sap*"), swung at someone's head, can be lethal. Even a finely rolled up newspaper can be turned into a makeshift weapon. It is precisely because inmates are so inventive that jail and prison cells are regularly inspected for hidden drugs, makeshift weapons, and other contraband items.

The most commonly used weapons used in prison are those prisoners have made themselves, though weapons have been known to be smuggled in by visitors and at times, corrections staff. Among homemade weapons are daggers and *shanks* or *shivs* (interchangeable terms for sharp objects made from everyday materials available to prisoners). Detainees and prisoners have also been known to use food items to fashion weapons, as in one example where Jolly Rancher® hard candies were melted down with contraband lighters and dried to shape a solid piece, which was then filed into a sharp object. Likewise candy bars can be allowed to go stale, becoming hard enough to either use as a sap weapon or sharpened into a makeshift knife.

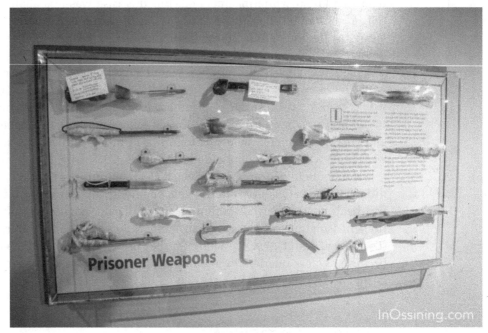

Display of Weapons Confiscated from Prisoners, Sing Sing Prison Exhibit and Museum. (*Source*: https://www.inossining.com/sing-sing-prison-exhibit-museum/)

Everyday items we take for granted have been modified for prisoner use, to reduce the chances of their being turned into a weapon. For instance, an ordinary toothbrush handle can be filed down to a sharp object that can do serious harm. Because of this, the handle of a jail or prison issued toothbrush is rounded, short, and flexible, as seen in the photo to the left.

The same precautions with eating utensils in psychiatric hospitals are taken in jails and prisons, where a conventional knife or fork, even if plastic, could do serious physical damage if sharpened. Jails and prisons take extra precautions with the utensils that are used in the kitchens, often chaining knives and other sharp objects to work stations where it is not uncommon for prisoners to provide the labor in food preparation, often in vocational programs.

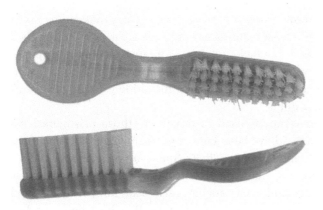

Example of Jail and Prison Toothbrushes. (*Source*: Security Dental Products, retrieved from https://www.securitydentalproducts.com/product/secure-care-flexible-security-tooth/)

Deadlier weapons created in prison, as reported by *Corrections 1* (2009), a website for corrections staff, and Lincoln, et al. (2006), include the following:

- Shotgun made from iron bedposts, using AA batteries to ignite it.
- *Shiv* disguised as a cross that had been fashioned in a prison woodworking shop.
- "*Knuckleduster*" made from a rasp stolen from a prison workshop.
- *Mace,* which is a club-like weapon generally consisting of a ball covered with spikes (e.g., nails) and sometimes attached to a chain or other materials that make the weapon easy to swing at victims and that can be made in a prison metal workshop.
- Whip made with razor blades.
- Hairbrush modified into a stabbing weapon.
- Weapons made out of prescribed medical devices, including knee braces.

Though not generally deadly, detainees and prisoners have gone so far as to using their bodily fluids, including spit, blood, urine, as well as feces as weapons against each other and corrections personnel (U.S. Department of Justice, Federal Bureau of Prisons, 2011). These bodily fluids can be knowingly infected with a number of bacterial or viral substances, including staph, tuberculosis, AIDS, hepatitis, the COVID-19 virus, and other infectious diseases. Correctional staff have to be regularly tested for a number of these conditions, as the dangers of violent physical injury is far exceeded by their exposure to illness and disease in the ordinary duties in their jobs (Ferdik and Smith, 2017).

GENERAL THEORIES TO EXPLAIN VIOLENCE IN PRISON

One of the most convincing theories to explain violence in prison is the general culture of violence. Some of the arrested and convicted have come from communities where violence is the norm, as in the example of cities where gangs are more prevalent. Even if detainees or inmates come from nonviolent communities, jails and higher security prisons represent a population that is more likely to have a mix of criminals accused of or convicted of a number of violent crimes, including assaults, rapes, and murder, as compared to low or medium security prisons. This is not to say that assaults do not happen in prisons that house nonviolent offenders. It just is more uncommon than in maximum security or supermax prisons.

There are a number of aspects of prison culture that can contribute to violence. The first and perhaps foremost, as we have mentioned, is overcrowding. Study after study indicate that overcrowded prisons are a recipe for interpersonal violence. This holds true when examining jails and prisons in the United States, as well as prisons in other parts of the world (Caravaca-Sànchez et al., 2019)

Other contributing factors are the prevalence of gangs in prisons. Yet another compelling argument is that prisons can be considered domestic space, similar to the insides of our homes, where there is a greater possibility of domestic violence, some resulting from failures in communication and petty arguments (Crawley and Crawley, 2008). After all, detainees and prisoners eat, sleep, work, and socialize within the same confined spaces, similar to the person who is working from home and has no escape, as in the case of widespread stay-at-home orders during the COVID-19 pandemic. Again, as we have noted, at least the person in quarantine confined at home has the freedom to take a walk around the block or in nature.

Using those conditions as an analogy to what prison life is like, just as we might anticipate an increase in domestic violence during the pandemic ("a pandemic within a pandemic"), we might surmise that same can be held true among the prisoner populations as well (Evans et al., 2020). Though the expected increase in intimate partner violence (IPV)—physical violence, stalking, or psychological harm by a current or former partner or spouse—did not materialize as anticipated early in the pandemic, experts still believe that an increase was inevitable and that there may be failure to report domestic violence incidences as victims are trapped with their tormentors (Evans et al., 2020). It is still also early in the data gathering process from the pandemic to have accurate rates of increases, if any, of domestic violence or assaults in prison.

We would be remiss if we did not include a discussion addressing the underlying issues that prisoners are fighting over that leads to violence. Conflicts between prisoners, whether verbal or physical, are generally over three things: *interests*, *values*, and *relationships*. According to Edgar (2008), interests include material goods, like tobacco, phone cards, and drugs. Values are things like respect, privacy, loyalty, and honesty (Edgar, 2008). Relationships are defined by whether individuals in conflict are strangers, acquaintances, or close friends (Edgar, 2008). These, coupled with the struggle for power among the powerless, can all be facilitators for violence exploding behind jail and prison walls.

IMPORTATION AND PRISONIZATION THEORIES

Two key theories, (1) *importation theory* and (2) *prisonization theory*, can help explain unacceptable and prohibited behavior that takes place in jail or prison, including prison violence. On the surface, the two theories may appear to contradict each other, but when applied together, they are useful in understanding the underlying reasons for violence in prison, whether it is directed at others or self-inflicted. We should note that both importation and prisonization research has been largely ignored in recent decades, with no explanation from theorists as to why that should be the case.

Importation theory proposes that bad behavior is brought into the jail or prison from the outside. The detainee or inmate already was antisocial or broke a number of social norms, and that is the reason they are in jail or prison in the first place. Prisoners are often required to complete anger management treatment while incarcerated. An example that illustrates importation theory is the gang member who has already been part of a violent subculture in their community before going to prison and brings violent tendencies with them into the institution.

Prisonization theory, a deprivation model, proposes that antisocial behavior is a result of the prison experience. In other words, experiences in jail or prison contribute to antisocial behavior and misconduct. In fact, it is the conditions of prison life and the prisonization process that makes reentry into society difficult for convicts on release, with the degree of difficulty growing greater along with the length of the sentence. These factors can also make transition from jail to the outside world difficult, even for suspects who are found to be not guilty at their trial, whether due to evidence or lack of evidence in the case, if they have been detained pretrial.

Prisonization processes are not immediate. And the prisonization happens differently for those who are incarcerated for the first time, as compared to those who are repeat offenders. In either case, there are two key variables that contribute to prisonization. The first is powerlessness. Once detained or incarcerated, the accused or convicted lose most of their civil liberties.

The second variable that applies to the detained and incarcerated in the prisonization process is negative post-release expectations. This is where the accused is found guilty in a court of law and sees no positive outcomes once they have left jail or prison (Thomas et al., 1978). There is the real fear that an arrest record and/or conviction narrows opportunities on the outside, including job prospects. In an age where most job applications require prospective employees to divulge criminal records and explain arrests even if the charges were dropped, many detainees and convicts resign themselves to the fact that their lives have forever been damaged, if not fully ruined. Of course, we have to consider that the fear may only be imagined, as in the case of the elite white collar criminal who might exit prison with a number of career avenues still open or financial means relatively intact, as in the example of Michael Milken who has since flourished in the nonprofit sector, after serving time in prison in the 1990s for security fraud[3]. But for the vast majority of the previously incarcerated, their life prospects after prison are limited.

In the face of such hopelessness, where the temptation to resort to violence to settle disputes may ordinarily be tempered outside of incarceration, the detainee or inmate may instead feel like they have nothing to lose. In addition to this, if inmates are hanging around others who possess violent tendencies, as in the case of those who have been convicted of violent crimes, the prisonization process comes full circle with negative behavior being reinforced or encouraged. If we consider that a good number of convicts are in prison for violent crimes, violence may be viewed as the normal way to settle arguments. But for the intervention of corrections officers and the physical design of jails and prisons, violence among the incarcerated might

---

[3] Milken's foundation can be found at https://www.mff.org/about-the-foundation/the-founders/michael-milken/.

become more commonplace than it is, at least in jails and prisons in the United States.

Part of the conditions of prisonization, particularly for males, is that definitions of what it means to be a man are constrained by the prison system. Having been stripped of many of the things that society characterize as being crucial to the male identity, including employment and normative sexual relationships, prisoners will resort to violence to reassert their masculinity. The conditions of prison life are so problematic to maintaining the masculine identity, heightened aggression is an adoptive response (Sykes, 1958). Violence can be a response to the powerlessness experienced in prison.

As we said earlier, importation and prisonization theories seem to contradict one another in some respects, but in all reality, for some inmates it can be the combination of the two factors. Most proponents of both theories would argue that the two should be integrated, as for many prisoners, it is the antisocial behavior brought into the prison and the conditions of prison that can contribute to misconduct while incarcerated (Gillespie, 2002). Of gravest concern is that both importation and prisonization processes become cyclical, where the values and violent tendencies are then exported into the community after release, resulting in recidivism and failed rehabilitation.

MENTAL HEALTH ISSUES AND VIOLENT BEHAVIOR BEHIND BARS

Certain psychiatric and psychological disorders can also contribute to violent behavior in jail and prisons. In fact, it can be the very reason why someone ends up in jail or prison in the first place, as further discussed in Chapter 11. A psychosis may already exist as in the case of those who suffer from one of the bipolar disorders or schizophrenia or can result from a new onset of mental health issues, due to the conditions of being incarcerated. Extreme violent behavior can also be brought on by the consumption of contraband substances, including prison-made alcoholic beverages where there is no control or regulation of strength of alcohol content and drugs that have been smuggled in or manufactured behind prison jail or prison walls.

Not all violence is directed at others. In some cases, the detainee or inmate turns the violence on themselves in self-harming. Suicide rates in general have been on the rise, but exponentially so in jails and prisons, as indicated but the Prison Policy Initiative (https://www.prisonpolicy.org/blog/2020/02/13/jaildeaths/). But self-harm is not limited to suicide.

Self-mutilation is not uncommon and can consist of self-inflicted cuts, a psychological condition that is seen outside of prison as well. Self-mutilators tend to be white, generally already have wrist or forearm scars upon admission to jail or prison, and are more likely to attempt suicide while incarcerated (Jones, 1986). This same population is also more likely to have been convicted of more felonies, had disciplinary action, charged with more assaults while in jail or prison (Jones,

1986), indicating that they are not limited to harming just themselves, but will hurt others as well.

It is very common for victims of violence to experience their own psychological crises. The prison experience itself can result in post-traumatic stress disorder (PTSD). There is a greater risk for someone who is a victim of violence, whether in or out of prison, to develop the symptoms of PTSD. The symptoms of PTSD can be heightened further for those who do not have strong friendship or family support systems in place (Scarpa et al., 2006), conditions that are present for most, if not all of those incarcerated.

A more detailed discussion of mental health issues in prison is discussed in the next chapter on all types of health issues found behind prison walls.

THE ROLE OF GANGS IN PRISON VIOLENCE

If we consider that gangs, or other organized crime groups for that matter, are predatory, violence is part and parcel to their cultures. Of course, all gangs are not equal, if we consider the differences between neighborhood crews and rates of violence, as compared to formal, established gangs, like MS-13, Crips, Bloods, etc., and a number of white supremacy groups. In a study of inmates in Nevada and Ohio, gang members were found to be more likely to have citations for violating prison rules, found guilty in disciplinary hearings, and be disciplined for drugs and/or fighting (Skarbeck, 2014; Sheldon, 1991).

Not all gang members who are in jails or prisons come in with gang affiliation. Many are recruited while incarcerated. As we have established in this chapter and others, inmates in men's prison very much self-segregate themselves along racial lines. This is due largely to self-preservation, with the belief that fellow gang members will protect them from violence. Self-segregation is not far off from what we see in street gangs as we rarely see gangs that are integrated by race, much less by gender. Gang members in prison, like those on the outside, are more frequently violent, more likely to use lethal weapons, and cause more injuries and accidents than nonmembers (Wood and Dennard, 2017; Decker and Pyrooz, 2010; Klein et al., 2006).

Membership to a gang or white supremacy group is not automatic in prison. In light of the need to maintain threats of violence plus the ability to run illegal enterprises, prison gangs look to recruit only "high quality" members (Skarbeck, 2014). Potential gang members must demonstrate some connection to existing members, by way of gang affiliation outside the prison or have neighborhood, community connections. To be a sponsor of a gang recruit can prove to be deadly in itself, as in the case of the Mexikanemi Hispanic prison gang in Texas in which, when a new recruit turned traitor, it was the responsibility of the sponsor to kill them (Skarbeck, 2014). Or gang members may turn on the recruiter, if the new member they have sponsored does not live up to expectations.

The illegal underground enterprises of gang members can also expose them to victimization. Because of fierce competition behind bars, drug dealers in prison have to overcome a number of obstacles, including assault (Skarbek, 2014). We have discussed the "convict code" elsewhere in this book. Many of the rules prescribed in the code are enforced by gangs (Skarbek, 2014). But as Skarbek (2014) notes, with the changes in inmate demographics in recent decades, where there are substantially more gang members incarcerated, whereas the convict code initially was created to instill order, honor, and cooperation between inmates, the code has been turned upside down. There is less incentive for inmates to get along and follow the code when they are split down racial or gang affiliations.

We should also note that part of the gang problem among the incarcerated, beyond the issue of violence, is that the larger the prison population, the more likely that gangs can flourish behind bars by bringing more members into the fold.

PRISON RIOTS

Though less common than incidents of individual assault, *riots* (disturbances that involve five or more detainees or inmates) can and do occur in jails and prisons. According to Barak-Glantz (1983), there is one major riot in a U.S. jail or prison each year. The Bureau of Justice Statistics, as well as the Bureau of Prisons, define riots or other major disturbances in jails or prisons as "incidents involving five or more inmates resulting in serious injury or significant property damage." (Stephan and Karsberg, 2003, p. 10; Byrne and Hummer, 2008). Though they are not regular occurrences, riots, when they do happen, create chaos that can last long after they have been suppressed. The greatest rates of deadly force use by corrections officers can be found, understandably so, during prison riots (Gibbs, 1981).

Most of what we see of violence in prisons are isolated incidences. However, in extreme cases when prison conditions are perceived to be intolerable to enough inmates, given the chance, they will collectively try to take over the prison. If you recall, prisoners do not have the constitutional right to peacefully assemble and protest their conditions. Other riots are a result of two or more competing factions in the prison population turning on one another in all out warfare. As a result, in some riots, prisoners are turning on corrections officers and staff. In others, they are targeting one another.

Riots, as to be expected, are not all equal. Some are momentary skirmishes, put down quickly by corrections officers. Others last for a number of days and result in millions of dollars in damage to the jail or prison facility, as well as costing a number of lives:

- Deadliest riot: New Mexico Penitentiary (1980).
- Longest riot: Southern Ohio Correctional Facility (1993).

■ Most recent reported in U.S. history: City Justice Center, St. Louis, Missouri (2021).[4]

As violent and deadly as jail and prison riots can be in the United States, there have been a number of riots in other countries that have been far greater in size and consequences. For example, in July 2019, 62 hostages were taken at the Centro de Recuperação Regional de Altamira prison in Brazil. By the end of the riot, at least 57 prisoners had been killed, 16 of whom had been beheaded (*Folha de S.Paulo*, 2019). This was on the heels of a riot in the previous year that resulted in 7 people killed in the same facility (*Folha de S.Paulo*, 2019). In both cases, the conditions that lead to the Brazil prison riots were similar to those in the United States but considerably worst: understaffing and overcrowding.

RESPONSES TO VIOLENCE IN PRISON: ADMINISTRATION AND CORRECTIONS OFFICERS PERPECTIVES

In prison administration, much like in law enforcement on the street, prevention is key in forestalling violence in prison. Unlike violence outside of prison walls, there are a number of ways that jails and prison are structured to prevent assaults from happening. The first and obvious is the way in which jails and prisons are constructed, building security into the physical structure, the topic of Chapter 3 and prison architecture. The second way in which jails and prisons can help prevent violence is to threaten to write up the detainee or prisoner who commits any type of transgression behind bars, which in many cases can delay parole or release and if the offense breaks additional laws, can result in additional sentences imposed on the convicted.

There are a number of ways that jails and prisons can respond to actual incidences of violence or the potential for violence. Byrne and Hummer (2008, p. 41) identify three broad categories of responses to violence and disorder:

1. *Inmate-focused strategies* (e.g., classification, offender profiling, and conflict resolution strategies).
2. *Staff-focused strategies* (including the National Institute of Corrections Culture Change Initiative).
3. *Management-focused strategies* (e.g., increased access to treatment programs, crowding reduction, and changes in situational context).

A controversial suggested policy to reduce violence in prison includes purposeful segregation by race. Besides possibly creating Civil Rights violations, there

---

[4] City Justice Center is a jail facility.

is concern as to whether this might result in unequal treatment of prisoners. The push for segregation policies has been motivated by the number of disturbances that are instigated by the race difference of prisoners. Whatever racial prejudices exist in society based on race as a whole becomes exaggerated and magnified in prison. One example out of California is a riot in 2000, involving approximately 300 inmates, allegedly started between competing Hispanic groups at Pelican Bay State Prison, resulting in a full lockdown of the facility (Spiegel, 2007). As in the Pelican Bay example, violence can be intra-racial and does not necessarily happen only between different racial groups.

The culture among those jailed and prisoners is not the only one that has consequences when it comes to the potential for violence to erupt in jails or prisons. The type of prison personnel is crucial as well. In earlier chapters we describe the styles of corrections officers, where some try to be mentors. While others can be particularly oppressive and abusive towards prisoners and viewed as tormentors, with inmates sometimes feeling that the only way to fight back is to resort to violence.

If you consider, again, that corrections personnel do not carry weapons within the cell units, it is a wonder that there is not more violence perpetrated against them by detainees or prisoners. And vice versa, that there are not more incidences of excessive use of force by prison staff using fists. After all, detainees and prisoners in facilities outnumber the corrections officers. If we take into consideration that with the exception of more recent years, the rise in the prison population in the past several decades, the demand for corrections officers has not been successfully satisfied to meet the safety requirement of most jails and prisons. As the Bureau of Prisons reports, jail corrections officers to inmate ratio is only a bit better than that of state facilities, at 4 to 1 (Bureau of Prisons, 2018).

Prison officials can and do put some prisoners in protective custody if they have already been victimized or reportedly are vulnerable to victimization. But the process in most cases is not automatic. Little has changed in recent decades on who might be put in protective custody. On the list of criteria, homosexual inmates, as well as inmates whose lives are in danger for other reasons (e.g., quitting a gang; informants) will be housed outside of general population. To a large extent, being in protective custody is similar to being in solitary confinement, with many in protective custody being held in single person cells. Essentially it may feel like additional punishment of solitary confinement for non-disciplinary purposes. Further damage to the psyche happens when prisoners become paranoid or develop anxiety disorders from real or imagined fear of victimization, while in or out of protective custody (Wood and Dennard, 2017).

RESPONSES TO VIOLENCE IN PRISON: PRISONERS' PERSPECTIVES

Darwinism dictates that one must attack and eat, before one falls prey to being eaten themselves. In other words, the best defense in avoid being a victim to violence in prison is a strong offense. For incarcerated men in particular, the sooner they can at least give the illusion of dominance, the less likely they will be victimized. For the fortunate few, their "street cred" or reputations from the streets precedes them and they can exert dominance in prison the minute that they arrive. Examples would be a gang leader or the head of an organized crime family, whose reputation for toughness and ruthlessness precedes their criminal conviction.

Even if a prisoner is not housed in a facility with a reputation for violence, by the very nature of incarceration, they may feel like they might be victimized. The perception of victimization drives many detainees and prisoners to connect with others that they believe will protect them. This includes formal and informal cliques, generally, as we have noted, divided down racial lines. The prisoner then may be subject to paying for "protective services" provided by other prisoners, with commissary items, illegal contraband including drugs, and/or sexual favors.

VIOLENCE IN WOMEN'S PRISONS

As we pointed out in Chapter 8, the topic of women in prison is still largely under-researched. The most obvious reason for this is that there are far fewer women in prison. The reality is that until recently, women have been ignored in a number of areas of research outside of criminal justice, including organizational theory. Even less is understood about women and violence in jails and prisons. The following data and information reported is what we do know at this juncture.

Most of what we see of violence in women's prisons involves interpersonal violence or intimate partner violence (IPV). As we saw in greater depth in Chapter 8, women form pseudo-families in prison. And similarly, to what we see in the outside world, domestic violence can take place between cellmates, friends, and romantic partners. This is somewhat different than what we see in men's prisons, where most of the violence is centered around retribution or disputes between rival racial groups, including gangs. Rates of violence in men's prisons is nearly ten times that of women's prisons (Harer and Langan, 2001). However, the risk factors for violent behavior in prison are the same for males and females, including low educational attainment and poverty (Harer and Langan, 2001).

Though women in general typically are not perceived to be as violent as men, largely due to socialization, some women will and do become violent in prison. Again, like men, in some cases this is due to mental health issues. However, with prison reflecting what we see on the streets, particularly in gangs, women are becoming more readily willing to resort to violence to settle disputes (Hansen, 2005).

As we noted in Chapter 8 on women in prison, if you ask a corrections officer whether they would prefer to supervise male or female inmates, most will report they would rather work in a men's jail or prison. Though women are less likely to have violent confrontations, they can be more difficult to break up once they get started. Women in and out of incarceration tend to hold on to grudges longer than males and are less likely to forgive (Chesler, 2009). It may be these attributes that are the very reason why it is more difficult to tackle the underlying causes for women's violence in prison.

SUMMARY

There are a number of reasons why violence occurs behind jail and prison walls. The most likely causes are due to overcrowding and the deprivations experienced in jail or prison. This coupled with contentious relationships between prisoners and sometimes between prisoners and corrections officers, violence is difficult to prevent. That is why for some prisoner populations, including gang members, the only alternative is to house them in maximum security facilities, even if the official reason (e.g., charges that stick, sentencing) for being incarcerated in the first place are for relatively minor offenses.

Violence in prison comes in a number of forms. These include simple assaults, aggravated assaults, sexual assaults, and in the extreme, homicides. Depending on the severity of the violence, prisoners can be written up and disciplinary action take, including being sent to solitary confinement or be formally charged and prosecuted, adding to their current sentence if found guilty. Parole or release can be delayed.

Detainees in jails and prisoners, except those who have regular jobs behinds bars or are required to attend in-house programs, have endlessly boring days. This coupled with limited liberties can result in producing inventive and deadly weapons. The most commonly used weapons are fists, but a number of types of makeshift weapons can be found during cell inspections. Some of the materials used to make these weapons are ordinary objects, including clothing, locks, toothbrushes and hair brushes, and soap. Commissary items can purposely made to go stale or melted, then filed down, as in the examples given of candy. Weapons can also be made out of materials found in metal or woodshops, both located in prisons that offer vocational training requiring the use of sharp tools.

The consequences, beyond physical injury, of violence in prisons can be felt both by prisoners and prison staff. The most common effect is PTSD, a condition felt by most if not all victims of violence, whether it happens in or out of prison. Victims of violence, including in prison, may resort to self-medication, or being violent themselves as a means of protection. Or they can resort to self-mutilation or other forms of self-harm.

One solution for detainees and prisoners, in an attempt to avoid victimization, is to join a prison gang, generally organized around geographically or racially divided lines, such as, according to the U.S. Department of Justice, the Texas

Syndicate, the Mexican Mafia, the Nuestra Familia, the Black Guerilla Family, and the Aryan Brotherhood, a white supremacy group. These mimic some of the same functions of organized crime found outside of prison. Members of prison gangs tend to be more violent and have more disciplinary action brought against them. Some of the violence for gang members and nonmembers functions to exert masculinity that has been perceived to have been neutered by the conditions of prison.

For the most part, women are less likely to join prison gangs and prefer to form pseudo families instead, as noted in Chapter 8. They can and will, however, become violent with their altercations, short of riots, and their disputes are more difficult to resolve. Women are less likely to fight over material stakes (e.g., drugs) and more likely to have conflicts over interpersonal relationships, as compared to men.

In the extreme, violence can result in prison riots. As we will see in our narrative of the New Mexico prison riot in 1980, in our *Stories from Behind Bars* section in this chapter and in the Bogota, Colombia prison protests in our *International Perspectives on Punishment and Corrections* section, some of these riots can be deadly. If we consider that a riot is defined as involving five or more prisoners, they may occur on a more frequent basis that we have knowledge of.

Though great efforts are made by the Bureau of Prisons and state prison systems to reduce violence in jails and prisons, these efforts are stymied by overcrowding. Conditions are not any better based on data from privately run, for-profit prisons, where there can equally be overcrowded, have understaffed conditions, and with less qualified personnel employed. Though violent crime has fallen in recent decades, the demographics of prisons have changed, with more potential for violence within jail and prison walls, however fortified against violence cells might be.

STORIES FROM BEHIND BARS

New Mexico Prison Riot, 1980.

Though there have been a number of noted riots in prisons since 1980s, there has never been another riot in contemporary history that was as deadly as the one that took place in February 1980 at the New Mexico Penitentiary, located 14 miles south of Santa Fe. For anyone who has ventured to the "Land of Enchantment," in particular, Santa Fe, this riot was certainly far removed from the magic of the city, well-known for artists' galleries, world class cuisine, and rich cultural history. By the end of the riot that took place over a day and a half, 33 prisoners had been killed, most in a gruesome manner. A dozen corrections officers were held captive by prisoners, some badly beaten, and in some cases, sodomized.

New Mexico State Penitentiary, Santa Fe County. (*Source*: Valley Daily Post, n.d., https://valleydailypost
.com/blog/the-forgotten-vet-of-the-new-mexico-prison-riot.)/)

As these things go, it is never one event that is the flashpoint of a prison riot. Generally, prison riots rise out of what is seen as the intolerable conditions experienced in prison. Of course these perceptions are subjective, with not all prisons being equal. As we have noted in other chapters, prisoners have sued departments of corrections for things as trivial as not receiving their preferred crunchy peanut butter or for the serving of broken cookies at meals. However, what may seem trivial to persons living their lives outside of prison, with no jail or prison experiences, it is difficult to understand just how meaningful some of these matters are to prisoners living behind bars 24 hours a day, seven days a week, some for the duration of what is left of their lifetime.

As then Governor Bruce King describes it in *Cowboy in the Roundhouse* (1998), he was awakened in the wee hours of February 2 by a call to his emergency phone line from Martin Vigil of the New Mexico State Police: "Governor, we've lost contact with the penitentiary. . . . It's possible we have a serious problem." What the governor didn't know at that moment is that guards had been taken hostage by prisoners, who had gained control of the prison. The state attorney general estimated that the prisoners were able to break into the control center within 3-5 minutes; controlled the prison within the first 22 minutes at the start of the riot.

Prisoners who were not involved in the capture of corrections officers and the destruction of prison property huddled together in frightened masses, self-segregating by race, proximity, and their alliances. Anything that could be used as a weapon was collected, including knives taken from the kitchen, plumbing pipes, and furniture parts. As to be expected, as chaos descended on the prison, food was stolen, as well as drugs from the pharmacy.

So, what were the factors that led to such a violent uprising within the walls of the prison? There are a number of theories as to what contributed to the breaking point. One of the biggest contributing factors, as stated by then U.S. Senator Bingaman, the prison had long been neglected, wasting away with understaffing, overcrowding, and growing rage among prisoners at the horrible living conditions. On top of these charges, there were allegations of corruption, with what little staff available being underpaid and undertrained at the time.

However, probably more of a contributor to the riot at the Penitentiary of New Mexico was the anger many prisoners had towards "jail house snitches"—prisoners who cooperate with the authorities in order to either get preferential treatment or in some cases, a reduced sentence. As the riot progressed, a "death squad" of a dozen inmates was formed with the intent of storming Cell Block 3, where prisoners who required protective custody were held, many of whom had become informants. One by one, these prisoners were dispatched, by burning them to death or in one case, beheading them.

As conditions deteriorated and police, the National Guard, and elite units of local law enforcement outfitted in riot gear gathered outside the prison in response, inmate demands were made:

- Federal prison officials were to be brought to the prison to ensure that there would be no retaliation directed at any inmate after the revolt ended.
- Prisoners were to be segregated so that first-timers with shorter sentences would not be housed with violent inmates with life sentences.
- An end to overcrowding of prisoners and harassment by corrections officers.
- Better food, better educational and recreational facilities.
- A new disciplinary committee formed.

As negotiations broke down between authorities and prisoners, some of the inmates were able to escape to the outside and report how conditions were unfolding in the prison. By mid-day on February 3d, some 800 prisoners, not all who had partaken in the riot, had surrendered to authorities. As Haywood reports it (2020), the prison was eventually secured, but the prison was in shambles, with some portions of the facility a smoky mess where fires had been set. New Mexico legislators were required to appropriate over $100 million to the cleanup efforts.

The negative long-term effects on prisoners, corrections officers, and their families is immeasurable. If there is any positive outcome to this story, New Mexico was forced to build more prisons to ease overcrowding, as directed by the Federal Bureau of Prisons. The main facility was eventually closed, and similarly to what happened to Alcatraz and other closed prisons, has become a tourist attraction and on occasion, a location for movies and television shows[5].

The following is an abbreviated timeline of how the events unfolded.[6]

FRIDAY, FEB. 1, 1980

8:30 pm:	Inmates begin drinking home brew in Dormitory E-2.
10: 30 pm:	Inmates are drunk, loud, and angry and begin talking about taking over the prison.

SATURDAY, FEB. 2, 1980

1:09 am:	Corrections officers begin to close the South Wing.
1:40 am:	Inmates jump corrections officers in Dormitory E-2. The guards are stripped and beaten.
2:00 am:	A group of 75-100 inmates reaches the penitentiary's control center and begin hitting the glass as two corrections officers flee.
2:01 am:	An officer tells the control tower to call state police.
2:15 am:	City and state police begin arriving.
2:30 am:	Maximum security prisoners in Cell Block 3 are set free and form an informal death squad with other violent inmates from E-2 who had sparked the riot.
2:35 am:	Gov. Bruce King is alerted.
2:40 am:	Gov. King alerts the National Guard.
4:00 am:	The so-called death squad begins cutting through a jammed door of Cell Block 4 where inmates in protective custody are held.
4:00 am-7:00 am:	Some of the most brutal murders and mutilations take place by the death squad.
6:40 am:	A prisoner demands to speak with the media and offers to set up a negations table.
7:00 am:	84 prisoners escape through a window and surrender.
7:02 am:	A badly beaten corrections officer hostage is released.
7:30 am:	First 50 New Mexico National Guard troops arrive.

---

[5] Some of the movies filmed at the New Mexico Penitentiary include *Doing Time* (1980), *All the Pretty Horses* (2000), *The Longest Yard* (2005), *The Astronaut Farmer* (2006), and *The Book of Eli* (2010). The prison is located at 4311 NM-14, Santa Fe, New Mexico, which is about 40 miles from the home of this author.

[6] Haywood (2020), complete timeline available at https://www.santafenewmexican.com/news/local_news/devastating-penitentiary-riot-of-1980-changed-new-mexico-and-its-prisons/article_be64a016-31ae-11ea-a754-fb85e49fca77.html)

8:30 am:	Twenty additional inmates escape the prison and surrender.
9:15 am:	Gov. King arrives at the penitentiary.
Noon:	An inmate negotiator demands to see media members and threatens to decapitate prisoners if the demand is not met.
2:48 pm:	Inmates meet with prison officials.
3:20 pm:	Gov. King is notified that corrections officers who were being held hostage are still alive.
5:10 pm:	An inmate threatens to kill corrections officers.
6:50 pm:	The first body of a prisoner is brought out of the prison by inmates.
7:12 pm:	An inmate negotiator meets with prison officials and radio journalist.
11:25 pm:	A beaten corrections officer is released, tied to a chair.

SUNDAY, FEB. 3, 1980

2:30 am:	New Mexico Corrections Secretary Adolph Saenz arrives.
8:00 am:	A headcount reveals about 800 inmates are outside the prison.
10:00 am:	Inmate negotiators meet with a TV drew and prison officials.
10:55 am:	A hostage escapes with the help of inmates.
12:34 pm:	The beheaded body of a mentally ill inmate is brought out.
1:26 pm:	The final two hostages are released.
1:30 pm:	State police and Santa Fe police enter and secure the facility.

SOURCE

Haywood, P, (2020), *Santa Fe New Mexican*, special section. Available at https://www.santafenewmexican.com/news/local_news/devastating-penitentiary-riot-of-1980-changed-new-mexico-and-its-prisons/article_be64a016-31ae-11ea-a754-fb85e49fca77.html)

INTERNATIONAL PERSPECTIVES ON PUNISHMENT AND CORRECTIONS: FRANCE

When most people think of France, they think about the romantic City of Lights, Paris, with its world class cuisine and dozens of museums devoted to the visual arts, including the Louvre. However, Paris has also been the setting of several violent periods in history, including the French Revolution, as well German occupation during World War II, from 1940 to liberation in 1944. More recently violence has broken out intermittently, due to union strikes, protests, and the November 15, 2015, coordinated terrorist attacks in several locations in the city. Paris is also the location of one of the most brutal prisons in the world, La Santé Prison, sometimes referred to as Maison d'arrêt de la Santé or Prison de la Santé (La Santé Prison, in English, or more literally, Prison on Santé Street).

Next to the Bastille, La Santé Prison is perhaps the second best known prison in France (Hussey, 2014). Ironically, the word *santé* means "health" in French, as the street is also home to a hospital, but prisoners have historically been far from enjoying healthy lives (*Geographics*, 2020).

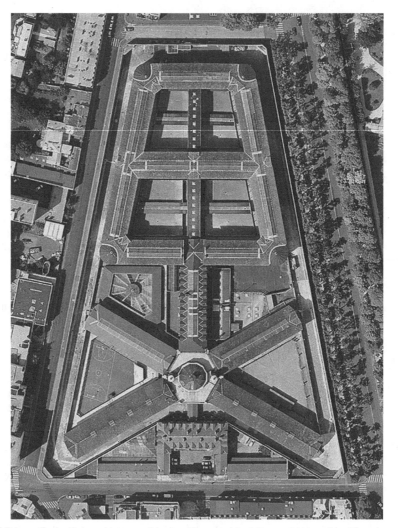

La Santé Prison, Paris. (*Sources*: Museum of Justice, Crime, and Punishment, 2014, retrieved from https://criminocorpus.org/en/exhibitions/jails/la-maison-darret-de-la-sante-une-prison-dans-paris/apres-le-choc-de-la-guerre-le-temps-de-la-reforme-et-de-la-renov/; Google Maps, 2021.)

Built in 1867 and in almost continued use for the last 153 years, the prison is located near the densely populated Montparnasse district of Paris. It coexists with some of the most quintessential of Parisian places, including street markets, outdoor cafés, and bookstores (Hussey, 2014). Reportedly the delighted laughter of school children enjoying recess on the playground nearby intermingled with the riotous screams of prisoners at La Santé Prison (*Geographics*, 2020; Hussey, 2014). This is the same part of the city where some of the titans of the surrealist and modernism movements in art emerged (Duchamp, Dalĺ, Braque, Matisse, Picasso, among others) and is seemingly an odd location for what is argued to be one of the most violent prisons in the world, much less a prison at all.

As to be expected in a city known for its beautiful buildings and structures, beyond function, the esthetics of the prison were taken into consideration during its construction. Built at a time when panopticon prison style favored in Britain[7] was in vogue, the prison was designed by famous church architect Joseph August Émile Vaudremer (*Geographics*, 2020). After construction, it was considered to be the best and most beautiful prison in Europe at the time, surpassing Bentham's design in Britain (*Geographics*, 2020). La Santé Prison, incongruously to its supposed beauty, has been witness to a number of riots, public executions by guillotine, and a number of suicides.

Housing prisoners both pretrial and conviction, the prison has been largely over-crowded up through modern day. During WWII under German occupation, the prison housed both criminals and resistance fighters. Resistance fighters were not treated as prisoners of war by the Germans, with French partisans subjected to particularly harsh conditions by the Gestapo, including 28 freedom fighters put to death by firing squad or guillotine (*Geographics*, 2020). Conditions, including overcrowding, were so bad in the prison during German occupation, that just prior to the liberation of France, resistance fighters incarcerated there attempted an escape, which was thwarted by French militia who were collaborating with the Nazis (*Geographics*, 2020).

Along with a violent history, the prison has been the home of a number of famous inmates. One of these included the gangster, ruthless killer, and master of disguises Jacques Mesrine. Mesrine frustrated both police and prison staff when he escaped from La Santé Prison, becoming a romantic folk hero to Parisians (Hussey, 2014).

La Santé Prison Modernization. (*Source*: Bertrand Guay, Getty Images, retrieved from https://www.shutterstock.com/editorial/image-editorial/french-police-officers-stand-front-paris'-mythic-10202571g.)

---

[7]Panopticon prison design based on Jeremy Bentham's social philosophy of punishment, is discussed in more detail in Chapter 3.

The conditions of the prison went largely ignored until the beginning of the 21st century. In 2000, Véronique Vasseur, the chief physician at La Santé Prison, published a scathing book, *Médecin-chef á la Prison de La Santé*, revealing just how deplorable conditions were for both inmates and staff. Among her charges and observations were the following (Hussey, 2014; Vasseur, 2012; Dorozynski, 2000):

- Descriptions of filthy cells infested with rats and cockroaches;
- Mattresses teeming with lice and other insects;
- Overcrowded conditions;
- Suicidal inmates left in chains;
- Skin conditions that had been virtually eradicated in the 19th century found on prisoners along with wounds that are ordinarily inflicted in wartime;
- Spoiled food with gastroenteritis common;
- Rape was frequent;
- Corrections officers beating up prisoners, with seasoned inmates preying on weaker ones;
- Corrections staff were involved in drug trafficking; and
- Suicides and attempted suicides, with ingestion of disinfectant the most commonly used method.

Keeping in mind that the prison served both to house suspects pretrial and those who had been convicted, it is no wonder that, as Dorozynski reported, in 1999 alone,

> *118 prisoners committed suicide, more than 1,000 attempted it, and there were 1,362 mutilations, including swallowing metallic objects—knives, forks, and even razor blades (usually tapped or wrapped in cloth. . . . There were 953 hunger strikes lasting at least seven days and 278 attacks by inmates on guards; mistreatment and beating of prisoners by guards also took place.* (2000, retrieved from https://www.ncbi.nlm.nih.gov/pmc/articles/PMC1127522/)

After Vasseur's book was published, the French public were horrified and outraged, resulting in more infamous and affluent white collar offenders, who had been housed in La Santé Prison, signing a petition for its closure or major overhaul and demanding that a commission be formed in order to investigate the living conditions of prisoners, as well as the working conditions of prison staff (Dorozynski, 2000).

The prison was closed in 2014 for a four-year modernization program, during which the public was invited to visit the prison, similar to tourism at other famous prison around in the world (Hussey, 2014). When the prison was reopened in 2019, it did so with a reduced capacity for 800 prisoners (Miller, n.d.). For obvious reasons, the prison no longer offers tours to the public.

SOURCES

Dorozynski, A. (2000) Doctor's book shames French prisons. *British Medical Journal*. Feb., Vol. 320, No. 7233:465.

Geographics (2020) *La Santé Prison: Serving Time in the Heart of Paris*. Video. Jan. 6. Retrieved from https://www.youtube.com/watch?v=nE5G97q7-Q0.

Hussey, A. (2014) La Santé prison: Visitors welcome. *The Guardian*. Dec. 7. Retrieved from https://www.theguardian.com/world/2014/dec/07/la-sante-prison-paris-visitors-welcome.

Miller, F. (n.d.) La Santé Prison. *Frank Falla Archive*. Retrieved from https://www.frankfalla archive.org/prisons/la-sante-prison/.

Vasseur, V. (2012) *Médecin-chef á la Prison de La Santé*. French ed. Paris, France: Cherche Midi.

GLOSSARY

Importation Theory A theory that proposes that antisocial behavior, including violence, is brought into prison by inmates from their lives prior to incarceration.

Intimate partner violence (IPV) Label used for any physical violence, stalking, or psychological harm by a current or former partner or spouse. (Center for Disease Control, available at https://www.cdc.gov/violenceprevention/intimatepartnerviolence/index.html)

Knuckleduster A makeshift weapon that can be used with a fist in hand-to-hand combat. An example would be brass knuckles, which would be contraband in prison.

Mace A medieval club-like weapon that can be made in prison, generally consisting of a ball covered with spikes (e.g., nails) and sometimes attached to a chain or other materials in order to make the mace easy to swing at victims.

Prison Rape Elimination Act (PREA) 2003 passed legislation in Congress that requires that the problem of rape in prison be addressed, including ways by which to protect prisoners from both fellow prisoners and prison staff.

Prisonization Theory A theory that proposes that antisocial behavior, including violence, is a result of the conditions of prison.

Protective custody A segregated portion of a jail or prison that is reserved for detainees or prisoners who have to be protected from other inmates for a number of reasons, including cases where they have witnessed crimes and turned evidence against other prisoners, are victims of violence, or due to their sexual orientation.

Riots Defined by the Bureau of Prisons as any disturbance in jail or prison that involves five or more detainees or inmates.

Sap Makeshift weapon where a hard object like a bar of soap or lock is placed in a sock and used against a fellow detainee or prisoner.

Shank   Prison-made sharp object, including knives, made from everyday materials available to prisoners. Pseudonym for *shiv.* .

Shiv   See *shank.*

REFERENCES AND SUGGESTED READINGS

Barak-Glantz, I. L. (1983) The anatomy of another prison riot. *The Prison Journal.* Spring/Summer, Vol. 63, No. 1:3-23

Beck, A., M. Berzofsky, R. Caspar, and C. Krebs (2013) Sexual victimization in prisons and jails reported by inmates 2011-2012 [NCJ241399]. Bureau of Justice Statistics (BJS). Washington, D.C.: U.S. Department of Justice.

Bieneck, S. and B. Krahé (2011) Blaming the victim and exonerating the perpetrator in cases of rape and robbery: Is there a double standard? *Journal of Interpersonal Violence.* Vol. 26:1785-1797.

Brown, J. A. and V. Jenness (2020) LGBT people in prison: Management strategies, human rights violations, and political mobilization. *Criminology and Criminal Justice.* June 30. Retrieved from https://oxfordre.com/criminology/view/10.1093/acrefore/9780190264079.001.0001/acrefore-9780190264079-e-647.

Bureau of Prisons (2020) Prison safety: *Chronic Disciplinary Records.* Retrieved from https://www.bop.gov/about/statistics/statistics_prison_safety.jsp?month=Oct&year=2020

Byrne, J. M. and D. Hummer (2008) The nature and extent of prison violence. *The Culture of Prison Violence,* J. M. Byrne, D. Hummer, and F. S. Taxman, eds. Ch. 1. Boston: Pearson Education, Inc.

Caracava-Sànchez, F., N. Wolff, and B. Teasdale (2019) Exploring associations between interpersonal violence and prison size in Spanish prisons. *Crime and Delinquency.* Vol. 65, No. 4:2019-2043.

Carson, E. A. and M. P. Cowhig (2020) Mortality in state and federal prisons, 2001-2016 – Statistical tables. U.S. Department of Justice. Feb., NCJ 251920. Retrieved from https://www.bjs.gov/content/pub/pdf/msfp0116st.pdf.

Chesler, P. (2009) *Woman's Inhumanity to Woman.* Chicago: Lawrence Hill Books.

Cleveland.com (2020) Cuyahoga County Jail officer convicted in inmate beating will likely serve prison time in protective custody. Feb. 29. Retrieved from https://www.cleveland.com/metro/2020/02/cuyahoga-county-jail-officer-convicted-in-inmate-beating-will-likely-serve-prison-time-in-protective-custody.html.

Crawley, E. and P. Crawley (2008) Culture, performance, and disorder: The communicative quality of prison violence. *The Culture of Prison Violence.* J. M. Byrne, D. Hummer, and F. S. Taxman, eds. Ch. 6. Boston: Pearson Education, Inc.

Decker, S. H. and D. C. Pyrooz (2010) On the validity of gang homicide: A comparison of disparate sources. *Homicide Studies.* Vol. 14:359-376.

Drago, F., R. Galbiati, and P. Vertova (2011) Prison conditions and recidivism. *American Law and Economics Review.* Spring, Vol. 13, No. 1:103-130.

Edgar, K. (2008) Cultural roots in England's prisons: An exploration for inter-prisoner conflict. *The Culture of Prison Violence.* J. M. Byrne, D. Hummer, and F. S. Taxman, eds. Ch. 9. Boston: Pearson Education, Inc.

Evans, M. L., M. Lindauer, and M. E. Farrell (2020) A pandemic within a pandemic—Intimate partner violence during COVID-19. *New England Journal of Medicine.* Sept. 16. Retrieved from https://www.nejm.org/doi/full/10.1056/NEJMp2024046.

Ferdik, F. V. and H. P. Smith (2017) Correctional officer safety and wellness literature synthesis. National Institute of Justice (NIJ). July. Retrieved from https://www.ncjrs.gov/pdffil es1/nij/250484.pdf.

Folha de S. Paulo (2019) Rebellion leaves at least 57 dead in prison in the interior of Pará: Suspicion is that factional fighting motivated the rebellion; 16 prisoners died beheaded. July. 29. Translation. Retrieved from https://translate.google.com/translate ?hl=en&sl=pt&u=https://www1.folha.uol.com.br/cotidiano/2019/07/rebeliao-deixa -52-mortos-em-presidio-no-interior-do-para.shtml&prev=search&pto=aue.

Gibbs, J. J. (1981) Violence in prison: Its extent, nature and consequences. *Critical Issues in Corrections*, R. R. Roberg and V. J. Webb, eds. St. Paul, MN: West Publishing Co. pp. 110-149.

Gillespie, W. (2002) *Prisonization: Individual and Institutional Factors Affecting Inmate Conduct.* New York: LFB Scholarly Publishing.

Gordon, M. T. and S. Riger (2011) *The Female Fear.* New York City, New York: The Free Press.

Gravelin, C. R., M. Biernat, and C. E. Bucher (2019) Blaming the victim of acquaintance rape: Individual, situational, and sociocultural factors. Frontiers in Psychology. Jan. 21. Retrieved from https://www.frontiersin.org/articles/10.3389/fpsyg.2018.02422/full.

Grierson, J. and P. Duncan (2019) Private jails more violent than public ones, data analysis shows. The Guardian. May 13. Retrieved from https://www.theguardian.com/society/ 2019/13/private-jails-more-violent-than-public-prisons-england-wales-data-analysis.

Hansen, L. L. (2005) "Girl 'Crew' Members Doing Gender, Boy 'Crew' Members Doing Violence: An Ethnographic and Network Analysis of Maria Hinojosa's New York Gangs." 2005. *Western Criminology Review.* Vol. 6, No. 1:134-44. Retrieved from http://www .westerncriminology.org/documents/WCR/v06n1/article_pdfs/hansen.pdf

Harer, M. D. and N. P. Langan (2001) Gender differences in predictors of prison violence: Assessing the predictive validity of a risk classification system. *Crime and Delinquency.* Oct., Vol. 47, No. 4:513-536.

Human Rights Watch (2020) Colombia: New evidence that prisoners were intentionally shot. Nov. 24. Retrieved from https://www.hrw.org/news/2020/11/24/colombia-new-evide nce-prisoners-were-intentionally-shot.

Jensen, V., L. Sexton, and J. Sumner (2018) Sexual victimization against transgender women in prison: Consent and coercion in context. *Criminology.* Vol. 57:603-631.

Jones, A. (1986) Self-mutilation in prison: A comparison of mutilators and nonmutilators. *Criminal Justice and Behavior.* Vol. 13, Iss. 3:286-296.

Klein, M. W. and C. L. Maxson (2006) *Street gang Patterns and Policies.* New Work, NY: Oxford University Press, Inc.

Kubiak, S. P., J. Brenner, D. Bybee, R. Campbell, C. E. Cummings, K. M. Darcy, G. Fedock, and R. Goodman-Williams (2017) Sexual misconduct in prison: What factors affect whether incarcerated women will report abuses committed by prison staff. *Faculty Scholarship,* California Western School of Law. p. 224. Available at https://scholarlycommons.law .cwsl.edu/fs/224.

Lincoln, J. M., L-H Chen, J. S. Mair, P. J. Biermann, and S. P. Baker (2006) Inmate-made weapons in prison facilities: Assessing the injury risk. *Injury Prevention.* June, Vol. 12, No. 3:195-198.

Lovlie, A. and P. Guruli (2021) Public or private administration of justice: Privatization of prisons. *Nordisk Tidsskirft for Kriminalvidenskab.* No. 1 (2021). Retrieved from https:// pdfs.semanticscholar.org/a3e8/aa901c64c7af515040955e16e6f0e073be4e.pdf

Malatesta, P. (2015) Inmate who killed Jeffrey Dahmer reveals why he murdered the serial killer. *WGN9,* Chicago. Apr. 29. Retrieved from https://wgntv.com/news/inmate-who-kil led-jeffrey-dahmer-reveals-why-he-murdered-the-serial-killer/.

National PREA Resource Center. (n.d.) Prison Rape Elimination Act. Retrieved from https://www.prearesourcecenter.org/about/prison-rape-elimination-act-prea

New Mexico Corrections Department (n.d.) Penitentiary of New Mexico. Retrieved from https://cd.nm.gov/divisions/adult-prison/nmcd-prison-facilities/penitentiary-of-new-mexico/

Ratkalkar, M. and C. A. Atkin-Plunk (2020) Can I ask for help? The relationship among incarcerated males' sexual orientation, sexual abuse history, and perceptions of rape in prison. *Journal of Interpersonal Violence*. Vol. 35:4117-4140.

Scarpa, A., S. C. Haden, and J. Hurley (2006) Community violence victimization and symptoms of posttraumatic stress disorder: The moderating effects of coping and social support. *Journal of Interpersonal Violence*. Apr., Vol. 21:446-69.

60 Minutes (2020) *60 Minutes* investigates the death of Jeffrey Epstein. CBS News. Jan. 5. Retrieved from https://www.cbsnews.com/news/did-jeffrey-epstein-kill-himself-60-minutes-investigates-2020-01-05/

Spiegel, S. (2007) "Race riots": An easy case for segregation? *California Law Review*. Dec., Vol. 95, No. 6:2261-2293.

Smith, E. L. (2019) Sexual victimization reported by youth in juvenile facilities, 2018. Bureau of Justice Statistics. Dec. 11. Retrieved from https://www.bjs.gov/index.cfm?ty=pbdetail&iid=6746#:~:text=Highlights%3A,that%20involved%20force%20or%20coercion.

Statista.com (2019) Reported aggravated assault rate in the United States from 1990 to 2019. Retrieved from https://www.statista.com/statistics/191231/reported-aggravated-assault-rate-in-the-us-since-1990/.

Stephan, J. and J. Karsberg (2003) *The Census of State and Federal Correctional Facilities*. Washington, D.C.: U.S. Department of Justice.

Sykes, G. M. (1958) *The Society of the Captives: A Study of a Maximum Security Prison*. Princeton, N.J.: Princeton University Press.

Thomas, C. W., D. M. Petersen, and R. M. Zingraff (1978) Structural and social psychological correlates of prisonization. *Criminology*. Nov., Vol. 16, No. 3:368-380.

United States Department of Justice. (2011) Inmate discipline program. Federal Bureau of Prisons. Retrieved from https://www.bop.gov/policy/progstat/5270_009.pdf

Widra, E. (2020) Deaths in state prisons are on the rise, new data shows. What can be done? Prison Policy Initiative. Feb 13. Retrieved from https://www.prisonpolicy.org/blog/2020/02/13/prisondeaths/.

Wood, J. and S. Dennard (2017) Gang membership: Links to violence exposure, PTSD, anxiety, and forced control of behavior in prison. *Psychiatry*. Vol. 80:30-41.

Chapter ELEVEN

Physical and Mental Health Issues in Corrections

As a provider of last resort, county jails (and prisons) have become the de facto mental health providers for our most critical needs patients. County jails are not equipped nor structured to have successful interventions with such a demanding population.

— Sheriff (Anonymous), Ohio[1]

Chapter Objectives

- Review types of mental and physical disorders that convicts experience before, during, and after incarceration.
- Inform readers of the legal rights of prisoners regarding their health care.
- Examine the different strategies and options available to treat criminals with mental health issues[2].
- Provide analysis of the roles of health care providers in and out of jails and prisons, including ethical issues.

Key Terms

Activities of daily
 living (ADLs)
Alcohol Use Disorder (AUD)
Americans with Disabilities
 Act (ADA, 1990)

Community-based corrections
Compassion-Based Therapy (CBT)
Compassionate release
Diagnostic and Statistical Manual of Mental
 Disorders (DSM-5)

---

[1] Retrieved from https://www.psychsearch.net/select-quotes-on-the-incarceration-of-the-mentally-ill/
[2] It has become more socially acceptable to say "mental health issues" instead of "mental illness."

End of life care (EOL)   Infirmary
Goldfish bowl effect   Mental health courts
Health care   Occupational therapy
Health Insurance Portability   Palliative care
    and Accountability Act   Physical therapy
    (HIPAA, 1996)   Risk-Need-Responsivity Principle (RNR)
Hoptowit v. Ray (1982)   Substance use disorders (SUDs)
Hospice care   Talk therapy

INTRODUCTION

Before we launch into discussions of the medical and mental health issues in jails and prisons, corrections in general, and community-based solutions, we need to distinguish the differences between *health care,* health-care, and healthcare. By dictionary and medical professions' definitions (Merriam-Webster Dictionary, 2021; *Docnotes*, 2020), health care refers to the efforts to maintain or restore either physical and/or mental health by trained/licensed professionals. Health-care refers to the professionals themselves, and healthcare refers to the administrative system that is business-focused. For many, even in the medical professions, it is simply a matter of semantics. Wherever possible, we will use the term "health care" to refer to the efforts taken in jails and prisons to address the physical and mental health issues experienced during detainment, incarceration, or any one of the *community-based corrections* (sentencing provisions that take place in the community, outside of jail or prison) options discussed in our next chapter.

Health care for prisoners hasn't just recently become a concern to the public, activists, or the courts. As early as 1792, in the infancy of the American nation, Delaware's state constitution contained a provision that required that the construction of jails and prisons must take into consideration the health of prisoners (Sonntag, 2017). By the time the Civil War ended in 1865, other states, including those newly admitted to the union, followed suit, turning health and general treatment of prisoners into constitutional concerns (Sonntag, 2017).

There is perhaps no bigger problem in jails and prisons today than the handling of the physical and mental health needs of prisoners, including costs to state and federal facilities, even if they are privately operated. Secondary to the challenges is the public perception that once someone is incarcerated that it is unfair they receive free health care, while here in the United States, health care costs for the average person have skyrocketed and make up a sizeable portion of household budgets. In 2020 terms, the average cost to individuals for health insurance alone was $456 a month per person; for family households, $1,152 a month (Porretta, 2020). That does not even include copayments for office visits, emergency room trips, or hospitalization costs not covered by insurance, not to mention the cost of prescription drugs, some of which are not fully covered by insurance.

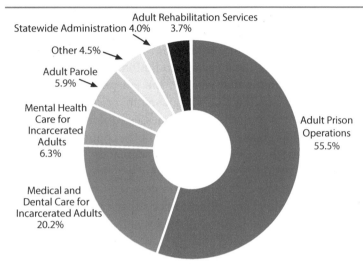

Over 80% of Spending on State Corrections Goes to Prison Operations or to Medical, Dental, and Mental Health Care

Proposed 2019-20 Spending on State Corrections = $12.7 Billion

Statewide Administration 4.0%
Adult Rehabilitation Services 3.7%
Other 4.5%
Adult Parole 5.9%
Mental Health Care for Incarcerated Adults 6.3%
Medical and Dental Care for Incarcerated Adults 20.2%
Adult Prison Operations 55.5%

Note: Reflects state operations and local assistance spending through the Board of State of Community Corrections (BSCC) and the California Department of Corrections and Rehabilitation. "Other" reflects the BSCC as well as adult contract facilities, state-level youth correctional operations and services, and certain California Department of Justice legal services. Figures do not sum to 100 due to rounding.
Source: Budget Center analysis of Department of Finance data

FIGURE 11.1 | **Health Care Costs, California Prison System.**
(*Source*: California Budget and Policy Center, 2019, retrieved from https://calbudgetcenter.org/resources/most-state-corrections-spending-supports-prison-operations-or-health-related-services-including-mental-health-care/)

Figure 11.1 provides a snapshot of typical costs of medical and mental health care in prisons, with California prison system as an example.

What the general public does not understand is that medical and psychiatric care is not 100 percent free to prisoners. According to Eisen (Brennan Center for Justice, 2015), prisoners are also required to pay copayments for treatment in a prison *infirmary*, ranging to a few dollars to as much as $100, depending on the services. That is still a considerable savings from the cost of care on the outside for convicts coming from lower-income households, who may not otherwise have had access to affordable health care in the first place prior to incarceration.

Training is another issue associated with health care in corrections, though that has somewhat improved, starting with more facilities requiring their corrections officer applicants to have completed some college and academy training. There is little in high school curricula to prepare future corrections officers and staff for the range and depth of physical and mental health issues from which convicted criminals suffer. Even college courses that address these issues, including the course you are currently taking in corrections, cannot fully prepare people in criminal justice professions for the realities. Certainly, the daily grind of working with detainees and inmates, parolees, and probationers with health issues can contribute to the high burnout rates in the corrections professions that we have discussed in this book.

Because sentencing laws began placing the convicted in prison for longer and longer sentences, as in the case of Three Strikes Laws (e.g., Washington and California), much of the prison population is aging. This translates into a disproportionate number of inmates suffering from a range of age-related health problems, psychiatric illnesses, and addictions (Goldstein, 2014). An additional challenge to corrections is that some of the jail population is transient, with detainees being released to the public or sent to prison after conviction with any number of untreated or undisclosed illnesses (Goldstein, 2014). This in turn creates a public health problem, if not a crisis, in the communities where the convicted are released to once they have served their sentences.

The life expectancy of many who have served time in jail or prison can be cut short. Some of this has to do with the fact that criminals in general are more likely to be risk-takers, with lifestyles that can shorten life expectancy. But a portion of the reduction in life expectancy can be explained by the physical and mental health of the incarcerated after they are detained. For those who have served part or all of their time in solitary confinement, the statistics are even more grim.

We are intentionally restricting this chapter to general health and psychological issues that affect all those who are incarcerated or are at the mercy of the correctional system. We have already covered in a bit more depth those issues that are unique to women. We also cover transgender population who are incarcerated in Chapter 8 in our discussions of the prisoners' perspective. However, we cannot emphasize enough that the needs of men and women, and every gender in between, are not only unique to the individual, but can be unique to their gender or sex. The criminal justice system, including corrections, have historically ignored this, both in policy and practice. Even medical schools can ignore these differences, though they are much more informed than they were a few decades ago (Hansen, 2006).

DETAINEES' AND PRISONERS' RIGHTS TO HEALTH CARE AND ACCOMMODATIONS

Only in the past 50 years have the rights of detainees and prisoners and their access to health care while incarcerated been seriously addressed. One factor driving interest in improving the health of those in custody is economics, as the cost of health care skyrockets. By preventing illness and disease, the state or federal government saves money in the long run in the care for the incarcerated. However, the main motive for concern is for humanitarian reasons, at least from the standpoint of criminal justice reformers. As Zalman noted in 1972 (p. 185), "no longer are prisoners said to be slaves to the state and entitled only to the rights granted them by basic humanity and whims of their jailers. Instead, it is recognized today that the prisoner is confined for the protection of the state," and as they cannot care for themselves, it becomes the responsibility of the jail or prison to do so, including health care.

Access to adequate health care, whether in or out of prison, is a human rights issue, whether in the United States or elsewhere in the world. The Universal Declaration of Human Rights states that jails and prisons have to provide adequate health care, as the detained and imprisoned have no control over the conditions behind bars (Reyes, 2001). However, to put this in better perspective, according to a study conducted at the beginning of the COVID-19 pandemic in 2020 (Collins et al., 2020), the U.S. health care system is already in crisis, with 43.4 percent of adults ages 19 to 64 inadequately insured, and 12.4 uninsured all together. It is one thing to make declarations on the human rights of detainees and prisoners, but it is another to provide adequate care in the face of a national health insurance crisis.

Increasingly in and out of prison, largely due to the COVID-19 pandemic, computer applications are being used in the treatment of clients and patients and in providing counseling services. These include the use of video calls which can be accessed on smart phones, tablets, or other electronic devices (Garofalo, 2020), though this still puts poorer patients, including probationers and parolees requiring psychiatric treatment, at a disadvantage if they do not have access to computer applications. However, as Garofalo (2020) notes, there is a great advantage in the use of computer applications for those in need of individual or family therapy who cannot drive the long distances to institutions offering face-to-face counseling.

To withhold health care is neglect and in the case of the detained or prisoners, a violation of the 8th Amendment. In our *Stories from Behind Bars* section of this chapter, we introduce a key U.S. Supreme Court case that tested the limits of the cruel and unusual punishment clause of the 8th Amendment as they apply to prisoners. We do have to consider that some people who end up behind bars already are suffering from some mental or physical ailment and there is the real possibility that they will receive better care, as imperfect that it might be, while incarcerated, as compared to the alternative of having to fend for oneself under conditions of poverty on the outside.

HIPAA and the Incarcerated

The average person outside of prison has privacy rights when it comes to their medical records. The Health Insurance Portability and Accountability Act (1996) or HIPAA, protects patients from having their sensitive health information or medical records disclosed to anyone without their consent or knowledge (CDC, n.d.). The HIPAA Privacy Rule, as part of the same law, "contains standards for individuals' rights to understand and control how their health information is used." (CDC, n.d., retrieved from https://www.cdc.gov/phlp/publications/topic/hipaa .html). However, it is a tricky proposition to retain the same rights while incarcerated.

Because detainees and prisoners lose much of their privacy, including their medical records, there is much controversy surrounding HIPAA as it applies to the incarcerated.

There are limitations on the extent to which HIPAA applies to inmates. In the final privacy rule of the act, inmates are not required to be given a "Notice of Privacy Practices" typically provided to patients on the outside. Health care facilities who treat inmates can release inmates' medical or psychiatric records without their consent in the following cases (Morris, 2004):

- The health and safety of the individual or other inmates are at stake.
- The health and safety of officers or other staff are at stake.
- It is necessary to release the information to jail or prison administrators in order to maintain the safety, security, and general good order of the correctional facility.

Inmates do retain the right to review their own medical records and request amendments where there are errors. The privacy of medical records poses an ethical dilemma for both doctors and nurses, and mental health professionals working in jails and prisons. For example, the Code of Ethics for Nurses, Provision 1, requires that a nurse practices with compassion; Provision 3 requires them to protect the rights of the patient (American Nurses Association, 2015). This can be in conflict with correctional facilities where the primary concern is for the safety and security of the facility and its inhabitants, where medical and psychiatric records may aid in those goals, as in the example of a violent inmate.

Most, if not all of medical records are now stored electronically. This leaves them vulnerable to breaches and cybertheft. States and the federal government have an astounding amount of data on the people they have in custody, including medical records, that have the potential of being unintentionally or intentionally released to the public.

Americans with Disabilities Act (ADA): Compliance in Jails and Prisons

As part of the U.S. Department of Justice Civil Rights Division, the *Americans with Disabilities Act (ADA,* 1990) requires that public buildings, whether they are state or federal, provide reasonable accommodations to those who need them due to physical or mental impairment. This includes courthouses, jails, and prisons, as well as parole and probation departments. Title III Regulations of the ADA (Part 36, 2017) also require nondiscrimination on the basis of disabilities in businesses, which means that private, nonprofit or for-profit jails and prisoners have to comply as well.

The Program Review Division (PRD) of the Bureau of Prisons (BOP) is the responsible entity for assuring that the provisions in the ADA are followed in jails and prisons. The PRD conducts all reviews of BOP programs, including examining if facilities are following laws, rules, regulation, and policies. ADA §504 provides a design guide for the construction of accessible cells, as the U.S. Department of Justice acknowledges that a number of inmates in state, federal, and local correctional facilities, as well as in private jails and prisons, have limited mobility (Civil Rights Division, U.S. Department of Justice, 2020). Design features can be viewed in Figure 11.2.

Further considerations in order to accommodate detainees and prisoners with disabilities, while still providing security in facilities, are as follows (Civil Rights

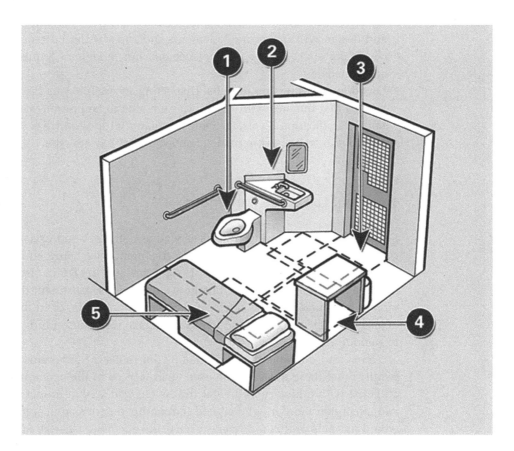

DRAWING NOTES:
1) Assessible toilet with grab bars.
2) Accessible sink with knee and toe space, facet accessibility with loose fist (e.g., for stroke patients), cleared floor for easy approach, lower mirror.
3) Doors with 32 inches of clearing space to accommodate wheelchairs.
4) Desk with knee and toe space.
5) Bed with clear floor space for a side approach to the bed.

FIGURE 11.2 | **Cell Design to Meet ADA Requirements for Inmates.**
(*Source*: Civil Rights Division, U.S. Department of Justice, 2020, retrieved from https://www.ada .gov/accessiblecells.htm)

Division, U.S. Department of Justice, 2020, retrieved from https://www.ada.gov/accessiblecells.htm):

- **Security.** Accessible cells do not compromise the security of prison personnel. In fact, having accessible cells increases security because they allow inmates with mobility issues to function independently, minimizing the need for assistance from corrections officers.
- **Basic Features.** Inmates with disabilities—including those who use wheelchairs—need to be able to enter their cells and move around inside them, using the cells' features without assistance. What makes this possible? Careful planning and design will incorporate elements such as a wider entrance door, adequate clear floor space, appropriate placement and models of fixtures and furniture, and grab bars.
- **Location or Dispersion of Cells.** Dispersing accessible cells throughout a facility insures that inmates with disabilities are able to be housed with inmates of the same classification levels. Generally, inmates with disabilities who are not ill do not need to be housed in medical areas unless they are receiving medical care or treatment.

The Right to Refuse Treatment

People outside of jails and prisons as well as detainees and prisoners, as a general rule, can refuse medical or psychiatric treatment after being informed of the consequences of refusing treatment. This right deviates in certain circumstances, such as when a mentally disturbed inmate wants to refuse treatment that subdues their violent tendencies for the safety of themselves or others, or in the administration of antipsychotic drugs pretrial in order to make the accused individual competent to stand trial.

Even forced medication is limited by the 1990s U.S. Supreme Court ruling that requires that these measures be used sparingly, as in the example of Charles Sell, a dentist with a history of mental illness charged with a number of fraud counts and attempted murder, who argued that on his doctor's advice, forced medication would not help and could have serious side effects or Charles Singleton, a death-row inmate, who was ordered to be medicated to make him sane enough for his execution (Ashraf, 2003).

PHYSICAL HEATH CARE IN JAIL AND PRISON

There are three ways that jails and prisons are bad for the health. One has to do with the living conditions that are conducive to developing chronic mental and physical ailments, including overcrowding. Overcrowding also leads to the faster spread of communicable diseases such as tuberculosis and, more recently, the COVID-19 virus. As Reyes notes (2001), catching a communicable disease is not part of the prison sentence. The second way has to do with the everyday reality of exposure to violence in many prisons as well as psychological bullying and intimidation from fellow prisoners and corrections officers (Reyes, 2001). Third, as in the general public, when instead of preventative measures, treatment of illness and disease is available only after the fact, it can become a public health crisis. It also adds additional economic burden on individuals once released and/or on state and federal government programs.

Hoptowit v. Ray (1982) is one of many cases that shed light on the fact that health care can potentially be callously ignored by prison staff (Douds et al., 2020). As part of a lawsuit brought against the Governor of the State of Washington and corrections officials, inmates contended, along with a number of general complaints about the Washington State Penitentiary, that the inadequate medical care they had received, including a blatant disregard for dental care, was in violation of the 8th Amendment (*Hoptowit v. Ray,* 1982). The district court found the following constitutionally deficiencies in the penitentiary, where the inmates won their case on appeal (*Hoptowit v. Ray*, 1982):

- Medical staffing was inadequate.
- Organization and administration of the medical care system was inadequate, with few, if any written procedures.
- Access to medical care was inadequate.
- Corrections officers were the gatekeepers to medical care, many of whom would fail to forward medical complaints to medical staff.
- Medication was prepared and dispensed by untrained, unlicensed personnel.
- Medical [and dental] facilities were ill-equipped and too small.
- There was little in the way of basic psychiatric and mental health care, staff and programs were insufficient.

Dental Care

The medical community and researchers are becoming increasingly aware of how oral health is closely associated with overall health. It is only in recent decades that dentists routinely checked for signs of oral cancer. Poor oral hygiene and health can contribute to any number of diseases and illnesses, including cardiovascular disease and pneumonia (Mayo Clinic Staff, 2019). For prisoners, regular dental care is one crucial component to successful reintegration into society after incarceration (Douds et al., 2020).

Even outside of prison, what dental insurance provides in the way of coverage is fairly limited in most cases, beyond routine preventative care and cleanings. For many detainees and prisoners, they may very well receive better dental care from behind bars, than what they could afford on the outside. Research indicates that poverty is associated with poor dental care and prisoners are more likely to suffer from decayed or missing teeth (Douds et al., 2020).

We should also consider that dental care is often cosmetic, beyond the health concerns. Dental disorders, including missing teeth, have a negative effect on self-esteem, particularly in adolescents and young adults, and can have long term effects on quality of life if not treated (Kaur et al., 2017). Cosmetic dentistry, unless necessary for health reasons (even then can be neglect), is generally not performed on prisoners. As is often the case, dental care is only done when there is a problem in jail or prison and not necessarily as preventative measures for the physical and mental well-being of the incarcerated individual.

We do know that neglect of dental care can have long-term effects. Access to health care after incarceration is challenging (Binswanger et al., 2011); access to dental care is doubly so (Douds et al., 2016). Neglect of dental care in prison is not completely due to intentional disregard for prisoners' well-being. Part of the problem lies in the shortage of dental health care professionals in jails and prisons (Douds et al., 2016; Ringgenberg, 2011; Robertson, 2011). However, neglect of oral hygiene and proper dental care, including routine screening and cleanings, can haunt ex-convicts long after their sentence is finished.

Physical Therapy

One primary goal of *physical therapy*, beyond the usual therapeutics for back injuries, is to help patients regain mobility. Outpatient (e.g., non-hospitalization) physical therapy may be necessary, but neglected, in the case of an individual being injured prior to, during, or after an arrest and incarceration. Treatment can be short term, as in the example of rehabilitation following orthopedic surgery, or can be long term for chronic conditions, as in the case of working with patients with rheumatoid arthritis.

Occupational Therapy

The name, *occupational therapy*, is a bit deceiving. One would think it would have something to do with teaching job skills. Occupational therapy, in actuality, is training individuals with any number of disabilities, to become more independent in their *activities of daily living* (ADLs). For example, if someone has suffered a stroke, occupational therapy can assist with relearning how to use eating utensils. As stated by the American Occupational Therapy Association (AOTA), providing occupational therapy to those who need it not only improves the life of individual but also helps prevent injury, illness, or further disabilities (AOTA, 2021).

The importance of occupational therapy programs in jails and prisons has more to do with the ability to reenter society than it has to do with managing day-to-day life behind bars. Programs for detainees and prisoners, including occupational therapy, demonstrate that many do help in reducing recidivism (Jaegers et al., 2020). By not providing these types of programs before reentry, without support, there will be an impact not only on the ex-convict, but on the community in general, including placing economic burdens on families and state, federal governments (Jaegers et al., 2020; Morenoff and Harding, 2014).

Whether prisoners are given physical or occupational therapy, it reduces the amount of work that corrections officers and staff have to spend helping inmates with disabilities take care of themselves, including showers, dressing, utilizing the library or visiting the prison commissary; some inmates with paralysis or after a stroke may even need help in feeding themselves (Morgan and Fellow, 2017). Any therapies or programs that increase the independence of disabled inmates are moves in the direction of freeing up correctional staff and preparing inmates for life outside of prison walls.

COMMON PHYSICAL HEALTH ISSUES IN JAIL AND PRISON

There are a number of illnesses that affect prisoners, often exacerbated by the stresses of incarceration. Compounded by questionable health care in jails and prisons, disease progression can be faster than on the outside. On the other hand, as we have already noted, for some they will receive better treatment on the inside than what they could afford on the outside. It is one thing to treat the common cold or a flu virus. It is another when an inmate/patient requires ongoing treatment for a chronic medical condition.[3]

Chronic Medical Conditions

There are a number of chronic diseases that can afflict people, whether they are in or out of prison. Some are preventable or at least manageable with lifestyle changes. Others are genetic disorders that require medication and/or treatment. The National Health Council reports (2013) that approximately 40 percent of Americans have suffered from one or more chronic health conditions. In comparison, the National Inmate Survey (NIS-3, 2011-2012) reveals that half of all state and federal prisoners and local jail inmates report suffering from a chronic condition at one time or another (Maruschak et al., 2016). And that is of the number who disclose their condition—there are untold others who do not.

Out of those with chronic conditions, 66 percent of prisoners and 40 percent of those who are jailed require prescription medication for their illnesses (Maruschak

---

[3] A chronic medical condition is an illness, disease, or debilitating condition that lasts three months or longer, and often is expected to be with the person for their lifetime. If left untreated, chronic conditions can be life-threatening.

et al., 2016). The most common chronic physical conditions found in the inmate population include arthritis (including the more debilitating rheumatoid arthritis), asthma, cancer, diabetes, heart disease, high blood pressure, cirrhosis of the liver, and stroke-related problems (Maruschak et al., 2016).

Neurological Disorders Associated with Aging

As we see a running theme of an aging prison population and the consequences of incarceration off and on in this chapter, we have to consider as well that a portion of older prisoners will develop neurological conditions including Alzheimer's, dementia, and other disorders that eventually erode cognitive processes. In other words, they may eventually have no recollection of why they are there, much less an understanding where they are, having lost considerable touch with reality as they lose their memory over time. They will increasingly lose ability to care for themselves even in the simplest of daily tasks, including eating, brushing their teeth, showering. Poor physical and mental health of prisoners puts them at higher risk of developing dementia (Maschi et al., 2012). Jails and prisons are generally poorly equipped to handle offenders with neurological disorders. The overall cost for caring for older adults in prison is three times that of younger inmates (Falter, 1999; 2006).

COMMUNICABLE ILLNESSES AND DISEASES IN JAIL AND PRISON

Beyond the common cold virus, upper respiratory illnesses, and seasonal flu, there are a great number of illnesses that inmates can pass on to one another while living close quarters, some of which are potentially deadly. Some are airborne, some can be caught by touching contaminated surfaces, and still others are sexually transmitted. There is also the possibility of vector-borne diseases[4] being present in prisons as well, though that is less likely to be present, at least in the United States.

Hepatitis

Hepatitis, translated, means the inflammation of the liver. The most common cause of hepatitis is a viral infection, but there are other causes as well, just like there are different types of hepatitis (World Health Organization, 2019, retrieved from https://www.who.int/news-room/q-a-detail/hepatitis):

---

[4] Vector-borne diseases are transmitted by parasites, bacteria, or viruses (WHO, 2020). Examples include malaria via mosquitos and Lyme disease via deer ticks.

- Hepatitis A (HAV) and E (HEV) are generally contracted when ingesting contaminated food or water, as when visiting a developing country. Hepatitis A virus is present in the feces of infected persons. Certain sexual acts can also transmit the viruses. There is an effective vaccine for HAV. There is a safe and effective vaccine for HEV, but it is not widely available.
- Hepatitis B (HBV), C (HCV), and D (HDV) result from contact with an infected parent, e.g., from mother to baby during birth (hepatitis B), receipt of contaminated blood or blood product, invasive medical procedures where contaminated equipment has been used. Hepatitis B, C, and D can also be transmitted by sexual contact, the more likely conduit in jails and prisons. There is an effective vaccine that protects against HBV and HDV. There is no vaccine for HCV.

The most commonly spread hepatitis in prison is HCV. This is accomplished through needle sharing and use of contaminated tattooing equipment, which is considered contraband (Krans, 2018). Left untreated, HCV can be deadly. As Krans (2018) cautions, the cure for HCV can cost up to $90,000 and is not always covered by insurance—for prisoners the cure is further out of reach and an estimated 97 percent of incarcerated patients with the disease are not getting the treatment they require. And as always, one big concern is bringing HCV or any disease into the community after release. The transmission of HCV from prisoners to people outside is illustrated in Figure 11.3.

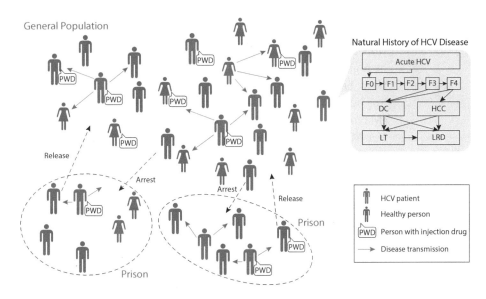

FIGURE 11.3 Social Network Transmission of HCV from Prison to People on the Outside.
(*Source*: Dalgic et al., 2019, Scientific Reports, Article number: 16849, retrieved from https://www.nature.com/articles/s41598-019-52564-0)

HIV/AIDS

Since the mid-1980s when HIV/AIDS or human immunodeficiency virus/acquired immunodeficiency syndrome was identified, seemingly being transmitted primarily in the gay community, there has been a concerted effort to find a cure. More recently, the first AIDS cases are now believed to have emerged as early as 1981, with unusual cases of pneumonia found in the homosexual community (Centers for Disease Control, 2001). Of concern for the prison population is the fact that "the prevalence of Human Immunodeficiency Virus (HIV) infection is three times higher in jails and prisons than in the general population. . . ." (Krieger et al., 2019, p. 602).

So far, the best medical intervention in treating HIV is with antiviral medications (sometimes described as a "cocktail") before it develops into the more serious (and deadly) AIDS virus. Before researchers understood the means of transmission and characteristics of the virus, contracting HIV pretty much spelled a death sentence. Today, individuals with HIV are living longer lives with a far greater period of time between contracting HIV and having it develop into AIDS, due to treatments currently available. This is similar to how in the beginning of the COVID-19 pandemic, an alarming number of people who contracted the virus ended up on ventilators in the hospital, many of whom tragically died, before treatments were developed that were more effective in combating the virus, along with vaccination.

MRSA

Methicillin-resistant Staphylococcus aureus or MRSA is a particularly nasty infection in the staph bacterial family that is resistant to antibiotic treatment. Those at highest risk live in nursing homes or work in medical facilities, with the bacteria being transmitted by contamination during invasive surgeries, IV tubing application, touching people with unclean hands, or touching unclean surfaces (Mayo Clinic Staff, 2020). Like hepatitis, there are a few variants of the bacteria, HA-MRSA and CA-MRSA. The risks for contracting either one are different (Mayo Clinic Staff, 2020, retrieved from https://www.mayoclinic.org/diseases-conditions/mrsa/symptoms-causes/syc-20375336):

Risk factors for HA-MRSA
- **Being hospitalized**. MRSA remains a concern in hospitals where it can attack the vulnerable—older adults and people with weakened immune systems.
- **Having an invasive medical device**. Medical tubing such as intravenous lines and catheters can provide a pathway for MRSA to travel into your body.
- **Residing in a long-term care facility [or in this case, jails or prisons]**. MRSA is prevalent in nursing homes. Carriers of MRSA have the ability to spread it, even if they are not sick themselves.

Risk factors for CA-MRSA
- **Participating in contact sports**. MRSA can spread easily through cuts and scrapes and skin-to-skin contact.
- **Living in crowded or unsanitary conditions**. MRSA outbreaks have occurred in military training camps, child care centers, and jails.
- **Men having sex with men.** Men who have sex with men have a higher risk of developing infections.
- **Having HIV infection.** People with HIV have a higher risk of developing MRSA infection.
- **Using illicit injected drugs.** People wo use illicit injected drugs have a higher risk for infection.

As in the case of the COVID-19, one of the best preventative measures for MRSA infections in jails and prisons is frequent handwashing. Fortunately, there is low risk for infections to be transmitted to visitors as long as any draining lesions are completely covered and no personal items are exchanged (e.g., towels); prisoners should also avoid sharing with other inmates any personal items that might be soiled with the bacteria (NCDHHS, n.d.).

Other Sexually Transmitted Diseases

There are a number of sexually transmitted diseases (STDs) that circulate in jail and prison populations. As we have indicated previously in this book, sex is prohibited in jails and prisons, with the exception of conjugal visits, but as we know from self-reporting surveys and other accounts, sex still occurs behinds bars. And in our discussions of violence in prison, sex is not always consensual, nor does it always represent a loving act.

The most common STDs found in jails and prisons, besides HIV/AIDS and hepatitis, are as follows, with the estimated rates within the incarceration population (Krieger, 2019; Altice and Springer, 2005):

- Gonorrhea (3%);
- Syphilis (21%); and
- Chlamydia (19%).

STDs are not limited to adult inmates. Of serious concern is the alarming rate of STDs in juvenile detention centers. Belanko et al. (2008) found in their study of adolescent and young adult offenders that they are at greater risk for STDs, including an estimated 60 percent annual incidences of documented cases of gonorrhea and 54 percent of cases of chlamydia occurring in 15-to-24-year olds. The Centers for Disease Control and Prevention (CDC) confirms these figures, and report that this age category represent almost half of all new STD infections, with males having sex with males representing the highest risk for transmission (CDC, 2021). The increase risk among juvenile offenders is explained by their higher rates of substance abuse, other health problems, plus limited access to preventive health care (Fitzgibbon, 2004; Forrester et al., 2000).

There are a few cities or states that allow condom distribution in their jails and prisons in order to provide some STD protection, meaning that much of the sex occurring in prison is unprotected. European prisons are more progressive, with condom provision viewed as one of the most effective means to prevent STD transmission (Moazen et al., 2021). Like other types of diseases, the concern is not simply for the health of inmates. It becomes an additional public health problem when STDs are exported to family members and intimate partners after release. Studies have found that women who date men who were previously incarcerated are at greater risk of contracting STD (Nowotny et al., 2020).

Tuberculosis

Tuberculosis (TB) is a highly contagious, airborne respiratory disease that is easily transmitted in the close quarters of jails and prisons. The symptoms of active TB include a prolonged cough, loss of appetite and weight loss, fever, chills, and night sweats (American Lung Association, 2020), some of which are symptoms that can be attributed to any number of illnesses or can be associated with drug or alcohol withdrawal. Though only 3 percent of TB cases can be found in correctional facilities (CDC, n.d.) and the number of cases has been dropping since 1994, the percent of cases relative to the general population has remained fairly steady, as demonstrated by the Centers for Disease Control and Prevention (CDC) graph in Figure 11.4.

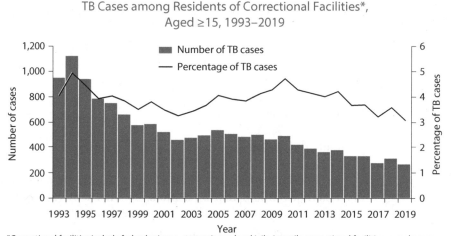

*Correctional facilities include federal prisons, state prisons, local jails, juvenile correctional facilities, or unknown type of correctional facility.

FIGURE 11.4 **Tuberculosis Cases, Residents of Correctional Facilities, 1993-2019.** (*Source:* Centers for Disease Control, n.d., retrieved from https://www.cdc.gov/tb/statistics/surv/surv2019/images/Slide46.PNG.)

In order to reduce cases and control TB in jails and prisons, the CDC (n.d., retrieved from https://www.cdc.gov/tb/topic/populations/correctional/default.htm) recommends that the following protocols be followed:

- Early identification of persons with TB disease through entry and periodic follow-up screening;
- Successful treatment of TB disease and latent TB infection;
- Appropriate use of airborne precautions (e.g., airborne infection isolation, environmental controls, and respiratory protection);
- Comprehensive discharge planning; and
- Thorough and efficient contact investigations when a TB case has been identified.

LOCKUP DURING PANDEMICS AND OTHER HEALTH CRISES

There are two types of mass disease and illness spread that is of concern for jail and prison administrators. Epidemics are localized spreads of disease or illness, which are alarming but easier to contain in comparison to pandemic outbreaks which are more serious and can potentially span the globe. If we were ever reminded of our vulnerability to potentially deadly illnesses, the COVID-19 pandemic spreading globally in late 2019 drove home the fact. For the incarcerated, the vulnerability is ten-fold, as the abilities to prevent the spread, including sanitation of surfaces and social distancing, are limited in the crowded conditions of jails and prisons. What we know of the COVID-19 virus is that it can survive for long periods of time on the type of surface materials found in jails and prisons, including nonporous and metallic surfaces, making disinfecting an almost impossible task (Franco-Paredes et al., 2020).

Even as infectious disease experts and medical personnel have learned much over the course of the COVID-19 pandemic, so have prison administrators. First and foremost, it became a priority to inoculate both inmates and prison workers with the vaccines as urgently as for those who spend time in hospitals and nursing homes, including employees and other frontline workers, in order to slow the spread of the virus. According Barnert and Williams (2021, p. 1099), the following are the main public health concerns found, based on the lessons learned from the COVID-19 cases in U.S. jails and prisons:

1. Accelerate [prison] population reduction coupled with community reentry support;
2. improve prison ventilation systems;
3. ensure appropriate mask use;
4. limit transfers between facilities;
5. strengthen partnerships between public health department and prison leadership;
6. introduce or maintain effective occupational health programs;

7. ensure access to advance care planning processes from incarcerated patients and delineation of patient health care rights;
8. strengthen partnerships between prison leadership and incarcerated people;
9. provide emergency mental health support for prison residents and staff; and
10. commit to public accountability and transparency.

The last priority is crucial, as in the cases of undisclosed diseases and illnesses making their way into the community if individuals are released without a plan for treatment or protection for those outside of jails and prisons.

Prison Hospice Care

Though someone may not technically have a life sentence in prison, for inmates with terminal illnesses, it may very well be one. On the rare occasion, someone might receive a *compassionate release* (early release from jail or prison on the basis of a documented mental or medical condition), which we will discuss in greater detail towards the end of this chapter. Inmates who are at the end of their lives may receive *end of life (EOL)* hospice or palliative care while incarcerated. While *hospice care* involves mentally preparing the patient for end of life after treatments to prolong life are terminated; *palliative care* includes the medical interventions from the beginning of diagnosis, including pain relief, to alleviate the worse symptoms that the dying might be experiencing.

With an ever-aging prison population, on the heels of longer sentences and three strikes convictions, ethical issues have emerged on the quality of the end of life that dying offenders experience. According to O'Connor (2004, p. 63), "few issues require more ethical attention and analysis than prisoner populations and terminal illness." Yet it is a topic that continues to be neglected in research and in practice (Stensland and Sanders, 2016). It can often put jail and prison policies in conflict with medical practices, as in the example of a terminally ill or pregnant inmate who is chained to a hospital bed during treatment.

The three ethical issues are as follows (Stensland and Sanders, 2016):

1. *Equity in the quality of care.* Terminally ill prisoners are not allowed to know when their outside appointments or treatments are scheduled, as it presents a security risk. They are not active participants in their care, as would normally be the case if they were outside of prison.
2. *Early release.* The terminally ill offender is not viewed as a threat to society, yet not all seriously ill or dying inmates are released from prison before completing their sentences or at least qualifying for parole.
3. *The terminally ill as a vulnerable population.* Inmates with terminal illnesses do not trust prison staff, who often oversee all medical decisions of the offender. Often their fear is that prison staff may make decisions that will hasten their death.

Hospice care has only emerged in popularity, in the general public, in the past half century, and it is no surprise that prisons are lagging behind this medical and social welfare trend. Hospice programs unfortunately rely heavily on volunteers, making it difficult to implement in prisons. Research on early hospice programs for prisoners in the United States found that there needs to be more stringent screening, as well as more training before interacting with the patients (Hoffman and Dickson, 2011), as additional precautions need to be taken for the security of the facility and the safety of the volunteers.

PSYCHOLOGICAL AND PSYCHIATRIC ISSUES

There continues to be the ongoing debate of where to put people who break the law, largely due to their mental health issues. To quote Patrick Kennedy (Founder of The Kennedy Forum, former U.S. Representative), "We don't throw people in jail for having cancer. We don't put people in prison for having diabetes. And yet, too often, our response to people with mental illness or addiction is to lock them up." (Kennedy, n.d., retrieved from https://www.nami.org/Personal-Stories/31-Stories-31-Days-Patrick-Kennedy). According to the American Psychiatric Association (APA), at least half of prisoners suffer from some form of mental illness, with 10-25 percent suffering from serious mental illnesses, including schizophrenia (Collier, 2014). Comparatively speaking, mental health issues are not uncommon in the United States, with one in five people experiencing some form or another during their lifetime (National Institute of Mental Health, 2021), but a disproportionate number of those with mental health issues are in custody.

As psychological and psychiatric conditions are on a spectrum, they can range from being mildly debilitating to completely incapacitating the sufferer. For an example, someone with an anxiety disorder might be able to cope well with day-to-day life, with good self-awareness, therapy, and/or medication. Others with anxiety may have such mild cases that the disorder may not have a major effect on their lives. However, someone with the symptoms of bipolar disorder or schizophrenia may have a much more difficult time managing in society without aggressive treatment and intervention. Jail and prison staff, as well as probation and parole officers, have to be prepared to handle any number of mental health issues in the course of their daily work.

Addiction

Addiction to alcohol and/or drugs continues to be one of the leading factors in offending. According to the National Institute on Drug Abuse (2020), the actual rate of inmate *substance use disorders (SUDs)* is unknown but an estimated 65 percent of the prison population has an active addiction. Others may suffer from *Alcohol*

Use Disorder (AUD) which includes a list of problematic drinking habits, including high-intensity drinking[5], binge drinking, and alcoholism (National Institute on Alcohol Abuse and Alcoholism, 2021). In some cases, offenders are abusing both alcohol and drugs.

More recently, one addiction that has increasingly become a public health crisis is opioid use and abuse, including heroin. One form of treatment (or in this case, non-treatment) of opioid dependency is forcing the detainee or inmate into unassisted withdrawal. As one jail corrections officer put it, their drug treatment program for detainees is "cold turkey"[6]. Addicts, on the most part, based on their behaviors, are not the most sympathetic characters, to their families, friends, and the community at large. In many cases, family and friends have been victimized by the addict, including by theft. And as Farrell et al. (2006) and Mumola and Beck (1997), as well as so many other research studies indicate, because of their behaviors (e.g., theft, sale of drugs), opioid dependent individuals often end up in the criminal justice and correctional systems.

While critics might say that addicts get what they deserve, including being forced off their drug of choice with no replacement medication to ease symptoms of withdrawal, others believe that it is more humane to treat withdrawal symptoms. In fact, withholding medication in itself from the incarcerated could be interpreted as cruel and unusual punishment, violating the 8th Amendment. Given the current opioid crisis which has landed a number of people in prisons, on the heels of the documented overprescribing of the drug OxyContin, opioid dependence in any form can lead to a chronic, relapsing disease which can be effectively treated medically with methadone and buprenorphine (Bruce and Schleifer, 2008).

Withholding treatment because someone is incarcerated is also viewed as a human rights violation. Yet most inmates who are addicted to heroin are left untreated while incarcerated (Gordon et al., 2016). More importantly, the use of medical interventions like methadone with opioid addicted prisoners reduces risks of death when they are released, as without treatment, they are more likely to return to illegal opioid use (Marsden et al., 2017). If left untreated in prison, they are much more likely to go untreated on release (Gordon, 2017). However, we should also acknowledge that any number of the opioid addicted might be dead in the streets but for having been arrested and sent to prison (Revier, 2019).

---

[5] According to the Mayo Clinic (n.d., retrieved from https://www.mayoclinic.org/healthy-lifestyle/nutrition-and-healthy-eating/in-depth/alcohol/art-20044551), "moderate alcohol use for healthy adults generally means up to one drink a day for women and up to two drinks a day for men. . . . Heavy or high-risk drinking is defined as more than three drinks on any day or more than seven drinks a week for women and for men older than age 65, and more than four drinks on any day or more than 14 drinks a week for men age 65 and younger."
[6] "Cold turkey" refers to an individual voluntarily or involuntarily stopping alcohol and/or drug consumption without any medical assistance (e.g., methadone during heroin addiction recovery), which often, if not always has serious and unpleasant withdrawal symptoms.

PSYCHOLOGICAL AND PSYCHIATRIC ISSUES DURING AND AFTER INCARCERATION

Since deinstitutionalization and the wholesale closing of psychiatric hospitals, there has been a sharp increase of individuals landing in jails and prisons over the past 50 years. "Persons with mental illnesses are overrepresented within the criminal justice system (Teplin 1994; Steadman et al. 2009) and most also have a co-occurring substance use disorder (Drake et al. 2004)." (Barrenger et al., 2017, p. 883) In the beginning of this chapter we noted the large expenditure that health care represents in jail and prison budgets. The care of the offender with mental health issues contributes to these costs.

For some individuals, they enter jail or prison clinically normal[7] but can exit with any number of psychiatric disorders. Normal is a relative term, if we consider that the American Psychiatric Association (APA) continues to expand the definition of mental illness, as witnessed by the changes over the past few decades to their *Diagnostic and Statistical Manual of Mental Disorders (DSM-5)*. However, it stands to reason that the incarcerated population are susceptible to developing disorders, including depression and anxiety, whether they are genetically predisposed to them or not.

There have been a number of mainstream journal articles and books as well that question whether anyone is "normal" with the proliferation of diagnostic labels and mental disorders, given the examples of *The Loss of Sadness: How Psychiatry Transformed Normal Sorrow into Depressive Disorder* (Horwitz and Wakefield, 2008; 2012), *The Last Normal Child* (Diller and Lawrence, 2006), and *Shyness: How Normal Behavior Became a Sickness* (Lane, 2007) (Kramer, 2009). Whether mental health issues, real or contrived, were lying dormant in the individual prior to incarceration, only to be awakened with the experience of being incarcerated or if they develop after arrest or conviction, the effects can stay with the individual, sometimes for a lifetime, without treatment.

More recently attention has been given to head injuries in football players, with some question as to whether they contributed to homicidal or suicidal behavior in National Football League (NFL) population, some of whom have ended up arrested, in prison, or dead (Cummings et al., 2018). In these cases, treatment of mental health issues and neurological disorders in and out of prison is much more difficult. It is similar to when an individual who prior to a stroke is a gentle, kind person, afterwards becomes belligerent, irritable, and difficult to engage in conversation depending on what part of the brain is affected.

---

[7] As the definition of normal in psychology is an individual who does not have a mental illness, it is difficult to say that anyone who commits a crime is really clinically "normal." The forces alone that drive people to commit crimes can bring on mental health issues, however mild, as in the example of an individual who steals in order to put food on the table for their child is no doubt suffering from extreme stress, if not undiagnosed depression.

One suspected case of consistent head trauma leading to crime is that of Aaron Hernandez, a star player on the New England Patriots NFL team, who while serving time in prison for a homicide and having not yet exhausted the appeals process, committed suicide while behind bars (Gallagher, 2019). Reportedly, doctors at Boston University determined that he suffered from an advanced form of chronic traumatic encephalopathy (CTE), a progressive disease that is similar to dementia, that can be the result of repeated head traumas, similar to that which is experienced in contact sports like football (Shah, 2017; Alzheimer's Association, n.d.). The number of offenders with prior serious head injuries is unknown, but is estimated that brain injury rates for prisoners is seven time greater than in the general public (Harmon, 2012).

Therapies and Medication

There are some questions as to whether the medical and psychiatric community is overmedicating individuals in general. There are even more controversies of overmedicating detainees and prisoners. As in the reports of teachers misdiagnosing (and unprofessionally) children with attention deficient disorders, it is well documented that non-medical personnel in jails and prisons regularly prescribe and overmedicate inmates with psychotropic drugs, whether needed or not (Black Youth Project, 2020). For all the grim statistics, over 60 percent of inmates do receive some type of treatment while incarcerated, as noted in Figure 11.5

Of course, the level of psychiatric care can differ from jurisdiction to jurisdiction and is not always given by the most qualified of individuals, as demonstrated in *Hoptowit v. Ray* (1982).

Mental Health Issues and Recidivism

Sociologists tend to blame societal problems for contributing to mental illness; psychologists are inclined to look to causes within the individual. The reality is that for those who commit crimes and suffer from mental health issues, it is probably a combination of both factors. Barrenger et al. (2017) observed that it is necessary to look at both environmental and interpersonal factors in order to understand how those with mental illness have increased risk for recidivism. Adjusting to life post-incarceration or conviction is difficult at best for the mentally healthy individual. It is doubly difficult for those who suffer from mental illness. If left untreated, mental illnesses among the convicted can lead to further offending, while on probation or after release from jail or prison.

Mental Health Issues and Community Corrections

As part of the prisoners' rights to health care, they are required, by law, to receive adequate mental health care as well. Yet as Zielinski et al. (2020) chastise the mental

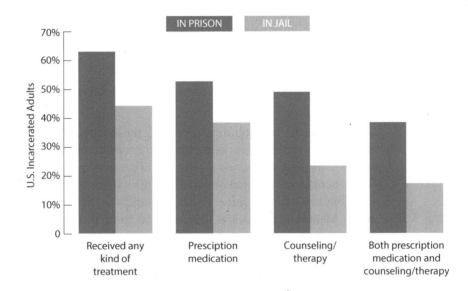

MENTAL HEALTH Treatment Among Incarcerated Adults

Many adults who are incarcerated experiencce at least one mental health issue, with some being undiagnosed or untreated when they are take into custody. The graphic below shows the percentage of individuals in U.S. jails and prisons who reported a history of mental health problems and received some king of mental health treatment once admitted to a correctional facility.

FIGURE 11-5 **Types of Mental Health Treatment, Incarcerated Adults.**
(*Sources*: U.S. Department of Justice; USC Suzanne Dworak Peck School of Social Work Department of Nursing, retrieved from https://nursing.usc.edu/blog/correctional-nurse -career/)

health care professionals in jails and prisons, there is little in the way of evidence-based mental health care practices applied in these settings. This may mean that the therapies available behind bars are largely outdated, vaguely tested, or rely too heavily on pharmaceuticals to address mental health issues, rather than addressing the underlying problems. It's like putting a band-aid over a wound, without applying an antiseptic topical to prevent infection.

When we examine the "sick role" through the lens of Talcott Parsons' theories (1975), someone who is ill, including those with mental health issues, is considered deviant and is expected by society to recover with or without the help of the medical community, which is much more difficult in the case of chronic than in that of temporary mental distress, as in the example of episodic depression after a loved one passes away. And even though mental illness has become less stigmatizing, those who suffer from it can still be marginalized, doubly so if they are convicted criminals, making it at times difficult to seek treatment in the community, even if court-ordered.

Not all those released will be eligible for programs in the community, including those with mental health issues, though in recent decades there has been a greater concerted effort made to provide services for offenders after incarceration. Again, this is dependent on jurisdiction. More recently correctional programming in and out of prison has followed the *Risk-Need-Responsivity Principle (RNR)* approach where offenders are evaluated for what services are appropriate for them, to help reduce recidivism rates (Garofalo, 2020). Instead of simply warehousing inmates, as was the practice in the 1990s, providing more evidence-based, effective programming instead improves the success rates of reentry and hopefully reduces prison overcrowding with fewer convicts reoffending (Garofalo, 2020).

Mental Health Courts

Like drug courts, one solution to keeping those with mental health issues out of jail and prison is trying these cases in *mental health courts* (MHC) instead of in criminal courts. This innovative concept, similar to drug courts, came about largely due to the sharp increase in the number of defendants with mental health issues being arrested since the 1990s in the United States (Loong, 2019; Schneider, 2010; Schneider et al., 2007). Mental health courts are designed to help criminals whose mental health conditions are the primary contributors to their criminal behavior (Loong, 2019). It is yet another means by which to keep convicted criminals out of jails and prisons, allowing them to live in the community in the hopes that they can be successfully treated and rehabilitated. At the very least, the goal and hope is that they can learn to manage their mental health issues more productively and proactively.

There is little research into just why and how MHC works to reduce recidivism. Researchers do have some ideas as why it is effective. It appears that combinations of therapies, including medication and outpatient mental health services, like individual and group therapies, may be what is contributing to the successes of MHCs. This seems to be primarily successful for those individuals who are actively involved in their recovery, rather than those resistant or forced into rehabilitation (Woojae and Redlich, 2016). This is certainly an area of criminal justice that researchers believe deserves more attention, in the same vein as drug courts.

What we also do know is key to success is in the completion of whatever program the court prescribes for the offender. For those who do not complete programs, recidivism rates remain high (Canada et al., 2019). Of considerable concern is for those who have permanent neurological damage, as in the case of mental illness caused by traumatic brain injury. Depending on the type of injury, it may result in the individual's inability to ever regulate their emotions or behavior if left unchecked, including bouts of uncontrollable anger, as in the cases of our previously discuss chronic and permanent disorders, including CTEs (Wagner, 2020).

Non-Pharmaceutical Treatment in the Community

There are also a number of non-pharmaceutical therapy solutions, although as we saw in the graph on combinations of treatments in this chapter, medication often accompanies other types of therapies, and patients cannot always be counted on to take the medications recommended by their physicians or psychiatrists. There are high rates of noncompliance as to patients taking medication—about 50 percent of all patients fail to take their medications as prescribed (DiMatteo et al., 2002).

Therapies can include referrals to individual or group psychotherapy, though medication seems to be the most common route for treatment of mental health issues. In a study of veterans suffering from PTSD, 79 percent were given medication, 39 percent were referred to individual psychotherapy, 24 percent were referred to group psychotherapy (Mott et al., 2014). Whatever combination of therapies are used in intervention, there are more positive outcomes for reduction of psychiatric and criminal recidivism with treatment, as compared to those who do not receive treatment (Morgan et al., 2012).

Those with severe mental illness are of particular challenge to community corrections personnel. For example, it is difficult to get compliance with parole officer meetings outside the home if the former inmate is agoraphobic, afraid to venture from their homes, much less help them to find employment if it is a condition of their release. It is also difficult if the severely mentally challenged do not have a support system in the community, including services, family, and friends. Some of those bridges often have been burned when they committed their crimes.

We should also caution that there can be reluctance to participate in individual or group therapy in general, especially if it is court ordered. Men in particular, as compared to women, are reluctant to seek out medical or psychiatric help until a disease has already significantly progressed and can no longer be ignored (Banks, 2001). In therapy, especially in the group setting, there is a tendency towards impression management, where the patient expresses enthusiasm towards the process or only pretends to participate (Colquhoun et al., 2018). Therapy, like any other type of rehabilitation, is only as good as the participant's willingness to change their behavior. Or at least come to some understanding as to how to manage their mental health issues, including addictions, if it is a chronic condition.

NON-PHARMACEUTICAL THERAPIES

Some of the generally used non-pharmaceutical therapies are discussed here, but as a disclaimer, this is not, by any means, an exhaustive list. New forms of therapies are being developed and tested on a fairly regular basis. However, classic talk therapy is still the most common in used today.

Individual Psychotherapy

There are a number of different forms of individual therapy, and much depends on the preferences and training of the social worker, counselor, or therapist. The most common, *talk therapy* (or psychotherapy), is where the therapist objectively leads the patient to discussions about their lives in depth and is designed to help the patient come to their own conclusions about solutions to resolving their behavioral and psychological problems. Psychotherapy is used for a number of different types of mental disorders, including depression, anxiety, and anger issues, all commonly experienced by offenders before, during, and after incarceration. There are four primary forms of psychotherapy (Gallagher, 2020), some of which we discuss elsewhere in this book, as they apply:

1. *Cognitive behavioral therapy (CBT)* used to target behavioral responses.
2. *Dialectical behavioral therapy (DBT)* used to help patients cope with interpersonal issues, including communication.
3. *Psychodynamic therapy* used to examine the patient's past experiences to better understand current patterns of behaviors and emotions.
4. *Humanistic therapy* used to address multi-faceted problems, where the patient has issues in a number of areas of their lives, including their actions, relationships, and physical feelings.

Though each type of psychotherapy is designed to target specific issues, there is little evidence that one type is better than another, in offenders or in the general public. What we do know is that in one-year follow up of patients, problem solving and mindfulness therapies, including CBT, seem to have better long term outcomes (Cujipers et al., 2021).

Beyond behavior-targeted therapies for individuals, there have been some promising results with therapies that target attitudes. Offenders often report that they felt little empathy for their victims at the time that a crime was committed, except when it may benefit them by pretending to look like they do, as in the example of showing remorse at parole board hearings. By promoting prosocial, empathetic attitudes in offenders in *Compassion-Focused Therapy (CFT)*, it guides them to understand the damage that they have done, through the eyes of the victim (Gilbert, 2017). This type of therapy, however, has its limitations in those offenders who have a genetic or neurological predisposition to antisocial behavior, as well as those who have psychopathic traits and those who focus on the benefits of the harming, abusing, or neglect of others, rather than concern for the harm done to victims (Gilbert, 2017).

Group Therapy

Group therapy is an efficient way to treat more than one patient (or client) at a time. There is also the philosophy that by bringing together individuals suffering from similar mental health issues or addictions, they may help one another, plus it helps to develop communication and socialization skills (American Addiction Centers, 2021).

However, there are some drawbacks. Not everyone responds equally well in the group therapy setting. In a study of sex offenders participating in group dramatherapy, some described their experiences with group therapy in the following ways (Colquhoun et al., 2018, pp. 363-365):

- *It didn't build my confidence, in fact it had the opposite effect. . . it knocked my confidence.*
- *It's different to think about it in front of people because I had to pick out the words, and pick out the right words. . . .*
- *I found it more difficult [in group therapy] because I didn't trust the other people in the group so I found it quite hard to do drama [e.g., role playing, dramatherapy] with them.*
- *I thought I was forced to be upset—not feel upset—you know what I mean, I felt that I should [appear to] feel upset, so I did.*
- *I had to make up a story that fit their manual.*

As Colquhoun et al. (2018) also discovered in their study, the sex offenders felt like they were under the microscope, in something called the *goldfish bowl effect*. In other words, participants are acutely aware that every word and gesture is being noted, not only by the therapist, but their fellow participants in group therapy. And like in a goldfish bowl, their perceptions and interpretations of others' opinions and actions, including those of the therapist, may be distorted.

Family Therapy

As we will note in our discussion of juveniles, it is not always the case of treating the individual offender. Adults can likewise benefit from family therapy. Often offenders will be released from jail or prison, returning to live with family members and their children (Garofalo, 2020). While incarcerated, offenders may fantasize about how conditions will be at home; in reality, they may not be prepared to face the conflict, substance abuse, and antisocial behaviors that exist in some families and contributed to their offending in the first place (Gendreau et al., 2004). And yet family therapy is not that common in the prisoner reentry process (Garofalo, 2020).

COMPASSIONATE RELEASE

When the health of a prisoner is so sorely compromised by illness and incarceration, they may apply or have someone apply on their behalf for a *compassionate release.*

This does not necessarily mean an unconditional release and may only mean a reduction in a sentence. The purposes of a compassionate release or a reduction in sentence, according to the Federal Bureau of Prisons (2019, retrieved from https://www.bop.gov/policy/progstat/5050_050_EN.pdf) are as follows:

> Under 18 U.S.C. 4205(g), a sentencing court, on motion of the Bureau of Prisons, may make an inmate with a minimum term sentence immediately eligible for parole by reducing the minimum term of the sentence to time served. . . . The Bureau uses 18 U.S.C. 4205(g) and 18 U.S.C. 3582(c)(1)(A) in particularly extraordinary or compelling circumstances which could not be reasonably foreseen by the court at the time of sentencing.

During the COVID-19 pandemic, a number of inmates applied for compassionate release under the circumstances. Federal wardens denied 98 percent of those requests, as in the example of 56-year old Marie Neba who was suffering from Stage 4 cancer during the pandemic and had three children at home; her application to be released from the Carswell medical prison in Texas where she had been serving her sentence for Medicare fraud, a white collar crime (Blakinger and Neff, 2020), was denied. Neba has since died in custody. Compassionate releases were never intended to release large numbers of inmates, even during a pandemic, and only 6 percent of the terminally ill who apply will be released, allowed to die outside of prison (Widra and Bertram, 2020).

SUMMARY

There is enough research and evidence that jails and prisons are bad for the health of the incarcerated. Some of this has to do with the ailments that alleged offenders and convicted already suffer from (e.g., addiction) but also has to do with the conditions of jails and prisons, including overcrowding. Those who have spent time in jail or prison, on average, are at greater risk for reduced life expectancy because of incarceration. Some of the more common illnesses experienced in prison, beyond communicable and sexually transmitted disease, are arthritis, asthma, cancer, diabetes, heart disease, high blood pressure, cirrhosis of the liver and stroke-related problems (Maruschak et al., 2016).

Throughout this chapter we have examined the ethical problems associated with the mental and physical care of the incarcerated, as well as community-based treatments. Any form of treatment is only as good as the provider, the partnership between health care provider and the patient, and the willingness of the patient to comply with recommended course of treatment. This holds true whether someone is a criminal or not. The challenge in the criminal justice system is providing a balance between punishment for crimes and compassionate care of the sick individual in custody.

Beyond considerations for compassionate care, there are the sizeable costs of health care for inmates in jails and prisons. With an aging prison population, as well as rising health care costs in general, these financial burdens are only going to become more challenging for state and federal corrections administrators. An additional consideration is in attracting quality medical personnel to work in correctional facilities, along with providing adequate training to non-medical corrections staff.

As we note in this chapter, there is a disproportionate number of inmates with age-related health problems, along with a number of psychiatric disorders, addictions. When offenders are released to the community after incarceration, whether or not they are still in the custody of corrections as in the case of parole, they can pose a public health and safety threat. There are a number of communicable diseases present in prison, some of which were brought in by prisoners, others that are contract during incarceration. The COVID-19 pandemic exacerbated heath conditions in jails and prisons, requiring additional precautions taken, including sanitation protocol, masks, social distancing, and vaccinations, all challenges when dealing with a jail or prison population.

Those in custody do retain certain rights as they apply to their medical and psychological care. Though prison staff have considerable control over their care, prisoners still retain a portion of HIPAA protections. However, the records of their medical and psychological diagnoses and treatments can be released to prison staff without their permission. There are also a number of ethical dilemmas for doctors and nurses, as they are required by their professional oaths to protect the rights of patients, some of which may be in conflict with the policies of correctional facilities. Those in custody can refuse treatment; however, they may be forced to be medicated in the event that their behavior threatens the safety and security of the facility, as well as the safety of fellow inmates and correctional staff.

Jails and prisons are required by law to comply with the Americans with Disabilities Act and provide accommodations to those with disabilities, including accessible cells. However, they are not always in compliance, particularly in older facilities. There have been a number of lawsuits brought before the U.S. Supreme Court that have shed light on the general problems of inadequate health care and accommodations in jails and prisons, some of which we examined in this chapter.

Along with physical ailments, mental health issues are almost insurmountable challenges both for the offender and correctional staff. They can also be a challenge in community-based corrections. Throughout this chapter we have emphasized that addiction to alcohol and/or drugs continues to be one of the leading causes of incarceration, a problem further complicated by the fact that both types of substances are illegally obtained or made in prison, as we see in our chapter on prison culture. Some jails and prisons prescribe to the "cold turkey" prescription for rehabilitation; others, but far too few, do provide treatment, including opioid substitution treatment (e.g., methadone).

One option for those with mental health issues who commit crimes is to have cases heard in mental health courts, rather than in the criminal court system. There are a number of options for community-based treatment of mental illness for offenders, whether they are on probation or newly released from prison. These include individual psychotherapies, group therapy, and family therapy. Therapies can target both behaviors and attitudes that landed the offender in the criminal justice system in the first place. Therapies can be used in conjunction with medication or are standalone treatments for mental health issues. But as we cautioned, therapies and rehabilitation strategies are only as good as the willingness for the individual to commit to change, as well as compliance with taking medications, if prescribed.

As a last resort, if an inmate is sick enough, as in the case of the terminally ill, they can apply for compassionate release. However, most cases will be denied and, as we have noted, even if someone is not sentenced to life in prison without the possibility of parole, they may end up spending the rest of their life in prison and dying there, depending at what age they offended or the state of their health. Even with hospice and palliative care available in prison, where offered, few would argue that this is an ideal way to spend the end days of one's life.

STORIES FROM BEHIND BARS

Estelle v. Gamble (1976)

For a number of reasons, the least of which is HIPAA regulations, we are deviating in this chapter from telling personal tales from behind bars. Because the ambiguity of laws surrounding health care and prisons, as well as the ethical issues and public opinion, we are reserving this section for examining legal precedent for changing health care conditions in jails and prisons.

One key case, *Estelle v. Gamble* (1976), the first of its kind, was eventually presented to the U.S. Supreme Court and addressed the constitutional rights of prisoners as they apply to health care. It does not by any means represent the last of legal actions taken against correctional facilities, states, and the federal government, when health care rights have been ignored or violated. Nearly 50 years after the ruling in *Estelle v. Gamble* (1976), with an aging prison population, as well as a system in the United States struggling to provide affordable and reliable medical care to the general population, the case is still hotly debated today.

Facts of the Case

While J. W. Gamble was a prisoner in a Huntington, Texas prison, he worked as prison labor in a textile mill. On November 9, 1973, a 600-pound bale of cotton fell on him, after which he returned to work for several hours. As these injuries sometime progress, it was not until some hours later that he experienced stiffness and pain, at which time he requested to go to the prison hospital. He was examined for a possible hernia, then sent back to his cell. His pain increased, including chest pain which could indicate a cardiac event, and the unit nurse simply gave him a pain reliever. On November 10th, he was placed on a cell-pass, cell-feed routine, meaning that he was allowed to stay in his cell to recover, receiving his meals there. Days later he would be placed on light work detail, though Gamble refused to work in the coming months after his injury, due to his continuing to experience pain. Each he time refused to work, he was disciplined. By December 6th, he was also diagnosed with high blood pressure.

In February 1974, Gamble signed a *pro se* (i.e., representing himself) complaint and brought a civil rights action lawsuit against the state corrections department medical director and two corrections officials, on the basis that his 8th Amendment rights had been violated. This was argued to be due to the lack of appropriate care for his injuries that he received in prison, interpreted as a form of cruel and unusual punishment, similar to our discussions of withholding treatment in this chapter. In defense of the Texas prison health care system in the 1970s, back injuries then, as they are today, are difficult to diagnose, treat, or document (Simon, 2013).

The complaint was dismissed at the district court level. However, The United States Court of Appeals reversed the ruling, acknowledging that the prison did not X-ray Gamble to make a proper diagnosis in a back injury, as well as failing to provide adequate treatment. The court also acknowledged that Gamble was placed in solitary confinement, not due to behavior or for his protection, but rather due to the substandard of medical care he was receiving in prison. The Court of Appeals held that the case could be reinstated. The court did determine, however, this was not a violation of the 8th Amendment, but rather a case of medical malpractice. This created a roadblock to holding non-medical personnel accountable, but they could be sued for neglect of general custodial care (Sonntag, 2017).

The U.S. Supreme Court, citing that Gamble was seen numerous times by medical personnel for his back injury, ruled that he couldn't necessarily claim this was cruel and unusual punishment. However, the court did set a precedent for callous indifference in medical care. As Justice Marshall wrote in the decision, "the denial of needed medical care might, in the most unfortunate cases, cause grave suffering akin to torture, and the infliction of such 'unnecessary suffering is inconsistent with contemporary standards of decency.'" (Simon, 2013, para 1; *Estelle v. Gamble*, 429 U.S. at 103-4) By the time the case reached the U.S. Supreme Court, it was vaguely an 8th Amendment rights case, and rather, a damnation of the health care delivery system in U.S. state and federal prisons and Gamble's claims were dismissed.

Postscript

Since the *Estelle v. Gamble* decision, lawsuits have expanded to include cases involving inmates with mental health issues and prisoner suicides. In one extreme example, in *Brown v. Plata* in California, the mental and health care system in state corrections was found to be so broken that a federal trial court "placed the entire California prison health care in receivership" (Simon, 2013, para 22) for violating the 8th Amendment. Though physical and mental health care is still a challenge in prisons today, it has vastly improved since the 1970s, aided by new technologies and better (but not perfect) training, including that of non-medical staff.

To address the rising costs of health care in jails and prison, there have been primarily three strategies: (1) Expansion of Medicaid access under the Affordable Care Act provides savings when released prisoners have access to health care, which is a factor in recidivism, (2) Enrollment of lower income adults in Medicaid reduces the need for them to commit crime in the first place, and (3) Outsourcing prison health care to outside contractors at a cost savings (Sonntag, 2017).

The U.S. Congress passed the Prison Litigation Reform Act (1995), discussed in Chapter 5, which limits frivolous lawsuits prisoners can file, including those seeking restitution after alleged malpractice committed by prison staff. In the absence of lawsuits, the fear is that the primary regulatory system for prison medical personnel is internally monitored or by the professional organizations they belong to (e.g., American Medical Association; American Nurses Association) which may further hide any medical malfeasance being committed behind bars (Sonntag, 2017).

SOURCES

Estelle v. Gamble (n.d.) *Oyez.* Retrieved from https://www.oyez.org/cases/1976/75-929.

Simon, J. (2013) REFORMING CALIFORNIA CORRECTION: From health to humanity: Re-reading *Estelle v. Gamble* after *Brown v. Plata. Federal Sentencing Reporter.* Vol. 25, Iss. 4:276.

Sonntag, H. (2017) Medicine behind bars: regulating and litigating prison healthcare under state law forty years after *Estelle v. Gamble. Case Western Reserve Law Review.* Winter, Vol. 68, Iss. 2:603-650.

INTERNATIONAL PERSPECTIVES IN PUNISHMENT AND CORRECTIONS: GUATEMALA

Guatemala is a Central American country which borders Mexico to the north, Honduras and El Salvador to the south. As a country with chronic internal conflict, plus as conduit for the illegal transport of people and drugs through Mexico to the United States, the country has been fraught with violence and corruption.

As a familiar refrain that we hear over and over again in this book, Guatemala prisons are overcrowded and underfunded. Male prisoners are dependent on female visitors to provide essential goods they cannot get in prison, including basic hygiene products and food (Fontes and O'Neill, 2019). Female prisoners are not so lucky and there is far more control over who may visit them in prison (Fontes and O'Neill, 2019).

What is of gravest concern in the international community of corrections watchdogs are the conditions in Guatemalan mental institutions, one of which, as a public hospital, also houses the criminally insane. As in the United States, when a convict's mental state is so deteriorated that they cannot function in a standard prison, they will be sentenced to a mental hospital for an indeterminate period of time.

Federico Mora Hospital Guatemala (*left*); Patients Left Unattended on Hospital Grounds (*right*).
(*Source*: Cunha, 2021, retrieved from https://casocriminal.org/en/pychiatric-hospitals/federico-mora
-the-worst-psychiatric-hospital-in-the-world/)

Federico Mora Hospital in Guatemala houses approximately 340 males and females together, with about 15 percent classified as violent and mentally-disturbed criminals (Rogers, 2014). The hospital is the only public psychiatric hospital in Guatemala (Larsson, 2020). The facility is described as run down, with hygiene not a priority and there are reports that prisoners are often left naked with their skin covered with their own feces and urine—"They look more like concentration camp prisoners than patients." (Larsson, 2020; Rogers, 2014, retrieved from https://www.bbc.com/news/magazine-30293880). Former patients of the hospital report that they have been raped while sedated, with the director confessing that the corrections officers sexually abuse patients and abuses are common knowledge (Cunha, 2021). Conditions have worsened during the COVID-19 pandemic, where insiders and advocates warn that patients in the hospital are simply left to die rather than treated (Larsson, 2020).

SOURCES

Cunha, J. (2021) Federico Mora: The worst psychiatric hospital in the world. July 22. *CasoCriminal*. Retrieved from https://casocriminal.org/en/pychiatric-hospitals/federico-mora-the-worst-psychiatric-hospital-in-the-world/.

Fontes, A.W. and K. L. O'Neill (2019) *La Visita*: Prisons and survival in Guatemala. *Journal of Latin American Studies*. Vol. 51:85-107.

Larsson, N. (2020) Officials conceal conditions at Guatemala mental health hospital during pandemic. The North American Congress on Latin America (NACLA). June 23. Retrieved from https://nacla.org/news/2020/06/23/guatemala-mental-health-hospital-covid.

Rogers, C. (2014) Inside the 'world's most dangerous' hospital. British Broadcasting Company (*BBC*). Dec 5. Retrieved from https://www.bbc.com/news/magazine-30293880.

GLOSSARY

Activities of daily living (ADLs)   The things we do in our daily lives that can affect quality of life, health, and mental well-being when we are unable to do them, including using utensils to eat, personal hygiene, brushing our teeth, and showering or bathing.

Alcohol Use Disorder (AUD)   Condition whereby a person has uncontrolled drinking habits and preoccupation with alcohol consumption. Also called alcoholism or alcohol dependency.

Americans with Disabilities Act (ADA, 1990)   Legislation that requires public spaces, buildings, and businesses to provide access and accommodations to those with physical or mental limitations. Applies to jail and prison construction. Also prohibits discrimination on the basis of physical or mental limitations.

Community-based corrections   Sentencing provisions that take place in the community, outside of jail or prison, including therapy, rehabilitation, conditions for release in the case of probation or parole.

Compassion-based therapy (CBT)   Psychotherapy that is based in developing empathy in the offender.

Compassionate release   Early release from jail or prison on the basis of a documented mental or medical condition, where continued incarceration would be considered unethical or cruel. Example: Early release for a terminally ill inmate.

Diagnostic and Statistical Manual of Mental Disorders (DSM-5)   The American Psychological Association's manual that provides a comprehensive list of recognized mental disorders and illnesses.

End of life care (EOL)   Medical and emotional support given to patients (in this case, inmates) who are terminally ill and near death. (See *Hospice*; *Palliative care*)

Goldfish bowl effect   There are two components of the goldfish bowl effect. First, it is the perception that everyone is looking at you. Second, that perception is distorted, as in the example of the curved sides of a goldfish bowl.

Health care   Efforts to restore or maintain the health and well-being of patients.

Health Insurance Portability and Accountability Act (HIPPA, 1996)   Legislation that protects individuals' medical records from being disclosed without their permission. Limited in jails and prisons due to concerns for safety and security.

***Hoptowit v. Ray* (1982)**   Lawsuit brought by inmates at the Washington State Penitentiary against the Governor and various officials, alleging that conditions (including medical, dental) in the prison violated the 8th Amendment, citing that it was cruel and unusual punishment.

Hospice care   Emotional and logistical support to terminal patients and their family as they cope with and adjust to the last days or weeks of the individual who is dying. (See *End of Life Care (EOL; Palliative care*)

Infirmary   Medical facilities at a jail or prison, borrowing the term from the military.

Libel (or defamation, Costa Rica)   Ordinarily more likely to be treated as a civil case in the United States, Costa Rica will prosecute for criminal libel or defamation, where someone has published unflattering or false stories about an individual, individuals, companies, or government entities.

Mental health courts   Alternatives to criminal court system for offenders with mental health issues, where they are more likely to be sentenced to treatment in the community.

Occupational therapy   Therapies aimed at improving a patient's ability to perform their activities of daily living after a serious injury or illness. (See *Activities of daily living (ADLs)*)

Palliative care   Medical intervention to ease the pain and discomfort that terminal patients experience towards the end of their lives.

Physical therapy   Rehabilitative therapy after a serious injury or illness to restore or improve the mobility of the patient.

Risk-Need-Responsivity Principle (RNR)   Used to test the appropriateness of treatments or services to reduce the convict's risk for reoffending.

Substance use disorders (SUDs)   Synonymous with drug addiction.

Talk therapy   Layperson's terms for psychotherapy that is individualized therapy used to treat a number of mental disorders or emotional issues.

REFERENCES AND SUGGESTED READINGS

Altice, F. L. and S. A. Springer (2005) Management of HIV/AIDS in correctional settings in *The AIDS Pandemic: Impact of Science and Society*, K. H. Mayer and H. F. Pizer, eds. Cambridge, MA: Academic Press. Ch. 18.

Alzheimer's Association (n.d.) Chronic traumatic encephalopathy (CTE). Retrieved from https://www.alz.org/alzheimers-dementia/what-is-dementia/related_conditions/chronic-traumatic-encephalopathy-(cte).

American Addiction Centers (2021) Psychotherapy guide: Group vs. individual therapy. Apr 2. Retrieved from https://americanaddictioncenters.org/therapy-treatment/group-individual.

American Lung Association (2020) Tuberculosis symptoms and diagnosis. Mar. 9. Retrieved from https://www.lung.org/lung-health-diseases/lung-disease-lookup/tuberculosis/symptoms-diagnosis.

American Nurses Association (ANA) (2015) Code of Ethics. Retrieved from https://nursing.rutgers.edu/wp-content/uploads/2019/06/ANA-Code-of-Ethics-for-Nurses.pdf.

American Occupational Therapy Association (2021) What is occupational therapy? Retrieved from https://www.aota.org/Conference-Events/OTMonth/what-is-OT.aspx.

Americans with Disabilities Act (2017) Title III Regulations, Part 36 Nondiscrimination on the basis of disability in public accommodations and commercial facilities. Jan. 17. Retrieved from https://www.ada.gov/regs2010/titleIII_2010/titleIII_2010_regulations.htm.

Ashraf, H. (2003) US Supreme Court limits forced drugging of mentally ill before trial. The Lancet. London, UK. June 21. Retrieved from https://eds-a-ebscohost-com.wne.idm .oclc.org/eds/pdfviewer/pdfviewer?vid=2&sid=c645e3cf-61de-4922-96f1-3e706e321 53c%40sessionmgr4007.

Banks, I. (2001) No man's land: Men, illness, and the NHS. *British Medical Journal*. Nov., Vol. 323(7320):1058-1060.

Barnert, E. and B. Williams (2021) Then urgent priorities based on lessons learned from more than half a million known COVID-19 cases in US prisons. *American Journal of Public Health*. June, Vol. 111, Iss. 6:1099-1106.

Barrenger, S. L., J. Draine, B. Angell, and D. Hermann (2017) Reincarceration risk among men with mental illnesses leaving prison: A risk environment analysis. *Community Mental Health Journal*. Vol. 53:883-892.

Belenko, S., R. Dembo, D. Weiland, M. Rollie, C. Salvatore, A. Hanlon, and K. Childs (2008) Recently arrested adolescents are at high risk for sexually transmitted diseases. *Sexually Transmitted Diseases*. Aug., Vol. 35, No. 8:758-763.

Binswanger, I. A., C. Nowels, K. F. Corsi, J. Long R. E. Booth, J. Kutner, and J. F. Steiner (2011) "From the prison door right to the sidewalk, everything went downhill": A qualitative study of the health experiences of recently released inmates. *International Journal of Law and Psychiatry*. Vol. 34:249-255.

Black Youth Project (2020) Big Pharma and the prison industry are colluding to overmed-icate incarcerated populations. Mar. 17. Retrieved from http://blackyouthproject.com/ big-pharma-and-the-prison-industry-are-colluding-to-overmedicate-incarcerated -populations/#:~:text=Overmedication%20of%20psychotropics%20is%20a,themsel ves%2C%20instead%20of%20medical%20doctors.&text=The%20increased%20vulner ability%20in%20women's,%2C%20sexual%2C%20and%20physical%20violence.

Blakinger, K. and J. Neff (2020) Thousands of sick federal prisoners sought compassionate release. 98 percent were denied. *Journalism and Justice*, The Marshall Project. Oct. 7. Retrieved from https://www.themarshallproject.org/2020/10/07/thousands-of-sick-federal -prisoners-sought-compassionate-release-98-percent-were-denied.

Bondurant, B. (2013) The privatization of prisons and prisoner healthcare: Addressing the extent of prisoners' right to healthcare. *New England Journal of Criminal and Civil Confinement*. Spring, Vol. 39, Iss. 2:407-426.

Bruce, R. D. and R. A. Schleifer (2008) Ethical and human rights imperatives to ensure med-ical treatment for opioid dependence in prisons and pre-trial detention. *International Journal of Drug Policy*. Vol. 19:17-23.

Canada, K., S. Barrenger, and B. Ray (2019) Bridging mental health and criminal justice sys-tems: A systematic review of the impact of mental health courts on individuals and communities. *Psychology, Public Policy, and Law*. Vol. 25, No. 2:73-91.

Centers for Disease Control and Prevention (CDC) (n.d.) Health Insurance Portability and Accountability Act of 1996 (HIPPA). *Public Health Professionals Gateway*, Public Health Law. Retrieved from https://www.cdc.gov/phlp/publications/topic/hipaa.html.

Centers for Disease Control and Prevention (CDC) (n.d.) TB control in correctional facilities. Retrieved from https://www.cdc.gov/tb/topic/populations/correctional/default.htm.

Centers for Disease Control and Prevention (CDC) (2001) First report of AIDS. *Morbidity and Mortality Weekly Report*. U.S. Department of Health and Human Services. June, Vol. 50, No. 21. Retrieved from https://www.cdc.gov/mmwr/pdf/wk/mm5021.pdf.

Centers for Disease Control and Prevention (CDC) (2021) Sexually transmitted disease surveillance, 2019. Apr. 13. Retrieved from https://www.cdc.gov/std/default.htm.

Collier, L. (2014) Incarceration nation. American Psychological Association. Oct., Vol. 45, No. 9. Retrieved from https://www.apa.org/monitor/2014/10/incarceration.

Collins, S. R., M. Z. Gunja, and G. N. Aboulafia (2020) U.S. health insurance coverage in 2020: A looming crisis in affordability. Commonwealth Fund Biennial Health Insurance Survey, 2020. Aug. 19. Retrieved from https://www.commonwealthfund.org/publications/issue-briefs/2020/aug/looming-crisis-health-coverage-2020-biennial.

Colquhoun, B., A. Lord, and A. M. Bacon (2018) A qualitative evaluation of recovery processes experienced by mentally disordered offenders following a group treatment program. *Journal of Forensic Psychology Research and Practice*. Vol. 18, No. 5:352-373.

Cujipers, P., S. Quero, H. Noma, M. Ciharova, C. Miguel, E. Karyotaki, A. Capriani, I. A. Cristea, and T. A. Furukawa (2021) Psychotherapies for depression: A network meta-analysis covering efficacy, acceptability and long-term outcomes of all main treatment types. *World Psychiatry*. Vol. 20, Iss. 2:283-293.

Cummings, P., A. G. Harbaug, and G. Farah (2018) Homicidal violence among National Football League athletes. *Academic Forensic Pathology*. Sept., Vol. 8, No. 3:808-711.

DiMatteo, M. R., P. J. Giordani, and H. S. Lepper (2002) Patient adherence and medical treatment outcome. *Medical Care*. Vol. 40, No. 9:794-811.

Docnotes (2020) Healthcare vs. health care. May 31. Retrieved from https://docnotes.net/2020/05/healthcare-vs-health-care.html.

Douds, A. S., E. M. Ahlin, P. R. Kauvanaugh, and A. Olaghere (2016) Decayed prospects: A qualitative study of prisoner dental care and its impact on former prisoners. *Criminal Justice Review*. Vol 4, No 1:21-40.

Douds, A. S., E. M. Ahlin, N. S. Fiori, and N. J. Barrish (2020) Why prison dental care matters: Legal, policy, and practical concerns. *Annals of Health Law*. Vol. 29:101.

Eisen, L. (2015) Charging Inmates Perpetuates Mass Incarceration. Report, The Brennan Center for Justice, New York University School of Law. Retrieved from https://www.brennancenter.org/sites/default/files/2019-08/Report_Charging_Inmates_Mass_Incarceration.pdf.

Falter, R. G. (1999) Selected predictors of health service needs of inmates over age 50. *Journal of Correctional Health Care*. Vol. 6:149-175.

Falter, R. G. (2006) Elderly inmates: An emerging correctional population. *Correctional Health Journal*. Vol. 1:52-69.

Farrell, M., A. Boys, N. Singleton, H. Meltzer, T. Brugha, and P. Bebbington (2006) Predictors of mental health service utilization in the 12 months before imprisonment: Analysis of results from a national prison survey. *Australian and New Zealand Journal of Psychiatry*. Vol. 40, Nos 6-7:548-553.

Federal Bureau of Prisons (BOP) (2019) Compassionate release/reduction in sentence: Procedures for implementation of 18 U.S.C. §§3582 and 4205(g). Program Statement, U.S. Department of Justice. Jan. 17. Retrieved from https://www.bop.gov/policy/progstat/5050_050_EN.pdf.

Fitzgibbon, J. J. (2004) Healthcare for adolescents in juvenile facilities: Increasing needs for adolescent females. *Journal of Pediatric Adolescent Gynecology*. Vol 17:3-5.

Forrester, C. B., E. Tambor, A. W. Riley, M.E. Ensminger, and B. Starfield (2000) The health profile of incarcerated male youth. *Pediatrics*. Jan., Vol. 105 (1 Pt 3):286-291.

Franco-Paredes, C., K. Jankousky, J. Schultz, J. Bernfeld, K. Cullen, N.G Quan, S. Kon, P. Hotez, A. F. Henao-Martinez, and M. Krsak (2020) COVID-19 in jails and prisons: A neglected infection in a marginalized population. Public Library of Science, *Neglected Tropical Diseases*. June 22, Vol. 14, No. 6:e0008409. Electronic Publication. Available at https://journals.plos.org/plosntds/article?id=10.1371/journal.pntd.0008409.

Gallagher, J. (2020) Talking it out: Talk therapy and how it can benefit you. *The Talkspace Voice*. Nov. 7. Retrieved from https://www.talkspace.com/blog/what-is-talk-therapy/.

Garofalo, M. (2020) Family therapy in corrections: implications for reentry into the community. *Journal of Correctional Health Care*. July, Vol. 26, No. 3. Retrieved from https://www.liebertpub.com/doi/full/10.1177/1078345820938350.

Gilbert, P. (2017). Exploring compassion focused therapy in forensic settings: An evolutionary and social-contextual approach, in *Individual psychological therapies in forensic settings: Research and practice,* J. Davies & C. Nagi, eds. Milton Park, UK: Routledge/Taylor & Francis Group. pp. 59-84.

Goldstein, M. M. (2014) Health information privacy and health information technology in the US correctional setting. *American Journal of Public Health*. Vol. 104, Iss. 5:803-809.

Gordon, M. S., T. W. Kinlock, R. P. Schwartz, K. E. O'Grady, T. T. Fitzgerald, and F. J. Vocci (2017) *Drug and Alcohol Dependence*. Vol. 172:34-42.

Hansen, L. L. (2006) Women disadvantaged in the workplace: The second shift, emotional labor, and the "good old boy network," in *The Women of Ophthalmology*, J. B. Pinto and E. A. Davis, eds. Fairfax, VA: American Society of Cataract and Refractive Surgery and American Society of Ophthalmic Administration. Ch. 5.

Harmon, K. (2012) Brain injury rate 7 times greater among U.S. prisoners. Scientific America. Feb 4. Retrieved from https://www.scientificamerican.com/article/traumatic-brain-injury-prison/.

Hoffman, H. C. and G. E. Dickson (2011) Characteristics of prison hospice programs in the United States. *American Journal of Hospice and Palliative Care*. June, Vol. 28, No. 4:245-52.

Jaegers, L. A., E. Skinner, B. Conners, C. Hayes, S. West-Bruce, M. B. Vaughn, D. L. Smith, and K. F. Barney (2020) Evaluation of jail-based occupational therapy transition and integration program for community reentry. *American Journal of Occupational Therapy*. May/June, Vol. 74, No. 3:1-11.

Kaur, P., S. Simapreet, A. Mathur, D. K. Makkar, V. P. Aggarwal, M. Batra, A. Sharma, and N. Goyal (2017) Impact of dental disorders and its influence on self-esteem levels among adolescents. *Journal of Clinical Diagnosis Research*. Apr., Vol. 11, No 4:ZC05-ZC08. Retrieved from https://www.ncbi.nlm.nih.gov/pmc/articles/PMC5449896/.

Krans, B. (2018) Why aren't prison officials treating inmates for hepatitis C? *Healthline*. July 24. Retrieved from https://www.healthline.com/health-news/why-arent-prison-officials-treating-inmates-for-hepatitis-c.

Krieger, D., C. Abe, A. Pottorff, X. Li, J. Rich, A. Nijhawan, and E. Ank (2019) Sexually transmitted infections detected during and after incarceration among people with Human Immonodeficiency Virus: Prevalence and implications for screening and prevention. *Sexually Transmitted Diseases*. Vol. 46, Iss. 9:602-607. Available at https://journals-lww-com.wne.idm.oclc.org/stdjournal/Fulltext/2019/09000/Sexually_Transmitted_Infections_Detected_During.7.aspx.

Loong, D., S. Bonato, J. Barnsley, and C. S. Dewa (2019) The effectiveness of mental health courts in reducing recidivism and police contact: A systematic review. *Community Mental Health Journal*. Vol. 55:1073-1098.

Marsden, J., G. Stillwell, H. Jones, A. Cooper, B. Eastwood, M. Farrell, T. Lowden, N. Maddalena, C. Metcalfe, J. Shaw, and M. Hickman (2017) Does exposure to opioid substitution treatment in prison reduce the risk of death after release? A national observational perspective study. *Addiction*. Aug., Vol. 112, Iss. 8:1408-1419.

Maruschak, L. M. and M. Berzofsky (2016) Medical problems of state and federal prisoners and jail inmates, 2011-2012. Special Report, U.S. Department of Justice, Office of Justice Programs, Bureau of Justice Statistics. Oct. 4. Retrieved from https://bjs.ojp.gov/content/pub/pdf/mpsfpji1112.pdf.

Maschi, T., J. Kwak, E. Ko, and M. B. Morrissey (2012) Forget me not: Dementia in prison. *Gerontologist*. Vol. 52, No. 4:441-451.

Mayo Clinic Staff (2019) Oral health: A window to your overall health. Healthy Lifestyle, Adult Health, Mayo Clinic. Rochester, MN. June 4. Retrieved from https://www.mayocli nic.org/healthy-lifestyle/adult-health/in-depth/dental/art-20047475.

Mayo Clinic Staff (2020) MRSA infection. Dec. 1. Retrieved from https://www.mayoclinic. org/diseases-conditions/mrsa/symptoms-.

Merriam-Webster Dictionary (2021) "Health care," "Health-care," and "Healthcare." Retrieved from https://www.merriam-webster.com/dictionary/health%20care.

Moazen, B., J. Mauti, P. Meireles, T. Cerniková, F. Neuhann, A. Jahn, and H. Stöver (2021) Principles of condom provision programs in prisons from the standpoint of European prison health experts: A qualitative study. *Harm Reduction Journal*. Vol. 18, Article No. 14. Available at https://harmreductionjournal.biomedcentral.com/track/pdf/10.1186/ s12954-021-00462-y.pdf.

Morenoff, J. D. and D. J. Harding (2014) Incarceration, prison reentry, and communities. *Annual Review of Sociology*. Vol 40:411-429.

Morgan, J. and A. L. Fellow (2017) Prisoners with physical disabilities are forgotten and neglected in America. *Speak Freely*, American Civil Liberties Union (ACLU). Jan. 12. Retrieved from https://www.aclu.org/blog/prisoners-rights/solitary-confinement/prison ers-physical-disabilities-are-forgotten-and.

Morgan, R. D., D. B. Flora, D. G. Kroner, J. F. Mills, F. Varghese, and J. S. Steffan (2012) Treating offenders with mental illness: A research synthesis. *Law and Human Behavior*. Feb., Vol. 36, No. 1:37-50.

Morris, K. (2004) Night shift nurse was videotaped as she conducted a client interview in segregation. Issues and Answers, in *Ohio Nurses Review*. Feb., Vol. 79, Iss. 2:16.

Mumola, C. and A. Beck (1997) *Bureau of Justice Statistics Bulletin*. Washington, D.C.: U.S. Department of Justice, Office of Justice Programs.

Mott, J. M., T. L. Barrera, C. Hernandez, D. P. Graham, and E. J. Teng (2014) Rates and pre-dictors of referral for individual psychotherapy, group psychotherapy, and medications among Iraq and Afghanistan veterans with PTSD. *Journal of Behavioral Health Services and Research*. Apr., Vol. 41, No. 2:99-109.

National Center for Health Statistics, Centers for Disease Control and Prevention. (2013) Summary Health Statistics for the U.S. Population: National Health Interview Survey, 2012. Retrieved from http://www.cdc.gov/nchs/data/series/sr_10/sr10_259.pdf

National Institute of Mental Health (NIMH) (2021) Mental illness. National Institute of Health (NIH). Jan. Retrieved from https://www.nimh.nih.gov/health/statistics/mental -illness.

National Institute on Alcohol Abuse and Alcoholism (NIAAA) (2021) Alcohol use in the United States. National Institute of Health. June. Retrieved from https://www.niaaa.nih .gov/publications/brochures-and-fact-sheets/alcohol-facts-and-statistics.

National Institute on Drug Abuse (2020) *Criminal Justice Drug Facts*. National Institute of Health. June. Retrieved from https://www.drugabuse.gov/publications/drugfacts/crimi nal-justice.

North Carolina Department of Health and Human Services (NCDHHS) (n.d.) Managing CA-MRSA in incarceration: N.C. Public Health recommendations. Disease and Topics: Community-Associated MRSA. Retrieved from https://epi.dph.ncdhhs.gov/cd/mrsa_ca/jails.html.

Nowotny, K. M., M. Omori, M. Mckenna, and J. Kleinman (2020) Incarceration rates and inci-dences of sexually transmitted infections in US counties, 2011-2016. *American Journal of Public Health*. Vol 110:130-136.

Parsons, T. (1975) The sick role and the role of physician reconsidered. The Milbank Memorial Fund Quarterly, *Health and Society*. Summer, Vol. 53, No. 3:257-278.

Porretta, A. (2020) How much does individual health insurance cost? *eHealth*. Nov. 24. Retrieved from https://www.ehealthinsurance.com/resources/individual-and-family/how-much-does-individual-health-insurance-cost.

Revier, K. (2019) "You'll either die or go to prison": Therapeutic surveillance and addiction narratives in drug court. Conference paper, American Sociological Association. 26 pp.

Reyes, H. (2001) Health and human rights in prisons. International Committee of the Red Cross, excerpt from HIV in Prisons: A reader with particular relevance to the newly developed states, in *World Health Organization-Europe, Health in Prison Project*. Chapter 2. Retrieved from https://www.icrc.org/en/doc/resources/documents/misc/59n 8yx.htm#a2.

Riggenberg, W. J. (2011) Initial dental needs and a projection of needed dental capacity in the Iowa Department of Corrections. *Journal of Correctional Health*. Vol. 17"150-159.

Robertson, J. E. (2011) Correctional case law: 2010. *Criminal Justice Review*. Vol. 36:232-244.

Schneider, R. D. (2010) Mental health courts and diversion programs: A global survey. *International Journal of Law and Psychiatry*. Vol. 33, No. 4:201-206.

Schneider, R. D., H. Bloom, and M. Heerema (2007) *Mental Health Courts: Decriminalizing the Mentally Ill*. Toronto, Canada: Irwin Law.

Shah, M. (2017) Aaron Hernandez's violent end: Was CTE to blame? ABC News. Sept. 22. Retrieved from https://abcnews.go.com/Health/aaron-hernandezs-violent-end-cte-blame/story?id=50025719.

Sonntag, H. (2017) Medicine behind bars: regulating and litigating prison healthcare under state law forty years after *Estelle v. Gamble. Case Western Reserve Law Review*. Winter, Vol. 68, Iss. 2:603-650.

Stensland, M. and S. Sanders (2016) Detained and dying: Ethical issues surrounding end-of-life care in prison. *Journal of Social Work in End-of-Life and Palliative Care*. Vol. 12, No. 3:259-276.

United States Court of Appeals (1982) *Hoptowit. v. Ray,* 682 F.2d 1237. No. 80-3366, Ninth Circuit. Retrieved from https://scholar.google.com/scholar_case?case=547207218557 5171255&q=hoptowit+v.+ray&hl=en&as_sdt=6,32&as_vis=1.

United States Department of Justice (DOJ) (2020) *ADA/Section 504 Design Guide: Accessible Cells in Correctional Facilities*. Disability Rights Section, Civil Rights Division. Feb. 25. Retrieved from https://www.ada.gov/accessiblecells.htm.

Wagner, A. R. (2020) Article and survey: The criminally damaged brain and the need to expand mental health courts: A look at the traumatized mind, unfortunate criminal consequences, and the divergent paths of prison or treatment. *Nova Law Review*. Vol. 44:403.

Woojae, H. and A. D. Redlich (2016) The impact of community treatment among mental health court participants. Psychiatric Services. Vol. 67, No. 4:385-390.

Widra, E. and W. Bertram (2020) Compassionate release was never designed to release large numbers of people. Prison Policy Initiative. May 29. Retrieved from https://www.priso npolicy.org/blog/2020/05/29/compassionate-release/.

World Health Organization (2019) Hepatitis. Q&A Detail. Sept. 1. Retrieved from https://www.who.int/news-room/q-a-detail/hepatitis.

World Health Organization (2020) Vector-borne diseases. Mar. 2. Retrieved from https://www.who.int/news-room/fact-sheets/detail/vector-borne-diseases.

Zalman, M. (1972) Prisoners' rights to medical care. *The Journal of Criminal Law, Criminology, and Police Science*. Vol. 63, No. 2:185-199.

Zielinski, M. J., M. K. Allison, L. Brinkley-Rubinstein, G. Curran, N. D. Zaller, and J. E. Kichner (2020) Making change happen in criminal justice settings: Leveraging implementation science to improve mental health care. *Health and Justice*. Vol. 9, Iss. 1:1-10.

Chapter TWELVE

Alternatives to Incarceration
Community-Based Corrections

> *I made my third parole and I believe if I had made it the first time, I wouldn't be here today. I still would've been out there doing stupid stuff.*
>
> — Derrick Lewis, American professional mixed martial arts fighter, who received parole after serving 3 ½ years of a 5-year sentence for aggravated assault

Chapter Objectives

- Distinguish the differences between probation and parole.
- Explore other alternatives to incarceration.
- Review the conditions of probation and parole.
- Introduce different philosophies in community-based corrections
- Discuss aftercare, after release to the community.

Key Terms

Actuarial risk
Adult transition centers
Cognitive Behavioral
    Treatment (CBT)
Diversion programs
Dosage (in Eight Principles of
    Intervention and Prevention)
Drug courts
Electronic monitoring (EM)
Faith-based programs
Good time earned

Intensive supervision probation (ISP)
Intermediate sanctions
Intrinsic motivation
Mandatory release
Multifactor Offender Readiness
    Model (MORM)
Need principle
Parole
Probation
Probation officer directives
Responsivity principle

Risk principle

Self-efficacy

Sex offender registry

Shaming and reintegration

Shock probation

Study-release programs

Substantive violations

Technical violation

Treatment principle

Work-release programs

INTRODUCTION

For as many people as there are in prison, the vast majority of both juveniles and adults who have had contact with the corrections system in the United States because of alleged or proven crimes are not incarcerated. Approximately 1 in 58 adults in the United States are living under some form of community-based corrections (Kaeble and Alper, 2020). We have seen a steady downward trend in the number of people in community-based supervision, with 1 in 45 adults in the system in 2008, a 22 percent decrease over 12 years (Kaeble and Alper, 2020). For those who are incarcerated, plans for reentry into society begin early on. According to the Federal Bureau of Prisons (n.d.), plans for release begin from the first day of incarceration.

There is a desperate need for evidence-based programs both in the juvenile justice system and in community-based corrections. As the main goal of community-based programs is to keep the offender from reoffending and out of jail or prison, the only way to assess whether they work is through empirical studies. But as we will see in this chapter in the section of evidence-based programs, this is easier said than done. The Crime and Justice Institute and the National Institute of Corrections (2009, pp. x-xii) advise that the success of community-based corrections programs requires considerable investment of resources, including personnel, time, and money, as indicated by the eight principles of effective intervention and prevention:

1. Assess *actuarial risk* (statistical and algorithmic instruments that assist in determining the level of risk an individual possess for reoffending).
2. Enhance *intrinsic motivation* (internal motivation to do things, including living a law abiding life for other than material rewards).
3. Target interventions:
   - ■ *Risk Principle*: Prioritize supervision and treatment resources for higher risk offenders.
   - ■ *Need Principle*: Target interventions to criminogenic (correlated to crime) needs.
   - ■ *Responsivity Principle*: Be responsive to temperament, learning style, motivation culture, and gender when assigning programs.
   - ■ **Dosage**: Structure 40-70 percent of high-risk offenders' time for three to nine months.
   - ■ *Treatment Principle*: Integrate treatment into the full sentence/sanction requirements.

4. Skill training with directed practice (e.g., use *cognitive behavioral treatment* methods).
5. Increase positive reinforcement.
6. Engage ongoing support in natural communities.
7. Measure relevant processes/practices.
8. Provide measurement feedback.

The realities in implementing any or all of these principles is that they are only as effective as there is willingness of the convicted to accept help, are staff available, adequacy of training, as well as funding. We will see these three themes again in our discussion of evidence-based programs later in this chapter.

There are a number of forms of community-based corrections. The more commonly known are *probation* and *parole.* Community-based corrections are operated by specialized agencies, but can also include reporting centers, halfway houses, residential facilities, *work-release programs*, as well as partnership with rehabilitation services (PEW Center on the States, 2007). There are also faith-based programs that rely on religion for rehabilitation and reintegration into society.

Some of the accused have been let out on bail pretrial, others have had their cases dismissed before they have been arrested or released from jail because of a lack of evidence. More than half of the people who have been convicted of a crime will be given probation, which means that a majority of the accused or convicted, whether before or after spending time in jail, will be serving their time somewhere out in the community.

The backbone of community-based corrections, probation and parole, are terms that are often confused, just like the terms jail and prison. They are not interchangeable. Probation is generally in lieu of incarceration. Parole is at the back end of incarceration. Probation can, but does not always, include both jail time and a period of time where the convicted is required to report to a probation officer. Either way, probation and parole is the difference between custodial (incarcerated) and non-custodial (community-based corrections) sanctions, where a review of studies comparing the two have found that there is no difference between the two when it comes to reoffending (Villettaz, et al., 2015).

Intermediate sanctions are interchangeable with the front-end punishments that people may receive in lieu of jail or prison time. As Tonry and Will (1990) noted, besides probation, intermediate sanctions fill in the gap between probation and prison. This can also include some time served behind bars, called *shock probation*. This should not be confused with juvenile programs like Scared Straight, as this is not simply a visit to jail or prison for the day to talk about the horrors of incarceration with inmates or to be yelled at by corrections officers to simulate the prison experience.

Shock probation is a protracted period of time that the convicted is incarcerated after which there is early release, in hopes that the experience is so unpleasant that it acts as a deterrence to reoffending. Shock probation has the similar intended purposes as juvenile boot camps. Though designed to reduce recidivism, studies have indicated that there is relatively little difference between shock and regular probation on reoffending (Vito, et al., 1985), though there has been little research in recent years to indicate if this holds true today.

One of the main purposes of probation or parole is to extend to the convicted the opportunity to start their lives anew, as a form of forgiveness. If we use the analogy of a child on their first offense, parents may give them a stern warning with the threat of punishment if they continue to display the bad behavior. We should not view any form of community corrections, including probation or parole, as a "get out of jail free" card. There are conditions to any and all forms of community corrections, many of which the convicted fail to meet. This one reason is why the recidivism rates are so high.

Even the language used for probationers and parolees is gentler, similar to how labeling is different for juvenile offenders who have contact with the criminal justice system. Probationers and parolees are generally called "clients" by the officers and the systems that oversee their cases. Throughout this chapter we will be using the term "client" to those who are under community supervision.

Beyond that distinction, it is very clear by the job requirements of probation and parole officers, which can be as stringent in many ways as those for police officers, including academy training, that they are not simply there to provide counseling to probationers and parolees. If we take the example of the New Mexico Corrections Department, the state requires a number of hours of required training in physical fitness, as well as training in defensive tactics, plus in the use of tasers and batons (New Mexico Corrections Department, 2021). This is a good indication that the role of probation or parole officer goes beyond acting as a specialized social worker.

More recently, there have been heated discussions on whether university campus police should carry sidearms and of practices of police officers on the street as they approach suspects. Likewise, there are also discussions as to whether probation or parole officers should carry guns. Evidence indicates that most probation and parole officers would prefer to carry a firearm during the course of their duties, with approximately 65 percent of federal officers armed (Brown, 1990). Some states allow probation and parole officers to carry firearms, often requiring additional training and certification, with some states finding that it is a dangerous staffing problem when officers are not armed (Ammann, 2015). Given the example of Florida, in some states, even if probation and parole officers are allowed to carry firearms, it is at their own expense (Ammann, 2015).

HISTORY OF COMMUNITY-BASED CORRECTIONS

Releasing convicted criminals into the community is a relatively new concept. The more recent activist push for community-based corrections as alternatives to incarceration began in the mid-1960s, in response to a "punitive turn" in sentencing when a marked increase in incarceration began (Evans, 2021; Blackmore, 1980). It is an ongoing challenge for practitioners and researchers to find what works to reduce reoffending, while still giving out punishment that will satisfy the law, courts, victim(s), and the public. There is of course always the consideration as to what is in the best interest in public safety. Today, there are a number of options that judges have in sentencing that will keep convicted offenders out of prison or at least out of long jail sentences.

If you consider that the basis of community-based corrections is like going to a restaurant with the option of choosing from different entrees, sides, desserts, etc., with any number of permutations in order to create a complete meal, from appetizer to dessert. Judges have the discretion of sentencing offenders to any combination of home confinement, community service, fines, probation, rehabilitation, and/or a brief stint in jail. As long as the individual complies with the conditions of release to the community, they will be allowed to serve their sentence, or in the case of parole, the rest of their sentence, outside of jail or prison walls.

There are both defenders and critics of community solutions as alternatives to jail or prison time. Progressives and scholars see community supervision as the lesser of two evils between living on the outside with restrictions and being incarcerated (Cullen, et al., 2002). This is from a standpoint of offering offenders a means by which to remain grounded in their community, retain their relationships with their families, and continue to maintain a job. Community supervision also translates to a cost savings when the state or federal government is not footing the bill for their room and board and medical expenses.

Proponents of a more conservative viewpoint place their focus more on public safety and "get tough on crime" policies, which translates to jail or prison time for the offender. There is also a concern that relying too heavily on community-based corrections places an intangible burden on that system, increasing average caseloads of probation and parole officers (Still, et al., 2016). The key is in building legitimacy into the system so as to satisfy the opinions of both sides, including adequate staffing in community-based corrections.

Supervisors working in community-based corrections act as a deterrent between the offender and reoffending. Besides enforcing the conditions of release, they also stand as a barrier between the offender and potential victims. In addition to recent initiatives about developing a new paradigm for policing, there have been discussions about the need to focus on the health and psychiatric issues of probationers and parolees while they are under the jurisdiction of community-based corrections. Specifically, there is a redoubled effort to reform corrections in and out of jail and prisons to include addressing health issues, like the recent pandemic, as part of the public safety role of corrections (Sperber, 2020).

More recently, even though community-based corrections was intended to be an alternative to incarceration, critics, including corrections staff, prosecutors, defense attorneys, and activists argue that it is ineffectual in its current form. Probation and parole caseloads grew exponentially in the past three decades and in studies of effectiveness, community corrections has been found to be as much a contributor to mass incarceration as those committing new criminal offenses (Columbia Justice Labs, 2018).

The COVID-19 pandemic made those working in community-based corrections rethink the model. During the pandemic, to reduce the risks of spreading the virus, case managers of probationers and parolees had to resort to virtual meetings instead of face-to-face interviews (Cardwell, 2021). It is still too soon to tell if virtual meetings will be the new model for case managers and their clients or whether it has any impact on the effectiveness of community-based corrections. One drawback is that clients who are struggling financially may not have the means to go online for virtual meetings, as it requires smart phone technology, a tablet, or a computer with Internet access. To further complicate matters, pursuant to 18 U.S.C. §3563(b)(23), sex offenders may be required to relinquish their electronic devices with any capability of electronic communication, data storage, or media access (United States Courts, 2016a). The upside is that neither case manager nor client, when video meetings are available, needs to occupy the same physical space in order to connect with one another.

SELF-EFFICACY OF COMMUNITY-BASED CORRECTIONS CLIENTS

As on the outside, *self-efficacy* of prisoners to accomplish educational, training, and therapy goals is largely dependent on their own ability to be self-motivated. Though self-efficacy can be nurtured with the right mentoring, it is a combination of factors that contribute to successful self-starters, including their social environment, their behaviors, and cognitions (Allerd, et al., 2013; Bandura, 1986). In other words, there are a number of social psychological aspects that may be beyond the capability of individuals to successfully fulfil the requirements of their community-based corrections sentencing.

A number of tests can be administered to prisoners before they are released in order to determine how successful they will be in managing their own behaviors outside of prison. Among these is the *Multifactor Offender Readiness Model* (MORM) which measures how receptive offenders will be to court-ordered treatment or community-based programs (Hatcher and Roberts, 2019). Instead of assuming that offenders want to change, or conversely, have no desire to, data points like those that can be collected from the MORM and similar instruments enable supervisors to better implement appropriate programs and treatment or at least recommend them to the courts.

Programs, unfortunately, often tend to be "one size fits all," not taking into consideration that offenders may vary greatly in their level of commitment to turn their lives around. Hatcher and Roberts (2019) suggest that programs should be flexible so that the treatment program or setting can be modified in order to increase offenders' self-efficacy. In addition to an integrated approach and more customization of programs, any attempts to promote self-efficacy should include positive reinforcement (Varghese, et al., 2017).

PERSPECTIVES OF PROBATION AND PAROLE OFFICERS

Earlier in this book, we discussed the jail and prison experience, as seen through the eyes of corrections staff and the incarcerated. In this chapter, we will additionally discuss the experience and stresses of working in community-based corrections on staff. It is a unique situation as compared to correctional officers working behind bars, as probation and parole officers are required to go out in the community, often visiting their clients in their homes. This has the potential of being a dangerous situation for community-based corrections staff, as well as for social workers who may be required to make home visits. As we noted regarding changes in office appointments, home visits were also greatly impacted by the coronavirus pandemic. Home visits were extremely problematic in the face of social distancing requirements recommended by the Centers for Disease Control, and state and federal government mandates to prevent the spread of the virus. In some cases, the pandemic resulted in foregoing jailing or return to prison, when the client committed a technical violation (Schwartzapfel, 2020), discussed later in this chapter in situations where probation or parole might be revoked.

Home Visits

During home visits, probation and parole officers are trained to take note of a number of things, including changes in the lives of their clients that might not be so evident in an office appointment. Probation and parole officers take note of any unexplained changes, including in financial situation, mental health, substance abuse relapse, or any number of crises that put the client at risk for reoffending (United States Courts, 2016b). This can be a dangerous situation for the probation or parole officer making a home visit, especially in the evening hours, sometimes requiring back up from a police officer, ideally with the police acting as a passive onlooker (Alarid, 2015; Alarid, et al., 2011). For probationers under intense supervision, there may be little relief from surveillance.

As in the case of many parts of the criminal justice system and criticism of invasion of privacy, there is the question as to at what point offenders can begin their post-incarceration lives without fear of constant surveillance. There is the added issue that if the probationer or parolee is living with family or friends, essentially everyone in the household is subject to a home visit. Probation or parole officers can exert pressure on other residents in the home to assist in surveillance, as well as being under surveillance themselves (Sandoval, 2020).

Home visits by parole officers is one of the reasons that some convicts choose to serve their complete sentence in prison and be released into the community without parole, so that they do not have to fear a corrections supervisor knocking on their door at all hours of the day or night for a home visit or making invasive phone calls.

ADULT PROBATION

As many people are incarcerated, far greater numbers are on *probation*. According to the PEW Charitable Trusts (2018), there are approximately 4.5 million people on probation in the United States. This figure more than tripled in the last four decades (The Pew Charitable Trusts, 2018). This is not an indication that judges are becoming more lenient, but rather a function of increased convictions, particularly for recreation drug use.

There is always the question as to whether the wealthy are more likely to get probation, whereas the poor get prison. After all, as we have noted elsewhere in the book, your legal representation often is only as good as what you can afford. Wealthy people are also in better positions to pay monetary fines. As Reiman and Leighton point out in their seminal work, *The Rich Get Richer and the Poor Get Prison* (2012), the poor are disadvantaged from start to finish in the criminal justice system.

Diversion Programs

Diversion programs can be part of the conditions of probation. The most common ones we see in adult community corrections are for anger management, domestic violence education, and drug treatment. Diversion programs or therapy may be set up as outpatient care or require voluntary or involuntary institutionalization for a period of time. After a client has completed a program or treatment, they are reassessed and may or may not continue to be on probation. In some cases, a client may have to complete more than one program as a condition of their probation, as in the example of someone who has substance abuse issues and also requires anger management therapy. Increasingly, states are mandating that police act as intermediaries and instead of arrest, will refer an individual on a first offense to behavior health professionals rather than booking them into jail (Kopak, 2020).

Diversion programs are not always successful, as any type of treatment program requires the willingness of the participant to change. Kopak's study (2020) indicates that those with more serious mental health problems are more likely to be rearrested, making practitioners and judges rethink the value of diversion programs for more severely affected individuals. For example, unless someone with schizophrenia is willing to take medication to control their illness, once they are out from under supervision, any program is useless in preventing them from ending up unhoused or in jail, without intervention. Another issue is that the offender can be required to pay for a diversion program, if there is no grant or public funding for it, in which case the poor are disadvantaged further.

Intensive Supervision Probation

Not all probation sanctions are equal. If we take the example of drunk driving offenses, in some states, on the first offense the convicted may never have to meet with a case manager, yet is still on probation. Depending on the offense, particularly in the case of drug convictions or other more serious offenses, the probation client has to see their probation officer much more often, sometimes a few times a week for both updates and drug testing. When there is much more supervision and surveillance of a convict on probation, we call this *intensive supervision probation* or *ISP*, for short. For obvious reasons, probation officers who handle these cases have fewer clients, but spend much more time with the ones that they have.

There are some thoughts that ISP is nearly as intrusive to one's life as time in jail or prison. The increased use of ISP for violent offenders rather than prison time is largely due to finding alternative forms of social control on convicts in recent decades because of prison overcrowding (Hyatt and Barnes, 2017). The higher the risk the client will reoffend, the greater likelihood they will be placed in ISP, which of course is only as effective as they are receptive to the supervision and treatment plans. Unfortunately, research has found that ISP has little to no effect on reoffending, as compared to other forms of community-based corrections (Hyatt and Barnes, 2017).

PAROLE

As much as the public may clamor for convicts to serve their full sentence, most have the opportunity to be released early, either due to a parole board decision, overcrowding, or for good behavior while incarcerated. Parole, like probation, does not mean that the individual is free to do anything they like. It is a conditional release with many of the same conditions as probation as discussed in the next section. Failure to comply with the conditions of parole will result in it being revoked and the individual will be returned to prison to serve more or all of their sentence.

There are two types of parole (1) *discretionary parole*, which is granted by a parole board, and (2) *mandatory release,* which means that as part of sentencing, prisoners are given credit for *good time earned*, and placed on community supervision for the remainder of their sentence. So if you consider a sentence of

25 years to life, it means that the convict will not be released on parole any sooner than after 25 years have been served, but could be held for the rest of their lives, depending on their behavior while incarcerated. Those who have been released on parole are required, in most cases, to serve a percentage of their original sentence behind bars.

Of course, there are those who are sentenced to life in prison, without the possibility of parole. Except for judges and juries who look at the statistical probability of whether someone will reoffend, much sentencing to life in prison is a bit arbitrary and dependent on which jurisdiction the offense took place. Life without the possibility of parole was viewed as a more merciful solution than the death penalty (Lerner, 2015). One of the condemnations of the current criminal justice system in America is that decisions on sentencing are political and possibly a function of the public's ignorance, including juries, of true crime rates, demanding severe punishment when it is not always deserved (Beale, 2006).

Parole Boards

Parole boards take into consideration a number of factors before releasing a convict into the community on parole. Even if a sentence promises the possibility of parole, there is no guarantee that it will be granted. If we take the infamous case of Charles Manson, during his incarceration he was up for conditional release a number of times after his sentence was reduced from the death penalty to life in prison with the possibility of parole. This held true as well with three members of his cult ("Manson Family") who were or are behind bars.

The public was horrified at the prospect of any of the Manson Family being released, especially since one of the victims, Sharon Tate, was eight months pregnant at the time of her murder. Because of the notoriety of the case and the brutality of the murders, as many times as Manson went before a parole board, sometimes contrite, sometimes making a mockery of the proceedings, he was forever denied parole. Manson died in prison at 82 years of age. A number of excerpts from his parole hearings can be viewed on YouTube.com:

- Charles Manson: 30 Years of Parole Hearings (2012), available at https://www .youtube.com/watch?v=rtWwdzD6vd0.
- Charles Manson_Parole hearing (1992), available at https://www.youtube.com/ watch?v=glU-xBxbZbo.
- Charles Manson_Parole Hearing (1997), available at https://www.youtube.com/ watch?v=xUaMTdDew1s.
- Charles Manson Parole Hearing (2012), available at https://www.youtube.com/ watch?v=3P1TbDRsUVo.

In total, Charles Manson was denied parole 11 times. His final in-person denial was in 2007; he chose not to appear at his 2012 parole hearing (Charlesmanson. com, n.d.).

Reentry

As we noted in Chapter 6 on prison culture, there are two times when prisoners are the most likely to feel a heightened sense of dread or fear. The first time is on their first day in prison. The second is when they are preparing to leave. For many of the newly released, there is much uncertainty, including whether they will be able to make it on the outside. *Reentry* into society is a complex process with a number of moving parts, including self-efficacy, discussed earlier, support systems, including family and friends, and availability of social services in the community where they are released.

The difficulty is in returning the offender back into the community where they offended in the first place. Much of this is well out of their control, based on the jurisdiction in charge of their probation, parole, or other community-based corrections, as well as where the offender considers to be home. As Simes (2019), observed, one's neighborhood is often inherited, based on life chances and economic status. If we consider that 57 percent of people in the United States have never lived outside their current state, and 37 percent have never even left their hometown, with only a small percentage of people experiencing some form of mobility (Cohn and Morin, 2008), it is probable that convicts will serve their community-based sentencing close to where they offended.

GENERAL CONDITIONS OF PROBATION AND PAROLE

There are some general conditions and requirements of probation and parole that are universal, although these might vary by jurisdiction[1]:

- Must pay all fees and/or fines ordered by the court.
- Must stay in the jurisdiction of the court and can only leave with written permission to do so.
- Must obey all court orders and conditions of probation or parole.
- Must obey all municipal, state, and federal laws.
- Must attend regular meetings with probation or parole officer, as mandated by court and as part of sentencing to probation.
- Probationers and parolees are expected to avoid others who are committing crimes.
- Probationers and parolees are required to contact their probation or parole officers if they have been arrested for a crime.
- Probation officer, parole officer, or law enforcement may enter and search the person or residence of the probationer or parole at any time with or without a warrant or probable cause, but on "reasonable grounds." (See *Griffin v. Wisconsin*, 483 U.S. 868, 1987; *United States v. Knights*, 534 U.S. 112, 2001)

---

[1] These conditions have been triangulated from a number of state websites, as well from the United States Courts (2016) and only include the conditions that are in common, in most jurisdictions.

- Same applies to the search of the probationer's or parolee's personal vehicle.
- Must notify the probation or parole officer if there is a change of residence or in employment.
- Often required to submit to random drug and alcohol tests, including breath, blood and urine collection, particularly in the case of drug or alcohol related offenses.
- Cannot possess any pharmaceutical drugs unless they are medically prescribed.
- May not possess fire arms.

Conditions of probation may also include directions from probation officers, or *probation officer directives.* However, any condition that a probation officer places on a client is temporary, and will only be made permanent if approved by the courts (Barklage, et al., 2006).

Substance abuse continues to be one of the main reasons that probationers and parolees fail to meet the conditions of their release to the community. Those who successfully complete drug and/or alcohol treatment programs are less likely to reoffend (Degiorgio and DiDonato, 2012; Huebner and Cobbina, 2007; Vito, et al., 1990). There are a number of other risk factors that are taken into consideration when granting probation or parole. One of the key factors is the amount to which the individual carries the weight of the responsibility for their offending. Other risks include the following (Degiorgio and DiDonato, 2012):

- The extent to which they are being truthful, not defensive or guarded, and are not attempting to fake being "good."
- The extent to which they harbor violent tendencies.
- The extent to which they display aggressive behavior.
- The extent to which they are antisocial, refusing to conform to social norms and mores.
- The extent to which they lack empathy for their victims.
- The extent to which they lack appropriate stress coping abilities.

Any one of these could be cause to fail conditions of probation or parole, with the risk of having probation or parole revoked increasing with every added risk factor.

SPECIAL CONDITIONS OF PROBATION AND PAROLE

In addition to general conditions of probation or parole, the following may also apply, along with other restrictions:

- Notifying probation or parole officer if probationer or parolee leaves the jurisdiction.

- May have to complete community service as a condition of probation.
- A nighttime curfew may be applied.
- May be required to be on house arrest and/or wear an ankle monitor to track their movements.
- Depending on the offense, may have limited driving privileges (e.g., only to and from work).
- Restitution may be required to the victim or victims.
- May have to enter treatment for alcohol/drug abuses, domestic violence, and/or anger management, at the cost of the probationer or parolee.
- May be required to complete a sex offender program and report as a sex offender to local police department.
- Must be actively seeking employment, if currently unemployed, or pursuing an educational degree or job training.
- May be required to sell personal assets in order to pay for restitution.

Special conditions of probation or parole can be tailored to the offender and to the offense, and is to the discretion of the court what these might be. We should also note that reporting to a probation or parole officer may be allowed in person, by mail, or by telephone, depending on the conditions of release to community-based supervision.

PROBATION AND PAROLE VIOLATIONS

There are two ways that a probationer or parolee can violate the conditions of their serving their time in the community, both of which can land the individual back into jail or prison. The most obvious reason for sending someone back to jail or prison is if they commit another crime, called *substantive violations*.

The second reason for having probation or parole revoked is called a *technical violation*. The individual has not committed a new crime, but rather simply has failed to do something that is part of the bureaucratic procedures required of them. These procedures include, for example, failing to report a change of address, missing a probation or parole meeting, failing to get or keep a job, or any number of violations that do not involve committing a new crime. Technical violations can include the prohibited use of alcohol, even if they are old enough to drink, if it is a condition of their release into the community. Probationers and parolees can be routinely tested for drug and alcohol use. It is particularly unfortunate that there are those individuals who find themselves back behind bars for a technical violation.

One of the most common ways that the convicted released to community corrections get into trouble is with their addictions. Any addiction, whether it is to alcohol, or to legal or illegal drugs, puts the addicted at risk for not only failing to hold down a job but needing an illegal means by which to pay for their habit. In more recent years, the greatest concern has been the use of heroin and prescription opioids among those who are in some part of community corrections. Those at greatest risk for concurrently using both opioids and benzodiazepines (e.g., valium, Xanax), for individuals with drug-related offenses are white females who are married, use cannabis[2], and have been prescribed psychiatric medications (Cropsey, et al., 2015). Substance abuse often reduces inhibitions, in which case the conditions of probation or parole become meaningless.

There are some probation or parole officers and judges who will forgive an indiscretion or two, letting the individual off with a warning if they fail to meet one or more conditions of their release from custody. However, if the probationer or parolee continues to show a pattern of disregarding the conditions of their release, they can find themselves behind bars once again. A great number of those taken into custody have committed probation or parole violations.

One notorious example of repeated probation violations is that of Darryl Strawberry, once a gifted baseball player who played for a number of major league teams, including the New York Yankees, whose actions landed him in a Florida prison in 2002 because he violated the conditions of his probation for 1999 convictions on drug and solicitation of prostitution charges (CBS News, 2002). Sent an extraordinary six times to rehabilitation by the courts instead of prison, he continued to violate the conditions of his probation sentencings, one time escaping a treatment center and embarking on a cross-state drug binge (CBS News, 2002). Strawberry's example of continued drug abuses is not an uncommon story for ordinary drug addicts, though there is some speculation that due to Strawberry's popularity as a professional athlete, he may have been given preferential treatment and more chances by the courts.

The same can hold true for those who are out on bail as well, though generally they have a bit more freedom than probationers or parolees. If they commit further crimes or violate conditions of their release (e.g., by leaving the jurisdiction without permission), they can find themselves in jail pretrial with their bail revoked. It is due to violations of conditions of release, whether for those out on bail, probationers or parolees, that the criminal justice system often looks like a revolving door with the same offenders.

ENVIRONMENTAL MODEL OF PROBATION AND PAROLE

With recidivism rates being what they are, looking for a solution has been a priority in the criminal justice system in the United States. In the overall push to reform the criminal justice system, experts argue that it is necessary to not only find solutions to prison overcrowding, but also to consider reinventing community supervision (Cullen, et al., 2002).

One solution in the quest to reduce recidivism is to look at conditions outside of the client that is contributing to criminal offending. Whereas traditional

---

[2] We should note that recreational cannabis use is legal in some states, though it continues to be illegal at the federal level in the United States.

approaches to probation and parole focus on the individual, environmental corrections focus on criminological theories that place the blame of crime on the environment in which the criminal lives (Schaefer, et al., 2015).

COMMUNITY SERVICE

Community service is an interesting construct in community-based corrections. When we ordinarily think of volunteers, we think of them as selfless philanthropists, devoting their extra time to favorite causes. For instance, a dog or cat lover may spend time volunteering at an animal rescue shelter. Or those who wish to lend a hand to the poor or unhoused may volunteer at a soup kitchen.

Some forms of community service, however, are stigmatizing_and not really voluntary. For example, a probationer or inmate may be ordered to pick up trash on the side of the road for the community service component of their sentence. They may have to wear Department of Corrections garb while doing so, traveling to the destination by a DOC van, as depicted in the following photo of inmates picking up trash. This visibility signals to observers traveling by on the highway that the individual did something bad to warrant community service hours, leaving it up to the imaginations of the passersby as to just how bad the offense may have been.

Prison Inmates Working on the Side of the Road to Cut Weeds, Trim Grass, Pick Up Trash. Work Release, Lincoln, Nebraska, USA. (*Source:* Petryszyn, Morning Journal, 2012, Retrieved from https://bit.ly/3L8Idme)

Community service is sometimes intended to act as a form of shock therapy. For example, the actress Lindsay Lohan, after failing at a number of attempts at probation for drunk driving and cocaine possession charges, was eventually ordered in 2011 to the Los Angeles County coroner's office, where she was assigned to cleaning toilets and emptying the trash (*Los Angeles Times*, 2011). The paparazzi predictably were staked out to catch her coming or going from the facility (*Los Angeles Times*, 2011). To some extent, this is a *shaming and reintegration* approach to community service. In spite of her community service, Lohan eventually was ordered to spend 90 days in jail, after failing to regularly attend mandatory meetings and drug treatment (Duke, 2012). Due to overcrowding in the L.A. County jail, Lohan only spent 14 days of her 90-day sentence behind bars (Duke, 2012).

There is, however, a public misconception that celebrities get off easy for drug or drunk-driving charges and that they are more likely to be sent to rehabilitation or receive community service. This is a function of two realities of the lives of celebrities. First, they very well may have the financial means to hire lawyers who are extremely knowledgeable about noncustodial options, including rehabilitation (American Addiction Centers, n.d.). Second, celebrities are relatively low-risk offenders, less likely to be dealing in drugs, and not presenting a major flight risk as it is much more difficult for them to simply disappear into a crowd because of the public's familiarity with them (American Addiction Centers, n.d.).

ELECTRONIC MONITORING AND OTHER FORMS OF SURVEILLANCE TECHNOLOGY

Electronic Monitoring

A rather expensive alternative to incarceration is *electronic monitoring* (EM), more specifically, the use of ankle bracelets. Though electronic monitoring of the accused and convicted seems like fairly new technology, it has been tested for a number of decades in a various forms, starting with experiments back in the early 1960s (Corbett and Pattavina, 2015). There are two forms of technologies used in electronic monitoring. The two types include utilizing radio frequency (RF) and global positioning (GPS) monitoring.

The more advanced of the two, GPS monitoring technology was released from strict military use in the 1990s and EM made the leap to satellite technology to monitor offenders. But as we know from using GPS in our automobiles or on devices used in hiking, GPS can fail in areas where satellite signals are blocked. As Goodman (2021, retrieved from https://axleaddict.com/safety/Disadvantages -of-GPS) cautions, the seven disadvantages of GPS[3], whether for our own personal use or in the monitoring of prisoners are:

---

[3] The disadvantages of GPS that directly affect probationer or parolee monitoring are noted with an *.

1. Inaccuracy;*
2. Lack of local knowledge;
3. Driving distraction;
4. Signal or battery failure;*
5. Reliance on the U.S. Department of Defense;*
6. Privacy issues and crime.* and
7. Commercial exploitation.

The original intent of the devices was to provide positive reinforcement of good behavior. It was viewed by one of the early innovators, Harvard researcher Ralph Schwitzgebel, as a tool to achieve rehabilitation goals with the use of behavioral modification methods, with a capability of supervisors having direct communication with their clients through the bracelets (Corbett and Pattavina, 2015; Fox, 1987). A side note, according to legend, it wasn't until 1977 that EM came into practical use in monitoring offenders as a result of a district court judge in Albuquerque, New Mexico, who was inspired by a Spider-Man comic that depicted a criminal attaching a bracelet to the crime fighter to keep electronic track of his whereabouts (Fox, 1987).

EM has various uses in community-based corrections. EM may be used for individuals who are pretrial, on probation, or in some cases, even on parole (Weiss, 2019). The purpose of EM is to support orders of house arrest or confinement and monitor the movement of the wearer. The ankle bracelet emits a trackable GPS signal and will be triggered if the wearer steps outside their designated area that is programmed into the device. For some offenders, they are strictly forbidden to leave their homes. Others are allowed to leave, but only for work. EM was infamously highlighted by Martha Stewart's post-prison experience, where she was ordered to wear an ankle bracelet, even though she was allowed to leave her Connecticut home to go to her offices in New York City.

Ankle bracelets are not just programmed to follow movement. One criticism of EM is that the ankle bracelets can also be used to call and record people's conversations without their consent, which questions whether this is a violation of 5th Amendment rights (Weiss, 2019). So when this ability is available to corrections supervisors, those on probation or parole may have even less conversation privacy than what they experience while incarcerated.

Like any technology, ankle bracelets require maintenance and are not always reliable, leaving many to question as to whether the cost of EM is worth it. Most of what we see in studies of whether EM is utilized are the financial and technological implications (Maglione, 2019). Ankle bracelets are subject to removal by the convicted, in which case they can leave it at home as they disregard orders to stay home and allows them to go out into the community. Historically monitors have been able to detect movement by the offender ordered to wear them, but not necessarily tampering. There is also the question as to whether they can still offend at home, as in the case of a drug addict having their supply brought to them by friends or family members.

Alcohol Breathalyzers

EM is not exclusively the only technology to monitor or modify the behavior of convicts who serve time in community-based corrections. As most of us are aware, particularly those who are studying criminal justice, *breathalyzers* are used by police officers to determine whether someone is driving with an alcohol level above legal limits (e.g., Driving While Intoxicated offense, commonly known as a DWI). Alcohol breathalyzers may also be ordered in the case of an individual who has been given probation, particularly on alcohol-related offenses. Some are programs to prevent vehicles from being started include installation of an *ignition interlock device*, as seen in the diagram below. The ignition interlock device is not meant to be punitive, but rather to try and prevent additional alcohol-related highway deaths.

A number of studies have demonstrated the effectiveness of requiring an ignition interlock, for obvious reasons. When the ignition interlock device works, as long as the offender does not try and drive someone else's vehicle, they will have an inoperable car if they fail the breathalyzer test, hence keeping them off the road. There are retest safeguards built in, as noted in the diagram below, that prevent someone else who has not been drinking alcohol to blow into the breathalyzer for (Shulman-Laniel, 2017). However, as the United States Government Accounting Office (2015) has argued, the problem continues to be in getting them installed in more vehicles. It is not for lack of trying: "According to NHTSA [National Highway Transportation Safety Administration], currently all states [in the United States]

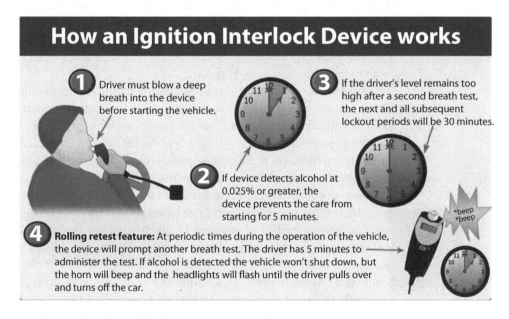

FIGURE 12.1 | **Ignition Interlock Devices.**
(*Source*: Fight DUI Charges, n.d., retrieved from https://www.fightduicharges.com/ignition-interlock-device/)

have enacted legislation requiring or permitting the use of ignition interlocks and they generally follow the same overall installation and removal process, according to Association of Ignition Interlock Program Administrators." (U.S. Government Accounting Office, 2015, p. 6). By 2016, all 50 states had ignition interlock laws in diverse forms. In 27 states, all convicted DWI offenders are required to install the device as part of their sentencing, while in 21 states, some, but not all offenders are mandated to have an ignition interlock device (Schulman-Laniel, et al., 2017). The good news is that ignition interlock devices reduce recidivism as much as 65 percent in the case of repeat DWI offenders, as compared to those who did not have one installed on their car (Shulman-Laniel, et al., 2017).

DRUG COURTS

For some decades, there has been a shift in thinking of drug dependence as strictly a criminal justice problem. More recently, drug addiction leading to arrest is viewed as a public health issue, as given the example of the recent rise in prescription drug abuses. Instead of going through the traditional criminal court system, nonviolent drug offenders are more frequently referred to *drug courts*. The first drug court was initiated in the state of Florida in 1989 (Csete, 2019). There have been, modestly speaking, some successes with the drug courts. For example, a 15-year study of Baltimore City's Drug Treatment Court found that there were "significantly fewer unique arrests, total charges and total drug, property, and person charges" (Kearley and Gottfredson, 2020, p. 419), signifying that it is a viable solution for drug addicted offenders.

Successful graduates of drug court programs have distinct advantages over individuals who have spent time in prison, instead being diverted to rehabilitation programs. They are more likely to remain crime-free, stabilize family relationships, and maintain employment as compared to individuals who have served prison time (Gibbs and Lytle, 2020). Successful graduates can also be rewarded by the court by having their charges dismissed, relieving them from the stigma of a conviction (Gibbs and Lytle, 2020).

The drug court model has been adopted in other countries across the globe. Since 2016, The United Nations has encouraged member states to take similar treatment over prison-oriented approaches used in the United States (Csete, 2019). However much encouraging that the drug court model has been in the United States, it has not been universally successful elsewhere. It has all but disappeared from England and Wales, after encountering institutional and operational failings during a brief pilot of the model in those U.K. countries (Collins, 2019).

In theory, drug courts are supposed to act as both an alternative to incarceration as well as finding help for the drug addicted (Csete, 2019). In reality, suspected offenders and reoffenders are not uniformly diverted to drug courts.

FURLOUGHS AND WORK-RELEASE PROGRAMS

Furloughs

Release from prison in advance of parole or completion of a sentence is rare, and it more commonly happens due to prison overcrowding. However, under certain circumstances, inmates can be issued a *furlough* or temporary release, in which they can leave the prison for a brief period of time. However, they are required to return to prison after the furlough runs out. It is one means through which prisoners have an opportunity to ease into life on the outside before their release back into the "real world," and it gives parole officers an opportunity to see how well they will adjust (Smith and Milan, 1973).

Some of the reasons why a person who is incarcerated in jail or prison might be allowed to leave a prison temporarily include for medical treatment that cannot be done in the facility or to encourage convicts to maintain family ties while incarcerated by means of a social furlough. There are two types of furloughs: escorted and unescorted. Furloughed prisoners who pose a minimal risk of reoffending or failing to report back to prison, particularly those housed in minimum security prisons, are most likely allowed an unescorted furlough (*Prisonology*™, n.d.). However, there are occasions when an individual does not meet the security or custodial requirements to be unescorted, in which case they will be accompanied by correctional staff (*Prisonology*™, n.d.). For example, a woman who is pregnant in prison and experiences complications requiring medical care in a hospital is most likely going to be escorted and, as we saw in the chapter on women in prison, cuffed to the hospital bed.

There is, however, as in the case of release on bail, the risk that the individual will fail to return to jail, unless they are closely monitored while on furlough. Furloughs are not automatic and have to be applied for, but only after the prisoner has served a substantial amount of their sentence.

Work-Release Programs

For the lucky few (and the trusted), inmates are allowed to keep their current employment or begin a new job in programs that are designed to encourage inmates to earn a living on the outside, while still serving their jail or prison sentences from behind bars. Employment placement of prisoners in work-release programs, it may very well be the turning point where former convicts have a legitimate alternative to returning to crime in order to make a living. Studies of causes of recidivism indicate that one of the primary reasons, beyond addiction, for offenders to return to prison after release is due to challenges in finding and keeping employment (Varghese, et al., 2017). If prisoners are allowed to get a head start in seeking employment in advance of their release, there is a greater chance that they will not return to jail or prison.

Work-release programs allow for the incarcerated to be in a better position to support their families as well as pay any court-ordered restitution. The ability to find work is not guaranteed with work-release programs without career counseling and some people have a greater capacity to find employment after incarceration. Women, younger offenders, and those who have had visitors while in prison have much better odds of finding employment post-release (Duwe, 2015).

Additional gender differences exist between men and women participating in work-release programs. Jones Young, et al. (2019) found the following as far as feelings of preparedness among men and women who are allowed to participate in these programs:

1. Women feel that their training is less valued. This could be due to general gender differences in employment, where women are more likely to occupy lower-paying positions.
2. Women and men feel differently about the level of occupational training help that they are receiving. Again, this may be a function of gendered work training, discussed in Chapter 6.
3. Women and men have different work experiences prior to being incarcerated.
4. Frequency of incarceration has an effect on how supported men and women feel in their work-release programs.

This complements Duwe's (2015) work, in that women may be more likely to find work after incarceration, as they have traditionally been paid less than men, in the absence of equal pay legislation (e.g. ratified Equal Rights Amendment). This makes them more attractive employees, as companies look to their profit margins and bottom line. That does not mean that women are happier in the jobs they find after incarceration, nor with their training options during work-release programs.

More recently, the COVID-19 pandemic has resulted in challenges to prison work-release programs. With convicts allowed out into the community, there was greater risk of their bringing back the virus to prison facilities. This in turn, sadly, resulted in greater infection and mortality rates in prisons where there are work-release programs (Dunne, et al., 2021).

In some cases, it is an impossibility for convicts to find meaningful work without job training beyond what can be provided in prison. In this case, particularly for prisoners who were enrolled in community college or university, they may be allowed to leave the prison to attend classes in *study-release programs*. But these are not common programs, as there are increased opportunities in recent decades, at least in some facilities, to complete GEDs or college courses.

Halfway Houses

One alternative to releasing individuals into the community with minimal or no supervision, is to release them to residential reentry facilities, more commonly known as *halfway houses*. These are group homes that provide continued support after prison as well as some supervision. This allows the individual to ease back into society with the safety net of more accountability. According to the Bureau of Prisons, residential reentry facilities reduce recidivism, by assisting with employment, housing, and substance abuse issues, plus continuity with mental and medical health treatments (U.S. Federal Bureau of Prisons, n.d.).

One controversy of halfway houses is that they are rarely welcomed in communities. In the same vein as where prisons are built, and as we discussed earlier in the book, there can be a "not in my backyard" (NIMBY) response from the community where proposed halfway houses are going to be located. There are misconceptions of the impact of halfway houses in neighborhoods. The general fears are that property values will plummet and they will attract more crime. However, a 2002 study conducted by George Washington University in conjunction with the Justice Policy Institute in Northeast Washington found that there is more crime around popular grocery stores and public libraries than around halfway houses; property values were not affected by their presence and, in fact, though not correlated, they went up as much as the general housing market did (Fern, 2002).

For some prisoners, if they have spent a longer time incarcerated, leaving prison can be as frightening as entering it. As one ex-convict explains, for some, prison feels safer than the streets where there are far more unknowns and uncertainties. Prison, to a large extent, offers a predictable routine. Counselors in reentry programs often times find that the biggest challenge is to finding predictability on the outside for ex-convicts, including housing and work.

The same problems that landed them in prison often haunt them in prison and after release. These include low education attainment, mental health issues, substance abuse, and communicable diseases. According to the TReND Wyoming organization, a group dedicated to working with ex-offenders with mental health and substance abuse issues, the four biggest challenges to those who are released from prison, are the following (Jackson, 2020, retrieved from https://www.trendwyoming .org/articles/biggest-challenges-after-prison-release/):

1. Not knowing where to begin because there are so many moving parts with reentry (e.g., reconnecting with family, friends, finding work, etc.).
2. Family strain because parolees and the released rely heavily on family for support and assistance with reentry. However, this can put emotional and financial strain on families of the formerly incarcerated.
3. Finding employment as most employers ask for information on criminal records. If these are not asked for, at the very least, offenders have to explain the gap in their employment records whether it is months or years.
4. Mental health issues plague a great number of ex-convicts, regardless of whether they existed prior to prison or arose due to the conditions of prison. These include depression, anxiety, and addiction, all of which are difficult for both the released and for the families and friends trying to support them as they attempt to transition back into society.

AFTERCARE FOR PROBATIONERS AND FORMER PRISONERS

Key to the success of community corrections is cooperation and partnership with community programs and local law enforcement agencies. Perhaps one of the most important partnerships is between mental health providers and community corrections. There is considerable overlap between those who are psychiatric practitioners and those who work in probation and parole, as well as with social workers. The partnerships are, however, only as successful as the clients are willing to be referred to mental health services, much less willing to benefit from treatment.

There are, some disconnects between mental health providers and probation and parole officers. As Lasher and Stinson note (2020), mental health providers and community corrections supervisors measure outcome differently: treatment providers focus on competence and ethical concerns whereas community corrections supervisors focus on measurable successes with their clients. Also, the level of training required for mental health providers with masters and Ph.D. or MD degrees generally differs from that of probation and parole officers who may only be required to have earned a bachelor's degree. However, it is becoming increasingly more common to see probation and parole officers with advanced degrees in psychology or criminal justice.

Faith-Based Programs

As we saw in our study of religion playing a role in the rehabilitation of prisoners in our chapter on the history of corrections, *faith-based programs* continue to be an alternative to secular programs. The earliest documented faith-based program is thought to be through the Roman Catholic Church, where beginning in 1488, condemned prisoners were given spiritual guidance and consoled in advance of their execution (Zimmer, 2004/2005). Faith-based programs continue to be a voluntary part of prisoner rehabilitation beyond for those condemned to death for their crimes. Since the mid-1970s, faith-based programs ran by private organizations have resulted in reduced rates of recidivism (Zimmer, 2004/2005).

Faith-based programs in community-based corrections can also include focus on family reunification. For example, the Celebrate Recovery program, in addition to bible studies, offers a 14-week Strengthen Family program that includes training in parenting and social/life skills (Roberts and Stacer, 2017). Again, like other programs, faith-based programs are only as effective as people believe it will work or in the case of religion, are open to a religious solution for change.

SEX OFFENDER REGISTRY

One type of offender who can virtually never live their crime down are those who have been convicted of a serious sex offense. For those who have been convicted of the most heinous of sex offenses, including rape, sex with a minor, child pornography, sex trafficking, and in some states, prostitution, cannot hide their crimes from the public eye. Those convicted of serious sex crimes are required as a condition of their release from custody, whether on probation or on parole, to register as a sex offender on the sex offender registry in their state.

EVIDENCE-BASED PROGRAMS IN ADULT COMMUNITY CORRECTIONS

If, as a criminal justice student, you are required to also take statistics courses, there is a very good reason you are being asked to do so. Increasingly every part of the criminal justice system relies on statistical analysis in order to find more effective ways to control crime. Data analysis is also critical in the course of grant writing, where there has to be some evidence that a new program will actually work. Hence, as noted by the U.S. Bureau of Justice contention, "impartial, timely, and accurate statistical data are essential to guide and inform federal, state, and local policymaking on crime and the administration of justice and to improve the quality of and access to information used for decision making." (U.S. Bureau of Justice Statistics, 2020, retrieved from https://www.ojp.gov/topics/research-statist ics-evaluation#:~:text=Impartial%2C%20timely%2C%20and%20accurate%20stat istical,information%20used%20for%20decision%20making. This holds true for corrections programs in and out of prison.

As frustration has mounted on the stagnanting numbers for recidivism, there has been demand since the 1970s to move away from "nothing works" to taking a closer look at "what works" in prison and community-based corrections, by turning to evidence-based programs with proven track records. However, we cannot emphasize enough that the vast majority of programs never receive rigorous testing or academic study to see if they are really working, beyond superficial evaluations or relying on anecdotal stories. In some cases, as is common elsewhere in social services, programs are abandoned before they have had adequate time to be evaluated as to whether they have potential to reduce recidivism. Other programs are so institutionalized that it is difficult to get policy makers to change course to try new ones.

We first discussed evidence-based programs or EBPs in our chapter on juvenile offenders. We should be cautioned that any empirical study of community corrections is only as good as the data, and what might seem promising today based on evidence, may be proven to be ineffectual under closer scrutiny. What we do know it that it is more difficult for researchers to get their hands on information about failed studies, as those inevitably do not get published in academic journals. The other problem is in selection biases, where because of the size of the programs, probability sampling is a challenge. And as Roberts and Stacer (2017) stated, there are generally no comparison groups to see whether programs really work, not to mention the ethics of having a control group that receives no treatment or that does not participate in pilot programs when it comes to attempts to reduce recidivism.

The key features of evaluating any corrections program, including those that are community based is risk prevention and risk reduction (Bryne and Pattavina, 2006). Within the past decade, there has been a heightened demand for evidence-based programs in and out of prison (Roberts and Stacer, 2017). More importantly, program evaluations have become increasingly crucial to funding opportunities, from both the government and private sectors. The double bind of program evaluations is that not only do the programs cost money, but the assessments themselves can be expensive as well, particularly if outside evaluators are called in. This is where valuable partnerships between research institutes, like universities, and community based-corrections, public health agencies are important to reduce costs, where academic scholars, including graduate students, may be willing to conduct the evaluations for free, in exchange for using the data in their research.

There is also the problem of a program working in one location, but not working elsewhere for a variety of reasons, the least of which is that they may not be uniformly implemented in all places where it is being used. This can be a function of inadequate or inconsistent training, as noted by Gottfredson and Gottfredson (1997) in their study of school-based gang prevention programs. Programs are only as good as those who run them, the faith of participants that they will work, or the funding available to support them.

We should also note that the vast majority of community-based correction programs have not been empirically tested for effectiveness. In an interview with the PEW Center on the States, Petersilia (2007) estimated that as many as 99 percent of all programs have not undergone scientific evaluation and it is impossible to know which programs really work. Unfortunately, whether we are discussing front-end preventative programs or aftercare, there is a tendency to latch on to whatever program looks to be the latest innovation, without necessarily having any evidence that they will work. What we mostly see evaluated are large-scale federally funded programs (PEW Center on the States 2007). What follows is a sample of some community-based programs that have been proven to be effective in evidence-based evaluations.

Using Statistics in Sentencing

Judges will often consider what type of community corrections is appropriate for the convicted, dependent on the severity of the crime, prior criminal record, work history, and the extent to which the victim may have been injured. Judges are also increasingly using classification decision algorithms. Translation: statistics and evidence based practices are being used in order to determine how appropriate the sentencing is, depending on certain data points of the offender.[4] The beauty of

---

[4] A *Ted Talk*® given by Anne Milgram (2018) helps explain this in simple terms, in "Why smart statistics are the key to fighting crime." The video can be viewed at https://www.ted.com/talks/anne_milgram_why_smart_statistics_are_the_key_to_fighting_crime/transcript?language=en.

using statistical probability and evidence-based programs, rather than relying on gut feelings about sentencing, is that there can be more consistency in sentencing to community-based corrections.

Combining Sanctions and Services

Community-based corrections are not an all or nothing proposition, with one program adequately addressing the problems of any one individual. As we noted, there may be any number of combinations of sanctions or therapies required of the convicted adult or the adjudicated juvenile. What appears to be the most effective is intensive community supervision, in combination with court-ordered rehabilitation, primarily in the case of drug-addicted felons (PEW Center on the States, 2007).

One example of the successful combining of services comes out of the Israeli prison system. In the evaluation of individuals participating in a work-release program, researchers concluded that the social environment into which offenders are release is also crucial, in which case intensive counseling and therapy is necessary alongside work-release programs, in addition to other privileges, including furloughs and cultural field trips, in something called "matched treatment" (Weisburd, et al., 2017). Weisburd, et al.'s (2017) work indicates that a broader, more integrative approach to program assignments is important in the reduction of recidivism.

Adult Transition Centers

Similar to a reporting center for employment post-incarceration, *adult transition centers* (ATCs) are not limited to serving the convict population. They are designed to help individuals transition to adult life in general, including those with special needs and disabilities. In an evaluation of the work-release programs in Illinois prisons, unsurprisingly, women in particular who completed the adult transition center program were more successful in finding employment, as well as increasing their earnings, as compared to those who dropped out of the program (Jung and Lalonde (2019).

SUMMARY

There continues to be a concerted effort to find alternatives to placing convicted criminals in jails and prisons. Unlike a century ago, judges have the discretion to sentence individuals to a number of community-based corrections options. These can include any combination of probation, parole (after serving time), community service, half-way houses, and diversion programs, as in the examples of drug and/or alcohol rehabilitation and anger management therapies. Unfortunately, the greatest contributors to the failure to thrive in community-based corrections continue to be drug and/or alcohol addiction. Much of the success in community-based corrections programs is dependent on the self-efficacy and self-motivation of the individual.

Though there are a number of intermediate sanctions that can be part of sentencing, the backbones of community-based corrections continue to be probation and parole. Probation in lieu of jail or prison time can be stand alone, or can be part of sentencing along with some jail time. Parole, on the other hand, is on the back end of incarceration, granted in a number of ways and under a number of conditions. However, we should note that some of the incarcerated will turn down the opportunity to be paroled into the community, choosing instead to serve the entirety of their sentence. The primary reason for this is that if they do serve their full sentence, they will be released into the community without it being under the cloud of the many conditions that are attached to parole, the least of which is the requirement to meet with a parole officer on a regular basis.

As well as new solutions to overcrowding in prisons with creative use of community-based corrections, those convicted of crimes associated with drug or alcohol use may have the opportunity to participate in rehabilitation programs. These types of programs can be required in sentencing from traditional courts, or increasingly, sentenced in drug courts. In this way the crime is more likely to be viewed a public health issue, rather than simply criminal.

When individuals do get sentenced to probation, though it is considered a form of forgiveness, it comes with a number of conditions. Same goes for those who are released on parole. All probationers and parolees have to follow a number of general conditions, including staying away from known criminals, holding down a job, and reporting on a regular basis to their probation or parole officer. However, other probationers and parolees may also be required to follow a number of special conditions as well. There can also be additional conditions that are ordered by the probation or parole officer.

Increasingly judges are using statistics in order to determine the likelihood an individual before them in their court is at risk of reoffending. This involves calculating the risk factors and characteristics of the convicted against those of individuals convicted on similar crimes. Again, this aids in providing more latitude in the combination of possible sanctions that can be utilized, with an eye, always, on reducing recidivism, while still doing what is perceived to be fair to victims and the community. All in all, the success of any form of community-based corrections rests in the cooperation and partnership between agencies and local law enforcement, beyond the willingness for the offender to be integrated into society without reoffending.

STORIES FROM BEHIND BARS

Against All Odds — Melissa Smylie

On the surface, Melissa Smylie, a Native American, is a very unlikely candidate for a criminal conviction. Living in Montana, she is a mother, served in the AmeriCorps, and is a college graduate. In spite of her seemingly stellar life, by her own words, she has three felony DUI convictions along with a number of probation violations. While on probation in 2008, she violated her community-based sanctions when she was caught drinking. And as she notes, one condition of probation was to avoid drinking establishments (e.g., bars), which she failed to do. After she had her probation revoked, she was required to complete a women's residential alcohol treatment program, but ended up incarcerated while waiting for a bed at the rehabilitation center when there was none to be had.

After successfully completing treatment, she was released to Great Falls Pre-Release Center, and from there received early release under a Montana law provision. With a job lined up, Smylie was also required to meet with the probation office within 24 hours, an office that was 85 miles away from home. The first job she lined up she had to quit because her probation officer did not allow her to drive. She had to also turn down the second job, a bookkeeping position for a casino, because being in or around a casino was prohibited, even though the accounting offices were offsite.

Smylie's impression of her probation officer is that she was being viewed as a burden and was subjected to threats to revoke her probation on the basis of needing to drive to work, even though Smylie had a valid driver's license. Having her transportation taken away from her[5], Smylie was ordered to quit her job and find one closer to home to which she did not have to drive and that was also closer to her probation officer in Shelby. This required that she move to another town in order to do so. Rapidly running out of options, Smylie found that her employment opportunities were limited.

The probation officer eventually put out a *"no bond" hold*, claiming that she was running "amok" and out of control, which meant the Smylie was picked up and sent to the women's prison, waiting for a hearing without access to a lawyer, witness, or supportive family members, including children. As Smylie's probation officer improperly issued the no bond hold, she was released. A new probation officer ordered her to move back to Great Falls, which meant that she now had to leave her daughter behind in Shelby, which also meant that her daughter would be now in child protective services. Smylie was unable to get food assistance while on probation and could not sign a lease agreement until the "amok" charges from the original probation officer could be resolved. Smylie found herself hungry, homeless, and impoverished while on probation.

Postscript

After several false starts, run-ins with the probation system, Melissa Smylie finally completed her sentence, largely due to her own self advocacy, including serving as her own legal counsel. In 2010, she completed a bachelor's degree program in paralegal studies. She believes that a secret to her success is that even with roadblocks

---

[5] This is an example of a probation officer directive.

during probation, she found ways to remain active in the community, including volunteering. She currently shares her story of her experiences in the probation system in Montana and she survived it, as she says, against all odds.

We tell Smylie's story not to condemn probation and parole officers, but rather to shine a spotlight at some of the contradictions in the system that make it difficult for offenders to fulfill the requirements of their probation.

SOURCES

American Civil Liberties Union (ACLU) Montana (2018). Against all odds: Melissa Smylie's success in spite of the criminal justice system. Sept. 10. Retrieved from https://www.aclumontana.org/en/melissasmylie.

Publication Admin (2019) Bad policies and systematic bias are driving huge increases in Native American incarceration rates. *Native American Roots*. Nov. 28. Retrieved from http://nativeamericannetroots.net/diary/Bad-policies-and-systemic-bias-are-driving-huge-increases-in-Native-American-incarceration-rates.

INTERNATIONAL PERSPECTIVES IN PUNISHMENT AND CORRECTIONS: UNITED KINGDOM

The countries of the United Kingdom (U.K.), comprised of England, Scotland, Wales, and Northern Ireland, have similar prison systems but decidedly different political histories, even though they are intertwined. Under one umbrella of prison systems, the U.K. categorizes prisoners in terms of the degree of danger they pose to the public and to national security (Silvestri, 2013). The most trusted of prisoners are housed in *open prisons*, similar to those found in Nordic countries, including Iceland. Instead of a warden, prisons are run by a governor that has similar duties as a warden.

Older prisons in the United Kingdom, some dating back to the 17th through the 19th centuries, have been replaced over time as they became too deteriorated to humanely house prisoners. Some former U.K. prisons are now tourist attractions, much as Alcatraz in California and Eastern State Penitentiary in Pennsylvania in the United States, for their historical significance. An example in the United Kingdom is the Crumlin Road Gaol[6] in Belfast, Northern Ireland, which operated from the Victorian Era through 1996 when it closed and was transformed into a prison museum.

Prison conditions in England were still horrendous, relatively speaking, until the late 20th century. Physical conditions were described as

---

[6] Earlier in the book we discussed "gaols," which today are called "jails." Gaols housed both detained suspects and convicted prisoners.

the daily degradation of hundreds of prisoners carrying foetid chamber pots along landings to stinking slop sinks. . . . As Lord Justice Woolf noted in 1991, [these] practices [were] uncivilized and degrading. . . . Destroyed the morale of prisoners and staff (Woolf 1991:24). (Coyle, 2016, p. 8)

Thankfully since Woolf's report in 1991, prison conditions in England have vastly improved (Coyle, 2016).

Like other countries around the world, the countries in the United Kingdom have a substantial number of people in prison who have learning disabilities. If left untreated with special education remedies, these individuals are disadvantaged from the moment they are in school. Poor school performance is linked to criminal behavior, though the learning disabilities in themselves is no measure of intellectual capabilities. Researchers in the United Kingdom acknowledge that prisoners with learning disabilities need special help both while incarcerated and when they return to their communities after release (Hayes et al., 2007).

GLOSSARY

Actuarial risk   Statistical and algorithmic instruments that assist in determining the level of risk an individual possess for reoffending.

Adult transition centers   Multipurpose centers for probationers, parolees, and other special populations, including the disabled, that help with developing adult skills.

Cognitive Behavioral Treatment (CBT)   Form of therapy that is used for a wide range of psychological issues, including behavioral, addiction, and severe mental illness.

Diversion programs   Pre-prison programs that are designed to change behavior so as the individual can remain in the community while addressing the problems that lead to crime, as in the example of drug addiction.

Drug courts   An alternative to traditional criminal court that seeks treatment solutions instead of incarceration.

Electronic monitoring (EM)   Any use of devices that will track the movements of offenders, most commonly the GPS-guided ankle bracelet.

Faith-based programs   Private programs that are designed by faith-based organizations in order to address any number of social problems that lead to criminal behavior.

Good time earned   "Earned time" or "meritorious credit" that will shorten a convict's time in jail or prison.

Intensive supervision probation (ISP)   Probation that requires more contact with probation supervisors, including several meetings a week and home visits. May be combined with electronic monitoring.

Intermediate sanctions   A facet of community-based corrections where a number of penalties may be imposed on the convicted, including fines, restitution, community service, and other punishments meant to keep the convicted out of prison and in the community.

Intrinsic motivation   The internal motivation to do things, including living a law abiding life for other than material rewards, like money.

Mandatory release   The required release date built into sentencing.

Multifactor Offender Readiness Model (MORM)   A survey used to determine just how prepared an offender is to successfully complete a program, including testing self-efficacy.

Need principle   A target principle: Target interventions to criminogenic (correlated to crime) needs.

Parole   A type of back-end correction that makes early release from prison possible for a number of reasons (e.g., overcrowding, "good time" served) but that still requires serving the sentence with supervision in the community.

Probation   A type of front-end correction that is intended to keep the convicted out of prison and under the community supervision.

Probation officer directives   Requirements that are imposed on the probationer by the probation officer, beyond those imposed by the court.

Responsivity Principle: Programs are assigned in order specifically to the temperament, learning style, motivation culture, and gender of the offender.

Risk Principle   Prioritizes supervision and treatment resources for higher risk offenders.

Self-efficacy   The ability of an individual to be self-motivated, built on individual social experiences, training, and mentoring.

Sex offender registry   The requirement that convicted sex offenders register their offense status with local law enforcement wherever they may live. The registry is publicly published so that the community is aware of the location of sex offenders within their neighborhoods.

Shaming and reintegration   An age-old strategy that has reemerged in criminal justice where the accused or convicted has to face their community and in some cases, confess their crimes, make apologies, and make restitution. After shaming phase is satisfactorily completed, the individual is then reintegrated in the community.

Shock probation   Sentencing that includes some jail time followed by probation, in the hopes that the experience is so traumatizing, that it will reduce reoffending.

Study-release programs   Much less common that work-release programs, inmates are allowed to leave the prison to attend college classes, but have to be in prison when they are not in school. (See *Work-release programs*)

Substantive violations   Violations of probation or parole that involve new criminal offenses that will revoke community-based supervision and send the individual back to jail or prison, to a new trial.

Technical violation   Noncriminal violations of the conditions of release, including failure to report to probation or parole meetings, a change of address, or a change of job.

Treatment Principle   Integrates treatment into the full sentence/sanction requirements of the sentence.

Work-release programs   Career and vocational programs that allow inmates to leave the prison in order to work on the outside, but under which they are required to be back in the prison when they are not working.

REFERENCES AND SUGGESTED READINGS

Alarid, L. F. (2015) Perceptions of probation and police officer home visits during intensive probation supervision. *Federal Probation*. Vol. 79, Iss. 1:11-16.

Alarid, L. F., B. A. Sims, and J. Ruiz (2011) School-based juvenile probation and police partnerships for truancy reduction. *Journal of Knowledge and Best Practices in Juvenile Justice and Psychology*. Vol. 5, No. 1:13-20.

Allerd, S. L., L. D. Harrison, D. J. O'Connell (2013) Self-efficacy: An important aspect of prison-based learning. *The Prison Journal*. Vol. 23, No. 2:211-233.

American Addiction Centers (n.d.) How do celebrity drug sentences compare with regular people's? Editorial Staff. Retrieved from https://www.rehabs.com/blog/how-do-celebrity-drug-arrest-sentences-compare-to-regular-peoples/.

Barklage, H., D. Miller, and G. Bonham (2006) Probation conditions versus probation officer directives: Where the twain shall meet. *Federal Probation*. Dec., Vol. 70, Iss. 32:37-41.

Beale, S. S. (2006) The news media's influence on criminal justice policy: How market-driven news promotes punitiveness. *William and Mary Law Review*. Vol. 48:397.

Blackmore, J. (1980) Community corrections. *Corrections Magazine*. Vol. 6, Iss. 5:4-14.

Brown, P.W. (1990) Guns and probation officers: The unspoken reality. *Federal Probation*. June, Vol. 54, Iss. 2:21-26

Bryne, J. M. and A. Pattavina (2006) Assessing the role of clinical and actuarial risk assessment in an evidence-based community corrections system: Issues to consider. *Federal Probation*. Sept., Vol. 70, Iss. 2:64-67.

Cardwell, C. (2021) Working virtually with community corrections clients. *Journal of Community Corrections*. Spring. Vol. 30, No. 3:7

Collins, J. (2019) Explaining the failure of drug courts in the United Kingdom, in in *Rethinking Drug Courts: International Experiences of a US Policy Export*, J. Collins, W. Agnew-Pauley, A. Soderholm, eds. London, UK: London School of Economics International Drug Policy Unit. Ch. 5.

CBS News (2002) Former baseball star Darryl Strawberry gets 18 months in prison for probation violation. *News on 6*. Apr. 29. Retrieved from https://www.newson6.com/story/5e3682cf2f69d76f620977c8/former-baseball-star-darryl-strawberry-gets-18-months-in-prison-for-probation-violation.

Charlesmanson.com (n.d.) Charles Manson parole hearings. Retrieved from https://www .charlesmanson.com/related/parole-hearings/.

Cohn, D. and R. Morin (2008) Who moves? Who stays put? Where is home? Pews Research Center. Dec. 29. Retrieved from https://www.pewresearch.org/social-trends/2008/12/17/ who-moves-who-stays-put-wheres-home/#:~:text=Among%20all%20respondents%20 to%20the,lived%20outside%20their%20current%20state. .

Columbia Justice Labs (2018) *Statement on the Future of Community Corrections*. Columbia University. May 17. Retrieved from https://justicelab.columbia.edu/statement-future -community-corrections.

Corbett, R. P. and A. Pattavina (2015) Promoting offender change in the community: Positive reinforcement through EM technology. *Journal of Community Corrections*. Summer, Vol. 24, Iss. 4:5-16.

Crime and Justice Institute at Community Resources for Justice (2009) *Implementing Evidence-based Policy and Practice in Community Corrections*, 2d ed. Washington, DC: National Institute of Corrections.

Cropsey, K. L., E. N. Stevens, P. Valera, C. B. Clark, H. W. Bulls, P. Nair, and P. S. Lane (2015) Risk factors for concurrent use of benzodiazepines and opioids among individuals under community corrections supervision. *Drug and Alcohol Dependence*. Vol. 154:152-157.

Csete, J. (2019) Drug courts in the United States: Punishment for "patients", in *Rethinking Drug Courts: International Experiences of a US Policy Export*, J. Collins, W. Agnew-Pauley, A. Soderholm, eds. London, UK: London School of Economics International Drug Policy Unit. Ch. 1.

Cullen, F. T., Eck, J. E., and C. T. Lowenkamp (2002) Environmental corrections: A New Paradigm for effective probation and parole supervisions. *Federal Probation*. Vol. 66, Iss. 2:28-37.

Degiorgio, L. and M. DiDonato (2014) Predicting probationer rates of reincarceration using dynamic factors from the Substance Abuse Questionnaire_Adult Probation III (SAQ-Adult Probation III). *American Journal of Criminal Justice*. Vol. 39:94-108.

Duke, A. (2012) Lindsay Lohan's troubled timeline. Entertainment, CNN. Mar. 29. Retrieved from https://www.cnn.com/2012/03/28/showbiz/lohan-troubled-timeline/index.html.

Dunne, E. M., E. Morgan, B. Wells-Moore, S. Pierson, S. Zakroff, L. Haskell, K. Link, J. Powell, I. Holland, K. Elgethun, C. Ball, R. Haugen, C. G. Hahn, K. K. Carter, and C. Starr (2021) COVID-19 outbreaks in correctional facilities with work-release programs_Idaho, July-November 2020. *MMWR Morbidity and Mortality Weekly Report*. Apr. 23, Vol. 70, No. 16:589-594.

Duwe, G. (2015) An outcome evaluation of a prison release program: Estimating its effects on recidivism, employment, and cost avoidance. *Criminal Justice Policy Review*. Vol. 26, No 6:531-554.

Evans, D. G. (2021) Will the pandemic be an opportunity for community corrections to reimagine its role in the provision of services? *Journal of Community Corrections*. Spring, Vol. 30, No 3:4.

Fern, M. (2002) Study disputes impact of halfway houses on neighborhoods. *Washington Post*. May 16. Retrieved from https://www.washingtonpost.com/archive/local/2002/05/ 16/study-disputes-impact-of-halfway-houses-on-neighborhoods/fc3b4949-3792-4d1c-ac34-40771dbc17b1/.

Gibbs, B. R. and R. Lytle (2020) Drug court participant and time to failure: An examination of recidivism across program outcome. *American Journal of Criminal Justice*. Apr., Vol. 45, Iss. 2:215-235.

Goodman, P. (2021) 7 disadvantages of GPS. *Axle Addict*. Apr. 30. Retrieved from https://axl eaddict.com/safety/Disadvantages-of-GPS.

Gottfredson, G. D. and D. C. Gottfredson (1997) Survey of school-based gang prevention and intervention programs: Preliminary findings. Report, Office of Justice Programs, U.S. Department of Justice. ERIC Number ED432652. 18 pp.

Huebner, B. M. and J. E. Cobbina (2007) The effect of drug use, drug treatment completion on probationer recidivism. *Journal of Drug Issues*. Vol. 37:619-642.

Hyatt, J. M. and G. Barnes (2017) An experimental evaluation of the impact of intensive supervision on recidivism of high-risk probationers. *Crime and Delinquency*. Vol. 63, Issue 1:3-38.

Jackson, S. (2020) The 4 biggest challenges facing the newly released from prison. TReND Wyoming. Apr. Retrieved from https://www.trendwyoming.org/articles/biggest-challenges-after-prison-release/.

Jones Young, N. C. J., J. N. Griffith, and K. S. Anazoda (2019) Exploring the impact of training on equitable access to employment: A gendered perspective of work release programs. *Journal of Human Resource Management*. Vol. 22, No. 2:70-86.

Jung, H. and R. J. LaLonde (2019) Prison work-release programs and incarcerated women's labor market outcomes. *Prison Journal*. Nov., Vol. 99, Iss. 5:535-558.

Kaeble, D. and M. Alper (2020) Probation and parole in the United States, 2017-2018. Bureau of Justice Statistics, Office of Justice Programs. Aug. 4. Retrieved from https://www.bjs.gov/index.cfm?ty=pbdetail&iid=6986.

Kearley, B. and D. Gottfredson (2020) Long term effects of drug court participation: Evidence from a 15-year follow-up of a randomized controlled trial. *Journal of Experimental Criminology*. Vol. 16, Iss. 1:27-47.

Kopak, A. M. (2020) Behavioral health indicators and time-to-arrest in adult pre-arrest diversion programs. *Behavioral Science and the Law*. Jan., Vol. 38, No. 1:66-76.

Lasher, M. P. and J. D. Stinson (2020) "Built on respect and good honest communication": A study of partnerships between mental health providers and community corrections. *Administration and Policy in Mental Health and Mental Health Services Research*. Vol. 47:617-631.

Lerner, C. S. (2015) Who's really sentenced to life without parole: Searching for "ugly disproportionalities" in the American criminal justice system. *Wisconsin Law Review*. Vol. 2015, Iss. 5:789-862.

Los Angeles Times (2011) Lindsay Lohan cleaning toilets, emptying trash at morgue. Oct. 21. Retrieved from https://latimesblogs.latimes.com/lanow/2011/10/lindsay-lohan-morgue-community-service.html.

New Mexico Department of Corrections (2021) Probation and parole officers. Retrieved from https://cd.nm.gov/divisions/training-academy/recruiting/probation-and-parole-officers/.

PEW Center on the States (2007) What works in community corrections: An interview with Dr. Joan Petersilia. Expert Q&A. Nov., No. 2. Retrieved from https://www.pewtrusts.org/-/media/legacy/uploadedfiles/wwwpewtrustsorg/reports/sentencing_and_corrections/qacommunitycorrectionspdf.pdf

PEW Charitable Trust (2018) Probation on parole systems marked with high stakes, missed opportunities. *Issue Brief*. Sept. 25. Retrieved from https://www.pewtrusts.org/en/research-and-analysis/issue-briefs/2018/09/probation-and-parole-systems-marked-by-high-stakes-missed-opportunities.

Prisonology™ (n.d.) Communication and visitation: Furlough. Retrieved from https://prisonologyx.com/prison/communication-visitation/furlough/.

Reiman, J. and P. Leighton (2012) *The Rich Get Richer and the Poor Get Prison*. New York, NY: Pearson North America.

Roberts, M. R. and M. J. Stacer (2017) Evaluating a faith-based diversion and reentry program: Who graduates and who is rearrested. *Offender Programs Report*. Mar./Apr., Vol. 20, Iss. 6:89-103.

Sandoval, J. R. (2020) "Everyone is on supervision": The function of home visits in structuring family dynamics and exerting continuous control. *Journal of Offender Rehabilitation*. Vol. 59, Iss. 4:177-197.

Schaefer, L., F. T. Cullen, and J. E. Eck (2015) Environmental Corrections: *A New Paradigm for Supervisors of Offenders in the Community*. Newbury Park, CA: SAGE Publishing.

Schwartzapfel, B. (2020) Probation and parole officers are rethinking their rules as the coronavirus spreads. The Marshall Project. Retrieved from https://www.themarshallproject.org/2020/04/03/probation-and-parole-officers-are-rethinking-their-rules-as-coronavirus-spreads.

Shulman-Laniel, J., J. S. Vernick, B. McGinty, S. Frattaroli, L. Rutkow (2017) U.S. State ignition interlock for alcohol impaired driving prevention: A 50 state survey and analysis. *Journal of Law, Medicine, and Ethics*. Summer, Vol. 45, Iss. 2: 221-230.

Simes, J. T. (2019) Place after prison: Neighborhood attainment and attachment during reentry. *Journal of Urban Affairs*. Vol. 41, No. 4:443-463.

Smith, R. R. and M. A. Milan (1973) A survey of the home furlough policies of American correctional agencies. *Criminology*. May, Vol. 11, Iss. 1:95-104.

Sperber, K. G. (2020) Contemplating the role of community corrections and the intersection of public health and public safety. *Journal of Community Corrections*. Summer, Vol. 29, Iss. 4:5-19.

Still, W., B. Broderick, and S. Raphael (2016) Building trust and legitimacy within community corrections. *New Thinking in Community Corrections*, National Institute of Justice. Dec., No. 3. Retrieved from https://www.ojp.gov/pdffiles1/nij/249946.pdf.

United States Bureau of Justice Statistics (2020) Statistics, in *Research, Statistics, and Evaluation*. Office of Justice Programs, U.S Department of Justice. Retrieved from https://www.ojp.gov/topics/research-statistics-evaluation#:~:text=Impartial%2C%20timely%2C%20and%20accurate%20statistical,information%20used%20for%20decision%20making.

United States Bureau of Prisons (n.d.) Completing the transition. Reentry assistance reduces recidivism. Retrieved from https://www.bop.gov/about/facilities/residential_reentry_management_centers.jsp.

United States Courts (2016a) Chapter 3: Computer and Internet Restrictions (Probation and Supervised Release Conditions), in *Overview of Probation and Supervised Release Conditions*. Administrative Office of The United States Courts, Probation and Pretrial Service Office. Retrieved from https://www.uscourts.gov/services-forms/computer-internet-restrictions-probation-supervised-release-conditions.

United States Courts (2016b) *Overview of Probation and Supervised Release Conditions*. Administrative Office of The United States Courts, Probation and Pretrial Service Office. Retrieved from https://www.uscourts.gov/sites/default/files/overview_of_probation_and_supervised_release_conditions_0.pdf.

United States Government Accounting Office (2015) Traffic safety: Alcohol ignition interlocks are effective while installed; less is known about how to increase installation rates, in *Alcohol Ignition Interlocks: Effectiveness and Case Studies of Six States*, T. Palmer, ed. New York: Nova Publishers. Ch. 1.

Varghese, F. P., K. M. Anderson, D. L. Cummings, and E. Fitzgerald (2017) The Offender Job Search Self-Efficacy Scale: Development and initial validation. *Psychological Services*. Vol. 15, No. 4:477-485.

Villettaz, P., G. Gillieron, and M. Killias (2015) The effects on re-offending of custodial vs. non-custodial sanctions: An updated systematic review of the state of knowledge. *Campbell Systematic Reviews*. Vol. 11, Iss. 1:1-92.

Vito, G. F., R. M. Holmes, and D. G. Wilson (1985) The effect of shock and regular probation upon recidivism: A comparative analysis. *American Journal of Criminal Justice*. Spring, Vol. 9, Iss. 2:152-162.

Vito, G. F., D. G. Wilson, and T. J. Keil (1990) Drug testing, treatment, and revocation: A review of program findings. *Federal Probation*. Vol. 3:37-43.

Weiss, D. C. (2019) GPS ankle monitors can call and record people without their consent; do they violate 5th Amendment. Privacy Law, *Daily News*, *American Bar Association Journal*. Apr. 9. Retrieved from https://www.abajournal.com/news/article/electro nic-monitoring-devices-can-call-and-record-people-accused-of-crimes-without-their -consent.

Zimmer, B. (2004/2005) The effect of faith-based programs in reducing recidivism and substance abuse of ex-offenders. *Journal of Community Corrections*. Winter, Vol. 14, Iss. 2:7-19.

COMMUNITY-BASED RESOURCES FOR REENTRY

The following is not an exhausted list, but a sample of resources available to convicts who are reentering society. Some are secular (e.g., government-run) and others are faith-based.

First Step Alliance. *Reducing recidivism: Creating a path to successful re-entry*. Available at https://www.firststepalliance.org/post/reducing-recidivism?gclid=CjwKCAjwtdeFB hBAEiwAKOIy5712-yfcdQRUliAf7af-Qg6Hxg1jYa4EoZLwIn2JjFU2MLcEDjLkHBoC egIQAvD_BwE.

Hope for Prisoners: *Transforming Lives, Transforming Communities*. Available at https:// hopeforprisoners.org/?gclid=CjwKCAjwtdeFBhBAEiwAKOIy58X3w9iW3aARcOqIuL JilFXFldvLXz0KFtEiW5dZRxvHjCb9sms4jxoCjgIQAvD_BwE

National Reentry Resource Center (NRRC). Available at https://nationalreentryresourcecen ter.org/.

Prison Fellowship. Resources for essential reentry resources. Available at https://www.priso nfellowship.org/resources/training-resources/reentry-ministry/ministry-tools-2/resour ces-for-essential-reentry-services/.

United States Department of Health and Human Services, Office of Minority Health. *Reentry Resources*. Available at https://www.minorityhealth.hhs.gov/omh/content.aspx?ID=10326.

Chapter THIRTEEN

The Death Penalty[1]

> *The death penalty is not about whether people deserve to die for the crimes they commit. The real question of capital punishment in this country [the U.S.] is, "Do we deserve to kill?"*
>
> — Bryan Stevenson, *Just Mercy: A Story of Justice and Redemption* (2014)

Chapter Objectives

- Discuss the history, methods, and controversies of the death penalty in depth.
- Review three key amendments connected to corrections and capital punishment.
- Review key Supreme Court cases and capital punishment.
- Introduce readers to the realities of life for Death Row inmates.
- Provide insight into the effects of working on Death Row for prison personnel.

Key Terms

5th Amendment of the U.S. Constitution

8th Amendment of the U.S. Constitution

14th Amendment of the U.S. Constitution

Capital punishment

Jim Crow laws

Lynching

Mandatory vs. discretionary death penalty

Old Testament

Pardons

Qu'ran (or Koran)

---

[1] **TRIGGER WARNING:** The topics we are discussing in this chapter may be disturbing to some readers. We recommend that you discuss with your professor or instructor as to how much or how little of this chapter you will be responsible for.

Reprieves   Stays of execution
Secrecy statutes   Symbolic executions
Sharia Law   Torah

INTRODUCTION

Many of the controversies discussed in this chapter have been touched upon briefly elsewhere in the book. Nowhere in this book do we most readily touch upon social justice issues as we do here. The intention of this chapter is not to necessarily influence your own views on the controversies, but to inform you of both sides of the arguments and encourage critical thinking skills on this and other topics in corrections.

The most controversial topic in corrections is the death penalty. It is the ultimate in punishments intended to be a deterrence. Executions are so controversial that the topic crept into the work of the famous artist Andy Warhol, in his *Death and Disaster* series (1960s) that included silkscreened photos of grisly subject matter, including the electric chair. Some of the controversy relates to the push/pull between *Old Testament* (also *Torah* or *Qu'ran*) scripture calling for "an eye for an eye" retribution and the views of proponents of social justice in contemporary life. As the death penalty is the ultimate retributive punishment, it has been subject of debate for several decades, not just in the United States but elsewhere in the world.

It may seem odd that we should spend one chapter on the death penalty, as it might seem more appropriate in a class on criminal law or the courts. The reality is that the death penalty, though recommended by prosecutors, then handed over to juries and judges to decide, ultimately has a greater impact within the criminal justice system on the prison staff and the condemned themselves. Facilities that carry out death penalty convictions are affected not only by the infrastructure needed to do so, but also by the social and psychological consequences of being responsible for carrying out the sentences. Another consideration is the effect executions has on inmates living on Death Row, as well as on any other inmates at those facilities when they are carried out.

HISTORY OF THE DEATH PENALTY

We suspect that the death penalty predates written history and laws and probably was used to punish those who violated a community's norms. Capital punishment has been universally used as punishment at some point in time by all known societies (Ward, 2015). It may very well have been used against offending individuals for a number of indiscretions besides murder, even for things we would consider to be relatively banal infringements today. Even banishment, though not a sentence of death per se, may end up having the same result if someone has been banished into the wilderness without human companionship or possibly with few skills or provisions with which to survive on their own.

The death penalty, referred to in current times as *capital punishment,* was and still is also used as a cruel political weapon in war. Untold innocent people through the centuries have been executed for no other reason than they were on the losing side of a war or skirmish. Most notably, the threats of death and rape have historically been weapons of war. We also know that the death penalty was imposed on populations who did not convert (or at least pretend to convert) to the dominant religion, as in the example of Catholicism and the Spanish Inquisition. Even more horrifically, as we have discussed in earlier chapters, the accused were often tortured in advance of their death.

Leading up to and after the American Revolution, punishment was brutal as we pointed out in Chapter 3. Much of what was seen in the colonies in the way of putting people to death was imported from Europe, primarily England. Soulatges (Foucault, 1995, p. 32) graphically described the means of punishment that most often led to death for the accused in the United States, sometimes handed out even before a trial took place:

> *Capital punishment comprises many kinds of death: some prisoners may be condemned to be hanged, others to have their hands cut off or their tongues cut out or pierced and then to be hanged; others, for more serious crimes, to be broken alive and to die on the wheel, after having their limbs broken; others to be broken until they die a natural death[2], others to be strangled and broken, others to be burnt alive, others to be burnt after first being strangled; others to be drawn by four horses[3], others to have their heads cut off, and others to have their heads broken (Soulatges, 169-171).*

After WWII, there was less worldwide support for capital punishment. In the *Universal Declaration of Human Rights* adopted by the United Nations General Assembly in 1948, under Article 3, governments who deny citizens the right to live, including criminals, are suspected of denying access to other basic human rights (Anckar, 2014; Center for Constitutional Rights, n.d.). In the 21st century, there has been ever-increasing criticism of the death penalty. In spite of pressures by international lawyers, some nations, and non-governmental organizations, there is continued resistance to the abolition of capital punishment, including in some regions of the United States (Anckar, 2014). As much opposition as there is to the death penalty in the United States, as of 2018, 54 percent of Americans were still in support of its use (Oliphant, 2018).

---

[2] By today's medical standards, these were not natural deaths.
[3] "Draw and quartering," where the accused has all four limbs tied by ropes to four horses, who then are spurred to ride off in four different directions. It essentially tears the limbs from the torso of the victim.

Capital punishment continued to be the norm in most countries around the world through the 19th century and well into the 20th century. One by one, countries, primarily in Western Europe, abandoned the death penalty for other means of punishing those who commit the most heinous crimes. Since the mid-1970s, 75 countries around the world have either abolished the death penalty for ordinary crimes, with others abolishing it all together. Though fewer countries are using the death penalty in punishment, those who do still employ it are executing more criminals in seemingly indiscriminate ways, including China (NPR, 2016).

CURRENT STATUS OF THE DEATH PENALTY IN AMERICA

Currently in the United States, the death penalty is not universally available in sentencing in all states. There are a number of states that have abolished the death penalty. Yet others have placed a moratorium on capital punishment. The death penalty is still an option in certain federal cases, for about 60 offenses including the following, beyond particularly horrific cases of homicide warranting a death sentence (Death Penalty Information Center, 2021):

- Air piracy;
- Treason;
- Espionage; and
- Murder or attempted murder of a witness, juror, or court official.

There had been an almost two decade long moratorium on the use of capital punishment at the federal level, since 2003. In 2019, the Department of Justice, under the direction of then Attorney General William Barr ordered the then Acting Director of the Bureau of Prisons to resume scheduling executions, including five federal Death Row inmates (U.S. Department of Justice, 2019). These orders included the following individuals, the crimes they were convicted of, and their dates of execution (U.S. Department of Justice, 2019):

- Daniel Lewis Lee robbed and murdered a family of three, including an eight-year-old girl. Convicted May 4, 1999. Executed July 14, 2020.
- Lezmond Mitchell murdered a 63-year-old grandmother, forcing her granddaughter to sit beside her lifeless body for a 30-40 mile drive, after which Mitchell crushed the granddaughter's head with a rock and buried both victims. Convicted May 8, 2008. Executed August 26, 2020.
- Wesley Ira Purkey raped, murdered, and dismembered a 16-year-old girl. Also convicted in state court of murdering an 80-year-old woman. Convicted November 5, 2003. Executed July 16, 2020.

- Alfred Bourgeois tortured, sexually molested, and then beat to death his two-and-a-half-year-old daughter. Convicted March 16, 2004. Executed December 11, 2020.
- Dustin Lee Honken shot and killed five people, including two men who planned to testify against him in another case. Convicted October 14, 2004. Executed July 17, 2020.

Between July 2020 and January 2021, 13 federal Death Row inmates had been executed, breaking a 130-year tradition of pausing executions in the middle of an election year and presidential transition in the United States (Honderich, 2021).

We should note that as the Death Penalty Information Center reports (2021), even though they are part of the United States, but not officially states of the union, the District of Columbia and Puerto Rico[4] have had the discretion to prohibit the death penalty. The states that currently have the death penalty are seen in Figure 13.1.

The reality is that in federal cases the death penalty is rarely used even in the most prescribed cases, and far rarer than in states that have capital punishment. Human rights and social justice groups have been calling for the end of the death penalty at the federal level for some time, more urgently so after the so-called "execution spree" that took place in 2020 and those scheduled for 2021 (Death Penalty

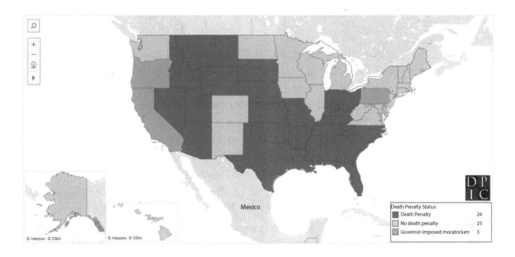

FIGURE 13-1 | **States That Currently Have the Death Penalty, 2021.**
(*Source*: Death Penalty Information Center, 2021, retrieved from https://deathpenaltyinfo.org/state-and-federal-info/state-by-state.)

---

[4] The District of Columbia is home of the U.S. Capital, Washington; Puerto Rico is a U.S. territory, but its inhabitants born there or naturalized are given the rights and privileges of American citizens.

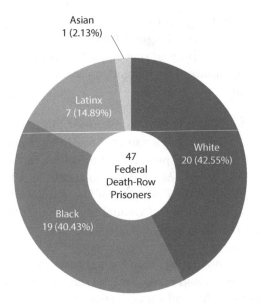

FIGURE 13-2 | **Proportion of Death Row Inmates by Race in the United States, 2020.** (*Source*: Death Penalty Information Center, 2020, retrieved from https://deathpenaltyinfo.org/state-and-federal-info/federal-death-penalty.)

Information Center, 2020). Of second and urgent concern is the disproportion number of persons of color sitting on federal Death Row, as seen in Figure 13.2.

Of the two most prominent minority groups in the United States, their representation on Death Row is vastly different. By the last U.S. census reported (2020), only 13.4 percent of Americans are Black, yet approximately 42 percent of those on Death Row in both federal and state facilities are Black, demonstrating a vast disparity in sentencing. Comparatively, Latinx/Hispanic inmates make up approximately 13 percent of the total Death Row population, compared to the 18.5 percent in the general population in the United States (U.S. Census Bureau, 2021; Noe-Bustamante et al., 2020; Death Penalty Information Center, n.d.b).

A death penalty conviction today in the United States does not necessarily mean that the punishment will be carried out before an inmate dies of natural causes in prison, as in the case of an older convict who is still working their way through a lengthy appeals process. There are also means by which a death penalty sentence will be set aside. The following reasons can bring about reprieves, commuted sentences, or pardons in death penalty cases, both on the federal and state levels:

- Faulty evidence;
- Unfair trials;
- Disproportionate sentences;

- Public opposition to the death penalty;
- Mental health issues of the accused; and
- Juvenile status of defendants at time of crime

Key Amendments, U.S. Constitution and the Death Penalty

Though the United States is a pluralistic society with a number of varying opinions about capital punishment and corrections in general, states that have the death penalty are still beholden to hold up the principles of the U.S. Constitution as they apply to the condemned. Even with the parameters of what is allowed constitutionally by states, the Constitution, and in particular, its amendments, have been used to argue against the use of the death penalty.

Even Supreme Court justices have not agreed on the validity of the death penalty. As recently as in the case of *Roper v. Simmons* (2005), The U.S. Supreme Court, with a decision written by Justice Anthony Kennedy, forbids the imposition of the death penalty on individuals who were juveniles at the time that they committed their crimes, while Judge Antonin Scalia, offering the dissenting opinion in the case, claimed that when the 8th Amendment was written, it did not prohibit capital punishment for 16- and 17-year-old offenders (U.S. Supreme Court, *Roper v. Simmons*, 2005). This is the difference between the justices (and scholars for that matter) interpreting the Constitution and Bill of Rights from the standpoint of the framers in the 18th and 19th centuries versus contemporary interpretations of the documents.

The amendments that hold the most sway in determining the ethics and humanity of punishment, including the death penalty, include the 5th, 8th, and 14th Amendments. Though these amendments tend to be used on both sides of the argument. Of course, just as the main body of the Constitution is open to interpretation, so are the amendments. And as with any interpretation, arguments on the intent of the originators of the Constitution and Amendments are subjective.

5th Amendment

The 5th Amendment is not always discussed in reference to the death penalty. However, it does address the legal particulars as to how one might be charged with a capital offence. The 5th Amendment, ratified in 1791, states that

> *No person shall be held to answer for a capital, or otherwise infamous crime, unless on a presentment or indictment of a Grand Jury. . . . Nor shall any person be subject to the same offense to be twice put in jeopardy of life or limb ["double jeopardy"]; nor compelled in any criminal case to be a witness against himself, nor be deprived of life, liberty, or property without due process of law.*

The bone of contention for those who oppose the death penalty, as it relates to the 5th Amendment, is that there is the risk for an unacceptable high rate of innocent people to be convicted on a number of offenses, including capital crimes. This could be because of the perception that they have been denied due process, either with hasty judgements perceived to have been made at time of arrest, no access to good legal representation, or a number of things that are built into a system that is inherently biased towards defendants with the economic means to hire the best lawyers to represent them in court (Rakoff, 2002). Proponents of the death penalty argue that there are a number of safeguards built into the system and that the Founders of the Constitution and Amendments supported the death penalty (Richardson et al., 2002).

8th Amendment

The part of the 8th Amendment, passed in 1791 while the U.S. was in its infancy, that applies to the death penalty is the prohibition of cruel and unusual punishment. Considering the era, what was considered humane treatment in the 18th century is not necessarily the same as we would interpret it today. The concerns that the framers of the Constitution had were that the same types of torture and punishment seen in Europe could be imposed as a means by which to oppress people in the newly formed country of America (Stevenson and Stinneford, n.d.). As we shall see further in this chapter, debates as to whether the death penalty is cruel and/or unusual punishment, including what life is like on Death Row, are complex.

The 8th Amendment is perhaps the most cited for argument against the death penalty. Essentially the state or federal government "smashes the convicted criminal into oblivions," with the executioner actively handing out punishment, which the condemned has no choice but to passively receive (Bedau, 1997). Even Socrates, as a political prisoner, was allowed to die at his own hand, peacefully passing away (according to the accounts of Plato and Xenophon) after drinking a cup of hemlock which had been ordered by the Athenian court that sentenced him to the options of death or banishment (Bedau, 1997).

14th Amendment

Opponents of the death penalty often cite the 14th Amendment, along with the 8th Amendment, to argue for the abolishment of the death penalty. In Amendment XIV, Section I of the U.S. Constitution (1868), it states that

> *No state shall make or enforce any law which shall abridge the privileges or immunities of citizens of the United States; nor shall any state deprive a person of life, liberty, or property, without due process of law; nor deny to any person its jurisdiction the equal protections of the laws.*

However, in the U.S. Supreme Court case of *Gregg v. Georgia* (1976), Justice Potter Stewart wrote in the court's judgment that a sentence of death does not violate the 8th or the 14th Amendment. This was based on the fact that the death penalty sentences in cases of murder have a long history of acceptance in the United States (U.S. Supreme Court, *Gregg v. Georgia*, 1976).

METHODS OF EXECUTION

The methods of execution have changed over the centuries, largely due to technological change. In the same way that we have learned better ways to keep people alive, we have also found better ways (which is debatable) to legally put people to death. The methods are on a continuum of what is unpleasant for the condemned as well as for the executioner. In the United States, the Constitution guarantees the condemned to be informed of what form of execution they can expect to receive. This constitutional right has been complicated in recent years after cases where lethal injection executions were particularly disturbing and failed to work as they were intended to, muddying the waters on what states will and will not divulge to those convicted of capital crimes as to what method of execution to expect, in so-called *secrecy statutes* (Mennemeir, 2017).

Executions are not necessarily automatic, even when the date arrives. The state or federal government has to issue a death warrant for the condemned which is often only good for 24 hours (Bowers, 2005a). If the execution does not take place on the appointed day due to a number of possible factors, including last minute appeals or *stays of execution*, a new death warrant has to be petitioned for through the courts (Bower, 2005a). It is primarily because of the fact that death warrants have an expiration date that executions are generally scheduled right after midnight, so as to not to have time run out with the last minute appeals process. Another reason is that this is the time when the rest of the prison population is in lockdown in their cells, with less disturbances expected to occur among inmates during an execution (Bower, 2005b). Bower (2005b) notes that a few states, including Texas and Arizona, have changed the execution time to afternoon or evening, as it makes it easier on judges who are standing by on appeals and stays, as well as on the corrections officers, other officials, and the families of victims that may be present to witness the execution.

In the United States, there are, in theory, five methods of execution. By far, lethal injection has been the most often used method in recent history, as indicated in the Figure 13.3.

Hanging

Hanging is one of the more ancient and familiar forms of executing criminals. We should note that in some cases, the accused was not necessarily legally executed but that it was done at the hands of vigilantes ahead of any formal arrest or due process in the United States. Here fictional movies, including Westerns, are not too far

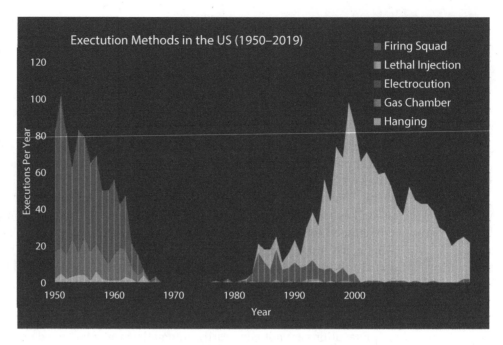

FIGURE 13.3 | **Execution Methods in the United States, 1950-2019.**
(*Source*: Litwin, 2021, The Science Survey, retrieved from https://thesciencesurvey.com/
editorial/2021/03/21/the-death-penalty-is-wrong-what-can-president-biden-do-about-it/)

off from the reality of the 19th century or early 20th century, where an ad hoc posse was thrown together to go after the alleged "bad guys."

More seriously disturbing was (and is) the *lynching* of people of color, primarily Blacks in the south, most often illegally committed by members of white supremacy groups, including the Ku Klux Klan (KKK). The vast majority of lynchings, which sadly still take place occasionally in the contemporary United States, were motivated only by the color of the individual's skin and/or some falsely accused slight or alleged offense. Perhaps the most famous example is that of Emmett Till, who at the age of 14 was lynched by a group of white vigilantes for allegedly whistling suggestively at a white woman.

Hanging was not always successful. The fall from a tree, ladder, or horse might be too gradual to be fatal. If you have had the good fortune to have taken a tour of Kilmainham Gaol in Dublin, Ireland, you may have heard the tour guide talk about the science of knowing just the right length of rope, the right height to drop the accused, based on their weight and height. Executioners were often professionals who conducted hangings for a living, going from town to town where they were hired for executions. Some of the accused were buried while they were still alive and conscious after their hanging, interred in premature burials. This is one of the most primal of human fears, particularly before the age where medicine more accurately identified the moment when someone dies by vital signs measurement. By the end of the 19th century, reformists started thinking about more humane ways of execution.

Even today, in parts of the world where hanging is still an option, the "long drop" requires professional executioners to weigh the prisoner the day before the execution, in order to assure the rope is the right length—too long, the individual may be decapitated in the process; too short and strangulation may take several minutes to occur (Young, 2015).

Firing Squad

The firing squad was viewed as a more humane form of execution, and unlike hanging, was more likely to be fatal. In some firing squads there is anonymity, where not all of the shooters are given live rounds of ammunition, so that no executioner is sure if they were the one to fire the fatal bullet. The condemned may or may not be blindfolded, as seen in the artist Goya's print, *Y No Hai Remedo* (1810, translated from Spanish: *And there is no help*). The subject of Goya's series of prints depicted in his series, *The Disasters of War*, were the tragedies of Napoleon's occupation of Spain, including execution of prisoners of war.

And There Is No Help, Francisco de Goya y Lucientes, 1810, The Metropolitan Museum of Art, NYC. (*Source*: National Galleries of Scotland, retrieved from https://www.nationalgalleries.org/art-and-artists/ 33979/and-there-no-help-y-no-hai-remedio-plate-15-disasters-war)

433

Today the condemned facing a firing squad is usually tied to a chair or pole, with a black hood over their heads. In some places in the world, the accused is simply made to kneel, either facing towards or away from the executioner, killed with a single shot or more to the head. The shooters in a firing squad are supposed to aim for the heart, but can miss the condemned, either by accident or intentionally, in which case the prisoner will slowly bleed to death (Young, 2015). This does not occur in the United States, as there are very specific protocols to assure that condemned dies as instantaneously as possible. The states of Mississippi, Oklahoma, South Carolina, and Utah are currently the only states that authorize the use of the firing squad in executions, with some arguing that it is a more humane way to execute people, in light of the controversies surrounding lethal injections (Sarat, 2021a), discussed later in this section.

Electric Chair

Before it was used to execute those convicted of capital crimes, electricity was used to discipline prisoners. This was accomplished by placing them in a few inches of water, naked, blindfolded, and cuffed, then transmitting the electricity through the water. These electrical devices originated from cattle prods and were used both by law enforcement and corrections officers (Hillman, 2003).

It would seem that on the surface, the electric chair was part of the ongoing search for a more humane method of execution. The reality is that the invention of the electric chair came about because of an economic war in the late 19th century between George Westinghouse and Thomas Edison who were competing for customers for their relatively new electric power sources. Westinghouse developed alternating current or AC power, whereas Edison had created direct current or DC power. In order to prove the alleged superiority of DC power, Edison toured the country executing thousands of animals in public demonstrations in a smear campaign, using AC power, which he was implying was more dangerous than DC. He was correct, to some extent as, according to electricians, it is somewhat safer to work with DC power, but both types of electricity can result in electrical shock leading to heart attacks or death (Evans, 2019).

To further demonize Westinghouse's AC electricity, Edison secured support from his political allies to develop an electric chair, using AC power (Pusey, 2019). By 1889, the first electrical execution law went into effect. To counter Edison's campaign to discredit AC electricity, Westinghouse offered to pay for the appeals for the first people sentenced to death by electrocution, citing cruel and unusual punishment.

There have been a number of bungled executions using the electric chair and procedures have evolved to address these issues that can lead to an excruciating death. Today, electrocution involves the condemned receiving between 2,400 to 3,000 volts of electricity, given in cycles of high and low shocks and takes about 2.5 minutes to death (Givens, 2013). Executioners, if given a choice, prefer electrocution over lethal injection as it is a shorter procedure in duration, as well as feeling like it is more hands off than the direct administration of drugs (Givens, 2013). However, the electric chair was and is one of the most barbaric forms of execution (Bedau, 1997).

Gas Chamber

Gassing was originally proposed by Dr. Allen McLean Hamilton who was a toxicologist. He suggested that it was an execution method that would be more humane than hanging or shooting which were the choices offered to condemned men in Nevada in the early part of the 20th century. However, by the later part of the century, the method was argued to be in violation of the 8th Amendment, as it was increasingly viewed as cruel and unusual punishment (Bedau, 1997).

First used in the euthanizing of injured or unwanted animals in the 19th century, lethal gas was viewed as a gentler way to put the condemned to death, by depriving them of oxygen after they had fallen into a deep sleep (Sarat, 2014). In 1921, the Nevada State Assembly proposed a change in the method of execution to the gas chamber that passed into law, ushering in a new, but brief era of executions (Sarat, 2014). The first death chamber in the United States using lethal gas was built at the Carson City Penitentiary, using cyanide gas (Sarat, 2014).

Lethal Injection

The gas chamber has rapidly been replaced with lethal injection as a means of execution. As the gas chamber was viewed in the 1930s, lethal injection was viewed as quick, painless, and reliable, as well as less disfiguring of the condemned during execution (Bedau, 1997). However, as what has transpired with other forms of execution used within the last century, lethal injection is now being questioned as to how humane it really is.

Lethal injection is the administration of drugs to euthanize the condemned. Some states and the federal government will only use lethal injections for executions while others offer a secondary method.

One major concern with lethal injection, beyond the fact that it can be a long, drawn out death for some people, is the problem with correctional facilities carrying out the executions acquiring the right drugs in the first place. Some states are looking at alternatives to lethal injection in the face of the shortage of the drugs. However, the shortage of the drugs for lethal injection seems to wax and wane, plus some drugs used in executions have expiration dates that come and go, before they are needed (Wamsley, 2021). One solution is to place a moratorium on carrying out death penalty warrants until the drugs are readily available. The second solution, as South Carolina has been debating and reported by *The Washington Post*, is as an alternative solution of forcing Death Row inmates to choose between the electric chair or firing squad if the drugs are not available (Salcedo, 2021a).

The condemned is typically given an intravenous injection of one to three drugs, depending on the state. According to the Death Penalty Information Center, the states that currently use only one injection, Arizona, Georgia, Idaho, Missouri, Ohio, South Dakota, Texas, and Washington, administer a lethal dose of anesthetic, generally pentobarbital. For those who use three injections, they will first administer an anesthetic, pancuronium bromide, second a paralytic agent, and finally, potassium chloride which stops the heart and causes death (Death Penalty Information Center, n.d.c). Death is expected to occur after 5 minutes; however, the whole procedure can take up to 45 minutes.

One of the great ironies of lethal injection is that the injection site where an IV is placed is first swabbed with isopropyl alcohol, used in the administration of shots (e.g., vaccinations) in order to avoid infection. One might assume that the precaution is taken in the very rare chance that there is a last minute reprieve. Another irony is that for some of the condemned, they were previously intravenous drug users, making it difficult to find a viable vein to insert the IV.

BOTCHED EXECUTIONS

Botched executions occur either when procedures are not strictly followed or when there is some issue that arises during the execution that those present are not prepared to handle. According to Sarat (2014), over the course of 120 years in the United States, approximately 3 percent of executions have gone wrong, with lethal injections having the highest rates of failures.

In 1924, Gee Jon, who had been convicted of murder, was executed in California, which amounted to a botched attempt to kill him in the gas chamber. The procedure did not go according to plan, as there was a malfunction of the heater inside the chamber, which had to be heated to a critical 79 degrees for the hydrocyanic acid (HCN) to turn lethal (Sarat, 2014). The witnesses and executioners entered the chamber only to find that Jon was still breathing, but he finally succumbed to the fumes within another six minutes (Sarat, 2014).

There have been a number of cases of lethal injections not working as planned, resulting in questions of just how humane this form of execution is compared to earlier methods. One of the most notable cases involved Clayton Lockett in Oklahoma, on Death Row for the murder of 19-year-old Stephanie Neiman. It was a particularly brutal murder in that Neiman had been kidnapped, raped, and assaulted, shot, and subsequently buried alive (United States Court of Appeals, *Estate of Clayton Lockett v. Fallin*, 2016). Just prior to his execution, Lockett made a number of attempts at suicide, including fashioning a noose out of sheets, using the blade out of a safety razor to make cuts into his arms, and swallowing pills that he had hoarded (Stern, 2015).

To make matters worse, Lockett's execution did not go as planned. In fact, it has now become a textbook case of botched executions. Once Lockett was strapped down and being prepped for his execution, the medical personnel assigned to inserting the IV line had difficulty finding a vein. They resorted to inserting a needle that was the incorrect size into a vein in Lockett's groin area, allegedly hitting an artery which resulted in blood splattering everywhere (Fretland, 2014). The execution proceeded, but not after a great deal of discomfort experienced by Lockett. We should note that a number of alternative procedures had to be used, as the drugs ordinarily used were difficult to come by and new protocols had been put into place prior to Lockett's execution.

The family of Clayton Lockett eventually sued a number of individuals, including the then Governor of Oklahoma, Mary Fallin, and Anita Trammell, the warden of the Oklahoma State Penitentiary (United States Court of Appeals, *Estate of Clayton Lockett v. Fallin,* 2016). In the court case, the lawyers for the family argued that one of the alternative drugs used in Lockett's execution, midazolam, which is intended to render the condemned unconscious, poses a risk that the subsequent two drugs could cause excruciating pain in the event that the dosage is not sufficient (United States Court of Appeals, *Estate of Clayton Lockett v. Fallin,* 2016). Even though the second drug, vecuronium bromide, and the third drug, potassium chloride, had been administered, Lockett was still conscious and attempted to rise off of the table (United States Court of Appeals, *Estate of Clayton Lockett v. Fallin,* 2016). As the court papers note, in response to Lockett's obvious consciousness and pain,

> *Dr. Doe examined the IV site and saw that the injection vein had collapsed, preventing some of the drugs from reaching Lockett's circulatory system. Responding to a question from Director Patton [Department of Oklahoma Corrections], Dr. Doe5 advised him that he believed insufficient drugs had entered Lockett's system to cause death. Dr. Doe also told Director Patton that no other vein was available and that insufficient drugs remained to complete the execution even if Dr. Doe could find another vein. . . . As events soon proved, Dr. Doe was mistaken that the drugs in Lockett's system might not cause death. At 7:06 p.m., Dr. Doe declared Lockett dead, 43 minutes after the executioners administered the first drug.* (United States Court of Appeals, *Estate of Clayton Lockett v. Fallin,* 2016, p. 8)

It was concluded in an Oklahoma state report that there were a number of errors made in the Lockett execution, including IV errors and poor training on the part of those involved in the administering of the drugs (Aspinwall and Branstetter, 2014). As a result, two subsequent executions had to be put on hold in 2014, as the prison continued to not have the necessary medical equipment nor a contingency plan yet in place in the event that things went wrong as in the Lockett case (Aspinwall and Branstetter, 2014).

---

[5] In some court cases, the respondents' names are anonymous in court documents. In the civil case against a number of individuals who were present at Lockett's execution, they are called "John" or "Jane" Doe, including the doctors and executioners, in order to protect them from retaliation, in the event that their real names become public.

Lockett was far from the only lethal injection execution going wrong. In the case of Dennis McGuire in Ohio, his execution has been described as a tortuous death. A reporter witnessing the execution, noted that McGuire gasping and convulsing for approximately ten minutes before expiring (Ford and Fantz, 2014). McGuire's execution was conducted using a new untested drug combination that, in his case, did not provide the humane and peaceful death promised by proponents of lethal injection. Students from Amherst College in Massachusetts (2021) discovered in their research collaboration[6] while studying lethal injections, that at least 3.7 percent of all executions between 2010 and 2020 resulted in problems while administering the drugs (Sarat, 2021b).

LIFE ON DEATH ROW — INMATES

We start with the sentencing in capital cases, where inmates are viewed by the jury, the courts, and by society in general, as being beyond redemption. Even during the course of appeals, except in the rare case of new evidence or problems with original trials or rulings, the condemned are viewed by the public as the most disposable of convicts in the "waste management" philosophy of corrections. Death Row inmates are not allowed to mingle with the general population of prisoners and are held in solitary confinement in special units of maximum security prisons.

Life on Death Row is a combination of monotony and anxiety. This is true for all prisoners, but both of these are heightened for the Death Row inmate. They are heavily guarded, ineligible for most prison jobs and programs, with little exception. There was a very popular television show, *Prison Break* (2005-2009; 2017, 20th Century Fox Television), where at the beginning of the series, one of the main characters was a Death Row inmate who was portrayed as having the freedom to spend large portions of their day out of his cell, including working with access to other parts of the prison and allowed to converse freely with non-Death Row inmates. Anyone who is not familiar with the facts of actual life on Death Row might believe that condemned inmates have that much mobility in the prison. The portrayals of Death Row on *Prison Break* and other television shows and movies, are more often far from the realities of Death Row life.

Social Death

A death penalty is intended to kill the offenders in two ways. The first "death" is both social and psychological, where the individual is separated from the general

---

[6] This is not the first time that college students have had a major impact in the death penalty debate. Journalism students at Northeastern raised the question of just how many innocent people were on Death Row for a class project in the 1990s. Their results influenced then Governor Ryan of Illinois to place a moratorium on executions until further investigations into their cases.

population, with little legitimate ability to even communicate with other Death Row inmates. Visits with friends and loved ones from the outside are limited.

The second death is virtual, if the convicted is not successful through the appeal process to have their original sentence either overturned or commuted by clemency, or if, when proven innocent in a new trial, released from prison. There is always the remote possibility of a pardon, but these are rare in death penalty cases. But by then, even if the individual has been released from prison or released into the general prison population in the case of commutations, the damage of social death has already taken place.

Last Day on Death Row

The stay on Death Row can be a long one. Depending on the state, the appeal process can take decades. Once all appeals have been exhausted, to no avail and no changes to the original sentence of death, the condemn faces a scheduled date of execution. Except in the cases of successful suicide or legal euthanasia of terminal patients, this is the only other situation where the individual is aware of the date and time of their death, sometimes several months in advance.

Bovey (n.d.), an editor for *The Versed* website, describes the last day of a Death Row inmate where the method of execution was the electric chair, paraphrased here:

- The Death Row inmate will be transferred the evening before their execution to the Death House. This prevents them from fighting or attacking corrections officers or staff during transit to their execution. They can also be more closely observed and prevent them, ironically, from taking their own life in advance.
- On the way to the Death House, barring any last minute appeal, this is the last time the condemned will see the light of day. Often the corridors leading to the Death House are open above to the sky for this very reason.
- The condemned are housed in a cell that contains a toilet and a shower, and is often more luxurious as compared to the Death Row cells, including a phone for their use just outside of the cell.
- The inmate is allowed to change their clothes into something that looks less like a prison uniform, but without a belt or laces or anything worn that could be used in a suicide attempt.
- Throughout that day as they settle into the Death House, they are allowed to speak with the prison chaplain, visit with family and/or use the phone. The only person they can use their last call to is the prison chaplain. They may be writing farewell letters as well.
- On the actual day of the execution, the inmate will have an early lunch, but this will not be their last meal with special requests.
- Late afternoon, preparation for the execution takes place, including requiring the condemned to shower and have their head shaved for the electric chair.

■ The inmate then has their last meal, with execution taking place within hours afterwards, again barring any last minute appeal or stay by the governor of the state.

We should note that even though the electric chair is viewed as an inhumane and painful way to execute an individual, it is still an option in a number of states in the United States. In 2018, Edmund Zagorski who was scheduled for execution, requested the use of the electric chair over lethal injection, based on the painful and scary side effects some people experience with one or more of the three drugs used (*The Independent*, 2018). His argument tested once again the 8th Amendment prohibition of cruel and unusual punishment.

The Last Meal

Few people entertain the thought of what they their wish actual last meal would be and certainly do not contemplate the unthinkable of that happening on Death Row. There are a lot of preconceived notions about the last meal that the condemned can order. The reality is that it would be impossible to fulfill all requests for the menu. For example, if a Death Row inmate requests a fruit or vegetable that is out of season, unless it is available canned or frozen, there is little chance of acquiring it.

There is generally a dollar limit placed on the last meal in a most states. Also, anything that is prohibited in prison is denied, including alcoholic beverages. It is very unlikely that the condemned will have much of an appetite just before their execution, so much of the food ordered may go untouched. The following is a list of last meals of famous criminals who have been executed in the United States (Capatides, 2015, retrieved from https://www.cbsnews.com/pictures/last-meals-of-death-row/):

■ Victor Feguer, put to death by hanging for a kidnapping and murder requested a single olive. (Iowa, 1963)

■ John Wayne Gacy (Pogo the Clown), put to death for rape and 33 counts of murder, requested 12 fried shrimp, a bucket of original recipe KFC® fried chicken, French fries, and a pound of strawberries. Gacy had managed 3 KFC® restaurants prior to his arrest. (Illinois, 1994)

■ Timothy McVeigh, one of the convicted Oklahoma City bombers, put to death by lethal injection after being sentenced on 168 counts of murder, ordered two pints of mint chocolate chip ice cream. (Indiana, 2001)

■ Ricky Ray Rector, put to death by lethal injection after being convicted on two counts of murder, requested a steak, fried chicken, cherry Kool-Aid®, and pecan pie. Rector, who was mentally incapacitated during his time on Death Row infamously left the pie uneaten, telling the correction officer he was "saving it for later." (Arkansas, 1992)

■ Stephen Anderson, put to death by lethal injection for burglary, assault, seven counts of murder, and escaping from prison, ordered two grilled cheese sandwiches, a pint of cottage cheese, a hominy/corn mixture,

The Last Meal (continued)

peach pie, chocolate chip ice cream, and radishes. (California, 2002)

- Angel Nieves Diaz, put to death by lethal injection for murder, kidnapping, and armed robbery, declined his last meal, so he was served the regular prison food, which he did not eat. (Florida, 2006)
- Ted Bundy, put to death in the electric chair for rape, necrophilia, prison escape, and 35 counts of murder, declined a special meal so was given the traditional last meal served in California that included a steak, eggs, hash browns, toast with butter and jelly, milk, and juice. (California, 1989)

- Teresa Lewis, put to death by lethal injection for murder, conspiracy, and robbery, requested fried chicken, peas with butter, apple pie, and a Dr. Pepper® soda. (Virginia, 2010)
- Ronnie Threadgill, put to death by lethal injection for murder, requested baked chicken, mashed potatoes with country vegetables, sweet peas, bread, tea, water, and punch. Unfortunately, Texas had abolished last meal choices in 2011 for the condemned so he was served the same meals as everyone else in his unit. (Texas, 2013)

Famous Last Words

Often the last words of the condemned before they lose consciousness include comments on one or more of three subjects: Apologies to family and/or victims, criticism of criminal justice system, and/or venting of one's frustrations. These are generally given in written statements, but can also be spoken in the death chamber.

Historically, in a number of cultures, there were *symbolic executions* with no intention of actually killing the accused. Last words, particularly when the offenders indicated repentance and made apologies for their crimes,

could mean being spared execution (Ward, 2015). However, a symbolic execution could result in a real execution, in the case of a prisoner who is not contrite. Symbolic executions, as seen prior to the 19th century, at least in the United States, no longer take place. No last words coming from the condemned will overturn the sentence, unless a legal mandated stay of execution occurs or a last minute pardon or commuted sentence.

Stimson (2020, retrieved from https://www.foxnews.com/us/death-row-inmates-last-words) and Batchelor (2020, retrieved from

Famous Last Words (continued)

https://www.newsweek.com/brandon-bernard -execution-final-words-death-row-inmate -1554026) reported on some of the statements made by Death Row inmates before their executions:

- Corey Johnson (executed on January 14, 2021, by lethal injection):
  I want to say that I'm sorry for my crimes. I wanted to say that to the families that I victimized. To my family I have always loved you. . . . On the streets, I was looking for shortcuts, I had some good role models, I was side tracking, I was blind and stupid. I am not the same man that I was.
- Billie Wayne Coble (executed on February 28, 2019, by lethal injection):
  . . . That'll be five dollars, take care.[7]

- Joseph Garcia (executed on December 5, 2019, by lethal injection):
  Dear heavenly Father, please forgive them, for they know not what they do.
- Robert Sparks (executed on September 25, 2019, by lethal injection):
  I am sorry for the hard times. And what hurts me is that I hurt y'all. . . . I love you all . . . I feel it.
- Don Johnson (executed on May 16, 2019, by lethal injection):
  No more dying here.
- Brandon Bernard (executed on December 10, 2020, by lethal injection)
  I wish I could take it all back, but I can't . . . I'm sorry, that's the only words that I can say that completely capture how I feel now and how I felt that day [for the kidnapping and killing of two youth ministers].

LIFE ON DEATH ROW — PRISON STAFF

The primary social interaction that Death Row inmates experience is with corrections officers. Most facilities discourage anything beyond professional interaction between corrections staff and inmates. Prison personnel are discouraged from acknowledging the humanity of these prisoners. This is really intended for the self-preservation of the corrections officers, as it is difficult to not become sympathetic to an inmate, particularly if they are on Death Row for a number of years, only to see them go to their execution, whether it is viewed as justified or not and irrespective of their personal views on the death penalty.

---

[7] While Cole was giving his statement, his son, a friend, and daughter-in-law, witnesses to his execution, became emotionally violent, including throwing fists and kicking at other witnesses — the two men were arrested (Stimson, 2020).

The Executioner

There is perhaps more research conducted on the history of executioners, particularly in the Middle Ages in Europe, than on corrections staff working on Death Row and executioners today. For example, in a published diary of Frantz Schmidt's life as an executioner, in his occupation from 1573 to 1618, he talked about his life living on the margins, where executioners were part of a dishonorable caste, but were well-compensated for their services (Harrington, 2013). It was basically a dirty job and executioners with their families often lived on the edges of "proper" society.

What we know about executioners today is more likely to be found in firsthand accounts from the executioners themselves. Descriptions of executions by the executioners can be sanitized, describing the condemned as having fallen asleep peacefully on "beds," instead of using the more sterile and correct term for what they are strapped down to, a hospital gurney (Tarm, 2021). Other witnesses to the same executions, including the media, paint a different picture, describing the prisoner as thrashing about, shaking, and shuddering as the pentobarbital takes effect (Tarm, 2021).

In one self-reporting of life as a contemporary executioner, Jerry Givens has discussed his regrets of working as a state executioner. Working 25 years for the Department of Corrections in Virginia, he administered the death penalty, by lethal injection and electric chair from 1982 to 1992 (Givens, 2013). Since leaving his position as state executioner, Givens now campaigns for the abolishment of the death penalty.

LIFE FOR THE FAMILY AND FRIENDS OF DEATH ROW INMATES

Durkheim and other social scientists believed that punishment is extended to family and friends of the accused. Children are condemned to live under the shadow of not only their parents' crimes, but the sentence they receive, including the death penalty. Examples include offspring of the infamous married couple, Julius and Ethel Rosenberg, executed during the 1950s in the United States, after having been convicted of spying for the Soviet Union during the Cold War. The offspring of the Rosenbergs' children, Michael and Robert[8], who were sent to live with relatives after their parents' arrest and subsequent conviction and execution, changed their last names to Meeropol and only in recent years publicly admitted who their real parents were (Blakemore, 2021).

There can be one of two primary reactions from the family members and friends of the condemned. Some react by emotionally withdrawing from the individual and

---

[8] Both brothers grew up to be college professors, with Michael having recently retired from Western New England University, where this author is a professor emerita.

others respond with renewed support (Radelet et al., 1983). Some of the horrors, emotions, and experiences that the condemneds' family and friends experience, according to Sharpe (2005) include the following:

- Projected loss of their loved one to execution;
- Alienation from the condemned;
- Alienation from their neighbors and friends who may shun them;
- Social isolation as additional stigma of being related to a capital crime offender, some of whom have been convicted of doing unspeakable crimes;
- Artificial atmosphere of prison visits, including in the last days; and
- Anguish of witnessing execution, if their request to be present is granted.

The means by which the loved ones of the accused cope with the impeding loss of their friend or relative may be expected to follow the classic Kübler-Ross (1969; Kübler-Ross and Kessler, 2014) stages of bereavement and grief model. (Figure 13.4)

Because most people do not know what to say to someone who is grieving the forthcoming execution of a loved one, far less emotional and social support can be expected. Though the Kübler-Ross model of grief recovery is still universally accepted, there are a number of criticisms as well for the model.

More recent scholars have warned health care professionals not to expect those in mourning to go through these stages strictly in order, nor to expect them to hit every grieving milestone. In fact, it can be more harmful to the bereaved if they are expected to adhere to these five stages during their recovery and fail to do so (Stroebe et al., 2017). Others see the stages as being more like a circular staircase than a straight line to acceptance of death and dying (Stroebe et al., 2017), including the grieving experiences of the convict, and will vacillate between stages in various orders. For example, even the condemned may one day accept the inevitable, as they grieve their own life coming to an end, but bounce back to bargaining and anger stages, as they move through the appeals process.

We should also note that there can be economic loss to the family of the condemned, when it is a primary breadwinner or ex-spouse who is incarcerated, including those on Death Row. If they have in the past provided child support or alimony, this generally goes away (if it hasn't happened already) when the ex-spouse is arrested and incarcerated. As in the case of a divorce, it is generally a single-female head of household who is left financially destitute, when ex-spouse or partner is no longer providing financial assistance.

However the people who are left behind grieve before and after an execution, many do not have the means to pay for professional help in dealing with their bereavement. Some may be haunted by the loss and the stigma for years, if not decades, as in the example of the Rosenberg sons after their parents' execution. Others may feel ashamed to seek professional help, even if they have the means to do so, as is all too common with people dealing with emotional stress and

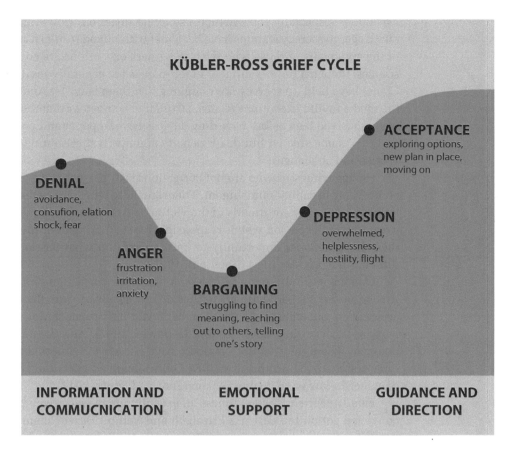

FIGURE 13.4 **Five States of Grief and Corresponding Therapy Needs.**
(*Source*: Grand Valley State University Counseling Center, 2020, retrieved from https://www
.gvsu.edu/counsel/grief-and-loss-week-two-335.htm.)

bereavement. Thankfully there is currently more public awareness of the benefits of seeking psychological or psychiatric help in difficult times including in bereavement.

WITNESSES TO EXECUTIONS

Right-to-view statutes for executions are intimately tied to earlier demands of the public to be allowed to witness the death of those who have committed capital crimes. Some of the interest in witnessing executions stems from reports of bungled executions, especially those which use lethal injection. However, in recent years, challenges to secrecy statutes have been met with mixed results (Gates, 2019). Many of the arguments of those who wish to witness executions are coming from media sources, though a limited number of journalists are generally invited (Gates, 2019). Courts have held up secrecy laws, arguing that there is no 1st Amendment right for the media to film executions (Gates, 2019). If you consider that the 1st Amendment was conceived long before recording devices beyond paper and pen, it makes sense that this is one area within death penalty arguments that continue to raise controversies and challenges.

Having witnesses who are not corrections staff present at executions is another controversy in capital punishment. There are those who believe that it is the right of the family members or friends of the victim or victims to be allowed to witness the execution of the person who is responsible for murdering their loved one. To allow them to do so is an opportunity to have closure on what has to be an extremely difficult time in their lives (Goodwin, 1997).

Opponents to allowing witnesses other than corrections officials to witness executions argue that victims' families do not necessarily get the closure that they are seeking, plus that the death chamber is not the proper setting for catharsis and may result in further victimization (Goodwin, 1997). And in the case of the condemned, where their family members have chosen to witness the execution, it is often traumatizing. In the case of McGuire's bungled execution, his children and daughter-in-law were visibly shaken (Ford and Fantz, 2014).

Family or friends who witness an execution may walk away believing that the convicted got off too easy. As Elizabeth and Vernon Harvey commented after witnessing their daughter's murderer, Robert Lee Willie, executed,

> He died an extremely lot easier than my daughter. . . . He got a spiritual advisor, the choice of a last meal. Know what they should've done to Willie? . . . They should've strapped him in that chair, count to ten, then at count of nine take him out of the chair and let him sit in his cell for a day or two and then strapped him in the chair again. (Goodwin, 1997, retrieved from https://www.pbs.org/wgbh/pages/frontline/shows/execution/readings/against.html)

COUNTRIES THAT CURRENTLY HAVE THE DEATH PENALTY

Amnesty International reported that there were at least 2,307 known death sentences in 56 countries in 2019 (Death Penalty Information Center, 2019). As we know from death penalty cases in the United States, not all death sentences mean immediate execution, though there are some countries that are hastier to carry out sentences than others. However, in keeping with our 2019 benchmark, that year the countries that carried out the most *known* executions were China, Iran, Saudi Arabia, Iraq, and Egypt, in that order (Amnesty International, 2020).

In some countries, because of a lack of transparency, we do not know the true figures of how many people have been put to death as punishment. The United States is currently the only western country to still have the death penalty. We should note that not all legal systems in the world are secular as in the United States. For instance, *Sharia Law* followed in Muslim countries has its basis in religious doctrine, including the use of the death penalty.

The forms of execution also vary around the world, though save Saudi Arabia, some of the same methods utilized in the United States are used elsewhere. In Saudi Arabia, beheading is also a method of execution carried out on the condemned, who sometimes is given a sedative and blindfolded, and also used for nonviolent crimes including adultery, blasphemy, sexual intercourse outside of marriage, homosexuality[9], and sorcery (Young, 2015).

The death penalty is less common in the world than it was a century ago. According to Anckar (2014), fewer than half of all countries in the world have the death penalty on the books; only 30 percent will actually apply it.

CURRENT DEBATES ON THE DEATH PENALTY

The debates centered on capital punishment continue to bring forth the same arguments for and against its use. Both sides of the argument use the Constitution to prove their points, which can result in mostly debates about semantics, as in the example of what constitutes "cruel and unusual punishment." Some of the debate is centered, as we saw earlier in this chapter, on the method used. We summarize both sides of the argument here within this section.

Comparisons of Life Sentences and the Death Penalty

Comparisons on pros and cons of life sentences versus the death penalty include:

- The death penalty is more expensive.
- The death penalty has not been proven to serve as a deterrent.
- Life sentences (without parole) provide the protection from repeat offenders that the public looks for.
- Even if paroled, an inmate who is released at 55 or 60 years old is statistically less likely to commit another crime.

---

[9]Until the 20th century, in most countries, homosexuality, if detected or suspected, whether factual or not, was considered deviant and punishable in criminal court. Homosexual acts between consenting adults only became officially legal in the United States in 2003, in *Lawrence v. Texas*.

- Life sentence inmates are some of the most well-behaved inmates; if released they can contribute to youth programs (e.g., Scared Straight).

Controversies Surrounding the Death Penalty

Here is a summary list of the some of the key controversies and questions surrounding capital punishment (American Civil Liberties Union, 2021):

- The death penalty is not fairly applied in cases.
- It is a waste of taxpayers' dollars, because of multiple appeals.
- Innocent people are too often sentenced to death.[10]
- Is there such a thing as a humane execution?
- Should jurors be given more choice of penalties in capital crime cases (e.g., *mandatory* vs. *discretionary death penalty* recommended sentencing).
- Prior to DNA evidence, how many innocent people ended up on Death Row or worse yet, executed?
- What should be done about the disproportionate number of people of color who are sentenced to Death Row? There is doubt on the guilt of some, but as to others, the sentence may well be due to charges of racism in sentencing.
- In the case of some murders, like crimes of passion, is the offender really unredeemable?

So as to be fair and balanced on the subject of the death penalty, here are some of the arguments generally given as to why the death penalty should be an option in sentencing (PEW Research Center, 2021):

- Most Americans (65 percent in 2021) favor the death penalty.
- The death penalty is morally justified (biblical; "an eye for an eye" retribution)
- The death penalty deters people from committing serious crimes.
- There are adequate safeguards in the criminal justice system to prevent innocent people from being executed.

We can note that there are more questions than answers swirling around the ethics and practicalities of the death penalty and the topic will no doubt continue to be a subject of debate for years to come in countries that still have capital punishment. Even those states and countries that have abolished the death penalty can reinstate it if the political winds blow in that direction. With U.S. opinion almost evenly split about the death penalty, it is highly unlikely that changes will be made, except perhaps in some states, on this, the most controversial topic in corrections.

---

[10] This is a tougher argument today in light of DNA evidence technology.

SUMMARY

The controversies surrounding capital punishment fall on the sides of constitution-ality, human rights, tough crime policies, ethics, and religion. Executions, legal or otherwise, for supposed or proven wrongdoings, are as old as time and no doubt predate written history. What we see in the United States, where just 55 percent approve of the death penalty, there is a vast divide between those who are for capi-tal punishment and who are against it, plus their reasons for their viewpoints.

There are several methods used in executions in the United States and around the world, including the more popular form in recent decades, lethal injection. Seen as a more humane way to execute the condemned, there have been a number of issues surrounding its use, including availability of the appropriate drugs, the fact that people will react differently to medication, and the ethics of administering the drugs by medical personnel whose very professions are based in life saving, not life taking. Other forms of execution used in the past or currently available in some places of the world are hanging, one of the oldest forms of execution, the electric chair, gas chamber, and firing squad. In Saudi Arabia, beheading is also an option.

Throughout this book, including in this chapter, an undercurrent for consid-eration in the information provided is whether jail or prison is the punishment of the soul or punishment of the body. We have to remember that it is not up to jail or prison administers to decide if the punishment fits the crime—that is the job of sentencing guidelines, judges, and juries. In the United States, within the court system, the U.S. Supreme Court is the final legal authority, except in the case of pardons or commutations by governors or the president.

Few would dispute the argument that punishment should by its very name be unpleasant, so as to be a deterrent or offer restitution to society. The controversies here will not be easily settled, if at all, as to whether the death penalty and other questioned practices in punishment serve their intended purposes. Either way, decisions made as to what is appropriate punishment inevitably affects the lives of the convicted, their corrections officers, and their families, friends.

STORIES FROM BEHIND BARS

The Killing of George Stinney, Jr, Youngest Death Row Inmate[11]

At age 14, George Stinney, Jr., a Black juvenile in South Carolina, was executed by the electric chair on June 16, 1944. He had been sentenced to death after an all-white male jury deliberated for minutes after a three-hour trial, not the usual days

---

[11] Because the primary sources for this *Stories from Behind Bars* section come from journalism, the author has reviewed a number of news stories in order to confirm or refute the information on any one website.

or weeks it takes for a murder conviction - There was virtually no Black person in the courthouse during his trial (Kulmala and Marchant, 2019; Chappell, 2014). Stinney was to be the youngest person ever to be executed in the United States. The crimes of which he was convicted included the murder of two white girls, ages seven and eleven (McLaughlin, 2014). His trial and execution were swiftly carried out less than three months after the girls' murder, unheard of by today's standards of due process (Kulmala and Marchant, 2019). According to his former cellmate, Stinney maintained his innocence until the end (Pan and Berry Hawes, 2020).

George Stinney, Jr., Youngest Death Row Inmate. (*Source*: NPR, 2014, retrieved from https://www.npr.org/sections/thetwo-way/2014/12/17/371534533/s-c-judge-says-boy -14-shouldn-t-have-been-executed.)

In 2014, the family of Kinney sought a new trial, claiming that while an exoneration would not bring him back, it would at least clear his name (McLaughlin, 2014). Their belief, as well as those of others, is that he had been coerced into making a confession. In fact, he had an alibi, and the fact that his jury consisted of all white males during a time of tremendous racial prejudices under *Jim Crow laws*[12] in the south left the arrest, trial, and sentencing suspect (McLaughlin, 2014).

The new trial took place at a time when the fate of a number of young Black males, who in recent years have died either while being pursued by or in the custody of police, has brought renewed attention to the inequalities and inherent racism built into the criminal justice system. The Stinney case also brought back into

---

[12] The laws were formally upheld by authorities and informally (and illegally) often carried out by vigilantes, including the Ku Klux Klan (KKK). And even though the 15th Amendment was ratified in 1870, there were a number of obstacles the Black community faced in order to have an active voice in politics or anything else for that matter, due to institutionalized racism. This included the imposition of poll taxes and mass incarceration in the south of Black males.

focus the post-Civil War era of denying livelihoods, voices in government, and suppression of voting rights of Black Americans and other people of color living in the United States, as the "new Jim Crow."

Long after Stinney was executed, he was finally exonerated in October 2014, on the basis that he did not received a fair trial. It is key to note that it was not on the basis of innocence, which would be difficult to prove with the absence of state-of-the-art scientific evidence. Circuit Judge Carmen Mullen, who ruled on the case, wrote that "fundamental, Constitutional violations of due process exist in the 1944 prosecution of George Stinney, Jr., and hereby vacates the judgement." (Chappell, 2014, retrieved from https://www.npr.org/sections/thetwo-way/2014/12/17/371534533/s-c-judge-says-boy-14-shouldn-t-have-been-executed).

There was considerable good logic in exonerating him, as Kinney was convicted under the shadow of Jim Crow laws in the south. There are still extreme prejudices and discrimination against people of color, even after the abolishment of the Jim Crow laws, including informal segregation and racial oppressions, in spite of the provisions laid out in the Civil Rights Act of 1964, promising to protect the rights of people of color, along with other disenfranchised minority groups.

SOURCES

Chappell, B. (2014) S.C. Judge says 1944 execution of 14-year-old boy was wrong. NPR. Dec. 17. Retrieved from https://www.npr.org/sections/thetwo-way/2014/12/17/371534533/s-c-judge-says-boy-14-shouldn-t-have-been-executed.

Kulmala, T. and B. Marchant (2019) 75 years ago today, SC executed a black teenager after a three-hour trial. Crime and Courts, The State. June 16. Retrieved from https://www.thestate.com/news/local/crime/article231467578.html.

McLaughlin, E. C. (2014) New trial sought for George Stinney, executed at 14. CNN. Jan. 23. Retrieved from https://www.cnn.com/2014/01/21/us/george-stinney-hearing/.

Pan, D. and Berry Hawkes, J. (2020) Quest to clear George Stinny's name draws scrutiny to another man. *The Post Courier.* Sept. 14. Retrieved from https://www.postandcourier.com/news/special_reports/quest-to-clear-george-stinneys-name-draws-new-scrutiny-to-another-man/article_1f4a8474-292b-11e8-bd9f-d334d74b4604.html.

INTERNATIONAL PERSPECTIVES ON PUNISHMENT AND CORRECTIONS: AFGHANASTAN

In August 2021, after nearly 20 years of intervention, the United States withdrew its military and civilians from Afghanistan. Why the United States was there in the first place is a long, complicated political and historical story and beyond the scope of this book. Suffice it to say, there have been a number of comparisons of the Afghanistan Wars (including a civil war and later American involvement) with the Vietnam War and their respective outcomes. However, it is an unfair comparison. One of the things that they do have in common is the type of media images that were published during both wars that uncovered and archived human suffering, including forms of capital punishment (George and Shoos, 2005).

To understand the reason why the United States was in Afghanistan is to understand what life was like under Taliban rule and al-Qaeda control. It also calls for understanding the reactions of the United States population and government to the events the 9/11 terrorist attacks on American soil. However, reactions to what was happening in Afghanistan also had to do with a number of documented international human rights violations. Some of the understanding of why the west had such a visceral reaction to conditions in Afghanistan can come from studying the means by which the death penalty was implemented under the Taliban.

The death penalty, as we see in this chapter, is absent from a number of other countries of the world that still have capital punishment, for cases of less serious crimes than murder. Again, we should note that the United States is the only country remaining among western countries that still has the death penalty in a number of states and at the federal level. However, since the 1930s in the United States, executions are exclusively conducted behind prison walls with a small audience witnessing the proceedings, all there on official business, or as the family members of the victim(s).

In a number of countries in the world, Afghanistan included, public executions and other punishments still take place. And some of these are horrific by human rights standards, though we should also be sensitive to the fact that due to cultural differences, any feelings we might have about public executions are subjective and not universally felt even in the United States. The amputation of limbs and other forms of mutilation are also commonplace, as punishment for theft, robbery, burglary and other offenses in countries that adhere strictly to Sharia laws, including Afghanistan under Taliban rule. Stoning is another means by which to carrying out a death sentence, for a number of offenses, including adultery.

During the 1990s, under Taliban rule, the Ghazi Stadium in Kabul was transformed into a scene of public executions and punishments for crimes, even as it was still being used as a sports arena. Mohammad Isaq, a soccer player who had left Afghanistan when civil war erupted in the early 1990s, came back to a country in 1996 to a different world than the one he left (Bezhan, 2012). Isaq, while serving as captain to the Afghan national soccer team at the time, describes his first training session at Ghazi Stadium in the late 1990s with the team:

> *We did some warm-ups and went to do some shooting practice. When I lifted a barrel that was in the middle of the pitch [playing surface], I found six amputated hands. . . . When I saw them it really affected me. I left the training session and the stadium and went home. I felt sick for one or two weeks.* (Fest, 2021, retrieved from https://www.infobae.com/aroundtherings/articles/2021/08/18/when-the -taliban-ruled-afghanistan-soccer-was-often-replaced-by-public-executions/)

The soccer field was said to be so blood-soaked that it was whispered that grass could not grow there (Bezhan, 2012).

Women were not spared the death penalty under Taliban rule. A woman only identified as Zarmeena (sometimes spelled Zarmina), a mother of seven children, was brought to the soccer field in Kabul by the Taliban in the bed of a pickup truck, forced to step off and walk to her execution in front of an audience of thousands in the stadium, some of whom were children (Fest, 2021; Miglani, 2008; Associated Press, 2002). She was forced to kneel, after which she was shot execution style in the back of the head. Up until her execution, Zarmeena believed that the only punishment she would receive for her crime would be 100 lashes and had borrowed extra dresses from her fellow inmates to wear under her burqa[13], in order to soften the blows (Fest, 2021).

Zarmeena's crime? She had beaten her husband to death. We do not have a clear picture of the circumstances of her crime, including the possibility of her being a victim of domestic violence. As the death penalty exists in the United States, even for some women who have been convicted of murder, what was so shocking to western eyes was the size of the public spectacle Zarmeena's execution was, where thousands had come out to lay witness to punishments handed out in the arena that day. The images of her execution became iconic representation of the general suffering of women under Taliban rule (Fest, 2021).

Woman Being Executed on Soccer Field in Afghanistan, 1999. (*Source*: *The Mirror*, 2002, retrieved from http://www.rawa.org/murder-w.htm)

---

[13] A burqa is a head to toe garment that women wear in Islamic countries to cover them entirely, sometimes including a veil to cover the face, as dictated by religious law and local customs.

For as haunting as images of the Ghazi Stadium executions in Kabul are to people in other countries around the world, they have likewise haunted the Afghan people as well. Though a number of sports are very popular in the country, few Afghans wish to visit the stadium at night as they fear that the ghosts of the executed still roam the grounds (Bezhan, 2012; Miglani, 2008). As Mohammad Nasim, a caretaker at the stadium observed, "Too much blood has flowed here." (Miglani, 2008, retrieved from https://www.reuters.com/article/us-afghan-stadium/taliban-executions-still-haunt-afghan-soccer-field-idUSSP12564220080913).

Even under the watchful eye of U.S. troops, the death penalty was still in use in Afghanistan, in accordance with criminal law and Islamic law (Sharia laws). However, at that time, there was an informal moratorium on the death penalty and punishments were no longer public spectacles (Qaane and Bjelica, 2016). Many of the executions that took place under American occupation were of convicted Taliban terrorists (Qaane and Bjelica, 2016). There are a number of fears now that these more brutal methods will return to the country, now that the United States has withdrawn its troops. The Taliban are reportedly claiming that they do not intend, at this time, to return to the same treatment of criminals and in particular, women in general, as they did in the 1990s. It is too soon at the time of this writing to predict which direction punishment, including death penalties, will go under the current Taliban regime.

SOURCES

Associated Press (2002) Taliban publicly execute woman. *The Mirror*. Nov. 17. Retrieved from http://www.rawa.org/murder-w.htm.

Bezhan, F. (2012) Afghans lift lid on sports under the Taliban. *Radio Free Europe*. July 11. Retrieved from https://www.rferl.org/a/afghans-recall-sports-under-the-taliban/24642278.html.

Fest, S. A. (2021) When the Taliban ruled Afghanistan soccer was often replaced by public executions. *Around the Rings*. Aug. 18. Retrieved from https://www.infobae.com/aroundtherings/articles/2021/08/18/when-the-taliban-ruled-afghanistan-soccer-was-often-replaced-by-public-executions/.

George, D. and D. Shoos (2005) Deflecting the political in the visual images of execution and the death penalty debate. College English. July, Vol. 67, Iss. 6:587-609.

Miglani, S. (2008) Taliban executions still haunt Afghan soccer field. Reuters. Sept. 12. Retrieved from https://www.reuters.com/article/us-afghan-stadium/taliban-executions-still-haunt-afghan-soccer-field-idUSSP12564220080913.

Qaane, E. and J. Bjelica (2016) Afghanistan's latest executions: Responding to calls for capital punishment. Rights and Freedoms, Afghanistan Analysts Network. May 11. Retrieved from https://www.afghanistan-analysts.org/en/reports/rights-freedom/afghanistans-latest-executions-responding-to-calls-for-capital-punishment/

GLOSSARY

5th Amendment of the U.S. Constitution   The so-called "due process" in a court of law amendment.

8th Amendment of the U.S. Constitution Cruel and unusual punishments are prohibited, along with excessive bail and fines.

14th Amendment of the U.S. Constitution An additional "due process" amendment that prohibits state and local governments from depriving persons of life, liberty, or property without a fair procedure

Black Jails (China) Secret detention centers throughout China that are notorious for holding political prisoners who are critical of the government.

Capital punishment The imposition of the death penalty in certain, particularly gruesome cases. Capital punishment is permitted on the federal level in the United States and in 27 states.

Dark tourism Tourism that is sometimes meant to satisfy the morbid curiosity of the visitors that places where human misery has taken place, including former jails and prisons. (See *grief tourism*.)

"Felon friendly" employers Employers who are willing to hire people with criminal records, including those with felony convictions. Some industries are more "felon friendly" than others.

Grief tourism Similar to dark tourism, but may include visits to places that have personal meaning, as in the case of the descendants of Holocaust survivors and victims visiting former concentration camps. ·

Jim Crow Laws State and local laws that prohibited integration of Blacks and whites and legalized institutional racism in the south.

Lynching The hanging by rope of an individual that has been targeted by a vigilante group, on the basis of their race and alleged crimes.

Mandatory vs. discretionary death penalty Cases where the death penalty is the only punishment allowed, if the individual has been found guilty as opposed to the discretion of a jury and/or a judge to impose the death penalty in a case.

Old Testament First part of the Christian Bible that is often cited as to why punishment should fit a crime. To paraphrase, "an eye for an eye" logic.

Pardons Powers of governors and presidents to "forgive" a crime and sets aside a judgement and sentence.

Qu'ran or Koran The primary religious writings in Islam.

Reprieves Cancellation or postponement of sentences, generally because new evidence has come to light. It does not necessarily mean that punishment won't eventually be handed out to the convicted, including in death penalty cases.

Right-to-view statutes The legal right to view and in the case of the media, record the proceedings during an execution. (See *Secrecy statutes*.)

Secrecy statutes   Law in some states to allow secrecy around the method of execution, even from the condemned. Also include the corrections department right to limit the number of witnesses at an execution. (See *Right-to-view statutes*.)

Sharia Law   Islamic religious laws.

Torah   First five books of the Hebrew Bible used in Judaism and thought to be the origins of the Old Testament in the Christian Bible.

Stays of execution   Similar to a reprieve, a delay in carrying out a court order, in the case of the death penalty, the execution.

Symbolic executions   Staged executions that were not intended to actually kill the accused. These were theatrical, public events, that allowed for the accused to show penitence and plead for their lives. For example, they might be brought to the gallows, even have a noose put around their necks, but were given a reprieve and pardon, after giving their "last words" speech.

REFERENCES AND SUGGESTED READINGS

Alcatraz Prison Cocktail Bar (n.d.) Available at https://www.alcotraz.co.uk/.

Amnesty International (2020) Death penalties in 2019: Facts and figures. Apr. 21. Retrieved from https://www.amnesty.org/en/latest/news/2020/04/death-penalty-in-2019-facts-and-figures/#:~:text=Global%20death%20penalty%20figures,in%20at%20least%20a%20decade.

Anckar, C. (2014) Why countries choose the death penalty. *Brown Journal of World Affairs*. Vol. 21, Iss. 1:7-26.

Aspinwall, C. and Z. Branstetter (2014) IV errors, lack of training cited in Oklahoma botched execution report. *Tulsa World*. Sept. 5. Retrieved from https://tulsaworld.com/news/local/crime-and-courts/iv-errors-lack-of-training-cited-in-oklahoma-botched-execution-report/article_daf3a9e5-6d7b-5a94-835c-951be33ac72a.html.

Batchelor, T. (2020) Brandon Bernard's final words before the execution of Death Row inmate. *Newsweek*. Dec. 11. Retrieved from https://www.newsweek.com/brandon-bernard-execution-final-words-death-row-inmate-1554026.

Bedau, H. A. (1997) *The Death Penalty in America: Current Controversies*. H. A. Bedau, ed. New York City, New York: Oxford University Press.

Blakemore, E. (2021) Why the Rosenbergs' sons eventually admitted their father was a spy. History Channel. Mar. 30. Retrieved from https://www.history.com/news/rosenberg-sons-admit-father-julius-guilty.

Bovey, L. J. (ed.) (n.d.) This is what your last day on Death Row would be like. *The Versed*. Retrieved from https://www.theversed.com/95849/last-day-death-row-like/#.J5Zah7LrIg.

Bowers, A. (2005a) Why executions happen at midnight: Capital punishment and the witching hour. SLATE. Dec. 13. Retrieved from https://slate.com/news-and-politics/2005/12/why-midnight-executions.html.

Bowers, A. (2005b) Slate's explainer: Early morning executions. NPR. Radio interview. Dec. 13. Retrieved from https://www.npr.org/templates/story/story.php?storyId=5051496.

Britan, D. B. (2017) Why tourist go to sites associated with death and suffering. *Salon*. Aug. 27. Retrieved from https://www.salon.com/2017/08/26/why-tourists-go-to-sites-associated-with-death-and-suffering_partner/.

Capatides, C. (2015) Last meals of death row inmates. CBS News. Nov. 2. Retrieved from https://www.cbsnews.com/pictures/last-meals-of-death-row/2/.

Center for Constitutional Rights (n.d.) Death Penalty is a Human Rights violation: An examination of the death penalty in the U.S. from a Human Rights perspective. Retrieved from https://ccrjustice.org/files/CCR%20Death%20Penalty%20Factsheet.pdf.

Crain's Cleveland Business (2021) University's prison program is embroiled in controversy; Most of Ashland's 2020 undergrad enrollees are distance learning inmates. Jan. 18, Vol. 42, Iss. 2:1.

Death Penalty Information Center (n.d.a) Countries that have abolished the death penalty since 1976. Retrieved from https://deathpenaltyinfo.org/policy-issues/international/countries-that-have-abolished-the-death-penalty-since-1976.

Death Penalty Information Center (n.d.b) Racial demographics: Current U.S. Death Row population by race. Retrieved from https://deathpenaltyinfo.org/death-row/overview/demographics.

Death Penalty Information Center (n.d.c) Overview of Lethal Injection Protocols. Retrieved from https://deathpenaltyinfo.org/executions/lethal-injection/overview-of-lethal-injection-protocols.

Death Penalty Information Center (2019) Executions around the World. Retrieved from https://deathpenaltyinfo.org/policy-issues/international/executions-around-the-world.

Death Penalty Information Center (2020) Federal death penalty: The federal government can seek death sentences for a limited set of crimes, but federal executions are much rarer than state executions. Retrieved from https://deathpenaltyinfo.org/state-and-federal-info/federal-death-penalty.

Evans, J. (2019) Alternating current or direct current? *Tips and Advice*, Electrical Installation Services. Retrieved from https://electricalinstallationservices.co.uk/alternating-current-or-direct-current/.

Ford, D. and A. Fantz (2014) Controversial execution in Ohio uses new drug combination. CNN. Jan. 17. Retrieved from https://www.cnn.com/2014/01/16/justice/ohio-dennis-mcguire-execution/index.html.

Flory, B. (2016) Jackson prison industries: competition breed controversy. Michigan History Magazine. Vol. 100Iss. 3. Retrieved from https://go-gale-com.wne.idm.oclc.org/ps/retrieve.do?tabID=T003&resultListType=RESULT_LIST&searchResultsType=SingleTab&hitCount=1&searchType=AdvancedSearchForm&currentPosition=1&docId=GALE%7CA452051963&docType=Article&sort=RELEVANCE&contentSegment=ZEAI-MOD1&prodId=EAIM&pageNum=1&contentSet=GALE%7CA452051963&searchId=R1&userGroupName=mlin_w_westnew&inPS=true.

Foucault, M. (1997) *Discipline and Punish: The Birth of the Prison*. A. Sheridan, trans. New York City, New York: Vintage Books.

Fretland, K. (2014) Scene at botched Oklahoma execution of Clayton Lockett was 'a bloody mess'. *The Guardian*. Dec. 13. Retrieved from https://www.theguardian.com/world/2014/dec/13/botched-oklahoma-execution-clayton-lockett-bloody-mess.

Gates, M. (2019) Drawing back the curtain: Executions and the First Amendment. Harvard Civil Rights—Civil Liberties Law Review. Oct. 24. Retrieved from https://harvardcrcl.org/drawing-back-the-curtain-executions-and-the-first-amendment/.

Givens, J. (2013) I was Virginia's executioner from 1982 to 1999. Any questions for me? *The Guardian*. Nov. 12. Retrieved from https://www.theguardian.com/commentisfree/2013/nov/21/death-penalty-former-executioner-jerry-givens.

Goodwin, M. L. (1997) An eye for an eye: An argument against allowing the families of murder victims to view executions. *Journal of Family Law*. Vol. 36, No. 4. On *Frontline*, *Public Broadcasting Service* (*PBS*), retrieved from https://www.pbs.org/wgbh/pages/frontline/shows/execution/readings/against.html.

Harrington, J. F. (2013) *The Faithful Executioner: Life and Death, Honor and Shame in the Turbulent Sixteenth Century*. New York: Farrar, Straus, and Giroux.

Hillman, H. (2003) Electrical devices used by prison officers, police and security forces. *Medicine, Conflict and Survival*. Vol. 19, Iss. 23:197-204.

Honderich, H. (2021) In Trump's final days, a rush of federal executions. British Broadcasting Company (BBC) News. Jan. 16. Retrieved from https://www.bbc.com/news/world-us-canada-55236260.

Independent, The (2018) Death Row inmate asks for electric chair execution instead of lethal injection. p. 3 retrieved from https://link.gale.com/apps/doc/A557518508/GPS?u=mlin_w_westnew&sid=GPS&xid=84f38efe

Johnson, K. (2016) Argument analysis: Immigrant detention and the Constitution. *SCOTUSblog*: Independent News and Analysis of the U.S. Supreme Court. Dec. 1. Retrieved from https://www.scotusblog.com/2016/12/argument-analysis-immigrant-detention-and-the-constitution/.

Kübler-Ross, E. (1969) *On Death and Dying*. New York, NY: Macmillan.

Kübler-Ross, E. and D. Kessler (2014) *On Grief and Grieving: Finding the Meaning of Grief Through the Five Stages of Loss*. New York, NY: Scriber.

May, L. C. (2020) Resilience and resistance: Fighting for higher education in prison. Inside Higher Education. Mar. 18. https://www.insidehighered.com/views/2020/03/18/prisoner-describes-his-and-other-inmates-struggles-access-higher-education-opinion.

Mennemeir, K. A. (2017) A right to know how you'll die: A First Amendment challenge to state secrecy statutes regarding lethal injection drugs. *Journal of Criminal Law and Criminology*. Summer, Vol. 107, Iss. 3:443-492.

Miller, K. (n.d.) 20 advantages and disadvantages of private prisons. *Future of Work*. Retrieved from https://futureofworking.com/6-advantages-and-disadvantages-of-private-prisons/.

National Public Radio (NPR) (2016) Fewer countries are relying on death penalty but they're executing more. Broadcast transcript. Jan. 7.

Noe-Bustamante, L., M. H. Lopez, and J. M. Krogstad (2020) U.S. Hispanic population surpasses 60 million in 2019, but growth has slowed. Pews Research Center. July 7. Retrieved from https://www.pewresearch.org/fact-tank/2020/07/07/u-s-hispanic-population-surpassed-60-million-in-2019-but-growth-has-slowed/

Old Prisons Magazine (2020) Prison tourism is a growing heritage travel niche around the world. Feb. 15. Retrieved from https://www.oldprisons.com/prison-tourism-is-a-growing-heritage-travel-niche-around-the-world/#:~:text=Prison%20tourism%20is%20a%20growing%20heritage%20travel%20niche%20around%20the%20world,-Posted%20by%20OldPrisons&text=Located%20in%20Philadelphia%2C%20America's%20most,been%20a%20museum%20since%201994.

Oliphant, J. B. (2018) Public support for the death penalty ticks up. Pew Research Center. June 11. Retrieved from https://www.pewresearch.org/fact-tank/2018/06/11/us-support-for-death-penalty-ticks-up-2018/.

PEW Research Center (2021) Report: Most Americans favor the death penalty despite concerns about its administration. Jun 2. Retrieved from https://www.pewresearch.org/politics/2021/06/02/most-americans-favor-the-death-penalty-despite-concerns-about-its-administration/.

Pusey, A. (2019) Aug. 6, 1890: First execution by the electric chair. *ABA Journal*. July/Aug., Vol. 105, Iss. 6:1.

Radelet, M. L., M. Vandiver, and F. M. Berardo (1983) Families, prisons, and men with death sentences: The human impact of structured uncertainty. *Journal of Family Issues*. Vol. 4, Iss. 4:593-612.

Rakoff, J. S. (2002) *United States v. Quinones* United States Court of Appeals, Second Circuit. Dec. 10.

Richardson, W., B. Hornsby, and M. Martinez (2002) Perspectives on the death penalty, in *The Leviathan's Choice: Capital Punishment in the 21st Century*, M. Martinez, W. Richardson, and B. Hornsby, eds. New York: Rowman and Littlefield Publishers, Inc. Introduction, xi-xxvii.

Rubinkam, M. (2020) Kids-for-cash judge loses bid for lighter sentence. *The Washington Post.* Aug. 26. Retrieved from https://www.washingtonpost.com/national/kids-for-cash-judge-loses-bid-for-lighter-prison-sentence/2020/08/26/a8e82fea-e7a8-11ea-bf44-0d31c85838a5_story.html.

Salcedo, A. (2021) South Carolina could force Death Row inmates to choose between electric chair, firing squad. *The Washington Post.* Mar. 2. Retrieved from https://go-gale-com.wne.idm.oclc.org/ps/i.do?v=2.1&u=mlin_w_westnew&it=r&id=GALE|A653627669&p=GPS&sw=w.

Sarat, A. (2014) *Gruesome Spectacles: Botched Executions and America's Death Penalty.* Stanford, CA: Stanford Law Books.

Sarat, A. (2021a) The return of firing squads shows death and its 'machinery' are grinding to a halt. *USA Today.* May 18. Retrieved from https://www.usatoday.com/story/opinion/policing/2021/05/18/firing-squads-gruesome-not-humane-death-penalty-fading/5120497001/.

Sarat, A. (2021b) The failure of lethal injections. *Verdict Justia.* Mar. 23. Retrieved from https://verdict.justia.com/2021/03/23/the-dreadful-failure-of-lethal-injection.

Soulatges, J. A. (1792) *Traité Des Crimes.* Vol. 1.

Stern, J. E. (2015) The cruel and unusual execution of Clayton Lockett. *The Atlantic.* June. Retrieved from https://www.theatlantic.com/magazine/archive/2015/06/execution-clayton-lockett/392069/.

Sharp, S. F. (2005) *Hidden Victims: The Effects of the Death Penalty on Families of the Accused.*

New Brunswick, NJ: Rutgers University Press.

Steinbuch, A. T. (2014) The movement away from solitary confinement in the United States. *New England Journal on Criminal and Civil Confinement.* Spring, Vol. 40, Iss. 2:499-534.

Stevenson, B. A. and J. F. Stinneford (n.d.) Common interpretation: The Eighth Amendment. Interactive Constitution, National Constitution Center. Retrieved from https://constitutioncenter.org/interactive-constitution/interpretation/amendment-viii/clauses/103#:~:text=In%201791%2C%20this%20same%20prohibition,prohibit%20cruel%20and%20unusual%20punishments.

Stroebe, M., H. Schut, and K. Boerner (2017) Cautioning health-care professionals: Bereaved persons are misguided through the stages of grief. OMEGA — *Journal of Death and Dying.* Vol. 74, No. 4:455-473.

Supreme Court of the United States (SCOTUS) (1976) *Gregg v. Georgia.* No. 74-6257. Decided July 2. Retrieved from https://deathpenalty.procon.org/wp-content/uploads/sites/45/greggvgeorgia.pdf.

Supreme Court of the United States (SCOTUS) (2005) *Roper v. Simmons.* No. 03-633. Retrieved from https://scholar.google.com/scholar_case?case=16987406842050815187&hl=en&as_sdt=6&as_vis=1&oi=scholarr.

Supreme Court of the United States (SCOTUS) (2018) *Jennings v. Rodriguez* October Term, 2017. Retrieved from https://www.supremecourt.gov/opinions/17pdf/15-1204_f29g.pdf.

Tarm, M (2021) Executioners sanitized accounts of deaths in federal cases. *AP News.* Feb. 17. Retrieved from https://apnews.com/article/executioners-sanitized-accounts-of-death-25d133f59039150c2e308ba1a2a5caef.

Tory, S. (2019) The case against immigration prisons. High Country News. Nov. 11. Retrieved from https://www.hcn.org/issues/51.19/interview-the-case-against-immigration-prisons.

United States Census Bureau (2021) 2020 census: Quick facts. Retrieved from https://www.census.gov/quickfacts/fact/table/US/RHI725219#RHI725219.

United States Court of Appeals (2016) *Estate of Clayton Lockett v. Fallin*. Tenth Circuit, No. 15-6134. Nov. 15. Retrieved from https://cases.justia.com/federal/appellate-courts/ca10/15-6134/15-6134-2016-11-15.pdf?ts=1479243718.

United States Department of Justice (2019) Federal government to resume capital punishment after nearly two decades. Press release, Office of Public Affairs. July 25. Retrieved from https://www.justice.gov/opa/pr/federal-government-resume-capital-punishment-after-nearly-two-decade-lapse.

Wamsley, L. (2021) With lethal injections harder to come by, some states are turning to firing squads. National Public Radio (NPR). May 19. Retrieved from https://www.npr.org/2021/05/19/997632625/with-lethal-injections-harder-to-come-by-some-states-are-turning-to-firing-squad.

Ward, R. (2015) Introduction, in *A Global History of Execution and the Criminal Corpse*, R. Ward, ed. Basingstoke, UK: Palgrave Macmillian.

Young, K. (2015) Death penalty: Methods of execution used around the world. Amnesty International. Retrieved from https://www.amnesty.org.au/death-penalty-methods-of-execution-used-around-the-world/.

Chapter FOURTEEN

Other Controversies in Punishment and Corrections[1]

> *Punishment no longer constitutes a marginal area of the larger economy....*
> *These vast immobilized armies supply labour to corporations, profits to private*
> *prison businesses and captive markets to suppliers.*
>
> —Angela Davis

Chapter Objectives

- Discuss some of the more uncomfortable issues in corrections.
- Introduce some of the most hotly debated topics in criminal justice and corrections.
- Provide instructors and students with topics that can spark wider debate in the classroom.
- Develop critical thinking skills in social justice and corrections.

Key Terms

Coed prison
Dark tourism
"Felon Friendly" employers
Grief tourism
Hawes-Cooper Act of 1929
Jennings v. Rodriguez

Omnibus Crime Control and Safe
   Streets Act of 1968
Open prisons
Violent Crime Control and Law
   Enforcement Act of 1994

---

[1]**TRIGGER WARNING**: The topics we are discussing in this chapter may be disturbing to some readers. We recommend that you discuss with your professor or instructor as to how much or how little of this chapter you will be responsible for.

INTRODUCTION

This chapter of the book explores some of the more obvious controversies, beyond the death penalty, that haunt corrections in the United States today. It is not an exhaustive list of controversies and the arguments for or against each controversy only offer a limited number of opinions. However, it is the hope that in reading these, that we return to the question asked in the first chapter of this book, "Is corrections 'corrective', as the name suggests, or is it both punishment of the body and soul?" Readers are also encouraged to think about more arguments for or against each controversy, including in class discussion and debate.

We have already covered a number of controversies surrounding corrections in other chapters. Some of these included the incarceration of women who are pregnant, prison births, and prison nurseries. Chapter 13 provides an overview of the problems that are inherent to capital punishment, whether it is ethical, forms of execution, and the effects of Death Row on inmates and prison staff. We have also discussed in some length the controversy of incarcerating the elderly.

This chapter explores both sides of the debates on a number of controversial topics we have yet to explore, including college courses for inmates and the incarceration of those who illegally migrate to the United States. Many of these topics elicit strong responses from proponents and opponents alike. We will also go into more depth on conversations centered on prison overcrowding, even though we have discussed the topic in a number of places in this textbook, including in the *International Perspectives in Punishment and Corrections* sections in chapters. As it is a universal theme, it bears repeating. We will also explore further the topic of private jails and prisons.

Some of the controversies have to do with practical matters. Others have to do with ongoing social justice issues. Whatever the arguments for and against in each controversy, there are disagreements that are not easily resolved, particularly in the United States, where at present time, the nation is highly polarized on a number of topics, including criminal justice reform.

CRUELTY BUILT INTO THE STRUCTURE OF JAILS AND PRISONS

In literature and real tales of infamous convicts, we rarely hear that jail or prison is a pleasant experience. Reportedly the Marquis de Sade[2] wanted to beat his brains out against his cell walls, Jean Genet[3] was moved to kiss them (Wilkinson, 2018).

---

[2] The Marquis de Sade, a French author, was imprisoned both for his erotic writings that included descriptions of sadistic acts and his alleged sexual assaults.
[3] Jean Genet, another French author, spent a number of years in the Mettray Penal Colony for Juveniles, in France, opened in 1840 in order to rehabilitate young male juvenile delinquents (Toth, 2019).

Foucault (1997) believed that the art of punishment is in its presentation. In order for punishment to act as a deterrent, both for the convicted and for those who have yet to commit crimes, jails and prisons inherently cannot be pleasant places. Conceivably, you could design a prison that is secure without the institutional décor and inevitable slump stone construction, not to mention the ever-present razor wire. Jails and prisons, beyond their stated purposes, are built to be intimidating and restrictive.

Female Inmate in Prison Cell. (*Source*: Chew, n.d., Center for Health Journalism, USC Annenberg, retrieved from https://centerforhealthjournalism.org/fellowships/projects/aging-prison-forgotten-plight-women-behind-bars-6.)

Even minimum security prisons and camps have minimal creature comforts, designed to be discomforting and not intended to be esthetically pleasing, except where the public demands it, at least on the outside. We see this example with jails and prisons built in cities. As Winona County Board member Marcia Ward stated, when plans were being made to build a new jail, "I want the ugliest jail in Minnesota. . . ." (Rogers, 2021, retrieved from https://www.winonapost.com/news/i-want-the-ugliest-jail-in-minnesota/article_f7b777ff-9316-5da5-b8ee-8b9dc6c250e3 .html). In later clarifying what she meant in her statement, Ward said, "It shouldn't be ugly, but it shouldn't be architecturally, a classic piece of architecture." (Rogers, 2021, retrieved from https://www.winonapost.com/news/i-want-the-ugliest-jail-in-minnesota/article_f7b777ff-9316-5da5-b8ee-8b9dc6c250e3 .html).

What is interesting to observe in Ward's statements, is that she is referring to jails. The fact that jails are rarely attractive places inside and out, to some, flies in the face of the values of the American criminal justice system. Suspects and the accused are assumed innocent, until proven guilty in a court of law. The reality is that jails still have to provide security for a wide variety of alleged criminals, whether they are guilty of the crimes they are accused of or not. And if we additionally consider that jails also house those convicted with shorter sentences, it would be difficult to provide two systems within one jail, particularly in jurisdictions with smaller populations, and hence, fewer detainees or inmates.

There are only a few key elements in jails and prisons that are absolutely necessary. Detainees and prisoners must have places where they can eat, bathe, dispose of excreta, and sleep—everything else is superfluous (Wilkinson, 2018). Granted, for those living on the street prior to incarceration, these may feel like creature comforts. However, even in the most comfortable of circumstances in jails and prisons, they are still intended to be miserable places, as exemplified by the nickname for United States Penitentiary Hazelton in West Virginia, "Misery Mountain," where James "Whitey" Bulger was killed (*CBS News*, 2018).

We should acknowledge that a great deal of what makes jails and prisons miserable is overcrowding, particularly when it leads to violence. There is little that can be done for overcrowded conditions, as infrastructures of most jails and prisons were not designed for the number of detainees and prisoners they presently hold. Many place the incarcerated in locations in the facility intended for recreational or educational purposes, further shrinking the number of areas in facilities that offer some form of escape from the monotony of living in a cramped cell.

Arguments for Austere Prisons

As Foucault noted, presentation, in this case, jails and prisons, is everything in order to frighten convicts and would be criminals. If we are to believe that punishments should act as deterrents to crime or reoffending, then the physical structure and day to day life in prison should be unpleasant.

Arguments against Austere Prisons

As we will see in the *International Perspectives in Punishment and Corrections* section in this chapter, in our profile of Halden Prison in Norway, proponents of more comfortable settings and structures of prisons, including those that look like college campus, claim that they provide an environment in which real rehabilitation can take place. Jails and prisons in the United States, in their present state, are described as being physical and moral blemishes on the face of American life (Gopnik, 2012). Some of the conditions in U.S. jails and prisons may violate the 8th Amendment, for cruel and unusual punishment, as in the example of no air conditioning in prisons located in regions where temperatures can top 100 degrees Fahrenheit in the summer (Ernst, 2018).

FUNDING SURPLUSES AND GAPS

We currently spend more in the United States on corrections than we do on public education. Approximately $81 billion is spent each by the U.S. government and states on jails, public, and private prisons (Prison Policy Initiative, 2021; Wagner and Rabuy, 2017). However, even with the size of the spending, there continue to be funding gaps, making budgeting precarious in some facilities. Even when the economy is good, corrections administrators rarely see an increase in their spending budgets and corrections also is an attractive place for budget cuts (Wallace, 2019).

Worst yet, not all states have the same consistent revenue flows, based on per capita income and the state taxes generated to partially fund jails and prisons. Some of the largest spending gaps can be found in prison programs, including education. Another problematic area of underfunding in corrections is in contributions to retiree health care for former corrections employees (Henrichson and Delaney, 2012). Keep in mind that like police officers, corrections officers leave the profession before they are eligible for social security payments and Medicare, generally retiring between the ages of 50 and 55.

And troubling, for prisoners, one place that budget cuts can be made is on food. Approximately one-fourth of what the average American spends on food each day is spent on prisoners' daily diet (Sawyer, 2017; Prison Policy Initiative, n.d.). In the long run, any deficiency in prisoners' diet may end up being a public health problem in the long run, with government money paying for any health issues that arise due to incarceration after prisoners are released, along with those that arise in prison (Sawyer, 2017).

On the other side of the coin, during the 1990s there was outrage at the financial incentives for keeping people behind bars, including the private prison debate we discuss further in this chapter. State and local agencies are subsidized by federal funding, which in turn is argued to have resulted in more arrests, probation and incarceration (Eisen, 2021). Eisen (2021) contends that the funding for corrections, including accusations that COVID-19 funding was diverted to building more prisons, that has fueled mass incarceration, beyond tough drug laws, reaches back to the *Omnibus Crime Control and Safe Streets Act of 1968*. Subsequent law and order bills, including the *Violent Crime Control and Law Enforcement Act of 1994*, offered increases in funding to law enforcement and corrections and has also been accused of contributing to increased numbers in prisons.

More recently, within the past decade, with a number of social justice activist groups, including the Black Lives Matter movement calling for the defunding of police, if fully coming to fruition, will result in a decease in the number of arrests and subsequent incarcerations. Though we are primarily speaking here of law enforcement funding, it is also intimately tied to corrections as well. What is generally misunderstood is that the motive behind defunding the police is to move funds to more community services, including those for mental health. In other words, it is suggested that funding should be directed at prevention, which, as we have already discovered elsewhere in this book, is the Achilles' heel of the criminal justice system in the United States and many other countries of the world.

Arguments for Increased Funding in Corrections

As we have noted time and again in this book, prisons are overcrowded. Unless there is a move to grant more early releases, or funds are shifted to mental health care options, there will continue to be a need to build more prisons and hire more corrections personnel.

Arguments for Decreased Funding in Corrections

Any decrease in funding for corrections can only happen with other changes in the criminal justice system that will put an end to mass incarceration. One way to acquire funding for preventative work and programs designed to lower causative factors that lead to crime and incarceration is to move money from policing and corrections into non-law enforcement service agencies. These agencies and programs are notoriously underfunded and often dependent on the insecurity of grants that may or may not be awarded or continued (UCLA School of Law, 2020).

A second weakness, beyond underfunding, is that programs are often not based in evidence from routine program evaluations. Meaning that programs can be implemented, without a real test as to whether they will work. Even if a program is evidence-based, it is often a challenge to get them funded for any extended period of time. Many are grant-based, requiring stakeholders to reapply for continued funding, with no guarantees that additional grants will be approved. Communities can also be in heated competition for what grant money is available.

COED PRISONS

In some jurisdictions, there are so few women who need to be incarcerated that it doesn't warrant having a separate facility to house only females. In such cases, they may be housed in unisex prisons, where male and female inmates are kept in separate units. However, the opposite problem can be the case, where the one facility available for female inmates may become overcrowded. One alternative in either case is the *coed prison*. But what happens where male and female[4] inmates are allowed to more freely interact with one another?

In 1987, Logan Correctional Center, a medium security prison in Illinois, became a coed facility. Initially the concerns were as silly as to whether enough men's cologne could be stocked in the commissary (Johnson, 1987). Male and female prisoners were allowed to interact during meals, recreation, work, or education programs (Smith, 1988).

Arguments for Coed Prisons

By allowing males and females to interact more freely during incarceration, it helps to normalize relationships and transitions to their post-incarceration lives. As one inmate at Logan Correctional Center observed, the men act more "gentlemanly," the warden confirming this by noting that the presence of female inmates had a calming effect on the men (Johnson, 1987). In the case of Logan Correctional Center, by moving women from the all-women Dwight prison, overcrowding was eased, as Dwight at the time housed 607 female inmates in a facility designed to hold 418 (Smith, 1988).

Arguments against Coed Prisons

In the 1970s, there were over 20 coed state and federal prisons (Smykla, 1979); by the late 1990s, few remained. Even in the 1970s, in examining the success of coed prisons, a number of problems were identified, including pregnancy, abortions, and prostitution happening behind bars (Smykla, 1979).

Corrections officers are left with more responsibilities, including making sure that sexual relations do not occur between male and female inmates. Within 11 months of going coed, 7 out of the 156 female inmates were pregnant at Logan Correctional Center (Smith, 1988). Corrections officers are required to act as chaperones, to assure that male and female inmates are not kissing, or engaging in any other sexual activities, writing them up on disciplinary actions when they have been caught (Smith, 1988).

---

[4] We are not assuming gender binary is correct, but rather referring to males and females, as people are classified (sometimes incorrectly) in jail and prison facilities.

PRISON COLLEGE PROGRAMS

Most would agree that offering GED programs in prison so that inmates can complete their high school education from behind bars is reasonable. There is enough evidence that possessing a high school degree is beneficial on the job market, if not a college degree, and the hope that if inmates earn at least the GED, they will be less likely to reoffend. There are enough strikes against them in finding a job after incarceration without the stigma of being high school dropouts.

However, more controversial inmate education programs that are offered at some prisons include face-to-face or distance learning for college credit. With the rising cost of college for undergraduates and their families, the controversy has grown in the past several decades. An example comes from a program through Ashland University, a private Christian university in Ohio. The university supports the inmate program through endowments and Pell Grant funding, a federal government grant program that offers tuition and fees assistance for students in financial need, including prisoners (*Crain's Cleveland Business*, 2021). According to *Crain's Cleveland Business* (2021), the majority of students in distance learning happening at Ashland University are inmates. To date, there are 26 states that do not offer higher education learning opportunities to inmates (May, 2020).

In conjunction with college behind bars, universities also offer career counseling on what types of industries and employers are *"felon friendly."* For example, the University of New Mexico, Albuquerque, offers a number of resources in their career center for ex-cons (See https://career.unm.edu/resources/ex-offenders.html). These resources include links at their website to a list of companies who will hire felons, tattoo removal programs[5], and college programs for ex-convicts.

Arguments for Distance Learning for Inmates

Studies indicate that having more education decreases the likelihood that an individual will offend or reoffend because more career opportunities are open to those with a college degree. Exposure to college also allows inmates to explore a number of career paths. In research conducted by the American Correctional Association in Indiana, those who had participated in education programs while incarcerated had lower recidivism rates: 20 percent lower for those with GED degrees and 44 percent lower for college graduates (*TBS* staff, 2021).

---

[5] Felons may often have visible tattoos that indicate gang affiliation and that were crudely and obviously done in prison. There is also the issue of people in general sporting racist (e.g., white supremacy) tattoos being turned down for jobs because of their messages.

Arguments against Distance Learning for Inmates

The opposing view for providing learning opportunities asserts that because college classes are so expensive today, inmates should not have access to a free university education. Part of their punishment should be denial of education opportunities beyond a high school diploma equivalency with the GED. And even in the Indiana study, education programs did not significantly lower recidivism rates among those who did receive their GED.

UNAUTHORIZED AND UNDOCUMENTED IMMIGRANT INCARCERATION

We should be clear as to what we mean by unauthorized or undocumented immigrant incarceration. Few would argue that someone who is an immigrant and present in a country legally or illegally should be above the law as far as committing crimes, along with citizens of the country. However there is considerable controversy surrounding the detention of immigrants whose only crime was to enter the country illegally.

Most of the concentration of detention centers is at the U.S.-Mexico border. However, there have been attempts by individuals who are illegally in the United States to seek asylum by crossing the border into Canada. In these cases, they are often turned away by Canadian authorities and if caught by U.S. Border Patrol agents on the U.S. side of the border, they will face detention and deportation (Jacobs, 2020).

The incarceration of immigrants who have been caught and detained by Border Patrol or U.S. Customs agents after making unauthorized border crossings and entering the country illegally is a controversial topic of debate that has raged on for decades. In some cases, the individual has been in the country for some time and subsequently is arrested by U.S. Immigration and Customs Enforcement (ICE) agents. Though the main concern of ICE is to prevent the illegal movement of people and drugs (U.S. Department of Homeland Security, 2020), many more who have committed no other crime than having entered the United States illegally have been sent to detention centers at the border before hearings and in most cases, deportation.

Arguments for Immigration Incarceration

One argument in support of incarceration is that people who enter the country illegally have broken the law and are therefore subject to criminal prosecution. Currently there is a mass immigration crisis in the United States, with no good solutions as to how to house, feed, prosecute, and deport people who enter the country illegally.

Nor are there any good deterrents to mass illegal immigration, save the threat of incarceration if, for some, the crossing into hostile desert conditions in southern California, Arizona, New Mexico, or Texas doesn't stop them; or, for those who try to come by boat, the risk of a watery death in a rickety boat, which many of them are. In some cases, detaining illegal immigrants at the border or at ports may very well spare them the trek across the desert or a dangerous water crossing and risk of death.

Jennings v. Rodriguez, a class-action challenge to detention centers brought before the U.S. Supreme Court, was based on the question as to whether anyone on U.S. soil should be guaranteed a bond hearing, along with other legal rights (Johnson, 2016). In the opinion written by Justice Alito, he determined that on the basis of not being U.S. citizens and therefore protected by the Constitution, illegal immigrants are not allowed the right to be released on bond and *shall be held in custody* until their case has been resolved and/or they can be deported (*Jennings v. Rodriguez,* 2018).

Arguments against Immigration Incarceration

Currently the United States incarcerates nearly 400,000 immigrants, including women, children, and infants. The latter are separated from their parents and placed in so called "baby jail" (Tory, 2019). It is inhumane to incarcerate people who are fleeing from extreme poverty, political violence, and unrest in their own countries. Law professor César Cuauhtémoc Garcia Hernández stated in an interview that even though it has been a federal misdemeanor since 1929 to enter the country illegally, until the early 1980s, people were rarely locked up for migrating to the United States from or through Mexico, with most undocumented individuals seeking seasonal work in agriculture (Tory, 2019).

Another consideration is that undocumented immigrants also contribute to the economy as they spend a good part of their earnings on U.S. goods and services within the borders, and the taxes they pay on those goods and services in turn benefit local and state governments. When not being paid under the table for their labor, as in the case of undocumented individuals who were able to obtain social security numbers prior to its prohibition, they are paying income taxes on their earnings, further benefiting state and federal governments. An alternative to incarcerating undocumented immigrants is to provide a path to citizenship, as in the current (though controversial) DACA program for people who were brought to the United States illegally during their infancy or childhood years.

INCARCERATION OF JUVENILES IN ADULT FACILITIES

Throughout history, there has always been the question as to when a child is an adult. Ceremonies around the time of puberty in some cultures mark the end of childhood (at least symbolically) and the beginnings of taking on more adult responsibilities. Yet older teens and young adults have become more dependent on their biological, adoptive, or substitute parents or guardians for a longer period now than in previous generations in the so called "extended adolescence." This is largely due to the rising costs of living over the last several decades, and because more young adults are entering college after high school, making it difficult for them to break free from financial dependency on their families.

Because laws have to determine at what age children are treated as adults for a number of reasons, including marriage, entering military service, and cigarette, marijuana, alcohol consumption, it has been generally legally accepted that the cutoff ages for adolescents are between 18 and 21. Some countries are more liberal in their cutoff ages, as in the example of alcohol consumption in some European countries, where children as young as 16 are allowed to at least drink beer and wine. Whatever the legal cutoff dates for childhood, it does not translate into an overnight transformation of the child into an adult. People generally reach emotional, psychological, and physical maturity at different rates, depending on genetics and environmental factors, among other variables.

Arguments for Incarceration of Juveniles in Adult Facilities

Some juveniles have committed such horrendous crimes, like premeditated murder, that it would not be healthy for other children in a juvenile facility to be exposed to them. By age 12 (prepubescent, pubescent), children have reached the age of reason when they should clearly know the difference between right and wrong, particularly with respect to crimes like murder, rape, and sexual assault. The only available solution is to place juveniles who have committed serious, violent crimes in adult prison.

Arguments against Incarceration of Juveniles in Adult Facilities

Proponents of theories in developmental and physiological psychology make several arguments for prohibiting the incarceration of juveniles in adult facilities, including that (1) children up to even young adulthood live in a world of "magical thinking" where there is little understanding of the consequences of their actions, (2) the frontal lobes of the brain, the center of impulse control, does not become fully developed before the age of 25, and (3) juveniles are a vulnerable population that can be victimized in adult prison. A further argument is that children in juvenile detention, where there is greater focus on rehabilitation, generally have access to adult mentors who are more likely to have a positive influence on them in their formative years, which is a better situation for them than being in the presence of and subject to influence from adult offenders.

PRISON INDUSTRIES

Though we have discussed in this book the merits of job training programs for prisoners, we have not discussed the controversies of prison industries. The difference is that job training programs act more like education programs. Prison industries are actually putting inmates to work to sell the fruits of their labors. The lines are blurred between the two.

This is not a new controversy. There has been the use of inmate labor for centuries, as well as poor houses where the indigent would provide labor in exchange for room and board, as meager as those accommodations might be. Earlier controversies included the hiring out of inmates to private industries, which in turn provided revenue to states, not income to the inmates providing the labor. As in the example of Jackson Prison in 19th century Michigan, as is the case today, inmates were paid far less than what the average worker outside of prison earned (Flory, 2016). After a number of complaints in several states, Congress passed the *Hawes-Cooper Act of 1929*, banning the sale of inmate made goods on the open market (Flory, 2016), primarily on the basis that it represented unfair competition with companies that did not use prison labor and could not sell their products at or below prices of goods made by prisoners.

Arguments for Prison Industries

Prison industries allow for inmates to learn work skills they can take outside of prison when they are released. It is also a way by which to give back to society, by defraying some of the costs of housing and feeding them. And though their incomes are meager, they have more buying power in the prison commissary.

Arguments against Prison Industries

Not all prisoners will be released from prison at an age when they can easily enter the workforce, as in the example of the convicted murderer who is released after a longer sentence. And it is one thing for the state to use prison labor to make things like furniture that is used in state facilities (e.g., schools, government offices). It is another thing to pay prisoners so little for their labor making items that are being sold, or in some cases, providing services for a profit.

PRISON OVERCROWDING

We have to remember that prison overcrowding is a function of policy and sentencing, not one of the jails or prisons themselves. There is little discretion by

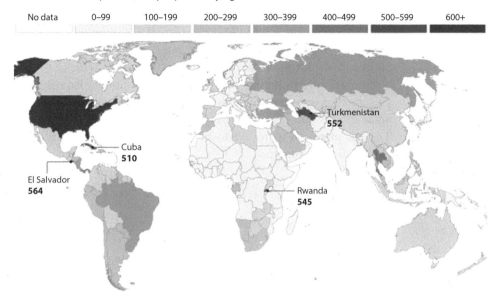

U.S. incarcerates a larger share of its population than any other country

Incarceration rate per 100,000 people of any age

No data   0–99   100–199   200–299   300–399   400–499   500–599   600+

Turkmenistan 552

Cuba 510

El Salvador 564

Rwanda 545

Note: Figures reflect most recent available data for each country. Territories are counted separately.
Data accessed Aug. 10, 2021.
Source: World Prison Brief, Institute for Crime & Justice Policy Research.

PEW RESEARCH CENTER

FIGURE 14.1 | **Countries with the Highest Incarceration Rates.**
(*Source*: America's incarceration rate falls to lowest level since 1995. Pew Research Center, Washington, D.C. (August 16, 2021) https://www.pewresearch.org/fact-tank/2021/08/16/americas-incarceration-rate-lowest-since-1995/.)

correctional administrators as to what or how many inmates will be housed at any one facility. As a result, if a jail or prison becomes overcrowded with detainees or prisoners, it is up to administrators to deal with the fallout. As we saw in the story of the New Mexico prison riot, overcrowding, along with truly miserable conditions that came with it, led to the worst prison riot in American history.

Arguments for Allowing Overcrowding in Prisons

Among the arguments for allowing overcrowding is that just because jails and prisons are overcrowded, it does not justify suspending the detention of suspected criminals or sentencing criminals to prison. Another argument is that truth in sentencing laws dictate that inmates must serve a substantial amount of their sentence before being released on parole and that they should not be let out sooner due to overcrowding. Yet another point of view is that prison is not meant to be a pleasant experience and that if overcrowding makes prisoners uncomfortable, it is not the fault of the sentencing judges or the prison staff.

Arguments against Overcrowding in Prison

Overcrowding contributes to higher rates of disease transmission, which is of special concern during a pandemic as we witnessed with COVID-19. Overcrowding also contributes to inmate unrest as tempers flare. It also results in using spaces in prisons that were not intended to be living spaces, like in the case of recreational areas of jails and prisons converted into dorms with rows and rows of bunkbeds. Though prison is expected to be unpleasant, the Constitution guarantees that it should also be humane.

PRISON TOURISM

Proponents of prison tourism feel that opening up former jails and prisons to educational tours and to the public, as in the cases of Eastern State Penitentiary in Philadelphia, the Old Charleston Jail in South Carolina, Kilmainham Gaol[6] in Dublin, Ireland, or even the prison where Nelson Mandela was held in South Africa, should not be controversial. For the uninitiated public, it may be the only glimpse that they get to peek behind bars, even if these facilities are crumbling and obsolete. They also provide important history lessons.

There are a few reasons why tourists might seek out jails and prisons specifically as part of their vacation experience. People generally want to visit former jails and prisons out of curiosity (*Old Prisons Magazine*, 2020). Others are scholars and historians, amateur or otherwise, looking to further their knowledge in prison history and architecture. *Old Prisons Magazine* proposed in a 2020 article that prison visits may very well be part of a popular niche in heritage tourism, where visitors can see where some of the most notorious criminals were held, including Al "Scarface" Capone.

However, what happens when jail and prison tours become commercial? One example is the conversion of jails and prisons into luxury hotels. *Trivago Magazine* lists a number of such establishments, where former cells have been converted into hotel suites (2019, https://magazine.trivago.com/prisons-converted-hotels/):

- Het Arresthuis, Roermond, Netherlands;
- Malmaison, Oxford, United Kingdom;
- Four Seasons Sultanahmet, Istanbul, Turkey;
- Långholmen, Sweden;

---

[6] As we found out earlier in the book, the terms "gaol," "gaiole," gaole," "jaiole,"or "jaile" originally from Middle English or French, are simply different names for jail.

- The Liberty, Boston, United States;
- Lloyd Hotel and Cultural Embassy, Amsterdam, Netherlands;
- Best Western Premier Katajanokka, Finland; and
- Clink78 Hostel, London, United Kingdom

Exterior, Malmaison Oxford Hotel (a former prison), Oxford, United Kingdom; *Interior*, Clink78 Hostel, London, United Kingdom. (*Source*: Uniq Hotels, n.d., retrieved from https://bit.ly/3KI2OYQ and Road Affair, 2021, retrieved from https://www.roadaffair.com/clink78-hostel-review/)

As Trivago asks its readers (2019, https://magazine.trivago.com/prisons-converted-hotels/),

Have you always wondered how is [sic] to sleep in a prison cell? Well, it's not necessary to commit any crime: there are plenty of nice and luxury prisons converted to luxury hotels around the globe. Today, many retain original features, making it possible to spend the night in a prison cell—with a little added comfort.

Though the inmates are long gone, some might question the tastefulness of tourists spending the night in a facility where very possibly so much human misery took place.

Another example of prison tourism does not even include spending time in a real jail or prison, but rather a facsimile of one. In the United Kingdom there is a bar at two locations, London and Brighton, called *Alcatraz Prison Cocktail Bar*. The name of the bar is a play on the name of the real former prison in San Francisco Bay, Alcatraz, which is now open to tours through the National Park Services. According to the bar's website (https://www.alcotraz.co.uk/), patrons are asked to don orange jumpsuits, have their mug shots taken, sit in metal cells while sipping their cocktails, and given means to "escape" by "crooked guards" (e.g., wait staff). To some, this might be all good fun, but to anyone who has ever been in prison for a crime, they may not find it in good taste.

Arguments for Prison Tourism

Tours of prison are educational, historically, sociologically and architecturally. It also allows people to peek inside former jails and prisons without having actual contact with detainees or inmates. Some tours even include talks by former inmates about what occasionally occurred there, such as at the former prison on Alcatraz in California; a talk that might in itself act as a deterrent to crime.

Arguments against Prison Tourism

As *Old Prisons Magazine* notes (2020), tourism connected to old prisons and jails is called *dark tourism* by some, as places that are identified with death and suffering, including battlefields, cemeteries, locations of disasters (e.g., the 9/11 Memorial in NYC), concentration camps, prisons, and other places that might be haunted by ghosts, real or imagined. It is also sometimes called *grief tourism* that is becoming more popular in recent decades, where those who were victims or whose family members were victims can have an immersive experience at the location of a tragedy (*Old Prisons Magazines*, 2020, retrieved from oldprisons.com; Bitran, 2017). For others, it is simply morbid curiosity and tourism has no place in encouraging this.

PRIVATE PRISONS

Since the beginnings of mass incarceration in the United States, the federal government and states have looked for solutions to defray the cost of guarding and caring for inmates. One solution is private prisons, which we have already discussed in this textbook. Suffice it to say that the use of private prisons had expanded exponentially over the course of decades along with the rise in mass incarceration, only to decline after 2012 (The Sentencing Project, 2021), as witnessed in the following graph. States do not equally use private facilities, with some more likely to do so than others. For example, Montana holds 47 percent of their prison population in private prisons; 20 states do not use for-profit prisons at all.

Arguments for Private Prisons

There is no evidence that prisoners misbehave more in private prisons. In fact, there are more instances of violence in public jails and prisons (Sayed et al., 2020). Private prisons provide a quick solution to overcrowding and more efficiently spends taxpayers' dollars (Miller, n.d.). Private prisons also provide economic opportunities in the communities where they are built, including jobs and commerce.

Arguments against Private Prisons

There are contradictory studies as to whether there is more violence in private prisons, though there is some indication that it occurs more frequently in private

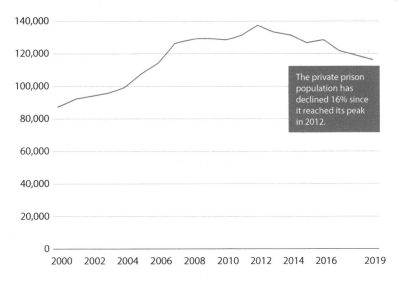

FIGURE 14.2 | **Private Prison Population, 2000-2019.**
(*Source*: The Sentencing Project, 2021, retrieved from https://www.sentencingproject.org/publications/private-prisons-united-states/)

facilities, exposing corrections officers to more danger (Miller, n.d.). This is supposedly due to the fewer personnel to prisoner ratio seen in private prisons. Even with fewer corrections officers, private prisons do not necessarily mean cost savings to the federal government or states (Sayed et al., 2020), even though their staff are paid less than in public facilities.

There have also been a number of cases where judges have been prosecuted for excessive sentencing of both juveniles and adults to for-profit private prisons, in exchange for bribes. For example, Judge Mark Ciavarella was convicted for a "cash for kids" scheme (Rubinkam, 2020). There is also the issue as to whether the competition for prisoners will heat up as prison populations decline and for-profit opportunities dry up (The Sentencing Project, 2021).

Also, there are questions as to whether prison staff at private prisons are as dedicated to their jobs as those working in public prisons, in light of the smaller salaries they earn, and also as to whether they are as well-trained as those in public prisons. There are also higher turnovers of personnel in private prisons, making for a less stable pool of corrections officers (Miller, n.d.).

SOLITARY CONFINEMENT

Throughout this book we have discussed solitary confinement, including the mental health effects on inmates. Solitary confinement, including life on Death Row, is perhaps the best example we have in order to answer the question as to whether incarceration is the punishment of the body or the soul.

Arguments for Solitary Confinement

Some inmates are unable to get along with other inmates and are required to be held in segregation away from the general prison population. There also has to be a separate unit for inmates who have to be disciplined, not unlike sending a child to their room for misbehaving, as in a "time out." This includes those with extreme mental health issues who are at greater risk of harming themselves and others and therefore require more intense supervision. It is also a solution to putting prisoners in protective custody, as in the example of former gang members or high profile inmates.

Arguments against Solitary Confinement

Humans are essentially social creatures and require interaction with others in order to remain mentally healthy. Solitary confinement with little exposure to sunlight and exercise can also contribute to physical deterioration. There is the question of the constitutionality of solitary confinement that could be interpreted to some as cruel and unusual punishment. There is also evidence that mental health issues will actually become worse for those who suffer from it, if they are held in solitary confinement (Steinbuch, 2014).

OPEN PRISONS

Open prisons (or open jails), like probation and parole, afford much more freedom to the convicted. These are facilities where prisoners are allowed to leave the facility during the day to go to work while serving their sentence. They are required to return to the facility at night and remain in prison or jail during their days off, with a strict curfew tied to their hours of employment. Open prisons are more likely to be found in the United Kingdom and Scandinavian countries, though they have some history in the United States.

There are a number of architectural concerns with the open prison concept. It is difficult on the prisoners left behind, if only a handful of inmates are allowed to go to work during the day outside of the prison walls. Ideally, an open prison should only house those who need minimal supervision. With still some key elements of social management, open prison architecture, similar to the Norwegian prison that we discuss at the end of this chapter, should offer environmental incentives for good behavior, including cells that look more like dorm rooms than part of a prison (Knoblauch, 2020).

Arguments for the Open Prison Concept

Allowing inmates to continue to work outside of prison walls while serving their sentences offers some form of normalcy. In addition to being of value to the convicted, the open prison concept can relieve overcrowding, when a great number, if not all inmates leave the facility during the day.

Arguments against the Open Prison Concept

There are three things of concern with the open prison concept. One, how much is this form of "punishment" really serving to pay the convict's debt to society? If they were so trustworthy in the first place, why not simply put them on probation?

The second concern is whether there is still the possibility of offending on the outside. For example, if the inmate has organized crime ties in the community, could they conduct illegal business during their workday?

The third concern is the undue burden this places on employers. How much responsibility should they have to make sure that the inmate employee is still following the conditions of their release from prison during their work hours?

SUMMARY

Beyond capital punishment, there are a number of other controversies in corrections. Some of the debates that were addressed in this chapter included college education for inmates, prison overcrowding (which has been a running theme throughout this book), and private prisons. The arguments for and against these other controversies are as strongly defended as those made in discussions of the death penalty, some resulting in more heated discussions than others.

Throughout this book, including in this chapter, we have asked you to consider whether jail and prison is the punishment of the soul or punishment of the body. We have to remember that it is not up to jail or prison administrators to decide if the punishment fits the crime—that is the job of the courts, sentencing guidelines, judges, and juries. Few would dispute the argument that punishment should by its very nature be unpleasant, so as to act as a deterrent or offer restitution to society. The controversies here will not be easily settled, if at all, as to whether the death penalty and other questioned practices in punishment serve their intended purposes. Either way, decisions made as to what is appropriate punishment inevitably affects the lives of the convicted, corrections staff, and their families, friends.

STORIES FROM BEHIND PRISON WALLS

College Behind Bars

In this chapter, you were introduced to the debate on whether the convicted should be allowed to pursue a college education while incarcerated. The PBS documentary *College Behind Bars* (2019) follows 12 inmates who participated in the Bard Prison Initiative at the Eastern New York Correctional Facility. Some of the participants were serving long sentences, as in the case of Salih Israil, who served 20 years beginning in 1998, for robbery, assault, and possession of a weapon (Gaines, 2019). Israil today is a software engineer, thanks largely to his degree earned from Bard College while incarcerated (Gaines, 2019). Bard College is only one of a number of colleges and universities that offer programs leading to course credit and degrees for the incarcerated.

In the Northwest New Mexico Correctional Center in Grants, New Mexico, college courses are also offered. Two inmates recently received bachelor's degrees in Christian Studies, through the University of the Southwest (CoreCivic, 2021). They did so in normative time, within five years[7], in an in-person program, that required that they earn their associate degrees first from a local community college program that is funded through the New Mexico Corrections Department (CoreCivic, 2021).

College programs are not always limited to younger inmates with shorter sentences. Saint Louis University in Missouri admitted an inmate to their prison program who was 51-years-old and still had 36 more years remaining on his sentence (Earhart, 2014). Deficits in high school educations, including lower scores on GED exams or anemic GPAs of high school graduates are not deterrents for the determined inmate (Karpowitz, 2017).

According to *The Best Schools* staff writers (2021), prison education offers a number of opportunities to have access to practical training and academic degrees. The challenge is in the fact that most inmates, both at the federal and state levels, have little Internet access, including in juvenile facilities, where some in detention are still required to complete an education (Tynan, 2016). The lack of Internet access translates to an additional burden in attempting face-to-face instruction in prisons and juvenile detention centers during the COVID-19 pandemic.

The good news is that tablets are becoming more readily available in prisons with staff having the capability of limiting the type of Internet use prisoners can access. However, some institutions have returned to the outdated correspondence methods of teaching during the pandemic, using pen and paper for assignments during the pandemic, which is a much more time consuming process involving mailing work and the use of proctors for exams (Burke, 2020).

SOURCES

Burke, L. (2020) College programs in prisons go remote. *Inside Higher Ed.* June 18. Retrieved from https://www.insidehighered.com/news/2020/06/18/college-programs-prisons-adapt-covid.

---

[7] According to National Student Clearinghouse Research Center (2016), the average time it takes for a student to complete their two-year degree is 3.3 years and a four-year degree is 5.1 years. Note that this statistic was pre-COVID-19 pandemic and we do not have the latest figures on how long it will take to finish four-year degrees, on average, if there is a disruption of studies for a yet unknown number of college students, for a number of reasons.

CoreCivic (2021) Inmates at Northwest New Mexico facility earn college degrees. Apr. 22. Retrieved from https://www.corecivic.com/news/inmates-at-northwest-new-mexico-facility-earn-college-degrees.

Earhart, J. (2014) Overcoming isolation: A college program challenges culture through engagement. *Saint Louis University Public Law Review*. Vol. 33, Iss. 2:329-342.

Gaines, P. (2019) PBS chronicles 12 inmates who value education in "College Behind Bars." *NBC News*. Nov. 25. Retrieved from https://www.nbcnews.com/news/nbcblk/pbs-chronicles-12-inmates-who-value-education-college-behind-bars-n1089921.

Karpowitz, D. (2017) *College in Prison: Reading in an Age of Mass Incarceration*. New Brunswick, NJ: Rutgers University Press.

Staff (2021) Prison education: Guide to college degrees for inmates and ex-offenders. *The Best Schools* (TBS). Apr. 22. Retrieved from https://thebestschools.org/magazine/prison-inmate-education-guide/.

INTERNATIONAL PERSPECTIVES IN PUNISHMENT AND CORRECTIONS: NORWAY

In the Nordic regions, Finland, Sweden, Norway, Denmark, and the island nation of Iceland, for all their similarities and common historical roots, have differences, the least of which is the periodic animosity between themselves and with Russia. Their criminal justice needs are different, as we compare a fairly homogeneous population in these countries, as compared to that of the United States. They have become more diverse in recent decades due to immigration and have never had legal racial segregation (Kyllingstad, 2017).

Within the past five decades, Norway has gained more immigrants, some of whom are minorities. However, immigrants still make up about 16 percent of the population; only 8.5 percent of the population in Norway belong to a minority group (*CIA World Factbook*, 2020). The prison rate is 54 per 100,000 residents, where 24.8 percent of those incarcerated are foreign born (World Prison Brief, n.d.). To a large extent, this mirrors the disparity of the disproportionate number of minorities incarcerated in the United States and elsewhere in the world.

Some prisons in Western Europe are more progressive than others. For instance, prisons in Nordic countries have decidedly placed more focus on rehabilitation and humane treatment. Some prison cells in these countries look more like dormitory rooms, similar to what you may be occupying at this moment while you are in college. Nordic countries, including Norway, aggressively tackled the spread of the COVID-19 virus in prison by abolishing the use of double and multi-bed cells (Nordic Policy Centre, 2020). Nordic countries have lower rates of incarceration and recidivism, which has minimized overcrowding, as well as reducing the transmission of infectious diseases (Nordic Policy Centre, 2020).

Norway has always had a reputation for progressive approaches to punishment and incarceration. Of prisons in Norway, Halden, a high-security prison, is arguably the most humane and comfortable prison in the world (Gentleman, 2012). The exterior of the prison is built with clean Scandinavian lines and the prison has been praised for being architecturally simpatico with Nordic tastes. The only part of the prison that identifies it as a house of corrections is the 25-foot high concrete wall surrounding it, but other than that, there is nothing to identify it as a prison, as there are no guard towers manned by corrections officers with guns, nor is there razor wire (Kofman, 2015). Prison cells, game rooms, and common areas look very similar to those found in apartment-style college dorms in the U.S (Gentleman, 2012). Each cell has a flat screen television, an en-suite bathroom with privacy, and unbarred windows looking out on forest scenery; prisoners are reportedly also provided with fluffy white towels (Gentleman, 2012). Inmates work a normal work week in a number of local industries, giving them routine and responsibility (*Sunday Today*, 2019).

Beyond the esthetics of the prison, inside and out, the focus in Norwegian corrections is rehabilitation, avoiding the prisonization process from setting in, and providing normalcy in preparation for life after incarceration. As Gentleman (2012) and Kofman (2015) have emphasized, prisoners in Halden are there after being convicted of serious crimes, including rape, pedophilia, and murder. However, according to Are Høidal, the governor[8] of Halden Prison and prison architects, the design of the prison makes inmates "softer" with little in the way of violence breaking out between them.

Relatively speaking, even the minimum security prisons in the United States holding nonviolent and white collar offenders and with a reputation of being more like summer camp than prison are far from being as luxurious as Halden. Recently there have been discussions as to whether the Norwegian model for incarceration would work in the United States. After a tour of Halden Prison, North Dakota prisons chief Leann Bertsch was convinced that something along the same lines could be tried in her state as part of the push for prison reform (Slater, 2017). By 2019, North Dakota State Penitentiary boasted softball tournaments, fish tanks in classrooms, poetry slams and barbeques—inmates are even allowed to take field trips to participate in community service projects, including serving food to the homeless and training service dogs (Janzer, 2019). As it is still early in the North Dakota prison experiment, it is too soon to say that there are the same positive effects of reducing recidivism, as seen in the inmates released from Halden Prison.

SOURCES

CIA World Factbook (2020) Norwegian Demographics Profile. Index Mundi. Retrieved from https://www.indexmundi.com/norway/demographics_profile.html.

Gentleman, A. (2012) Inside Halden, the most humane prison in the world. *The Guardian.* May 18. Retrieved from https://www.theguardian.com/society/2012/may/18/halden-most-humane-prison-in-world.

---

[8] A prison governor in Norway is the same as a prison warden in the United States.

Janzer, C. (2019) North Dakota reforms prisons, Norwegian style. *U.S. News and World Report.* Feb. 22. Retrieved from https://www.usnews.com/news/best-states/articles/2019-02-22/inspired-by-norways-approach-north-dakota-reforms-its-prisons.

Killingstad, J. R. (2017) The absence of race in Norway? *Journal of Anthropological Sciences.* Vol. 95:319-327.

Nordic Policy Centre (2020) Prison during covid-19: Nordic approaches. The Australia Institute. Apr. 30. Retrieved from https://www.nordicpolicycentre.org.au/prison_during _covid_19_nordic_approaches.

Slater, D. (2017) North Dakota's Norway experiment. *Mother Jones.* July/Aug. Retrieved from https://www.motherjones.com/crime-justice/2017/07/north-dakota-norway-prisons -experiment/.

World Prison Brief (n.d.) World Prison Brief data: Norway. Institute for Crime and Justice Policy Research (ICPR), University of London, Birkbeck. Retrieved from https://www .prisonstudies.org/country/norway.

Sunday Today (2019) Go inside one of the most humane prisons in the world. Video, *NBC.* Sept. 8. Retrieved from https://www.youtube.com/watch?v=sCZt2YipiIs

GLOSSARY

Coed prison   Any prison that houses both males and females who are allowed to interact with one another rather than being held in separate sections of the facility and having no contact with one another.

Dark tourism   Tourism that places visitors in locations such as former jails and prisons where human misery has taken place; sometimes meant to satisfy the morbid curiosity of the visitors. (See *grief tourism.*)

Felon friendly **employers**   Prospective employers, organizations, and companies that will hire people with criminal records, including those with felony convictions. Some industries are more "felon friendly" than others.

Grief tourism   Similar to dark tourism, but may include visits to places that have personal meaning, as in the case of the descendants of Holocaust survivors and victims visiting former concentration camps.

Hawes-Cooper Act of 1929   Act that bans the sale of inmate made goods on the open market, primarily on the basis that it represented unfair competition with companies that did not use prison labor and could not sell their products at or below prices of goods made by prisoners.

Jennings v. Rodriguez   2018 Supreme Court case ruling that it is constitutional to hold illegal or undocumented immigrants in detention until a hearing and/or deportation.

Omnibus Crime Control and Safe Streets Act of 1968   Designed to assist State and local in the reduction of crime, as well as assist law enforcement and criminal justice systems at all levels of government. (See U.S. Department of Justice, Office of Justice Programs, https://www.ojp.gov/ncjrs/virtual-library/abstracts/omnibus-

crime-control-and-safe-streets-act-1968#:~:text=The%20Omnibus%20Crime%20
Control%20and,at%20all%20levels%20of%20government)

Open prisons (United Kingdom, Iceland)   Prisons that house more trusted, low-risk prisoners who are allowed more freedom and do not spend as much time in their cells as in higher security prisons. Also called "training prisons" for their focus on rehabilitation, including job training.

Violent Crime Control and Law Enforcement Act of 1994   Anti-crime bill that provided 100,000 new police officers, $9.7 billion in funding for prisons and $6.1 billion in funding for prevention programs. The bill also provided $2.6 billion in funding for the FBI, United States Attorneys, and other Justice Department agencies. (For summary of criminal provisions, see National Criminal Justice Reference Service, https://www.ncjrs.gov/txtfiles/billfs.txt)

REFERENCES AND SUGGESTED READINGS

Alcatraz Prison Cocktail Bar (n.d.) Available at https://www.alcotraz.co.uk/.

Australian Capital Territory (2021) *Crimes Act 1900*. Republication No 133. ACT Parliamentary Counsel. Apr. 20.

Bitran, D. B. (2017) Why tourists go to sites associated with death and suffering. *Salon*. Aug. 27. Retrieved from https://www.salon.com/2017/08/26/why-tourists-go-to-sites-associated-with-death-and-suffering_partner/.

CBS News (2018) "Misery Mountain": Violence plagued West Virginia prison before Whitey Bulger killing. Associated Press (AP). Nov. 1. Retrieved from https://www.cbsnews.com/news/whitey-bulger-dead-misery-mountain-violence-plagued-west-virginia-prison-hazelton/.

Crain's Cleveland Business (2021) University's prison program is embroiled in controversy; Most of Ashland's 2020 undergrad enrollees are distance learning inmates. Jan. 18, Vol. 42, Iss. 2:1.

Eisen, L. B. (2021). Breaking down Biden's order to eliminate DOJ private prison contracts. Brennan Center for Justice. Oct 23. Retrieved from https://www.brennancenter.org/our-work/analysis-opinion/alabama-using-covid-funds-build-new-prisons

Ernst, A. (2018) The awful thing I saw in prison that stunned me into silence. The Marshall Project. Aug. 23. Retrieved from https://www.themarshallproject.org/2018/08/23/the-awful-thing-i-saw-in-prison-that-stunned-me-into-silence.

Flory, B. (2016) Jackson prison industries: competition breed controversy. *Michigan History Magazine*. Vol. 100, Iss. 3. Retrieved from https://go-gale-com.wne.idm.oclc.org/ps/retrieve.do?tabID=T003&resultListType=RESULT_LIST&searchResultsType=SingleTab&hitCount=1&searchType=AdvancedSearchForm&currentPosition=1&docId=GALE%7CA452051963&docType=Article&sort=RELEVANCE&contentSegment=ZEAI-MOD1&prodId=EAIM&pageNum=1&contentSet=GALE%7CA452051963&searchId=R1&userGroupName=mlin_w_westnew&inPS=true.

Foucault, M. (1997) *Discipline and Punishment: The Birth of the Prison*. New York City, NY: Vintage Press.

Gobnik, A. (2012) The caging of America: Why do we lock up so many people? *The New Yorker*. Jan. 22. Retrieved from https://www.newyorker.com/magazine/2012/01/30/the-caging-of-america.

Henrichson, C. and R. Delaney (2012) *The Price of Prison: What Incarceration Costs Taxpayers.* Center on Sentencing and Corrections. Brooklyn, NY: Vera Institute for Justice.

Jacobs, E. (2020) Asylum seekers turned back from Canada face detention, deportation. WBFO-FM 88.7, NPR. Dec. 20. Retrieved from https://www.wbfo.org/binational/2020 -12-30/asylum-seekers-turned-back-from-canada-face-detention-deportation.

Johnson, D. (1987) Women blend in with men at Illinois prison. *The New York Times.* June 1.

Johnson, K. (2016) Argument analysis: Immigrant detention and the Constitution. *SCOTUSblog*: Independent News and Analysis of the U.S. Supreme Court. Dec. 1. Retrieved from https://www.scotusblog.com/2016/12/argument-analysis-immigrant -detention-and-the-constitution/.

May, L. C. (2020) Resilience and resistance: Fighting for higher education in prison. Inside Higher Education. Mar. 18. https://www.insidehighered.com/views/2020/03/18/priso ner-describes-his-and-other-inmates-struggles-access-higher-education-opinion.

Miller, K. (n.d.) 20 advantages and disadvantages of private prisons. *Future of Work*. Retrieved from https://futureofworking.com/6-advantages-and-disadvantages-of-private-prisons/.

National Student Clearinghouse Research Center (2016) Time to Degree—2016. Sept. 18. Retrieved from https://nscresearchcenter.org/signaturereport11/.

Noe-Bustamante, L., M. H. Lopez, and J. M. Krogstad (2020) U.S. Hispanic population surpasses 60 million in 2019, but growth has slowed. Pews Research Center. July 7. Retrieved from https://www.pewresearch.org/fact-tank/2020/07/07/u-s-hispanic -population-surpassed-60-million-in-2019-but-growth-has-slowed/

Old Prisons Magazine (2020) Prison tourism is a growing heritage travel niche around the world. Feb 15. Retrieved from https://www.oldprisons.com/prison-tourism-is- a-growing-heritage-travel-niche-around-the-world/#:~:text=Prison%20tourism%20 is%20a%20growing%20heritage%20travel%20niche%20around%20the%20world, -Posted%20by%20OldPrisons&text=Located%20in%20Philadelphia%2C%20 America's%20most,been%20a%20museum%20since%201994.

Prison Policy Initiative (2021) Economics of incarceration: The economic drivers and consequences. Retrieved from https://www.prisonpolicy.org/research/economics_of_incarc eration/.

Prison Policy Initiative (n.d.) Daily cost to feed prisoners and the average American. Retrieved from https://www.prisonpolicy.org/graphs/foodcosts.html.

Rakoff, J. S. (2002) *United States v. Quinones et al.* United States Court of Appeals, Second Circuit. Dec. 10.

Rogers, C. (2021) "I want the ugliest jail in Minnesota. Winona Post. Aug. 16. Retrieved from https://www.winonapost.com/news/i-want-the-ugliest-jail-in-minnesota/article_f7b77 7ff-9316-5da5-b8ee-8b9dc6c250e3.html.

Rubinkam, M. (2020) Kids-for-cash judge loses bid for lighter sentence. *The Washington Post.* Aug. 26. Retrieved from https://www.washingtonpost.com/national/kids-for-cash-judge -loses-bid-for-lighter-prison-sentence/2020/08/26/a8e82fea-e7a8-11ea-bf44-0d31c85 838a5_story.html.

Sawyer, W. (2017) Food for thought: Prison food is a public health problem. Prison Policy Initiative. Mar. 3. Retrieved from https://www.prisonpolicy.org/blog/2017/03/03/prison -food/.

Sayed, S. A., R. G. Morris, and R. A. DeShay (2020) Comparing the rates of misconduct between private and public prisons in Texas. *Crime and Delinquency*. Vol. 66, No. 9:1217-1241.

Sentencing Project, The (2021) Report: Private prisons in the United States. Mar. 3. Retrieved from https://www.sentencingproject.org/publications/private-prisons-united-states/.

Smith, W. (1988) Male, female prison having baby boom. *Chicago Tribune*. Jan. 12. Retrieved from https://www.chicagotribune.com/news/ct-xpm-1988-01-12-8803210740-story.html.

Steinbuch, A. T. (2014) The movement away from solitary confinement in the United States. *New England Journal on Criminal and Civil Confinement*. Spring, Vol. 40, Iss. 2:499-534.

Smykla, J. O. (1979) Does coed prison work? *Prison Journal.* Vol. 59, Iss. 1:61-72.

Supreme Court of the United States (SCOTUS) (2005) *Roper, Superintendent, Potosi Correctional Center v. Simmons.* No. 03-633. Retrieved from https://scholar.google.com/scholar_case?case=16987406842050815187&hl=en&as_sdt=6&as_vis=1&oi=scholarr.

Tory, S. (2019) The case against immigration prisons. High Country News. Nov. 11. Retrieved from https://www.hcn.org/issues/51.19/interview-the-case-against-immigration-prisons.

Toth, S. A. (2019) Mettray: A History of France's Most Venerated Carceral Institution. Ithaca, NY: Cornell University Press.

United States Department of Homeland Security (DHS) (2020) Immigration and customs enforcement. Retrieved from https://www.dhs.gov/topic/immigration-and-customs-enforcement.

University of California, Los Angeles (UCLA) (2020) What happens after we defund police? Criminal Justice Program. June. Retrieved from https://law.ucla.edu/sites/default/files/PDFs/Academics/What%20Happends%20After%20We%20Defund%20Police--June%202020.pdf.

Wagner, P. and B. Rabuy (2017) Following the money of mass incarceration. Prison Policy Initiative. Jan. 25. Retrieved from https://www.prisonpolicy.org/reports/money.html.

Wallace, R. (2019) 5 of the biggest challenges facing corrections in 2019. *Corrections 1,* American Military University. Dec. 11. Retrieved from https://www.corrections1.com/2018-review/articles/5-of-the-biggest-challenges-facing-corrections-in-2019-b9Afg8ZhS84p06uT/.

Wilkinson, T. (2018) Typology: Prison. *The Architectural Review.* June 11. Retrieved from https://www.architectural-review.com/essays/typology/typology-prison.

GLOSSARY

ACLU National Prison Project An initiative and cause of the American Civil Liberties Union to protect and defend prisoners' civil, human, and Constitutional rights. (See *American Civil Liberties Union*)

Activities of daily living (ADLs) The things we do in our daily lives that can affect quality of life, health, and mental well-being when we are unable to do them, including using utensils to eat, personal hygiene, brushing our teeth, and showering or bathing.

Actuarial risk Statistical and algorithmic instruments that assist in determining the level of risk an individual poses for reoffending.

Administrative-security level A facility, generally in the federal corrections system, that houses a mixture of inmates, including those needing specialized medical care, those prone to escape, and more violent offenders needing more supervision.

Adult transition centers Multipurpose centers for probationers, parolees, and other special populations, including the disabled, that help with developing adult skills.

Alcohol Use Disorder (AUD) Condition whereby a person has uncontrolled drinking habits and preoccupation with alcohol consumption. Also called alcoholism or alcohol dependency.

Alternative school Also called continuation school in some places, these are schools where students who have been expelled from a traditional school or have been referred to for behavior problems can go to complete their compulsory education.

American Civil Liberties Union (ACLU) Founded in 1920, the ACLU's mission is to work with lawmakers to protect individual rights

Americans with Disabilities Act (ADA, 1990) Legislation that requires public spaces, buildings, and businesses to provide access and accommodations to those with physical or mental limitations. Applies to jail and prison construction. Also prohibits discrimination on the basis of physical or mental limitations.

Antebellum In American history, the period prior to the Civil War, usually referring to the southern states.

Apartheid (South Africa) A policy that calls for institutional racial segregation, where there is discrimination against nonwhite people even if they are in the majority by population numbers. An example is South Africa, from 1948 after the National Party took over with an all-white government, until negotiations to end apartheid were finalized in 1994.

B

Bail   An amount set by the court that allows the accused to be conditionally released from jail prior to trial.

Banishment   Punishment by which the guilty party is ordered to leave the community, generally to never return again, as a form of social death.

Benevolent sexism   Overly positive and affectionate attitudes towards females, promoting male superiority (Ragatz and Russell, 2010).

Biophilic design   A prison design that allows for more green spaces, natural light, and open concept interiors.

Black Jails (China)   Secret detention centers throughout China that are notorious for holding political prisoners who are critical of the government.

Blackout cells   Prison cells used for solitary confinement that do not have any windows and where the prisoner is held in nearly, if not complete, blackout conditions with no light.

Branding   A common punishment during the Colonial Era, involving the use of a hot iron to mark the accused indicating their convict status for life.

Buccaneers   Spanish term for pirates who operated primarily off of the Spanish American coasts, as well as off the coasts of southeastern America.

Bureaucracy   According to Weber (1922), the most efficient way to run an organization, including the military, or in this case, corrections. Bureaucracy has a number of characteristics, which include hiring people with expertise and specialization, keeping written records, and clear hierarchy. (See *Chain of command*)

Bureaucratic control   From Edwards (1979) and Weber (1922), a system where control of workers and the running of an organization is built into the rules and regulations.

C

Capital punishment   The imposition of the death penalty in certain, particularly gruesome cases. Capital punishment is permitted on the federal level in the United States and in 27 states.

Case petitioning   Court procedure in which the court is asked to assume jurisdiction over an alleged juvenile delinquent, allowing them to be transferred to criminal court for prosecution.

Chain of command   As demonstrated by an organizational chart, the chain of command shows the clear lines of leadership and front line staff.

Child Protective Services (CPS)   The term for a number of agencies (names differs from state to state) that are responsible, along with the courts, to remove juveniles from the homes of unfit parents, relatives, or guardians. The juveniles removed may become wards of the state, in which case they may be placed in foster care or, in extreme cases, put up for adoption. (See *Ward of the Courts*). In the case of foster care, removal of the child may be temporary. In the case of adoption, the severing of legal ties between parent or guardian and the child is permanent.

Cliques   Subgroups or alliances of individuals who are part of a larger group whose members have the same values, beliefs, and/or goals. Gangs within in prisons are an example of a clique.

Coed prison   Any prison that houses both males and females who are allowed to interact with one another rather than being held in separate sections of the facility and having no contact with one another.

Cognitive Behavioral Therapy (CBT)   A form of behavior therapy that targets negative thinking by teaching patients how to recognize their distortions of reality. Example: Understanding the differences between real and perceived threats in anxiety and panic disorders.

Cognitive Behavioral Treatment (CBT)   Form of therapy that is used for a wide range of psychological issues, including behavioral, addiction, and severe mental illness.

Community corrections   Punishment or rehabilitation other than incarceration that is served in the community. Examples would be community service, probation, or court-ordered drug treatment.

Community-based corrections   Sentencing provisions that take place in the community, outside of jail or prison, including therapy, rehabilitation, and conditions for release in the case of probation or parole.

Compassionate release   Early release from jail or prison on the basis of a documented mental or medical condition, where continued incarceration would be considered unethical or cruel. Example: Early release for a terminally ill inmate.

Compassion-based therapy (CBT)   Psychotherapy that is based in developing empathy in the offender.

Conjugal visitation   Sanctioned visits to prisoners by spouses where sexual relationships are allowed. Held in housing separate from the main prison facility.

Corporal punishment   Any form of physical punishment (e.g. whipping, branding).

Crew   A subgroup similar to gangs, but generally are more neighborhood oriented. Not all crews are demonstratively criminal, as compared to street gangs.

D

Dark tourism   Tourism that places visitors in locations such as former jails and prisons where human misery has taken place; sometimes meant to satisfy the morbid curiosity of the visitors. See *grief tourism.*

De-escalate (or de-escalation)   To defuse a potentially violent or deadly situation, in this case in a jail or prison. Learning techniques to de-escalate a situation takes specialized training, generally in psychology.

Detention officer   Synonymous with corrections officer.

Deterrence   In context of punishment, the philosophy that the punishment should be so painful that the guilty will not commit the crime again, nor will others in the community.

Diagnostic and Statistical Manual of Mental Disorders (DSM-5)   The American Psychiatric Association's manual that provides a comprehensive list of recognized mental disorders and illnesses.

Differential association Theory (Sutherland)   In summary, Sutherland's theory that if individuals, in this case, juveniles, hang around with criminal or deviant family or friends, they themselves will become criminal or deviant because they are more likely to be rewarded with acceptance when they commit crimes, than if they have good behavior, where they might be teased or bullied.

Diversion programs   Pre-prison programs that are designed to change behavior so as the individual can remain in the community while addressing the problems that lead to crime, as in the example of drug addiction.

Drug courts   An alternative to traditional criminal court that seeks treatment solutions instead of incarceration.

DUI (or DWI)   Driving under the influence or driving while intoxicated charges.

Dysphoria   Feeling very unhappy, uneasy, or dissatisfied with life. See *Gender dysphoria*.

E

Eighth Amendment of the U.S. Constitution   The most commonly used clause in prisoners' civil lawsuits is prohibition of cruel or unusual punishment.

Electronic monitoring (EM)   Any use of devices that will track the movements of offenders, most commonly the GPS-guided ankle bracelet.

Emotional labor   Based on Hochschild's research (1983), when part of the conditions of working requires the display of certain emotions, as in the example of prison personnel having to not only look "tough" but also impartial.

End of life care (EOL)   Medical and emotional support given to patients (in this case, inmates) who are terminally ill and near death. See *Hospice*; *Palliative care*

***Estelle v. Gamble* (1976)**   Eighth Amendment case brought by an inmate, J. W. Gamble, against the Texas Department of Corrections after he was not given proper care after a back injury while doing prison work and instead was placed in solitary confinement when he refused to return to light work, citing the Eighth Amendment for cruel and unusual punishment.

Evidence-based programs Programs that have been tested in pilot programs or have been demonstrated to provide their intended outcomes, as in the example of programs that target recidivism.

F

Faith-based programs Private programs that are designed by faith-based organizations in order to address any number of social problems that lead to criminal behavior.

Felon friendly **employers** Prospective employers, organizations, and companies that are willing to hire people with criminal records, including those with felony convictions. Some industries are more "felon friendly" than others.

Fifth Amendment of the U.S. Constitution The so-called "due process" in a court of law amendment. (See *Fourth Amendment*)

First Amendment of the U.S. Constitution As it relates to detainees and prisoners, they have the rights to freedom of religion, freedom of speech, and freedom to sue the government, all of which have certain restrictions for prisoners where the safety and security of the facility is concerned.

Food insecurity The condition of not having predictable or having limited access to enough food to maintain an active, healthy life.

Fourteenth Amendment of the U.S. Constitution Cited for equal protection of detainees and prisoners under the law, as well as depriving a person of life, as in the case of the death penalty.

Fourth Amendment of the U.S. Constitution Usually cited in cases where detainees believe that there has been an unreasonable search of their cell or during a strip-search or pat down. (See *strip-search*)

G

GED A high school equivalency diploma available for people who have dropped out of high school that requires classes and testing.

Gender dysphoria The disconnect between the sex that one is identified as at birth and the expected gender roles linked to that sex, resulting in a number of psychological disorders, including depression and distress. Transgender individuals who have not as yet allowed themselves or are not allowed by others to manifest the gender that they identify with are said to suffer from gender dysphoria. Treatments include hormone therapy and sex reassignment surgery. See *Transgender*.

General deterrence   Punishment or barriers to prevent crimes in general and not any one specific crime.

Geneva Convention   Signed in 1950, a unilateral agreement brought by the United Nations to require that prisoners of war be treated with dignity and are not subject to torture or abuses.

Goldfish bowl effect   There are two components of the goldfish bowl effect. First, it is the perception that everyone is looking at you. Second, that perception is distorted, as in the example of the curved sides of a goldfish bowl.

Good time earned   "Earned time" or "meritorious credit" that will shorten a convict's time in jail or prison.

Grief tourism   Similar to dark tourism, but may include visits to places that have personal meaning, as in the case of the descendants of Holocaust survivors and victims visiting former concentration camps.

H

Habeas corpus   Legal right for someone who has been arrested to be brought before a judge in a timely matter (which is subjective) and provide provisions for release, unless there are legal grounds to detain the accused before trial.

Habeas privileges   From the Constitution, habeas corpus is the right to be brought before a judge before being detained or imprisoned. This is why arraignments and formal charges brought against a suspect have to take place quickly after someone has been arrested.

Hawes-Cooper Act of 1929   Act that bans the sale of inmate made goods on the open market, primarily on the basis that it represented unfair competition with companies that did not use prison labor and could not sell their products at or below prices of goods made by prisoners.

Health care   Efforts to restore or maintain the health and well-being of patients.

Health Insurance Portability and Accountability Act (HIPPA, 1996)   Legislation that protects individuals' medical records from being disclosed without their permission. Limited in jails and prisons due to concerns for safety and security.

Healthcare   The system that controls and manages health care. Generally, is more business focused on the costs, legal issues, and general management of health care.

High security prisons   Correctional facilities that house the most violent offenders, those with gang affiliations, and the criminally insane that are not housed in psychiatric hospitals. Inmates need the highest degree of supervision at all times, many of whom are kept in solitary confinement.

Hootch   Homemade alcoholic beverage that is made in prison cells illegally with little or no control over the percentage of alcohol contained.

Hoptowit v. Ray (1982) Lawsuit brought by inmates at the Washington State Penitentiary against the Governor and various officials, alleging that conditions (including medical, dental) in the prison violated the 8th Amendment, citing that it was cruel and unusual punishment.

Hospice care Emotional and logistical support to terminal ill patients and their families as they cope with and adjust to the last days or weeks of the individual who is dying. See *End of Life Care (EOL); Palliative care*

I

Importation Theory Theory that proposes that anti-social behavior, including violence, is brought into the prison by inmates from their lives prior to incarceration.

Incapacitation Punishment that is intended to temporarily stop further criminal behavior, including imprisonment or in extreme cases of violent crimes, permanently with the death penalty.

Incarceration Punishment that includes time in jail or prison as part of sentencing.

Indentured servant An individual in Colonial times who voluntarily enters a contract to work for an employer for free, save room and board, in return for payment of travel expenses. Example: An immigrant cannot afford to travel to the American Colonies, so promises to work for free in return for the payment of passage to America.

Individuals with Disabilities Education Act (IDEA) 1997 law that requires that a free, appropriate public education must be made available for eligible children with disabilities, including special education with individualized learning plans.

Infirmary Another name for the medical facilities at a jail or prison, borrowing the term from the military.

Inmate code The set of rules made up by prisoners themselves on how to behave in prison.

Intake Process by which a juvenile is referred to the juvenile justice system, including screening to determine what type of programs may be appropriate, as well as other strategies to avoid juvenile detention, whenever possible.

Intensive supervision probation (ISP) Probation that requires more contact with probation supervisors, including several meetings a week and home visits. May be combined with electronic monitoring.

Intermediate sanctions A facet of community-based corrections where a number of penalties may be imposed on the convicted, including fines, restitution, community service, and other punishments meant to keep the convicted out of prison and in the community.

Intimate partner violence (IPV) Domestic violence, stalking, sexual assault, or psychological harm perpetrated against or between romantic partners and/or spouses.

Intrinsic motivation   The internal motivation to do things, including living a law abiding life for other than material rewards, like money.

Iron Cage of Bureaucracy   Weber's concept of bureaucracy becoming so rule-bound that it becomes difficult to get anything accomplished. Same thing as the proverbial "red tape."

J

Jailhouse snitches   Individuals who will act as informants to report criminal activities of prisoners or inform on prisoners who are suspected of being involved in criminal activities yet to be reported to prosecutors or authorities.

Jennings v. Rodriguez 2018   Supreme Court case ruling that it is constitutional to hold illegal or undocumented immigrants in detention until a hearing and/or deportation.

Jim Crow Laws   State and local laws that prohibited integration of Blacks and whites and legalized institutional racism in the south.

Jurisdictional roles   Same as "job descriptions" that clearly state exactly what duties someone has in a particular position.

"Just deserts"   Kant's philosophy of punishment that criminals get what they deserve, even with harsh sentencing.

Juvenile boot camps   Military-styled residential programs for juvenile delinquents or at-risk youth, focused on physical fitness, behavioral modification, and discipline.

K

Knuckleduster   A makeshift weapon that can be used with a fist in hand-to-hand combat. An example would be brass knuckles, which would be contraband in prison.

Koran   The primary religious writings in Islam.

L

Labeling Theory (Tannenbaum)   Theory that proposes that once someone is stigmatized (e.g., labeled a juvenile delinquent), it is very difficult to get rid of the negative reputation in society.

Libel (or defamation, Costa Rica)   Ordinarily more likely to be treated as a civil case in the United States, Costa Rica will prosecute for criminal libel or defamation, where someone has published unflattering or false stories about an individual, individuals, companies, or government entities.

Lifers   Individuals who have been sentenced to life in prison. This could include individuals with life with or without the possibility of parole.

Lockdowns   Emergency events in jails or prison when there is a real or reported threat of violence, rioting, or escape. Detainees and inmates are required to be locked in their cells until the emergency has passed and prison administration end the lockdown.

Low security prisons   Prisons intended for low level offenders, including nonviolent drug offenders and white collar criminals.

Lynching   An unsanctioned, illegal hanging of an accused individual, whether they are guilty or not of their offense, usually by an angry mob.

M

Mace   A medieval club-like weapon that can be made in prison, generally consisting of a ball covered with spikes (e.g., nails) and sometimes attached to a chain or other materials in order to make the mace easy to swing at victims.

Mandatory release   The required release date built into sentencing.

Mandatory vs. discretionary death penalty   Cases where the death penalty is the only punishment allowed, if the individual has been found guilty as opposed to the discretion of a jury and/or a judge to impose the death penalty in a case.

Master status   The main identity that we identify with. For prisoners, whether they commit to that status or not, prison staff see them, generally, as only detainees or prisoners, guilty of their crimes.

Medium security prisons   Prisons for inmates who do not need as much supervision as in a high security facility but cannot necessarily be trusted in a low security facility.

Mental health courts   Alternatives to criminal court system for offenders with mental health issues, where they are more likely to be sentenced to treatment in the community.

Micromanage, micromanagement   An inefficient, hands-on approach to management where a supervisor wants to handle all aspects of operations themselves. A more efficient way of managing is to trust your employees and that you have hired the best people for their jobs.

Model Sentencing and Corrections Act (1978)   Legislation that was intended to unify correctional systems, in order to more efficiently use scarce resources.

Multifactor Offender Readiness Model (MORM)   A survey used to determine just how prepared an offender is to successfully complete a program, including testing self-efficacy.

N

National Survey of Youth in Custody (NSYC)   A survey conducted by the Bureau of Justice Statistics (BJS) as part of the BJS's National Rape Statistics program, which gathers data on sexual assault and abuses in juvenile facilities.

Nelson Mandela Rules (South Africa)   United Nations policies and rules that are given to mandate the expected treatment of prisoners, including prohibiting torture, excessive time in solitary confinement, and denial of health care. Named for Nelson Mandela who served 27 years in South African prisons for being an anti-apartheid activist. Mandela was later elected President of South Africa after his release from prison.

Nepotism   Practice of hiring family and friends, even though they may not be qualified for the job they are filling.

New Jim Crow   Continued use of a caste system in post-Jim Crow southern states, which disadvantages Blacks and other minorities by discrimination and prejudice.

Norm   The expected, lawful behaviors that society requires of its members, generally agreed upon by most people in the population.

Not in my backyard (NIMBY)   The concerns of residents and businesses have when faced with the possibility of a jail or prison being built in the community, the fear being that it will negatively affect property values and bring crime to the area.

O

Occupational therapy   Therapies aimed at improving a patient's ability to perform their activities of daily living after a serious injury or illness. See *Activities of daily living (ADLs)*

Office of Juvenile Justice and Delinquency Prevention (OJJDP)   U.S. government agency established as part of the Juvenile and Delinquency Prevention Act of 1974 and the Juvenile Justice and Delinquency Prevention Act Reauthorization (2018) whose mission is to prevent delinquency and improve the juvenile justice system in the United States.

Old Testament   First half of the Christian Bible that is often cited as to why punishment should fit a crime. To paraphrase, "an eye for an eye" logic. Basis of the Old Testament is in the Torah, the sacred text of Judaism.

Open prisons (United Kingdom, Iceland)   Prisons that house more trusted, low-risk prisoners who are allowed more freedom and do not spend as much time in their cells as in higher security prisons. Also called "training prisons" for their focus on rehabilitation, including job training.

P

Palliative care   Medical intervention to ease the pain and discomfort that terminal patients experience towards the end of their lives.

Paramilitary   Not to be confused with extremist groups, paramilitary operations, like in jails and prisons, are organized similarly as the military with a clear chain of command and ranks. (See *Chain of command*)

Pardons   Powers of governors and presidents to "forgive" a crime and set aside a judgement and sentence.

Parole   A type of back end correction that makes early release from prison possible for a number of reasons (e.g., overcrowding, "good time" served) but that still requires serving the sentence with supervision in the community.

Patient-to-prisoner pipeline   Not to be confused with the school-to-prison pipeline described in our chapter on juveniles in custody, the patient-to-prison pipeline is the path that many people with mental illness take if they do not have intervention and/or help from family or friends (Onah, 2018).

Peer mediation   Programs in primary and secondary schools where fellow students, with adult supervision of teachers and guidance counselors, stand in objective judgement when there is conflict between students. Used in conflict resolution to avoid further escalation of interpersonal issues into violence.

Penal colonies (United States and Australia)   Off shore communities housing prisoners established in more remote parts of the world, as in the example of 19th-century England's Australian penal colony. Not all criminals sent to penal colonies were hardened, violent criminals. Some worked as servants to settlers who could eventually become part of the larger community after serving their time. Others were/are used as forced labor, including on chain gangs.

Penitence   The display of regret and apology for wrongdoings, usually with some form of religious request for forgiveness.

Penologists   Trained professionals who work in prisons to study the efficiency and effectiveness of incarceration and programs.

Penology   The study of the purposes and types of punishment.

Physical therapy   Rehabilitative therapy after a serious injury or illness to restore or improve the mobility of the patient.

Piracy   The attacking and robbing of ships on the seas and along coastlines.

Pirates   Robbers and pillagers who travel by sea, launching attacks both on land and sea with the goal of illegal financial gain.

Pity booking   The arrest and detaining of unhoused individuals in jail on extremely cold or hot days/nights. These bookings usually include charges of vagrancy that are often dropped once weather conditions outside improve for the unhoused.

Pods   A collection of jail or prison cells, used to keep similar offender populations together, whenever possible, of those who are undergoing rehabilitation.

Post-traumatic stress disorder (PTSD) Psychological disorder that is experienced by some people who have lived through traumatic events in their lives. For example, veterans who were actively engaged in war.

Prison Litigation Reform Act (PLRA, 1996) Legislation that was intended to stop or at least slow down the number of frivolous lawsuits that were taking up court time as well as court resources.

Prison Rape Elimination Act (PREA) 2003 passed legislation in Congress that requires that the problem of rape in prison be addressed, including ways by which to protect prisoners from both fellow prisoners and prison staff.

Prison slang A special vocabulary that has been created by prisoners or, in some cases, brought in from the outside.

Prisoners of war (POWs) Individuals who are captured by an enemy in the course of war. POWs can include both civilian and military captives.

Prisonization Theory A theory that proposes that antisocial behavior, including violence, is a result of the conditions of prison.

Privateers Pirates who are operating on the high seas with the blessing of a government, including military activities along with robbery.

Pro bono The offer of an attorney to provide legal services free of charge.

Pro se Representing oneself in a court of law or in a legal matter.

Probation A type of front end correction that is intended to keep the convicted out of prison and under community supervision.

Probation officer directives Requirements that are imposed on the probationer by the probation officer, beyond those imposed by the court.

Procunier v. Martinez (1974) Case that defined the freedoms and limits of inmates' First Amendment rights to free speech.

Protective custody A segregated portion of a jail or prison that is reserved for detainees or prisoners who have to be protected from other inmates for a number of reasons, including cases where they have witnessed crimes and turned evidence against other prisoners, are victims of violence, or due to their sexual orientation.

Pruno See *Hootch*.

Pseudo-families A group of people who are not related by the legal definition of family by blood, marriage, or adoption, but for all intents and purposes, consider themselves to be a family unit. Examples would be a house full of roommates or a cohabitating couple, who, even though they are not legally related, still rely one each other for financial and emotional support within the household, similarly to the way that legal families do.

"Publisher only" rule   Requirement of both detainees and prisoners to only receive publications from the outside directly from the publisher.

Pure restitution   Philosophy of punishment whereby the guilty party is only responsible for restitution to the victims and generally not excessively fined or required to serve time in prison.

Q

Qur'an   See *Koran*.

R

Recidivism   Reoffending by individuals who have spent time in prison.

Rehabilitation   Programs that are directed at the behaviors that land people in prison in the first place.

Reprieves   Cancellation or postponement of sentences, generally because new evidence has come to light. It does not necessarily mean that punishment won't eventually be handed out to the convicted, including in death penalty cases.

Responsivity Principle   A target principle: Be responsive to temperament, learning style, motivation culture, and gender when assigning programs.

Restitution   Usually fines paid to victims. Can also include fines to the state or federal government as a means by which to monetarily pay for a crime.

Restorative justice   Philosophy of punishment by which the act of facing one's crime victim and asking for forgiveness will be beneficial for both the criminal and the victim.

Retribution   Revenge based punishment whereby the punishment should be similar to the crime committed. Example: An eye for an eye from the Bible.

Right-to-view statutes   The legal right to view and in the case of the media, record the proceedings during an execution. See *Secrecy statutes*.

Riots   Defined by the Bureau of Prisons as any disturbance in jail or prison that involves five or more detainees or inmates.

Risk Principle   A target principle: Prioritize supervision and treatment resources for higher risk offenders.

Risk-Need-Responsivity Principle (RNR)   Used to test the appropriateness of treatments or services to reduce the convict's risk for reoffending.

S

Sally port   "Sally" meaning to go out and "port," the French word for door, together are still used today to describe the double doored entrance by which the arrested and prisoners are escorted in and out of jail or prison. Most sally ports today lead directly to the processing (or intake) offices of the facility. Like other terms used in corrections, sally port comes from the military, used for the gate or door that soldiers went out of during a siege.

Sap Makeshift weapon where a hard object like a bar of soap or lock is placed in a sock and used against a fellow detainee or prisoner.

Secrecy statutes Law in some states to allow secrecy around the method of execution, even from the condemned. Also include the corrections department right to limit the number of witnesses at an execution. See *Right-to-view statutes*.

Seditious libel An artifact brought over from England to the American colonies, making it a criminal offense to publish or make statements that are anti-government.

Self-efficacy The ability of an individual to be self-motivated, built on individual social experiences, training, and mentoring.

Self-fulfilling prophecy (Merton) Social psychological phenomenon where other people's expectations of the individual, whether positive or negative, eventually result in that individual living up to those expectations. Example: If a child is constantly accused of stealing, even when they are not doing so, they may begin to start stealing.

Sentencing Project, The From their website, a nonprofit that "promotes effective and humane responses to crime that minimize imprisonment and criminalization of youth and adults by promoting racial, ethnic, economic, and gender justice."

Sex offender registry The requirement that convicted sex offenders register their offense status with local law enforcement wherever they may live. The registry is publicly published so that the community is aware of the location of sex offenders within their neighborhoods.

Shaming and reintegration Form of restorative justice that requires the guilty party to publicly admit their crime to their victim(s) and to the community so that they may be forgiven and become law abiding members of the community again.

Shank Prison-made sharp object, including knives, made from everyday materials available to prisoners. Synonymous for *shiv*.

Sharia Law Islamic religious laws.

Shiv See *shank*.

Shock probation Sentencing that includes some jail time followed by probation, in the hopes that the experience is so traumatizing, that it will reduce reoffending.

Simple control Management style described by Edwards (1979) in smaller operations where supervision is up close and personal; it can at times be arbitrary, as in the example of a family-run business.

Situational homosexuality Same-sex relationships that occur when individuals who ordinarily identify as heterosexual are housed only with the same sex.

Social capital offenders Women who grew up in rural settings in poor households, with low victimization histories, serving time for drug offenses (DeHart, 2018).

Social identity theories Sociological and social psychological theories that address issues around how we identify ourselves on the basis of what groups we belong to.

Social Learning Theory (Akers) A theory that can be applied to both juvenile and adult offenders, where the environment and who you associate with, including family members and peer groups, may result in learning how to be deviant and/or delinquent. Similar to Sutherland's *Differential Association Theory*.

Solitary confinement Cells with single-person occupancy, used either in protective custody, or as discipline when there has been serious rule violations or violence committed by an inmate. Prisoners with extreme mental disorders are also housed in solitary confinement for their safety and the safety of others.

Span of control The number of people that someone can effectively supervise. That number is dependent on the industry. In corrections, it refers to the number of staff that a supervisor can manage or the number of prisoners that a corrections officer can safely handle.

Specific deterrence A punishment or barrier that is targeting a specific type of crime. Example: burglar alarms.

Staties The term used in law enforcement circles to refer to the state police. In some states, they are considered to be the elite of the elite in law enforcement at the state level. County and State Police are generally responsible for running local jails.

Stays of execution Similar to a reprieve, a delay in carrying out a court order, in the case of the death penalty, the execution

Stigma The negative attitudes and discrimination against individuals who do not appear to conform to society's norms, standards, and expectations. Stigma is difficult to get rid of as whatever it is, it is viewed as the master status of the individual. Example: Ex-convict.

Stolen Generations (Australia) Similar to practices in North America with respect to Native American and First Nations children placed in "Indian schools," children of indigenous people of Australia were taken from their homes from 1910 to the 1970s under the guise of the Aboriginal Protection Act of 1869. The policy was instated to forcibly assimilate them into the dominant white culture and eventually erase the native language, culture, and religious practices from the continent of Australia and surrounding islands.

Strain Theory (Merton) A multifaceted theory where individuals who cannot meet society's goals or find the means by which to achieve those goals, may find alternative, deviant goals and/or means to do so. Other responses may be to reject society's goals and means and become, as Merton termed them, "retreatists."

Strip-searches   Searching a person's body while they are either partially or fully undressed.

Study-release programs   Much less common than work-release programs, inmates are allowed to leave the prison to attend college classes, but have to be in prison when they are not in school. (see *Work-release programs*)

Substance use disorders (SUDs)   Synonymous with drug addiction.

Substantive violations   Violations of probation or parole that involve new criminal offenses that will revoke community-based supervision and send the individual back to jail or prison, to a new trial.

Summary discipline   Punishment that does not have purpose; is arbitrary.

"Supermax" prisons   Highest security level prisons where inmates generally spend up to 23 hours a day in their cells.

T

Talk therapy   Layperson's terms for psychotherapy that is individualized therapy used to treat a number of mental disorders or emotional issues.

Technical control   Edward's term (1979) where control of employees, and in this case, the incarcerated as well, is built into the physical structure of the building. In jails and prisons, this includes mechanized or computerized security doors and cells.

Technical violation   A violation of a condition of probation or parole that is not criminal, but can still result in having probation or parole revoked and the juvenile or adult taken into back into custody, sent to a detention center, jail, or prison to complete their original sentence. Examples: Continually violating court ordered curfews, missing hearings for updates on progress.

Thirteenth Amendment of the U.S. Constitution   Section 1, Exception Clause, as it relates to corrections: "Neither slavery nor involuntary servitude, except as a punishment for crime...."

***Three strikes* rule, PLRA**   After inmates have had three civil lawsuits denied on the basis of being frivolous, they are not able to file further lawsuits, unless they can prove that it is an emergency or that they are in eminent danger.

Torah   First five books of the Hebrew Bible used in Judaism and thought to be the origins of the Old Testament in the Christian Bible.

Total institutions   Places where there are limited liberties for the individuals who are housed there voluntarily or involuntarily, e.g., prisoners, the institutionalized mentally ill, the military, and monasteries.

Transgender   An individual whose self-identification by sex and gender is in conflict with the sex they were born with. For instance, a trans woman is born male, but identifies as female; a trans male is born female, but identifies as male. See *Dysphoria, Gender dysphoria*

Treatment Principle   A target principle: Integrate treatment into the full sentence/sanction requirements.

Tree jumper **school**   Protective custody housing for individuals who have been convicted of certain sex crimes, including sexual abuse and/or murder of children.

U

Units   See *Pods.*

V

Vengeful, vengeance   Punishment that is intended to "get even" with the accused, as in the example of torture before killing a suspect.

Vitek v. Jones   U.S. Supreme Court case that requires inmates who are going to be transferred to mental hospitals or facilities to be notified and given a hearing, under the due process clause of the Fourteenth Amendment.

W

Wards of the Court   Used in both cases of juvenile delinquency and child maltreatment, the juvenile will be taken under the protection of the court and parental or guardian rights are diminished. Similar to becoming a *ward of the state,* which has broader implications, such as having a guardian assigned or being referred to child protective services.

Waste management model   A punishment philosophy in the United States that promotes the removal of convicted criminals, sequestering them far from the rest of society, where they and the prisons they are housed in cannot be seen by the general population.

Wilderness programs   Outdoor programs set in the mountains, seaside, or desert that are intended to foster self-esteem, team building, and interpersonal communication skills. An example would be Outward Bound, a program that targets both adults and juveniles.

Work-release programs   Prison programs where the convicted are allowed out in the community to work during the day, but need to return to prison after their shift, typically at night and have to be incarcerated over the weekend and/or their days off from work.

Wraparound programs   Multipronged approach to reducing juvenile delinquency that includes treating both the offender and the family in community-based corrections (e.g., probation) and rehabilitation.

Y

Yellow journalism   News that is based less on fact than on sensationalism and exaggerations in order to draw a bigger audience, and in turn, generate more revenue for the source.

TABLE OF REFERENCES

Ababi, M. (2018) 11 American work habits other countries avoid at all costs. *Business Insider*. Mar. 8. Retrieved from https://www.businessinsider.com/unhealthy-american-work-habits-2017-11.

Abbott, J. H. (1981) *In the Belly of the Beast: Letters from Prison*. New York: Random House.

ABC News (2016) *Rikers Correction Officer/A Day in the Life*. Available at https://www.youtube .com/watch?v=4X0xKSBvqvE.

ABC News (2018) Interview: John McCain on the horrors he endured as a POW. Video. Aug. 26. Retrieved from https://www.youtube.com/watch?v=RYxMRiftYuY.

Abram, K. M., L. A. Teplin, and D. R. Charles. (2004) Posttraumatic stress disorder and trauma in youth in juvenile detention. *Archives of General Psychiatry*. Vol. 61, No. 4:403-410.

Abram, K. M., L. A. Teplin, and G. M. McClelland (2003) Comorbid psychiatric disorders in youth in juvenile detention. *Archives of General Psychiatry*. Vol. 60, No. 11:1097-1108.

Acevedo, J. F. (2017) Dignity Takings in the Criminal Law of Seventeenth-Century England and the Massachusetts Colony. *Chicago-Kent Law Review*. Summer, Vol. 92, Iss. 3:743-767.

Acosta, L. (2015) *Please Don't Take My Daddy*! Bloomington, IN: Xlibris US.

AFP News Agency (2013) Mexico: Yoga classes to steer young offenders away from crime. Sept. 30. Video. Retrieved from https://www.youtube.com/watch?v=2LcK2lPOVao&t=6s.

Agoff, C., S. Sandberg, and G. Fondevilla (2020) Women providing and men free riding: Work, visits and gender roles in Mexican prisons. *Victims and Offenders*. Nov. 19. Available at https://www.researchgate.net/profile/Sveinung_Sandberg/publication/346979143_Women _Providing_and_Men_Free_Riding_Work_Visits_and_Gender_Roles_in_Mexican_Prisons/ links/5fd74409299bf140880a87e1/Women-Providing-and-Men-Free-Riding-Work-Visits-and -Gender-Roles-in-Mexican-Prisons.pdf.

Aguayo, T. (2006) Youth who killed at 12 gets 30 years for violating probation. *New York Times*. May 19. Retrieved from https://www.nytimes.com/2006/05/19/us/youth-who-killed-at-12 -gets-30-years-for-violating-probation.html.

Ahlin, E. M. and D. Barberi (2019) Addressing sexual assault and victimization in detention facili- ties: Fifteen years post-PREA. *Juvenile Justice Update*. Winter, Vol. 24, Iss. 4:9-18.

Akkan, G. (2018) *Midnight Express* as a product of Hollywood Orientalism. *E-Revista de Estudos Interculturais do CEI—ISCAP (E-Journal of Intercultural Studies)*. May, No. 6:1-6. Retrieved from https://www.iscap.pt/cei/e-rei/n6/artigos/Goksu-Akkan_Midnight-Express-Hollywood .pdf.

A.L. (2007) Review, Santa Monica Jail. *Yelp.com*. Mar. 29. Retrieved from https://www.yelp.com/ biz/santa-monica-jail-santa-monica?hrid=_J8uoqZdUtMbXCj2Ntk7vw&osq=Jails+%26+ Prisons.

Alarid, L. F. (2015) Perceptions of probation and police officer home visits during intensive proba- tion supervision. *Federal Probation*. Vol. 79, Iss. 1:11-16.

Alarid, L. F., B. A. Sims, and J. Ruiz (2011) School-based juvenile probation and police partner- ships for truancy reduction. *Journal of Knowledge and Best Practices in Juvenile Justice and Psychology*. Vol. 5, No. 1:13-20.

Albert Corbarrubias Justice Project (2012) Supreme Court rules any offense, however minor, allows for a strip search. Apr. 3. Retrieved from https://acjusticeproject.org/2012/04/03/supreme -court-rules-any-offense-however-minor-allows-for-a-strip-search/.

Alexander, M. (2017) Forward: Standing without sweet company, in *Inside This Place, Not of It: Narratives from Women's Prisons*, R. Levi and A. Waldman, eds. Voice of Witness© (VOW). Brooklyn, NY: Verso Books. Kindle ed.

Alexander, M. (2020) *The New Jim Crow: Mass Incarceration in the Age of Colorblindness*. New York, NY: The New Press.

Allerd, S. L., L. D. Harrison, D. J. O'Connell (2013) Self-efficacy: An important aspect of prison- based learning. *The Prison Journal*. Vol. 23, No. 2:211-233.

Alper, M., M. R. Durose, and J. Markman (2018) 2018 Update on prisoner recidivism: A nine-year follow-up period (2004-2015). Office of Justice Programs, *Bureau of Justice Statistics*, U. S. Department of Justice. May. NCJ 250975. 23 pp.

Altice, F. L. and S. A. Springer (2005) Management of HIV/AIDS in correctional settings in *The AIDS Pandemic: Impact of Science and Society*, K. H. Mayer and H. F. Pizer, eds. Cambridge, MA: Academic Press. Ch. 18.

American Addiction Centers (2022) Corrections officers: Addiction, stressors, and problems they face. By ed. staff. Jan 31. Retrieved from https://americanaddictioncenters.org/rehab-guide/corrections-officers.

American Bar Association (ABA) (2011) Criminal justice standards: Treatment of prisoners.

American Bar Association (ABA) Treatment of Prisoners: https://www.americanbar.org/groups/criminal_justice/publications/criminal_justice_section_archive/crimjust_standards_treatmentprisoners/.

American Civil Liberties Union (ACLU) (2017) *Dockery v. Hall*. Mar. 2. Retrieved from https://www.aclu.org/cases/prisoners-rights/dockery-v-hall.

American Civil Liberties Union (ACLU) (2021) Facts about the over-incarceration of women in the United States. Retrieved from https://www.aclu.org/other/facts-about-over-incarceration-women-united-states.

American Civil Liberties Union (ACLU) (2021) Juveniles and the death penalty. Retrieved from https://www.aclu.org/other/juveniles-and-death-penalty#:~:text=The%20United%20States%20Supreme%20Court,death%20sentences%20have%20been%20imposed.

American Civil Liberties Union (ACLU), National Prison Project: https://www.aclu.org/issues/prisoners-rights?redirect=prisoners-rights.

American Civil Liberties Union (ACLU) (n.d.) ACLU National Prison Project. Retrieved from https://www.aclu.org/other/aclu-national-prison-project.

American History X (New Line Cinema, The Turman-Morrissey Co., 1998) Movie.

American Me (Universal Pictures, 1992) Movie.

American University Washington College of Law (n.d.) Project on addressing prison rape. Retrieved from https://www.wcl.american.edu/impact/initiatives-programs/endsilence/research-guidance/nprec-says-bop-policy-change-endangers-transgender-people-in-custody/.

Anckar, C. (2014) Why countries choose the death penalty. *Brown Journal of World Affairs*. Vol. 21, Iss. 1:7-26.

Annas, G. J. (2006) Hunger strikes at Guantanamo—Medical Ethics and Human Rights in a "Legal Black Hole." *The New England Journal of Medicine*. Vol. 355, No. 13:1377-1382.

Annie E. Casey Foundation (2011) *No Place for Kids: The Case for Reducing Juvenile Incarceration*. Baltimore, MD: Anne E. Casey Foundation.

Annie E. Casey Foundation (2020) New reports finds many families with children are depressed, uninsured, hungry and at risk of foreclosure or eviction. Dec. 4. Retrieved from https://www.aecf.org/blog/new-report-finds-many-families-with-children-are-depressed-uninsured-hungry.

Anton-Solanas, A., B. V. O'Neill, T. E. Morris, and J. Dunbar (2016) Physiological and cognitive response to an Antarctic Expedition: A case report. *International Journal of Sports Physiology and Performance*. Vol. 11:11053-1059.

Armstrong, M. (2019) In sickness and in health—and in prison. *Looking Back*, The Marshall Project. Aug. 19. Retrieved from https://www.themarshallproject.org/2019/08/19/in-sickness-in-health-and-in-prison.

Arts & Entertainment (A&E) (2018) *Born Behind Bars*. Television series. Season 1. Retrieved from https://play.aetv.com/shows/born-behind-bars.

Arts & Entertainment (A&E) (2019) *Behind Bars: Rookie Year: Is it Worth It*. Available at https://www.youtube.com/watch?v=Ugz5xFLlnkc.

Arts & Entertainment (A&E) (2019) *Behind Bars: Rookie Year: Little Lilly Shows She's Tough*. Available at https://www.youtube.com/watch?v=6mrsWuOPdDs.

Ashraf, H. (2003) US Supreme Court limits forced drugging of mentally ill before trial. *The Lancet*. London, UK. June 21. Retrieved from https://eds-a-ebscohost-com.wne.idm.oclc.org/eds/pdfviewer/pdfviewer?vid=2&sid=c645e3cf-61de-4922-96f1-3e706e32153c%40sessionmgr4007.

Asim, F. and V. Shree (2020) Biophilic architecture for restoration and therapy within the built environment: A review. Visions for Sustainability. Vol. 15. Retrieved from https://www.preprints.org/manuscript/201907.0323/v1.

Aspinwall, C., K. Blakinger, and J. Neff (2020) What women dying in prison from COVID-19 tell us about female incarceration. The Marshall Project. May 14. Retrieved from https://www.themarshallproject.org/2020/05/14/what-women-dying-in-prison-from-covid-19-tell-us-about-female-incarceration.

Aspinwall, C. and Z. Branstetter (2014) IV errors, lack of training cited in Oklahoma botched execution report. *Tulsa World*. Sept. 5. Retrieved from https://tulsaworld.com/news/local/crime-and-courts/iv-errors-lack-of-training-cited-in-oklahoma-botched-execution-report/article_daf3a9e5-6d7b-5a94-835c-951be33ac72a.html.

Associated Press (2002) Taliban publicly execute woman. *The Mirror*. Nov. 17. Retrieved from http://www.rawa.org/murder-w.htm.

Associated Press (2021) Federal prisons forced to use cooks, nurses to guard inmates due to staff shortages. *U.S. News*, NBC News. May 21. Retrieved from https://www.nbcnews.com/news/us-news/federal-prisons-forced-use-cooks-nurses-guard-inmates-due-staff-n1268138.

Associated Press (2021) Nebraska inmates' fight to wed ends after one of them dies. ABC News. May 24. Retrieved from https://abcnews.go.com/US/wireStory/nebraska-inmates-fight-wed-ends-dies-77877572.

Au, J. (2016) A remedy for male-to-female transgender inmates: Applying disparate impact to prison placement. *American University Journal of Gender, Social Policy and the Law*. Vol. 24, Iss. 3:371-400.

Austin, J., K. D. Johnson, and M. Gregoriou (2000) *Juveniles in Adult Prisons and Jails*. NCJ 182503. Washington D.C.: Institute on Crime, Justice and Corrections at George Washington University and National Council on Crime and Delinquency.

Australian Capital Territory (2021) *Crimes Act 1900*. Republication No 133. ACT Parliamentary Counsel. Apr. 20.

Australians Today (2020) The Stolen Generations: The forcible removal of Aboriginal and Torres Strait Islander children from their families. Nov. 17. Retrieved from https://australianstogether.org.au/discover/australian-history/stolen-generations#stolengenref5.

Avalon Project, The (n.d.) Alabama: Constitution of 1819. Lillian Goldman Law Library, Yale Law School. Retrieved from https://avalon.law.yale.edu/19th_century/ala1819.asp.

AZYEP (2020) Restorative justice: Is there a way to decrease recidivism within the criminal justice system? KDNK 88 Community Radio. Jul. 13 airdate. Retrieved from https://www.kdnk.org/post/restorative-justice-there-way-decrease-recidivism-within-criminal-justice-system.

Babbar, M. (2021) The Fourth Amendment stripped bare: Substantiating prisoners' reasonable right to bodily privacy. *Northwestern University Law Review*. Vol. 115, Iss. 6:1737-1779.

Baglivio, M. T., K. T. Wolff, M. DeLisi, and K. Jackowski (2020) The role of adverse childhood experience (ACEs) and psychopathic features on juvenile offending criminal careers to 18. *Youth Violence and Juvenile Justice*. Vol. 18, No. 4:337-364.

Baker, S. U. (2017) *Transgender behind prison walls*. Hook, Hampshire, UK: Waterside Press.

Baker, T., M. M. Mitchell, J. A. Gordon (2021) Prison visitation and concerns about reentry: variations in frequency of visits are associated with reentry concerns among people incarcerated. *International Journal of Offender Therapy and Comparative Criminology*. Electronic publication. May 4: 306624X211013516.

Balahur, D. and G. M. Ichim (2019) Women and gendered penalties: Risks and needs of female prisoners. *Scientific Annals of Al. I. Cuza University*, Department of Sociology and Social Work. Dec., Vol. 12, Iss. 2:15-24.

Banks, I. (2001) No man's land: Men, illness, and the NHS. *British Medical Journal*. Nov., Vol. 323(7320):1058-1060.

Barak-Glantz, I. L. (1983) The anatomy of another prison riot. *The Prison Journal*. Spring/Summer, Vol. 63, No. 1:3-23.

Barnert, E. and B. Williams (2021) Then urgent priorities based on lessons learned from more than half a million known COVID-19 cases in US prisons. *American Journal of Public Health*. June, Vol. 111, Iss. 6:1099-1106.

Barr, J. (2020) Harvey Weinstein leaves Rikers Island for state prison facility. *The Hollywood Reporter*. Mar. 18. Retrieved from https://www.hollywoodreporter.com/thr-esq/harvey-weinstein-leaves-rikers-island-state-prison-facility-1284504.

Barrenger, S. L., J. Draine, B. Angell, and D. Hermann (2017) Reincarceration risk among men with mental illnesses leaving prison: A risk environment analysis. *Community Mental Health Journal*. Vol. 53:883-892.

Barry, E. M. (2000) Women prisoners on the cutting edge: Development of the activist Women's Prisoners' Rights Movement. *Social Justice*. Vol. 27, Iss. 3:168-175.

Bartash, J. (2020) U.S. poverty rate fell to record low in 2019 but the coronavirus is reversing the gains. *Market Watch*. Sept. 15. Retrieved from https://www.marketwatch.com/story/us-pove rty-rate-fell-to-record-low-in-2019-but-the-coronavirus-is-reversing-the-gains-2020-09-15.

Barton, (2014) *Literary Executions: Capital Punishment and American Culture, 1820-1925*. Baltimore, MD: Johns Hopkins University Press.

Batchelor, T. (2020) Brandon Bernard's final words before the execution of Death Row inmate. *Newsweek*. Dec. 11. Retrieved from https://www.newsweek.com/brandon-bernard-execution -final-words-death-row-inmate-1554026.

Bayer, P. and D. E. Pozen (2004) The effectiveness of juvenile correctional facilities: Public versus private management. Center Discussion Paper No. 863. Economic Growth Center Yale University. New Haven, CT: Yale University. Retrieved from http://www.econ.yale.edu// growth_pdf/cdp863.pdf.

Bayer, P. and D. E. Pozen (2005) The effectiveness of juvenile correctional facilities: Public versus private management. *Journal of Law and Economics*. Vol. 48, Iss. 2:549-589.

Baylor, A. (2018) Centering women in prisoners' rights litigation. *Michigan Journal of Gender and Law*. Vol. 25, Iss. 2:109-159.

BBC Three (2017) *What's It Like Being a Prison Guard in America?* Available at https://www.youtube .com/watch?v=9-VgEymhKSY.

Beale, S. S. (2006) The news media's influence on criminal justice policy: How market-driven news promotes punitiveness. *William and Mary Law Review*. Vol. 48:397.

Beam, A. (2020) California will house transgender inmates by gender identity. Associated Press. Sept. 26. Retrieved from https://apnews.com/article/prisons-gender-identity-california-gavin -newsom-archive-14cd954b06360d21349b77233318369e.

Beccaria, C. (1764; 2009) *On Crime and Punishment*. Scotts Valley, AZ: CreateSpace Independent Publishing Platform. Trans. from Italian.

Bedau, H. A. (1997) *The Death Penalty in America: Current Controversies*. H. A. Bedau, ed. New York City, New York: Oxford University Press.

Beijersbergen, K. A., A. J. E. Dirkzwager, P. H. van der Lann, and P. Nieuwbeerta (2014) A social building? Prison architecture and staff-prisoner relationships. *Crime and Delinquency*. Vol. 62:1-32.

Beit, C. (2020) Legal, ethical, and developmental considerations concerning children in prison nursery programs. *Family Court Review*. Oct., Vol. 58, Iss. 4:1040-1048.

Belenko, S., R. Dembo, D. Weiland, M. Rollie, C. Salvatore, A. Hanlon, and K. Childs (2008) Recently arrested adolescents are at high risk for sexually transmitted diseases. *Sexually Transmitted Diseases*. Aug., Vol. 35, No. 8:758-763.

Belknap, J. (2020) *The Invisible Woman: Gender, Crime, and Justice*. Newbury Park, CA: SAGE Publishing. 5th ed.

Bernstein, L. (2013) The Hudson River School of Incarceration: Sing Sing Prison in antebellum New York. *American Nineteenth Century History*. Vol. 14, No. 3:261-292.

Bezhan, F. (2012) Afghans lift lid on sports under the Taliban. *Radio Free Europe*. July 11. Retrieved from https://www.rferl.org/a/afghans-recall-sports-under-the-taliban/24642278.html.

Bieneck, S. and B. Krahé (2011) Blaming the victim and exonerating the perpetrator in cases of rape and robbery: Is there a double standard? *Journal of Interpersonal Violence*. Vol. 26:1785-1797.

Bilder, R. B. (1966) Control of criminal conduct in Antarctica. *Virginia Law Review*. Vol. 52, No. 2:231-285.

Binswanger, I. A., C. Nowels, K. F. Corsi, J. Long R. E. Booth, J. Kutner, and J. F. Steiner (2011) "From the prison door right to the sidewalk, everything went downhill": A qualitative study of the health experiences of recently released inmates. *International Journal of Law and Psychiatry*. Vol. 34:249-255.

Bisby, M., E. Kimonis, and N. Goutler (2017) Maternal warmth mediates the relationship between emotional neglect and callous-unemotional traits among juvenile offenders. *Journal of Child and Family Studies*. Vol. 26, No. 7:1790-1798.

Bitran, D. B. (2017) Why tourists go to sites associated with death and suffering. *Salon*. Aug. 27. Retrieved from https://www.salon.com/2017/08/26/why-tourists-go-to-sites-associated-with -death-and-suffering_partner/.

Bizic, M. R., M. Jeftovic, S. Pusica, B. Stojanovic, D. Duisin, S. Vujovic, V. Rakic, and M. L. Djordjevic (2018) Gender Dysphoria: Bioethical aspects of medical treatment. *BioMed Research International*. June 13. Retrieved from https://www.ncbi.nlm.nih.gov/pmc/articles/PMC6020665/.

Black, D. W. (2016) *Ending Zero Tolerance: The Crisis of Absolute School Discipline*. Families, Law, and Society Series. New York, NY: New York University Press.

Black, H. L. et al. (1993) "Life after prison": Successful community reintegration programs, reduced recidivism in Illinois. Southeastern Illinois College, Correctional Education Division. Report. May. Retrieved from https://files.eric.ed.gov/fulltext/ED362674.pdf. 19 pp.

Blackman, P. H. and V. McLaughlin (2004) Mass legal executions in America up to 1865, in *Crime, Histoire and Société/Crime, History, and Societies*. International Association for the History of Crime and Criminal Justice. Vol. 8, No. 2:33-61.

Blackman, P. H. and V. McLaughlin (2014) The dog that stopped barking: Mass legal executions in 21st-century America. *Laws*. Vol. 3, Iss. 1:153-162.

Blackmore, J. (1980) Community corrections. *Corrections Magazine*. Vol. 6, Iss. 5:4-14.

Blakely, C. R. and V. Bumphus (2004) Private and public sector prisons—A comparison of select characteristics. *Federal Probation*. Vol. 68, No. 1:27-31.

Blakinger, K. and J. Neff (2020) Thousands of sick federal prisoners sought compassionate release. 98 percent were denied. *Journalism and Justice*, The Marshall Project. Oct. 7. Retrieved from https://www.themarshallproject.org/2020/10/07/thousands-of-sick-federal-prisoners-sou ght-compassionate-release-98-percent-were-denied.

Blau, J. R., S. C. Light, and M. Chamlin (1986) Individual and contextual effects on stress and job satisfaction. *Work and Occupations*. Vol. 13, No. 1:131-156.

Blau, P. (1968) The hierarchy of authority in organizations. *American Journal of Sociology*. Vol. 73, Iss. 4:453-467.

Board of State and Community Corrections (BSCC) A new kind of jail inspires staff, offenders alike. The State of California. Retrieved from https://www.bscc.ca.gov/s_countyfacilitiesconstruction/.

Bobbit, M. and M. Nelson (2004) The front line: Building programs that recognize families' role in reentry. Vera Institution of Justice. Sept. Retrieved from https://www.prisonpolicy.org/scans/ vera/249_476.pdf.

Bogdan, M. (2000) The law of the Republic of Cape Verde 25 years of independence. *Journal of African Law*. Vol. 44, No. 1:86-95.

Bohm, R. (1999) *Deathquest: An Introduction to the Theory and Practice of Capital Punishment in the United States*. Cincinnati, OH: Anderson Publishing.

Bondurant, B. (2013) The privatization of prisons and prisoner healthcare: Addressing the extent of prisoners' right to healthcare. *New England Journal of Criminal and Civil Confinement*. Spring, Vol. 39, Iss. 2:407-426.

Bouclin, S. (2009) Women in prison movies as jurisprudence. *Canadian Journal of Women and the Law*. Vol. 21, Iss. 1:19-34.

Bountress, K., S. H. Aggen, and W. Kliewer (2021) Is delinquency associated with subsequent victimization by community violence in adolescents? A test of risky behavior in a primarily African American sample. *Psychology of Violence*. May, Vol. 11, No. 3:234-243.

Bovey, L. J. (ed.) (n.d.) This is what your last day on Death Row would be like. *The Versed*. Retrieved from https://www.theversed.com/95849/last-day-death-row-like/#.J5Zah7LrIg.

Brewster, K. R. and K. M. Cumiskey (2017) Girls in juvenile detention facilities: Zones of abandonment, in *Gender, Psychology, and Justice: The Mental Health of Women and Girls in the Legal System*, C. C. Datchi and J. R. Ancis, eds. New York, NY: New York University Press. Ch. 6.

BricTV (2017) Maisha Yearwood's "9 Grams" retells the story of being locked up abroad. June 12. Retrieved from https://www.youtube.com/watch?v=DODkhcpQa30.

British Broadcasting Company (BBC) (2016) Mexico dismantles 'luxury cells' in Topo Chico riot jail. Feb. 15. Retrieved from https://www.bbc.com/news/world-latin-america-35578390.

Broadbridge, C. (2017) Mother's Day Series: Being Mum. Campaign for Youth Justice. May 4. Retrieved from http://www.campaignforyouthjustice.org/voices/item/mother-s-day-series-being-mum.

Brooks, T. (2001) Corlett on Kant, Hegel, and retribution. *Philosophy*. Vol. 76, No. 298:561-580.

Brown, A. (2018) Suicide and the fear of flogging. Social History Society. Sept. 17. Retrieved from https://socialhistory.org.uk/shs_exchange/suicide-and-the-fear-of-flogging/.

Brown, J. A. and V. Jenness (2020) LGBT people in prison: Management strategies, human rights violations, and political mobilization. *Criminology and Criminal Justice*. June 30. Retrieved from https://oxfordre.com/criminology/view/10.1093/acrefore/9780190264079.001.0001/acrefore-9780190264079-e-647.

Brown, P.W. (1990) Guns and probation officers: The unspoken reality. *Federal Probation*. June, Vol. 54, Iss. 2:21-26.

Bruce, R. D. and R. A. Schleifer (2008) Ethical and human rights imperatives to ensure medical treatment for opioid dependence in prisons and pre-trial detention. *International Journal of Drug Policy*. Vol. 19:17-23.

Bunker, E. (2011) *No Beast So Fierce*.

Bureau of Labor Statistics (BLS) (2021) Plumbers, pipefitters, and steamfitters. Apr. 9. Retrieved from https://www.bls.gov/ooh/construction-and-extraction/plumbers-pipefitters-and-steamfitters.htm.

Bureau of Prisons (2020) Prison safety: *Chronic Disciplinary Records*. Retrieved from https://www.bop.gov/about/statistics/statistics_prison_safety.jsp?month=Oct&year=2020.

Burke, A. S. (2021) The structure of the juvenile justice system, in *Introduction to the American Criminal Justice System*, A. S. Burke, D. Carter, B. Fedorek, T. Morey, L. Rutz-Burri, and S. Sanchez, contributors. Ch. 10, Section 10. Open Oregon Education Resources. Available at https://openoregon.pressbooks.pub/ccj230/.

Burke, L. (2020) College programs in prisons go remote. *Inside Higher Ed*. June 18. Retrieved from https://www.insidehighered.com/news/2020/06/18/college-programs-prisons-adapt-covid.

Burton, C. S. (2019) Child savers and unchildlike youth: Class, race, and juvenile justice in the early twentieth century. *Law & Social Inquiry*. Nov., Vol. 44, Iss. 4:1251-1269.

Butler, N. (2018) The pirate executions of 1718. Charleston County Public Library. Dec. 8. Retrieved from https://www.ccpl.org/charleston-time-machine/pirate-executions-1718.

Butterworth, O. (1993) *A Visit to the Big House*. Boston, MA: Houghton Mifflin Harcourt.

Byrne, J. M. and D. Hummer (2008) The nature and extent of prison violence. *The Culture of Prison Violence*, J. M. Byrne, D. Hummer, and F. S. Taxman, eds. Ch. 1. Boston: Pearson Education, Inc.

Byrne, J. M. and A. Pattavina (2006) Assessing the role of clinical and actuarial risk assessment in an evidence-based community corrections system: Issues to consider. *Federal Probation*. Sept., Vol. 70, Iss. 2:64-67.

Cain, S. and M. Speed (1999) *Dad's in Prison*. London, UK:A&C Black.

Caldera, C. (2020) Fact check: 'Hangover' refers to aftereffects, not the practice of sleeping over a rope. *USA Today*. Oct. 23. Retrieved from https://www.usatoday.com/story/news/factcheck/2020/10/23/fact-check-hungover-refers-aftereffects-not-sleeping-over-rope/3732337001/.

California Department of Corrections (CDCR) (n.d.) Details and history, California Institute for Men (CIM). Retrieved from https://www.cdcr.ca.gov/facility-locator/cim/.

Camarena, P. (2017) Yoga as a tool for rehabilitation. Fairfly Project. Apr. 25. Retrieved from https://www.fairflyproject.com/yoga-as-a-tool-for-rehabilitation/.

Cameron, J. (2021) Cooks, nurses, helping to guard inmates in US prisons amid shortage. *The Hill*. May 21. Retrieved from https://thehill.com/homenews/news/554741-cooks-and-nurses-helping-to-guard-inmates-in-us-prisons-amid-officer-shortage.

Canada, K., S. Barrenger, and B. Ray (2019) Bridging mental health and criminal justice systems: A systematic review of the impact of mental health courts on individuals and communities. *Psychology, Public Policy, and Law*. Vol. 25, No. 2:73-91.

Caple, L. (2004) *Mama Loves Me From Away*. New York, NY: Astra Publishing House.

Caracava-Sànchez, F., N. Wolff, and B. Teasdale (2019) Exploring associations between interpersonal violence and prison size in Spanish prisons. *Crime and Delinquency*. Vol. 65, No. 4:2019-2043.

Cardwell, C. (2021) Working virtually with community corrections clients. *Journal of Community Corrections*. Spring. Vol. 30, No. 3:7.

Cary, J. H. (1958) France looks to Pennsylvania. *The Pennsylvania Magazine of History and Biography*. Apr., Vol. 82, No. 2:186-203.

Casella, E. C. (2007) *The Archeology of Institutional Confinement: An American Experience in Archeological Perspective*. Gainesville, FL.: University Press of Florida.

Castillo, T. (2019) Incarcerated women in Thailand face issues seen worldwide. *Filter Magazine*. Nov. 26. Retrieved from https://filtermag.org/incarcerated-women-thailand/.

Cavanaugh, C. and E. Cauffman. Longitudinal association of relationship quality and reoffending among first-time juvenile offenders and their mothers. *Journal of Youth and Adolescence*. Vol. 46, No. 7:1533-1546.

CBS News (2002) Former baseball star Darryl Strawberry gets 18 months in prison for probation violation. *News on 6*. Apr. 29. Retrieved from https://www.newson6.com/story/5e3682cf2f69d 76f620977c8/former-baseball-star-darryl-strawberry-gets-18-months-in-prison-for-probation -violation.

CBS News (2018) "Misery Mountain": Violence plagued West Virginia prison before Whitey Bulger killing. Associated Press (AP). Nov. 1. Retrieved from https://www.cbsnews.com/news/ whitey-bulger-dead-misery-mountain-violence-plagued-west-virginia-prison-hazelton/.

Center on Juvenile and Criminal Justice (n.d.) Wraparound Program. San Francisco, CA. Retrieved from http://www.cjcj.org/Direct-services/Wraparound-Program.html.

Centers for Disease Control and Prevention (CDC) (2001) First report of AIDS. *Morbidity and Mortality Weekly Report*. U.S. Department of Health and Human Services. June, Vol. 50, No. 21. Retrieved from https://www.cdc.gov/mmwr/pdf/wk/mm5021.pdf.

Centers for Disease Control and Prevention (CDC) (n.d.) Health Insurance Portability and Accountability Act of 1996 (HIPPA). *Public Health Professionals Gateway*, Public Health Law. Retrieved from https://www.cdc.gov/phlp/publications/topic/hipaa.html.

Chappell, B. (2021) A former college professor accused of serial arson is denied bail in California. NPR. Aug. 11. Retrieved from https://www.npr.org/2021/08/11/1026700103/former-college -professor-arson-charges-california-dixie-fire.

Chappell, B. (2021) U.S. Birthrate dropped by 4% in 2020 hitting another record low. NPR. May 5. Retrieved from https://www.npr.org/2021/05/05/993817146/u-s-birth-rate-fell-by-4-in-2020 -hitting-another-record-low#:~:text=The%20number%20of%20babies%20born,according %20to%20the%20provisional%20data.

Charriere, H. (2006) *Papillon*. New York William Morrow Paperbacks.

Chase, R. T. (2021) VOICES: Prison violence like Alabama's demands a national reckoning. *Facing South*. June 18. Retrieved from https://www.facingsouth.org/2021/06/voices-prison -violence-alabamas-demands-national-reckoning.

Chase, S. (2017) Sarah Chase, in *Inside This Place, Not of It: Narratives from Women's Prisons*, R. Levi and A. Waldman, eds. Voice of Witness© (VOW). Brooklyn, NY: Verso Books. Kindle ed.

Cheek, F. E. and M. S. Di Miller (1983) Experience of stress for correction officers: Double-Bind Theory of correctional stress. *Journal of Criminal Justice*. Vol. 1, Iss. 2:105-120.

Chesler, P. (2009) *Woman's Inhumanity to Woman*. Chicago: Lawrence Hill Books.

Children of Incarcerated Parents: https://youth.gov/youth-topics/children-of-incarcerated-parents.

Children's Society (1989) *Penal Custody for Juveniles: The Line of Least Resistance*. London, UK: Children's Society.

Chokprajakchat, S. and W. Techagaisiyavanit (2019) Women prisons in North-Eastern Thailand: How well do they meet international human rights standards? *International Journal for Crime, Justice, and Social Democracy*. Vol. 8, Iss. 4:123-136.

Christian, E. R. (2002) TIGER in Antarctica: Crime and punishment. National Aeronautics and Space Administration, Goddard Space Flight Center. Retrieved from https://asd.gsfc.nasa.gov/ archive/tiger/crime.html.

Chron Contributor (2020) What kinds of hour shifts do correctional deputies work? Work/Career Advice/Frustrations at Work, *Chron*. Oct. 15. Retrieved from https://work.chron.com/kind -hour-shifts-correctional-deputies-work-24189.html.

Chuck, E. (2018) Prison nurseries give incarcerated mothers a chance to raise their babies—behind bars. NBC News. Aug. 17. Retrieved from https://www.nbcnews.com/news/us-news/prison -nurseries-give-incarcerated-mothers-chance-raise-their-babies-behind-n894171.

CIA World Factbook (2020) Norwegian Demographics Profile. Index Mundi. Retrieved from https://www.indexmundi.com/norway/demographics_profile.html.

Clark, E. B. (1995) 'The sacred right of the weak': Punishment and the culture of individual rights in Antebellum America. *Journal of American History*. Sept., Vol. 82, Iss. 2:423.

Clark, P. (2014) Types of facilities, in *Desktop Guide to Quality Practice for Working with Youth in Confinement*. National Partnership for Juvenile Services and Office of Juvenile Justice and Delinquency Prevention (OJJDP). Ch. 2. Retrieved from https://info.nicic.gov/dtg/node/4.

Clarke J. G. and E. Y. Adashi (2011) Prenatal care for incarcerated patients: A 25 year old woman pregnant in jail. *Journal of the American Medical Association*. Vol. 305, No. 9:939-929.

Clarke, J. G. and R. E. Simon (2013) Shackling and separation: Motherhood in prison. *American Medical Association Journal of Ethics*. Sept., Vol. 15, No. 9:779-785.

Clinton, H. (2012) *It Takes a Village*. New York, NY: Simon and Schuster.

Cloward, R. A., D. R. Cressey, G. H. Grosser, R. McCleery, L. E. Ohlin, G. E. Sykes, and S. E. Messenger (1960) *Theoretical Studies in Social Organization of the Prison*. New York City, NY: Social Science Research Council.

Codd, H. (2020) Prisons, older people, and age-friendly cities and communities: Towards an inclusive approach. *International Journal of Environmental Research and Public Health*. Dec. 9, Vol. 17, No. 24:1-14.

Collica, K. (2010) Surviving incarceration: Two prison-based peer programs build communities of support for female offenders. *Deviant Behavior*. Vol. 31:314-347.

Collins, C. and G. Alvarez (2015) Prison Ramen: Recipes and Stories from Behind Doors. New York: Workman Publishing.

Collins, J. (2019) Explaining the failure of drug courts in the United Kingdom, in *Rethinking Drug Courts: International Experiences of a US Policy Export*, J. Collins, W. Agnew-Pauley, A. Soderholm, eds. London, UK: London School of Economics International Drug Policy Unit. Ch. 5.

Colquhoun, B., A. Lord, and A. M. Bacon (2018) A qualitative evaluation of recovery processes experienced by mentally disordered offenders following a group treatment program. *Journal of Forensic Psychology Research and Practice*. Vol. 18, No. 5:352-373.

Columbia Justice Labs (2018) *Statement on the Future of Community Corrections*. Columbia University. May 17. Retrieved from https://justicelab.columbia.edu/statement-future -community-corrections.

Comfort, M. K. E. Krieger, J. Landwehr, T. McKay, C. H. Lindquist, R. Feinberg, E. K. Kennedy, and A. Bir (2018) Partnership after prison: Couple relationships during reentry. *Journal of Offender Rehabilitation*. Vol. 57, No. 2:188-205.

ConflictNerd (2018) Prison Architect/Strong Foundations (#1). Video. Sept. 25, retrieved from https://www.youtube.com/watch?v=qWSbVZbVxRE.

Connelly, S. (2015) Ex-Rikers guard, who served time for selling drugs to inmates, also pimped out female officers as 'copstitutes': book. *Daily News*. Mar. 14. Retrieved from https://www .nydailynews.com/new-york/nyc-crime/ex-rikers-guard-sold-drugs-pimped-female -officers-book-article-1.2149561.

Conrad, S. (2011) A restorative environmental justice for e-waste recycling. *Peace Review*. Jul.-Sept., Vol. 23, Iss. 3:348-355.

Constitutional Center (2021) Fourth Amendment: Search and Seizure. Retrieved from https:// constitutioncenter.org/interactive-constitution/amendment/amendment-iv#:~:text=The %20right%20of%20the%20people,and%20the%20persons%20or%20things.

Cook, C. L. and J. Lane (2014) Professional orientation and pluralistic ignorance among jail correctional officers. *International Journal of Offender Therapy and Comparative Criminology*. Vol. 58, No. 6:735-757.

Cooke, B. K., R. C. W. Hall, S. H. Friedman, A. Jain, and R. Wagoner (2019) Professional boundaries in corrections. *The Journal of the American Academy of Psychiatry and the Law*. Mar., Vol. 47, No. 1:91-99.

Cooks, S. (2020) Students need more life skills courses. *Pulse*, Kenosha Unified School District, Wisconsin. Oct. 29. Retrieved from https://www.kusd.edu/indiantrailpulse/?p=8522.

Corbett, R. P. and A. Pattavina (2015) Promoting offender change in the community: Positive reinforcement through EM technology. *Journal of Community Corrections*. Summer, Vol. 24, Iss. 4:5-16.

Corcoran, C. S. (1991) Communication: The key to survival for American prisoners of war in Vietnam. *Air Power History*. Vol. 28, No. 4:48-54.

Corley, C. (2018) Programs help incarcerated moms bond with their babies in prison. *National Public Radio (NPR)*. Dec. 6. Retrieved from https://www.npr.org/2018/12/06/663516573/ programs-help-incarcerated-moms-bond-with-their-babies-in-prison.

Correctional Officer Education (n.d.) Corrections officer jobs in New Mexico. Retrieved from https://www.correctionalofficeredu.org/new-mexico/.

Correctional Officer Education (n.d.) Job requirements for state and federal corrections officers. Retrieved from https://www.correctionalofficeredu.org/correctional-officer-requirements/#:~:text=General%20Requirements,high%20school%20diploma%20or%20GED.

Correctional Services of Canada (CSC) (2019) The Prison Needle Exchange Programme. Aug. 28. Retrieved from https://www.csc-scc.gc.ca/health/002006-2004-en.shtml.

Corrections1 (2019) Seven mistakes that rookie correctional officers consistently make. Nov. 25. Retrieved from https://www.corrections1.com/corrections-jobs-careers/articles/7-mistakes-that-rookie-correctional-officers-consistently-make-OTfsx0ixwIkkvIBw/.

Corrections Today. Trade publication for the American Correctional Assocation (ACA). Available at http://www.aca.org/ACA_Prod_IMIS/ACA_Member/correctionstoday.

Corsetti, G. (2020) Social distancing – not an introvert's dream. Blog. *Mental Agility*. Mar. 24. Retrieved from https://mentallyagile.com/blog/2020/3/24/social-distancing-not-an-introverts-dream.

Corston, J. (2007) *The Corston Report: A review of women with particular vulnerabilities in the criminal justice system*. HM Department of Corrections (UK). Retrieved from https://www.nicco.org.uk/directory-of-research/the-corston-report#:~:text=The%20Corston%20Report%20is%20a,2006%20by%20Baroness%20Jean%20Corston.&text=The%20Corston%20report%20is%20useful,having%20a%20mother%20in%20prison.

Cox, J. A. (2003) Bilboes, brands and branks: Colonial crimes and punishment. *Colonial Williamsburg Journal*. Spring. Retrieved from https://research.colonialwilliamsburg.org/Foundation/journal/spring03/branks.cfm.

Craft, J. L. (2013) Living in the gray: Lessons on ethics from prison. *Journal of Business Ethics*. Vol. 115:327-339.

Crain's Cleveland Business (2021) University's prison program is embroiled in controversy; Most of Ashland's 2020 undergrad enrollees are distance learning inmates. Jan. 18, Vol. 42, Iss. 2:1.

Crawley, E. and P. Crawley (2008) Culture, performance, and disorder: The communicative quality of prison violence. *The Culture of Prison Violence*. J. M. Byrne, D. Hummer, and F. S. Taxman, eds. Ch. 6. Boston: Pearson Education, Inc.

Creasey, H., M. R. Sulway, O. Dent, G. A. Broe, A. Jorm, and C. Tennant (1999) Is experience as a prisoner of war a risk factor for accelerated age-related illness and disability? *Journal of American Geriatrics Society*. Vol. 1, No. 1:60-64.

Crime and Justice Institute at Community Resources for Justice (2009) *Implementing Evidence-based Policy and Practice in Community Corrections*, 2d ed. Washington, DC: National Institute of Corrections.

Criminal Justice U.S. Jobs (2020) Learn how to be a penologist. Feb. 2. Retrieved from https://cjusjobs.com/penologist-career-guide/.

Cripe, C. A. (1997) *Legal Aspects of Corrections Management*. Gaithersburg, MD: Aspen Publishers, Inc.

Cropsey, K. L., E. N. Stevens, P. Valera, C. B. Clark, H. W. Bulls, P. Nair, and P. S. Lane (2015) Risk factors for concurrent use of benzodiazepines and opioids among individuals under community corrections supervision. *Drug and Alcohol Dependence*. Vol. 154:152-157.

Csete, J. (2019) Drug courts in the United States: Punishment for "patients," in *Rethinking Drug Courts: International Experiences of a US Policy Export*, J. Collins, W. Agnew-Pauley, A. Soderholm, eds. London, UK: London School of Economics International Drug Policy Unit. Ch. 1.

Csukai, M. and P. Ruzsonyi (2018) Juvenile boot camps in the shadow of tragedies. *Academic and Applied Research in Military and Public Management Science*. Vol. 17, No. 1:5-12.

Cujipers, P., S. Quero, H. Noma, M. Ciharova, C. Miguel, E. Karyotaki, A. Capriani, I. A. Cristea, and T. A. Furukawa (2021) Psychotherapies for depression: A network meta-analysis covering efficacy, acceptability and long-term outcomes of all main treatment types. *World Psychiatry*. Vol. 20, Iss. 2:283-293.

Cullen, F. T., Eck, J. E., and C. T. Lowenkamp (2002) Environmental corrections: A New Paradigm for effective probation and parole supervisions. *Federal Probation*. Vol. 66, Iss. 2:28-37.

Cummings, P., A. G. Harbaug, and G. Farah (2018) Homicidal violence among National Football League athletes. *Academic Forensic Pathology*. Sept., Vol. 8, No. 3:808-711.

Cunha, J. (2021) Federico Mora: The worst psychiatric hospital in the world. July 22. *CasoCriminal*. Retrieved from https://casocriminal.org/en/pychiatric-hospitals/federico-mora-the-worst-psychiatric-hospital-in-the-world/.

D. A. (2017) Midnight express: A black lesbian's play tackles her time in a Turkish prison. *Advocate.* Oct./Nov., Iss. 1092:29.

d'Abbs, P. (Jamijin)13 (2019) Aboriginal alcohol policy and practice in Australia: A case study of unintended consequences. *International Journal of Drug Policy.* Apr., Vol. 66:9-14.

Dagger, R. (1991) Restitution: Pure or punitive? *Criminal Justice Ethics.* Vol. 10, Iss. 2:29-39.

Daley, J. (2018) Russian researcher charged with attempted murder in Antarctica. *Smithsonian Magazine.* Oct. 25. Retrieved from https://www.smithsonianmag.com/smart-news/russ ian-faces-antarctica-attempted-murder-charge-180970632/.

Dalrymple-Blackburn, D. (1995) Comment: AIDS, prisoners, and the American Disabilities Act. *Utah Law Review.* Vol. 1995, No. 3:839-886.

Da Silva, C. (2020) Judge says conditions at U.S. border holding cells violated the Constitution in 'Monumental' ruling. *Newsweek.* Feb. 20. Retrieved from https://www.newsweek.com/ judge-says-conditions-us-border-holding-cells-violated-constitution-monumental-ruling -1488281.

Davies, K. (2007) Telephone pole design, in *Encyclopedia of Prisons and Correctional Facilities,* M. Bosworth, ed. Sage Publications. Newbury Park, CA: SAGE Publications.

Davis, A. M. (1895) The law of adultery and ignominious punishments with especial reference to the penalty of wearing a letter affixed to the clothing. *Proceedings of the American Antiquarian Society.* Vol. 10, Iss. 1:97-126.

Day, A., A. Gerace, C. Oster, D. O'Kane, and S. Casey (2018) The views of women in prison about help-seeking for intimate partner violence: At the intersection of survivor and offender. *Victims and Offenders.* Vol. 13, No. 7:974-994.

Debczak, M. (2019) Death at the South Pole: The mystery of Antarctica's unsolved poisoning case. *Mental Floss.* June 25. Retrieved from https://www.mentalfloss.com/article/579732/mysteri ous-death-rodney-marks-scientist-who-was-poisoned-antarctica.

Decker, S., C. Melde, and D. C. Pyrooz (2013) What do we know about gangs and gang members and where do we go from here? *Justice Quarterly.* Vol. 30, No. 3:369-402.

Decker, S. H. and D. C. Pyrooz (2010) On the validity of gang homicide: A comparison of disparate sources. *Homicide Studies.* Vol. 14:359-376.

Defranco, J. and T. Duncan (2017) *Life as a Jailer.* Morrisville, North Carolina: Lulu Publishing Services.

Degiorgio, L. and M. DiDonato (2014) Predicting probationer rates of reincarceration using dynamic factors from the Substance Abuse Questionnaire _ Adult Probation III (SAQ-Adult Probation III). *American Journal of Criminal Justice.* Vol. 39:94-108.

DeHart, D. D. (2018) Women's pathways to crime: A heuristic typology of offenders. *Criminal Justice and Behavior.* Oct., Vol. 45, No. 10:1461-1482.

Delaney, J. (2013) *Ghost Prison.* Sourcebooks Fire. Naperville, ILL: Sourcebook Fire. Juvenile Fiction.

Delap, N. (2020) What does COVID-19 mean for new mothers in prison? *British Journal of Midwifery.* Aug., Vol. 28, No. 8:460-461.

Delay, Chris (2001) *Prison Architect.* Video Game. Stockholm, Sweden: Paradox Interactive, Introversion Software, Double Eleven. Available at https://www.prisonarchitect.com/.

Delisi, M., M. T. Berg, and A. Hochstetler (2004) Gang members, career criminals and prison vio-lence: Further specification of the importation model of inmate behavior. Criminal Justice Studies. *A Critical Journal of Crime, Law and Society.* Vol. 17, No. 4:369-383.

Dervan, L. E. (2011) Symposium: Prison policy: American prison culture in an international con-text: An examination of prisons in America, the Netherlands, and Israel. *Stanford Law and Policy Review.* Vol. 22:413.

Destination Hope (2012) Recovering addicts as addiction counselors. Nov. 1. Retrieved from https:// destinationhope.com/recovering-addicts-as-addiction-counselors/.

DiMatteo, M. R., P. J. Giordani, and H. S. Lepper (2002) Patient adherence and medical treatment outcome. *Medical Care.* Vol. 40, No. 9:794-811.

Dir, A. L., L. A. Magee, R. L. Clifton, F. Ouyang, W. Tu, S. E. Wiehe, and M. C. Aaslma (2021) Diminishing returns in juvenile probation: Probation requirements and risk of technical pro-bation violations among first time probation-involved youth. *Psychology, Public Policy, and Law.* Vol. 27, No. 2:283-291.

District of Columbia (D.C.) Metropolitan Police Department (n.d.) Understanding and avoiding gangs. DC.gov. Retrieved from https://mpdc.dc.gov/page/understanding-and-avoiding-gangs#:~:text=What%20is%20a%20Gang%20or,often%20based%20on%20a%20neighborhood.

Dittmann, M. (2003) Braving the ice: Psychologists journey to Antarctica to evaluate those stationed there during the severe winters. *Monitor on Psychology*. Mar., Vol. 34, No. 3:56.

Dizikes, P. (2015) Study: Juvenile incarceration yields less schooling, more crime. MIT News. June 9. Retrieved from https://news.mit.edu/2015/juvenile-incarceration-less-schooling-more-crime-0610.

Docnotes (2020) Healthcare vs. health care. May 31. Retrieved from https://docnotes.net/2020/05/healthcare-vs-health-care.html.

Doleac, J. L. (2019) Wrap-around services don't improve prisoner reentry. *Journal of Policy Analysis and Management*. Mar. Vol. 38, Iss. 2:508-514.

Dolin, E. J. (2018) Turning the tide against piracy in America: Pardons, punishments, British Naval Power, and plenty of hanging. *Crime Reads*. Oct. 15. Retrieved from https://crimereads.com/turning-the-tide-against-piracy-in-america/.

Dorozynski, A. (2000) Doctor's book shames French prisons. *British Medical Journal*. Feb., Vol. 320, No. 7233:465.

Douds, A. S., E. M. Ahlin, N. S. Fiori, and N. J. Barrish (2020) Why prison dental care matters: Legal, policy, and practical concerns. *Annals of Health Law*. Vol. 29:101.

Douds, A. S., E. M. Ahlin, P. R. Kauvanaugh, and A. Olaghere (2016) Decayed prospects: A qualitative study of prisoner dental care and its impact on former prisoners. *Criminal Justice Review*. Vol. 4, No 1:21-40.

Drago, F., R. Galbiati, and P. Vertova (2011) Prison conditions and recidivism. *American Law and Economics Review*. Spring, Vol. 13, No. 1:103-130.

Dunn, C. G., E. Kenney, S. Fleischhacker, and Sara N. Bleich (2020) Feeding low-income children during the COVID-19 pandemic. *New England Journal of Medicine*. Apr. 30. 382:e40. Retrieved from https://www.nejm.org/doi/full/10.1056/nejmp2005638.

Dunne, E. M., E. Morgan, B. Wells-Moore, S. Pierson, S. Zakroff, L. Haskell, K. Link, J. Powell, I. Holland, K. Elgethun, C. Ball, R. Haugen, C. G. Hahn, K. K. Carter, and C. Starr (2021) COVID-19 outbreaks in correctional facilities with work-release programs _ Idaho, July-November 2020. *MMWR Morbidity and Mortality Weekly Report*. Apr. 23, Vol. 70, No. 16:589-594.

Durham, A. M. (1989) Managing the costs of modern corrections: Implications of Nineteenth-Century privatized prison-labor programs. *Journal of Criminal Justice*. Vol. 17:441-455.

DuRose, M. R., A. D. Cooper, H. N. Snyder (2014) Recidivism of prisoners released in 30 states in 2005: Patterns from 2005 to 2010. Bureau of Justice Statistics, NJS 244205.

Duwe, G. (2015) An outcome evaluation of a prison release program: Estimating its effects on recidivism, employment, and cost avoidance. *Criminal Justice Policy Review*. Vol. 26, No 6:531-554.

Dwyer, C. (2017) Ex-sheriff Joe Arpaio convicted of criminal contempt. NPR. Jul. 31. Retrieved from https://www.npr.org/sections/thetwo-way/2017/07/31/540629884/ex-sheriff-joe-arpaio-convicted-of-criminal-contempt.

E2BN (2006) Convict life in Australia. *Victorian Crime and Punishment*. Retrieved from http://vcp.e2bn.org/justice/page11384-convict-life-in-australia.html.

Earhart, J. (2014) Overcoming isolation: A college program challenges culture through engagement. *Saint Louis University Public Law Review*. Vol. 33, Iss. 2:329-342.

Earl, J. (2017) "It's the shame effect": Judge orders public humiliation for domestic abuser. CBS News. Mar. 31. Retrieved from https://www.cbsnews.com/news/its-the-shame-effect-judge-orders-public-humiliation-for-domestic-abusers/.

Earle, A. M. (1896) *Curious Punishments of Bygone Days*. New York: Macmillan. Available at https://www.gutenberg.org/files/34005/34005-h/34005-h.htm.

Eaton, K. (2015) This is what it's like to get a massage in a Thai prison. NBC News. May 8. Retrieved from https://www.nbcnews.com/news/asian-america/what-its-get-massage-thai-prison-n348986.

Edgar, K. (2008) Cultural roots in England's prisons: An exploration for inter-prisoner conflict. *The Culture of Prison Violence*. J. M. Byrne, D. Hummer, and F. S. Taxman, eds. Ch. 9. Boston: Pearson Education, Inc.

Edgerton, K. (2004) *Montana Justice: Power, Punishment and the Penitentiary*. Seattle, WA: University of Washington Press.

Edwards, R. (1979) *Contested Terrain: The Transformation of the Workplace in the Twentieth Century*. New York: Basic Books.

Eisenchlas, S. A. (2013) Gender roles and expectations: Any changes online? *SAGE Open*. Oct.-Dec.:1-11. Retrieved from https://journals.sagepub.com/doi/pdf/10.1177/2158244013506446.

Elderbroom, B. and J. Durnan (2018) Reclassified: State drug law reforms to reduce felony convictions and increase second chances. *Urban Institute*. Oct. Retrieved from https://www.urban.org/sites/default/files/publication/99077/reclassified_state_drug_law_reforms_to_reduce_felony_convictions_and_increase_second_chances.pdf.

Eldridge, D. (2016) Bennett, Breen, and the Birdman of Alcatraz: A case study of collaborative censorship between the Production Code Administration and the Federal Bureau of Prisons. Film History. Vol. 28, No. 2:1-31.

Ellis, A. (2003) A deterrence theory of punishment. *The Philosophical Quarterly*. Vol. 53, No. 212:337-351.

Ellis, D. (2007) *Jakeman*. Markham, Ontario, CA: Fitzhenry and Whiteside.

El-Saadawi, N. (2018) Foreword, in *Unveiling Desire: Fallen Women in Literature, Culture, and Film*. D. Das and C. Morrow, eds. New Brunswick, Camden, Rutgers University Press.

Equal Justice Initiative (n.d.) Children in adult prison. Retrieved from https://eji.org/issues/children-in-prison/.

Evans, D. G. (2021) Will the pandemic be an opportunity for community corrections to reimagine its role in the provision of services? *Journal of Community Corrections*. Spring, Vol. 30, No 3:4.

Evans, D. N., G. Moreno, K. T. Wolff, and J. A. Butts (2020) Easily overstated: Estimating the relationship between state justice policy environments and falling rates of youth confinement. John Jay College of Criminal Justice Research and Evaluation Center. Jan. 1. Retrieved from https://johnjayrec.nyc/2020/01/01/easilyoverstated2020/#findings.

Evans, J. (2019) Alternating current or direct current? *Tips and Advice*, Electrical Installation Services. Retrieved from https://electricalinstallationservices.co.uk/alternating-current-or-direct-current/.

Evans, M. L., M. Lindauer, and M. E. Farrell (2020) A pandemic within a pandemic—Intimate partner violence during COVID-19. *New England Journal of Medicine*. Sept. 16. Retrieved from https://www.nejm.org/doi/full/10.1056/NEJMp2024046.

EverFi (n.d.) The state of financial literacy. Retrieved from https://everfi.com/financial-education/., 310

Fadel, L. (2016) As Egypt's jails fill, growing fears of a rise in radicalization. Broadcast, NPR, *Morning Edition*. Aug. 24. Retrieved from https://www.npr.org/sections/parallels/2016/08/24/491170122/as-egypt.

Failinger, M. A. (2006) Lessons unlearned: Women offenders, the ethics of are and the promise of restorative justice. *Fordham Urban Law Journal*. Jan. Vol. 33, Iss. 2:487-526.

Fairweather, L. and S. McConville, eds. (2000) *Prison Architecture: Policy, design, and experience*. Woburn, MA: Reed.

Falter, R. G. (1999) Selected predictors of health service needs of inmates over age 50. *Journal of Correctional Health Care*. Vol. 6:149-175.

Falter, R. G. (2006) Elderly inmates: An emerging correctional population. *Correctional Health Journal*. Vol. 1:52-69.

Farmer, J. A. (1990) Juvenile exploitation of juvenile correctional workers: A content analysis. *Journal of Correctional Education*. Vol. 41, Iss. 3:118-119.

Farrell, M., A. Boys, N. Singleton, H. Meltzer, T. Brugha, and P. Bebbington (2006) Predictors of mental health service utilization in the 12 months before imprisonment: Analysis of results from a national prison survey. *Australian and New Zealand Journal of Psychiatry*. Vol. 40, Nos 6-7:548-553.

Federal Bureau of Prisons (2011) Marriages of Inmates. U.S. Department of Justice. Sept. 22. Retrieved from https://www.bop.gov/policy/progstat/5326_005.pdf.

Federal Bureau of Prisons (n.d.) General visiting information. Retrieved from https://www.bop.gov/inmates/visiting.jsp.

Felbab-Brown, V. (2020) Mexico's prisons, COVID-19, and the amnesty law. *Order from Chaos*, The Brookings Institute. May 22. Retrieved from https:// www.brookings.edu/blog/order-from-chaos/ 2020/05/26/mexicos-prisons-covid-19-and-the-amnesty-law/#:~:text=Mexican%20prisons%20 are%20notoriously%20overcrowded,hygienic%20facilities%2C%20and%20health%20care.

Fern, M. (2002) Study disputes impact of halfway houses on neighborhoods. *Washington Post*. May 16. Retrieved from https://www.washingtonpost.com/archive/local/2002/05/16/study-disputes -impact-of-halfway-houses-on-neighborhoods/fc3b4949-3792-4d1c-ac34-40771dbc17b1/.

Ferranti, S. (2013) *Prison Stories*. Rock Hill, SC: Strategic Media Books.

Fest, S. A. (2021) When the Taliban ruled Afghanistan soccer was often replaced by public executions. *Around the Rings*. Aug. 18. Retrieved from https://www.infobae.com/aroundtherings/ articles/2021/08/18/when-the-taliban-ruled-afghanistan-soccer-was-often-replaced-by -public-executions/.

Fine, A. D., Z. R. Rowan, and E. Cauffman (2020) Parents or adversaries? The relation between juvenile diversion supervision and parenting. *Law and Human Behavior*. Vol. 44, No. 6:461-473.

Finn, P. (1998) Correctional officer stress: A cause for concern and additional help. *Federal Probation*. Vol. 62 Iss. 2:65-74.

Finn, P. (2000) Addressing correctional officers programs and strategies. U.S. Department of Justice Office of Justice Programs, NCJ Number 183474. Dec. Retrieved from https://www.ojp.gov/ ncjrs/virtual-library/abstracts/addressing-correctional-officer-stress-programs-and-strategies.

First Step Alliance. *Reducing recidivism: Creating a path to successful re-entry*. Available at https:// www.firststepalliance.org/post/reducing-recidivism?gclid=CjwKCAjwtdeFBhBAEiwAKOIy5 712-yfcdQRUliAf7af-Qg6Hxg1jYa4EoZLwIn2JjFU2MLcEDjLkHBoCegIQAvD_BwE.

Fitzgibbon, J. J. (2004) Healthcare for adolescents in juvenile facilities: Increasing needs for adolescent females. *Journal of Pediatric Adolescent Gynecology*. Vol. 17:3-5.

Fitzpatrick, T. and *Chicago Sun Times* (1979) Ten years locked up. *The Washington Post*. Mar. 11. Retrieved from https://www.washingtonpost.com/archive/lifestyle/1979/03/11/ten-years-loc ked-up/98de988b-22a1-42b5-a227-c63e7a130c64/.

Flagg, A. and A. Calderón (2020) Million hours: Trump's vast expansion of child detention. The Marshall Project. Oct. 30. Retrieved from https://www.themarshallproject.org/2020/10/30/ 500-000-kids-30-million-hours-trump-s-vast-expansion-of-child-detention.

Flores, J. (2013) "Staff here let you get down": The cultivation and co-optation of violence in a California juvenile detention center. *Signs*. Vol. 39, No. 1:221-241.

Flores, J. (2016) *Caught Up: Girls, Surveillance, and Wraparound Incarceration*. Oakland, CA: University of California Press.

Flory, B. (2016) Jackson prison industries: competition breed controversy. *Michigan History Magazine*. Vol. 100, Iss. 3. Retrieved from https://go-gale-com.wne.idm.oclc.org/ps/retrieve.do?tabID= T003&resultListType=RESULT_LIST&searchResultsType=SingleTab&hitCount=1&searchType =AdvancedSearchForm&currentPosition=1&docId=GALE%7CA452051963&docType=Article &sort=RELEVANCE&contentSegment=ZEAI-MOD1&prodId=EAIM&pageNum=1&contentSet= GALE%7CA452051963&searchId=R1&userGroupName=mlin_w_westnew&inPS=true.

Flynn, B. (2013) Expect to be caught . . . and do yoga in jail, Midnight Express author to tell Fringe. *The Times* (London, England). Aug. 22. Retrieved from https://go-gale-com.wne.idm.oclc.org/ ps/i.do?v=2.1&u=mlin_w_westnew&it=r&id=GALE%7CA340354709&p=GPS&sw=w.

Folha de S. Paulo (2019) Rebellion leaves at least 57 dead in prison in the interior of Pará: Suspicion is that factional fighting motivated the rebellion; 16 prisoners died beheaded. July 29. Translation. Retrieved from https://translate.google.com/translate?hl=en&sl=pt&u=https://www1.folha .uol.com.br/cotidiano/2019/07/rebeliao-deixa-52-mortos-em-presidio-no-interior-do-para .shtml&prev=search&pto=aue.

Fontes, A. W. and K. L. O'Neill (2019) *La Visita*: Prisons and survival in Guatemala. *Journal of Latin American Studies*. Vol. 51:85-107.

Forrester, C. B., E. Tambor, A. W. Riley, M. E. Ensminger, and B. Starfield (2000) The health profile of incarcerated male youth. *Pediatrics*. Jan., Vol. 105 (1 Pt. 3):286-291.

Forsyth, C. J. and R. D. Evans (2003) Reconsidering the pseudo-family/gang gender distinction in prison research. *Journal of Police and Criminal Psychology*. Vol. 18:15-23.

Foucault, M. (1975) *Discipline and Punish: The Birth of the Prison*. Trans. New York: Pantheon Books.

Foucault, M. (1997) *Discipline and Punishment: The Birth of the Prison*. New York City, NY: Vintage Press.

Foucault, M. (2007) *Discipline and Punish: The Birth of the Prison*. A. Sheridan, trans. New York, NY: Random House.

Franco-Paredes, C., K. Jankousky, J. Schultz, J. Bernfeld, K. Cullen, N. G. Quan, S. Kon, P. Hotez, A. F. Henao-Martinez, and M. Krsak (2020) COVID-19 in jails and prisons: A neglected infection in a marginalized population. Public Library of Science, *Neglected Tropical Diseases*. June 22, Vol. 14, No. 6:e0008409. Electronic Publication. Available at https://journals.plos .org/plosntds/article?id=10.1371/journal.pntd.0008409.

Fretland, K. (2014) Scene at botched Oklahoma execution of Clayton Lockett was 'a bloody mess.' *The Guardian*. Dec. 13. Retrieved from https://www.theguardian.com/world/2014/dec/13/ botched-oklahoma-execution-clayton-lockett-bloody-mess.

Friedman, A. (2014) Lowering recidivism through family communication. *Prison Legal News*. Apr. p. 24.

Friedman, L. M. (1993) *Crime and Punishment in American History*. New York, NY: Basic Books.

Gaines, P. (2019) PBS chronicles 12 inmates who value education in "College Behind Bars." NBC News. Nov. 25. Retrieved from https://www.nbcnews.com/news/nbcblk/pbs-chronicles-12 -inmates-who-value-education-college-behind-bars-n1089921.

Gallagher, J. (2020) Talking it out: Talk therapy and how it can benefit you. *The Talkspace Voice*. Nov. 7. Retrieved from https://www.talkspace.com/blog/what-is-talk-therapy/.

Gallagher, S. (2016) The limits of pure restitution. *Social Theory and Practice*. Jan., Vol. 42, No. 1:74-96.

Gamel, K. (2019) 'The torture stopped': 1969 brought temporary changes to infamous Hanoi Hilton. Vietnam at 50. *Stars and Stripes*. Aug, 15. Retrieved from https:// www.stripes.com/ news/special-reports/vietnam-stories/1969/the-torture-stopped-1969-brought-temporary -changes-to-infamous-hanoi-hilton-1.593300.

Garcia, J. (2020) *Riker's Island: Patrolling the toughest precients [sic] in New York City, as a CO: Life in the Bing (Central Punitive Segregation Unit)*. Apr. 30. New York: Self-published, Amazon Kindle Edition.

Gardner, B., P. Lally, J. Wardle (2012) Making health habitual: the psychology of 'habit-formation' and general practice. *British Journal of General Practice*. Vol. 62, No. 605:664-666.

Garland, D. (2001) *The Culture of Control: Crime and Social Order in Contemporary Society*. Oxford: Oxford University Press.

Garofalo, M. (2020) Family therapy in corrections: implications for reentry into the community. *Journal of Correctional Health Care*. July, Vol. 26, No. 3. Retrieved from https://www.liebert pub.com/doi/full/10.1177/1078345820938350.

Garvey, T. M. (2012) Routine strip-searches upheld. *Sexual Assault Report*. Vol. 16, No. 2:28.

Gaskew, T. (2014) *Rethinking Prison Reentry: Transforming Humiliation into Humility*. Latham, NY: Lexington Books.

Gates, M. (2019) Drawing back the curtain: Executions and the First Amendment. *Harvard Civil Rights—Civil Liberties Law Review*. Oct. 24. Retrieved from https://harvardcrcl.org/draw ing-back-the-curtain-executions-and-the-first-amendment/.

Gay and Lesbian Alliance Against Defamation (GLAAD) (n.d.) What does transgender mean? Retrieved from https://www.glaad.org/transgender/transfaq.

Genealogy Trails (n.d.) History of Montana's State Penitentiary. Powell County, Montana: Genealogy and History. Retrieved from http://genealogytrails.com/mon/powell/prison.html.

Gentleman, A. (2012) Inside Halden, the most humane prison in the world. *The Guardian*. May 18. Retrieved from https://www.theguardian.com/society/2012/may/18/halden-most-humane -prison-in-world.

Geographics (2020) *La Santé Prison: Serving Time in the Heart of Paris*. Video. Jan. 6. Retrieved from https://www.youtube.com/watch?v=nE5G97q7-Q0.

George, D. and D. Shoos (2005) Deflecting the political in the visual images of execution and the death penalty debate. *College English*. July, Vol. 67, Iss. 6:587-609.

Gibbs, B. R. and R. Lytle (2020) Drug court participant and time to failure: An examination of recidivism across program outcome. *American Journal of Criminal Justice*. Apr., Vol. 45, Iss. 2:215-235.

Gibbs, J. J. (1981) Violence in prison: Its extent, nature and consequences. *Critical Issues in Corrections*, R. R. Roberg and V. J. Webb, eds. St. Paul, MN: West Publishing Co. pp. 110-149.

Gilbert, P. (2017). Exploring compassion focused therapy in forensic settings: An evolutionary and social-contextual approach, in *Individual psychological therapies in forensic settings: Research and practice*, J. Davies & C. Nagi, eds. Milton Park, UK: Routledge/Taylor & Francis Group. pp. 59-84.

Gillespie, W. (2002) *Prisonization: Individual and Institutional Factors Affecting Inmate Conduct*. New York: LFB Scholarly Publishing.

Gillett, G. (2010) A world without Internet: A new framework for analyzing a supervised release condition that restricts computer and Internet access. *Fordham Law Review*. Oct., Vol. 79, Iss. 1:217.

Gil-Monte, P. R., H. Figueiredo-Ferraz, H. Valdez-Bonilla (2013) Factor analysis of the Spanish Burnout Inventory among Mexican prison employees. *Canadian Journal of Behavioural Science*. Vol. 45, No. 2:96-104.

Givens, J. (2013) I was Virginia's executioner from 1982 to 1999. Any questions for me? *The Guardian*. Nov. 12. Retrieved from https://www.theguardian.com/commentisfree/2013/nov/21/death-penalty-former-executioner-jerry-givens.

Gladfelter, A. S., B. Lantz, and R. B. Ruback (2018) Beyond ability to pay: Procedural justice and offender compliance with restitution orders. *International Journal of Offender Therapy and Comparative Criminology*. Vol. 63, No. 13:4314-4331.

Gobnik, A. (2012) The caging of America: Why do we lock up so many people? *The New Yorker*. Jan. 22. Retrieved from https://www.newyorker.com/magazine/2012/01/30/the-caging-of-america.

Godfrey, B. (2019) Prison versus Western Australia: Which worked best, the Australian penal colony or the English prison system? *British Journal of Criminology*. Vol. 59:1139-1160.

Goffman, E. (1961) *Asylums: Essays on the Social Situation of Mental Patients and Other Inmates*. New York City, NY: Anchor Books (Doubleday).

Goffman, E. (1969; 2009) *Stigma: Notes on the Management of Spoiled Identity*. New York, NY: Touchstone Books.

Gold Buscho, A. (2019) Divorce, emergency responders, and special circumstances. *Psychology Today*. Nov. 11. Retrieved from https://www.psychologytoday.com/us/blog/better-divorce/201911/divorce-emergency-responders-and-special-circumstances.

Goldberg, E. (2018) Women often can't afford tampons, pads in federal prisons. That's about to change. *Huffpost*. Dec. 20. Retrieved from https://www.huffpost.com/entry/the-new-criminal-justice-bill-provides-free-tampons-pads-in-federal-prisons_n_5c1ac0a0e4b08aaf7a84ac38.

Goldberg, P., S. Simone, M. F. Landre, M. Goldberg, S. Dassa, and R. Fuhrer (1996) Work conditions and mental health among staff in France. *Scandinavian Journal of Work, Environment, and Health*. Vol. 22, No. 1:45-54.

Goldsmith, L. (1999) "To profit by his skill and to traffic on his crime": Prison labor in Early 19th-Century Massachusetts. *Labor History*. Vol. 40, No. 4:439-457.

Goldson, B. (2002) New punitiveness: The politics of child incarceration, in *Youth Justice: Critical Readings*. J. Muncie, G, Hughes, and E. McLaughlin, eds. London, UK: SAGE Publishing.

Goldstein, M. M. (2014) Health information privacy and health information technology in the US correctional setting. *American Journal of Public Health*. Vol. 104, Iss. 5:803-809.

Gonzales, R. (2019) Felicity Huffman begins prison term at 'Club Fed' in East Bay in College Admissions Scandal. KQED, NPR. Oct. 19. Retrieved from https://www.kqed.org/news/11780480/felicity-huffman-begins-prison-term-at-club-fed-in-east-bay-in-college-admissions-scandal.

Gonzalez, K. (2020) A timeline on the closure of Rikers Island. *City & State New York*. Oct. 20. Retrieved from https://www.cityandstateny.com/articles/policy/criminal-justice/timeline-closure-rikers-island.html#:~:text=Alongside%20New%20York%20City%20Council,and%20smaller%20criminal%20justice%20system.

Goodman, P. (2021) 7 disadvantages of GPS. *Axle Addict*. Apr. 30. Retrieved from https://axleaddict.com/safety/Disadvantages-of-GPS.

Goodwin, M. L. (1997) An eye for an eye: An argument against allowing the families of murder victims to view executions. *Journal of Family Law*. Vol. 36, No. 4. On *Frontline, Public Broadcasting Service* (*PBS*), retrieved from https://www.pbs.org/wgbh/pages/frontline/shows/execution/readings/against.html.

Gordon, M. S., T. W. Kinlock, R. P. Schwartz, K. E. O'Grady, T. T. Fitzgerald, and F. J. Vocci (2017) *Drug and Alcohol Dependence*. Vol. 172:34-42.

Gordon, M. T. and S. Riger (2011) *The Female Fear*. New York City, New York: The Free Press.

Government Jobs (2021) Detention officer: Job description. Retrieved from https://www.governmentjobs.com/jobs/2914094-0/detention-officer?utm_campaign=google_jobs_apply&utm_source=google_jobs_apply&utm_medium=organic.

Gradman, T. J. (1990) *Does Work Make the Man: Masculine Identity During the Transition to Retirement*. Santa Monica, CA: Rand Corporation.

Grant, B. A. (1995) Impact of working rotating schedules on family life of correctional staff. Forum on Corrections Research. May, Vol. 7, Iss. 2:40-42.

Grasso, D. J., C. Doyle, and R. Koon (2019) Two rapid screens for detecting probable post-traumatic stress disorder and interpersonal violence exposure: Predictive utility in a juvenile justice sample. *Child Maltreatment*. Vol. 24, No. 1:113-120.

Gravelin, C. R., M. Biernat, and C. E. Bucher (2019) Blaming the victim of acquaintance rape: Individual, situational, and sociocultural factors. *Frontiers in Psychology*. Jan. 21. Retrieved from https://www.frontiersin.org/articles/10.3389/fpsyg.2018.02422/full.

Green, W. M. (1929) An ancient debate on capital punishment. *The Classical Journal*. Jan., Vol. 24, No. 4:267-275.

Greene, B. (2000) The executioners who live among us. Chicago Tribune. July 16. Retrieved from https://www.chicagotribune.com/news/ct-xpm-2000-07-16-0007160138-story.html.

Greifinger, R. (2006) Disabled prisoners and reasonable accommodations. *Criminal Justice Ethics*. Winter/Spring, Vol. 25, Iss. 1:2-55.

Grierson, J. and P. Duncan (2019) Private jails more violent than public ones, data analysis shows. *The Guardian*. May 13. Retrieved from https://www.theguardian.com/society/2019/13/private-jails-more-violent-than-public-prisons-england-wales-data-analysis.

Griffiths, A. (1897) Egyptian prisons. *The North American Review*. Sept., Vol. 165, No. 490:276-287.

Griffiths, A. (2016) "For the amusement of the shutins": The vicissitudes of film viewing in prison. Film History. Vol. 28, No. 3:1-23.

Grisham, J. *The Brethren*.

The Guardian (2019) The Guardian view on Morsi's death in Egypt: shocking because foreseen. *Editorial*. Jun. 18. Retrieved from https://www.theguardian.com/commentisfree/2019/jun/18/the-guardian-view-on-morsis-death-in-egypt-shocking-because-foreseen.

Gundjonsson, G. H., J. F, Sigurdsson, O. O. Bragason, E. Einarsson, and E. B. Validiarsdottir (2004) Compliance and personality: The vulnerability of the unstable introvert. *European Journal of Personality*. Jul./Aug., Vol. 18, Iss. 5:435-443.

Gupte, P. (1975) Escapee from Turkey describes return. *The New York Times*. Oct. 25. Retrieved from https://www.nytimes.com/1975/10/25/archives/escapee-from-turkey-describes-return.html.

Hacaoglu, S. (2018) U.S. pastor faces 35 years in Turkish prison as coup suspect. *Bloomberg*. Mar. 13. Retrieved from https://www.bloomberg.com/news/articles/2018-03-13/u-s-pastor-faces-life-in-turk-prison-as-coup-suspect-tv-saysj.

Hamilton, O. (2017) Olivia Hamilton, in *Inside This Place, Not of It: Narratives from Women's Prisons*, R. Levi and A. Waldman, eds. Voice of Witness© (VOW). Brooklyn, NY: Verso Books. Kindle ed.

Hanneman, M. (2017) Mother's Day Series: Mad, overwhelmed, trying, helpless, emotional, resilient. Campaign for Youth Justice. Retrieved from http://www.campaignforyouthjustice.org/voices/item/mother-s-day-series-2.

Hansen, L. L. (2005) "Girl 'Crew' Members Doing Gender, Boy 'Crew' Members Doing Violence: An Ethnographic and Network Analysis of Maria Hinojosa's New York Gangs." 2005. *Western Criminology Review*. Vol. 6, No. 1:134-44. Retrieved from http://www.westerncriminology.org/documents/WCR/v06n1/article_pdfs/hansen.pdf.

Hansen, L. L. (2006) Women disadvantaged in the workplace: The second shift, emotional labor, and the "good old boy network," in *The Women of Ophthalmology*, J. B. Pinto and E. A. Davis, eds. Fairfax, VA: American Society of Cataract and Refractive Surgery and American Society of Ophthalmic Administration. Ch. 5.

Hansen, L. P. (2020) *White Collar and Corporate Crime: A Case Study Approach*. Riverwoods, IL: Wolters Kluwer United States, Inc.

Hanson, K. and D. Stipek (2014) Schools v. prisons: Education's the way to cut prison population. Stanford Graduate School of Education; *San Jose Mercury News*. May 16. Retrieved from https://ed.stanford.edu/in-the-media/schools-v-prisons-educations-way-cut-prison-population-op-ed-deborah-stipek.

Harer, M. D. and N. P. Langan (2001) Gender differences in predictors of prison violence: Assessing the predictive validity of a risk classification system. *Crime and Delinquency*. Oct., Vol. 47, No. 4:513-536.

Harizanova, S. and R. Stoyanova (2020) Burnout among nurses and correctional officers. *Work*. Vol. 65, No. 1:71-77.

Harmon, K. (2012) Brain injury rate 7 times greater among U.S. prisoners. *Scientific American*. Feb 4. Retrieved from https://www.scientificamerican.com/article/traumatic-brain-injury-prison/.

Harmon, T. (2010) Violence on the rise in state prisons: Problem is attributed to gangs and high security inmates in medium-security prisons. *Pueblo Chieftain*. Jan. 27. Retrieved from https://go-gale-com.wne.idm.oclc.org/ps/i.do?v=2.1&u=mlin_w_westnew&it=r&id=GALE%7CA217514840&p=GPS&sw=w.

Harrington, J. F. (2013) *The Faithful Executioner: Life and Death, Honor and Shame in the Turbulent Sixteenth Century*. New York: Farrar, Straus, and Giroux.

Harris, D. H. (n.d.) The Convict Code of Conduct—From a True Convict. Prison Writers. Retrieved from https://prisonwriters.com/convict-code-of-conduct/.

Harris, H. M., K. Nakamura, K. B. Bucklen (2018) Do cellmates matter: A causal test of the Schools of Crime hypothesis with implications for differential association and deterrence theories. *Criminology*. Feb., Vol. 56, Iss. 1:87-122.

Hartwell, S. W. Fisher, X. Deng, D. A Pinals, and J. Siegfriedt. (2016) Intensity of offending following state prison release among persons treated for mental health problems while incarcerated. *Psychiatric Services*. Jan., Vol. 67, No. 1:49-54.

Harvard Law Review (2013) Recent cases: First Amendment – Free exercise in prison – Fifth Circuit holds that prison's prohibition on all objects over twenty-five dollars did not violate prisoner's First Amendment rights or substantially burden his religion under RLUOPA – *McFaul v. Valenzuela*, 684 F.3d 564 (5th Cir. 2012). Feb., Vol. 126, Iss. 4:1154-1161.

Haslam, S. A. and S. D. Reicher (2006) On the agency of individuals and groups: Lessons from the BBC Prison Study, in *Individuality and the Group: Advances in Social Identity*, T. Postmes and J. Jetten, eds. London, UK: Sage. 237-257.

Haslam, S. A. and S. D. Reicher (2012) When prisoners take over the prison: A social psychology of resistance. *Personality and Social Psychology Review*. Vol. 16, No. 2:154-179.

Hassine, V. (2007) *Life Without Parole: Living in Prison Today*. R. Johnson and A. Dobrzanska, eds. Oxford: Oxford University Press.

Haverkate, D. L. and K. A. Wright (2020) The differential effects of prison contact on parent-children relationship quality and child behavioral changes.

Hawthorne, N. (1850) *The Scarlet Letter*.

Hayes, S. C. (2007) Women with learning disabilities who offend: What do we know? *British Journal of Learning Disabilities*. Sept., Vol. 35, No. 3:187-191.

Haywood, P, (2020), *Santa Fe New Mexican*, special section. Available at https://www.santafenewmexican.com/news/local_news/devastating-penitentiary-riot-of-1980-changed-new-mexico-and-its-prisons/article_be64a016-31ae-11ea-a754-fb85e49fca77.html., 339

Heilbrun, K., K. Durham, A. Thornewill, R, Schiedel, V. Pietruszka, S. Phillips, B. Locklair, and J. Thomas. (2018) Life-sentenced juveniles: Public perceptions of risk and need for incarceration. *Behavioral Science and the Law*. Vol. 36, No. 5:587-596.

Henrichson, C. and R. Delaney (2012) *The Price of Prison: What Incarceration Costs Taxpayers*. Center on Sentencing and Corrections. Brooklyn, NY: Vera Institute for Justice.

Henrico County Sheriff's Office, VA (2019) *What's it Like to be a Jailor?* Available at https://www.youtube.com/watch?v=8ZddzDXa140.

Herman, J. W. and J. S. Sexton (2017) Girls leaving detention: Perceptions of transition to home after incarceration. *Journal of Juvenile Justice* Spring, Vol. 6, Iss. 1:33-47.

Hersh, J. (2014) Journalism becomes a crime in Egypt. *The New Yorker*. Jan. 31. Retrieved from https://www.newyorker.com/news/news-desk/journalism-becomes-a-crime-in-egypt.

Heyward, G. L. (2015) *Corruption Officer: From Jail Guard to Perpetrator Inside Rikers Island*. New York: Atria Books.

HG Legal Resources (n.d.) Burglary charges under California Penal Code 459. Retrieved from https://www.hg.org/legal-articles/burglary-charges-under-california-penal-code-459-25139.

HG.org (n.d.) Do inmates have rights? If so, what are they? *Legal Resources*. Retrieved from https://www.hg.org/legal-articles/do-inmates-have-rights-if-so-what-are-they-31517.

Higgins, M. (2014) *The Night Dad Went to Jail: What to Expect When Someone You Love Goes to Jail (Life's Challenges)*. Bloomington, MN: Picture Window Books.

Hill, T. E. (1999) Kant on wrongdoing, desert, and punishment. *Law and Philosophy*. Vol. 18:407-441.

Hillman, H. (2003) Electrical devices used by prison officers, police and security forces. *Medicine, Conflict and Survival*. Vol. 19, Iss. 23:197-204.

Hillman, K. and A. Caballero (2017) As a boy in an adult prison, his mother's letters 'were everything.' *Morning Edition*, NPR. Aug. 11. Retrieved from https://www.npr.org/2017/08/11/542648319/as-a-boy-in-an-adult-prison-his-mothers-letters-were-everything.

Hipp, J. R. and D. K. Yates (2011) Ghettos, thresholds, and crime: Does concentrated poverty really have an accelerated increasing effect on crime? *Criminology*. Vol. 49, No. 4:955-990.

Hixson, C. and Paul Mitchell (2019) "Tarrafal Never Again!" exhibition in Lisbon exposes horrors of Portugal's fascist concentration camp. *World Socialist Web Site*, International Committee of the Fourth International (ICFI). Apr. 9. Retrieved from https://www.wsws.org/en/articles/2019/04/09/port-a09.html.

Hochschild, A. (1983) *The Managed Heart: Commercialization of Human Feeling*. Berkeley: University of California Press.

Hodgson, J. (2014) Guantánamo Bay: The hunger strikes: Based on the personal statements of five detainees at Guantánamo prison camp. *Art Journal*. Vol. 73, No. 2:5-12.

Hodgson, J. (2019) Feminising restorative justice: A critical exploration of offending girls' experiences participating in restorative justice conferences. Thesis, Liverpool John Moores University.

Hoffman, H. C. and G. E. Dickson (2011) Characteristics of prison hospice programs in the United States. *American Journal of Hospice and Palliative Care*. June, Vol. 28, No. 4:245-52.

Holiday, J. S. (1999) *Rush for Riches: Gold Fever and the Making of California*. Oakland, CA: Oakland Museum of California; Berkeley, CA: University of California Press.

Hope for Prisoners. *Transforming Lives, Transforming Communities*. Available at https://hopeforprisoners.org/?gclid=CjwKCAjwtdeFBhBAEiwAKOIy58X3w9iW3aARcOqIuLJilFXFldvLXz0KFtEiW5dZRxvHjCb9sms4jxoCjgIQAvD_BwE.

Hopkins, A., L. Bartels, and L. Oxman (2019) Lessons in flexibility: Introducing a yoga program in an Australian prison. *International Journal of Crime, Justice and Social Democracy*. Vol. 8, No. 4:47-61.

Horowitz, J. M., K. Parker, and R. Stepler (2017) Wide partisan gaps in U.S. over how far the country has come on equality. Pews Research. Oct. 18. Retrieved from https://www.pewresearch.org/social-trends/2017/10/18/wide-partisan-gaps-in-u-s-over-how-far-the-country-has-come-on-gender-equality/.

Howard League (2008) *Growing Up, Shut Up Factsheet*. London, UK: Howard League.

Huebner, B. M. and J. E. Cobbina (2007) The effect of drug use, drug treatment completion on probationer recidivism. *Journal of Drug Issues*. Vol. 37:619-642.

Hughett, A. B. (2019) A "safe outlet" for prisoner discontent: How prison grievance procedures helped stymie prison organizing during the 1970s. *Law and Social Inquiry*. Nov., Vol. 44, Iss. 4:893-921.

Human Rights Watch (1996) All too familiar: Sexual abuse of women in U.S. state prisons. Report. Dec. Retrieved from https://www.hrw.org/reports/1996/Us1.htm.

Human Rights Watch (2018) In the freezer: Abusive conditions for women and children in US immigration holding cells. Feb. 28. Retrieved from https://www.hrw.org/report/2018/02/28/freezer/abusive-conditions-women-and-children-us-immigration-holding-cells#.

Human Rights Watch (2018) Q&A: Guantanamo Bay, U.S. Detentions and the Trump Administration. June 27. Retrieved from https://www.hrw.org/news/2018/06/27/qa-guantanamo-bay-us-detentions-and-trump-administration.

Hussey, A. (2014) La Santé prison: Visitors welcome. *The Guardian*. Dec. 7. Retrieved from https://www.theguardian.com/world/2014/dec/07/la-sante-prison-paris-visitors-welcome.

Hyatt, J. M. and G. Barnes (2017) An experimental evaluation of the impact of intensive supervision on recidivism of high-risk probationers. *Crime and Delinquency*. Vol. 63, Issue 1:3-38.

Ibsen, A. Z. (2013) Ruling by favors: Prison guards' informal exercise of institutional control. *Law and Social Inquiry.* Vol. 38, Iss. 2:342-363.

Immarigeon, R. (2016) Does anger management work? *Offender Programs Report.* Jan./Feb., Vol. 19, Iss. 5:71-80.

The Independent (2018) Death Row inmate asks for electric chair execution instead of lethal injection. p. 3 retrieved from https://link.gale.com/apps/doc/A557518508/GPS?u=mlin_w_westnew &sid=GPS&xid=84f38efe.

Independent Lens (2017) The prison economy: How do prisons affect the places we live? Public Broadcasting Service (PBS). May 5. Retrieved from https://www.pbs.org/independentlens/blog/prison-economy-how-do-prisons-affect-the-places-we-live/.

The Informer (Thunder Road Pictures, 2019) Movie.

International Corrections and Prisons Association (n.d.) Time to better protect our corrections and prison officers. Retrieved from https://icpa.org/time-to-better-protect-our-corrections-and-prison -officers/.

International Federation for Human Rights (2019) Not so model: The reality of women incarcerated in Thailand's 'model' prisons. Nov. 12. Retrieved from https://www.fidh.org/en/region/asia/thailand/not-so-model-the-reality-of-women-incarcerated-in-thailand-s-model.

Israel Ministry of Foreign Affairs (2013) 1967-1993: Major Terror Attacks. Retrieved from https://mfa.gov.il/mfa/aboutisrael/maps/pages/1967-1993-%20major%20terror%20attacks.aspx.

Iverson, K. (2017) A guide to Thailand's strange laws. *Culture Trip.* Feb. 16. Retrieved from https://theculturetrip.com/asia/thailand/articles/a-guide-to-thailands-strange-laws/.

Jablonski, R. K., J. Leszek, J. Rosinczuk, I. Uchmanowicz, and B. Panaszek (2015) Impact of incarceration in Nazi concentration camps on multimorbidity of former prisoners. *Neuropsychiatric Disease and Treatment.* Vol. 11:668-674.

Jackson, D. B. and K. Turney (2021) Sleep problems among mothers of youth stopped by police. *Journal of Urban Health.* Vol. 98:163-171.

Jacob, R. (2017) How prison architecture can transform inmates' lives. *Pacific Standard Magazine.* May 3. Retrieved from https://psmag.com/news/jail-prison-architecture-inmates-crime-design-82968.

Jacobs, J. B. (1980) The Prisoners' Rights Movement and its impact, 1960-1980. *Crime and Justice.* Vol. 2:429-470.

Jacobs, M., ed. (2020) Surviving Andersonville: A Civil War soldier's story. *America's Civil War.* Nov., Vol. 33, Iss. 5:40-49.

Jacobson, J., B. Bhardwa, T. Gyateng, G. Hunter, and M. Hough (2010) *Punishing Disadvantage: A Profile of Children in Custody.* London, UK: Prison Reform Trust.

Jaegers, L. A., E. Skinner, B. Conners, C. Hayes, S. West-Bruce, M. B. Vaughn, D. L. Smith, and K. F. Barney (2020) Evaluation of jail-based occupational therapy transition and integration program for community reentry. *American Journal of Occupational Therapy.* May/June, Vol. 74, No. 3:1-11.

Jafari, F., M. H. Hadizadeh R. Zabihi, and K. Ganji (2014) Comparison of depression, anxiety, quality of life, vitality and mental health between premenopausal and postmenopausal women. *Climacteric.* Vol. 17:660-665.

Jaffe, E. F., A. E. L. Palmquist, A. Knittel (2021) Experiences of menopause during incarceration. *Menopause: The Journal of The North American Menopause Society.* Vol. 28, No. 7:1-4.

Janzer, C. (2019) North Dakota reforms prisons, Norwegian style. *U.S. News and World Report.* Feb. 22. Retrieved from https://www.usnews.com/news/best-states/articles/2019-02-22/inspi red-by-norways-approach-north-dakota-reforms-its-prisons.

Jeffries and Newbold (2016) Analysing trends in the imprisonment of women in Australia and New Zealand. *Psychiatry, Psychology and Law.* Vol. 23:184-206.

Jeffries, S., C. Chuenurah, and T. Russell (2020) Expectations and experiences of women imprisoned for drug offending and returning to communities in Thailand: Understanding women's pathways into, through, and post-imprisonment. *Criminology and Criminal Justice.* June 2020. Open Access. Available at https://www.mdpi.com/2075-471X/9/2/15/htm.

Jensen, V., L. Sexton, and J. Sumner (2018) Sexual victimization against transgender women in prison: Consent and coercion in context. *Criminology.* Vol. 57:603-631.

Jobs for Felons Hub (2021) Can a felon become a plumber? Apr. 20. Retrieved from https://www .jobsforfelonshub.com/rights/can-felon-become-plumber/.

Johnson, D. (1987) Women blend in with men at Illinois prison. *The New York Times*. June 1.

Johnson, K. (2016) Argument analysis: Immigrant detention and the Constitution. *SCOTUSblog*: Independent News and Analysis of the U.S. Supreme Court. Dec. 1. Retrieved from https://www.scotusblog.com/2016/12/argument-analysis-immigrant-detention-and-the-constitution/.

Johnston, N. (2000). *Forms of Constraint: A history of Prison Architecture*. Chicago, IL: University of Illinois Press.

Jones, A. (1986) Self-mutilation in prison: A comparison of mutilators and nonmutilators. *Criminal Justice and Behavior*. Vol. 13, Iss. 3:286-296.

Jones Young, N. C. J., J. N. Griffith, and K. S. Anazoda (2019) Exploring the impact of training on equitable access to employment: A gendered perspective of work release programs. *Journal of Human Resource Management*. Vol. 22, No. 2:70-86.

Jung, H. and R. J. LaLonde (2019) Prison work-release programs and incarcerated women's labor market outcomes. *Prison Journal*. Nov., Vol. 99, Iss. 5:535-558.

Jurik, N. C. and M. C. Musheno (2006) The internal crisis of corrections: Professionalization and the work environment. *Justice Quarterly*. Vol. 3, Iss. 4:457-480.

Justia (2021) *Bell v. Wolfish*, 441 U.S. 520 (1979). Retrieved from https://supreme.justia.com/cases/federal/us/441/520/.

Justice, W. W. (1990) Origin of *Ruiz v. Estelle*. *Stanford Law Review*. Vol. 43, Iss. 1:1-12. Retrieved from https://www.ojp.gov/ncjrs/virtual-library/abstracts/origin-ruiz-v-estelle.

Justice Policy Institute (2020) *Sticker Shock 2020: The Cost of Youth Incarceration*. July. Retrieved from https://www.justicepolicy.org/uploads/justicepolicy/documents/Sticker_Shock_2020.pdf.

The Justice Project (2007) Jailhouse snitch testimony: A policy review. Retrieved from https://www.pewtrusts.org/~/media/legacy/uploadedfiles/wwwpewtrustsorg/reports/death_penalty_reform/jailhouse20snitch20testimony20policy20briefpdf.pdf.

Kageyama, B. (n.d.) America's last public execution. *History of Yesterday*. Retrieved from https://historyofyesterday.com/americas-last-public-execution-bb4b86c019ed.

Kanaboshi, N. (2014) Prison inmates' right to hunger strike: Its use and its limits under the U.S. Constitution. *Criminal Justice Review*. Vol. 39, No. 2:121-139.

Kang, R. (n.d.) Welcome to the dark web: A plain English introduction. International Association of Privacy Protection. Retrieved from https://iapp.org/news/a/welcome-to-the-dark-web-a-plain-english-introduction/.

Karpowitz, D. (2017) *College in Prison: Reading in an Age of Mass Incarceration*. New Brunswick, NJ: Rutgers University Press.

Kashatus, W. (1999) "Punishment, penitence, and reform": Eastern Penitentiary and the controversy over solitary confinement. *Pennsylvania Heritage*. Winter. Retrieved from http://paheritage.wpengine.com/article/punishment-penitence-reform-eastern-state-penitentiary-controversy-solitary-confinement/.

Kaufman, C. (2019) Solutions to a national problem of correctional officer turnover in the U.S. *Brief Policy Perspectives*. Dec. 18. Retrieved from https://policy-perspectives.org/2019/12/18/solutions-to-a-national-problem-correctional-officer-turnover-in-the-u-s/.

Kaur, P., S. Simapreet, A. Mathur, D. K. Makkar, V. P. Aggarwal, M. Batra, A. Sharma, and N. Goyal (2017) Impact of dental disorders and its influence on self-esteem levels among adolescents. *Journal of Clinical Diagnosis Research*. Apr., Vol. 11, No 4:ZC05-ZC08. Retrieved from https://www.ncbi.nlm.nih.gov/pmc/articles/PMC5449896/.

Kearley, B. and D. Gottfredson (2020) Long term effects of drug court participation: Evidence from a 15-year follow-up of a randomized controlled trial. *Journal of Experimental Criminology*. Vol. 16, Iss. 1:27-47.

Keary, I. (2015) *Prison Architect* review—once you're in you can't get out. *The Guardian*. Oct. 9. Retrieved from https://www.theguardian.com/technology/2015/oct/09/prison-architect-review-once-youre-in-you-cant-get-out.

Keehn, E. N. and A. Nevin (2018) Health, human rights and the transformation of punishment: South African litigation to address HIV and tuberculosis in prisons. *Health and Human Rights Journal*. Vol. 20, No. 1:213-224.

Kelly, A. (2017) President Trump pardons former Sheriff Joe Arpaio. NPR. Aug. 25. Retrieved from https://www.npr.org/2017/08/25/545282459/president-trump-pardons-former-sheriff-joe-arpaio.

Kenis, P., P. M. Kruyen, J. Baaijens, and P. Barneveld (2010) *The Prison Journal*. Vol. 90, No. 3:313-330.

Kerman, P. (2010) *Orange is the New Black*.

Khachatryan, N., K. M. Heide, E. V. Hummel, M. Ingraham, and J. Rad (2016) Examination of long-term postrelease outcome of juvenile homicide offenders. *Journal of Offender Rehabilitation*. Vol. 55, No. 8:503-524.

Khan, H. N. (2018) The trope of the "fallen women" in the fiction of Bangladeshi women writers, in *Unveiling Desire: Fallen Women in Literature, Culture, and Film*. D. Das and C. Morrow, eds. New Brunswick, Camden, Rutgers University Press.

Killingstad, J. R. (2017) The absence of race in Norway? *Journal of Anthropological Sciences*. Vol. 95:319-327.

Kimme, D. A., G. M. Bowker, and R. G. Deichman (2011) Jail Design Guide, 3d ed. National Institute of Corrections, U.S. Department of Justice. Mar., NIC Accession Number 04806. Champaign, IL: Kimme and Associates, Inc.

King, B. (2020) *The 15 Fundamental Laws of De-Escalation: How to Put Out Fires, Not Start Them*. Self-published.

King, M. J. and J. G. Boyle (2011) The theme park: The art of time and space, in *Disneyland and Culture: Essays on the Park and Their Influences*, K. M. Jackson and M. I. West, eds. Jefferson, North Carolina: McFarland and Co., Inc. Ch 1.

King, M. T. (2012) *A history of private prisons, in Prison Privatization: The Many Facets of a Controversial Industry*, Vol. 1, B. E. Price and J. C. Morris, eds. Westport, CT: Praeger Publishers.

King, S. (2017) *The Green Mile*, Illustrated edition New York Pocket Books. Movie adaptation: *The Green Mile* (Warner Bros. and Universal Pictures, 1999).

King, S. (2020) *Rita Hayworth and Shawshank Redemption*. New York City, NY: Scribner. Movie adaptation: *Shawshank Redemption* (Castle Rock Entertainment, 1994).

Kjellstrand, J., J. Cearley, J. M. Eddy, D. Foney, C. R. Martinez (2012) Characteristics of incarcerated fathers and mothers: Implications for preventive interventions targeting children and families. *Child Youth Services Review*. Dec. 1:2409-2415.

Klein, M. W. and C. L. Maxson (2006) *Street Gang Patterns and Policies*. New Work, NY: Oxford University Press, Inc.

Klemmer, C. L., S. Arayasirikul, H. F. Raymond (2021) Transphobia-based violence, depression and anxiety in transgender women: The role of body satisfaction. *Journal of Interpersonal Violence*. Vol. 36, No. 5-6:2633-2655.

Knochel, K. S. (1980) Fourteenth Amendment. Due process for prisoners in commitment proceedings. *The Journal of Criminal Law and Criminology*. Vol. 71, No. 4:579-592.

Ko, S. J., N. Kassam-Adams, C. Wilson, J. D. Ford, S. J. Berkowitz, M. Wong, and M. J. Brymer, C. M. Layne (2008) Creating trauma-informed systems: Child welfare, education, first responders, heath care, juvenile justice. *Professional Psychology, Research and Practice*. Aug, Vol. 39, No. 4:396-405.

KOAT, Channel 7, New Mexico (2012) Inmates using Aztec language to speak in code. Apr. 19. Retrieved from https://www.youtube.com/watch?v=8O9iRUWWMbQ.

Kolb, A. and T. Palys (2018) Playing the part: Pseudo-families, wives, and the politics in women's prisons in California. *Prison Journal*. Dec., Vol. 98, Iss. 6:678-699.

Konstan, D. (2003) Strategies of status, in *Ancient Anger: Perspectives from Homer to Galen*, S. Braud and G. W. Most, eds. Yale Classical Studies XXII. Cambridge: Cambridge University Press. 99-120.

Koonce, L. (2012) *Correction Officer's Guide to Understanding Inmates*. Atlanta, GA: Koonce Publishing.

Kopak, A. M. (2020) Behavioral health indicators and time-to-arrest in adult pre-arrest diversion programs. *Behavioral Science and the Law*. Jan., Vol. 38, No. 1:66-76.

Kovarsky, L. (2014) Prisoners and habeas privileges under the Fourteenth Amendment. *Vanderbilt Law Review*. Vol. 67:609.

Krajicek, D. J. (2015) How a hippie hash runner from Long Island escaped from Turkey's Alcatraz and inspired 'Midnight Express.' *New York Daily News*. June 20. Retrieved from https://www.nydailynews.com/news/crime/hed-hed-article-1.2264795.

Krans, B. (2018) Why aren't prison officials treating inmates for hepatitis C? *Healthline*. July 24. Retrieved from https://www.healthline.com/health-news/why-arent-prison-officials-treating-inmates-for-hepatitis-c.

Kraut, M. E. (n.d.) Supervised juvenile probation. Child Crime Prevention and Safety Center. Retrieved from https://childsafety.losangelescriminallawyer.pro/supervised-juvenile-probation.html#:~:text=Possible%20terms%20and%20conditions%20of,driver's%20license%20restrictions%2C%20fines%20and.

Kremer, K. P. and M. Vaughn (2019) College aspirations among incarcerated juvenile offenders: Importance of maternal education and neglect. *Youth Violence and Juvenile Justice*. Vol. 17, No. 4:431-447.

Krieger, D., C. Abe, A. Pottorff, X. Li, J. Rich, A. Nijhawan, and E. Ank (2019) Sexually transmitted infections detected during and after incarceration among people with Human Immonodeficiency Virus: Prevalence and implications for screening and prevention. *Sexually Transmitted Diseases*. Vol. 46, Iss. 9:602-607. Available at https://journals-lww-com.wne.idm.oclc.org/stdjournal/Fulltext/2019/09000/Sexually_Transmitted_Infections_Detected_During.7.aspx.

Kruml, S. M. and D. Geddes (2000) Exploring the dimensions of emotional labor. *Management Communication Quarterly*. Aug., Vol. 14, No. 1:8-49.

Kruzman, D. (2018) In U.S. prisons, tablets open window to outside world. Reuters. July 18. Retrieved from https://www.reuters.com/article/us-usa-prisons-computers/in-u-s-prisons-tablets-open-window-to-the-outside-world-idUSKBN1K813D.

Kuang, X., H. Liu, G. Guo, and H. Cheng (2019) The nonlinear effect of financial and fiscal poverty alleviation in China—An empirical analysis of Chinese 382 impoverished counties with PRSR models. *Plos One*. Nov. 5. Retrieved from https://journals.plos.org/plosone/article?id=10.1371/journal.pone.0224375#:~:text=In%20the%20nonlinear%20models%2C%20the,as%20the%20transition%20functions%20diminish.

Kubiak, S. P., J. Brenner, D. Bybee, R. Campbell, C. E. Cummings, K. M. Darcy, G. Fedock, and R. Goodman-Williams (2017) Sexual misconduct in prison: What factors affect whether incarcerated women will report abuses committed by prison staff. *Faculty Scholarship*, California Western School of Law. p. 224. Available at https://scholarlycommons.law.cwsl.edu/fs/224.

Kübler-Ross, E. (1969) *On Death and Dying*. New York, NY: Macmillan.

Kübler-Ross, E. and D. Kessler (2005, 2014) *On Grief and Grieving: Finding Meaning of Grief Through the Five States of Loss*. New York: Scribner.

Kumar, K. (2012) Greece and Rome in the British Empire: Contrasting role models. *Journal of British Studies*. Jan., Vol. 51, No. 1:76-101.

Kunda, Z. and B. Sherman-Williams (1993) Stereotypes and the construal of individuating information. *Personality and Social Psychology Bulletin*. Vol. 19:90-99.

Kyprianides, A. (2019) We need to rethink the way we treat ex-prisoners. Character and Context, Society for Personality and Social Psychology. June 12. Retrieved from https://www.spsp.org/news-center/blog/kyprianides-exprisoners.

Lacey, N. and H. Pickard (2015) The chimera of proportionality: Institutionalising limits on punishment in contemporary social and political systems. *Modern Law Review*. Mar., Vol. 78, No. 2:216-240.

Lacombe, D. (2013) "Mr. S., you do have sexual fantasies?" The parole hearing and prison treatment of a sex offender at the turn of the 21st Century. *Canadian Journal of Sociologie/Cahiers Canadièn de Sociologie*. Vol. 38, No. 1:33-63.

Larkin, S. (2020) Addressing the gap within the gap. *Journal of Indigenous Wellbeing*. May, Vol. 5, Iss. 1, Art. 6:72-78.

Lasher, M. P. and J. D. Stinson (2020) "Built on respect and good honest communication": A study of partnerships between mental health providers and community corrections. *Administration and Policy in Mental Health and Mental Health Services Research*. Vol. 47:617-631.

La Vigne, N. G. (2014) The cost of keeping prisoners hundreds of miles from home. Urban Institute. Feb.3. Retrieved from https://www.urban.org/urban-wire/cost-keeping-prisoners-hundreds-miles-home#:~:text=For%20state%20prisoners%2C%20the%20distance,but%20averages%20about%20100%20miles.

Law Explorer (2015) Crime and punishment. General Law. Nov. 30. Retrieved from https://lawexplores.com/crime-and-punishment/.

Lawrence, C. (2020) The ride of his life: Billy Hayes never tires of telling tale that inspired film 'Midnight Express.' Las Vegas Review-Journal Magazine. Mar. 15. Retrieved from https://www.reviewjournal.com/rj-magazine/meet-the-summerlin-resident-whose-drug-arrest-led-to-midnight-express-1966972/.

Ledesma, E. and C. L. Ford (2020) Health implications of housing assignments for incarcerated transgender women. *American Journal of Public Health.* May, Vol. 110, No. 5:650-654.

Lee, J. Y., A. C. Grogan-Kaylor, S. J. Lee, T. Ammari, A. Lu, and P. Davis-Kean (2020) A qualitative analysis of stay-at-home parents' spanking tweets. *Journal of Child and Family Studies.* Mar., Vol. 29, Iss. 3:817-830.

Lee, V. (2012) Prisoner participation in clinical research trials: A fundamental right under the Eighth Amendment. *Journal of Legal Medicine.* Vol. 33, Iss. 4:541-ii.

LeFlouria, T. L. (2015) *Chained in Silence: Black Women and Convict Labor in the New South.* Chapel Hill, NC: The University of North Carolina Press.

Legal Information Institute (n.d.) 28 CFR §97.14—Guard to prisoner ratio. Cornell Law School. Retrieved from https://www.law.cornell.edu/cfr/text/28/97.14.

Legal Information Institute (n.d.) Prisoners' rights: Overview. Cornell Law School. Retrieved from https://www.law.cornell.edu/lii/about/who_we_are.

Legal Information Institute (n.d.) Rights of prisoners. Cornell Law School. Retrieved from https://www.law.cornell.edu/constitution-conan/amendment-14/section-1/rights-of-prisoners#fn12 66amd14.

Legal Services for Prisoners with Children (LSPC): https://prisonerswithchildren.org/.

Leonard, J. (2020) What are the effects of solitary confinement on health? *Medical News Today.* Aug. 6. Retrieved from https://www.medicalnewstoday.com/articles/solitary-confinement-effects.

Lerner, C. S. (2015) Who's really sentenced to life without parole: Searching for "ugly disproportionalities" in the American criminal justice system. *Wisconsin Law Review.* Vol. 2015, Iss. 5:789-862.

Levi, R. and A. Waldman, eds. (2017) *Inside This Place, Not of It: Narratives from Women's Prisons.* Voice of Witness©. Brooklyn, NY: Verso Books. Kindle ed.

Levin, D. J., P. A. Langan, and J. M. Brown (2000) State court sentencing of convicted felons, 1996. Office of Justice Programs and Bureau of Justice Statistics, U.S. Department of Justice. Feb. Retrieved from https://www.bjs.gov/content/pub/ascii/scscf96.txt#:~:text=*%20Average %20elapsed%20time%20from%20date,trials%20took%20about%206%20months.

Levin, E. (2020) California Supreme Court orders Scott Peterson's murder conviction reexamined. *New England Public Media*, NPR. Oct. 15. Retrieved from https://www.npr.org/2020/10/15/ 923995078/california-supreme-court-scott-peterson-murder-conviction.

Levinson, E. and C. Mossburg (2020) Lori Loughlin released from prison after 2-month sentence for college admissions scam. *CNN.* Dec. 28. Retrieved from https://www.cnn.com/2020/12/28/us/ lori-loughlin-prison-release/index.html.

Levy, J. (2004) *Finding the Right Spot: When Kids Can't Live With their Parents.* Washington, D.C.: Magination Press.

Lewis, G. H. (1980) Social groupings in organized crime: The case of La Nuestra Familia. *Deviant Behavior.* Vol. 1, Iss. 2:129-143.

Lewis, K. and S. C. Hayes (1998) Intellectual functioning of women ex-prisoners. *Australian Journal of Forensic Science.* Vol. 30:19-28.

Lexington County Sheriff Department, SC (2015) *A Day in the Life of a Correctional Officer.* Available at https://www.youtube.com/watch?v=9-VgEymhKSY.

Lincoln, J. M., L-H Chen, J. S. Mair, P. J. Biermann, and S. P. Baker (2006) Inmate-made weapons in prison facilities: Assessing the injury risk. *Injury Prevention.* June, Vol. 12, No. 3:195-198.

Linders, A. (2002) The execution spectacle and state legitimacy: The changing nature of the American execution audience, 1833-1937. *Law and Society Review.* Vol. 36, No. 3:607-656.

Lithoxoidou, A., E. Seira, A. Vrantsi, and C. Dimitriadou (2021) Promoting resiliency, peer mediation and citizenship in schools: Outcomes of a three-fold research intervention. *Participatory Education Research.* Vol. 8, No. 2:109-128.

Lobel, J. (2020) Mass solitary and mass incarceration: Explaining the dramatic rise in prolonged solitary in America's prisons. *Northwestern University Law Review.* Vol. 115, Iss.1:159-209.

Lockwood, B. and N. Lewis (2019) The long journey to visit a family member in prison. The Marshall Project. Dec. 18. Retrieved from https://www.themarshallproject.org/2019/12/18/the -long-journey-to-visit-a-family-member-in-prison.

Lohman, J. (2000) School dropout age. *OLR Research Report*, 2000-r-0503. Apr. 24. Hartford, CT: Connecticut General Assembly.

Lommel, J. (2004) Turning around turnover. *Corrections Today Magazine.* Vol. 66, Iss. 5: 54-57.

Loong, D., S. Bonato, J. Barnsley, and C. S. Dewa (2019) The effectiveness of mental health courts in reducing recidivism and police contact: A systematic review. *Community Mental Health Journal*. Vol. 55:1073-1098.

Lovlie, A. and P. Guruli (2021) Public or private administration of justice: Privatization of prisons. *Nordisk Tidsskirft for Kriminalvidenskab*. No. 1 (2021). Retrieved from https://pdfs.semantic scholar.org/a3e8/aa901c64c7af515040955e16e6f0e073be4e.pdf.

Lubben, T. (2019) Caring for youth in juvenile detention centers: A story of hope. *The Permanente Journal*. May, Vol. 23:18-203.

Luyt, D. (2008) Governance, accountability, and poverty alleviation in South Africa. Paper, United Nations Social Forum. Sept. 2. Geneva, Switzerland.

Mailer, N. (1980) *The Executioner's Song*.

Malatesta, P. (2015) Inmate who killed Jeffrey Dahmer reveals why he murdered the serial killer. WGN9, Chicago. Apr. 29. Retrieved from https://wgntv.com/news/inmate-who-killed -jeffrey-dahmer-reveals-why-he-murdered-the-serial-killer/.

Malone, P. (2008) Long sentence goes against precedent: Woman gets six years for accessory to murder; six others charged this decade for same crime got far lighter sentences. *Pueblo Chieftain*. Sept. 3.

Mann, N. (2012) Ageing child sex offenders in prison: Denial, manipulation and community. *The Howard Journal of Criminal Justice*. Sept. Vol. 51, No. 4:345-358.

Marder-Spiro, J. (2020) Special factors counselling action: Why courts should allow people detained pretrial to bring Fifth Amendment *Bivens* claims. *Columbia Law Review*. June, Vol. 120, Iss. 5:1295-1331.

Marquart, J. W. and B. M. Crouch (1985) Judicial reform and prison control: The impact of *Ruiz v. Estelle* on a Texas penitentiary. *Law and Society Review*. Vol. 19, No. 4:557-586.

Marsden, J., G. Stillwell, H. Jones, A. Cooper, B. Eastwood, M. Farrell, T. Lowden, N. Maddalena, C. Metcalfe, J. Shaw, and M. Hickman (2017) Does exposure to opioid substitution treatment in prison reduce the risk of death after release? A national observational perspective study. *Addiction*. Aug., Vol. 112, Iss. 8:1408-1419.

The Marshall Project (2020) How prisons in each state are restricting visits due to coronavirus. Mar. 17. Retrieved from https://www.themarshallproject.org/2020/03/17/tracking-prisons-response -to-coronavirus.

Martinez, D. J. and J. Christian (2009) The familial relationships of former prisoners: Examining the link between residence and informal support mechanisms. *Journal of Contemporary Ethnography*. Vol. 38, No. 2:201-224.

Martinez, M. (2019) Deadly job: No rush to join Mexico's new police force. News, *British Broadcasting Company* (BBC). Sept. 11. Retrieved from https://www.bbc.com/news/world -latin-america-49551033.

Marusic, K. (2016) The sickening truth about what it's like to get your period in prison. *Women's Health Magazine*. July 7. Retrieved from https://www.womenshealthmag.com/life/a19997 775/women-jail-periods/.

Maschi, T., J. Kwak, E. Ko, and M. B. Morrissey (2012) Forget me not: Dementia in prison. *Gerontologist*. Vol. 52, No. 4:441-451.

Massachusetts Supreme Judicial Court (2018) Americans with Disabilities Act and parole – Massachusetts Supreme Judicial Court Observes that Americans with Disabilities Act applies to parole. *Harvard Law Review*. Jan., Vol. 131, Iss. 3:910-917.

Mayo, B. (2015) *Growing up on 21st Street, Northeast Washington, DC: A Memoir*. Scotts Valley, CA: Createspace Independent Publishing Platform.

Mayo Clinic (n.d.) Understanding menopause and discover relief from symptoms. Retrieved from https://www.mayoclinic.org/landing-pages/womens-health-menopause?mc_id=google &-campaign=12413826146&geo=9001666&kw=menopause%20symptoms&ad=504867715813 &network=g&sitetarget=&adgroup=125043279344&extension=&target=kwd-52076033 &matchtype=p&device=c&account=6033656803&invsrc=consult&placementsite= minnesota&gclid=Cj0KCQjw4ImEBhDFARIsAGOTMj_nBPjyGX2oKrJoiTkqHD27Ltz1nCw4v 9lzhO8REKKhj9APM9N-ydAaAuC0EALw_wcB.

McCain, J. (2008) John McCain, prisoner of war: A first person account. *U.S. News and World Report*. Jan. 28. Retrieved from https://www.usnews.com/news/articles/2008/01/28/john-mccain -prisoner-of-war-a-first-person-account.

McCall-Smith, K. (2016) Introductory Note to United Nations Standard Minimum Rules for the Treatment of Prisoners (Mandela Rules). International Legal Materials. Vol. 55, Iss. 6:1183-1205.

McCoy, S. P. and M. G. Aamodt (2010) A comparison of law enforcement divorce rates with those of other occupations. Mar., Vol. 25, No. 1:1-16.

McDonald, D. C. (1992) Private penal institutions. *Crime and Justice*. Vol. 16:361-419.

McElligott, G. (2017) Investment in prisons: Prison expansion and community development in Canada. *Studies in Social Justice*. Vol. 11, Iss, 1:86-112.

McGeachan, C. (2019) "A prison within a prison"? Examining the enfolding spatialities of care and control in the Barlinnie special units. *Area*. Jun., Vol. 51, Iss. 2:200-2007.

MeetUp.com – Support groups for families of prisoners: https://www.meetup.com/topics/support-group-for-families-of-prisoners/.

Mennel, R. (1973) *Thorns and Thistles: Juvenile Delinquents in the United States, 1825-1940*. Hanover, NH: University of New Hampshire.

Mennemeir, K. A. (2017) A right to know how you'll die: A First Amendment challenge to state secrecy statutes regarding lethal injection drugs. *Journal of Criminal Law and Criminology*. Summer, Vol. 107, Iss. 3:443-492.

Merikangas, K. R., J. P. He, D. Brody, P. W. Fisher, K. Bourdon, and D. S. Koretz (2010) Prevalence and treatment of mental disorders among US children in 2001-2004 NHANES. *Pediatrics*. Vol. 125:75-81.

Mervis, J. (2006) South Pole death probed. *Science*. Dec. 22., Vol. 314, Iss. 5807:1861.

Michigan Department of Corrections (2021) Marriage—Marrying a Prisoner. Retrieved from https://www.michigan.gov/corrections/0,4551,7-119-9741_12798-228401--,00.html.

Miller, F. (n.d.) La Santé Prison. *Frank Falla Archive*. Retrieved from https://www.frankfallaarchive.org/prisons/la-sante-prison/.

Miller, K. (n.d.) 20 advantages and disadvantages of private prisons. *Future of Work*. Retrieved from https://futureofworking.com/6-advantages-and-disadvantages-of-private-prisons/.

Miller, W. R., ed. (2012) Introduction, in *The Social History of Crime and Punishment in America: An Encyclopedia*. London, UK: SAGE Publications, Inc.

Miller-Perrin, C. L. and R. D. Perrin (2013) *Child Maltreatment: An Introduction*. 3d ed. Newbury Park, CA: SAGE Publishing.

Mitchell, D. (2003) Prisoners' constitutional rights. *Criminal Justice Studies*. Vol. 16, Iss. 3:245-264.

Mitchell, M. M., C. Fahmy, D. C. Pyrooz, and S. H. Decker (2017) Criminal crews, codes, and contexts: Differences and similarities across the Code of the Street, Convict Code, street gangs, and prison gangs. *Deviant Behavior*. Vol. 38, No. 10:1197-1222.

Mitra, E. (2021) She killed 7 members of her own family while pregnant. Now her son could be orphaned by execution. KAKE, Wichita, KS, ABC. Apr. 25. Retrieved from https://www.kake.com/story/43744092/she-killed-7-members-of-her-own-family-while-pregnant-now-her-son-could-be-orphaned-by-execution.

Mmari, K., A., S. G. Offiong, and T. Mendelson. (2019) How adolescents cope with food insecurity in Baltimore City: An exploratory study. Cambridge University Press. May 24. Retrieved from https://www-cambridge-org.wne.idm.oclc.org/core/journals/public-health-nutrition/article/how-adolescents-cope-with-food-insecurity-in-baltimore-city-an-exploratory-study/ED0FFEE3A73B015CEBE66C7EEAC891BC.

Moazen, B., J. Mauti, P. Meireles, T. Cerniková, F. Neuhann, A. Jahn, and H. Stöver (2021) Principles of condom provision programs in prisons from the standpoint of European prison health experts: A qualitative study. *Harm Reduction Journal*. Vol. 18, Article No. 14. Available at https://harmreductionjournal.biomedcentral.com/track/pdf/10.1186/s12954-021-00462-y.pdf.

Modrowski, C. A., D. C. Bennett, S. D. Chaplo, and P. K. Kerig (2017) Screening for PTSD among detained adolescents: Implication of the changes in the DSM-5. *Psychological Trauma: Theory, Research, Practice, and Policy*. Vol. 9:10.

Montagne, R. (2001) The last public execution in America. NPR, *Morning Edition*. May 1. Retrieved from https://legacy.npr.org/programs/morning/features/2001/apr/010430.execution.html#:~:text=Rainey%20Bethea%20was%20hanged%20on,last%20public%20execution%20in%20America.

Moreau, J. (2018) Bureau of prisons rolls back Obama-era transgender inmate protections. May 14. Retrieved from https://www.nbcnews.com/feature/nbc-out/bureau-prisons-rolls-back-obama-era-transgender-inmate-protections-n873966.

Morenoff, J. D. and D. J. Harding (2014) Incarceration, prison reentry, and communities. *Annual Review of Sociology*. Vol. 40:411-429.

Morgan, J. and A. L. Fellow (2017) Prisoners with physical disabilities are forgotten and neglected in America. *Speak Freely*, American Civil Liberties Union (ACLU). Jan. 12. Retrieved from https://www.aclu.org/blog/prisoners-rights/solitary-confinement/prisoners-physical-disabilities-are-forgotten-and.

Morgan, R. D., D. B. Flora, D. G. Kroner, J. F. Mills, F. Varghese, and J. S. Steffan (2012) Treating offenders with mental illness: A research synthesis. *Law and Human Behavior*. Feb., Vol. 36, No. 1:37-50.

Morris, K. (2004) Night shift nurse was videotaped as she conducted a client interview in segregation. Issues and Answers, in *Ohio Nurses Review*. Feb., Vol. 79, Iss. 2:16.

Morris, R. G. and J. L. Worrall (2014) Prison architecture and inmate misconduct: A multi-level assessment. *Crime and Delinquency*. Vol. 60, No. 7:1083-1109.

Morris, R. J. and K. C. Thompson (2008) Juvenile delinquency and special education laws: Policy implementation issues and directions for future research. *Journal of Correctional Education*. June, Vol. 59, No. 2:173-190.

Moss, H. (2009) Invisible aggression, impossible abuse: Female inmate-on-inmate sexual assault. *Georgetown Journal of Gender and Law*. Vol. 10, Iss. 3:979-985.

Mott, J. M., T. L. Barrera, C. Hernandez, D. P. Graham, and E. J. Teng (2014) Rates and predictors of referral for individual psychotherapy, group psychotherapy, and medications among Iraq and Afghanistan veterans with PTSD. *Journal of Behavioral Health Services and Research*. Apr., Vol. 41, No. 2:99-109.

Moughni, N. and N. Krinitsky (2020) Incarcerated body, liberated mind: The life of Mary Heinen McPherson. *Story Maps*, Carceral State Project: Documenting Criminalization and Confinement. Dec. 28. Retrieved from https://storymaps.arcgis.com/stories/d2552b27f3784308a25ff6273242bb1c.

MST Services (2019) Detention Centers. Nov. 6. Retrieved from https://info.mstservices.com/blog/gang-presence-juvenile#:~:text=Of%20the%20general%20population%20within,having%20a%20place%20to%20belong.

Mujuzi, J. D. (2009) The evolution of the meaning(s) of penal servitude for life (life imprisonment) in Mauritius: The Human Rights and jurisprudential challenges confronted so far and those ahead. *Journal of African Law*. Vol. 53, No. 2:222-248.

Mumola, C. and A. Beck (1997) *Bureau of Justice Statistics Bulletin*. Washington, D.C.: U.S. Department of Justice, Office of Justice Programs.

Muncie, J. (2021) *Youth and Crime*. 5th ed. London, UK: SAGE Publishing.

Murtha, E. (2021) Menendez brothers case back in spotlight thanks to TikTok teens: Reporter's notebook. News, ABC13. Apr. 3. Retrieved from https://abc13.com/menendez-brothers-now-abc-2020-lyle-erik-2020-episode/10480073/#:~:text=The%20brothers%20have%20now%20served,t%20changed%20all%20too%20much.

NAACP (n.d.) Criminal justice fact sheet. Retrieved from https:// www.naacp.org/criminal-justice-fact-sheet/.

Nadel, M. R. and D. P. Mears (2020) Building with no end in sight: The theory and effects of prison architecture. *Corrections*. Vol.5, Iss. 3:188-205.

NARCO (2003) A Failure of Justice: Reducing Child Imprisonment. London, UK: NARCO.

National Geographic (2016) Stories of Life in Solitary Confinement/Short Film Showcase. Aug. 6. Retrieved from https://www.youtube.com/watch?v=Q7ajzsh-i54.

National Institute of Corrections (n.d.) Corrections rankings: Measuring the efficiency of state prison systems. U.S. Department of Justice. Retrieved from https://nicic.gov/corrections-rankings-measuring-efficiency-state-prison-systems.

National Institute on Drug Abuse (2020) *Criminal Justice Drug Facts*. National Institute of Health. June. Retrieved from https://www.drugabuse.gov/publications/drugfacts/criminal-justice.

National Juvenile Defender Center (NJDC) (2017) The cost of juvenile probation: A critical look into juvenile supervision fees. Issue brief. Retrieved from https://njdc.info/wp-content/uploads/2017/08/NJDC_The-Cost-of-Juvenile-Probation.pdf.

National Juvenile Defender Center (NJDC) (n.d.) Violation of probation. Retrieved from https://njdc.info/violation-of-probation/.

National Public Radio, Inc. (NPR) (2014) A view on the torture and terror of Egyptian prison. Broadcast, *All Things Considered*. Mar. 21. Retrieved from https://go-gale-com.wne.idm.oclc .org/ps/i.do?p=LitRC&u=mlin_w_westnew&id=GALE%7CA362745818&v=2.1&it=r&sid=ebsco.

National Research Council of the National Academies (2014) *The Growth of Incarceration in the United States: Exploring Causes and Consequences*. Retrieved from https://www.nap.edu/ read/18613/chapter/1. Summary:2.

Neary, L. and R. Siegel (2002) Profile: Conditions inside Mexican prisons, and how they differ from those in American prisons. *All Things Considered*, National Public Radio, Inc. (NPR) June 25.

Neuman, A. E. (2021) 13 famous prisoners of Rikers Island. Unspeakable Times, *Ranker*. Feb. 26. Retrieved from https://www.ranker.com/list/famous-prisoners-at-rikers-island/treadlightly.

Newman, W. J. and C. L. Scott (2012) *Brown v. Plata*: Prison overcrowding in California. *Journal of the American Academy of Psychiatry and Law*. Vol. 40, No. 4:547-52.

Newsday (2012) Interview: Billy Hays revisits *Midnight Express*. June 22. Video. Retrieved from *Newsday*, 2012.

News Staff Editor (2016) Researchers at National University of Ireland, Galway target social work. *Politics and Government Business*. Jan. 14. P. 144.

News Talk 1460 (n.d.) Top 10 most notorious prisons in the U.S. KION (AM radio), Worldnews Staff. Salinas, CA. Retrieved from https://worldcnews.com/944822/top-10-most-notorious -prisons-in-the-u-s/.

The New York Times (2022) The Guantánamo docket. Mar 11. Retrieved from https://www.nytimes .com/interactive/2021/us/guantanamo-bay-detainees.html.

Nolo (n.d.) Exceptions to confidentiality of juvenile court records. *Legal Encyclopedia*. Retrieved from https://www.nolo.com/legal-encyclopedia/exceptions-confidentiality-juvenile-criminal -records.html.

Nowotny, K. M., M. Omori, M. Mckenna, and J. Kleinman (2020) Incarceration rates and incidences of sexually transmitted infections in US counties, 2011-2016. *American Journal of Public Health*. Vol. 110:130-136.

Nurse Practitioner Schools (2020) Nurse Practitioner vs. Doctor (Physician). Staff Writers. Oct. 26. Retrieved from https://www.nursepractitionerschools.com/faq/np-vs-doctor/.

Nussbaum, A. F. (1973) Let me tell you about prison movies. *Cinéaste*. Vol. 5, No. 4:45-47.

Odle, N. (2007) Privilege through prayer: Examining Bible based prison rehabilitation programs under the Establishment Clause. *Texas Journal on Civil Liberties and Civil Rights*. Spring, Vol. 12, Iss. 2:277-312.

Office of Juvenile Justice and Delinquency Prevention (2011) Wilderness camps. *Literature Review*: A product of the Model Programs Guide. Mar. Retrieved from https://ojjdp.ojp.gov/ sites/g/files/xyckuh176/files/media/document/Wilderness_Camp.pdf.

Office of Juvenile Justice and Delinquency Prevention (n.d.) Case flow diagram: Juvenile justice system structure and process. Office of Justice Programs, U.S. Department of Justice. Retrieved from https://www.ojjdp.gov/ojstatbb/structure_process/case.html.

Old Prisons Magazine (2020) Prison tourism is a growing heritage travel niche around the world. Feb. 15. Retrieved from https://www.oldprisons.com/prison-tourism-is-a-growing-heritage-travel-niche -around-the-world/#:~:text=Prison%20tourism%20is%20a%20growing%20heritage%20 travel%20niche%20around%20the%20world,-Posted%20by%20OldPrisons&text=Located%20 in%20Philadelphia%2C%20America's%20most,been%20a%20museum%20since%201994.

Onah, M. E. (2018) The patient-to-prisoner pipeline: The IMD exclusion's adverse impact on incarceration in the United States. *American Journal of Law and Medicine*. Vol. 44, No. 1:119-144.

Ondeck, M. (2019) Healthy birth practice #2: Walk, move around, change positions throughout labor. *The Journal of Perinatal Education*. Vol. 28, Iss. 2:188-193.

Owens-Schiele, E. and D. Eldeib (2011) Prisoners of love: Marrying an inmate brings challenges. *Chicago Tribune*. Dec. 21. Retrieved from https://www.chicagotribune.com/news/ct-xpm -2011-12-21-ct-x-1221-prison-wives-20111221-story.html.

Oyez (n.d.) *Estelle v. Gamble*. Retrieved from https://www.oyez.org/cases/1976/75-929.

Oyez (n.d.) *Robinson v. California*. Retrieved from https://www.oyez.org/cases/1961/554.

Pak, E. (2020) 10 iconic Wild West figures. *Biography*. Apr. 30. Retrieved from https://www.biography .com/news/wild-west-figures.

Pan, D. and Berry Hawkes, J. (2020) Quest to clear George Stinny's name draws scrutiny to another man. *The Post Courier*. Sept. 14. Retrieved from https://www.postandcourier.com/news/special _reports/quest-to-clear-george-stinneys-name-draws-new-scrutiny-to-another-man/article _1f4a8474-292b-11e8-bd9f-d334d74b4604.html.

Paperny, J. (2016) White Collar 101: Life in federal prison. *White Collar Advice*. Dec. 18. Retrieved from https://www.whitecollaradvice.com/white-collar-101-life-in-federal-prison/.

Parents with Incarcerated Children: http://prisonmoms.net/index.php.

Paris, J. E. (2008) Why prisoners deserve health care. Medicine and Society, *AMA Journal of Ethics*. Feb. Retrieved from https://journalofethics.ama-assn.org/article/why-prisoners-deserve -health-care/2008-02.

Parsons, T. (1975) The sick role and the role of physician reconsidered. The Milbank Memorial Fund Quarterly, *Health and Society*. Summer, Vol. 53, No. 3:257-278.

Paynter, M. J. and E. Snelgrove-Clarke (2017) Breastfeeding support for criminalized women in Canada. *Journal of Human Lactation*. Vol. 33, No. 4:672-676.

Payton, J. M. (2013) Alexander Oliver Exquemelin's The Buccaneers of America and the disen-chantment of Imperial history. *Early American Literature*. Spring, Vol. 48, Iss. 2:337-364.

Pennsylvania Prison Society (n.d.) Our history. Retrieved from https://www.prisonsociety.org/ history.

Peralta, E. (2011) Pa. judge sentenced to 28 years in massive juvenile justice bribery scandal. *The Two-Way*. NPR. Aug 11. Retrieved from https://www.npr.org/sections/thetwo-way/ 2011/08/11/139536686/pa-judge-sentenced-to-28-years-in-massive-juvenile-justice-bribery -scandal.

Pereboom, D. (2020) Incapacitation, reintegration limited general deterrence. *Neuroethics*. Vol. 13:87-97.

Perrin, P. and W. Coleman (1998) *Crime and Punishment: The Colonial Period to the New Frontier*. Carlisle, MA: Discovery Enterprises, Ltd.

Petek, G. (2019) *Improving California's Prison Inmate Classification System*. Legislative Analyst's Office, California Department of Corrections and Rehabilitation. May.

Peters, M., D. Thomas, C. Zamberlan, and Caliber Associates (1997) *Boot Camps for Juvenile Offenders: Program Summary*. Washington, DC: Office of Juvenile and Delinquency Prevention, U.S. Department of Justice.

Petersilia, J. (2011) Beyond prison bubble. National Institute of Justice, U.S. Department of Justice, Office of Justice Programs. Nov. 2. Retrieved from https://nij.ojp.gov/topics/articles/ beyond-prison-bubble#:~:text=Rehabilitation%20programs%20reduce%20recidivism%20 if,to%20get%20jobs%20after%20release.

Peté, S. and A. Devenish (2005) Flogging, fear, and food: Punishment and race in colonial Natal. *Journal of African Studies*. Vol. 31, No. 1:3-21.

PEW Charitable Trust (2018) Probation on parole systems marked with high stakes, missed oppor-tunities. *Issue Brief*. Sept. 25. Retrieved from https://www.pewtrusts.org/en/research-and -analysis/issue-briefs/2018/09/probation-and-parole-systems-marked-by-high-stakes-missed -opportunities.

Pfeiffer, S. (2020) Trial of Sept. 11 defendants at Guantánamo Bay delayed until August 2021. *Investigations*, NPR. Sept. 30. Retrieved from https://www.npr.org/2020/09/30/918454831/ trial-of-sept-11-defendants-at-guant-namo-delayed-until-august-2021.

Pickett, J. T. (2017) Blame their mothers: Public opinion about maternal employment as cause of juve-nile delinquency. *Feminist Criminology*. Available at https://doi.org/10.1177/1557085115624759.

Popp, R. K. (2018) From *Marrakesh Express* to *Midnight Express*: Backpackers, drug culture, and incarceration. *Journalism and Communication Monographs*. Vol. 20, No. 3:248-253.

Porche, C. (2015) A correctional officer reviews *Prison Architect*: How does the popular game stack up to really running a prison. From *Under the Phoenix Sun*, published at Corrections1. Apr. 28. Retrieved from https:// www.corrections1.com/corrections/articles/a-correctional-officer -reviews-prison-architect-4o1d2DreIXnyp9RV/.

Porretta, A. (2020) How much does individual health insurance cost? *eHealth*. Nov. 24. Retrieved from https://www.ehealthinsurance.com/resources/individual-and-family/how-much-does -individual-health-insurance-cost.

Positive Action (n.d.) Research outcomes, Evidence-based life skills curriculum and program. Retrieved from https://www.positiveaction.net/life-skills-curriculum-program.

Postmedia News (2015) Baby born in Ottawa jail cell dies one year after birth, sparking investigation into 'sudden death.' *National Post*. Jan, 25. Retrieved from https://nationalpost.com/news/canada/baby-born-in-ottawa-jail-cell-dies-one-year-after-birth-sparking-investigation-into-sudden-death.

Prater, N. (2021) 'It's hard to find the words to describe how bad it is right now'. Intelligencer, *New York Magazine*. Sept 27. Retrieved from https://nymag.com/intelligencer/2021/09/hard-to-find-the-words-to-describe-how-bad-it-is-on-rikers.html.

Pratt, T. C. and J. Maahs (1999) Are private prisons more cost-effective than public prisons? A meta-analysis of evaluation research studies. *Crime and Delinquency*. July, Vol. 45, Iss. 2:358-371.

Prejean, Sister Helen (1993) *Dead Man Walking: An Eyewitness Account of the Death Penalty in the United States.*

Prison Activist Resource Center (PARC): https://www.prisonactivist.org/.

Prison Families Anonymous: https://www.pfa-li.com/.

Prison Mindfulness Institute (2013) Prison yoga in Mexico. Jul. 15. Retrieved from https://www.prisonmindfulness.org/prison-yoga-practice-in-mexico/.

Prisonology™ (n.d.) Communication and visitation: Furlough. Retrieved from https://prisonologyx.com/prison/communication-visitation/furlough/.

PrisonPro (n.d.) Visiting an inmate: Answers to common questions and things you should know. Retrieved from https://www.prisonpro.com/content/visiting-inmate-answers-common-questions-things-you-should-know.

Prison Reform Trust/INQUEST (2012) *Fatally Flawed: Has the State Learned Lessons from the Deaths of Children and Young People in Prison?* London, UK: Prison Reform Trust.

Priyadarshi, N. (2014) A socio-legal study of prison system and its reforms in India. *International Journal of Enhanced Research in Educational Development*. Nov.-Dec., Vol. 2, Iss. 6:1-5.

Publication Admin (2019) Bad policies and systematic bias are driving huge increases in Native American incarceration rates. *Native American Roots*. Nov. 28. Retrieved from http://nativeamericannetroots.net/diary/Bad-policies-and-systemic-bias-are-driving-huge-increases-in-Native-American-incarceration-rates.

Purvis, J. (2009) Suffragette hunger strikes, 100 years on. *The Guardian*. July 6. Retrieved from https://www.theguardian.com/commentisfree/libertycentral/2009/jul/06/suffragette-hunger-strike-protest.

Pusey, A. (2019) Aug. 6, 1890: First execution by the electric chair. *ABA Journal*. July/Aug., Vol. 105, Iss. 6:1.

Pyrooz, D. C., S. H. Decker, and E. Owens (2020) Do prison administrative and survey data sources tell the same story? A multitrait, multimethod examination with application to gangs. *Crime and Delinquency*. Vol. 66, No. 5:627-662.

Quinn, K. (2015) Billy Hayes: Convicted drug smuggler tells the true story of *Midnight Express. The Sydney Morning Herald*. Mar. 24. Retrieved from https://www.smh.com.au/entertainment/movies/billy-hayes-convicted-drug-smuggler-tells-the-true-story-behind-midnight-express-20150324-1m6ole.html.

Radelet, M. L., M. Vandiver, and F. M. Berardo (1983) Families, prisons, and men with death sentences: The human impact of structured uncertainty. *Journal of Family Issues*. Vol. 4, Iss. 4:593-612.

Ragatz, L. L. and B. Russell (2010) Sex, sexual orientation, and sexism: What influence do these factors have on verdicts in a crime-of-passion case? *The Journal of Social Psychology*. Vol. 150, No. 4:341-360.

Raine, G. (2012) Inmates' "ridiculous" lawsuits rile officials. *San Francisco Gate*. Feb. 8. Retrieved from https://www.sfgate.com/news/article/Inmates-ridiculous-lawsuits-rile-officials-3151589.php.

Rakoff, J. S. (2002) *United States v. Quinones et al.* United States Court of Appeals, Second Circuit. Dec. 10.

Ransom, J. (2018) Women describe invasive strip searches on visits to city jails. *The New York Times*. Apr. 26. Retrieved from https://www.nytimes.com/2018/04/26/nyregion/strip-search-new-york-city-jails-lawsuits.html.

Ratkalkar, M. and C. A. Atkin-Plunk (2020) Can I ask for help? The relationship among incarcerated males' sexual orientation, sexual abuse history, and perceptions of rape in prison. *Journal of Interpersonal Violence*. Vol. 35:4117-4140.

Rawls, J. J. (1999) *A Golden State: Mining and Economic Development in Gold Rush California*. Berkeley, CA: University of California Press.

Region 13 Education Service Center (2019) What is peer mediation? *Behavior*. Mar. 18. Retrieved from https://blog.esc13.net/what-is-peer-mediation/#:~:text=Peer%20mediation%20is%20a%20process,ways%20of%20resolving%20a%20conflict.

Rehavi, M. M. and S. B. Starr. Racial disparity in federal criminal charging and its sentencing consequences. University of Michigan Law and Economy, Empirical Legal Studies Center, Paper No. 12-002. June 2. Retrieved from https://papers.ssrn.com/sol3/papers.cfm?abstract_id=1985377.

Reilly, S. B. (2021) Where is the strike zone? Arguing uniformly narrow interpretation of Prison Litigation Reform Act's "three strikes" rule. Vol. 70, Iss. 3:755-796.

Reiman, J. and P. Leighton (2012) *The Rich Get Richer and the Poor Get Prison*. New York, NY: Pearson North America.

Reinhart, C. (2003) Prisons and prisoners; litigation. OLR Research Report, State of Connecticut. Oct. 10. Retrieved from https://www.cga.ct.gov/PS98/rpt%5Colr%5Chtm/98-R-0822.htm.

Reyes, H. (2001) Health and human rights in prisons. International Committee of the Red Cross, excerpt from HIV in Prisons: A reader with particular relevance to the newly developed states, in *World Health Organization-Europe, Health in Prison Project*. Chapter 2. Retrieved from https://www.icrc.org/en/doc/resources/documents/misc/59n8yx.htm#a2.

Richardson, S. (2018) Interview with Angela Zombek: North and South behind bars. HistoryNet. Dec. Retrieved from https://www.historynet.com/interview-angela-zombek.htm.

Richardson, W., B. Hornsby, and M. Martinez (2002) Perspectives on the death penalty, in *The Leviathan's Choice: Capital Punishment in the 21st Century*, M. Martinez, W. Richardson, and B. Hornsby, eds. New York: Rowman and Littlefield Publishers, Inc. Introduction, xi-xxvii.

Rideau, Wilbert (2010) *In the Place of Justice*.

Ridge, M. (1999) Disorder, crime, and punishment in the California Gold Rush. *Montana: The Magazine of Western History*. Autumn, Vol. 49, No. 3 (Gold Rush Issue):12-27.

Riggenberg, W. J. (2011) Initial dental needs and a projection of needed dental capacity in the Iowa Department of Corrections. *Journal of Correctional Health*. Vol. 17:150-159.

Riley, N. S. (2019) On prison nurseries. National Affairs. Spring. Retrieved from https://www.nationalaffairs.com/publications/detail/on-prison-nurseries.

Ríos-Figueroa, J. (2012) Justice System institutions and corruption control: Evidence from Latin America. *The Justice System Journal*. Vol. 33, No. 2:194-214.

Riyad, Z. A. E. (2021) Ritual curse in Egypt during prehistoric and early dynastic periods. *Journal of General Union of Arab Archaeologists*. Vol. 22, Iss. 1:125-155.

Rizzoli, M. and L. Stanca (2012) Judicial errors and crime deterrence theory and experimental evidence. *The Journal of Law and Economics*. Vol. 55, No. 2:311-338.

Roberts, J. V. and M. Hough (2005) The state of prisons: Exploring public knowledge and opinion. *The Howard Journal*. Jul. Vol. 44, No. 3:286-306.

Roberts, M. R. and M. J. Stacer (2017) Evaluating a faith-based diversion and reentry program: Who graduates and who is rearrested. *Offender Programs Report*. Mar./Apr., Vol. 20, Iss. 6:89-103.

Robertson, J. E. (2011) Correctional case law: 2010. *Criminal Justice Review*. Vol. 36:232-244.

Rogers, C. (2014) Inside the 'world's most dangerous' hospital. British Broadcasting Company (BBC). Dec 5. Retrieved from https://www.bbc.com/news/magazine-30293880.

Roush, D. and M. McMillen (2000) Construction, operation, and staff training for juvenile confinement facilities. *Bulletin*, Juvenile Accountability Incentive Block Grants Program, U.S. Department of Justice, Office of Justice Programs. Jan. Retrieved from https://www.ojp.gov/pdffiles1/ojjdp/178928.pdf.

Roush, K. (2021) Prison health services fail to meet the needs of incarcerated women. *American Journal of Nursing*. Apr. Vol. 121, Iss. 4:14.

Roy, S. and A. Avidija (2012) The effect of prison security levels on job satisfaction and job burnout among staff in the USA: An assessment. *International Journal of Criminal Justice Sciences*. Jul.-Dec., Vol. 7, No. 2:524-538.

Rubinkam, M. (2020) Kids-for-cash judge loses bid for lighter prison sentence. *The Washington Post*. Aug. 26. Retrieved from https://www.washingtonpost.com/national/kids-for-cash-judge-loses-bid-for-lighter-prison-sentence/2020/08/26/a8e82fea-e7a8-11ea-bf44-0d31c85838a5_story.html.

Russo, J. (2019) Workforce issues in corrections. National Institute of Justice, U.S. Department of Justice. Dec. 1. Retrieved from https://nij.ojp.gov/topics/articles/workforce-issues-corrections#figure1.

Ryder, J. A. (2020) Enhancing female prisoners' access to education. *International Journal for Crime, Justice, and Social Democracy.* Vol. 9, Iss. 1:139-149.

Salcedo, A. (2021) South Carolina could force Death Row inmates to choose between electric chair, firing squad. *The Washington Post.* Mar. 2. Retrieved from https://go-gale-com.wne.idm.oclc .org/ps/i.do?v=2.1&u=mlin_w_westnew&it=r&id=GALE|A653627669&p=GPS&sw=w.

Salisbury, E. J., J. D. Dabney, and K. Russell (2015) Diverting victims of commercial sexual exploitation from juvenile detention: Development of the InterCSECt Screening Protocol. *Journal of Interpersonal Violence.* Vol. 30, No. 7:1247-1276.

Sampson, R. J. and J. L. Lauritsen (1997) Racial and ethnic disparities in crime and criminal justice in the United States. *Crime and Justice.* Vol. 21 (Crime and Immigration: Comparative and Cross-National Perspectives):311-374.

Sandberg, S., C. Agoff, and G. Fondevilla (2020) Stories of the "good father": The role of fatherhood among incarcerated men in Mexico. *Punishment and Society.* Nov. 5. 0(0):1-21.

Sanders, J. (n.d.) Convict or inmate? (There's a huge difference, by the way.). Prison Writers. Retrieved from https://prisonwriters.com/convict-or-inmate/.

Sanderson, M. (2017) Marilyn Sanderson. *Inside This Place, Not of It: Narratives from Women's Prisons.* Voice of Witness©. Brooklyn, NY: Verso Books. Kindle ed.

Sandoval, J. R. (2020) "Everyone is on supervision": The function of home visits in structuring family dynamics and exerting continuous control. *Journal of Offender Rehabilitation.* Vol. 59, Iss. 4:177-197.

Sanger, M. E. (2009) Mexico: Presumed guilty: Based on an untrue story. Berkeley Review of Latin American Studies, Center for Latin American Studies, University of California, Berkeley. Retrieved from https://clas.berkeley.edu/research/mexico-presumed-guilty-based-untrue-story.

Sarat, A. (2014) *Gruesome Spectacles: Botched Executions and America's Death Penalty.* Stanford, CA: Stanford Law Books.

Sarat, A. (2021a) The return of firing squads shows death and its 'machinery' are grinding to a halt. *USA Today.* May 18. Retrieved from https://www.usatoday.com/story/opinion/policing/2021/ 05/18/firing-squads-gruesome-not-humane-death-penalty-fading/5120497001/.

Sarat, A. (2021b) The failure of lethal injections. *Verdict Justia.* Mar. 23. Retrieved from https:// verdict.justia.com/2021/03/23/the-dreadful-failure-of-lethal-injection.

Sarkin, J. (2008) Prisons in Africa: An evaluation from a human rights perspective. *International Journal of Human Rights.* Jan. Retrieved from https://sur.conectas.org/en/prisons-in-africa/.

Saunders, V. (2017) Children of prisoners – children's decision making about contact. *Child and Family Social Work.* Vol. 22:63-72.

Sayed, S. A., R. G. Morris, and R. A. DeShay (2020) Comparing the rates of misconduct between private and public prisons in Texas. *Crime and Delinquency.* Vol. 66, No. 9:1217-1241.

Scarpa, A., S. C. Haden, and J. Hurley (2006) Community violence victimization and symptoms of posttraumatic stress disorder: The moderating effects of coping and social support. *Journal of Interpersonal Violence.* Apr., Vol. 21:446-69.

Schaefer, L., F. T. Cullen, and J. E. Eck (2015) Environmental Corrections: *A New Paradigm for Supervisors of Offenders in the Community.* Newbury Park, CA: SAGE Publishing.

Schlanger, M. (2016) The just barely sustainable California Prisoners' rights ecosystem. *The Annals of the American Academy of Political and Social Science.* Vol. 664, 62. https:// advance-lexis-com.wne.idm.oclc.org/api/document?collection=analytical-materials&id= urn:contentItem:5JCP-HD70-00CV-J160-00000-00&context=1516831.

Schneider, R. D. (2010) Mental health courts and diversion programs: A global survey. *International Journal of Law and Psychiatry.* Vol. 33, No. 4:201-206.

Schneider, R. D., H. Bloom, and M. Heerema (2007) *Mental Health Courts: Decriminalizing the Mentally Ill.* Toronto, Canada: Irwin Law.

Scott, D. (2018) A comparison of gang- and non-gang-related violent incidents from the incarcerated youth perspective. *Deviant Behavior.* Vol. 39, No. 10:1336-1356.

Secure World News Team (2018) 2 cases of cybercrime behind bars. July 30. Retrieved from https:// www.secureworldexpo.com/industry-news/cybercrime-behind-bars.

Sellers, J. B. and H. E. Amos Doss (1994) Crimes and punishments of slaves, in *Slavery in Alabama*. Tuscaloosa, AL: University of Alabama Press. Ch. 7.

Semple, J. (1993). *Bentham's Prison: A Study of the Panopticon Penitentiary*. New York, NY: Oxford University Press.

The Sentencing Project: https://www.sentencingproject.org/.

Sestanovich, C. (2015) Prison bling. The Marshall Project. Apr. 3. Retrieved from https://www.themarshallproject.org/2015/04/03/prison-bling#:~:text=The%20Rule%3A%20Inmates%20are%20only,or%20a%20Star%20of%20David.

Settembre, J. (2018) For less than $7 a month you could never run out of tampons again. *Market Watch*. Aug. 1. Retrieved from https://www.marketwatch.com/story/for-less-than-7-a-month-you-could-never-run-out-of-tampons-again-2018-08-01-888812.

7 Helpful Programs for Children of Incarcerated Parents: https://web.connectnetwork.com/programs-for-children-of-incarcerated-parents/.

Shanahan, R. and S. V. Agudelo (2012) Family and recidivism. *American Jails*. Sept./Oct.:17-24.

Sharp, S. F. (2005) *Hidden Victims: The Effects of the Death Penalty on Families of the Accused*. New Brunswick, NJ: Rutgers University Press.

Shepherd, S. M., J. R. P. Ogloff, and S. D. M. Thomas (2016) Are Australian prisons meeting the needs of Indigenous offenders? *Health and Justice*. Vol. 4:13-22.

Shulman-Laniel, J., J. S. Vernick, B. McGinty, S. Frattaroli, L. Rutkow (2017) U.S. State ignition interlock for alcohol impaired driving prevention: A 50 state survey and analysis. *Journal of Law, Medicine, and Ethics*. Summer, Vol. 45, Iss. 2: 221-230.

Siemionow, J. (2020) A model of social rehabilitation treatment for juveniles: Cognitive and behavioral perspective—practical aspects. *Juvenile and Family Court Journal*. Mar, Vol. 712, Iss. 1:31-44.

Siennick, S. E., E. A. Steward, and J. Staff (2014) Explaining the association between incarceration and divorce. *Criminology*. Vol. 52, No. 3:371-398.

Sigelman, L., S. A. Tuch, and J. K. Martin (2005) What's in a name: Preference for "black" versus "African American" among Americans of African descent. *Public Opinion Quarterly*. Fall, Vol. 69, No. 3:429-438.

Sigler, M. (2010) Private prisons, public functions, and the meaning of punishment. *Florida State University Law Review*. Article 4. Vol. 38, Iss. 1:149-178.

Simes, J. T. (2019) Place after prison: Neighborhood attainment and attachment during reentry. *Journal of Urban Affairs*. Vol. 41, No. 4:443-463.

Simon, J. (2013) REFORMING CALIFORNIA CORRECTION: From health to humanity: Re-reading *Estelle v. Gamble* after *Brown v. Plata*. *Federal Sentencing Reporter*. Vol. 25, Iss. 4:276.

Sindel, P. E. (1991) Fourteenth Amendment—the right to refuse antipsychotic drugs masked by prison bars. *The Journal of Criminal Law and Criminology*. Winter, Vol. 81, No. 4:952-980.

Sing Sing Prison Museum (n.d.) History. Retrieved from http://www.singsingprisonmuseum.org/history-of-sing-sing-prison.html.

60 Minutes (2020) *60 Minutes* investigates the death of Jeffrey Epstein. CBS News. Jan. 5. Retrieved from https://www.cbsnews.com/news/did-jeffrey-epstein-kill-himself-60-minutes-investigates-2020-01-05/.

Skiba, R. J., R. S. Michael, A. C. Nardo, and R. Peterson (2000) *The Color of Discipline: Sources of Racial and Gender Disproportionality in School Punishment*. Bloomington, IN: Indiana Education Policy Center, University of Indiana.

Sklansky, A. (2011) New perspectives in policing. Harvard Kennedy School, Program in Criminal Justice Police and Management; National Institute of Justice. Mar. Retrieved from https://www.ojp.gov/pdffiles1/nij/232676.pdf.

Slater, D. (2017) North Dakota's Norway experiment. *Mother Jones*. July/Aug. Retrieved from https://www.motherjones.com/crime-justice/2017/07/north-dakota-norway-prisons-experiment/.

Slyker, J. E. (2020) *Outside Looking In: Navigating My 29 Year Career as a Federal Employee of the Federal Bureau of Prisons*. Kindle Edition. New Providence, NJ: Bowker.

Smith, B. (1921) Efficiency vs. reform in prison administration. *Journal of the American Institute of Criminal Law and Criminology*. Feb., Vol. 11, Iss. 4:587-597.

Smith, B. L. (2012) The case against spanking: Physical discipline is slowly declining as some studies reveal lasting harms of children. *Monitor on Psychology*. Apr., Vol. 43, No. 4:60.

Smith, C., ed. (2016) *The Life and Adventures of a Haunted Convict, Austin Reed*. New York, NY: Random House. Digital.

Smith, R. R. and M. A. Milan (1973) A survey of the home furlough policies of American correctional agencies. *Criminology*. May, Vol. 11, Iss. 1:95-104.

Smith, W. (1988) Male, female prison having baby boom. *Chicago Tribune*. Jan. 12. Retrieved from https://www.chicagotribune.com/news/ct-xpm-1988-01-12-8803210740-story.html.

Smith Pangle, L. (2009) Moral and criminal responsibilities in Plato's "Laws." *The American Political Science Review*. Vol. 103, No. 3:456-473.

Smykla, J. O. (1979) Does coed prison work? *Prison Journal*. Vol. 59, Iss. 1:61-72.

Söderlund, J. and P. Newman (2017) Improving mental health in prisons through biophilic design. *The Prison Journal*. Vol. 97, No. 6:750-772.

Soniak, M. (2012) 50 prison slang words to make you sound like a tough guy. *Mental Floss*. Oct. 17. Retrieved from https://www.mentalfloss.com/article/12794/50-prison-slang-words-make-you -sound-tough-guy.

Sonntag, H. (2017) Medicine behind bars: regulating and litigating prison healthcare under state law forty years after *Estelle v. Gamble. Case Western Reserve Law Review*. Winter, Vol. 68, Iss. 2:603-650.

Soulatges, J. A. (1792) *Traité Des Crimes*. Vol. 1.

South, D. B. (2009) Monolithic domes make perfect jails and prisons. Commercial Monolithic Dome Structures, Momolithicdomes.com. May 26. Retrieved from https://www.monolithic.org/ commercial/monolithic-domes-make-perfect-jails-and-prisons.

Sowell, E. R., P. M. Thompson, C. J. Holmes, T. L. Jernigan, and A. W. Toga (1999) In vivo evidence for post-adolescent brain maturation in frontal and striatal regions. *Nature Neuroscience*. Vol. 2, No. 10:859-861.

Spanne, A., N. McCarthy, and L. Longhine (2010) *Wish You Were Here: Teens Write About Parents in Prison*. New York, NY: Youth Communication, New York Center.

Sperber, K. G. (2020) Contemplating the role of community corrections and the intersection of public health and public safety. *Journal of Community Corrections*. Summer, Vol. 29, Iss. 4:5-19.

Spetalnick, M., T. Hunnicutt, and P. Steward (2021) Biden launches review of Guantanamo prison, aims to close it before leaving office. Reuters. Feb 12. Retrieved from https://www .reuters.com/article/us-usa-biden-guantanamo-exclusive/biden-launches-review-of-guantan amo-prison-aims-to-close-it-before-leaving-office-idUSKBN2AC1Q4.

Spiegel, S. (2007) "Race riots": An easy case for segregation? *California Law Review*. Dec., Vol. 95, No. 6:2261-2293.

Spitzer, S. (1975) Punishment and social organization: A study of Durkheim's theory of penal evolution. *Law and Society Review*. Summer, Vol. 9, No. 4:613-638.

Staff (2021) Prison education: Guide to college degrees for inmates and ex-offenders. *The Best Schools* (TBS). Apr. 22. Retrieved from https://thebestschools.org/magazine/prison -inmate-education-guide/.

Stahlkopf, C., M. Males, and D. Macallair (2010) Testing incapacitation theory: Youth crime and incarceration in California. *Crime and Delinquency*. Vol. 56, No. 2:253-268.

Starr, S. B. (2012) Estimating gender disparities in federal criminal cases. University of Michigan Law and Economy, Empirical Legal Studies Center, Paper No. 12-018. Aug. 29. Retrieved from https://papers.ssrn.com/sol3/papers.cfm?abstract_id=2144002.

Stauffacher, S. (2009) *Harry Sue*. New York, NY: Yearling Books.

Steele, J. L., R. Bozick, and L. M. Davies (2016) Education for incarcerated juveniles: A Meta-analysis. *Journal of Education for Students Placed at Risk* (JESPAR). Vol. 21, No. 2:65-89.

Steinbuch, A. T. (2014) The movement away from solitary confinement in the United States. *New England Journal on Criminal and Civil Confinement*. Spring, Vol. 40, Iss. 2:499-534.

Stelter, L. and C. Evetts (2020) The impact of an occupational-based program for incarcerated women with intellectual and developmental disabilities. *American Journal of Occupational Therapy*. Aug., Vol. 74, Iss. 2, Sup 1.

Stensland, M. and S. Sanders (2016) Detained and dying: Ethical issues surrounding end-of-life care in prison. *Journal of Social Work in End-of-Life and Palliative Care*. Vol. 12, No. 3:259-276.

Stephan, J. and J. Karsberg (2003) *The Census of State and Federal Correctional Facilities*. Washington, D.C.: U.S. Department of Justice.

Stern, J. E. (2015) The cruel and unusual execution of Clayton Lockett. *The Atlantic*. June. Retrieved from https://www.theatlantic.com/magazine/archive/2015/06/execution-clayton-lockett/392069/.

Still, W., B. Broderick, and S. Raphael (2016) Building trust and legitimacy within community corrections. *New Thinking in Community Corrections*, National Institute of Justice. Dec., No. 3. Retrieved from https://www.ojp.gov/pdffiles1/nij/249946.pdf.

Stritoff, S. (2019) How to marry a prisoner. Aug. 4. Retrieved from https://www.thespruce.com/how-to-marry-a-prisoner-2300890#:~:text=Regulations%20for%20marrying%20a%20prisoner,permission%20to%20marry%20the%20prisoner.&text=Once%20the%20forms%20are%20completed,facility%20with%20the%20requested%20fees.

Stroebe, M., H. Schut, and K. Boerner (2017) Cautioning health-care professionals: Bereaved persons are misguided through the stages of grief. OMEGA — *Journal of Death and Dying*. Vol. 74, No. 4:455-473.

Stroud, Robert (1962) *The Birdman of Alcatraz*.

Suffolk County Sheriff's Department (2018) Common ground. Newsletter. Apr. Retrieved from http://www.scsdma.org/wp-content/uploads/2018/04/1804.pdf.

Sullivan, K. (2018) Education systems in juvenile detention centers. *Education and Law Journal*, Brigham Young University. Vol. 2018, Iss. 2:71-100.

Sultan, B. (n.d.) Working behind the Wall: Mental health of correctional-based staff. *PsychAlive*. Retrieved from https://www.psychalive.org/working-behind-the-wall-mental-health-of-correctional-based-staff/#:~:text=Twenty%2Dfive%20percent%20of%20correctional,report%20hopelessness%20and%2For%20worthlessness.

Sunday Today (2019) *Go inside one of the most humane prisons in the world*. Video, NBC. Sept. 8. Retrieved from https://www.youtube.com/watch?v=sCZt2YipiIs.

Superior Court of California (1962) *Robinson v. California*, No. 554. Appellate Department, Los Angeles County. Decided June 25. Retrieved from https://tile.loc.gov/storage-services/service/ll/usrep/usrep370/usrep370660/usrep370660.pdf.

Supreme Court of the United States (SCOTUS) (1976) *Gregg v. Georgia*. No. 74-6257. Decided July 2. Retrieved from https://deathpenalty.procon.org/wp-content/uploads/sites/45/greggvgeorgia.pdf.

Supreme Court of the United States (SCOTUS) (1987) *Turner v. Safley*, 482 U.S. 78. Justia. Retrieved from https://supreme.justia.com/cases/federal/us/482/78/.

Supreme Court of the United States (SCOTUS) (1994) *Farmer v. Brennan*. United States Court of Appeals for the Seventh Circuit. No. 92-7247.

Supreme Court of the United States (SCOTUS) (2005) *Roper, Superintendent, Potosi Correctional Center v. Simmons*. No. 03-633. Retrieved from https://scholar.google.com/scholar_case?case=16987406842050815187&hl=en&as_sdt=6&as_vis=1&oi=scholarr.

Supreme Court of the United States (SCOTUS) (2018) *Jennings v. Rodriguez*. October Term, 2017. Retrieved from https://www.supremecourt.gov/opinions/17pdf/15-1204_f29g.pdf.

Susi, M. (2020) Stories from mothers of incarcerated youth. Campaign for Youth Justice. May 7. Retrieved from http://www.campaignforyouthjustice.org/news/blog/item/stories-from-mothers-of-incarcerated-youth.

Sutherland, E. H. (1931) The prison as a criminological laboratory. *Annals of the American Academy of Political and Social Sciences*. Vol. 157:131-136.

Sutherland, E. H. (1955) *Principles of Criminology*, revised by D. R. Cressey. New York City, NY: J B Lippincott Co.

Swenson, D. (2019) Opinion: Dwindling population and disappearing jobs is the fate that awaits much of rural America. *Market Watch*. May 24. Retrieved from https://www.marketwatch.com/story/much-of-rural-america-is-fated-to-just-keep-dwindling-2019-05-07.

Sykes, G. M. (1958) *The Society of the Captives: A Study of a Maximum Security Prison*. Princeton, N.J.: Princeton University Press.

Taijfel, H. and J. C. Turner (1979) An integrative theory of intergroup conflict, in *The Social Psychology of Intergroup Relations*, W. G. Austin and S. Worchel, eds. Monterey, CA: Brooks and Cole.

Takei, C. (2018) The East Mississippi Correctional Facility is 'hell on earth.' *Speak Freely*, American Civil Liberties Union (ACLU). Mar. 5. Retrieved from https://www.aclu.org/blog/prisoners-rights/medical-and-mental-health-care/east-mississippi-correctional-facility-hell.

Tangney, J. P. (2014) After committing a crime, guilt and shame predict re-offense. Association for Psychological Science. Feb. 11. Retrieved from https://www.psychologicalscience.org/news/releases/after-committing-a-crime-guilt-and-shame-predict-re-offense.html.

Tarm, M (2021) Executioners sanitized accounts of deaths in federal cases. AP News. Feb. 17. Retrieved from https://apnews.com/article/executioners-sanitized-accounts-of-death-25d133f59039150c2e308ba1a2a5caef.

Tasca, M., M. L. Griffin, and N. Rodriguez (2010) The effect of importation and deprivation factors in violent misconduct: An examination of black and Latino youth in prison. *Youth Violence and Juvenile Justice*. Vol. 8, No. 3:234-249.

Tata, C. and N. Hutton, eds. (2016) *Sentencing and Society*. London: Routledge, Taylor and Francis Group.

Taylor, M. (2017) Maria Taylor, in *Inside This Place, Not of It: Narratives from Women's Prisons*, R. Levi and A. Waldman, eds. Voice of Witness© (VOW). Brooklyn, NY: Verso Books. Kindle ed.

Teal, J. A. (2020) *My Journey to Prison: A Story of Failure, Struggle, Discipline, and Gratitude*.

Temko, D. (2013) Prisoners and the press: The First Amendment Antidote to civil death after PLRA. *California Western Law Review*. Article 3, Vol. 49, No. 2:195-229.

Terrible Things Happening in Cold Places (2019) The Bellingshausen stabbing: An update and some background. Aug. 24, 7:33 pm. Retrieved from http://www.terriblethingshappeningincoldplaces.com/bellingshausen-stabbing-update.

Thomas, C. W., D. M. Petersen, and R. M. Zingraff (1978) Structural and social psychological correlates of prisonization. *Criminology*. Nov., Vol. 16, No. 3:368-380.

Thompson, T. (2016) Arrest, detention, and beyond juvenile probation overview. Power Point presentation. Alameda County Probation Department Juvenile Field Services Division. Courtesy of Berkeley Law, University of California. Sept. Retrieved from https://www.law.berkeley.edu/wp-content/uploads/2016/09/Juvenile-Services-Overview-Powerpoint-Judge-Thompson-Edition.pdf.

Tier Talk (2020) *What's It Like Being a Female Correctional Officer?* Available at https://www.youtube.com/watch?v=dk0clnB7vL4.

Torrey, E. F., M. T. Zdanowicz, A. D. Kennard, H. R. Lamb, D. F. Eslinger, M. C. Biasotti, and D. A. Fuller (2014) *The Treatment of Persons with Mental Illness: A State Survey*. Treatment Advocacy Center. Apr. 8. Retrieved from https://www.treatmentadvocacycenter.org/storage/documents/treatment-behind-bars/treatment-behind-bars.pdf.

Toth, S. A. (2019) *Mettray: A History of France's Most Venerated Carceral Institution*. Ithaca, NY: Cornell University Press.

Trammell, R. (2009) Values, rules, and keeping the peace: How men describe order and the inmate code in California prisons. *Deviant Behavior*. Vol. 30:746-771.

Trammell, R. (2012) *Enforcing the Convict Code: Violence and Prison Culture*. Boulder, CO: Lynne Rienner Publishers.

Trammell, R. and M. Rundle (2015) The inmate as a nonperson: Examining staff conflict from the inmate's perspective. *The Prison Journal*. Vol. 95, No. 4:472-492.

Tran, T. T., C. Dubost, S. Baggio, L. Gétaz, and Hans Wolff (2018) Safer tattooing interventions in prisons: A systematic review and call to action. *BMC Public Health*. Vol. 18:015.

Travis, A. (2011) Short jail sentence preferable to community service, say prisoners. *The Guardian*. June 7. Retrieved from https://www.theguardian.com/society/2011/jun/08/prisoners-prefer-jail-sentence-to-community-service.

Travisono, A. P. (ed.) (1978) *The American Prison: From the Beginning: A Pictorial History*. College Park, MD: American Correctional Association.

Trulson, C. R., J. M. Craig, J. W. Caudill, and M. Delisi (2020) The impact of adult prison transfer on the recidivism outcomes of blended-sentenced juvenile delinquents. *Crime and Delinquency*. Vol. 66, Nos. 6-7:887-914.

Umphres, E. (2019) 150% wrong: The Prison Litigation Reform Act and attorney's fees. *American Criminal Law Review*. Winter, Vol. 56, Iss. 1:261-293.

Umpierre, M. (2014) Rights and responsibilities of youth, families and staff, in *Desktop Guide to Quality Practice for Working with Youth in Confinement*. Washington, D.C.: National Partnership for Juvenile Services and Office of Juvenile Justice and Delinquency Prevention. Ch. 5.

United Nations Office on Drugs and Crime (2018) Cabo Verde cooperation with Portugal and UNODC on strengthening its juvenile justice system. Retrieved from https://www.unodc.org/westandcentralafrica/en/2018-02-23-cabo-verde-in-portugal-justice.html.

United States 2020 Census (2021) Quick facts. Retrieved from https://www.census.gov/quickfacts/fact/table/US/PST045219.

United States Bureau of Justice Statistics (2020) Statistics, in *Research, Statistics, and Evaluation*. Office of Justice Programs, U.S Department of Justice. Retrieved from https://www.ojp.gov/topics/research-statistics-evaluation#:~:text=Impartial%2C%20timely%2C%20and%20accurate%20statistical,information%20used%20for%20decision%20making.

United States Bureau of Labor Statistics (2020) Correctional officers and bailiffs—Work environment. Sept. 1. Retrieved from https://www.bls.gov/ooh/protective-service/correctional-officers.htm#tab-3.

United States Bureau of Labor Statistics (2020) Probation officers and correctional treatment specialists. Sept. 1. Retrieved from https://www.bls.gov/ooh/community-and-social-service/probation-officers-and-correctional-treatment-specialists.htmd.

United States Bureau of Prisons (2013) BOP holds first ever Universal Children's Day. Dec. 11. Retrieved from https://www.bop.gov/resources/news/20131210_childrensDay.jsp.

United States Bureau of Prisons (2014) Management of new prison activations can be improved. U.S. Government Accountability Office. Aug. Retrieved from https://www.gao.gov/assets/gao-14-709.pdf#?.

United States Bureau of Prisons (2019) Change Notice: Inmate security designation and custody classification. U.S. Department of Justice. Sept 4. Retrieved from https://www.bop.gov/policy/progstat/5100_008cn.pdf.

United States Bureau of Prisons (2021) Inmate gender. Statistics. Apr.10. Retrieved from https://www.bop.gov/about/statistics/statistics_inmate_gender.jsp.

United States Bureau of Prisons (n.d.) About our facilities: Administrative-level security. U.S. Department of Justice. Retrieved from https://www.bop.gov/about/facilities/federal_prisons.jsp#:~:text=Administrative%20facilities%20are%20institutions%20with,%2C%20or%20escape%2Dprone%20inmates.

United States Court of Appeals (1982) *Hoptowit. v. Ray*, 682 F.2d 1237. No. 80-3366, Ninth Circuit. Retrieved from https://scholar.google.com/scholar_case?case=5472072185575171255&q=hoptowit+v.+ray&hl=en&as_sdt=6,32&as_vis=1.

United States Court of Appeals (2003) *Ford v. McGinnis*, 352 F.3d 582, Docket No. 02-0205. Decided Dec. 15. Retrieved from https://scholar.google.com/scholar_case?case=8144509061522185362&hl=en&as_sdt=6&as_vis=1&oi=scholarr.

United States Court of Appeals (2013) *Stacy Graham v. Sheriff of Logan County*; *Rahmel Frances Jefferies*; *Alexander Alicides Mendez*. Tenth Circuit. Dec. 20. Retrieved from https://cases.justia.com/federal/appellate-courts/ca10/12-6302/12-6302-2013-12-20.pdf?ts=1411095953.

United States Court of Appeals (2016) *Estate of Clayton Lockett v. Fallin*. Tenth Circuit, No. 15-6134. Nov. 15. Retrieved from https://cases.justia.com/federal/appellate-courts/ca10/15-6134/15-6134-2016-11-15.pdf?ts=1479243718.

United States Courts (2016b) *Overview of Probation and Supervised Release Conditions*. Administrative Office of The United States Courts, Probation and Pretrial Service Office. Retrieved from https://www.uscourts.gov/sites/default/files/overview_of_probation_and_supervised_release_conditions_0.pdf.

United States Department of Health and Human Services (HHS) (2021) Annual update of the HHS poverty guidelines. Feb. 1. Retrieved from https://www.federalregister.gov/documents/2021/02/01/2021-01969/annual-update-of-the-hhs-poverty-guidelines.

United States Department of Health and Human Services (HHS), Office of Minority Health. *Reentry Resources*. Available at https://www.minorityhealth.hhs.gov/omh/content.aspx?ID=10326.

United States Department of Justice (2014) Manhattan U.S. attorney finds pattern and practice of excessive force and violence at NYC jails on Rikers Island that violates the Constitutional Rights of adolescent male inmates. Press release, U.S. Attorney's Office, Southern District. Aug. 4. Retrieved from https://www.justice.gov/usao-sdny/pr/manhattan-us-attorney-finds-pattern-and-practice-excessive-force-and-violence-nyc-jails.

United States Department of Justice (2020) *ADA/Section 504 Design Guide: Accessible Cells in Correctional Facilities*. Disability Rights Section, Civil Rights Division. Feb. 25. Retrieved from https://www.ada.gov/accessiblecells.htm.

United States Department of Justice (2020) Tribal Law and Order Act. Jan. 2. Retrieved from https://www.justice.gov/tribal/tribal-law-and-order-act.

United States Department of Labor (2021) Correctional officers and bailiffs. Occupational Outlook Handbook. Apr. 9. Retrieved from https://www.bls.gov/ooh/protective-service/correctional -officers.htm#:~:text=in%20May%202020.-,Job%20Outlook,to%20keep%20order%20in%20 courtrooms.

United States Department of Labor (n.d.) Child labor. Wage and Hour Division. Retrieved from https://www.dol.gov/agencies/whd/child-labor#:~:text=The%20federal%20child%20 labor%20provisions,well%2Dbeing%20or%20educational%20opportunities.

United States District Court (2009) *Inscoe v. Yates.* Eastern District of California, 9th Circuit. Case 1:08-cv-01588-DLB PC.

United States District Court (2019) *Dockery v. Hall*, Civil Action No. 3:13-cv-326-WHB-JCG. Southern District Mississippi, Northern Division. Decided Dec. 31.

United States Government Accounting Office (2015) Traffic safety: Alcohol ignition interlocks are effective while installed; less is known about how to increase installation rates, in *Alcohol Ignition Interlocks: Effectiveness and Case Studies of Six States*, T. Palmer, ed. New York: Nova Publishers. Ch. 1.

United States National Park Services (NPS) (n.d.) History of Andersonville Prison. Retrieved from https://www.nps.gov/ande/learn/historyculture/camp_sumter_history.htm.

United States Senate (1995) *Senate Bill S.984.* 104th Congress, 1st Session. June 29. Retrieved from https://www.congress.gov/104/bills/s984/BILLS-104s984is.pdf.

United States Senate (2004) *Juvenile Detention Centers: Are They Warehousing Children with Mental Illness?* Hearing before the Committee on Governmental Affairs. One Hundred Eighth Congress, Second Session. Washington, DC: U.S. Government Printing Office.

University of Minnesota, Human Rights Library (n.d.) Geneva Convention relative to the Treatment of Prisoners of War, 75 U.N.T.S. 135, entered into force Oct. 21, 1950. Retrieved from http://hrlibrary.umn.edu/instree/y3gctpw.htm.

University of Wisconsin-Madison (n.d.) About Restorative Justice. UWM Law School. Retrieved from https://law.wisc.edu/fjr/rjp/justice.html.

Urbina, I. (2009) For runaways, sex buys survival. *The New York Times*. Oct. 26. Retrieved from https://www.nytimes.com/2009/10/27/us/27runaways.html.

U.S. News and World Report (2012) Best states 2021: How they rank. Mar. 9. Retrieved from https://www.usnews.com/news/best-states/articles/methodology.

U.S. News and World Report (n.d.) Corrections rankings: Measuring the efficiency of state prison systems. Retrieved from https://www.usnews.com/news/best-states/rankings/crime-and -corrections/corrections?src=usn_tw.

van der Leun, Justine (2021) "No choice but to do it": Why women go to prison. *New Republic*. Jan./ Feb., Vol. 252, Iss. 1-2:28-37.

van der Vyver, J. D. (2003) Torture as crime under international law. *Albany Law Review*. Vol. 67:427.

Varghese, F. P., K. M. Anderson, D. L. Cummings, and E. Fitzgerald (2017) The Offender Job Search Self-Efficacy Scale: Development and initial validation. *Psychological Services*. Vol. 15, No. 4:477-485.

Vasseur, V. (2012) *Médecin-chef á la Prison de La Santé*. French ed. Paris, France: Cherche Midi.

Venters, H. (2019) *Life and Death in Rikers Island*. 1st ed. Baltimore, MD: Johns Hopkins University Press.

Verdugo, R. R. and B. C. Glenn (2006) Race and alternative schools. Conference paper, annual meeting of the Alternatives to Expulsion, Suspension, and Dropping Out of School Conference. Feb. 16-18, Orlando, FL. Washington, DC: Office of Justice Programs. Retrieved from https://www.ojp.gov/pdffiles1/ojjdp/grants/226234.pdf.

Villettaz, P., G. Gillieron, and M. Killias (2015) The effects on reoffending of custodial vs. non-custodial sanctions: An updated systematic review of the state of knowledge. *Campbell Systematic Reviews*. Vol. 11, Iss. 1:1-92.

Vito, G. F., R. M. Holmes, and D. G. Wilson (1985) The effect of shock and regular probation upon recidivism: A comparative analysis. *American Journal of Criminal Justice*. Spring, Vol. 9, Iss. 2:152-162.

Vito, G. F., D. G. Wilson, and T. J. Keil (1990) Drug testing, treatment, and revocation: A review of program findings. *Federal Probation*. Vol. 3:37-43.

Vivanco, J. M. (2020) Covid-19: The risk in Mexican prisons. Human Rights Watch and *El Universal*. June 4. Retrieved from https://www.hrw.org/news/2020/06/04/covid-19-risk-mexican-prisons.

Wagner, A. R. (2020) Article and survey: The criminally damaged brain and the need to expand mental health courts: A look at the traumatized mind, unfortunate criminal consequences, and the divergent paths of prison or treatment. *Nova Law Review*. Vol. 44:403.

Waid, C. A. and C. B. Clements (2001) Correctional facility design: Past, present and future. American Correctional Association, Inc., Corrections Compendium. Nov., Vol. 26, Iss. 11:1-29.

Wainwright, O. (2019) New York's high-rise jails: What could go wrong? *The Guardian*. Dec. 9. Retrieved from https://www.theguardian.com/cities/2019/dec/09/new-yorks-high-rise-prisons-what-could-go-wrong.

Wakai, S., S. Sampl, L. Hilton, and B. Ligon (2014) Women in prison: Self-injurious behavior, risk factors, psychological function and gender specific interventions. *The Prison Journal*. Vol. 94, No. 3:347-364.

Walker, J. (2006) *An Inmate's Daughter*. Norris, MT: Raven Publishing.

Walker, J. (2015) *Romar Jones Takes a Hike*. Gig Harbor, WA: Plicata Press, LLC.

Wallace, R. (2019) 5 of the biggest challenges facing corrections in 2019. *Corrections 1*, American Military University. Dec. 11. Retrieved from https://www.corrections1.com/2018-review/articles/5-of-the-biggest-challenges-facing-corrections-in-2019-b9Afg8ZhS84p06uT/.

Wallin and Klarich Law Corporation (n.d.) Involuntary manslaughter punishment sentencing – California Penal Code 192(b). Retrieved from https://www.wklaw.com/involuntary-manslaughter-sentencing/#:~:text=If%20convicted%2C%20you%20could%20spend,%2C%20three%2C%20or%20four%20years.

Walters, D. California's per-inmate cost has skyrocketed to $75,000 a year. *The Mercury News*. May 21. Retrieved from https://www.mercurynews.com/2018/05/20/walters-why-californias-per-inmate-cost-has-skyrocketed-to-about-75000-a-year/.

Ward, G. K. (2012) *The Black Child Savers: Racial Democracy and Juvenile Justice*. Chicago, IL: University of Chicago Press.

Ward, R. (2015) Introduction, in *A Global History of Execution and the Criminal Corpse*, R. Ward, ed. Basingstoke, UK: Palgrave Macmillian.

The Washington Post (n.d.) Prison writer Jack H. Abbott dies. Retrieved from https://www.washingtonpost.com/archive/local/2002/02/12/prison-writer-jack-h-abbott-dies/b12e2969-a2e7-4530-bc72-d78af089023f/.

Webb, W. F. and S. A. Brody (1968) The California Gold Rush and the mentally ill. *Southern California Quarterly*. Mar., Vol. 50, No. 1:430-50.

Weber, M. (1922, 1978) *Economy and Society: An Outline of Interpretive Sociology*. Vols. 1&2. Berkeley, CA: University of California Press.

Webster, P. (2018) Canada reveals needle exchange programme in prisons. *The Lancet*. May 26. Retrieved from https://www.thelancet.com/journals/lancet/article/PIIS0140-6736(18)31170-X/fulltext.

Wedding Stats (2021) Finance: Average cost of a wedding band. Jan. 16. Retrieved from https://www.weddingstats.org/cost-of-a-wedding-ring/.

Weegels, J. (2020) Prison riots in Nicaragua: Negotiating co-governance amid creative violence and public secrecy. *International Criminal Justice Review*. Vol. 30, No. 1:61-82.

Weiss, D. C. (2019) GPS ankle monitors can call and record people without their consent; do they violate 5th Amendment. Privacy Law, *Daily News, American Bar Association Journal*. Apr. 9. Retrieved from https://www.abajournal.com/news/article/electronic-monitoring-devices-can-call-and-record-people-accused-of-crimes-without-their-consent.

Wellford, C. (1967) Factors associated with adoption of the inmate code: A study of normative socialization. *The Journal of Criminal Law, Criminology, and Police Science*. Vol. 58, No. 2:197-203.

Wener, R. E. (2006) Effectiveness of direct supervision system of correctional design and management: A review of the literature. *Criminal Justice and Behavior*. Vol. 33:392-410.

Wener, R. E. (2012) *The Environmental Psychology of Prisons: Creating Spaces in Secure Settings. Environment and Behavior* series. Cambridge: Cambridge University Press.

Wennerstrom, A., B. Reilly, M. Sugarman, N. Henderson, and A. Niyogi (2020) Promoting health equity and criminal justice reform: The Louisiana experience. *American Journal of Public Health*. Jan., Vol. 11, Series 1:39-40.

Whissel, K. (2015) The spectacle of punishment and the "melodramatic imagination" in the classical-era prison film: *I am a Fugitive from a Chain Gang* (1932) and *Brute Force* (1947), in *Punishment in Popular Culture*. C. J. Ogletree, Jr. and A. Sarat, eds. New York: New York University Press. Ch. 3.

White, L. M., E. D. Holloway, M. Aalsma, and E. L. Adams (2015) Job-related burnout among juvenile probation officers: Implications for mental health stigma and competency. *Psychological Services*. Aug, Vol. 12, No. 3:291-302.

Wilkinson, T. (2018) Typology: Prison. *The Architectural Review*. June 11. Retrieved from https://www.architectural-review.com/essays/typology/typology-prison.

Williams, S. N. and S. A. LaTess (2020) Increasing cultural awareness in detained youth: Implications for intergroup relationships. *Professional Psychologist: Research and Practice*. Vol. 51, No. 3:291-296.

Willow, C. (2015) *Children Behind Bars: Why the Abuse of Child Imprisonment Must End*. Bristol, UK: Policy Press.

Wills, C. D. (2017) Caring for juveniles with mental disorders in adult prisons. *International Review of Psychiatry*. Vol. 29, No:25-33.

Wilson, R. M. (2013) *Crime and Punishment in Early Arizona*. Sacramento, CA: Stagecoach Publishing.

Wilson, W. J. (1987) *The Truly Disadvantaged: The Inner City, the Underclass, and Public Policy*. Chicago, IL: University of Chicago Press.

Winter, C. (2016) Spare the rod: Amid evidence zero tolerance doesn't work, schools reverse themselves. *APM Reports*. Aug. 25. Radio Broadcast. Retrieved from https://www.apmreports.org/episode/2016/08/25/reforming-school-discipline.

Witthold, M. (1998) *Let's Talk about when Your Parent Is in Jail*. New York, NY: Power Kids Press.

Wongsamuth, N. (2020) In prison, with periods and no pads: Life in a Thai jail. Reuters. Nov. 26. Retrieved from https://www.reuters.com/article/us-thailand-prison-women-trfn/in-prison-with-periods-and-no-pads-life-in-a-thai-jail-idUSKBN2861HT.

Wood, J. and S. Dennard (2017) Gang membership: Links to violence exposure, PTSD, anxiety, and forced control of behavior in prison. *Psychiatry*. Vol. 80:30-41.

Wood, M. (2018) This Medal of Honor recipient was executed for singing "God Bless America." Warfare History, *History Collection*. Mar. 26. Retrieved from https://historycollection.com/this-medal-of-honor-recipient-was-executed-for-singing-god-bless-america/2/., needs closing quotes after America

Woodfox, Albert (2019) *Solitary: Unbroken by Four Decades in Solitary Confinement*.

Woodruff, L. (2017) Prison reform: The origin of contemporary jail standards. *Lexipol*. Feb. 22. Retrieved from https://www.lexipol.com/resources/blog/prison-reform-origin-contempor ary-jail-standards/.

Woojae, H. and A. D. Redlich (2016) The impact of community treatment among mental health court participants. *Psychiatric Services*. Vol. 67, No. 4:385-390.

World Bank, The (2020) Population total – Canada. *DataBank*. Retrieved from https://data.world bank.org/indicator/SP.POP.TOTL?locations=CA.

World Monuments Fund (n.d.) Tarrafal Concentration Camp. Retrieved from https://www.wmf .org/project/tarrafal-concentration-camp.

World Population Review (2020) Cape Verde Population. Retrieved from https://worldpopulation review.com/countries/cape-verde-population.

World Population Review (2021) Public school rankings by state 2021. Retrieved from https://worldpopulationreview.com/state-rankings/public-school-rankings-by-state.

World Prison Brief (n.d.) World Prison Brief data, Canada. Institute for Crime and Justice Policy Research, University of London, Birkbeck. Retrieved from https://www.prisonstudies.org/country/canada.

Worth, R. F. (2002) Jailhouse author helped by Mailer found dead. *New York Times*. Feb. 11. Retrieved from https://www.nytimes.com/2002/02/11/nyregion/jailhouse-author-helped-by -mailer-is-found-dead.html.

WriteAPrisoner.com (Correspondence and Reintegration) (n.d.) Why write a prisoner? Retrieved from https://writeaprisoner.com/why-writeaprisoner.

WTOK Staff (2021a) Autopsy ordered after inmate death at EMCF. News Center, ABC 11. Jan. 16. Retrieved from https://www.wtok.com/2021/01/16/autopsy-ordered-after-inmate-death-at -emcf/.

WTOK Staff (2021b) Inmate deaths under investigation at EMCF. News Center, ABC 11. May 2. Retrieved from https://www.wtok.com/2021/05/02/inmate-deaths-under-investigation-at -emcf/.

Wyatt, R. (2006) Male rape in U.S. prisons: Are conjugal visits the answer. *Case Western Reserve Journal International.* Vol. 37, Iss. 2, Art. 20:579-614.

Yanofski, J. (2019) Prisons v. prisons: A history of mental health rights. *Psychiatry.* Vol. 7, No. 10:41-44.

Yoder, S. (2020) Sticker shock: The cost of New York youth prisons approaches $1 million per kid. Youth and Family News, *The Imprint.* Nov. 22. Retrieved from https://imprintnews.org/justice/ sticker-shock-cost-new-york-youth-prisons-approaches-million/49580.

Young, D. S. and R. F. Mattucci (2006) Enhancing the vocational skills of incarcerated women through a plumbing maintenance program. *Journal of Correctional Education.* Vol. 57, No. 2:126-140.

Zahn, M. A., J. C. Day, S. F. Mihalic, and L. Tichavsky (2009) Determining what works for girls in the Juvenile Justice System: A summary of evaluation evidence. *Crime and Delinquency.* Vol. 55, No. 2:266-93.

Zalman, M. (1972) Prisoners' rights to medical care. *The Journal of Criminal Law, Criminology, and Police Science.* Vol. 63, No. 2:185-199.

Zaumer, J. (2019) Released from Turkish prison, Pastor Andrew Brunson urges Congress to heed others being held. *The Washington Post.* Feb. 6. Retrieved from https://www.washingtonpost .com/religion/2019/02/06/released-turkish-prison-pastor-andrew-brunson-urges -congress-heed-other-prisoners/.

Zehr, H. (2015) *The Little Book of Restorative Justice: Revised and Updated.* 2d ed. Brattleboro, VT, Good Books.

Ziegler, E. M. (2014) *Harlots, Hussies, and Poor Unfortunate Women: Crime, Transportation, and Servitude of Female Convicts, 1718-1783.* Tuscaloosa, AL: University of Alabama Press.

Zielinski, M. J., M. K. Allison, L. Brinkley-Rubinstein, G. Curran, N. D. Zaller, and J. E. Kichner (2020) Making change happen in criminal justice settings: Leveraging implementation science to improve mental health care. *Health and Justice.* Vol. 9, Iss. 1:1-10.

Zillow (2021) Chino Hills home values. Feb. 28. Retrieved from https://www.zillow.com/chino -hills-ca/home-values/.

Zimmer, B. (2004/2005) The effect of faith-based programs in reducing recidivism and substance abuse of ex-offenders. *Journal of Community Corrections.* Winter, Vol. 14, Iss. 2:7-19.

Zimmer, W. C. (1916) Model jail architecture. *Journal of the American Institute of Criminal Law and Criminology.* Jan., Vol. 6, Iss. 5:717-713.

Zoetti, P. A. (2014) *Morabeza,* cash or body: Prison, violence and the state in Praia, Cape Verde. *International Journal of Cultural Studies.* Vol. 19, No. 4:391-406.

INDEX